Digital Design

with RTL Design, VHDL, and Verilog

SECOND EDITION

FRANK VAHID
University of California, Riverside

A John Wiley & Sons, Inc., Publication

To my family, Amy, Eric, Kelsi, and Maya;
and to all engineers who apply their skills
to improve the human condition.

VP and EXECUTIVE PUBLISHER	Don Fowley
ASSOCIATE PUBLISHER	Dan Sayre
EDITORIAL ASSISTANT	Katie Singleton
SENIOR PRODUCTION MANAGER	Micheline Frederick
SENIOR PRODUCTION EDITOR	Kerry Weinstein
EXECUTIVE MARKETING MANAGER	Christopher Ruel
COVER DESIGNER	Jim O'Shea
MEDIA EDITOR	Lauren Sapira
COVER PHOTO	Comstock Images/Getty Images, Inc.; iStockphoto

This book was set in 10/12 Times Roman by Frank Vahid. The text and cover were printed by Donnelley/Crawfordsville.

ISBN 978-0-470-53108-2

Printed in the United States of America
10 9 8 7 6 5 4 3 2 1

Contents

Preface

TO STUDENTS ABOUT TO STUDY DIGITAL DESIGN

Digital circuits form the basis of general-purpose computers and also of special-purpose devices like cell phones or video game consoles. Digital circuits are dramatically changing the world. Studying digital design not only gives you the confidence that comes with fundamentally understanding how digital circuits work, but also introduces you to an exciting possible career direction. This statement applies regardless of whether your major is electrical engineering, computer engineering, or computer science; in fact, the need for digital designers with strong computer science skills continues to increase. I hope you find digital design to be as interesting, exciting, and useful as I do.

Throughout this book, I have tried not only to introduce concepts in the most intuitive manner, but I have also tried to show how those concepts can be applied to real-world systems, such as pacemakers, ultrasound machines, printers, automobiles, or cell phones.

Young and capable engineering students sometimes leave their major, claiming they want a job that is more "people-oriented." Yet we need those people-oriented students more than ever, as engineering jobs are increasingly people-oriented, in several ways. First, engineers usually work in *tightly integrated groups* involving numerous other engineers, rather than "sitting alone in front of a computer all day" as many students believe. Second, engineers often work *directly with customers*, such as business people, doctors, lawyers, or government officials, and must therefore be able to connect with those customers. Third, and in my opinion most importantly, *engineers build things that dramatically impact people's lives*. Needed are engineers who combine their enthusiasm, creativity, and innovation with their solid engineering skills to invent and build new products that improve people's quality of life.

I have included "Designer Profiles" at the end of most chapters. The designers, whose experience levels vary from just a year to several decades, and whose companies range from small to huge, share with you their experiences, insights, and advice. You will notice how commonly they discuss the people aspects of their jobs. You may also notice their enthusiasm and passion for their jobs.

TO INSTRUCTORS OF DIGITAL DESIGN

This book has several key features that distinguish it from existing digital design books.

- *RTL design.* In the 1970s/1980s, chips had hundreds or thousands of gates, and hence digital design emphasized gate-level minimization. Today's chips hold millions of gates, and modern design is thus dominated by ***register-transfer level (RTL)*** design. A student exposed to RTL design in a first course will have a more relevant view of the modern digital design field, leading not only to a better appreciation of modern computers and other digital devices, but to a more accurate understanding of careers involving digital design. Such an accurate understanding is critical to attract computing majors to digital design careers, and to create a cadre of engineers with the comfort in both "software" and "hardware" necessary in modern embedded computing system design. Chapter 5 is entirely devoted to RTL design and is one of the only concise introductions to basic RTL design concepts and examples to be found anywhere.

- *Comprehensive and flexible HDL coverage.* HDLs are an important part of modern digital design, but they must be introduced carefully, such that students continue to learn fundamental digital design concepts along with the appropriate role of HDLs. Thus, this book covers HDLs in a separate chapter (Chapter 9), whose subsections each correspond to an earlier chapter, such that Section 9.2 can directly follow Chapter 2, Section 9.3 can follow Chapter 3, Section 9.4 can follow Chapter 4, and Section 9.5 can follow Chapter 5. This approach provides instructors the flexibility to cover HDLs in the latter part of a course only, or intermixed throughout, but in either case clearly showing students that HDLs are a mechanism for supporting digital design while being distinct from basic concepts. Furthermore, rather than the book choosing just one of the popular languages—VHDL, Verilog, or the relatively new SystemC—the book provides equal coverage of all three of those HDLs. We use our extensive experience in synthesis with commercial tools to create HDL descriptions well suited for synthesis, in addition to being suitable for simulation. Furthermore, for courses that cover HDLs in more depth or that have a follow-up course emphasizing more HDL design, two low-cost books have been created (one for VHDL, one for Verilog) specifically to accompany this book. Those HDL-introduction books use the same chapter structure and examples from this textbook, eliminating the common situation of students struggling to correlate their distinct and sometimes contradicting HDL book and digital design book. Our HDL-introduction books discuss language, simulation, and testing concepts in more depth than digital design books that incorporate HDL coverage, providing numerous HDL examples. The HDL books are also usable by themselves for HDL learning or reference. The HDL-introduction books improve upon the plethora of existing HDL books by emphasizing use of the language for real design, clearly distinguishing HDL use for synthesis from HDL use for testing, and by using extensive examples and figures throughout to illustrate concepts. The HDL-introduction books also come with complete PowerPoint slides that use graphics and animations to serve as an easy-to-use tutorial on the HDL.

- *Top-down design versus optimization.* Digital design and logic-size optimization were inseparably intertwined in the 1970s/1980s' small-capacity chip era. This book cleanly distinguishes design concepts from optimization concepts by using a distinct chapter for optimization (Chapter 6), expanding optimization coverage to also include tradeoffs and to include RTL topics. Nevertheless, the book provides an instructor maximum flexibility to introduce optimization at the times and to the extent desired by the instructor. In particular, the optimization chapter's subsections each correspond directly to one earlier chapter, such that Section 6.2 can directly follow Chapter 2, Section 6.3 can follow Chapter 3, Section 6.4 can follow Chapter 4, and Section 6.5 can follow Chapter 5. The book also emphasizes the modern approach of top-down design, involving capturing desired behavior and then converting to a circuit. At the same time, this book, like other books, uses a concrete bottom-up approach, starting from transistors, and building incrementally up to gates, flip-flops, registers, controllers, datapath components, and RTL.

- *Extensive use of applied examples and figures.* After describing a new concept and providing basic examples, the book provides examples that apply the concept to applications recognizable to a student, like a "seat belt unfastened" warning system, a computerized checkerboard game, a color printer, or a digital video camera. Furthermore, the end of most chapters includes a product profile, intended to give students an even broader view of the applicability of the concepts, and to introduce clever application-specific concepts the students may find interesting—like the idea of beamforming in an ultrasound machine or of filtering in a cellular phone. The book extensively uses figures to illustrate concepts; it contains over 600 figures.

- *Learning through discovery.* The book emphasizes understanding the need for new concepts, which not only helps students learn and remember the concepts, but develops reasoning skills that can apply the concepts to other domains. For example, rather than just defining a carry-lookahead adder, the book shows intuitive but inefficient approaches to building a faster adder, eventually solving the inefficiencies and leading to ("discovering") the carry-lookahead design.

- *Introduction to FPGAs.* The book includes a fully bottom-up introduction to FPGAs, showing students concretely how a circuit can be converted into a bitstream that programs the individual lookup tables, switch matrices, and other programmable components in an FPGA. This concrete introduction eliminates the mystery of the increasingly common FPGA devices.

- *Author-created graphical animated PowerPoint slides.* A rich set of PowerPoint slides is available to instructors. The slides were created by the textbook's author, resulting in consistency of perspective and emphasis between the slides and book. The slides are designed to be a truly effective teaching tool for the instructor. Most slides are graphical, avoiding slides consisting of just bulleted lists of text. The slides make extensive use of animation, where appropriate, to gradually unveil concepts or build up circuits, yet animated slides are carefully created so they can be printed out and understood. Nearly every figure, concept, and example from this book is included in the set of almost 500 slides.

- *Complete solutions manual.* Instructors may obtain a complete solutions manual (about 200 pages) containing solutions to every end-of-chapter exercise in this book. The manual extensively utilizes figures to illustrate solutions.

Many of the above features can be seen in the sample book materials available at http://www.ddvahid.com. Materials are available to instructors via the instructors site.

The second edition of this book includes a rewrite of the RTL design introduction in Chapter 5 to more intuitively introduce the subject, a further emphasis of top-down design (capture and convert) throughout Chapters 2–5, and improvements and additions to the descriptions, examples, and exercises in all chapters of the book.

HOW TO USE THIS BOOK

This book was designed to allow flexibility for instructors to choose among the most common approaches of material coverage. We describe several approaches below.

RTL-Focused Approach

An RTL-focused approach would simply cover the first 6 chapters in order:

1. Introduction (Chapter 1)
2. Combinational logic design (Chapter 2)
3. Sequential logic design (Chapter 3)
4. Combinational and sequential component design (Chapter 4)
5. RTL design (Chapter 5)
6. Optimizations and tradeoffs (Chapter 6), to the extent desired
7. Physical implementation (Chapter 7) and/or processor design (Chapter 8), to the extent desired

We think this is a great way to order the material, resulting in students doing interesting RTL designs in about seven weeks. HDLs can be introduced at the end if time permits, or left for a second course on digital design (as done at UCR), or covered immediately after each chapter—all three approaches are common.

Traditional Approach with Some Reordering

This book can be readily used in a traditional approach that introduces optimization along with basic design, with a slight difference from the traditional approach being the swapping of coverage of combinational components and sequential logic, as follows:

1. Introduction (Chapter 1)
2. Combinational logic design (Chapter 2) followed by combinational logic optimization (Section 6.2)
3. Sequential logic design (Chapter 3) followed by sequential logic optimization (Section 6.3)
4. Combinational and sequential component design (Chapter 4) followed by component tradeoffs (Section 6.4)
5. RTL design (Chapter 5) to the extent desired, followed by RTL optimization/tradeoffs (Section 6.5)
6. Physical implementation (Chapter 7) and/or processor design (Chapter 8), to the extent desired

This is a reasonable and effective approach, completing all discussion of one topic (e.g., FSM design as well as optimization) before moving on to the next topic. The reordering from a traditional approach introduces basic sequential design (FSMs and controllers) before combinational components (e.g., adders, comparators, etc.). Such reordering may lead into RTL design more naturally than a traditional approach, following instead an approach of increasing abstraction rather than the traditional approach that separates combinational and sequential design. HDLs can again be introduced at the end, left for another course, or integrated after each chapter. This approach could also be used as an intermediary step when migrating from a traditional approach to an RTL approach. Migrating might involve gradually postponing the Chapter 6 sections—for example, covering Chapters 2 and 3, and then Sections 6.2 and 6.3, before moving on to Chapter 4.

Traditional Approach

This book could also be used in a traditional approach, as follows:

1. Introduction (Chapter 1)

2. Combinational logic design (Chapter 2) followed by combinational logic optimization (Section 6.2)

3. Combinational component design (Sections 4.1, 4.3–4.8) followed by combinational component tradeoffs (Section 6.4—Faster Adders)

4. Sequential logic design (Chapter 3) followed by sequential logic optimization (Section 6.3)

5. Sequential component design (Sections 4.9, 4.10) followed by sequential component tradeoffs (Section 6.4—Smaller Multiplier)

6. RTL design (Chapter 5) to the extent desired, followed by RTL optimization/tradeoffs (Section 6.5)

7. Physical implementation (Chapter 7) and/or processor design (Chapter 8), to the extent desired.

Coverage of the first five topics has been the most widespread approach during the past two decades, with the above adding RTL design towards the end of the approach. Although the emphasized distinction between combinational and sequential design may no longer be relevant in the era of RTL design (where both types of design are intermixed), some people believe that such distinction makes for an easier learning path. HDLs can be included at the end, left for a later course, or integrated throughout.

ACKNOWLEDGEMENTS

Many people and organizations contributed to the making of this book.

- Staff members at John Wiley and Sons Publishers extensively supported the book's development. Dan Sayre inspired and oversaw the development of the second edition, and Micheline Frederick oversaw production. Kelly Applegate and Foti Kutil from Publication Services assisted greatly with composition and formatting of the second edition. Bill Zobrist supported my earlier "Embedded System Design" book, and motivated me to write the first edition of the book.

- Ryan Mannion contributed many items, including the appendices, numerous examples and exercises, several subsections, the complete exercise solutions manual, fact-checking, extensive proofreading, tremendous assistance during production, help with the slides, plenty of ideas during discussions, and much more.

- Roman Lysecky developed numerous examples and exercises, contributed most of the content of the HDL chapter, and co-authored our accompanying HDL-introduction books. Scott Sirowy contributed some of the HDL code for the second edition. Francesca Perkins did extensive proofreading of the second edition. Scott Sirowy, David Sheldon, and Bailey Miller helped with proofreading also.

- Numerous reviewers provided outstanding feedback on various versions of the book. Special thanks go to first-edition adopters who have provided great feedback, including Greg Link, Mark Brehob, Sharon Hu, Nikil Dutt, Eli Bozorgzadeh, and Jay Brockman (who has also made his lectures available on the web).

- The importance of the support provided to my research and teaching career by the National Science Foundation cannot be overstated.

ABOUT THE COVER

The cover's image of shrinking chips is more than just a nice visual; the image graphically depicts the amazing real-life phenomenon of digital circuits ("computer chips") shrinking in size by about one half every 18 months, for several decades now, a phenomenon referred to as Moore's Law. Such shrinking has enabled incredibly powerful computing circuits to fit inside tiny devices, like modern cell phones, medical devices, and portable video games.

ABOUT THE AUTHOR

Frank Vahid is a Professor of Computer Science and Engineering at the University of California, Riverside. He received his bachelor's degree in electrical engineering from the University of Illinois at Urbana-Champaign, and his master's and doctoral degrees in computer science from the University of California, Irvine. He has worked for Hewlett Packard and AMCC, and has consulted for Motorola, NEC, Atmel, Cardinal Health, and several other engineering firms. He is the inventor on three U.S. patents, has published over 150 research papers and two books on embedded systems, and helped establish the Embedded Systems Week conference. He established UCR's Computer Engineering program, and has received several UCR teaching awards. His research includes incorporating FPGAs into embedded systems, and networked sensor blocks that ordinary people can configure to monitor their surroundings.

See this book's website at http://www.ddvahid.com for additional book materials, for access to the publisher's book website and instructor materials, or to submit comments, corrections, or suggestions.

Reviewers and Evaluators

Rehab Abdel-Kader	Georgia Southern University
Otmane Ait Mohamed	Concordia University
Hussain Al-Asaad	University of California, Davis
Rocio Alba-Flores	University of Minnesota, Duluth
Bassem Alhalabi	Florida Atlantic University
Zekeriya Aliyazicioglu	California Polytechnic State University, Pomona
Vishal Anand	SUNY Brockport
Bevan Baas	University of California, Davis
Noni Bohonak	University of South Carolina, Lancaster
Don Bouldin	University of Tennessee
David Bourner	University of Maryland Baltimore County
Elaheh Bozorgzadeh	University of California, Irvine
Frank Candocia	Florida International University
Ralph Carestia	Oregon Institute of Technology
Rajan M. Chandra	California Polytechnic State University, Pomona
Ghulam Chaudhry	University of Missouri, Kansas City
Michael Chelian	California State University, Long Beach
Russell Clark	Saginaw Valley State University
James Conrad	University of North Carolina, Charlotte
Kevan Croteau	Francis Marion University
Sanjoy Das	Kansas State University
James Davis	University of South Carolina
Edward Doering	Rose-Hulman Institute of Technology
Travis Doom	Wright State University
Jim Duckworth	Worcester Polytechnic Institute
Nikil Dutt	University of California, Irvine
Dennis Fairclough	Utah Valley State College
Paul D. Franzon	North Carolina State University
Subra Ganesan	Oakland University
Zane Gastineau	Harding University
J. David Gillanders	Arkansas State University
Clay Gloster	Howard University
Ardian Greca	Georgia Southern University
Eric Hansen	Dartmouth College
Bruce A. Harvey	FAMU-FSU College of Engineering
John P. Hayes	University of Michigan
Michael Helm	Texas Tech University
William Hoff	Colorado School of Mines
Erh-Wen Hu	William Paterson University of New Jersey
Xiaobo Sharon Hu	University of Notre Dame
Baback Izadi	SUNY New Paltz

Jeff Jackson	University of Alabama
Anura Jayasumana	Colorado State University
Bruce Johnson	University of Nevada, Reno
Richard Johnston	Lawrence Technological University
Rajiv Kapadia	Minnesota State University, Mankato
Bahadir Karuv	Fairleigh Dickinson University
Robert Klenke	Virginia Commonwealth University
Clint Kohl	Cedarville University
Hermann Krompholz	Texas Tech University
Timothy Kurzweg	Drexel University
Jumoke Ladeji-Osias	Morgan State University
Jeffrey Lillie	Rochester Institute of Technology
David Livingston	Virginia Military Institute
Hong Man	Stevens Institute of Technology
Gihan Mandour	Christopher Newport University
Diana Marculescu	Carnegie Mellon University
Miguel Marin	McGill University
Maryam Moussavi	California State University, Long Beach
Olfa Nasraoui	University of Memphis
Patricia Nava	University of Texas, El Paso
John Nestor	Lafayette College
Rogelio Palomera	Garcia University of Puerto Rico, Mayaguez
James Peckol	University of Washington
Witold Pedrycz	University of Alberta
Andrew Perry	Springfield College
Denis Popel	Baker University
Tariq Qayyum	California Polytechnic State University, Pomona
Gang Qu	University of Maryland
Mihaela Radu	Rose-Hulman Institute of Technology
Suresh Rai	Louisiana State University, Baton Rouge
William Reid	Clemson University
Musoke Sendaula	Temple University
Martha Sloan	Michigan Technological University
Scott Smith	Boise State University
Gary Spivey	George Fox University
Larry Stephens	University of South Carolina
James Stine	Illinois Institute of Technology
Philip Swain	Purdue University
Shannon Tauro	University of California, Irvine
Carlos Tavora	Gonzaga University
Marc Timmerman	Oregon Institute of Technology
Hariharan Vijayaraghavan	University of Kansas
Bin Wang	Wright State University
M. Chris Wernicki	New York Institute of Technology
Shanchieh Yang	Rochester Institute of Technology
Henry Yeh	California State University, Long Beach
Kathleen Whitehorn	Colorado School of Mines
Naeem Zaman	San Jaoquin Delta College

Introduction

▷ 1.1 DIGITAL SYSTEMS IN THE WORLD AROUND US

Meet Arianna. Arianna is a five-year-old girl who lives in California. She's a cheerful, outgoing kid who loves to read, play soccer, dance, and tell jokes that she makes up herself.

One day, Arianna's family was driving home from a soccer game. She was in the middle of excitedly talking about the game when suddenly the van in which she was riding was clipped by a car that had crossed over to the wrong side of the highway. Although the accident wasn't particularly bad, the impact caused a loose item from the rear of the van to project forward inside the van, striking Arianna in the back of the head. She became unconscious.

Arianna was rushed to a hospital. Doctors immediately noticed that her breathing was very weak—a common situation after a severe blow to the head—so they put her onto a ventilator, which is a medical device that assists with breathing. She had sustained brain trauma during the blow to the head, and she remained unconscious for several weeks. All her vital signs were stable, except she continued to require breathing assistance from the ventilator. Patients in such a situation sometimes recover, and sometimes they don't. When they do recover, sometimes that recovery takes many months.

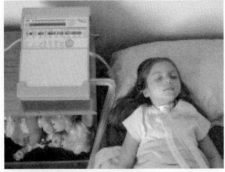

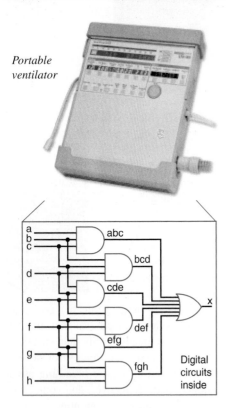

Portable ventilator

Digital circuits inside

Thanks to the advent of modern portable ventilators, Arianna's parents were given the option of taking her home while they hoped for her recovery, an option they chose. In addition to the remote monitoring of vital signs and the daily at-home visits by a nurse and respiratory therapist, Arianna was surrounded by her parents, brother, sister, cousins, other family, and friends. For the majority of the day, someone was holding her hand, singing to her, whispering in her ear, or encouraging her to recover. Her sister slept nearby. Some studies show that such human interaction can indeed increase the chances of recovery.

And recover she did. Several months later, with her mom sitting at her side, Arianna opened her eyes. Later that day, she was transported back to the hospital. She was weaned from the ventilator. Then, after a lengthy time of recovery and rehabilitation, Arianna finally went home. Today, six-year-old Arianna shows few signs of the accident that nearly took her life.

What does this story have to do with digital design? Arianna's recovery was aided by a portable ventilator device, whose invention was possible thanks to digital circuits. Over the past three decades, the amount of digital circuitry that can be stored on a single computer chip has increased dramatically—by nearly 100,000 times, believe it or not. Thus, ventilators, along with almost everything else that runs on electricity, can take advantage of incredibly powerful and fast yet inexpensive digital circuits. The ventilator in Arianna's case was the Pulmonetics LTV 1000 ventilator. Whereas a ventilator of the early 1990s might have been the size of a large copy machine and cost about $100,000, the LTV 1000 is not much bigger or heavier than this textbook and costs only a few thousand dollars—small enough, and inexpensive enough, to be carried in medical rescue helicopters and ambulances for life-saving situations, and even to be sent home with a patient. The digital circuits inside continually monitor the patient's breathing, and provide just the right amount of air pressure and volume to the patient. *Every breath* that the device delivers requires *millions* of computations for proper delivery, computations which are carried out by the digital circuits inside.

Photo courtesy of Pulmonetics

Photo courtesy of Pulmonetics

Portable ventilators help not only trauma victims, but even more commonly help patients with debilitating diseases, like multiple sclerosis, to gain mobility. Today, such people can move about in a wheelchair, and hence do things like attend school, visit museums, and take part in a family picnic, experiencing a far better quality of life than was feasible just a decade ago when those people would have been confined to a bed connected to a large, heavy, expensive ventilator. For example, the young girl pictured on the left will likely require a ventilator for the rest of her life—but she will be able to move about in her wheelchair quite freely, rather than being mostly confined to her home.

The LTV 1000 ventilator described above was conceived and designed by a small group of people, pictured on the left, who sought to build a portable and reliable ventilator in order to help people like Arianna and thousands of others like her (as well as to make some good money doing so!). Those designers probably started off like you, reading textbooks and taking courses on digital design, programming, electronics, and/or other subjects.

The ventilator is just one of literally *tens of thousands* of useful devices that have come about and continue to be created thanks to the era of digital circuits. If you stop and think about how many devices in the world are made possible because of digital circuits, you may be quite surprised. A few such devices include:

> Antilock brakes, airbags, autofocus cameras, automatic teller machines, aircraft controllers and navigators, camcorders, cash registers, cell phones, computer networks, credit card readers, cruise controllers, defibrillators, digital cameras, DVD players, electric card readers, electronic games, electronic pianos, fax machines, fingerprint identifiers, hearing aids, home security systems, modems, pacemakers, pagers, personal computers, personal digital assistants, photocopiers, portable music players, robotic arms, scanners, televisions, thermostat controllers, TV set-top boxes, ventilators, video game consoles—the list goes on.

One indicator of the rate that new inventions are developed is the number of new patents granted: nearly 200,000 in 2008 alone (from about 500,000 total applications).

Those devices were created by hundreds of thousands of designers, including computer scientists, computer engineers, electrical engineers, mechanical engineers, and others, working with people like scientists, doctors, business people, and teachers. One thing that seems clear is that new devices will continue to be invented for the foreseeable future—devices that in another decade will be hundreds of times smaller, cheaper, and more powerful than today's devices, enabling new applications that we can barely dream of. Already, we see new applications that seem futuristic but that exist today, like tiny digital-circuit-controlled medicine dispensers implanted under the skin, voice-controlled appliances, robotic self-guiding household vacuum cleaners, laser-guided automobile cruise control, handheld phones with full Internet access, and more. What's not clear is what new and exciting applications will be developed in the future, or who those devices will benefit. Future designers, like yourself perhaps, will help determine that.

▶ 1.2 THE WORLD OF DIGITAL SYSTEMS

Digital versus Analog

A *digital* signal, also known as a discrete signal, is a signal that at any time can have one of a finite set of possible values. In contrast, an *analog* signal can have one of an infinite number of possible values, and is also known as a continuous signal. A signal is just some physical phenomenon that has a unique value at every instant of time. An everyday example of an analog signal is the temperature outside, because physical temperature is a continuous value—the temperature may be 92.356666... degrees. An everyday example of a digital signal is the number of fingers you hold up, because the value must be either 0, 1, 2, 3, 4, 5, 6, 7, 8, 9, or 10—a finite set of values. In fact, the term "digital" comes from the Latin word for "digit" (digitus), meaning finger.

In computing systems, the most common digital signals are those that can have one of only two possible values, like on or off (often represented as 1 or 0). Such a two-valued representation is known as a *binary* representation. A *digital system* is a system that takes digital inputs and generates digital outputs. A *digital circuit* is a connection of digital components that together comprise a digital system. In this textbook, the term "digital" will refer to systems with binary-valued signals. A single binary signal is known as a binary digit, or *bit* for short (*b*inary dig*it*). Digital electronics became extremely popular in the mid-1900s after the invention of the transistor, an electric switch that can be turned on or off using another electric signal. We'll describe transistors further in the next chapter.

Figure 1.1 (a) General-purpose computer

Digital Circuits are the Basis for Computers

The most well-known use of digital circuits in the world around us is probably to build the microprocessors that serve as the brain of general-purpose computers, like the personal computer or laptop computer that you might have at home, illustrated in Figure 1.1(a). General-purpose computers are also used as servers, which operate behind the scenes to implement banking, airline reservation, web search, payroll, and similar such systems. General-purpose computers take digital input data, such as letters and numbers received from files or keyboards, and output new digital data, such as new letters and numbers stored in files or displayed on a monitor. Learning about digital design is therefore useful in understanding how computers work "under the hood," and hence has been required learning for most computing and electrical engineering majors for decades. Based on material in upcoming chapters, we'll design a simple computer in Chapter 8.

Digital Circuits are the Basis for Much More

Increasingly, digital circuits are being used for much more than implementing general-purpose computers. More and more new applications convert analog signals to digital ones, and run those digital signals through customized digital circuits, to achieve numerous benefits. Such applications, such as those in Figure 1.1(b), include cell phones, automobile engine controllers, TV set-top boxes, music instruments, digital cameras and camcorders, video game consoles, and so on. Digital circuits found inside applications other than general-purpose computers are often called *embedded systems,* because those digital systems are embedded inside another electronic device.

(b) Embedded systems

About 100,000 unique new digital circuits were designed in 2008.

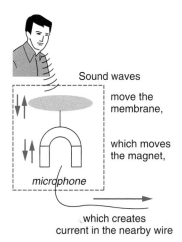

Sound waves move the membrane,

which moves the magnet,

microphone

which creates current in the nearby wire

Figure 1.2 Analog audio with a microphone.

The world is mostly analog, and therefore many applications were previously implemented with analog circuits. However, many implementations have changed or are changing over to digital implementations. To understand why, notice that although the world is mostly analog, humans often benefit from converting analog signals to digital signals before "processing" that information. For example, a car horn is actually an analog signal—the volume can take on infinite possible values, and the volume varies over time due to variations in the battery strength, temperature, etc. But humans neglect those variations, and instead "digitize" the sound heard into one of two values: the car horn is "off," or the car horn is "on" (get out of the way!).

Converting analog phenomena to digital for use with digital circuits can also yield benefits. Let's examine a particular example—audio recording. Audio is clearly an analog signal, with infinite possible frequencies and volumes. Consider recording an audio signal like music through a microphone, so that the music can later be played over speakers in an electronic stereo system. One type of microphone, a dynamic microphone, works based on a principle of electromagnetism—moving a magnet near a wire causes changing current (and hence voltage) in the wire, as illustrated in Figure 1.2. The more the magnet moves, the higher the voltage on the wire. A microphone thus has a small membrane attached to a magnet near a wire—when sound hits the membrane, the magnet moves, causing current in the wire. Likewise, a speaker works on the same principle in reverse—a changing current in a wire will cause a nearby magnet to move, which if attached to a membrane will create sound. (If you get a chance, open up an old speaker—you'll find a strong magnet inside.) If the microphone is attached directly to the speaker (through an amplifier that strengthens the microphone's output current), then no digitization is required for sound to be captured by the microphone and played by the speaker. But what if the sound should be saved on some sort of media so that a song can be recorded now and played back later? The sound can be recorded using analog methods or digital methods, but digital methods have many advantages.

One advantage of digital methods is lack of deterioration in quality over time. In the 1970s and 1980s, the audio cassette tape, an analog method, was a common method for recording and playing songs. Audio tape contains on its surface huge numbers of magnetic particles that can be moved to particular orientations using a magnet. Those particles hold that orientation even after the magnet is removed. Thus, magnetism can be used to change the tape's magnetic particles, some of them up, some higher, some down, etc. This is similar to how you can spike your hair, some up, some sideways, some down, using hair gel. The possible orientations of the tape's magnetic particles, and your hair, are infinite, so the tape is definitely analog. Recording onto a tape is done by passing the tape under a "head" that generates a magnetic field based on the electric current on the wire coming from a microphone. The tape's magnetic particles would thus be moved to particular orientations. To play a recorded song back, one would pass the tape under the head again, but this time the head operates in reverse, generating current on a wire based on the changing magnetic field of the moving tape. That current then gets amplified and sent to the speakers.

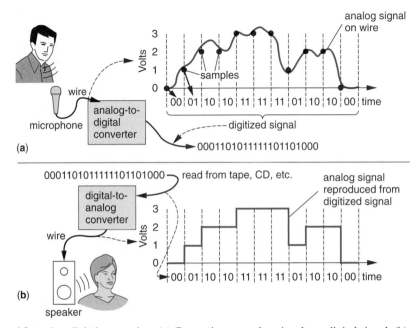

Figure 1.3 Analog-digital conversion: (a) Converting an analog signal to a digital signal, (b) converting a digital signal to an analog signal. Notice some quality loss in the reproduced signal—the signal (in blue) in (b) roughly follows but does not exactly match the signal in (a).

A problem with audio tape is that the orientations of the particles on the tape's surface change over time—just like a spiked hairdo in the morning eventually flattens out throughout the day. Thus, audio tape quality deteriorates over time. Such deterioration is a problem with many analog systems.

Digitizing the audio can reduce such deterioration. Digitized audio works as shown in Figure 1.3(a). The figure shows an analog signal on a wire during a period of time. We *sample* that signal at particular time intervals, shown by the dashed lines. Assuming the analog signal can range from 0 Volts to 3 Volts, and that we plan to store each sample using two bits, then we must round each sample to the nearest Volt (0, 1, 2, or 3). Each sample appears as a point in the figure. We can store 0 Volts as the two bits 00, 1 Volt as the two bits 01, 2 Volts as the two bits 10, and 3 Volts as the two bits 11. Thus, the shown analog signal would be converted into the following digital signal: 0001101011111101101000. This process is called ***analog-to-digital conversion*** or just ***digitization***.

To record this digital signal, we just need to store 0s and 1s on the recording media. Regular audio tape could be used, recording a short beep to represent a 1 and no beep to represent a 0, for example. While the audio signal on the tape will deteriorate over time, we can still certainly tell the difference between a beep and no beep, just like we can tell the difference between a car horn being on or off. A slightly quieter beep is still a beep. You've likely heard digitized data communicated using a manner similar to such beeps when you've picked up a phone being used by a computer modem or a fax machine. Even better than audio tape, the digital signal could be recorded using a media specifically designed to store 0s and 1s. For example, the surface of a CD (compact disc) or DVD (digital video disc) can be configured to reflect a laser beam to a sensor either strongly or weakly, thus storing 1s and 0s easily. Likewise, hard disks in computers use magnetic particle orientation to store 0s and 1s, making such disks similar to tape, but enabling faster access to random parts of the disk since the head can move sideways across the top of the spinning disk.

To play back this digitized audio signal, the digital value of each sampling period can simply be converted to an analog signal, as in Figure 1.3(b). The process is known as *digital-to-analog conversion*. The reproduced signal is not an exact replica of the original analog signal. The faster the analog signal is sampled and the more bits used for each sample, the closer the reproduced analog signal will be to the original analog signal—at some point, humans can't notice the difference between an original audio signal and one that has been digitized and then converted back to analog.

Another advantage of digitized audio is compression. Suppose that each sample will be stored with ten bits, rather than just two bits, to achieve better quality due to less rounding. The result is many more bits for the same audio—the signal in Figure 1.3 has eleven samples, and at ten bits per sample, one hundred ten bits would be required to store the audio. Sampling thousands of times a second results in huge numbers of bits. However, suppose that a particular audio recording has many samples that have the value 0000000000 or the value 1111111111. We could compress the digital file by creating new words using the following scheme: if the first bit of a word is *0*, the next bit being 0 means the word should be expanded to the sample 0000000000; the next bit being 1 means the word should be expanded to 1111111111. So *00* is shorthand for 0000000000 because the first bit is *0* and the next bit is 0, and *01* is shorthand for 1111111111. If instead the first bit of a word is a *1*, then the next ten bits represent the actual sample. So for *10000001111*, the first bit is *1*, and thus the actual sample is the next ten bits, or 0000001111. Using this compression scheme, the digitized signal "0000000000 0000000000 0000001111 1111111111" would be compressed to "00   00   10000001111   01." The receiver, which must know the compression scheme, would decompress that compressed signal into the original uncompressed digitized signal. There are many other schemes that can be used to compress digitized audio. Perhaps the mostly widely known audio compression scheme is known as *MP3*, which is popular for compressing digitized songs. A typical song might require many tens of megabytes uncompressed, but compressed usually only requires about 3 or 4 megabytes. Thanks to compression (combined with higher-capacity disks), today's portable music players can store tens of thousands of songs—a capability undreamt of by most people in the 1990s.

Digitized audio is widely used not only in music recording, but also in voice communications. For example, digital cellular telephones, called cell phones or mobile phones, digitize a person's voice and then compress the digital signal before transmitting that signal. Such digitization enables far more cell phones to operate in a particular region than is possible using analog cell phones. Pictures and video can be digitized in a manner similar to that described for audio. Digital cameras and video recorders, for example, store pictures and video in compressed digital form.

Digitized audio, pictures, and video are just a few of the thousands of past and future applications that benefit from digitization of analog phenomena. As shown in

	Satellites		DVD players		Video recorders		Musical instruments
Portable music players		Cell phones		Cameras		TVs	???

| 1995 | 1997 | 1999 | 2001 | 2003 | 2005 | 2007 |

Figure 1.4 More and more analog products are becoming primarily digital.

Figure 1.4, over the past decade numerous products that were previously analog have converted primarily to digital technology. Portable music players, for example, switched from cassette tapes to digital CDs in the middle 1990s, and recently to MP3s and other digital formats. Early cell phones used analog communication, but in the late 1990s digital communication, similar in idea to that shown in Figure 1.3, became dominant. In the early 2000s, analog VHS video players gave way to digital video disc (DVD) players, and then to hard-drive-based digital video recorders (DVRs). Portable video cameras have begun to digitize video before storing the video onto tape or a hard drive, while still picture cameras have eliminated film and store photos on digital cards. Musical instruments are increasingly digital-based, with electronic drums, keyboards, and electric guitars including more digital processing. Analog TV is also giving way to digital TV. Hundreds of other devices have converted from analog to digital in past decades, such as clocks and watches, household thermostats, human temperature thermometers (which now work in the ear rather than under the tongue or other places), car engine controllers, gasoline pumps, hearing aids, and more. Many other devices were never analog, instead being introduced in digital form from the very start. For example, video games have been digital since their inception.

The above devices use digitization, and digitization requires that phenomena be encoded into 1s and 0s. Computations using digital circuits also require that numbers be digitized into 1s and 0s. The next section describes how to encode items digitally.

▶ *THE TELEPHONE.*

The telephone, patented by Alexander Graham Bell in the late 1800s (though invented by Antonio Meucci), operates using the electromagnetic principle described earlier—your speech creates sound waves that move a membrane, which moves a magnet, which creates current on a nearby wire. Run that wire to somewhere far away, put a magnet connected to a membrane near that wire, and the membrane will move, producing sound waves that sound like you talking. Much of the telephone system today digitizes the audio to improve quality and quantity of audio transmissions over long distances. A couple of interesting facts about the telephone:

• Believe it or not, Western Union actually turned down Bell's initial proposal to develop the telephone, perhaps thinking that the then-popular telegraph was all people needed.

• Bell and his assistant Watson disagreed on how to answer the phone: Watson wanted "Hello," which won, but Bell wanted "Hoy hoy" instead. (Fans of the TV show *The Simpsons* may have noticed that Homer's boss, Mr. Burns, answers the phone with a "hoy hoy.")

An early-style telephone.

(Source of some of the above material: www.pbs.org, transcript of "The Telephone").

Digital Encodings and Binary Numbers—0s and 1s

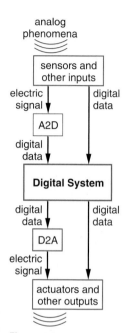

Figure 1.5 A typical digital system.

The previous section showed an example of a digital system, which involved digitizing an audio signal into bits that could then be processed using a digital circuit to achieve several benefits. Those bits *encoded* the data of interest. Encoding data into bits is a central task in digital systems. Some of the data to process may already be in digital form, while other data may be in analog form (e.g., audio, video, temperature) and thus require conversion to digital data first, as illustrated at the top of Figure 1.5. A digital system takes digital data as input, and produces digital data as output.

Encoding Analog Phenomena

Any analog phenomena can be digitized, and hence applications that digitize analog phenomena exist in a wide variety of domains. Automobiles digitize information about the engine temperature, car speed, fuel level, etc., so that an on-chip computer can monitor and control the vehicle. The ventilator introduced earlier digitizes the measure of the air flowing into the patient, so that a computer can make calculations on how much additional flow to provide. Digitizing analog phenomena requires:

* A **sensor** that measures the analog physical phenomena and converts the measured value to an analog electrical signal. One example is the microphone (which measures sound) in Figure 1.3. Other examples include video capture devices (which measure light), thermometers (which measure temperature), and speedometers (which measure speed).

* An **analog-to-digital converter** that converts the electrical signal into binary encodings. The converter must sample (measure) the electrical signal at a particular rate and convert each sample to some value of bits. Such a converter was featured in Figure 1.3, and is shown as the *A2D* component in Figure 1.5.

Likewise, a **digital-to-analog converter** (shown as *D2A* in Figure 1.5) converts bits back to an electrical signal, and an **actuator** converts that electrical signal back to physical phenomena. Sensors and actuators together represent types of devices known as **transducers**—devices that convert one form of energy to another.

Many examples in this book will utilize idealized sensors that themselves directly output digitized data. For instance, an example might use a temperature sensor that reads the present temperature and sets its 8-bit output to an encoding representing the temperature as a binary number, as in Figure 1.6 (see next sections for binary number encodings).

Encoding Digital Phenomena

Other phenomena are inherently digital. Such phenomena can only take on one value at a time from a finite set of values. Some digital phenomena can take on only one of two possible values at a time, and thus can be straightforwardly encoded as a single bit. For example, the following types of sensors may output an electrical signal that takes on one of two values at a time:

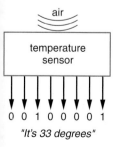

Figure 1.6 Idealized sensor that outputs digital data.

- Motion sensor: outputs a positive voltage (say +3 V) when motion is sensed, 0 volts when no motion is sensed.
- Light sensor: outputs a positive voltage when light is sensed, 0 V when dark.
- Button (sensor): outputs a positive voltage when the button is pressed, 0 V when not pressed.

We can straightforwardly encode each sensor's output to a bit, with 1 representing the positive voltage and 0 representing 0 V, as for the button in Figure 1.7. Examples throughout this book utilize idealized sensors that directly output the encoded bit value. Other digital phenomena can assume several possible values. For example, a keypad may have four buttons, colored red, blue, green, and black, as in Figure 1.8. A designer might create a circuit such that when red is pressed, the keypad's three-bit output has the value 001; blue outputs 010, green 011, and black 100. If no button is pressed, the output is 000.

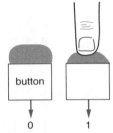

Figure 1.7 A button is easily encoded as a bit.

An even more general digital phenomenon is the English alphabet. Each character comes from a finite set of characters, so typing on a keyboard results in digital, not analog, data. The digital data can be converted to bits by assigning a bit encoding to each character. A popular encoding of English characters is known as ASCII, which stands for American Standard Code for Information Interchange, and is pronounced as "askey." ASCII encodes each character into seven bits. For example, the ASCII encoding for the uppercase letter 'A' is "1000001," and for 'B' is "1000010." A lowercase 'a' is "1100001," and 'b' is "1100010." Thus, the name "ABBA" would be encoded as "1000001 1000010 1000010 1000001." ASCII defines 7-bit encodings for all 26 letters (upper- and lowercase), the numerical symbols 0 through 9, punctuation marks, and even a number of encodings for nonprintable "control" operations. There are 128 encodings total in ASCII. A subset of ASCII encodings is shown in Figure 1.9. Another encoding, Unicode, is increasing in popularity due to its support of international languages. Unicode uses 16 bits per character, instead of just the 7 bits used in ASCII, and represents characters from a diversity of languages in the world.

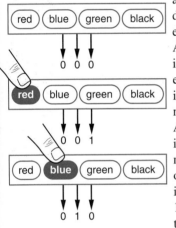

Figure 1.8 Keypad encodings.

Encoding	Symbol
010 0000	<space>
010 0001	!
010 0010	"
010 0011	#
010 0100	$
010 0101	%
010 0110	&
010 0111	'
010 1000	(
010 1001	)
010 1010	*
010 1011	+
010 1100	,
010 1101	-
010 1110	.
010 1111	/

Encoding	Symbol
100 0001	A
100 0010	B
100 0011	C
100 0100	D
100 0101	E
100 0110	F
100 0111	G
100 1000	H
100 1001	I
100 1010	J
100 1011	K
100 1100	L
100 1101	M

Encoding	Symbol
100 1110	N
100 1111	O
101 0000	P
101 0001	Q
101 0010	R
101 0011	S
101 0100	T
101 0101	U
101 0110	V
101 0111	W
101 1000	X
101 1001	Y
101 1010	Z

Encoding	Symbol
110 0001	a
110 0010	b
...	
111 1001	y
111 1010	z
011 0000	0
011 0001	1
011 0010	2
011 0011	3
011 0100	4
011 0101	5
011 0110	6
011 0111	7
011 1000	8
011 1001	9

Figure 1.9 Sample ASCII encodings.

Encoding Numbers as Binary Numbers

Perhaps the most important use of digital circuits is to perform arithmetic computations. In fact, a key driver of early digital computer design was the arithmetic computation of ballistic trajectories in World War II. To perform arithmetic computations, we need a way to encode numbers as bits—we need binary numbers.

To understand binary numbers, first refreshing our understanding of decimal numbers can help. Decimal numbers use a base ten numbering system. Base ten is a numbering system where the rightmost digit represents the number of ones (10^0) present, the next digit represents the number of groups of tens (10^1) present (meaning that the digit's place has a *weight* of 10^1), the next digit's place has a weight of (10^2), and so on, as illustrated in Figure 1.10. So the digits "523" in base 10 represent $5*10^2 + 2*10^1 + 3*10^0$.

With an understanding of base ten numbers, we can introduce base two numbers, known as **binary numbers**. Because digital circuits operate with values that are either "on" or "off," such circuits need only two symbols, rather than ten symbols. Let those two symbols be 0 and 1. If we need to represent a quantity more than 1, we'll use another digit, whose weight will be 2^1. So "10" in base two represents 1 two and 0 ones. Be careful not to call that 10 "ten" or "ten, base two" (which makes no sense)—instead, you might say "one zero, base two." If we need a bigger quantity, we'll use another digit, whose weight will be 2^2. The weights for the first few digits in base two are shown in Figure 1.11. For a given binary number, the lowest-weight (rightmost) digit is called the **least significant bit**, and the highest-weight (leftmost) digit is the **most significant bit**.

For example, the number 101 in base two equals $1*2^2 + 0*2^1 + 1*2^0$, or 5 in base ten. 101 can be spoken as "one zero one, base two." Definitely do *not* say "one hundred one, base two." 101 is one hundred one if in base ten, but the leftmost 1 does not represent one hundred when in base two.

When we are writing numbers of different bases and the base of the number is not obvious, we can indicate the base with a subscript, as follows: $101_2 = 5_{10}$. We might speak this as "one zero one in base two equals five in base ten." This book usually displays binary numbers using a different font, e.g., 101, to readily distinguish binary numbers from decimal numbers.

Note that because binary isn't as popular as decimal, people haven't created short names for its weights of 2^1, 2^2, and so on, like they have for weights in base ten (hundreds, thousands, millions, etc.). Instead, people just use the equivalent base ten name for each base two group—a source of confusion to some people just learning binary. Nevertheless, it may still be easier to think of each weight in base two using base ten names—one, two, four, eight—rather than increasing powers of two, as in Figure 1.12.

		5	2	3
10^4	10^3	10^2	10^1	10^0

Figure 1.10 Base ten number system.

		1	0	1
2^4	2^3	2^2	2^1	2^0

Figure 1.11 Base two number system.

I saw the following on a T-shirt, and found it rather funny:

"There are 10 types of people in the world: those who get binary, and those who don't."

		1	0	1
16	8	4	2	1

Figure 1.12 Base two number system showing weights in base ten.

▶ *WHY BASE TEN?*

Humans have ten fingers, so they chose a numbering system where each digit can represent ten possible values. There's nothing magical about base ten. If humans had nine fingers, they would probably use a base nine numbering system. It turns out that base twelve was used somewhat in the past too, because by using our thumb, we can easily point to twelve different spots on the remaining four fingers on that thumbs's hand—the four tops of those fingers, the four middle parts of those fingers, and the four bottoms of those fingers. That may partly explain why twelve is common in human counting today, like the use of the term "dozen," and the twelve hours of a clock.

(*Source: Ideas and Information*, Arno Penzias, W.W. Norton and Company.)

▶ *NAMES IN BASE TEN.*

Indian English has a name for 10^5*: lakh. In 2008, the Indian car company Tata Motors unveiled the "one lakh car," costing a mere 100,000 rupees, or about $2,500.*

The Web search tool name **Google** *comes from the word "googol" —a 1 followed by 100 zeroes, apparently implying that the tool can search a lot of information.*

English speakers use names for various quantities in base ten, names that are useful but can hamper gaining an intuitive understanding of base ten. 10^2 has its own name: *hundred*. 10^3 has the name *thousand*. There is no name (in American English) for 10^4 or 10^5. 10^6 has the name *million*, and subsequent groups that are multiples of 1,000 have the names *billion, trillion, quadrillion,* etc. English speakers also use abbreviated names for groups of tens—the numbers 10, 20, 30, ..., 90 could be called one ten, two ten, up to nine ten, but instead have abbreviated names: one ten as just "ten," two ten is "twenty," up to nine ten being "ninety." You can see how "ninety" is a shortening of "nine ten." Special names are also used for the numbers between 10 and 20. 11 could be "one ten one," but is instead "eleven," while 19 could be "one ten nine" but is

instead "nineteen." Table 1.1 indicates how one might count in base ten without these various names, to emphasize the nature of base ten. 523 might be spoken as "five hundred two ten three" rather than "five hundred twenty-three." Kids may have a harder time learning math because of the arbitrary base ten names—for example, carrying a one from the ones column to the tens column makes more sense if the ones column sums to "one ten seven" rather than to "seventeen"—"one ten seven" obviously adds one to the tens column. Likewise, learning binary may be slightly harder for some students due to a lack of a solid understanding of base ten. To help remedy the situation, perhaps when a store clerk tells you "That will be ninety-nine cents," you might say "You mean nine ten nine cents." If enough of us do this, perhaps it will catch on?

Table 1.1 Counting in base ten without the abbreviated or short names.

0 to 9	As usual: "zero," "one," "two," ..., "nine."
10 to 99	10, 11, 12, ... 19: "one ten," "one ten one," "one ten two," ... "one ten nine" 20, 21, 22, ..., 29: "two ten," "two ten one," "two ten two," ... "two ten nine" 30, 40, ... 90: "three ten," "four ten," ... "nine ten"
100 to 900	As usual: "one hundred," "two hundred," ... "nine hundred." Even clearer would be to replace the word "hundred" by "ten to the power of 2."
1000 and up	As usual. Even clearer for understanding bases: replace "thousand" by "ten to the (power of) 3", "ten thousand" by "ten to the 4," etc., eliminating the various names.

Example 1.1 Using digital data in a digital system

A digital system is desired that reads the value of a temperature sensor and shows the letter "F" (for "freezing") on a display if the temperature is 32 degrees Fahrenheit or below, shows "N" (for "normal") if the temperature is between 32 and 212 degrees, and shows the letter "B" (for "boiling") if the temperature is 212 or greater. The temperature sensor has an 8-bit output representing the temperature as a binary number between 0 and 255. The display has a 7-bit input that accepts an ASCII bit encoding and displays the corresponding symbol.

Figure 1.13 shows the temperature sensor output connected to the input of the desired digital system. Each wire can have

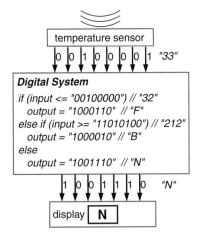

Figure 1.13 Digital system with bit encoded input (an 8-bit binary number) and 7-bit output (ASCII). The desired behavior of the digital system is shown.

the value of 1 or 0. The figure also shows a 7-bit output from the digital system connected to the display's 7-bit input.

The desired behavior for the digital system is shown in the figure: if the input is less than or equal to binary 00100000, which is 32 in base ten, then the output should be set to 1000110, which is the letter "F" in ASCII, as seen from Figure 1.9. Likewise, if the input is greater than or equal to binary 11010100, which is 212 in base ten, then the output should be 1000010, which is "B" in ASCII. For any other input value (which means the value is between 32 and 212), the output should be 1001110, which is "N" in ASCII. An example input of 00100001, which is 33 in base ten, is shown. For that input, the digital system outputs "N," as shown.

This example demonstrates how a digital system operates on digital input bits—0s and 1s—and creates digital output bits. We'll later see how to build circuits to implement desired digital system behavior.

Converting from Binary to Decimal

Because humans deal primarily with decimal numbers, a common digital design task is to convert a binary number to decimal, or to convert a decimal number to binary. Converting a binary number to decimal is straightforward: we simply sum the weights of each digit having a 1, as in the following example.

Example 1.2 Binary to decimal

Convert these binary numbers to decimal numbers: 1, 110, 10000, 10000111, and 00110.

1_2 is just $1*2^0$, or 1_{10}.

110_2 is $1*2^2 + 1*2^1 + 0*2^0$, or 6_{10}. We might think of this using the weights shown in Figure 1.12: $1*4 + 1*2 + 0*1$, or 6.

10000_2 is $1*16 + 0*8 + 0*4 + 0*2 + 0*1$, or 16_{10}.

10000111_2 is $1*128 + 1*4 + 1*2 + 1*1 = 135_{10}$. Notice this time that we didn't bother to write the weights having a 0 bit.

00110_2 is the same as 110_2 above — the leading 0's don't change the value.

1
2
4
8
16
32
64
128
256
512
1024
2048

Figure 1.14 Memorizing powers of two helps in working with binary.

When converting from binary to decimal, people often find it useful to be comfortable knowing the powers of two, shown in Figure 1.14, because each successive place to the left in a binary number is two times the previous place. In binary, the first, rightmost place is 1, the second place is 2, then 4, then 8, 16, 32, 64, 128, 256, 512, 1024, 2048, and so on. You might stop at this point to practice counting up by powers of two: 1, 2, 4, 8, 16, 32, 64, 128, 256, 512, 1024, 2048, etc., a few times. Now, when you see the number 10000111, you might move along the number from right to left and count up by powers of two for each bit to determine the weight of the leftmost bit: 1, 2, 4, 8, 16, 32, 64, *128*. The next highest 1 has a weight of (counting up again) 1, 2, *4*; adding 4 to 128 gives 132. The next 1 has a weight of 2; adding that to 132 gives 134. The rightmost 1 has a weight of 1; adding that to 134 gives 135. Thus, 10000111 equals 135 in base ten.

Being comfortable counting up in binary can also be helpful when working with binary. Counting up in binary goes as follows (using three digits): 000, 001, 010, 011, 100, 101, 110, 111. You might practice writing out this sequence several times to become more comfortable with it, doing so for four or even five digits also. Note that a binary number whose digits are all 1s has a base ten value exactly one less than the value of the next higher digit; for example, 111 is 7 in base ten, which is one less than 1000.

An interesting fact about binary numbers is that you can quickly determine whether a binary number is odd just by checking if the least-significant (i.e., rightmost) digit has a 1. If the rightmost digit is a 0, the number must be even, because the number is the sum of even numbers, as the only odd-weighted digit is the rightmost digit with a weight of 1.

Converting from Decimal to Binary Using the Addition Method
As seen earlier, converting a binary number to decimal is easy—just add the weights of each digit having a 1. Converting a decimal number to binary takes slightly more effort. One method for converting a decimal number to a binary number by hand is the *addition method*, in which we put a 1 in the highest place whose weight doesn't exceed the number, add that number to a sum, and repeat until the sum equals the desired number. For example, we can convert the decimal number 12 to binary as shown in Figure 1.15.

	Desired decimal number: **12**	Current sum	Binary number
(a)	16 > 12, too big; Put 0 in 16's place	0	0 ___ / 16 8 4 2 1
(b)	8 <= 12, so put 1 in 8's place, current sum is 8	8	0 1 ___ / 16 8 4 2 1
(c)	8+4=12 <= 12, so put 1 in 4's place, current sum is 12	12	0 1 1 ___ / 16 8 4 2 1
(d)	Reached desired 12, so put 0s in remaining places	done	0 1 1 0 0 / 16 8 4 2 1

Figure 1.15 Converting the decimal number 12 to binary using the addition method: (a) putting a 1 in place 16 would exceed 12, so we put a 0 there, (b) putting a 1 in place 8 gives us a sum of 8 so far, (c) putting a 1 in place 4 gives a sum of 8+4=12, the desired value, (d) because 12 has already been reached, we put 0s in the remaining places. The answer is thus 01100, or just 1100.

We can check our work by converting 1100 back to decimal: 1*8 + 1*4 + 0*2 + 0*2 = 12.

As another example, Figure 1.16 illustrates the addition method for converting the decimal number 23 to binary, using a more compact representation of the calculations. We can check our work by converting the result, 10111, back to decimal: 1*16 + 0*8 + 1*4 + 1*2 + 1*1 = 23.

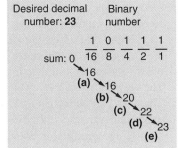

Figure 1.16 Decimal 23 to binary with the addition method: (a) 32 too big, put 1 in place 16, (b) 16+8=24 is too much, put 0 in place 8, (c) 16+4=20, (d) 20+2=22, (e) 22+1=23.

Example 1.3 Decimal to binary

Convert the following decimal numbers to binary using the addition method: 8, 14, 99.

To convert 8 to binary, we start by putting a 1 in the 8's place, yielding 1000 (putting 0s in the lower places not yet considered). The current sum is 8, so we are done—the answer is 1000.

To convert 14 to binary, we start by putting a 1 in the 8's place (16 is too much), yielding 1000 and a sum of 8. We put a 1 in the 4's place, yielding 1100 and a sum of 8+4=12. We put a 1 in the 2's place, yielding 1110, and a sum of 12+2=14, so we are done—the answer is 1110. We can check our work by converting back to decimal: 8 + 4 + 2 = 14.

To convert 99 to binary, we start by putting a 1 in the 64's place (the next higher place, 128, is too big—notice that being able to count by powers of two is quite handy in this problem), yielding 1000000 and a sum of 64. We put a 1 in the 32's place, yielding 1100000 and a sum of 64+32=96. Putting a 1 in the 16's place yield a sum of 96+16=112, which is too much, so we put a 0 in the 16's place. Likewise, we put 0s in the 8's place and the 4's place. Putting a 1 in the 2's place yields 1100010 and a sum of 96+2=98. Finally, we put a 1 in the 1's place, yielding the final answer of 1100011 and a sum of 98+1=99. We can check our work by converting back to decimal: 64 + 32 + 2 + 1 = 99.

Note that the addition method must be conducted starting from the highest weight place rather than starting from the lowest weight—in other words from left to right. Starting from the lowest weight, or from right to left, does not work. For example, for the decimal number 8, starting from the lowest weight would put a 1 in the 1's place, then a 1 in the 2's place yielding a sum of 3, and then a 1 in the 4's place yielding a sum of 7. Putting a 1 in the 8's place would then yield a sum of 15, which is too much, and thus the procedure would fail.

Example 1.4 Converting from decimal to binary to set a DIP-switch controlled channel

This example illustrates converting decimal to binary to configure a digital household appliance. A ceiling fan is a common household appliance that often comes with a remote controller that can be used to turn the fan on or off, as illustrated in Figure 1.17(a). All the fans and remote controllers may operate on the same wireless frequency. Because one house may have multiple such ceiling fans, a method is needed to prevent the remote controller of one fan from affecting another fan. A common method is to encode a channel number in the wireless signal, such that each ceiling-fan/remote-controller pair in a home shares a unique channel. When a ceiling fan's module detects the remote control wireless frequency, it checks whether the detected channel matches its own channel before responding. A common means for setting the channel is to use a DIP switch inside the remote controller and another DIP switch inside the ceiling fan module. An 8-pin DIP switch has eight switches that each can be either in an up or down position, and eight outputs that each will be either a 1 if its corresponding switch is up or a 0 if its switch is down. Thus, such a DIP switch can represent 2^8 = 256 distinct values.

Suppose the ceiling fan manufacturer wishes to set a particular ceiling-fan/remote-controller channel to 73. The manufacturer first converts 73 to binary, shown in Figure 1.17(b) to be 01001001. The manufacturer can then set the DIP switch inside the ceiling fan module, as well as inside the remote controller, to the up/down settings shown in Figure 1.17(c). Then, that ceiling fan module will only respond (by turning the fan on or off, in this case shown merely as setting its output to 1), if it detects the remote controller's frequency AND the encoded channel matches its DIP switch's value.

In case a homeowner happens to purchase two fan/controller pairs that are set to the same channel (the chances of which are 1 in 256), noticing this when one remote controller affects two fans, then the homeowner can remedy the problem without having to remove and exchange one of the fans.

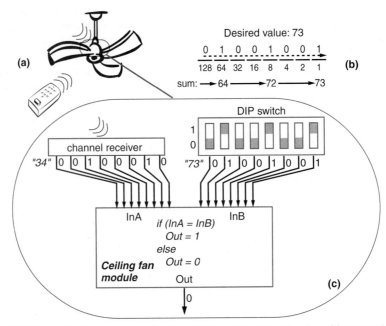

Figure 1.17 Decimal to binary conversion for a DIP switch: (a) ceiling fan with remote control, both having DIP switches to set their communication channel, (b) setting the fan's channel to "73" requires first converting 73 to binary, then setting the DIP switch to represent that binary value, (c) ceiling fan module only outputs 1 if the received channel matches DIP switch setting.

Instead, he/she can open the ceiling fan module and the remote controller of one pair, and simply change the DIP switch settings for that pair, ensuring that both DIP switches match after the change.

While this section introduced the addition method for converting from decimal to binary, many books and web resources introduce the **subtraction method**, wherein we start by setting a current number to the desired decimal number, put a 1 in the highest binary number place that doesn't exceed the current number, subtract that place's weight from the current number, and repeat until the current number reaches zero. The two methods are fundamentally the same; the addition method may be more intuitive when converting by hand.

Hexadecimal and Octal Numbers

Base sixteen numbers, known as **hexadecimal numbers** or just **hex**, are also popular in digital design, mainly because one base sixteen digit is equivalent to four base two digits, making hexadecimal numbers a nice shorthand representation for binary numbers. In base sixteen, the first digit represents up to fifteen ones—the sixteen symbols commonly used are 0, 1, 2, ..., 9, A, B, C, D, E, F (so A = ten, B = eleven, C = twelve, D = thirteen, E = fourteen, and F = fifteen). The next digit represents the number of groups of 16^1, the next digit the number of groups of 16^2, etc., as shown in Figure 1.18. So $8AF_{16}$ equals $8*16^2 + 10*16^1 + 15*16^0$, or 2223_{10}.

Because one digit in base 16 represents 16 values, and four digits in base two represents 16 values, then each digit in base 16 represents four digits in base two, as shown at the bottom of Figure 1.18. Thus, to convert $8AF_{16}$ to binary, we convert 8_{16} to 1000_2, A_{16} to 1010_2, and F_{16} to 1111_2, resulting in $8AF_{16} = 100010101111_2$. You can see why hexadecimal is a popular shorthand for binary: 8AF is a lot easier on the eye than 100010101111.

To convert a binary number to hexadecimal, we just substitute every four bits with the corresponding hexadecimal digit. Thus, to convert 101101101_2 to hex, we group the bits into groups of four starting from the right, yielding 1 0110 1101. We then replace each group of four bits with a single hex digit. 1101 is D, 0110 is 6, and 1 is 1, resulting in the hex number $16D_{16}$.

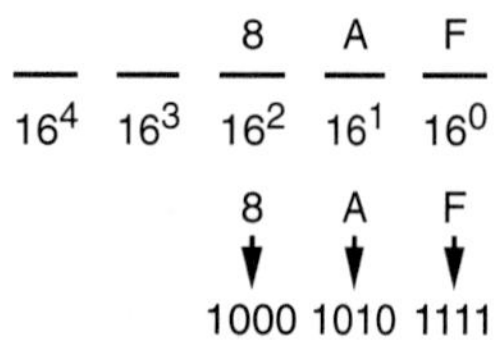

$$\frac{8}{16^4} \quad \frac{}{16^3} \quad \frac{8}{16^2} \quad \frac{A}{16^1} \quad \frac{F}{16^0}$$

$$\begin{array}{ccc} 8 & A & F \\ \downarrow & \downarrow & \downarrow \\ 1000 & 1010 & 1111 \end{array}$$

hex	binary	hex	binary
0	0000	8	1000
1	0001	9	1001
2	0010	A	1010
3	0011	B	1011
4	0100	C	1100
5	0101	D	1101
6	0110	E	1110
7	0111	F	1111

Figure 1.18 Base sixteen number system.

Example 1.5 Hexadecimal to/from binary

Convert the following hexadecimal numbers to binary: FF, 1011, A0000. You may find it useful to refer to Figure 1.18 to expand each hexadecimal digit to four bits.

FF_{16} is 1111 (for the left F) and 1111 (for the right F), or 11111111_2.

1011_{16} is 0001, 0000, 0001, 0001, or 0001000000010001_2. Don't be confused by the fact that 1011 didn't have any symbols but 1 and 0 (which makes the number look like a binary number). We said it was base 16, so it was. If we said it was base ten, then 1011 would equal one thousand and eleven.

$A0000_{16}$ is 1010, 0000, 0000, 0000, 0000, or 10100000000000000000_2.

Convert the following binary numbers to hexadecimal: 0010, 01111110, 111100.

0010_2 is 2_{16}.

01111110_2 is 0111 and 1110, meaning 7 and E, or $7E_{16}$. 111100_2 is 11 and 1100, which is 0011 and 1100, meaning 3 and C, or $3C_{16}$. Notice that we start grouping bits into groups of four from the right, not the left.

If a decimal number needs to be converted to hexadecimal, one can use the addition method. Sometimes, though, it is easier to first convert from decimal to binary using the addition method, and then converting from binary to hexadecimal by grouping sets of four bits.

Example 1.6 Decimal to hexadecimal

Convert 99 base 10 to base 16.

To perform this conversion, we can first convert 99 to binary and then convert the binary result to hexadecimal. Converting 99 to binary was done in Example 1.3, yielding `1100011`. Converting `1100011` to hexadecimal can be done by grouping sets of four bits (starting from the right), so `1100011` is `110` and `0011`, meaning 6 and 3, or 63_{16}. We can check our work by converting 63_{16} to decimal: $6*16^1 + 3*16^0 = 96 + 3 = 99$.

Example 1.7 RFID tag with identifier in hexadecimal

An RFID tag (radio frequency identification tag) is a chip that automatically responds to a radio signal by sending back a signal containing a unique identification number. RFID tags have been used since the 1990s with automobile toll transponders, dairy cows (as in Figure 1.19(a)), and dogs (in which the tag may be implanted under the skin). An RFID tag typically has an electronic circuit that uses the radio signal to power the chip, thus eliminating the need for a battery, decreasing the tag size, and increasing tag longevity.

In 2004, a Barcelona club began allowing customers to implant RFID tags under their skin to gain access to VIP lounges and to pay their bill. The U.S. F.D.A. approved human RFID implants in 2004. Source: www.theregister.co.uk

Figure 1.19(b) illustrates how the identifier in a cow tag might be structured as a 32-bit stored value where the first 8 bits correspond to a province (or state) number and the next 8 bits to a city number (thus representing the cow's birthplace), and the last 16 bits correspond to the animal's unique number. The device that wirelessly programs that identifier into the tag may require that the identifier be input in hex, even though the programming device will actually write `0`s and `1`s into the tag's 32-bit storage—typing 8 hex digits is less error-prone than typing 32 bits. Figure 1.19(c) provides sample desired values in decimal, Figure 1.19(d) shows those values converted to binary, and Figure 1.19(e) shows the binary values converted to hex. Finally, Figure 1.19(f) shows the 8-digit hex value that would be entered into the programming device, which would then program a specific tag with the corresponding 32-bit value. Once that value is programmed into the tag, the tag can be attached to the cow, and subsequently read countless times by an RFID reader, perhaps to help ensure that each cow is milked no more than once per day.

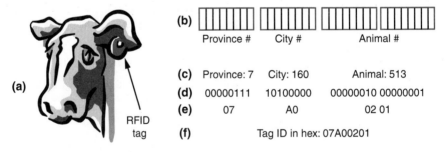

Figure 1.19 Hex used to configure RFID tag: (a) RFID tag attached to cow's ear, (b) 32-bit value inside tag stores unique identifier, the first 8 bits indicating a province number, the second 8 bits indicating a city number, and the remaining 16 bits being the animal's unique number, (c) sample values in decimal, (d) binary equivalents, (e) hex equivalents obtained from binary, (f) final 32-bit identifier in hex.

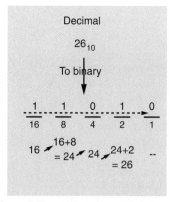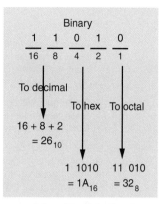

Figure 1.20 Methods for converting to binary and from binary by hand.

Base eight numbers, known as *octal numbers*, are sometimes used as a binary short-hand too, because one base eight digit equals three binary digits. 503_8 equals $5*8^2 + 0*8^1 +3*8^0 = 323_{10}$. We can convert 503_8 directly to binary simply by expanding each digit into three bits, resulting in 503_8 = 101 000 011, or 101000011_2. Likewise, we can convert binary to octal by grouping the binary number into groups of three bits starting from the right, and then replacing each group with the corresponding octal digit. Thus, 1011101_2 yields 1 011 101, or 135_8.

Figure 1.20 summarizes the methods for converting decimal to binary, and for converting binary to decimal, hex, or octal. Converting from decimal to hex or octal can be done by first converting to binary and then from binary to hex or octal. Converting from hex or octal to binary is a straightforward expansion of each digit to its four- or three-bit equivalent, respectively.

Automatic Conversion from Decimal to Binary Using the Divide-by-2 Method
The addition method is intuitive when converting from decimal to binary by hand, but if we wish to perform the conversion automatically with a computer program, another method, known as the divide-by-2 method, is well-suited. The *divide-by-2 method* involves repeatedly dividing the decimal number by 2; the remainder at each step, which will be either 0 or 1, becomes a bit in the binary number, starting from the least significant (rightmost) digit. For example, the process of converting the decimal number 12 to binary using the divide-by-2 method is shown in Figure 1.21.

Example 1.8 Decimal to binary using the divide-by-2 method

Convert the following numbers to binary using the divide-by-2 method: 8, 14, 99.

To convert 8 to binary, we start by dividing 8 by 2: 8/2=4, remainder 0. Then we divide the quotient, 4, by 2: 4/2=2, remainder 0. Then we divide 2 by 2: 2/2=1, remainder 0. Finally, we divide 1 by 2: 1/2=0, remainder 1. We stop dividing because the quotient is now 0. Combining all the remainders, least significant digit first, yields the binary number 1000. We can check this answer by multiplying each binary digit by its weight and adding the terms: $1*2^3 + 0*2^2 + 0*2^1 + 0*2^0 = 8$.

To convert 14 to binary, we follow a similar process: 14/2=7, remainder 0. 7/2=3, remainder 1. 3/2=1, remainder 1. 1/2=0, remainder 1. Combining the remainders gives us the binary number

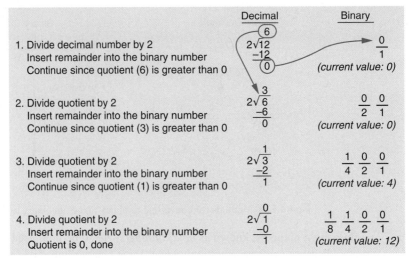

Figure 1.21 Converting the decimal number 12 to binary using the divide-by-2 method.

1110. Checking the answer shows that 1110 is correct: $1*2^3 + 1*2^2 + 1*2^1 + 0*2^0 = 8 + 4 + 2 + 0 = 14$.

To convert 99 to binary, the process is the same but naturally takes more steps: 99/2 = 49 remainder 1. 49/2 = 24, remainder 1. 24/2 = 12, remainder 0. 12/2 = 6, remainder 0. 6/2 = 3, remainder 0. 3/2 = 1, remainder 1. 1/2 = 0, remainder 1. Combining the remainders together gives us the binary number 1100011. We know from Example 1.3 that this is the correct answer.

We can use the same basic method to convert a base 10 number to a number in *any* base. To convert a number from base 10 to base *n*, we repeatedly divide the number by *n* and place the remainder in the new base *n* number, starting from the least significant digit. The method is called the ***divide-by-n method***.

Example 1.9 Decimal to arbitrary bases using the divide-by-*n* method

Convert the number 3439 to base 10 and to base 7.

We know the number 3439 is 3439 in base 10, but let's use the divide-by-*n* method (where *n* is 10) to illustrate that the method works for any base. We start by dividing 3439 by 10: 3439/10 = 343, remainder 9. We then divide the quotient by 10: 343/10 = 34, remainder 3. We do the same with the new quotient: 34/3 = 3, remainder 4. Finally, we divide 3 by 10: 3/10 = 0, remainder 3. Combining the remainders, least significant digit first, gives us the base 10 number 3439.

To convert 3439 to base 7, the approach is similar, except we now divide by 7. We begin by dividing 3439 by 7: 3439/7 = 491, remainder 2. Continuing our calculations, we get 491/7 = 70, remainder 1. 70/7 = 10, remainder 0. 10/7 = 1, remainder 3. 1/7 = 0, remainder 1. Thus, 3439 in base 7 is 13012. Checking the answer verifies that we have the correct result: $1*7^4 + 3*7^3 + 0*7^2 + 1*7^1 + 2*7^0 = 2401 + 1029 + 7 + 2 = 3439$.

Conversion between any two bases can be done by first converting to base ten, then converting the base ten number to the desired base using the divide-by-*n* method.

Bytes, Kilobytes, Megabytes, and More

When discussing bits, the term *byte* is commonly used to refer to a group of 8 bits. The term is used regardless of whether those bits encode a character, a binary number, an audio sample, or something else. Note that the term *byte* therefore just refers to the number of bits, not to a value in base two (in contrast to the term *hundred* in base ten, for example, which refers to a value).

Because digital systems often store large quantities of bits, metric prefixes like *kilo* (referring to a thousand, or 10^3), *mega* (million, or 10^6), *giga* (billion, or 10^9), and *tera* (trillion, or 10^{12}) are commonly used. Sometimes those prefixes are used when describing the number of bits. For example, a typical several minute song might be encoded as 24 megabits. More commonly, those prefixes are used when describing the number of bytes. So that same song would be encoded as 24/8 = 3 megabytes. A feature length movie might be encoded as about 2 gigabytes. A computer hard drive might have a capacity of 1 terabyte. Kilobytes, megabytes, gigabytes, and terabytes are commonly written as Kbytes or KB, Mbytes or MB, Gbytes or GB, and Tbytes or TB, respectively.

Seeking to solve the problem, the International Electrotechnical Commission (IEC) in 1999 introduced standard names, known as binary prefixes, for these power-of-two sizes: "kibi" for 1024 (2^{10}), "mebi" for 1,048,576 (2^{20}), then "gibi," "tebi," and more. Those prefixes haven't quite caught on yet.

Unfortunately, an inaccurate naming convention developed in digital system terminology. Quantities in digital systems, especially memory sizes, are often powers of two, such as 1024 (2^{10}), 2048 (2^{11}), or 4096 (2^{12}). Engineers began referring to 1024 as 1K, 2048 as 2K, 4096 as 4K, and so on. For example, one of the first personal computers was the Commodore 64, named due to its having $2^{16} = 65,536$ bytes of memory, or about 64 kilobytes of memory. This inaccurate use of metric prefixes is common today when referring to computer memory sizes, so a 1 megabyte memory actually has 1,048,576 (2^{20}) bytes rather than 1,000,000 bytes, and a 1 gigabyte memory actually has 1,073,741,824 (2^{30}) bytes rather than 1,000,000,000 bytes.

Another unfortunate convention is the use of Kb to represent kilobits, Mb for megabits, etc. Note the lower-case "b" to represents *bits*, in contast to the upper-case "B" to represent bytes as in KB or MB. The difference is easy to overlook.

In case you are curious, the metric prefixes that follow *tera* are *peta* (10^{15}), *exa* (10^{18}), *zetta* (10^{21}), and *yotta* (10^{24}). Do you think your computer will ever have a yotta-byte-sized hard drive?

Appendix A discusses number representations further.

▶ *INTERNET PROTOCOL (IP) ADDRESSES*

Internet domain names have an IP (Internet Protocol) address that is 32 bits long (for IPv4, the most common IP addressing used today). To aid in human readability, the 32 bits are divided into four bytes, and each byte is written as its decimal number equivalent, with each number separated by a period. You may have therefore seen an address like 192.168.1.1. That address in binary is 11000110 10101000 00000001 00000001 (spaces are added for readability; they don't exist in the actual binary address). Given a website's domain name, a web browser looks up the domain name's IP address and then contacts that address.

32 bits can represent 2^{32}, or about 4 billion, unique addresses, which you might imagine soon may not be sufficient for all the computers and sites on the Internet. The newer IPv6 therefore uses 128 bit addresses, and is slowly being adopted.

▶ 1.3 IMPLEMENTING DIGITAL SYSTEMS: MICROPROCESSORS VERSUS DIGITAL CIRCUITS

Designers can implement a digital system for an application by choosing one of two common digital system implementation methods—programming a microprocessor, or creating a custom digital circuit, which is known as digital design.

As an example of this choice, consider a simple application that turns on a lamp whenever there is motion in a dark room. Assume a motion detector has an output wire named *a* that outputs a 1 bit when motion is detected, and a 0 bit otherwise. Assume a light sensor has an output wire *b* that outputs a 1 bit when light is sensed, and a 0 bit otherwise. And assume a wire *F* turns on the lamp when *F* is 1, and turns off the lamp when 0. A drawing of the system is shown in Figure 1.22(a).

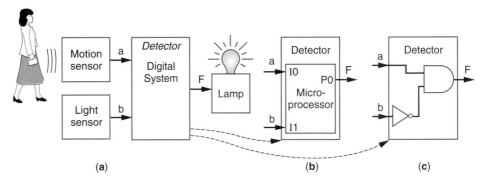

(a)　　　　　　　　　　　　**(b)**　　　　　　　**(c)**

Figure 1.22 Motion-in-the-dark-detector system: (a) system block diagram, (b) implementation using a microprocessor, (c) implementation using a custom digital circuit.

The design problem is to determine what to put inside the block named *Detector*. The *Detector* block takes wires *a* and *b* as inputs, and generates a value on *F*, such that the light should turn on when motion is detected when dark. The *Detector* application is readily implemented as a digital system, because the application's inputs and outputs obviously are digital, having only two possible values each. A designer can implement the *Detector* block by programming a microprocessor (Figure 1.22(b)) or by creating a custom digital circuit (Figure 1.22(c)).

Software on Microprocessors: The Digital Workhorse

Designers who work with digital phenomena commonly buy an off-the-shelf microprocessor and write software for that microprocessor, rather than design a custom digital circuit. Microprocessors are really the "workhorse" of digital systems, handling most digital processing tasks. A ***microprocessor*** is a programmable digital device that executes a user-specified sequence of instructions, known as a *program* or as *software*. Some of those instructions read the microprocessor's inputs, others write to the microprocessor's outputs, and other instructions perform computations on the input data.

A "processor" processes, or transforms, data. A "microprocessor" is a programmable processor implemented on a single computer chip—the "micro" just means small here. The term "microprocessor" became popular in the 1980s when processors shrank down from multiple chips to just one. The first single-chip microprocessor was the Intel 4004 chip in 1971.

Figure 1.23(a) illustrates a basic microprocessor with eight input pins named *I0, I1, ..., I7*, and eight output pins named *P0, P1, ..., P7*. A photograph of a microprocessor package with such pins is shown in Figure 1.23(b) (the ninth pin on this side is for power, and on the other side for ground).

A microprocessor-based solution to the motion-in-the-dark detector application is illustrated in Figure 1.22(b), and a photograph of a physical implementation is shown in Figure 1.24. The designer connects the a wire to the microprocessor input pin *I0*, the b wire to input pin *I1*, and output pin *P0* to the *F* wire. The designer could then specify the instructions for the microprocessor by writing the following C code:

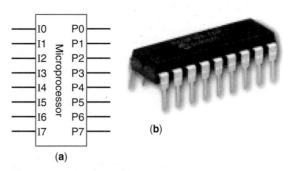

(a)   **(b)**

Figure 1.23 A basic microprocessor: (a) with eight outputs *P0-P7* that each can be set to a 0 or 1, and eight inputs *I0-I7* too, (b) photograph of a real microprocessor package.

```
void main()
{
    while (1) {
        P0 = I0 && !I1; // F = a and !b,
    }
}
```

C is one of several popular languages for describing the desired instructions to execute on the microprocessor. The above C code works as follows. The microprocessor, after being powered up and reset, executes the instructions within main's curly brackets { }. The first instruction is "while (1)" which means to forever repeat the instructions in the while's curly brackets. Inside those brackets is one instruction, "P0 = I0 && !I1," which assigns the microprocessor's output pin *P0* with a 1 if the input pin *I0* is 1 *and* (written as &&) the input pin *I1* is not 1 (meaning *I1* is 0). Thus, the output pin *P0*, which turns the lamp on or off, forever gets assigned the appropriate value based on the input pin values, which come from the motion and light sensors.

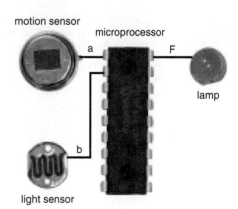

Figure 1.24 Physical motion-in-the-dark detector implementation using a microprocessor.

Figure 1.25 shows an example of the values of signals *a*, *b*, and *F* over time, with time proceeding to the right. As time proceeds, each signal may be either 0 or 1, illustrated by each signal's associated line being either low or high. We made *a* equal to 0 until time 7:05, when we made *a* become 1. We made *a* stay 1 until 7:06, when we made *a* return back to 0. We made *a* stay 0 until 9:00, when we made *a* become 1 again, and then we made *a* become 0 at 9:01. On the

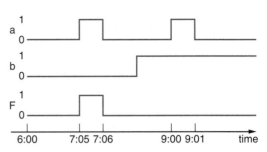

Figure 1.25 Timing diagram of motion-in-the-dark detector system.

other hand, we made *b* start as 0, and then become 1 between 7:06 and 9:00. The diagram shows what the value of *F* would be given the C program executing on the microprocessor—when *a* is 1 and *b* is 0 (from 7:05 to 7:06), *F* will be 1. A diagram with time proceeding to the right, and the values of digital signals shown by high or low lines, is known as a ***timing diagram***. We draw the input lines (*a* and *b*) to be whatever values we want, but then the output line (*F*) must describe the behavior of the digital system.

Example 1.10 Outdoor motion notifier using a microprocessor

Let's use the basic microprocessor of Figure 1.23 to implement a system that sounds a buzzer when motion is detected at any of three motion sensors outside a house. We connect the motion sensors to microprocessor input pins *I0*, *I1*, and *I2*, and connect output pin *P0* to a buzzer (Figure 1.26). (We assume the motion sensors and buzzers have appropriate electronic interfaces to the microprocessor pins.) We can then write the following C program:

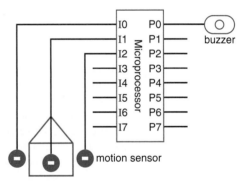

Figure 1.26 Motion sensors connected to microprocessor.

```
void main()
{
    while (1) {
        P0 = I0 || I1 || I2;
    }
}
```

The program executes the statement inside the while loop repeatedly. That statement will set *P0* to 1 if *I0* is 1 *or* (written as || in the C language) *I1* is 1 or *I2* is 1, otherwise the statement sets *P0* to 0.

Example 1.11 Counting the number of active motion sensors

This example uses the basic microprocessor of Figure 1.23 to implement a simple digital system that outputs in binary the number of motion sensors that presently detect motion. Assume two motion sensors, meaning a two-bit binary number will need to be output to represent the possible counts 0 (00), 1 (01), and 2 (10). The motion sensors are connected to microprocessor input pins *I0* and *I1*, and the binary number is output onto output pins *P1* and *P0*. We can write the following C program to achieve the desired behavior:

```c
void main()
{
    while (1) {
        if (!I0 && !I1) {
            P1 = 0; P0 = 0; // output 00, meaning zero
        }
        else if ( (I0 && !I1) || (!I0 && I1) ) {
            P1 = 0; P0 = 1; // output 01, meaning one
        }
        else if (I0 && I1) {
            P1 = 1; P0 = 0; // output 10, meaning two
        }
    }
}
```

Designers like to use microprocessors in their digital systems because microprocessors are readily available, inexpensive, easy to program, and easy to reprogram. It may surprise you to learn that you can buy certain microprocessor chips for under $1. Such microprocessors are found in places like telephone answering machines, microwave ovens, cars, toys, certain medical devices, and even in shoes with blinking lights. Examples include the 8051 (originally designed by Intel), the 68HC11 (made by Motorola), the PIC (made by MicroChip), and the AVR (made by Atmel). Other microprocessors may cost tens of dollars, found in places like cell phones, portable digital assistants, office automation equipment, and medical equipment. Such processors include the ARM (made by the ARM corporation),

Intel named their evolving 1980s/90s desktop processors using numbers: 80286, 80386, 80486. As PCs became popular, Intel switched to catchier names: the 80586 was called a Pentium ("penta" means 5), followed by the Pentium Pro, the Pentium II, Core 2 Due, and others. Eventually, the names dominated over the numbers.

Figure 1.27 Microprocessor chip packages: (a) PIC and 8051 microprocessors, costing about $1 each, (b) a Pentium processor with part of its package cover removed, showing the silicon chip inside.

the MIPS (made by the MIPS corporation), and others. Other microprocessors, like the well-known Pentium or Core 2 Quad processors from Intel, may cost several hundred dollars and may be found in desktop computers. Some microprocessors may cost several thousand dollars and are found in a mainframe computer running, perhaps, an airline reservation system. There are many hundreds of different microprocessor types available, differing in performance, cost, power, and other metrics. And many of the small low-power processors cost under $1.

Some readers of this book may be familiar with software programming of microprocessors, others may not. Knowledge of microprocessor programming is not essential to learning the material in this book. We will occasionally compare custom digital circuits with their corresponding microprocessor implementations—the conclusions of those comparisons can be understood without knowledge of programming itself.

Digital Design—When Microprocessors Aren't Good Enough

With a variety of microprocessors readily available, why would anyone ever need to design new digital circuits, other than those relatively few people designing microprocessor digital circuits themselves? The reason is that software running on a microprocessor isn't always good enough for a particular application. In many cases, software may be too slow. Microprocessors only execute one instruction or a few instructions at a time. But a custom digital circuit can execute hundreds or thousands of computations in parallel. Many applications, like picture or video compression, face recognition, voice command detection, or graphics display, require huge numbers of computations to be done in a short period of time in order to be practical—after all, who wants a voice-controlled phone that requires 5 minutes to decode your voice command, or a digital camera that requires 15 minutes to take each picture? In other cases, microprocessors are too big, or consume too much power, or would be too costly, thus making custom digital circuits preferable.

For the motion-in-the-dark-detector application, an alternative to the microprocessor-based design uses a custom digital circuit inside the *Detector* block. A ***circuit*** is an interconnection of electric components. We must design a circuit that, for each different combination of inputs *a* and *b*, generates the proper value on *F*. One such circuit is shown in Figure 1.22(c). We'll describe the components in that circuit later; briefly, the triangular component inverts the value on *b*, and the bullet-shaped component outputs a 1 only if both its inputs are 1, so *F* will be 1 only if *a* is 1 and *b* is 0. But you've now seen one simple example of designing a digital circuit to solve a design problem. A microprocessor also has a circuit inside, but because that circuit is designed to execute programs rather than just detect motion at night, a small microprocessor's circuit may contain about ten thousand components, compared to just two components in our custom digital circuit of Figure 1.22(c). Thus, our custom digital circuit may be smaller, cheaper, and faster, and consume less power than an implementation on a microprocessor.

Example 1.12 Deciding among a microprocessor and custom digital circuit

We are asked to design a digital system to control a fighter jet's aircraft wing. In order to properly control the aircraft, the digital system must execute a computation task 100 times per second that adjusts the wing's position based on the aircraft's present and desired speeds, pitch, yaw, and other flight factors. Suppose we estimate that software on a microprocessor would require 50 ms (milliseconds) for each execution of the computation task, whereas a custom digital circuit would require 5 ms per execution.

Executing the computation task 100 times on the microprocessor would require 100 * 50 ms = 5000 ms, or 5 seconds. But we require those 100 executions to be done in 1 second, so the microprocessor is not fast enough. Executing the task 100 times with the custom digital circuit would require 100 * 5 ms = 500 ms, or 0.5 seconds. As 0.5 seconds is less than 1 second, the custom digital circuit can satisfy the system's performance constraint. We thus choose to implement the digital system as a custom digital circuit rather than by using a microprocessor.

Many applications use both microprocessors and custom digital circuits to attain a system that achieves just the right balance of performance, cost, power, size, design time, flexibility, etc.

Example 1.13 Partitioning tasks in a digital camera

A digital camera captures pictures digitally using several steps. When the shutter button is pressed, a grid of a few million light-sensitive electronic elements capture the image, each element storing a binary number (perhaps 16 bits) representing the intensity of light hitting the element. The camera then performs several tasks: the camera *reads* the bits of each of these elements, *compresses* the tens of millions of bits into perhaps a few million bits, and *stores* the compressed bits as a file in the camera's flash memory, among other tasks. Table 1.2 provides sample task execution times running on an inexpensive low-power microprocessor versus executing as a custom digital circuit.

Table 1.2 Sample digital camera task execution times (in seconds) on a microprocessor versus a digital circuit.

Task	Microprocessor	Custom digital circuit
Read	5 s	0.1 s
Compress	8 s	0.5 s
Store	1 s	0.8 s

We need to decide which tasks to implement on the microprocessor and which to implement as a custom digital circuit, subject to the constraint that we should strive to minimize the amount of custom digital circuitry in order to reduce chip costs. Such decisions are known as ***partitioning***. Three partitioning options are shown in Figure 1.28. If we implement all three tasks on the microprocessor, the camera will require 5 + 8 + 1 = 14 seconds to take a picture—too much time for the camera to be popular with consumers. We could implement all the tasks as custom digital circuits, resulting in 0.1 + 0.5 + 0.8 = 1.4 seconds. We could instead implement the read and compress tasks

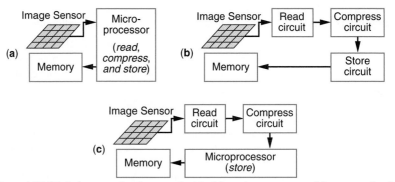

Figure 1.28 Digital camera implemented with: (a) a microprocessor, (b) custom circuits, and (c) a combination of custom circuits and a microprocessor.

with custom digital circuits, while leaving the store task to the microprocessor, resulting in 0.1 + 0.5 + 1, or 1.6 seconds.

We might decide on this last implementation option, to save cost without much noticeable time overhead.

▶ 1.4 ABOUT THIS BOOK

Section 1.1 discussed how digital systems now appear nearly everywhere and significantly impact the way we live. Section 1.2 highlighted how learning digital design accomplishes two goals: showing us how microprocessors work "under the hood," and enabling us to implement systems using custom digital circuits instead of (or along with) microprocessors to achieve better implementations. This latter goal is becoming increasingly significant since so many analog phenomena, like music and video, are becoming digital. That section also introduced a key method of digitizing analog signals, namely binary numbers, and described how to convert between decimal and binary numbers, as well as between numbers of any two bases. Section 1.3 described how designers may prefer to implement digital systems by writing software that executes on a microprocessor, yet designers often use custom digital circuits to meet an application's performance requirements or other requirements.

In the remainder of this book you will learn about the exciting and challenging field of digital design, wherein we convert desired system functionality into a custom digital circuit. Chapter 2 will introduce the most basic form of digital circuit, combinational circuits, whose outputs are each a function of the present values on the circuit's inputs. That chapter will show how to use a form of math called Boolean algebra to describe our desired circuit functionality, and will provide clear steps for converting Boolean equations to circuits. Chapter 3 will introduce a more advanced type of circuit, sequential circuits, whose outputs are a function not only of the present input values, but also of previous input values—in other words, sequential circuits have memory. Such circuits are commonly referred to as controllers. That chapter will show us how to use another mathematical abstraction, known as a finite-state machine, to represent desired sequential functionality, and will provide clear steps for converting finite-state machines to circuits. As with any form of design, we often use pre-designed building blocks, or components, to make our design task easier. Chapter 4 describes several such components, known as datapath components, including registers (for storing digital data), adders, comparators, multipliers, and small memories called register files, among other blocks. Chapter 5 introduces the modern approach to digital design, known as register-transfer level design, wherein we design systems consisting of datapath components controlled by controllers, to implement interesting and useful custom digital circuits. In fact, that chapter shows how to convert a C program to a custom digital circuit—clearly demonstrating that any desired function can be implemented as software on a microprocessor or as a custom digital circuit. That chapter also introduces some additional components, including ROM and RAM memories, and queues. Chapters 1 through 5 form the core of this book—after those five chapters, the reader can specify a wide variety of desired functionality and can convert that functionality to a working custom digital circuit.

Chapter 6 introduces methods for designing *better* digital circuits. The chapter describes methods for improving basic combinational circuits, basic sequential circuits, datapath components, and register-transfer level designs. That chapter emphasizes the important notion of *tradeoffs*, wherein we might make one aspect of the design better, but at the expense of worsening another aspect. Tradeoffs are the essence of design.

Chapter 7 describes different physical devices on which we can implement our digital circuits, including application-specific integrated circuits, field-programmable gate-arrays (FPGAs), simple programmable logic devices, and cheap off-the-shelf ICs.

Chapter 8 applies the digital design methods of earlier chapters to build a common type of digital circuit—a programmable microprocessor. The chapter demystifies the workings of a microprocessor, using a very simple design to illustrate the concepts.

Chapter 9 introduces hardware description languages, which are widely used in modern digital design for describing desired circuit functionality as well as for representing the final custom digital circuit design. Hardware description languages, looking much like software programming languages but with important extensions and differences, serve as the input to most modern digital design tools.

▶ 1.5 EXERCISES

SECTION 1.2: THE WORLD OF DIGITAL SYSTEMS

1.1 What is a digital signal, and how does it differ from an analog signal? Give two everyday examples of digital phenomena (e.g., a window can be open or closed) and two everyday examples of analog phenomena.

1.2 Suppose an analog audio signal comes in over a wire, and the voltage on the wire can range from 0 Volts (V) to 3 V. You want to convert the analog signal to a digital signal. You decide to encode each sample using two bits, such that 0 V would be encoded as 00, 1 V as 01, 2 V as 10, and 3 V as 11. You sample the signal every 1 millisecond and detect the following sequence of voltages: 0V 0V 1V 2V 3V 2V 1V. Show the signal converted to digital as a stream of 0s and 1s.

1.3 Assume that 0 V is encoded as 00, 1 V as 01, 2 V as 10, and 3 V as 11. You are given a digital encoding of an audio signal as follows: 1111101001010000. Plot the re-created analog signal with time on the *x*-axis and voltage on the *y*-axis. Assume that each encoding's corresponding voltage should be output for 1 millisecond.

1.4 Assume that a signal is encoded using 12 bits. Assume that many of the encodings turn out to be either 000000000000, 000000000001, or 111111111111. We thus decide to create compressed encodings by representing 000000000000 as 00, 000000000001 as 01, and 111111111111 as 10. 11 means that an uncompressed encoding follows. Using this encoding scheme, decompress the following encoded stream:

00 00 01 10 11 010101010101 00 00 10 10

1.5 Using the same encoding scheme as in Exercise 1.4, compress the following unencoded stream:

000000000000 000000000001 100000000000 111111111111

1.6 Encode the following words into bits using the ASCII encoding table in Figure 1.9.
(a) LET
(b) RESET!
(c) HELLO $1

1.7 Suppose you are building a keypad that has buttons A through G. A three-bit output should indicate which button is currently being pressed. 000 represents no button being pressed. Decide on a 3-bit encoding to represent each button being pressed.

1.8 Convert the following binary numbers to decimal numbers:
(a) 100
(b) 1011
(c) 0000000000001
(d) 111111
(e) 101010

1.9 Convert the following binary numbers to decimal numbers:
(a) 1010
(b) 1000000
(c) 11001100
(d) 11111
(e) 10111011001

1.10 Convert the following binary numbers to decimal numbers:
(a) 000011
(b) 1111
(c) 11110
(d) 111100
(e) 0011010

1.11 Convert the following decimal numbers to binary numbers using the addition method:
(a) 9
(b) 15
(c) 32
(d) 140

1.12 Convert the following decimal numbers to binary numbers using the addition method:
(a) 19
(b) 30
(c) 64
(d) 128

1.13 Convert the following decimal numbers to binary numbers using the addition method:
  (a) 3
  (b) 65
  (c) 90
  (d) 100

1.14 Convert the following decimal numbers to binary numbers using the divide-by-2 method:
  (a) 9
  (b) 15
  (c) 32
  (d) 140

1.15 Convert the following decimal numbers to binary numbers using the divide-by-2 method:
  (a) 19
  (b) 30
  (c) 64
  (d) 128

1.16 Convert the following decimal numbers to binary numbers using the divide-by-2 method:
  (a) 3
  (b) 65
  (c) 90
  (d) 100

1.17 Convert the following decimal numbers to binary numbers using the divide-by-2 method:
  (a) 23
  (b) 87
  (c) 123
  (d) 101

1.18 Convert the following binary numbers to hexadecimal:
  (a) 11110000
  (b) 11111111
  (c) 01011010
  (d) 1001101101101

1.19 Convert the following binary numbers to hexadecimal:
  (a) 11001101
  (b) 10100101
  (c) 11110001
  (d) 1101101111100

1.20 Convert the following binary numbers to hexadecimal:
  (a) 11100111
  (b) 11001000
  (c) 10100100
  (d) 011001101101101

1.21 Convert the following hexadecimal numbers to binary:
  (a) FF
  (b) F0A2
  (c) 0F100
  (d) 100

1.22 Convert the following hexadecimal numbers to binary:
  (a) 4F5E
  (b) 3FAD
  (c) 3E2A
  (d) DEED

1.23 Convert the following hexadecimal numbers to binary:
  (a) B0C4
  (b) 1EF03
  (c) F002
  (d) BEEF

1.24 Convert the following hexadecimal numbers to decimal:
  (a) FF
  (b) F0A2
  (c) 0F100
  (d) 100

1.25 Convert the following hexadecimal numbers to decimal:
  (a) 10
  (b) 4E3
  (c) FF0
  (d) 200

1.26 Convert the decimal number 128 to the following number systems:
  (a) binary
  (b) hexadecimal
  (c) base three
  (d) base five
  (e) base fifteen

1.27 Compare the number of digits necessary to represent the following decimal numbers in binary, octal, decimal, and hexadecimal representations. You need not determine the actual representations—just the number of required digits. For example, representing the decimal number 12 requires four digits in binary (1100 is the actual representation), two digits in octal (14), two digits in decimal (12), and one digit in hexadecimal (C).
  (a) 8
  (b) 60
  (c) 300
  (d) 1000
  (e) 999,999

1.28 Determine the decimal number ranges that can be represented in binary, octal, decimal, and hexadecimal using the following numbers of digits. For example, 2 digits can represent decimal number range 0 through 3 in binary (00 through 11), 0 through 63 in octal (00 through 77), 0 through 99 in decimal (00 through 99), and 0 through 255 in hexadecimal (00 through FF).
  (a) 1
  (b) 3
  (c) 6
  (d) 8

1.29 Rewrite the following bit quantities as byte quantities, using the most appropriate metric quantity; e.g., 16,000 bits is 2,000 bytes, most appropriately written as 2 Kbytes.
   (a) 8,000,000
   (b) 32,000,000,000
   (c) 1,000,000,000

SECTION 1.3: IMPLEMENTING DIGITAL SYSTEMS: PROGRAMMING MICROPROCESSORS VERSUS DESIGNING DIGITAL CIRCUITS

1.30 Use a microprocessor like that in Figure 1.23 to implement a system that sounds an alarm whenever there is motion detected at the same time in three different rooms. Each room's motion sensor is an input to the microprocessor; a 1 means motion, a 0 means no motion. The microprocessor can sound the alarm by setting an output wire "alarm" to 1. Show the connections to and from the microprocessor, and the C code to execute on the microprocessor. Hint: this problem is similar to Example 1.10.

1.31 A security camera company wishes to add a face recognition feature to their cameras such that the camera only broadcasts video when a human face is detected in the video. The camera records 30 video frames per second. For each frame, the camera would execute a face recognition application. The application implemented on a microprocessor requires 50 ms. The application implemented as a custom digital circuit requires 1 ms. Compute the maximum number of frames per second that each implementation supports, and indicate which implementation is sufficient for 30 frames per second.

1.32 Suppose that a particular banking system supports encrypted transactions, and that decrypting each transaction consists of three sub-tasks A, B, and C. The execution times of each task on a microprocessor versus a custom digital circuit are 50 ms versus 1 ms for A, 20 ms versus 2 ms for B, and 20 ms versus 1 ms for C. Partition the tasks among the microprocessor and custom digital circuitry, such that you minimize the amount of custom digital circuitry, while meeting the constraint of decrypting at least 40 transactions per second. Assume that each task requires the same amount of digital circuitry.

1.33 How many possible partitionings are there of a set of N tasks, where each task can be implemented either on a microprocessor or as a custom digital circuit? How many possible partitionings are there of a set of 20 tasks (expressed as a number without any exponents)?

Kelly first became interested in engineering while attending a talk about engineering at a career fair in high school. "I was dazzled by the interesting ideas and the cool graphs." While in college, though, she learned that "there was much more to engineering than ideas and graphs. Engineers *apply* their ideas and skills to build things that really make a difference in people's lives, for generations to come."

In her first few years as an engineer, Kelly has worked on a variety of projects that may help numerous individuals. One project was a ventilator system like the one mentioned earlier in this chapter. "We designed a new control system that may enable people on ventilators to breathe with more comfort while still getting the proper amount of oxygen." In addition, she examined alternative implementations of that control system, including on a microprocessor, as a custom digital circuit, and as a combination of the two. "Today's technologies, like FPGAs, provide so many different options. We examined several options to see what the tradeoffs were among them. Understanding the tradeoffs among the options is quite important if we want to build the best system possible."

She also worked on a project that developed small self-explanatory electronic blocks that people could connect together to build useful electronic systems involving almost any kind of sensor, like motion or light sensors. "Those blocks could be used by kids to learn basic concepts of logic and computers, concepts which are quite important to learn these days. Our hope is that these blocks will be used as teaching tools in schools. The blocks can also be used to help adults set up useful systems in their homes, perhaps to monitor an aging parent, or a child at home sick. The potential for these blocks is great—it will be interesting to see what impact they have.

"My favorite thing about engineering is the variety of skills and creativity involved. We are faced with problems that need to be solved, and we solve them by applying known techniques in creative ways. Engineers must continually learn new technologies, hear new ideas, and track current products, in order to be good designers. It's all very exciting and challenging. Each day at work is different. Each day is exciting and is a learning experience.

"Studying to be an engineer can be a great deal of work, but it's worth it. The key is to stay focused, to keep your mind open, and to make good use of available resources. Staying focused means to keep your priorities in order—for example, as a student, studying comes first, recreation second. Keeping your mind open means to always be willing to listen to different ideas and to learn about new technologies. Making good use of resources means to aggressively seek information, from the Internet, from colleagues, from books, and so on. You never know where you are going to get your next important bit of information, and you won't get that information unless you seek it."

CHAPTER 2

Combinational Logic Design

▶ 2.1 INTRODUCTION

A digital circuit whose output value depends solely on the *present combination of the circuit inputs' values* is called a **combinational circuit**. For example, Figure 2.1(a) shows a doorbell system; if the button is pressed, the bell sounds. Figure 2.1(b) shows a motion-in-the-dark lamp; if there is motion and it is dark, the lamp turns on. In contrast, in a *sequential* circuit, the output value depends on the present *and past* input values, such as the toggle lamp in Figure 2.1(c); pressing the button turns the lamp on, which stays on even after the button is released. Pressing the button again would turn the lamp off.

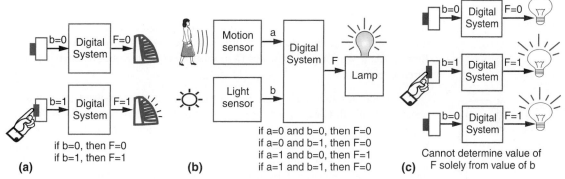

Figure 2.1 Combinational systems like (a) and (b) are such that the output value can be determined solely from the present input values. In contrast, a sequential system as in (c) has some internal "memory" that also impacts the output.

Combinational circuits are a basic class of digital circuits that are able to implement some systems, but that importantly make up part of more complex circuits. This chapter introduces the basic building blocks of combinational circuits, known as logic gates, and also introduces a form of mathematics known as Boolean algebra that is useful for working with combinational circuits. The chapter will describe a process for designing basic combinational circuits, wherein a designer first captures the desired circuit behavior, and then converts that behavior into a circuit of logic gates. Chapter 3 will introduce sequential circuits and a process for their design, and Chapter 4 will describe more complex combinational components.

▶ 2.2 SWITCHES

Electronic switches form the basis of all digital circuits, so make a good starting point for the discussion of digital circuits. You use a type of switch, a light switch, whenever you turn lights on or off. To understand a switch, it helps to understand some basic electronics.

Electronics 101

You're probably familiar with the idea of electrons, or let's just say charged particles, flowing through wires and causing lights to illuminate or stereos to blast music. An analogous situation is water flowing through pipes and causing sprinklers to pop up or turbines to turn. We now describe three basic electrical terms:

Although understanding the electronics underlying digital logic gates is optional, many people find that a basic understanding satisfies much curiosity and also helps in understanding some of the non-ideal digital gate behavior later on.

- *Voltage* is the difference in electric potential between two points. Voltage is measured in volts (V). Convention says that the earth, or *ground*, is 0 V. Informally, voltage tells us how "eager" the charged particles on one side of a wire are to get to ground (or any lower voltage) on the wire's other side. Voltage is analogous to the pressure of water trying to flow through a pipe—water under higher pressure is more eager to flow, even if the water can't actually flow, perhaps because of a closed faucet.

- *Current* is a measure of the flow of charged particles. Informally, current indicates the rate that particles are actually flowing. Current is analogous to the volume of water flowing through a pipe. Current is measured in amperes (A), or amps for short.

- *Resistance* is the tendency of a wire (or anything, really) to resist the flow of current. Resistance is analogous to a pipe's diameter—a narrow pipe resists water flow, while a wide pipe lets water flow more freely. Electrical resistance is measured in ohms (Ω).

Consider a battery. The particles at the positive terminal want to flow to the negative terminal. How "eager" are they to flow? That depends on the voltage difference between the terminals—a 9 V battery's particles are more eager to flow than a 1.5 V battery's particles, because the 9 V battery's particles have more potential energy. Now suppose you connect the positive terminal through a light bulb back to the negative terminal as shown in Figure 2.2. The 9 V battery will result in more current flowing, and thus a brighter lit light, than the 1.5 V battery. Precisely how much current will flow is determined using the equation

$$V = IR \text{ (known as Ohm's Law)}$$

where V is voltage, I is current, and R is resistance (in this case, of the light bulb). So if the resistance were 2 ohms, a 9 V battery would result in 4.5 A (since $9 = I*2$) of current, while a 1.5 V battery would result in 0.75 A.

Rewriting the equation as $I = V/R$ might make more intuitive sense—the higher the voltage, the more current; the higher the resistance, the less current. Ohm's Law is perhaps the most fundamental equation in electronics.

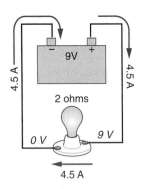

Figure 2.2 9V battery connected to a light bulb.

The Amazing Shrinking Switch

Now back to switches. Figure 2.3(b) shows that a switch has three parts—let's call them the source input, the output, and the control input. The source input has higher voltage than the output, so current tries to flow from the source input through the switch to the output. The whole purpose of a switch is to block that current when the control sets the switch "off," and to allow that current to flow when control sets the switch "on." For example, when you flip a light switch up to turn the switch on, the switch causes the source input wire to physically touch the output wire, so current flows. When you flip the switch down to turn the switch off, the switch physically separates the source input from the output. In our water analogy, the control input is like a faucet valve that determines whether water flows through a pipe.

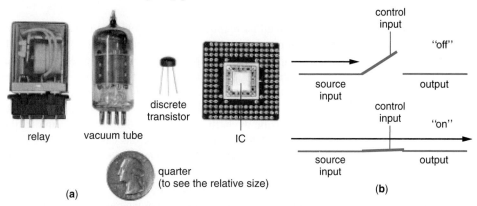

Figure 2.3 Switches: (a) Evolution, starting with relays (1930s), then vacuum tubes (1940s), discrete transistors (1950s), and integrated circuits (ICs) containing transistors (1960s–present). ICs originally held about ten transistors; now they can hold several billion. (b) Simple view of a switch.

Switches are what cause digital circuits to utilize binary numbers made from bits—the on or off nature of a switch corresponds to the 1s and 0s in binary. We now discuss the evolution of switches over the 1900s, leading up to the CMOS transistor switches commonly used today in digital circuits.

1930s—Relays

Engineers in the 1930s tried to devise ways to compute using electronically controlled switches—switches whose control input was another voltage. One such switch, an electro-magnetic relay like that in Figure 2.3(a), was already being used by the telephone industry for switching telephone calls. A relay has a control input that is a type of magnet, which becomes magnetized when the control has a positive voltage. In one type of relay, that magnet pulls a piece of metal down, resulting in a connection from the source input to the output—akin to pulling down a drawbridge to connect one road to another. When the control input returns to 0 V, the piece of metal returns up again (perhaps pushed by a small spring), disconnecting the source input from the output. In telephone systems, relays enabled calls to be routed from one phone to another, without the need for those nice human operators that previously would manually connect one phone's line to another.

▶ *"DEBUGGING"*

In 1945, a moth got stuck in one of the relays of the Mark II computer at Harvard. To get the computer working properly again, technicians found and removed the bug. Though the term "bug" had been used for decades before by engineers to indicate a defect in mechanical or electrical equipment, the removal of that moth in 1945 is considered to be the origin of the term "debugging" in computer programming. Technicians taped that moth to their written log (shown in the picture to the right), and that moth is now on display at the National Museum of American History in Washington, D.C.

1940s—Vacuum Tubes

Relays relied on metal parts moving up and down, and thus were slow. In the 1940s and 1950s, vacuum tubes, which were originally used to amplify weak electric signals like those in a telegraph, began to replace relays in computers. A vacuum tube, shown in Figure 2.3(a), is similar in design to a light bulb. In a light bulb, electrons flow through a filament in a vacuum inside the bulb, causing the filament to become hot and emit light—but not burn due to the lack of oxygen in the vacuum. In a vacuum tube, an extra terminal is added inside the bulb, separated by the vacuum from the filament. If a positive voltage is applied at that terminal, then electrons can flow from the filament to the extra terminal through the vacuum; i.e., a positive voltage at the extra terminal causes a "connection" between the filament and the extra terminal. Vacuum tubes had no moving parts, so the tubes were much faster than relays.

The machine said to be the world's first general-purpose computer, the ENIAC (electronic numerical integrator and computer), was completed in the U.S. in 1946. ENIAC contained about 18,000 vacuum tubes and 1500 relays, weighed over 30 tons, was 100 feet long and 8 feet high (so it likely would not fit in any room of your house, unless you have an absurdly big house), and consumed 174,000 watts of power. Imagine the heat generated by a room full of 1740 100-watt light bulbs. That's hot. For all that, ENIAC could compute about 5000 operations per second—compare that to the billions of operations per second of today's personal computers, and even the tens of millions of computations per second by a handheld cell phone.

Although vacuum tubes were faster than relays, they consumed a lot of power, generated a lot of heat, and failed frequently.

Vacuum tubes were commonplace in many electronic appliances in the 1960s and 1970s. I remember taking trips to the store with my dad in the early 1970s to buy replacement tubes for our television set. Vacuum tubes still live today in a few electronic devices. One place you might still find tubes is in electric guitar amplifiers, where the tube's unique-sounding audio amplification is still demanded by rock guitar enthusiasts who want their versions of classic rock songs to sound just like the originals.

1950s—Discrete Transistors

The invention of the transistor in 1947, credited to William Shockley, John Bardeen, and Walter Brattain of Bell Laboratories (the research arm of AT&T), resulted in smaller and lower-power computers. A solid-state (discrete) transistor, shown in Figure 2.3(a), uses a small piece of silicon, "doped" with some extra materials, to create a switch. Since these switches used "solid" materials rather than a vacuum or even moving parts in a relay, they were commonly referred to as solid-state transistors. Solid-state transistors were smaller, cheaper, faster, and more reliable than tubes, and became the dominant computer switch in the 1950s and 1960s.

1960s—Integrated Circuits

Jack Kilby of Texas Instruments and Robert Noyce of Fairchild Semiconductors are often credited with each having independently invented the IC.

The invention of the *integrated circuit (IC)* in 1958 revolutionized computing. An IC, a.k.a. a chip, packs numerous tiny transistors on a fingernail-sized piece of silicon. So instead of 10 transistors requiring 10 discrete electronic components on a board, 10 transistors can be implemented on one component, the chip. Figure 2.3(a) shows a picture of an IC having a few million transistors. Though early ICs featured only tens of transistors, improvements in IC technology have resulted in *several billion* transistors on a chip today. IC technology has shrunk transistors down to a totally different scale. A vacuum tube (about 100 mm long) is to a modern IC transistor (about 100 nm) as a skyscraper (about 0.5 km) is to the thickness of a credit card (about 0.5 mm).

I've been working in this field for two decades, and the amount of transistors on a chip still amazes me. The number 1 billion is bigger than most of us have an intuitive feel for. Consider the volume that 1 billion pennies would occupy. Would they fit in your bedroom? The answer is probably no, as a typical bedroom is about 40 cubic meters, while 1 billion pennies would occupy about 400 cubic meters. So a billion pennies would occupy about 10 bedrooms, roughly the size of a house, packed from wall to wall, floor to ceiling. If we stacked the pennies, they would reach nearly 1000 miles into the sky—for comparison, a jet flies at an altitude of about 5 miles. But we manage to fit 1 billion transistors onto silicon chips of just a few square centimeters. Truly amazing. The wires that connect all those transistors on a chip, if straightened into one straight wire, would be several miles long.

IC transistors are smaller, more reliable, faster, and less power-hungry than discrete transistors. IC transistors are now by far the most commonly used switch in computing.

ICs of the early 1960s could hold tens of transistors, and are known today as small-scale integration (*SSI*). As transistor sizes shrank, in the late 1960s and early 1970s, ICs could hold hundreds of transistors, known as medium-scale integration (*MSI*). The 1970s saw the development of large-scale integration (*LSI*) ICs with thousands of transistors, while very large-scale integration (*VLSI*) chips evolved in the 1980s. Since then, ICs have continued to increase in their capacity, to several billion transistors. To calibrate your understanding of this number, a processor in a 2009 laptop computer, like an Intel

---

► *A SIGNIFICANT INVENTION*

We now know that the invention of the transistor was the start of the amazing computation and communication revolutions that occurred in the latter half of the 20th century, enabling us today to do things like see the world on TV, surf the web, and talk on cell phones. But the implications of the transistor were not known by most people at the time of its invention. Newspapers did not headline the news, and most stories that did appear predicted simply that transistors would improve things like radios and hearing aids. One may wonder what recently invented but unnoticed technology might significantly change the world once again.

▶ *HOW TRANSISTORS ARE MADE SO SMALL—USING PHOTOGRAPHIC METHODS*

If you took a pencil and made the smallest dot that you could on a sheet of paper, that dot's area would hold many thousands of transistors on a modern silicon chip. How can chip makers create such tiny transistors? The key lies in photographic methods. Chip makers lay a special chemical onto the chip—special because the chemical changes when exposed to light. Chip makers then shine light through a lens that focuses the light down to extremely small regions on the chip—similar to how a microscope's lens lets us see tiny things by focusing light, but in reverse. The chemical in the small illuminated region changes, and then a solvent washes away the chemical—but some regions stay because of the light that changed that region. Those remaining regions form parts of transistors. Repeating this process over and over again, with different chemicals at different steps, results not only in transistors, but also wires connecting the transistors, and insulators preventing crossing wires from touching.

Photograph of a Pentium processor's silicon chip, having millions of transistors. Actual size is about 1 cm each side.

Atom or Celeron processor, requires only about 50 million transistors, and the processor in a cell phone, like an ARM processor, may have only a few million transistors. Many of today's high-end chips, like chips inside Internet routers, contain tens or hundreds of such microprocessors, and can conceivably contain thousands of even smaller microprocessors (or just a few very big microprocessors).

IC density has been doubling roughly every 18 months since the 1960s. The doubling of IC density every 18 months is widely known as *Moore's Law*, named after Gordon Moore, a co-founder of Intel Corporation, who made predictions back in 1965 that the number of components per IC would double every year or so. At some point, chip makers won't be able to shrink transistors any further. After all, the transistor has to at least be wide enough to let electrons pass through. People have been predicting the end of Moore's Law for two decades now, but transistors keep shrinking, though in 2009 many observers noted a slowdown.

Not only do smaller transistors and wires provide for more functionality in a chip, but they also provide for faster circuits, in part because electrons need not travel as far to get from one transistor to the next. This increased speed is the main reason why personal computer clock speeds have improved so drastically over the past few decades, from kilohertz frequencies in the 1970s to gigahertz frequencies in the 2000s.

▶ 2.3 THE CMOS TRANSISTOR

The most popular type of IC transistor is the CMOS transistor. A detailed explanation of how a CMOS transistor works is beyond the scope of this book, but nevertheless a simplified explanation may satisfy much curiosity.

A chip is made primarily from the element silicon. A chip, also known as an integrated circuit, or IC, is typically about the size of a fingernail. Even if you open up a computer or other chip-based device, you would not actually see the silicon chip, since chips are actually inside a larger, usually black, protective package. But you certainly

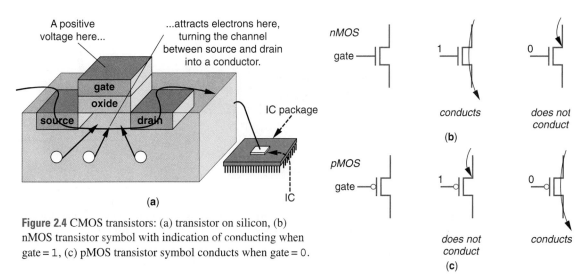

Figure 2.4 CMOS transistors: (a) transistor on silicon, (b) nMOS transistor symbol with indication of conducting when gate = 1, (c) pMOS transistor symbol conducts when gate = 0.

should be able to see those black packages, mounted on a printed circuit board, inside a variety of household electronic devices.

Figure 2.4(a) illustrates a cross section of a tiny part of silicon chip, showing the side view of one type of CMOS transistor—an nMOS transistor. The transistor has the three parts of a switch: (1) the *source* input; (2) the output, which is called the *drain*, perhaps because electric particles flow to the drain like water flows to a drain; and (3) the control input, which is called the *gate*, perhaps because the gate blocks the current flow like a gate blocks a dog from escaping the backyard. A chip maker creates the source and drain by injecting certain elements into the silicon. The region between the source and drain is the *channel*. The gate is separated from the channel by an insulation layer made from silicon dioxide, known as *oxide*. Figure 2.4(b) shows the electronic symbol of an nMOS transistor.

Suppose the drain was connected to a small positive voltage (modern technologies use about 1 or 2 V) known as the "power supply," and the source was connected through a resistor to ground. Current would thus try to flow from drain to source, and on to ground. (Unfortunately, convention is that current flow is defined using positive charge, even though negatively charged electrons are actually flowing—so notice we say current flows from drain to source, even though electrons flow from source to drain.) However, the silicon channel between source and drain is not normally a *conductor*, which is a substance that allows electrons to flow readily. Instead, the channel is normally an *insulator*, which is a substance that resists the flow of electrons. Think of an insulator as an extremely large resistance. Since $I = V/R$, then I will essentially be 0. The switch is off.

A feature of silicon is that the channel can be changed from an insulator to a conductor just *by applying a small positive voltage to the gate*. That gate voltage doesn't result in current flow from the gate to channel, because the insulating oxide layer between the gate and the channel blocks such flow. But that gate voltage does create a positive electric field that passes through the oxide and attracts electrons, which have a negative charge, from the larger silicon region into the channel region—akin to how you can move paper clips on a tabletop by moving a magnet under the table, whose magnetic field passes through the table. When enough electrons gather into the channel, the channel suddenly becomes a conductor. A conductor has extremely low resistance, so current flows almost freely between drain and source. The switch is now on. Thus, silicon is not quite a

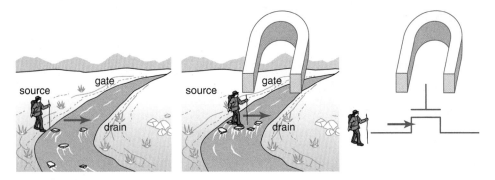

Figure 2.5 CMOS transistor operation analogy—A person may not be able to cross a river until just enough stepping stones are attracted into one pathway. Likewise, electrons can't cross the channel between source and drain until just enough electrons are attracted into the channel.

conductor but not quite an insulator either, rather representing something in between—hence the term *semiconductor*.

An analogy to the current trying to cross the channel is a person trying to cross a river. Normally, the river might not have enough stepping stones for the person to to walk across. But if we could attract stones from other parts of the river into one pathway (the channel), the person could easily walk across the river (Figure 2.5).

nMOS is one type of CMOS transistor. The other type is pMOS, which is similar, except that the channel has the opposite functionality—the channel is a conductor normally, and *doesn't* conduct when the gate has a positive voltage. Figure 2.4(c) shows the electronic symbol for a pMOS transistor. The use of these two "complementary" types of transistors is where the C comes from in CMOS. The MOS stands for metal oxide semiconductor; the reasons for that name should be clear from above, as MOS transistors use metal (to connect transistors), oxide (to insulate), and semiconductor material.

▶ SILICON VALLEY, AND THE SHAPE OF SILICON

Silicon Valley is not a city, but refers to an area in Northern California, about an hour south of San Francisco, that includes several cities like San Jose, Mountain View, Sunnyvale, Milpitas, Palo Alto, and others. The area is heavily populated by computer and other high-technology companies, and to a large extent is the result of Stanford University's (located in Palo Alto) efforts to attract and create such companies. **What shape is silicon?** Once, as my plane arrived in Silicon Valley, the person next to me asked "What shape is a silicon, anyway?" I realized he thought silicon was a type of polygon, like a pentagon or an octagon. Well, the words do sound similar. Silicon is not a shape, but an element, like carbon or aluminum or silver. Silicon has an atomic number of 14, has a chemical symbol of "Si," and is the second most abundant element (next to

oxygen) in the earth's crust, found in items like sand and clay. Silicon is used to make mirrors and glass, in addition to chips. In fact, to the naked eye, a silicon chip actually looks like a small mirror.

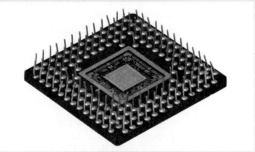

A chip package with its chip cover removed—you can see the mirror-like silicon chip in the center.

▷ 2.4 BOOLEAN LOGIC GATES—BUILDING BLOCKS FOR DIGITAL CIRCUITS

You've seen that CMOS transistors can be used to implement switches on an incredibly tiny scale. However, trying to use switches as building blocks to build complex digital circuits is akin to trying to use small rocks to build a bridge, as illustrated in Figure 2.6. Sure, you could probably build something from rudimentary building blocks, but the building process would be a real pain. Switches (and small rocks) are just too low-level as building blocks.

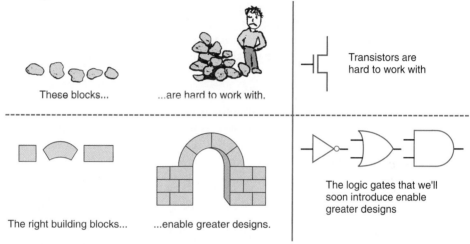

Figure 2.6 Having the right building blocks can make all the difference when building things.

Boolean Algebra and its Relation to Digital Circuits

Fortunately, Boolean logic gates aid the design task by representing digital circuit building blocks that are much easier to work with than switches. Boolean logic was developed in the mid-1800s by the mathematician George Boole, not to build digital circuits (which weren't even a glimmer in anyone's eye back then), but rather as a scheme for using algebraic methods to formalize human logic and thought.

Algebra is a branch of mathematics that uses letters or symbols to represent numbers or values, where those letters/symbols can be combined according to a set of known rules. *Boolean algebra* uses variables (known as Boolean variables) whose values can only be 1 or 0 (representing true or false, respectively). Boolean algebra's operators, like AND, OR, and NOT, operate on such variables and return 1 or 0. So we might declare Boolean variables x, y, and z, and then say that z = x OR y, meaning z will equal 1 if x is 1 or y is 1, else z will equal 0. Contrast Boolean algebra with the regular algebra you're familiar with, perhaps from high school, in which variable values could be integers (for example), and operators could be addition, subtraction, and multiplication.

The basic Boolean operators are AND, OR, and NOT:

- AND returns 1 if *both* its operands are 1. So the result of a AND b is 1 if both a=1 and b=1, otherwise the result is 0.

"ab=01" is
shorthand for
"a=0, b=1."

- OR returns 1 if *either or both* of its operands are 1. So the result of a OR b is 1 in any of the following cases: ab=01, ab=10, ab=11. Thus, the only time a OR b is 0 is when ab=00.

- NOT returns 1 if its operand is 0. So NOT(a) returns 1 if a is 0, and returns 0 if a is 1.

We use Boolean logic operators frequently in everyday thought, such as in the statement "I'll go to lunch if Mary goes OR John goes, AND Sally does not go." To represent this using Boolean concepts, let F represent my going to lunch (F=1 means I'll go to lunch, F=0 means I won't go). Let Boolean variables m, j, and s represent Mary, John, and Sally each going to lunch (so s=1 would represent Sally going to lunch, else s=0). Then we can translate the above English sentence into the Boolean equation:

$$F = (m \text{ OR } j) \text{ AND NOT}(s)$$

So F will equal 1 if either m or j is 1, and s is 0. Now that we've translated the English sentence into a Boolean equation, we can perform several mathematical activities with that equation. One thing we can do is determine the value of F for different values of m, j, and s:

- m=1, j=0, s=1 → F = (1 OR 0) AND NOT(1) = 1 AND 0 = 0
- m=1, j=1, s=0 → F = (1 OR 1) AND NOT(0) = 1 AND 1 = 1

In the first case, I don't go to lunch; in the second, I do.

A second thing we could do is apply some algebraic rules (discussed later) to modify the original equation to the equivalent equation:

$$F = (m \text{ and NOT}(s)) \text{ OR } (j \text{ and NOT}(s))$$

In other words, I'll go to lunch if Mary goes AND Sally does not go, OR if John goes AND Sally does not go. That statement, as different as it may look from the earlier statement, is nevertheless equivalent to the earlier statement.

A third thing we could do is formally prove properties about the equation. For example, we could prove that if Sally goes to lunch (s=1), then I don't go to lunch (F=0) no matter who else goes, using the equation:

$$F = (m \text{ OR } j) \text{ AND NOT}(1) = (m \text{ OR } j) \text{ AND } 0 = 0$$

No matter what the values of m and j, F will equal 0.

Noting all the mathematical activities we can do using Boolean equations, you can start to see what Boole was trying to accomplish in formalizing human reasoning.

Example 2.1 Converting a problem statement to a Boolean equation

Convert the following problem statements to Boolean equations using AND, OR, and NOT operators. F should equal 1 only if:

1. a is 1 and b is 1. *Answer:* F = a AND b

2. either of a or b is 1. *Answer:* F = a OR b

3. both a and b are not 0. *Answer:* F = NOT(a) AND NOT(b)

4. a is 1 and b is 0. *Answer:* F = a AND NOT(b)

Convert the following English problem statements to Boolean equations:

1. A fire sprinkler system should spray water if high heat is sensed and the system is set to enabled. *Answer:* Let Boolean variable h represent "high heat is sensed," e represent "enabled," and F represent "spraying water." Then an equation is: F = h AND e.

2. A car alarm should sound if the alarm is enabled, and either the car is shaken or the door is opened. *Answer:* Let a represent "alarm is enabled," s represent "car is shaken," d represent "door is opened," and F represent "alarm sounds." Then an equation is: F = a AND (s OR d).

   (a) Alternatively, assuming that the door sensor d represents "door is closed" instead of open (meaning d=1 when the door is closed, 0 when open), we obtain the following equation: F = a AND (s OR NOT(d)).

Example 2.2 Evaluating Boolean equations

Evaluate the Boolean equation F = (a AND b) OR (c AND d) for the given values of variables a, b, c, and d:

- a=1, b=1, c=1, d=0. *Answer:* F = (1 AND 1) OR (1 AND 0) = 1 OR 0 = 1.

- a=0, b=1, c=0, d=1. *Answer:* F = (0 AND 1) OR (0 AND 1) = 0 OR 0 = 0.

- a=1, b=1, c=1, d=1. *Answer:* F = (1 AND 1) OR (1 AND 1) = 1 OR 1 = 1.

Shannon, by the way, is also considered the father of information theory, due to his later work on digital communication.

One might now be wondering what Boolean algebra has to do with building circuits using switches. In 1938, an MIT graduate student named Claude Shannon wrote a paper (based on his master's thesis) describing how Boolean algebra could be applied to switch-based circuits, by showing that "on" switches could be treated as a 1 (or true), and "off" switches as a 0 (or false), by connecting those switches in a certain way (Figure 2.7). His thesis is widely considered as the seed that developed into modern digital design. Since Boolean algebra comes with a rich set of axioms, theorems, postulates, and rules, we can use all those things to manipulate digital circuits using algebra. In other words:

We can build circuits by doing math.

That's an extremely powerful concept. We'll be building circuits by doing math throughout this chapter.

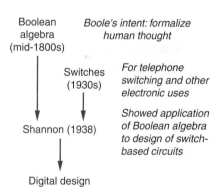

Figure 2.7 Shannon applied Boolean algebra to switch-based circuits, providing a formal basis to digital circuit design.

AND, OR, & NOT Gates

To build digital circuits that can be manipulated using Boolean algebra, we first implement the Boolean operators AND, OR, and NOT using small circuits of switches, and call those circuits Boolean *logic gates.* Then, *we forget about switches, and instead use Boolean logic gates as building blocks.* Suddenly, the power of Boolean algebra is at our fingertips for designing more complex circuits! This is like first assembling rocks into three shapes of bricks, and then building structures like a bridge from those bricks, as in Figure 2.6. Trying to build a bridge from small rocks is harder than building a bridge from the three basic brick shapes. Likewise, trying to build a motion-in-the-dark circuit (or any circuit) from switches is harder than building a circuit from Boolean logic gates.

Earlier we said a "gate" was the switch control input of a CMOS transistor, but now we're talking about "logic gates." In an unfortunate naming similarity, the same word (gate) refers to two different things. Don't worry, though; after the next section, we'll be using the word "gate" to refer only to a logic gate.

Let's first implement Boolean logic gates using CMOS transistors, shown in Figure 2.8 and soon to be described, and then a later section will show how Boolean algebra helps build better circuits. You really don't *have* to understand the underlying transistor implementations of logic gates to learn the digital design methods in the rest of this book, and in fact many textbooks omit the transistor discussion entirely. But an understanding of the underlying transistor implementation can be quite satisfying to a student, leaving no "mysteries." Such an understanding can also help in understanding the nonideal behavior of logic gates that one may later have to learn to deal with in digital design.

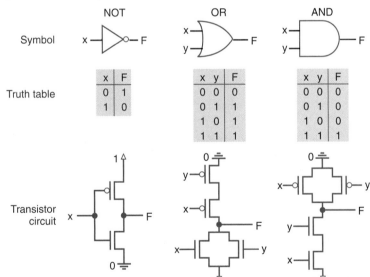

Figure 2.8 Basic logic gates' symbols, truth tables, and transistor circuits: (a) NOT (inverter) gate, (b) 2-input OR gate, (c) 2-input AND gate. Warning: real AND and OR gates *aren't* built this way, but rather in a more complex manner—see Section 2.8.

Figure 2.9 Sample voltage ranges for 1s and 0s.

1 will represent the power supply's voltage level, which today is usually around 1 V to 2 V for CMOS technology (e.g., 0.9 V, or 1.6 V). 0 will represent ground. Note that any two symbols or words could be used rather than 1 and 0 to represent power and ground voltage levels. For example, alternatives could be true and false, or H and L. Furthermore, 1 and 0 typically each represents a voltage *range*, such as 1 representing any voltage between 1.2 V to 1.8 V and 0 representing between 0 V and 0.6 V, as in Figure 2.9.

NOT Gate

A *NOT gate* has an input x and an output F. F should always be the opposite, or inverse, of x—for this reason, a NOT gate is commonly called an *inverter*. We can build a NOT gate using one pMOS and one nMOS transistor, as shown in Figure 2.8(a). The triangle at the top of the transistor circuit represents the positive voltage of the power supply, which we represent as 1. The series of lines at the bottom of the circuit represents ground, which we represent as 0. When the input x is 0, the pMOS transistor will conduct, but the nMOS will not, as shown in (a). In that case, we can think of the circuit as a wire from 1 to F, so when x = 0, then F = 1. On the other hand, when x is 1, the nMOS will conduct, but the pMOS will not, as shown in (b). In that case, we can think of the circuit as a wire from 0 to F, so when x=1, then F=0. The table in Figure 2.8, called a *truth table*, summarizes the NOT gate's behavior by listing the gate's output for every possible input.

Figure 2.10 shows a timing diagram for an inverter (See Section 1.3 for an introduction to timing diagrams.) When the input is 0, the output is 1; when the input is 1, the output is 0.

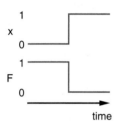

Figure 2.10 Inverter timing diagram.

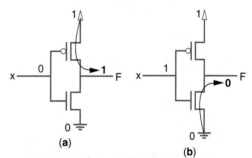

Figure 2.11 Inverter conduction paths when: (a) the input is 0, and (b) the input is 1.

Combining pMOS and nMOS in this way has the benefit of low power consumption. Figure 2.11 shows that for any value of x, either the pMOS or nMOS transistor will be nonconducting. Thus, current never flows (at least in theory) from the power source to ground, which will also be true for the AND and OR gates to be defined next. This feature makes CMOS circuits consume less power than other transistor technologies, and partly explains why CMOS is the most popular logic gate transistor technology today.

OR Gate

A basic *OR gate* has two inputs x and y and an output F. F should be 1 only if at least one of x or y is 1. We can build an OR gate using two pMOS transistors and two nMOS transistors, as shown in Figure 2.8(b). (Section 2.8 explains that OR gates are actually built in a more complex manner.) If at least one of x or y is 1, then a connection occurs from 1 to F, but no connection from 0 to F, so F is 1, as shown in Figure 2.12(a). If both x and y are 0, then a connection occurs from 0 to F, but no connection from 1 to F, so F is 0, as shown in Figure 2.12(b). The truth table for the OR gate appears in Figure 2.8(b).

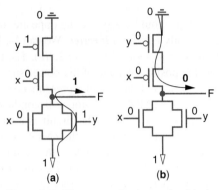

(a) **(b)**

Figure 2.12 OR gate conduction paths: (a)when one input is 1, and (b) when both inputs are 0.

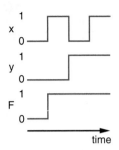

Figure 2.13 OR gate timing diagram.

Figure 2.13 shows a timing diagram for an OR gate. The table lists all possible value combinations of inputs x and y, and shows that F will be 1 if either or both inputs is a 1.

Larger OR gates having more than two inputs are also possible. If at least one of the OR gate's inputs are 1, the output is 1. For a three-input OR gate, the transistor circuit Figure 2.8(b) would have three pMOS transistors on top and three nMOS transistors on the bottom, instead of two transistors of each kind.

AND Gate

A basic **AND gate** has two inputs x and y and an output F. F should be 1 only if both x and y are 1. We can build an AND gate using two pMOS transistors and two nMOS transistors, as shown in Figure 2.8(c) (again, Section 2.8 will show that AND gates are actually built in a more complex manner). If both x and y are 1, then a connection occurs from 1 to F, but no connection from ground to F, so F is 1, as shown in Figure 2.14(a). If at least one of x or y is 0, then a connection occurs from 0 to F, but no connection from 1 to F, so F is 0, as shown in Figure 2.14(b). The truth table for the AND gate appears in Figure 2.8(c).

Figure 2.15 shows a timing diagram for an AND gate. We set inputs x and y to each possible combination of values, and show that F will be 1 only if both inputs are a 1.

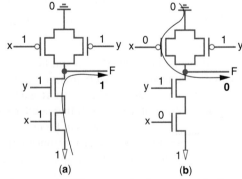

(a) **(b)**

Figure 2.14 AND gate conduction paths: (a) when all inputs are 1, and (b) when any input is 0.

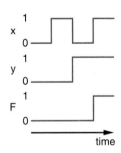

Figure 2.15 AND gate timing diagram.

Larger AND gates having more than two inputs are also possible. The output is 1 only if all the inputs are 1. For a three-input AND gate, the transistor circuit in Figure 2.8(b) would have three pMOS transistors on top and three nMOS transistors on the bottom, instead of two transistors of each kind.

Building Simple Circuits Using Gates

Having built logic gate building blocks from transistors, we now show how to build useful circuits from those building blocks. Recall the digital system example of Chapter 1, the motion-in-the-dark detector. a=1 meant motion, and b=0 meant dark, so we wanted F = a AND NOT(b). We can connect b through an inverter to get NOT(b), and connect the result along with a into an AND gate, whose output is F. The resulting circuit appears in Chapter 1, shown again in Figure 2.16 for convenience. We now provide more examples.

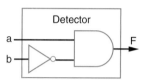

Figure 2.16 Motion-in-the-dark detector circuit.

Example 2.3 Converting a Boolean equation to a circuit with logic gates

Convert the following equation to a circuit:

$$F = a \text{ AND NOT}(\ b \text{ OR NOT}(c)\ )$$

We start by drawing F on the right, and then working toward the inputs. (We could instead start by drawing the inputs on the left and working toward the output.) The equation for F ANDs two items: a, and the output of a NOT. We thus begin by drawing the circuit of Figure 2.17(a). The NOT's input comes from an OR of two items: b, and NOT(c). We complete the drawing in Figure 2.17(b) by including an OR gate and NOT gate as shown.

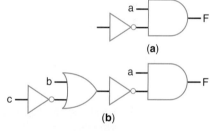

Figure 2.17 Building the circuit for F: (a) partial, (b) complete.

Example 2.4 More examples converting Boolean equations to gates

Figure 2.18 shows two more examples converting Boolean equations to circuits using logic gates. We again start from the output and work back to the inputs. The figure shows the correspondence between equation operators and gates, and the order in which we added each gate to the circuit.

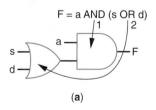

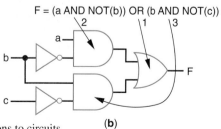

Figure 2.18 Examples of converting Boolean equations to circuits.

Example 2.5 Using AND and OR gates with more than two inputs

Figure 2.19(a) shows an implementation of the equation F = a AND b AND c, using two-input AND gates. However, designers would typically instead implement such an equation using a single three-input AND gate, shown in (b). The function is the same, but the three-input AND gate uses fewer transistors, 6 rather than $4+4=8$ (as well as having less delay—more on delay later). Likewise, F = a AND b AND c AND d would typically be implemented using a four-input AND gate.

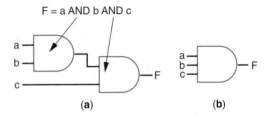

F = a AND b AND c

Figure 2.19 Using multiple-input AND gates: (a) using 2-input AND gates, (b) using a 3-input AND gate.

(a)   (b)

The same approach applies to OR gates. For example, F = a OR b OR c would typically be implemented using a single three-input OR gate.

Below are examples starting from English problem descriptions, each of which is first converted to a Boolean equation, and then implemented as a circuit.

Example 2.6 Seatbelt warning light

Suppose you want to design a system for an automobile that illuminates a warning light whenever the driver's seatbelt is not fastened and the key is in the ignition. Assume the following sensors:

- a sensor with output s indicates whether the driver's belt is fastened (s = 1 means the belt is fastened), and

- a sensor with output k indicates whether the key is in the ignition (k = 1 means the key is in).

Assume the warning light has a single input w that illuminates the light when w is 1. So the inputs to our digital system are s and k, and the output is w. w should equal 1 when both of the following occur: s is 0 and k is 1.

Let's first write a C program executing on a microprocessor to solve the design problem. If s connects to I0, k to I1, and w to P0, then the code inside the C program's main() function would be:

```
while (1) {
    P0 = !I0 && I1;
}
```

The code repeatedly checks the sensors and sets the warning light.

A Boolean equation describing a circuit implementing the design is:

$$w = \text{NOT(s) AND k}$$

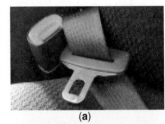

(a)

(b)

Figure 2.20 Seatbelt warning light: (a) unfastened, (b) warning light illuminated.

Using the AND and NOT logic gates introduced earlier, the design can be completed by connecting s to a NOT gate, and connecting the resulting NOT(s) and k to the inputs of a 2-input AND gate, as shown in Figure 2.21.

Figure 2.22 provides a timing diagram for the circuit. In a timing diagram, we can set the inputs to whatever values we want, but then we must draw the output line to match the circuit's function. In the figure, we set s and k to 00, then 01, then 10, then 11. The only time that the output w will be 1 is when s is 0 and k is 1, as shown in the figure.

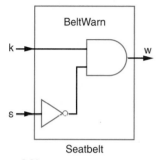

Figure 2.21 Seatbelt warning circuit.

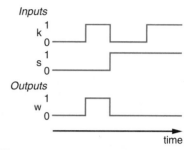

Figure 2.22 Timing diagram for seatbelt warning circuit.

We stated earlier that logic gates are more appropriate than transistors as building blocks for designing digital circuits. Note, however, that the logic gates are ultimately implemented using transistors, as shown in Figure 2.23. For C programmers, an analogy is that writing software in C is easier than writing in assembly, even though the C ultimately gets implemented using assembly. Notice how much less intuitive and less descriptive is the transistor-based circuit in Figure 2.23 than the equivalent logic gate-based circuit in Figure 2.21.

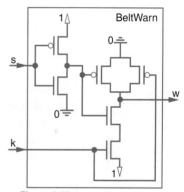

Figure 2.23 Seat belt warning circuit using transistors.

Example 2.7 Seat belt warning light with driver sensor

This example extends the previous example by adding a sensor, with output p, that detects whether a person is actually sitting in the driver's seat, and by changing the system's behavior to only illuminate the warning when a person is detected in the seat (p=1). The new circuit equation is:

w = p AND NOT(s) AND k

In this case, a 3-input AND gate is used. The circuit is shown in Figure 2.24.

Be aware that the order of the AND gate's inputs does not matter.

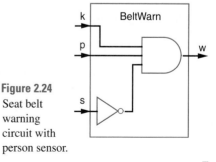

Figure 2.24 Seat belt warning circuit with person sensor.

Example 2.8 Seat belt warning light with initial illumination

Let's further extend the previous example. Automobiles typically light up all their warning lights when you first turn the key, so that you can check that all the warning lights are working. Assume that the system receives an input t that is 1 for the first 5 seconds after a key is inserted into the ignition, and 0 afterward (don't worry about who or what sets t in that way). So the system should set w=1 when p=1 and s=0 and k=1, OR when t=1. Note that when t=1, the circuit should illuminate the light, regardless of the values of p, s, and k. The new circuit equation is:

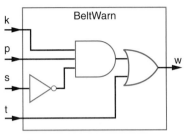

Figure 2.25 Extended seat belt warning circuit.

$$w = (p \text{ AND NOT}(s) \text{ AND } k) \text{ OR } t$$

The circuit is shown in Figure 2.25.

Some circuit drawing rules and conventions

There are some rules and conventions that designers commonly follow when drawing circuits of logic gates, as shown in Figure 2.26.

- Logic gates have one or more inputs and one output, but each input and output is typically not labeled. Remember: the order of the inputs into a gate doesn't affect the gate's logical behavior.

- Each wire has an implicit direction, from one gate's output to another gate's input, but we typically don't draw arrows showing each direction.

- A single wire can be branched out into two (or more) wires going to multiple gate inputs—the branches have the same value as the single wire. But two wires can NOT be merged into one wire—what would be the value of that one wire if the incoming two wires had different values?

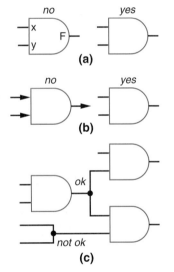

Figure 2.26 Circuit drawing rules.

▶ 2.5 BOOLEAN ALGEBRA

Logic gates are useful for implementing circuits, but equations are better for manipulating circuits. The algebraic tools of Boolean algebra enable us to manipulate Boolean equations so we can do things like simplify the equations, check whether two equations are equivalent, find the inverse of an equation, prove properties about the equations, etc. Since a Boolean equation consisting of AND, OR, and NOT operations can be straightforwardly transformed into a circuit of AND, OR, and NOT gates, manipulating Boolean equations can be considered as manipulating digital circuits. We'll informally introduce some of the most useful algebraic tools of Boolean algebra. Appendix A provides a formal definition of Boolean algebra.

Notation and Terminology

This section defines notation and terminology for describing Boolean equations. These definitions will be used extensively throughout the book.

Operators

Writing out the AND, OR, and NOT operators as words in equations is cumbersome. Thus, Boolean algebra uses simpler notation for those operators:

* "NOT(a)" is typically written as a' or $\bar{a}$. This book uses a', which one speaks as "a ***prime***." a' is also known as the ***complement*** of a, or the ***inverse*** of a.
* "a OR b" is typically written as "a + b," specifically intended to look similar to the addition operator in regular algebra. "a + b" is even referred to as the ***sum*** of a and b. "a + b" is usually spoken as "a or b."
* "a AND b" is typically written as "a * b" or "a•b" specifically intended to look similar to the multiplication operator in regular algebra, and even referred to as the ***product*** of a and b. Just as in regular algebra, we can even write "ab" for the product of a and b, as long as the fact that a and b are separate variables is clear. "a*b" is usually spoken as "a and b" or even just as "a b."

Mathematicians often use other notations for Boolean operators, but the above notations seem to be the most popular among engineers, likely due to the intentional similarity of those operators with regular algebra operators.

Using the simpler notation, the earlier seat belt example:

$$w = (p \text{ AND NOT}(s) \text{ AND } k) \text{ OR } t$$

could be rewritten more concisely as:

$$w = ps'k + t$$

which would be spoken as "w equals p s prime k, or t."

Example 2.9 Speaking Boolean equations

Speak the following equations:

1. F = a'b' + c. *Answer:* "F equals a prime b prime or c."
2. F = a + b * c'. *Answer:* "F equals a or b and c prime."

Convert the following spoken equations into written equations:

1. "F equals a b prime c prime." *Answer:* F = ab'c'.
2. "F equals a b c or d e prime." *Answer:* F = abc + de'.

The rules of Boolean algebra require that we evaluate expressions using the precedence rule that * has precedence over +, that complementing a variable has precedence over * and +, and that we of course compute what is in parentheses first. We can make the earlier equation's order of evaluation explicit using parentheses as follows: w = (p * (s') * k) + t.

Table 2.1 summarizes Boolean algebra precedence rules.

TABLE 2.1 **Boolean algebra precedence, highest precedence first.**

Symbol	Name	Description
( )	Parentheses	Evaluate expressions nested in parentheses first
'	NOT	Evaluate from left to right
*	AND	Evaluate from left to right
+	OR	Evaluate from left to right

Conventions

Although we borrowed the multiplication and addition operations from regular algebra and even use the terms sum and product, we *don't* say "times" for AND or "plus" for OR.

Digital design textbooks typically name each variable using a single character, because using a single character makes for concise equations like the equations above. We'll be writing many equations, so conciseness will aid understanding by preventing equations that wrap across multiple lines or pages. Thus, we'll usually follow the convention of using single characters. However, when you describe digital systems using a hardware description language or a programming language like C, you should probably use much more descriptive names so that your code is readable. So instead of using "s" to represent the output of a seat-belt-fastened sensor, you might instead use "SeatBeltFastened."

Example 2.10 Evaluating Boolean equations using precedence rules

Evaluate the following Boolean equations, assuming a=1, b=1, c=0, d=1.

1. F = a * b + c. *Answer:* * has precedence over +, so we evaluate the equation as F = (1 * 1) + 0 = (1) + 0 = 1 + 0 = 1.

2. F = ab + c. *Answer:* the problem is identical to the previous problem, using the shorthand notation for *.

3. F = ab'. *Answer:* we first evaluate b' because NOT has precedence over AND, resulting in F = 1 * (1') = 1 * (0) = 1 * 0 = 0.

4. F = (ac)'. *Answer:* we first evaluate what is inside the parentheses, then we NOT the result, yielding (1*0)' = (0)' = 0' = 1.

5. F = (a + b') * c + d'. *Answer:* The parentheses have highest precedence. Inside the parentheses, NOT has highest precedence. So we evaluate the parentheses part as (1 + (1')) = (1 + (0)) = (1 + 0) = 1. Next, * has precedence over +, yielding (1 * 0) + 1' = (0) + 1'. The NOT has precedence over the OR, giving (0) + (1') = (0) + (0) = 0 + 0 = 0.

Variables, Literals, Terms, and Sum of Products

This section defines a few more concepts, using the example equation: F(a,b,c) = a'bc + abc' + ab + c.

- *Variable:* A variable represents a quantity (0 or 1). The above equation has three variables: a, b, and c. We typically use variables in Boolean equations to represent the inputs of our systems. Sometimes we explicitly list a function's variables as above ("F(a,b,c) = ..."). Other times we omit the explicit list ("F = ...").

- *Literal:* A literal is the appearance of a variable, in either true or complemented form. The above equation has 9 literals: a', b, c, a, b, c', a, b, and c.

- *Product term:* A product term is a product of literals. The above equation has four terms: a'bc, abc', ab, and c.

- *Sum of products:* An equation written as an ORing of product terms is known as being in sum-of-products form. The above example equation for F is in sum-of-products form. The following equations are also in sum-of-products form:

      abc + abc'
      ab + a'c + abc
      a + b' + ac (note that a product term can have just one literal).

The following equations are NOT in sum-of-products form:

      (a + b)c
      (ab + bc)(b + c)
      (a')' + b
      a(b + c(d + e))
      (ab + bc)'

People seem to prefer working with Boolean equations in sum-of-products form, and thus that form is very common.

Some Properties of Boolean Algebra

This section lists some of the key rules of Boolean algebra. Assume a, b, and c are Boolean variables, which each holds the value of either 0 or 1.

Basic Properties

The following properties, known as postulates, are assumed to be true:

- *Commutative*

      a + b = b + a
      a * b = b * a

  This property should be obvious. Just try it for different values of a and b.

- *Distributive*

      a * (b + c) = a * b + a * c
      a + (b * c) = (a + b) * (a + c) (This one is tricky!)

  Careful, the second one may not be obvious. It's different than regular algebra. But you can verify that both of the distributive properties hold simply by evaluating both sides for all possible values of a, b, and c.

- *Associative*

      (a + b) + c = a + (b + c)
      (a * b) * c = a * (b * c)

  Again, try it for different values of a and b to see that this holds.

- *Identity*

$$0 + a = a + 0 = a$$
$$1 * a = a * 1 = a$$

This one should be intuitive. ORing a with 0 (a+0) just means that the result will be whatever a is. After all, $1+0$ is 1, while $0+0$ is 0. Likewise, ANDing a with 1 (a*1) results in a. $1*1$ is 1, while $0*1$ is 0.

- *Complement*

$$a + a' = 1$$
$$a * a' = 0$$

This also makes intuitive sense. Regardless of the value of a, a' is the opposite, so you get a 0 and a 1, or you get a 1 and a 0. One of (a, a') will always be a 1, so ORing them (a+a') must yield a 1. Likewise, one of (a, a') will always be a 0, so ANDing them (a*a') must yield a 0.

The following examples apply these basic properties to some digital design examples to see how the properties can help.

Example 2.11 Applying the basic properties of Boolean algebra

Use the properties of Boolean algebra for the following problems:

- Show that abc' is equivalent to c'ba.
  The commutative property allows swapping the operands being ANDed, so $a*b*c' = a*c'*b = c'*a*b = c'*b*a = c'ba$.

- Show that abc + abc' = ab.
  The first distributive property allows factoring out the ab term: $abc + abc' = ab(c+c')$. Then, the complement property allows replacing the c+c' by 1: $ab(c+c') = ab(1)$. Finally, the identity property allows removal of the 1 from the AND term: $ab(1) = ab*1 = ab$.

- Show that the equation $x + x'z$ is equivalent to $x + z$.
  The second distributive property (the tricky one) allows replacing x+x'z by $(x+x')*(x+z)$. The complement property allows replacing (x+x') by 1, and the identity property allows replacing $1*(x+z)$ by x+z.

- Show that (a+a')bc is just bc.
  The complement property states that (a+a') is 1, yielding 1*bc. The identity property then results in bc.

- Multiply out $(w + x)(y + z)$ into sum-of-products form.
  First writing (w + x) as A will make clear that the distributive property can be applied: $A(y+z)$. The first distributive property yields $Ay + Az$. Expanding A back yields $(w+x)y + (w+x)z$. Applying the first distributive property again yields $wy + xy + wz + xz$, which is in sum-of-products form.

Example 2.12 Simplification of an automatic sliding door system

Suppose you wish to design a system to control an automatic sliding door, like one that might be found at a grocery store's entrance. An input p to the system indicates whether a sensor detects a person in front of the door (p=1 means a person is detected). An input h indicates whether the door should be manually held open (h=1) regardless of whether a person is detected. An input c indicates whether the door should be forced to stay closed (like when the store is closed for business)—c = 1 means the door should stay closed. The latter two would normally be set by a manager with the proper keys. An output f opens the door when f is 1.

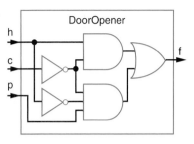

Figure 2.27 Initial door opener circuit.

The door should be opened if the door is set to be manually held open, OR if the door is not set to be manually held open but a person is detected. However, in either case, the door should only be opened if the door is not set to stay closed. These requirements can be translated into a Boolean equation:

$$f \;=\; hc' \;+\; h'pc'$$

A circuit to implement this equation could then be created, as in Figure 2.27.

The equation can be manipulated using the properties described earlier. Looking at the equation, we might try to factor out the c'. We might then be able to simplify the remaining h+h'p part too. Let's try some transformations, first factoring out c':

f = hc' + h'pc'	
f = c'h + c'h'p	(by the commutative property)
f = c'(h + h'p)	(by the first distributive property)
f = c'((h+h')*(h+p))	(by the 2nd distributive property—the tricky one)
f = c'((1)*(h + p))	(by the complement property)
f = c'(h+p)	(by the identity property)

Note that the simpler equation still makes intuitive sense—the door should be opened only if the door is not set to stay closed (c'), AND either the door is set to be manually held open (h) OR a person is detected (v). A circuit implementing this simpler equation is shown in Figure 2.28. Applying the algebraic properties led to a simpler circuit. In other words, we used math to simplify the circuit.

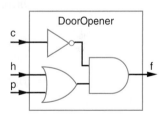

Figure 2.28 Simplified door opener circuit.

Simplification of logic circuits is the focus of Section 2.11.

Example 2.13 Equivalence of two automatic sliding door systems

Suppose you found a really cheap device for automatic sliding door systems. The device had inputs c, h, and p and output f, as in Example 2.12, but the device's documentation said that:

```
f = c'hp + c'hp' + c'h'p
```

Does that device do the same as that in Example 2.12? One way to check is to see if the above equation can be manipulated into the equation in Example 2.12:

```
f = c'hp + c'hp' + c'h'p
f = c'h(p + p') + c'h'p        (by the distributive property)
f = c'h(1) + c'h'p             (by the complement property)
f = c'h + c'h'p                (by the identity property)
f = hc' + h'pc'                (by the commutative property)
```

That's the same as the original equation in Example 2.12, so the device should work.

Additional Properties

This section introduces some additional properties, which happen to be known as theorems because they can be proven using the above postulates:

- *Null elements*

$$a + 1 = 1$$
$$a * 0 = 0$$

These should be fairly obvious. 1 OR anything is going to be 1, while 0 AND anything is going to be 0.

- *Idempotent Law*

$$a + a = a$$
$$a * a = a$$

Again, this should be fairly obvious. If a is 1, 1+1=1 and 1*1=1, while if a is 0, 0+0=0 and 0*0=0.

- *Involution Law*

$$(a')' = a$$

Fairly obvious. If a is 1, the first negation gives 0, while the second gives 1 again. Likewise, if a is 0, the first negation gives 1, while the second gives 0 again.

- *DeMorgan's Law*

$$(a + b)' = a'b'$$
$$(ab)' = a' + b'$$

These are not as obvious. Their proofs are in Appendix A. Let's consider both equations intuitively here. Consider (a + b)' = a'b'. The left side will only be 1 if (a + b) evaluates to 0, which only occurs when both a AND b are 0, meaning a'b' — the right side. Likewise, consider (ab)' = a' + b'. The left side will only be 1 if (ab) evaluates to 0, meaning at least one of a OR b must be 0, meaning a' + b'— the right side. DeMorgan's Law can be stated in English as follows: The complement of a sum equals the product of the complements; the complement of a product equals the sum of the complements. DeMorgan's Law is widely used, so take the time now to understand it and to remember it.

The following examples apply some of these additional properties.

Example 2.14 Applying the additional properties

- Convert the equation `F = ab(c+d)` into sum-of-products form.
  The distributive property allows us to "multiply out" the equation to `F = abc + abd`.

- Convert the equation `F = wx(x'y + zy' + xy)` into sum-of-products form, and make any obvious simplifications.
  The distributive property allows us to "multiply out" the equation: `wx(x'y + zy' + xy) = wxx'y + wxzy' + wxxy`. That equation is in sum-of-products form. The complement property allows us to replace `wxx'y` by `w*0*y`, and the null element property means that `w*0*y = 0`. The idempotent property allows us to replace `wxxy` by `wxy` (because `xx = x`). The resulting equation is therefore `0 + wxzy' + wxy = wxzy' + wxy`.

- Prove that `x(x' + y(x'+y'))` can never evaluate to 1.
  Repeated application of the first distributive property yields: `xx' + xy(x'+y') = xx' + xyx' + xyy'`. The complement property tells us that `xx'=0` and `yy'=0`, yielding `0 + 0*y + x*0`. The null element property leads to `0 + 0 + 0`, which equals `0`. So the equation always evaluates to 0, regardless of the actual values of x and y.

- Determine the opposite function of `F = (ab' + c)`.
  The desired function is `G = F' = (ab'+c)'`. DeMorgan's Law yields `G = (ab')' * c'`. Applying DeMorgan's Law again to the first term yields `G = (a'+(b')') * c'`. The involution property yields `(a' + b) * c'`. Finally, the distributive property yields `G = a'c' + bc'`.

Example 2.15 Applying DeMorgan's Law in an aircraft lavatory sign

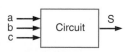

Figure 2.29 Aircraft lavatory sign block diagram.

Commercial aircraft typically have an illuminated sign indicating whether a lavatory (bathroom) is available. Suppose an aircraft has three lavatories. Each lavatory has a sensor outputting 1 if the lavatory door is locked, 0 otherwise. A circuit will have three inputs, a, b, and c, coming from those sensors, as shown in Figure 2.29. If *any* lavatory door is unlocked (whether one, two, or all three doors are unlocked), the circuit should illuminate the "Available" sign by setting the circuit's output S to 1.

With this understanding, we recognize that the OR function suits the problem, as OR outputs 1 if any of its inputs are 1, regardless of how many inputs are 1. We begin writing an equation for S. S should be 1 if a is 0 OR b is 0 OR c is 0. Saying a is 0 is the same as saying a'. Thus, the equation for S is:

$$S = a' + b' + c'$$

We translate the equation to the circuit in Figure 2.30.

DeMorgan's Law can be applied (in reverse) to the equation by noting that `(abc)' = a'+b'+c'`, so we can replace the equation by:

$$S = (abc)'$$

The circuit for that equation appears in Figure 2.31.

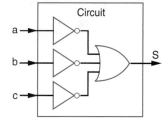

Figure 2.30 Aircraft lavatory sign circuit.

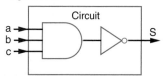

Figure 2.31 Circuit after applying DeMorgan's Law.

Example 2.16 Proving a property of the automatic sliding door system

A famous digital circuit error was the error found in the floating point unit of Intel's Pentium processor. It was found after the processor was already being widely sold in 1994, ultimately costing Intel $475 million. Thus, using Boolean techniques to <u>prove</u> correct behavior of circuits is a growing trend.

Your boss wants you to *prove* that the automatic sliding door circuit of Example 2.12 ensures that the door will stay closed when the door is supposed to be forced to stay closed, namely, when c=1. If the function f = c'(h+p) describes the sliding door, you can prove the door will stay closed (f=0) using properties of Boolean algebra:

$$
\begin{aligned}
&\texttt{f = c'(h+p)} \\
&\texttt{Let c = 1} && \text{(door forced closed)} \\
&\texttt{f = 1'(h+p)} \\
&\texttt{f = 0(h+p)} \\
&\texttt{f = 0h + 0p} && \text{(by the distributive property)} \\
&\texttt{f = 0 + 0} && \text{(by the null elements property)} \\
&\texttt{f = 0}
\end{aligned}
$$

Therefore, no matter what the values of h and p, if c=1, f will equal 0—the door will stay closed.

Example 2.17 Automatic sliding door with opposite polarity

Example 2.12 computed the function to open an automatic sliding door as:

```
f = c'( h + p )
```

Suppose our function will control an automatic door control that has the opposite polarity: the function should output 0 to open the door, and 1 to close the door. The function g that opens the door can be computed and simplified as follows:

$$
\begin{aligned}
&\texttt{g = f'} \\
&\texttt{g = (c'(h+p))'} && \text{(by substituting the equation for f)} \\
&\texttt{g = (c')' + (h+p)'} && \text{(by DeMorgan's Law)} \\
&\texttt{g = c + (h+p)'} && \text{(by the Involution Law)} \\
&\texttt{g = c + h'p'} && \text{(by DeMorgan's Law)}
\end{aligned}
$$

Complementing a Function

A common task is to compute the complement of a Boolean function, as was done in Example 2.17. A function's **complement**, also known as the **inverse** of a function, evaluates to 1 whenever the function would evaluate to 0, and evaluates to 1 whenever the function would evaluate to 0.

▶ *YOUR PROBLEM IS MY PROBLEM*

Boolean algebra was not invented for digital design, but rather for the different problem of formalizing human logic and thought. Digital design progressed slowly until Claude Shannon showed how Boolean algebra could be applied. In other words, powerful techniques from some other problem were applied to the digital design problem. Such borrowing of techniques from different problem domains is common in various fields engineering, and can lead to major breakthroughs.

The equation for a function's complement can be simplified by repeated use of DeMorgan's Law followed by other simplfications. Note that DeMorgan's Law applies to any number of variables, not just two. Specifically, for three variables:

```
(a + b + c)' = (abc)'
(abc)' = (a' + b' + c')
```

Likewise for four variables, five variables, and so on.

For example, the complement of the function $f = w'xy + wx'y'z'$ is $f' = (w'xy + wx'y'z')'$. DeMorgan's Law can then be applied as follows:

```
f' = (w'xy + wx'y'z')'
f' = (w'xy)'(wx'y'z')'          (by DeMorgan's Law)
f' = (w+x'+y')(w'+x+y+z)        (by DeMorgan's Law)
```

The equation can then be expanded into sum-of-products form as follows:

```
f' = w(w'+x+y+z) + x'(w'+x+y+z) + y'(w'+x+y+z)
f' = ww' + wx + wy + wz + x'w' + x'x + x'y + x'z +
     y'w' + y'x + y'y + y'z
f' = wx + wy + wz + w'x' + x'y + x'z + w'y' + xy' + y'z
```

▶ 2.6 REPRESENTATIONS OF BOOLEAN FUNCTIONS

A **Boolean function** is a *mapping* of each possible combination of values for the function's variables (the inputs) to either a 0 or 1 (the output). Figure 2.32(a) provides two alternative English descriptions of a particular Boolean function. There are several better representations than English for describing a Boolean function, including equations, circuits, and truth tables, as shown in Figure 2.32(b), (c), and (d). Each representation has its own advantages and disadvantages, and each is useful at different times during design. Yet all the representations, as different as they look from one another, represent the very same function. Such is akin to how there are different ways to represent a particular recipe for chocolate chip cookies: written words, pictures, or even a video. But no matter how the recipe is represented, it's the same recipe.

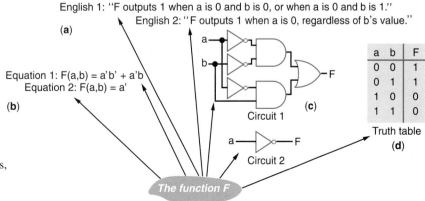

English 1: "F outputs 1 when a is 0 and b is 0, or when a is 0 and b is 1."
English 2: "F outputs 1 when a is 0, regardless of b's value."
(a)

Equation 1: F(a,b) = a'b' + a'b
Equation 2: F(a,b) = a'
(b)

Circuit 1
Circuit 2
(c)

a	b	F
0	0	1
0	1	1
1	0	0
1	1	0

Truth table
(d)

The function F

Figure 2.32 Seven representations of the same function F(a,b): (a) Two English descriptions, (b) two equations, (c) two circuits, (d) a truth table.

Equations

One way to represent a Boolean function is by using an equation. An *equation* is a mathematical statement equating one expression with another. $F(a,b) = a'b' + a'b$ is an example of an equation. The right-hand side of the equation is often referred to as an *expression*, which evaluates to either 0 or 1.

Different equations can represent the same function. The two equations in Figure 2.32(b), $F(a,b) = a'b' + a'b$ and $F(a,b) = a'$, represent the same function. Both equations perform exactly the same mapping of the input values to output values—pick any input values (e.g., a=0 and b=0), and both equations map those input values to the same output value (e.g., a=0 and b=0 would be mapped to F=1 by either equation).

One advantage of an equation as a Boolean function representation compared to other representations (such as English) is that equations can be manipulated using properties of Boolean algebra, enabling simplification of an equation, or proving that two equations represent the same function, or proving properties about a function, and more.

Circuits

Another way to represent a Boolean function is using a circuit of logic gates. A *circuit* is an interconnection of components. Because each logic gate component has a predefined mapping of input values to output values, and because wires just transmit their values unchanged, a circuit describes a function.

Different circuits can represent the same function. The two circuits in Figure 2.32(c) both represent the same function F. The bottom circuit uses fewer gates, but the function is exactly the same as the function of the top circuit.

One advantage of a circuit as a Boolean function representation compared to other representations is that a circuit may represent an actual physical implementation of a Boolean function. Another advantage is that a circuit drawn graphically can enable quick and easy comprehension of a function by humans.

Truth Tables

Another way to represent a Boolean function is using a *truth table*. A truth table's left side lists the input variables, and shows *all possible value combinations of those inputs*, with one row per combination, as shown in Figure 2.33. A truth table's right side lists the function's output value (1 or 0) for each row's particular combination of input values, as in Figure 2.32(d). Any function of two variables will have those four input combinations on the left side. People usually list the input combinations in order of increasing binary value (00=0, 01=1, 10=2, 11=3), though strictly speaking, the combinations could be listed in any order as long as all possible combinations are included. For any combination of input values (e.g., a=0, b=0), one merely needs to look at the corresponding value in the output column to determine the function's output. In the case of a=0, b=0, the output shown in Figure 2.32(d) is 1.

Inputs		Output
a	b	F
0	0	
0	1	
1	0	
1	1	

Figure 2.33 Truth table structure for a two-input function $F(a,b)$.

The word "truth" in truth table comes from Boolean algebra's use of two values "true" and "false"—the table shows when a function returns true.

a	b	F
0	0	
0	1	
1	0	
1	1	

(a)

a	b	c	F
0	0	0	
0	0	1	
0	1	0	
0	1	1	
1	0	0	
1	0	1	
1	1	0	
1	1	1	

(b)

a	b	c	d	F
0	0	0	0	
0	0	0	1	
0	0	1	0	
0	0	1	1	
0	1	0	0	
0	1	0	1	
0	1	1	0	
0	1	1	1	
1	0	0	0	
1	0	0	1	
1	0	1	0	
1	0	1	1	
1	1	0	0	
1	1	0	1	
1	1	1	0	
1	1	1	1	

(c)

Figure 2.34 Truth table structures for: (a) a two-input function $F(a,b)$, (b) a three-input function $F(a,b,c)$, and (c) a four-input function $F(a,b,c,d)$. Defining a specific function involves filling in the rightmost column for F with a 0 or a 1 for each row.

Figure 2.34 shows the truth table structures for a two-input function, a three-input function, and a four-input function.

Truth tables are not only found in digital design. If you've studied basic biology, you've likely seen a type of truth table describing the outcome of various gene pairs. For example, the table in Figure 2.35 shows outcomes for different eye color genes. Each person has two genes for eye color, one (labeled M) from the mom, one (labeled D) from the dad. Assuming only

Gene pair		Outcome
M	D	F
blue	blue	blue
blue	brown	brown
brown	blue	brown
brown	brown	brown

Figure 2.35 Truth table used to describe outcomes for gene pairs.

two possible values for each gene, blue and brown, the table lists all possible combinations of eye color gene pairs that a person may have. For each combination, the table lists the outcome. Only when a person has two blue eye genes will they have blue eyes; having one or two brown eye genes results in brown eyes, due to the brown eye gene being dominant over the blue eye gene.

Unlike equations and circuits, a Boolean function has only *one* truth table representation (neglecting the trivial differences obtained by reordering the inputs or by not listing the input combinations in increasing binary order).

One advantage of a truth table as a Boolean function representation compared to other representations is the fact that a function has only one truth table representation, so any other Boolean function representation can be converted to a truth table to determine whether different representations represent the same function—if two representations represent the same function, then their truth tables will be identical. Truth tables can also be quite intuitive to human readers for some functions, as a truth table clearly shows the output for every possible input. Thus, notice that truth tables were used in Figure 2.8 to describe in an intuitive manner the behavior of basic logic gates.

A drawback of truth tables is that for a large number of inputs, the number of truth table rows can be very large. Given a function with n inputs, the number of input combinations is 2^n. A function with 10 inputs would have $2^{10} = 1024$ possible input combinations—you can't easily see much of anything in a table having 1024 rows. A function with 16 inputs would have 65,536 rows in its truth table.

Example 2.18 Capturing a function as a truth table

TABLE 2.2 Truth table for 5-or-greater function.

a	b	c	F
0	0	0	0
0	0	1	0
0	1	0	0
0	1	1	0
1	0	0	0
1	0	1	1
1	1	0	1
1	1	1	1

Create a truth table describing a function that detects whether a three-bit inputs' value, representing a binary number, is 5 or greater. Table 2.2 shows a truth table for the function. We first list all possible combinations of the three input bits, which we've labeled a, b, and c. We then enter a 1 in the output row if the inputs represent 5, 6, or 7 in binary, meaning the last three rows. We enter 0s in all the other rows.

Converting among Boolean Function Representations

Given the above representations, converting from one representation to another is sometimes necessary or useful. For the three representations discussed so far (equations, circuits, and truth tables), there are six possible conversions from one representation to another, as shown in Figure 2.36, which will now be described.

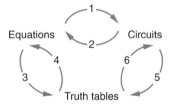

Figure 2.36 Possible conversions from one Boolean function representation to another.

1. Equations to Circuits

Converting an equation to a circuit can be done straightforwardly by using an AND gate for every AND operator, an OR gate for every OR operator, and a NOT gate for every NOT operator. Several examples of such conversions appear in Section 2.4.

2. Circuits to Equations

Converting a circuit into an equation can be done by starting from the circuit's inputs, and then writing the output of each gate as an expression involving the gate's inputs. The expression of the last gate before the output represents the expression for the circuit's function.

For example, consider the circuit in Figure 2.37. To convert to an equation, we start with the inverter, whose output will represent `c'`. We continue with the OR gate—note that we can't determine the output for the AND gate yet until we create expressions for all that gate's inputs. The OR gate's output represents `h+p`. Finally, we write the output of the AND as `c'(h+p)`. Thus, the equation `F(c,h,p)` = `c'(h+p)` represents the same function as the circuit.

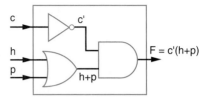

Figure 2.37 Converting a circuit to an equation.

3. Equations to Truth Tables

Converting an equation to a truth table can be done by first creating a truth table structure appropriate for the number of function input variables, and then evaluating the right-hand side of the equation for each combination of input values. For example, to convert the equation `F(a,b)` = `a'b' + a'b` to a truth table, we would first create the truth table structure for a two-input function, as in Figure 2.34(a). We would then evaluate the right-hand side of the equation for each row's combination of input values, as follows:

Inputs		Output
a	b	F
0	0	1
0	1	1
1	0	0
1	1	0

Figure 2.38 Truth table for F(a,b)=a'b'+a'b.

- `a=0 and b=0, F = 0'*0' + 0'*0 = 1*1 + 1*0 = 1 + 0 = 1`
- `a=0 and b=1, F = 0'*1' + 0'*1 = 1*0 + 1*1 = 0 + 1 = 1`
- `a=1 and b=0, F = 1'*0' + 1'*0 = 0*1 + 0*0 = 0 + 0 = 0`
- `a=1 and b=1, F = 1'*1' + 1'*1 = 0*0 + 0*1 = 0 + 0 = 0`

We would therefore fill in the table's right column as in Figure 2.38. Note that we applied properties of Boolean algebra (mostly the identity property and null elements property) to evaluate the equations.

Notice that converting the equation `F(a,b)=a'` to a truth table results in exactly the same truth table as in Figure 2.38. In particular, evaluating the right-hand side of the equation for each row's combination of input values yields:

- `a=0 and b=0, F = 0' = 1`
- `a=0 and b=1, F = 0' = 1`
- `a=1 and b=0, F = 1' = 0`
- `a=1 and b=1, F = 1' = 0`

Some people find it useful to create intermediate columns in the truth table to compute the equation's intermediate values, thus filling each column of the table from left to right, moving to the next column only after filling all rows of the current column. An example for the equation `F(a,b)` = `a'b' + a'b` is shown in Figure 2.39.

Inputs				Output
a	b	a' b'	a' b	F
0	0	1	0	1
0	1	0	1	1
1	0	0	0	0
1	1	0	0	0

Figure 2.39 Truth table for `F(a,b)` = a'b'+a'b with intermediate columns.

4. Truth Tables to Equations

Converting a truth table to an equation can be done by creating a product term for each 1 in the output column, and then ORing all the product terms. Doing so for the table of Figure 2.40 would yield the terms shown in the rightmost column. ORing those terms yields F = a'b' + a'b. This conversion will be very frequently used; take the time to understand it now.

Inputs		Outputs	Term
a	b	F	F = sum of
0	0	1	a' b'
0	1	1	a' b
1	0	0	
1	1	0	

Thus: F = a' b' + a' b

Figure 2.40 Converting a truth table to an equation.

5. Circuits to Truth Tables

A combinational circuit can be converted to a truth table by first converting the circuit to an equation (described earlier), and then converting the equation to a truth table (described earlier).

6. Truth Tables to Circuits

A truth table can be converted to a circuit by first converting the truth table to an equation (described earlier), and then converting the equation to a circuit (described earlier).

Example 2.19 Parity generator circuit design starting from a truth table

Nothing is perfect, and digital circuits are no exception. Sometimes a bit on a wire changes even though it is not supposed to change. So a 1 becomes a 0, or a 0 becomes a 1, accidentally. For example, a 0 may be traveling along a wire, when suddenly some electrical noise comes out of nowhere and changes the 0 to a 1. The likelihood of such errors can be reduced by methods such as using well-insulated wires, but such errors can't be completely prevented. Nor can all such errors be detected and corrected—but we can detect *some* of them. Designers typically look for situations where errors are likely to occur, such as data being transmitted between two chips over long wires—like from a computer over a printer cable to a printer, or from a keyboard over a wireless channel to a computer. For those situations, designers add circuits that at least try to detect that an error has occurred, in which case the receiving circuit can request that the sending circuit resend the data.

One common method of detecting an error is called *parity*. Say we have 7 data bits to transmit. We add an extra bit, called the parity bit, to make 8 bits total. The sender sets the parity bit to a 1 if that would make the total number of 1s even—that's called *even parity*. For example, if the 7 data bits were 0000001, then the parity bit would be 1, making the total number of 1s equal to 2 (an even number). The complete 8 bits would be 0000001*1*, where we've italicized the parity bit. If the 7 data bits were 1011111, then the parity bit would be 0, making the total number of 1s equal to 6 (an even number). The complete 8 bits would be 1011111*0*.

The receiver now can detect whether a bit has changed during transmission by checking whether there is an even number of 1s in the 8 bits received. If there is an even number of 1s, the transmission is assumed correct. If not even, an error occurred during transmission. For example, if 00000011 is received, the transmission is assumed to be correct, and the parity bit can be discarded, leaving 0000001. Suppose instead that 10000011 is received. Seeing the odd number of 1s, the receiver knows that an error occurred—note that the receiver does *not* know which bit is erroneous. Likewise, 00000010 would represent an error too.

Let's describe a function that generates an even parity bit P for 3 data bits a, b, and c. Starting from an equation is hard—what's the equation? For this example, starting with a truth table is the natural choice, as shown in Table 2.3. For each configuration of data bits (i.e., for each row in the

For this example, starting from a truth table is a more natural choice than an equation.

truth table), the value of the parity bit is set such as to make the total number of 1s even. The rows labeled 1, 2, 3, and 4 have two, two, two, and four 1s, respectively—all being even numbers of 1s.

From the truth table, the following equation for P can be derived:

TABLE 2.3 Even parity for 3-bit data.

$$P = a'b'c(1) + a'bc'(2) + ab'c'(3) + abc(4)$$

We used the numbers *1*, *2*, *3*, and *4* to show the correspondence between each 1 in the table and each term in the equation. For example, the input values for the row numbered *(3)* in the table are 1 0 0, which means ab'c'. This equation could then be converted to a circuit having four 3-input AND gates and one 4-input OR gate.

Note that receiving data that has an even number of 1s and that is supposed to have even parity doesn't mean for sure that the received data is really correct (note that we were careful to say earlier that the transmission was "assumed" to be correct if the parity was correct). In particular, if two errors occur on different bits, then the parity will still be even. For example, the sender may send 0110, but the receiver may receive 1111. 1111 has even parity and thus looks correct.

a	b	c	P
0	0	0	0
0	0	1	1 *(1)*
0	1	0	1 *(2)*
0	1	1	0
1	0	0	1 *(3)*
1	0	1	0
1	1	0	0
1	1	1	1 *(4)*

Undetected incorrect transmissions are sometimes why an email or webpage is received with garbled text, or why a computer, printer, or mobile phone might execute incorrectly or freeze up.

More powerful error detection methods are possible to detect multiple errors, but at the price of adding extra bits.

Odd parity is also a common kind of parity—the parity bit value makes the total number of 1s odd. There's no quality difference between even parity and odd parity—the key is simply that the sender and receiver must both use the same kind of parity, even or odd.

A popular representation of letters and numbers is known as ASCII, which encodes each character into 7 bits. ASCII adds one bit for parity, for a total of 8 bits per character.

Example 2.20 Converting a combinational circuit to a truth table

Convert the circuit depicted in Figure 2.41(a) into a truth table.

We begin by converting the circuit to an equation. Starting from the gates closest to the inputs—the leftmost AND gate and the inverter in this case—we label each gate's output as an expression of the gate's inputs. We label the leftmost AND gate's output, for example, as ab. Likewise, we label the leftmost inverter's output as c'. Continuing through the circuit's gates, we label the rightmost inverter's output as (ab)'. Finally, we label the rightmost AND gate's output as (ab)'c', which corresponds to the Boolean equation for F. The fully labeled circuit is shown in Figure 2.41(b).

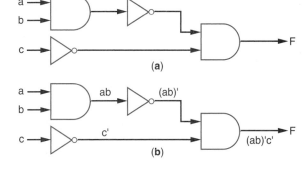

Figure 2.41 Converting a circuit to an equation: (a) original circuit, and (b) circuit with gates' output expressions labeled.

Inputs			ab	(ab)'	c'	Outputs
a	b	c				F
0	0	0	0	1	1	1
0	0	1	0	1	0	0
0	1	0	0	1	1	1
0	1	1	0	1	0	0
1	0	0	0	1	1	1
1	0	1	0	1	0	0
1	1	0	1	0	1	0
1	1	1	1	0	0	0

Figure 2.42 Truth table for the circuit's equation.

From the Boolean equation, we can now construct the truth table for the combinational circuit. Since our circuit has three inputs—a, b, and c—there are $2^3 = 8$ possible combinations of inputs (i.e., abc = 000, 001, 010, 011, 100, 101, 110, 111), so the truth table has the eight rows shown in Figure 2.42. For each input, we compute the value of F and fill in the corresponding entry in the truth table. For example, when a=0, b=0, and c=0, F is (00)'*0' = (0)'*1 = 1*1 = 1. We compute the circuit's output for the remaining combinations of inputs using a truth table with intermediate values, shown in Figure 2.42.

Standard Representation and Canonical Form

Standard Representation—Truth Tables

As stated earlier, although there are many equation representations and circuit representations of a Boolean function, there is only one possible truth table representation of a Boolean function. Truth tables therefore represent a *standard representation* of a function—for any function, there may be many possible equations, and many possible circuits, but there is only *one* truth table. The truth table representation is unique.

One use of a standard representation of a Boolean function is for comparing two functions to see if they are equivalent. Suppose you wanted to check whether two Boolean equations represented the same function. One way would be to try to manipulate one equation to be the same as the other equation, like we did in the automatic sliding door example of Example 2.13. But suppose we were not successful in getting them to be the same—is that because they really are not the same, or because we just didn't manipulate the equation enough? How do we really know the two equations do not represent the same function?

A conclusive way to check whether two items represent the same function is to create a truth table for each, and then check whether the truth tables are identical. So to determine whether F = ab + a' is equivalent to F = a'b' + a'b + ab, we could generate truth tables for each, using the method described earlier of evaluating the function for each output row, as Figure 2.43.

F = ab + a'		
a	b	F
0	0	1
0	1	1
1	0	0
1	1	1

F = a'b' + a'b + ab		
a	b	F
0	0	1
0	1	1
1	0	0
1	1	1

Figure 2.43 Truth tables showing equivalence.

We see that the two equations are indeed equivalent, because the outputs are identical for each input combination. Now let's check whether $F = ab + a'$ is equivalent to $F = (a+b)'$ by comparing truth tables.

As seen in Figure 2.44, those two equations are clearly not equivalent. Comparing truth tables leaves no doubt.

F = ab + a'				F = (a+b)'		
a	b	F		a	b	F
0	0	1		0	0	1
0	1	1		0	1	0
1	0	0		1	0	0
1	1	1		1	1	0

Figure 2.44 Non-equivalence proven.

While comparing truth tables works fine when a function has only 2 inputs, what if a function has 5 inputs, or 10, or 32? Creating truth tables becomes increasingly cumbersome, and in many cases unrealistic, since a truth table's number of rows equals 2^n, where n is the number of inputs. 2^n grows very quickly. 2^{32} is approximately 4 billion, for example. We can't realistically expect to compare 2 tables of 4 billion rows each.

However, in many cases, the number of output 1s in a truth table may be very small compared to the number of output 0s. For example, consider a function G of 5 variables a, b, c, d, and e: G = abcd + a'bcde. A truth table for this function would have 32 rows, but only three 1s in the output column—one 1 from a'bcde, and two 1s from abcd (which covers rows corresponding to abcde and abcde'). This leads to the question:

Is there a more compact but still *standard* representation of a Boolean function?

Canonical Form—Sum-of-Minterms Equation
The answer to the above question is yes. The key is to create a standard representation that only describes the situations where the function outputs 1, with the other situations assumed to output 0. An equation, such as G = abcd + a'bcde, is indeed a representation that only describes the situations where G is 1, but that representation is not unique, that is, the representation is not standard. We therefore want to define a standard form of a Boolean equation, known as a **canonical form**.

You've seen canonical forms in regular algebra. For example, the canonical form of a polynomial of degree two is: $ax^2 + bx + c$. To check whether the equation $9x^2 + 3x + 2 + 1$ is equivalent to the equation $3*(3x^2 + 1 + x)$, we convert each to canonical form, resulting in $9x^2 + 3x + 3$ for both equations.

One canonical form for a Boolean function is known as a sum of minterms. A *minterm* of a function is a product term whose literals include every variable of the function *exactly once*, in either true or complemented form. The function F(a,b,c) = a'bc + abc' + ab + c has four terms. The first two terms, a'bc and abc', are minterms. The third term, ab, is not a minterm since c does not appear. Likewise, the fourth term, c, is not a minterm, since neither a nor b appears in that term. An equation is in *sum-of-minterms form* if the equation is in sum-of-products form, and every product term is a minterm.

Converting any equation to sum-of-minterms canonical form can be done by following just a few steps:

1. First, manipulate the equation until it is in sum-of-products form. Suppose the given equation is F(a,b,c) = (a+b)(a'+ac)b. We manipulate it as follows:

```
F = (a+b)(a'+ac)b
F = (a+b)(a'b+acb)                    (by the distributive property)
F = a(a'b+acb) + b(a'b+acb)           (distributive property)
F = aa'b + aacb + ba'b + bacb         (distributive property)
F = 0*b + acb + a'b + acb             (complement, commutative,
                                          idempotent)
F = acb + a'b + acb                   (null elements)
F = acb + a'b                         (idempotent)
```

2. Second, expand each term until every term is a minterm:

```
F = acb + a'b
F = acb + a'b*1                       (identity)
F = acb + a'b*(c+c')                  (complement)
F = acb + a'bc + a'bc'                (distributive)
```

3. (Optional step.) For neatness, arrange the literals within each term to a consistent order (say, alphabetical), and also arrange the terms in the order they would appear in a truth table:

```
F = a'bc' + a'bc + abc
```

The equation is now in sum-of-minterms form. The equation is in sum-of-products form, and every product term is a minterm because each term includes every variable exactly once.

An alternative canonical form is known as product of maxterms. A ***maxterm*** is a sum term in which every variable appears exactly once in either true or complemented form, such as (a + b + c') for a function of three variables a, b, and c. An equation is in ***product-of-maxterms form*** if the equation is the product of sum terms, and every sum term is a maxterm. An example of a function (different from that above) in product-of-maxterms form is J(a,b,c) = (a + b + c')(a' + b' + c'). To avoid confusing the reader, we will not discuss the product-of-maxterms form further, as sum-of-minterms form is more common in practice, and sufficient for our purposes.

Example 2.21 Comparing two functions using canonical form

Suppose we want to determine whether the functions G(a,b,c,d,e) = abcd + a'bcde and H(a,b,c,d,e) = abcde + abcde' + a'bcde + a'bcde(a' + c) are equivalent. We first convert G to sum-of-minterms form:

```
G = abcd + a'bcde
G = abcd(e+e') + a'bcde
G = abcde + abcde' + a'bcde
G = a'bcde + abcde' + abcde
```

We then convert H to sum-of-minterms form:

```
H = abcde + abcde' + a'bcde + a'bcde(a' + c)
H = abcde + abcde' + a'bcde + a'bcdea' + a'bcdec
H = abcde + abcde' + a'bcde + a'bcde + a'bcde
H = abcde + abcde' + a'bcde
H = a'bcde + abcde' + abcde
```

Clearly, G and H are equivalent.

Note that checking the equivalence using truth tables would have resulted in two rather large truth tables having 32 rows each. Using sum of minterms was probably more appropriate here.

Compact sum-of-minterms representation

A more compact representation of sum-of-minterms form involves listing each minterm as a number, with each minterm's number determined from the binary representation of its variables' values. For example, a'bcde corresponds to 01111, or 15; abcde' corresponds to 11110, or 30; and abcde corresponds to 11111, or 31. Thus, we can say that the function H represented by the equation

$$H = a'bcde + abcde' + abcde$$

is the sum of the minterms 15, 30, and 31, which can be compactly written as:

$$H = \Sigma m(15,30,31)$$

The summation symbol means the sum, and then the numbers inside the parentheses represent the minterms being summed on the right side of the equation.

Multiple-Output Combinational Circuits

The examples above showed combinational circuits with only one output, but many circuits have multiple outputs. The simplest approach to handling a multiple-output circuit is to treat each output separately, leading to a separate circuit for each output. Actually, the circuits need not be completely separate—they could share common gates. The following examples show how to handle multiple-output circuits.

Example 2.22 Two-output combinational circuit

Design a circuit to implement the following two equations of three inputs a, b, and c:

$$F = ab + c' \qquad G = ab + bc$$

We can design the circuit by simply creating two separate circuits, as in Figure 2.45(a).

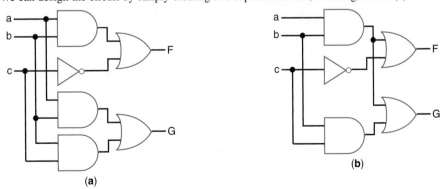

Figure 2.45 Multiple-output circuit: (a) treated as two separate circuits, and (b) with gate sharing.

We might instead notice that the term ab is common to both equations. Thus, the two circuits can share the gate that computes ab, as shown in Figure 2.45(b).

Example 2.23 Binary number to seven-segment display converter

Many electronic appliances display a number for us to read. Example appliances include a clock, a microwave oven, and a telephone answering machine. A popular and simple device for displaying a single digit number is a ***seven-segment display***, illustrated in Figure 2.46.

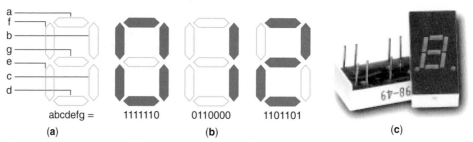

abcdefg =   1111110   0110000   1101101

(a)   **(b)**   **(c)**

Figure 2.46 Seven-segment display: (a) connections of inputs to segments, (b) input values for numbers 0, 1, and 2, and (c) a pair of real seven-segment display components.

The display consists of seven light segments, each of which can be illuminated independently of the others. A desired digit can be displayed by setting the signals a, b, c, d, e, f, and g appropriately. So to display the digit 8, all seven signals must be set to 1. To display the digit 1, b and c are each set to 1. A few letters can be displayed too, like a lower case "b."

Commonly, a microprocessor outputs a 4-bit binary number intended to be shown on a seven-segment display as a decimal (base ten) digit. Outputing four rather than seven signals conserves scarce pins on the microprocessor. Thus, a useful combinational circuit converts four bits w, x, y, and z of a binary number to the seven-segment display signals a–g, as in Figure 2.47.

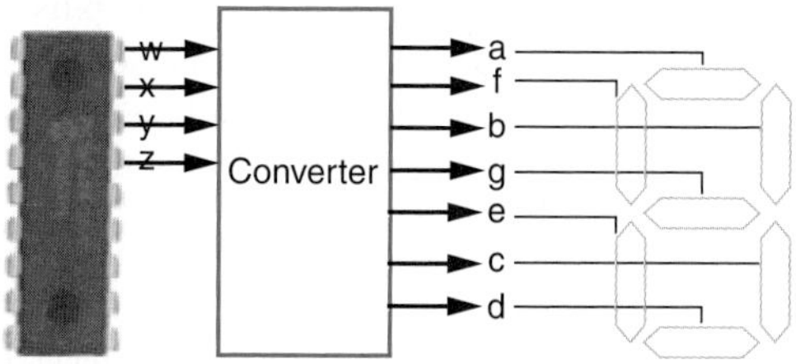

Figure 2.47 Binary to seven-segment converter.

The desired circuit behavior is easily captured as a table, shown in Table 2.4. In case the microprocessor outputs a number greater than 9, no segments are activated.

For this example, starting from a truth table is a more natural choice than an equation.

We can create a custom logic circuit to implement the converter. Note that Table 2.4 is in the form of a truth table having multiple outputs (a through g). We can treat each output separately, designing a circuit for a, then for b, etc. Summing the terms corresponding to the 1s in the a column (as was done in Figure 2.40) leads to the following equation for a:

$$a = w'x'y'z' + w'x'yz' + w'x'yz + w'xy'z + w'xyz'$$
$$+ w'xyz + wx'y'z' + wx'y'z$$

Likewise, summing the terms for the 1s in the b column leads to the following equation for b:

$$b = w'x'y'z' + w'x'y'z + w'x'yz' + w'x'yz + w'xy'z'$$
$$+ w'xyz + wx'y'z' + wx'y'z$$

Equations could similarly be created for the remaining outputs c through g. Finally, a circuit could be created for a having 8 4-input AND gates and an 8-input OR gate, another circuit for b having 8 4-input AND gates and an 8-input OR gate, and so on for c through g. We could, of course, have minimized the logic for each equation before creating each of the circuits.

You may notice that the equations for a and b have several terms in common. For example, the term w'x'y'z' appears in both equations. So it would make sense for both outputs to share one

TABLE 2.4 4-bit binary number to seven-segment display truth table.

w	x	y	z	a	b	c	d	e	f	g
0	0	0	0	1	1	1	1	1	1	0
0	0	0	1	0	1	1	0	0	0	0
0	0	1	0	1	1	0	1	1	0	1
0	0	1	1	1	1	1	1	0	0	1
0	1	0	0	0	1	1	0	0	1	1
0	1	0	1	1	0	1	1	0	1	1
0	1	1	0	1	0	1	1	1	1	1
0	1	1	1	1	1	1	0	0	0	0
1	0	0	0	1	1	1	1	1	1	1
1	0	0	1	1	1	1	1	0	1	1
1	0	1	0	0	0	0	0	0	0	0
1	0	1	1	0	0	0	0	0	0	0
1	1	0	0	0	0	0	0	0	0	0
1	1	0	1	0	0	0	0	0	0	0
1	1	1	0	0	0	0	0	0	0	0
1	1	1	1	0	0	0	0	0	0	0

AND gate generating that term. Looking at the truth table, we see that the term $w'x'y'z'$ is in fact needed for outputs a, b, c, e, f, and g, and thus the one AND gate generating that term could be shared by all six of those outputs. Likewise, each of the other required terms is shared by several outputs, meaning each gate generating each term could be shared among several outputs.

▶ 2.7 COMBINATIONAL LOGIC DESIGN PROCESS

The previous sections lead to the definition of a two-step process for designing combinational logic, summarized in Table 2.5. The first step is to describe the desired behavior of the logic, known as *capturing* the behavior. The behavior might be most naturally captured as a truth table or as equations, depending on particular problem. The second step is *converting* that behavior into a circuit. If the behavior was captured as a truth table, equations are first created from the truth table. A circuit is then created for each equation. These two steps of capturing the behavior and converting to a circuit will appear for more complex circuits in subsequent chapters too, though their details will differ.

TABLE 2.5 Combinational logic design process.

Step		Description
Step 1: Capture behavior	***Capture** the function*	Create a truth table or equations, whichever is most natural for the given problem, to describe the desired behavior of each output of the combinational logic.
Step 2: Convert to circuit	2A ***Create** equations*	This substep is only necessary if you captured the function using a truth table instead of equations. Create an equation for each output by ORing all the minterms for that output. Simplify the equations if desired.
	2B ***Implement** as a gate-based circuit*	For each output, create a circuit corresponding to the output's equation. (Sharing gates among multiple outputs is OK optionally.)

Below are several examples demonstrating the combinational logic design process. We normally create equations that are in sum-of-products form. Directly converting a sum-of-products equation into a circuit results in a column of AND gates (possibly preceded by some NOT gates) that feeds into a single OR gate, which is known as a ***two-level circuit*** or ***two-level logic***.

Example 2.24 Three 1s pattern detector

This example implements a circuit that can detect whether a pattern of at least three adjacent 1s occur anywhere in an 8-bit input, and that outputs a 1 in that case. The inputs are a, b, c, d, e, f, g, and h, and the output is y. So for an input of abcdefgh = 00011101, y should be 1, since there are three adjacent 1s, on inputs d, e, and f. For an input of 10101011, the output should be 0, since there are not three adjacent 1s anywhere. An input of 11110000 should result in y = 1, since having more than three adjacent 1s should still output a 1. Such a circuit is an extremely simple example of a general class of circuits known as pattern detectors. Pattern detectors are widely used in image processing to detect objects like humans or tanks in a digitized video image, or to detect specific spoken words in a digitized audio stream, for example.

For this example, starting from an equation is a more natural choice than a truth table.

Step 1: *Capture behavior.* We could capture the function as a rather large truth table, listing out all 256 combinations of inputs, and entering a 1 for y in each row where at least three 1s occur. However, a simpler method for capturing this particular function is to create an equation that lists the possible occurrences of three 1s in a row. One possibility is that of abc=111. Another is that of bcd=111. Likewise, if cde=111, def=111, efg=111, or fgh=111, we should output a 1. For each possibility, the values of the other inputs don't matter. So if abc=111, we output a 1, regardless of the values of d, e, f, g, and h. Thus, an equation describing y is simply:

$$y = abc + bcd + cde + def + efg + fgh$$

Step 2A: *Create equations.* We skip this substep because an equation was already created above.

Step 2B: *Implement as a gate-based circuit.* No simplification of the equation is possible. The resulting circuit is shown in Figure 2.48.

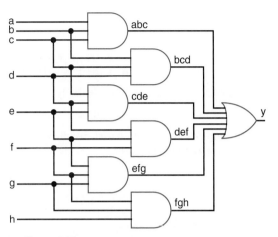

Figure 2.48 Three 1s pattern detector.

Example 2.25 Number-of-1s counter

For this example, starting from a truth table is a more natural choice than an equation.

This example designs a circuit that counts the number of 1s present on three inputs a, b, c, and outputs that number in binary using two outputs, y and z. An input of 110 has two 1s, so the circuit should output 10. The number of 1s on three inputs can range from 0 to 3, so a 2-bit output is sufficient, since 2 bits can represent 0 to 3. A number-of-1s counter circuit is useful in various situations, such as detecting the density of electronic particles hitting a collection of sensors by counting how many sensors are activated.

Step 1: Capture behavior. Capturing the behavior for this example is most naturally achieved using a truth table. We list all the possible input combinations, and the desired output number, as in Table 2.6.

TABLE 2.6 Truth table for number-of-1s counter.

Inputs			(# of 1s)	Outputs	
a	b	c		y	z
0	0	0	(0)	0	0
0	0	1	(1)	0	1
0	1	0	(1)	0	1
0	1	1	(2)	1	0
1	0	0	(1)	0	1
1	0	1	(2)	1	0
1	1	0	(2)	1	0
1	1	1	(3)	1	1

Step 2A: Create equations. We create equations (as was done in Figure 2.40) for each output as follows:

$$y = a'bc + ab'c + abc' + abc$$
$$z = a'b'c + a'bc' + ab'c' + abc$$

We can simplify the first equation algebraically:

$$y = a'bc + ab'c + ab(c' + c) = a'bc + ab'c + ab$$

Step 2B: Implement as a gate-based circuit. We then create the final circuits for the two outputs, as shown in Figure 2.49.

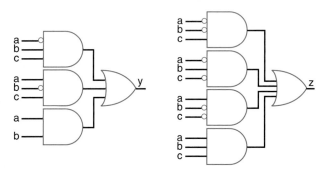

Figure 2.49 Number-of-1s counter gate-based circuit.

Simplifying Circuit Notations

Some new simplifying notations were used in the circuits in the previous example. One simplifying notation is to list the inputs multiple times, as in Figure 2.50(a). Such listing reduces lines in a drawing crossing one another. An input listed multiple times is assumed to have been branched from the same input.

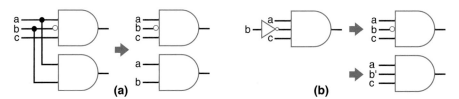

Figure 2.50 Simplifying circuit notations: (a) listing inputs multiple times to reduce drawing of crossing wires, (b) using inversion bubbles or complemented input to reduce NOT gates drawn.

Another simplifying notation is the use of an inversion bubble at the input of a gate, rather than the use of an inverter, as in Figure 2.50(b). An *__inversion bubble__* is a small circle drawn at the input of a gate as shown, indicating that the signal is inverted. An external input that has inversion bubbles at many gates is assumed to feed through a single inverter that is then branched out to those gates. An alternative simplification is to simply list the input as complemented, like b' shown in the figure.

Example 2.26 12-button keypad to 4-bit code converter

You've probably seen 12-button keypads in many different places, like on a telephone or at an ATM machine as shown in Figure 2.51. The first row has buttons 1, 2, and 3, the second row has 4, 5, and 6, the third row has 7, 8, and 9, and the last row has *, 0, and #. The outputs of such a keypad consist of seven signals—one for each of the four rows (r1, r2, r3, and r4), and one for each of the three columns (c1, c2, and c3). Pushing a particular button causes exactly two outputs to become 1, corresponding to the row and column of that button. So pushing button "1" causes r1=1 and c1=1, while pushing button "#" causes r4=1 and c3=1.

A useful circuit converts the seven signals from the keypad into a 4-bit output wxyz that indicates which button is pressed, as in Figure

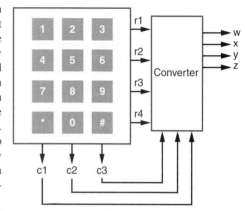

Figure 2.51 Converter for 12-button keypad.

For this example, starting from equations is a more natural choice than a truth table, although we used an informal table (not a truth table) to help us determine the equations.

2.51; the output may be connected to a microprocessor or other device. Buttons "0" to "9" should be encoded as 0000 through 1001 (0 through 9 in binary), respectively. Button "*" should be encoded as 1010, and # as 1011. 1111 will mean that no button is pressed. Assume for now that only one button can ever be pressed at a given time.

Step 1: Capture behavior. We could capture the behavior for w, x, y, and z using a truth table, with the seven inputs on the left side of the table, and the four outputs on the right side, but that table would have $2^7 = 128$ rows, and most of those rows would correspond merely to multiple buttons being pressed. Let's try instead to capture the functions using equations. The informal table in Table 2.7 might help us get started.

TABLE 2.7 Informal table for the 12-button keypad to 4-bit code converter.

Button	Signals		4-bit code outputs			
			w	x	y	z
1	r1	c1	0	0	0	1
2	r1	c2	0	0	1	0
3	r1	c3	0	0	1	1
4	r2	c1	0	1	0	0
5	r2	c2	0	1	0	1
6	r2	c3	0	1	1	0
7	r3	c1	0	1	1	1

Button	Signals		4-bit code outputs			
			w	x	y	z
8	r3	c2	1	0	0	0
9	r3	c3	1	0	0	1
*	r4	c1	1	0	1	0
0	r4	c2	0	0	0	0
#	r4	c3	1	0	1	1
(none)			1	1	1	1

Guided by this table, we can create equations for each of the four outputs, as follows:

w = r3c2 + r3c3 + r4c1 + r4c3 + r1'r2'r3'r4'c1'c2'c3'

x = r2c1 + r2c2 + r2c3 + r3c1 + r1'r2'r3'r4'c1'c2'c3'

$$y = r1c2 + r1c3 + r2c3 + r3c1 + r4c1 + r4c3 +$$
$$r1'r2'r3'r4'c1'c2'c3'$$

$$z = r1c1 + r1c3 + r2c2 + r3c1 + r3c3 + r4c3 +$$
$$r1'r2'r3'r4'c1'c2'c3'$$

Step 2B: Implement as gate-based circuit. (We skip substep 2A, as we already created equations). We can now create a circuit for each output. Obviously, the last term of each equation could be shared by all four outputs. Other terms could be shared too (like $r2c3$).

Note that this circuit would not work well if multiple buttons can be pressed simultaneously. Our circuit will output either a valid or invalid code in that situation, depending on which buttons were pressed. A preferable circuit would treat multiple buttons being pressed as no button being pressed. We leave the design of that circuit as an exercise.

Circuits similar to what we designed above exist in computer keyboards, except that there are a lot more rows and columns.

▶ SLOW DOWN! THE QWERTY KEYBOARD

Inside a standard computer keyboard is a small microprocessor and a ROM. The microprocessor detects which key is being pressed, looks up the 8-bit code for that key (much like the 12-button keypad in Example 2.26) from the ROM, and sends that code to the computer. There's an interesting story behind the way the keys are arranged in a standard PC keyboard, which is known as a QWERTY keyboard because those are the keys that begin the top left row of letters. The QWERTY arrangement was made in the era of typewriters (shown in the picture below), which, in case you haven't seen one, had each key connected to an arm that would swing up and press an ink ribbon against paper.

Arms stuck!

An annoying problem with typewriters was that arms would often get jammed side-by-side up near the paper if you typed too fast—like too many people getting jammed side-by-side while they all try to simultaneously walk through a doorway. So typewriter keys were arranged in the QWERTY arrangement to *slow down* typing by *separating* common letters, since slower typing reduced the occurrences of jammed keys. When PCs were invented, the QWERTY arrangement was the natural choice for PC keyboards, as people were accustomed to that arrangement. Some say the differently-arranged Dvorak keyboard enables faster typing, but that type of keyboard isn't very common, as people are just too accustomed to the QWERTY keyboard.

Keys connected to arms.

Example 2.27 Sprinkler valve controller

Automatic lawn sprinkler systems use a digital system to control the opening and closing of water valves. A sprinkler system usually supports several different zones, such as the backyard, left side yard, right side yard, front yard, etc. Only one zone's valve can be opened at a time in order to maintain enough water pressure in the sprinklers in that zone. Suppose a sprinkler system supports up to 8 zones. Typically, a sprinkler system is controlled by a small, inexpensive microprocessor executing a program that opens each valve only at specific times of the day and for specific durations. Suppose the microprocessor only has 4 output pins available to control the valves, not 8 outputs as required for the 8 zones. We can instead program the microprocessor to use 1 pin to indicate whether a valve should be opened, and use the 3 other pins to output the active zone (0, 1, ..., 7) in binary. Thus, we need to design a combinational circuit having 4 inputs, e (the enabler) and a, b, c (the binary value of the active zone), and having 8 outputs d7, d6, ..., d0 (the valve controls), as shown in Figure 2.52. When e=1, the circuit should decode the 3-bit binary input by setting exactly one output to 1.

Step 1: **Capture behavior.** Valve 0 should be active when abc=000 and e=1. So the equation for d0 is:

$$d0 = a'b'c'e$$

Likewise, valve 1 should be active when abc=001 and e=1, so the equation for d1 is:

$$d1 = a'b'ce$$

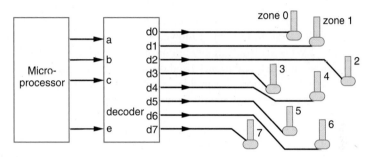

Figure 2.52 Sprinkler valve controller block diagram.

For this example, starting from equations is a more natural choice than a truth table.

The equations for the remaining outputs can be determined similarly:

$$d2 = a'bc'e$$
$$d3 = a'bce$$
$$d4 = ab'c'e$$
$$d5 = ab'ce$$
$$d6 = abc'e$$
$$d7 = abce$$

Step 2A: **Create equations.** Equations were already created.

Step 2B: **Implement as a gate-based circuit.** The circuit implementing the equations is shown in Figure 2.53. The circuit is actually a commonly used component known as a *decoder with enable*. Decoders as a building block will be introduced in an upcoming section.

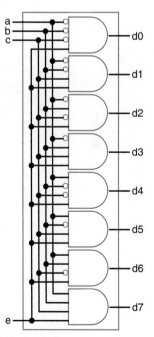

Figure 2.53 Sprinkler valve controller circuit (actually a 3x8 decoder with enable).

▶ 2.8 MORE GATES

Designers use several other types of gates beyond just AND, OR, and NOT. Those gates include NAND, NOR, XOR, and XNOR.

NAND & NOR

NAND

A *NAND* gate (short for "not AND") has the opposite output of an AND gate, outputting a 0 only when all inputs are 1, and outputting a 1 otherwise (meaning at least one input is 0). A NAND gate has the same behavior as an AND gate followed by a NOT gate. Figure 2.54(a) illustrates a NAND gate.

NOR

A *NOR* gate ("not OR") has the opposite output as an OR gate, outputting a 0 if at least one input is 1, and outputting 1 if all inputs are 0. A NOR gate has the same behavior as an OR gate followed by a NOT gate. Figure 2.54(b) shows a NOR gate.

Whereas Boolean algebra has the symbols "*" and "+" for the AND and OR operations, no such commonly-used operator symbols exist for NAND and NOR. Instead, the NAND operation on variables a and b would be written as (a*b)' or just (ab)', and the NOR operation would be written as (a + b)'.

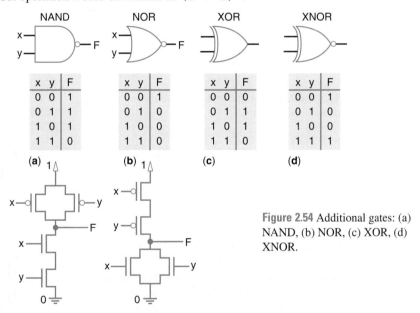

Figure 2.54 Additional gates: (a) NAND, (b) NOR, (c) XOR, (d) XNOR.

Section 2.4 warned that the shown CMOS transistor implementations of AND and OR gates were not realistic. The reason is because pMOS transistors don't conduct 0s very well, but they conduct 1s just fine. Likewise, nMOS transistors don't conduct 1s well, but they conduct 0s just fine. The reasons for these asymmetries are beyond this book's scope. The implications are that the AND and OR gates in Figure 2.8 are not feasible, as they rely on pMOS transistors to conduct 0s (but pMOS conducts 0s poorly) and nMOS transistors to conduct 1s (but nMOS conducts 1s poorly). However, if we switch the locations of power and ground in the AND and OR circuits of Figure 2.8, the results are the NAND and NOR gate circuits shown in Figure 2.54(a) and Figure 2.54(b).

An AND gate can still be implemented in CMOS, by appending a NOT gate at the output of a NAND gate (NAND followed by NOT computes AND), as in Figure 2.55. Likewise, an OR gate is implemented by appending a NOT gate at the output of a NOR gate. Those gates are obviously slower than NAND and NOR gates due to the extra NOT gate at the output. Fortunately, straightforward methods can convert any AND/OR/NOT circuit to a NAND-only circuit, or to a NOR-only circuit. Section 7.2 describes such methods.

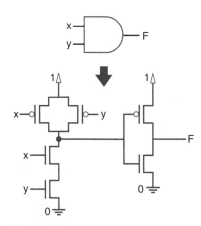

Figure 2.55 AND gate in CMOS.

Example 2.28 Aircraft lavatory sign using a NAND gate

Example 2.15 created a lavatory available sign using the following equation:

$$S = (abc)'$$

Noticing that the term on the right side corresponds to a NAND, the circuit can be implemented using a single NAND gate, as shown in Figure 2.56.

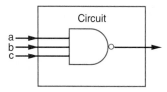

Figure 2.56 Circuit using NAND.

XOR & XNOR

A 2-input XOR gate, short for "exclusive or" and pronounced as "ex or," outputs a 1 if *exactly* one of the two inputs has a value of 1. So if such a gate has inputs a and b, then the output F will be 1 if a=1 and b=0, or if b=1 and a=0. A 2-input XOR gate is equivalent to the function F = ab' + a'b. In other words, one or the other input is 1, but not both. Figure 2.54(c) illustrates an XOR gate (for simplicity, we omit the transistor-level implementation of an XOR gate). For XOR gates with three or more inputs, the output is 1 only if the number of input 1s is odd.

An XNOR gate, short for "exclusive nor", and pronounced "ex nor," is simply the opposite of XOR. A 2-input XNOR is equivalent to F = a'b' + ab. In other words, F will be 1 if both input values are 0s, or if both input values are 1s. Figure 2.54(d) illustrates an XNOR gate, omitting the transistor-level implementation for simplicity. For XNOR gates with 3 or more inputs, the output is 1 only if the number of input 1s is even.

The XOR operation applied to variables a and b is written as $a \oplus b$; three variables would be $a \oplus b \oplus c$. There is no commonly used symbol for XNOR; instead, XNOR would be written as $(a \oplus b)'$

Interesting Uses of these Additional Gates

Detecting Binary 0 Using NOR

Figure 2.57 Detecting binary 0 with NOR.

A NOR gate can detect the situation of an *n*-bit binary number being equal to 0, because NOR outputs a 1 only when all *n* inputs are 0. For example, suppose a byte (8-bit) input to your system is counting down from 99 to 0, and when the byte reaches 0, you wish to sound an alarm. You can detect the byte being equal to 0 by simply connecting the 8 bits of the byte into an 8-input NOR gate. Figure 2.57 shows such detection for a 3-bit binary number.

Detecting Equality Using XNOR

XNOR gates can be used to compare two *n*-bit data items for equality, since a 2-input XNOR outputs a 1 only when the inputs are both 0 or are both 1. For example, suppose a byte input A (a7a6a5...a0) to your system is counting down from 99, and you want to sound an alarm when A has the same value as a second byte input B (b7b6b5...b0). You can detect such equality using eight 2-input XNOR gates, by connecting a0 and b0 to the first XNOR gate, a1 and b1 to the second XNOR gate, etc., as in Figure 2.58. Each XNOR gate indicates whether the bits in that particular position are equal. ANDing all the XNOR outputs indicates whether every position is equal.

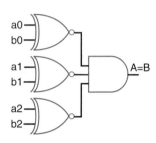

Figure 2.58 Detecting equality with 2-input XNORs.

Generating and Detecting Parity Using XOR

An XOR gate can be used to generate a parity bit for a set of data bits (see Example 2.19). XORing the data bits results in a 1 if there is an odd number of 1s in the data, so XOR computes the correct parity bit for even parity, because the XOR's output 1 would make the total number of 1s even. Notice that the truth table for generating an even parity bit in Table 2.3 does in fact represent a 3-bit XOR. Likewise, an XNOR gate can be used to generate an odd parity bit.

XOR can also be used to detect proper parity. XORing the incoming data bits along with the incoming parity bit will yield 1 if the number of 1s is odd. Thus, for even parity, XOR can be used to indicate that an error has occurred, since the number of 1s is supposed to be even. XNOR can be used to detect an error when odd parity is used.

Completeness of NAND and of NOR

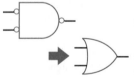

Figure 2.59 AND and NOT gates can form OR.

It should be fairly obvious that if you have AND gates, OR gates, and NOT gates, you can implement any Boolean function. This is because a Boolean function can be represented as a sum of products, which consists only of AND, OR, and NOT operations. The set of AND, OR, and NOT gates are thus **complete** with respect to implementing Boolean functions.

What might be slightly less obvious is that if you had only AND and NOT gates, you could still implement any Boolean function. Why? Here's a simple explanation—to obtain an OR, just put NOT gates at the inputs and output of an AND, as in Figure 2.59 (showing NOT gates as inversion bubbles). The resulting output computes OR, because F = (a'b')' = a'' + b'' (by DeMorgan's Law) = a + b.

Likewise, if you had only OR and NOT gates, you could implement any Boolean function. To obtain an AND, you could simply invert the inputs and output of an OR, since F = (a'+b')' = a''*b'' = ab.

It follows that if you *only* had NAND gates available, you could still implement any Boolean function. Why? We just saw above that we can implement any Boolean function using just NOT and AND gates. A NOT gate is a 1-input NAND gate. An AND gate can be implemented as a NAND gate followed by a 1-input NAND. Thus, we can implement any Boolean function using just NAND. A NAND gate is thus known as a **universal** gate.

Likewise, if you had only NOR gates, you could implement any Boolean function, because a NOT gate is a 1-input NOR gate, and an OR gate can be implemented as a NOR gate followed by a 1-input NOR. Since NOT and OR can implement any Boolean function, so can just NOR. A NOR gate is thus also known as a universal gate.

Number of Possible Logic Gates

Having seen several different types of basic 2-input logic gates (AND, OR, NAND, NOR, XOR, XNOR), one might wonder how many possible 2-input logic gates exist. That question is the same as asking how many Boolean functions exist for two variables. To answer the question, first note that a two-variable function's truth table will have $2^2 = 4$ rows. For each row, the function could output one of two possible values (0 or 1). Thus, as illustrated in Figure 2.60, there are $2 * 2 * 2 * 2 = 2^4 = 16$ possible functions.

a	b	F		
0	0	0 or 1	2 choices	2
0	1	0 or 1	2 choices	2
1	0	0 or 1	2 choices	2
1	1	0 or 1	2 choices	2

$2^4 = 16$ possible functions

Figure 2.60 Counting the number of possible Boolean functions of two variables.

Figure 2.61 lists all 16 such functions. The figure labels the 6 familiar functions (AND, OR, NAND, NOR, XOR, XNOR). Some of the other functions are 0, a, b, a', b', and 1. The remaining functions are uncommon functions, but each could be useful for some application. Thus, logic gates may not be built to represent those functions, but instead those functions, when needed, might be built as a circuit of the basic logic gates.

a	b	f0	f1	f2	f3	f4	f5	f6	f7	f8	f9	f10	f11	f12	f13	f14	f15
0	0	0	0	0	0	0	0	0	0	1	1	1	1	1	1	1	1
0	1	0	0	0	0	1	1	1	1	0	0	0	0	1	1	1	1
1	0	0	0	1	1	0	0	1	1	0	0	1	1	0	0	1	1
1	1	0	1	0	1	0	1	0	1	0	1	0	1	0	1	0	1
		0	a AND b		a		b	a XOR b	a OR b	a NOR b	a XNOR b	b'		a'		a NAND b	1

Figure 2.61 The 16 possible Boolean functions of two variables.

A more general question of interest is how many Boolean functions exist for a Boolean function of *N* variables. This number can be determined by first noting that an

N-variable function will have 2^N rows in its truth table. Then, note that each row can output one of two possible values. Thus, the number of possible functions will be $2 * 2 * 2 *\text{—}2^N$ times. Therefore, the total number of functions is:

$$2^{2^N}$$

So there are: $2^{2^3} = 2^8 = 256$ possible Boolean functions of 3 variables, and $2^{2^4} = 2^{16} = 65536$ possible functions of 4 variables.

▶ 2.9 DECODERS AND MUXES

Two additional components, a decoder and a multiplexer, are also commonly used as digital circuit building blocks, though they themselves can be built from logic gates.

Decoders

A decoder is a higher-level building block commonly used in digital circuits. A *decoder* decodes an input n-bit binary number by setting exactly one of the decoder's 2^n outputs to 1. For example, a 2-input decoder, illustrated in Figure 2.62(a), would have $2^2 = 4$ outputs, d3, d2, d1, d0. If the two inputs i1i0 are 00, d0 would be 1 and the remaining outputs would be 0. If i1i0=01, d1 would be 1. If i1i0=10, d2 would be 1. If i1i0=11, d3 would be 1. One and only one output of a decoder will ever be 1 at a given time, corresponding to the particular current value of the inputs, as shown in Figure 2.62(a).

The internal design of a decoder is straightforward. Consider a 2x4 decoder. Each output d0, d1, d2, and d3 is a distinct function. d0 should be 1 only when i1=0 and i0=0, so d0 = i1'i0'. Likewise, d1=i1'i0, d2=i1i0', and d3=i1i0. Thus, we build the decoder with one AND gate for each output, connecting the true or complemented values of i1 and i0 to each gate, as shown in Figure 2.62.

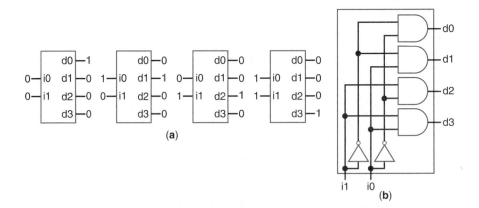

Figure 2.62 2x4 decoder: (a) outputs for possible input combinations, (b) internal design.

The internal design of a 3x8 decoder is similar: `d0=i2'i1'i0'`, `d1=i2'i1'i0`, etc.

A decoder often comes with an extra input called *enable*. When enable is `1`, the decoder acts normally. But when enable is `0`, the decoder outputs all `0`s—no output is a `1`. The enable is useful when sometimes you don't want to acti-vate any of the outputs. Without an enable, one output of the decoder *must* be a `1`, because the decoder has an output for every possible value of the decoder's *n*-bit input. We earlier created and used a decoder with enable in Figure 2.53. A block diagram and illustrated behavior of a decoder with enable appear in Figure 2.63.

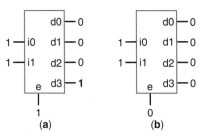

Figure 2.63 Decoder with enable: (a) `e=1`: normal decoding, (b) `e=0`: all outputs `0`.

When designing a particular system, we check whether part (or all) of the system's functionality could be carried out by a decoder. Using a decoder reduces the amount of required combinational logic design, as you'll see in Example 2.30.

Example 2.29 Basic questions about decoders

1. What would be a 2x4 decoder's output values when the inputs are `00`? *Answer:* `d0=1`, `d1=0`, `d2=0`, `d3=0`.

2. What would be a 2x4 decoder's output values when the inputs are `11`? *Answer:* `d0=0`, `d1=0`, `d2=0`, `d3=1`.

3. What input values of a 2x4 decoder cause more than one of the decoder's outputs to be `1` at the same time? *Answer:* No such input values exist. Only one of a decoder's outputs can be `1` at a given time.

4. What would the input values of a decoder be if the output values are `d0=0`, `d1=1`, `d2=0`, `d3=0`? *Answer:* The input values must be `i1=0`, `i0=1`.

5. What would the input values of a decoder be if the output values are `d0=1`, `d1=1`, `d2=0`, `d3=0`? *Answer:* This question is not valid. A decoder only has one output equal to `1` at any time.

6. How many outputs would a 5-input decoder have? *Answer:* 2^5, or 32.

7. A 2-input decoder with enable having inputs `i1=0`, `i0=1`, and `e=0`, would have what output values? *Answer:* All outputs would be `0`.

Example 2.30 New Year's Eve countdown display

A New Year's Eve countdown display could make use of a decoder. The display may have 60 light bulbs going up a tall pole, as in Figure 2.64. We want one light per second to illuminate (with the previous one turning off), starting from bulb 59 at the bottom of the pole, and ending with bulb 0 at the top. We could use a microprocessor to count down from 59 to 0, but the microprocessor probably doesn't have 60 output pins that we could use to control each light. Our microprocessor program could instead output the numbers 59, 58, ..., 2, 1, 0 in binary on a 6-bit output port (thus outputting `111011`, `111010`, ..., `000010`, `000001`, `000000`). Assume each light bulb has a signal that illuminates the bulb when set to 1. Thus, the problem is to design a circuit that, for each binary number that could be input, illuminates the appropriate light bulb.

Designing a circuit using gates could be done, but would require a design for each of the 60 bulb signals. Instead, we could connect those six bits coming from the microprocessor to a 6-input, 64 (2^6)-output decoder, with decoder output d59 lighting bulb 59, d58 lighting bulb 58, etc.

We'd probably want an enable on our decoder in this example, since all the lights should be off until we started the countdown. The microprocessor would initially set enable to 0 so that no lights would be illuminated. When the 60 second countdown begins, the microprocessor would set enable to 1, and then output 59, then 58 (1 second later), then 57, etc. The final system would look like that in Figure 2.64.

Figure 2.64 Using a 6x64 decoder to connect a microprocessor and a column of lights for a New Year's Eve display. The microprocessor sets e = 1 when the last minute countdown begins, and then counts down from 59 to 0 in binary on the pins i5..i0. Note that the microprocessor should never output 60, 61, 62, or 63 on i5..i0, and thus those outputs of the decoder go unused.

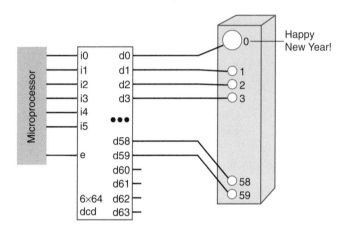

Notice that we implemented this system without having to design any gate-level combinational logic—we merely used a decoder and connected it to the appropriate inputs and outputs.

Whenever you have outputs such that exactly one of those outputs should be set to 1 based on the value of inputs representing a binary number, think about using a decoder.

Multiplexers (Muxes)

A multiplexer ("mux" for short) is another higher-level building block in digital circuits. An *Mx1* **multiplexer** has *M* data inputs and 1 output, and allows only one input to pass through to that output. A set of additional inputs, known as select inputs, determines which input to pass through. Multiplexers are sometimes called *selectors* because they select one input to pass through to the output.

A mux is like a railyard switch that connects multiple input tracks to a single output track, as shown in Figure 2.65. The switch's control lever causes the connection of the appropriate input track to the output track. Whether a train appears at the output depends on whether a train exists on the presently selected input track. For a mux, the switch's control is not a lever, but rather select inputs, which represent the desired connection in binary. Rather than a train appearing or not appearing at the output, a mux outputs a 1 or a 0 depending on whether the connected input has a 1 or a 0.

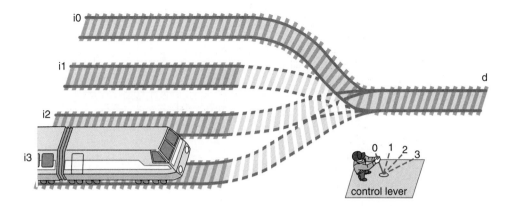

Figure 2.65 A multiplexer is like a railyard switch, determining which input track connects to the single output track, according to the switch's control lever.

A 2-input multiplexer, known as a 2x1 multiplexer, has two data inputs i1 and i0, one select input s0, and one data output d, as shown in Figure 2.66(a). As shown in Figure 2.66(b), if s0=0, i0's value passes through; if s0=1, i1's value passes through.

The internal design of a 2x1 multiplexer is shown in Figure 2.66(c). When s0=0, the top AND gate outputs 1*i0=i0, and the bottom AND gate outputs 0*i1=0. Thus, the OR gate outputs i0+0=i0. So i0 passes through as desired. Likewise, when s0=1, the bottom gate passes i1 while the top gate outputs 0, resulting in the OR gate passing i1.

A 4-input multiplexer, known as a 4x1 multiplexer, has four data inputs i3, i2, i1, and i0, two select inputs s1 and s0, and one data output d. A mux *always* has just one data output, no matter how many inputs. A 4x1 mux block diagram is shown in Figure 2.67(a).

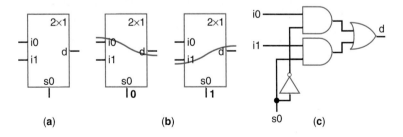

Figure 2.66 2x1 multiplexer: (a) block symbol, (b) connections for s0=0, and s0=1, and (c) internal design.

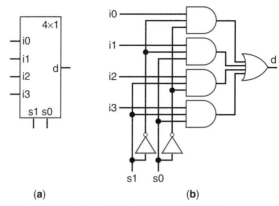

Figure 2.67 4x1 multiplexer: (a) block symbol and (b) internal design.

The internal design of a 4x1 multiplexer is shown in Figure 2.67(b). When s1s0=00, the top AND gate outputs i0*1*1=i0, the next AND gate outputs i1*0*1=0, the next gate outputs i2*1*0=0, and the bottom gate outputs i3*0*0=0. The OR gate outputs i0+0+0+0=i0. Thus, i0 passes through, as desired. Likewise, when s1s0=01, the second AND gate passes i1, while the remaining AND gates all output 0. When s1s0=10, the third AND gate passes i2, and the other AND gates output 0. When s1s0=11, the bottom AND gate passes i3, and the other AND gates output 0. For any value on s1s0, only 1 AND gate will have two 1s for its select inputs and will thus pass its data input; the other AND gates will have at least one 0 for its select inputs and will thus output 0.

An 8x1 multiplexer would have 8 data inputs (i7...i0), 3 select inputs (s2, s1, and s0), and one data output. More generally, an Mx1 multiplexer has M data inputs, $\log_2(M)$ select inputs, and one data output. Remember, a multiplexer always has just one output.

Example 2.31 Basic questions about multiplexers

Assume a 4x1 multiplexer's data inputs have the following present values: i0=1, i1=1, i2=0, and i3=0. What would be the value on the multiplexer's output d for the following select input values?

1. s1s0 = 01. *Answer:* Because s1s0=01 passes input i1 through to d, then d would have the value of i1, which presently is 1.

2. s1s0 = 11. *Answer:* That configuration of select line input values passes i3 through, so d would have the value of i3, which presently is 0.

3. How many select inputs must be present on a 16x1 multiplexer? *Answer:* Four select inputs would be needed to uniquely identify which of the 16 inputs to pass through to the output since $\log_2(16)=4$.

4. How many select lines are there on a 4x2 multiplexer? *Answer:* This question is not valid—there is no such thing as a 4x2 multiplexer. A multiplexer has exactly one output.

5. How many data inputs are there on a multiplexer having five select inputs? *Answer:* Five select inputs can uniquely identify one of $2^5=32$ inputs to pass through to the output.

Example 2.32 Mayor's vote display using a multiplexer

Consider a small town with a very unpopular mayor. During every town meeting, the city manager presents four proposals to the mayor, who then indicates his vote on the proposal (approve or deny). Very consistently, right after the mayor indicates his vote, the town's citizens boo and shout profanities at the mayor—no matter which way he votes. Having had enough of this abuse, the mayor sets up a simple digital system (the mayor happens to have taken a course in digital design), shown in Figure 2.68. He provides himself with four switches that can be positioned up or down, outputting 1 or 0, respectively. When the time comes during the meeting for him to vote on the first proposal, he places the first switch either in the up (accept) or down (deny) position—but nobody else can see the position of the switch. When the time

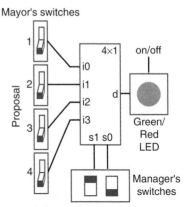

Figure 2.68 Mayor's vote display system implemented using a 4x1 mux.

comes to vote on the second proposal, he votes on the second proposal by placing the second switch up or down. And so on. When he has finished casting all his votes, he leaves the meeting and heads home. With the mayor gone, the city manager powers up a large green/red light. When the input to the light is 0, the light lights up red. When the input is 1, the light lights up green. The city manager controls two "select" switches that can route any of the mayor's switch outputs to the light, and so the manager steps through each configuration of the switches, starting with configuration 00 (and calling out "The mayor's vote on this proposal is ..."), then 01, then 10, and finally 11, causing the light to light either green or red for each configuration depending on the positions of the mayor's switches. The system can easily be implemented using a 4x1 multiplexer, as shown in Figure 2.68.

N-bit Mx1 Multiplexer

Muxes are often used to selectively pass through not just single bits, but N-bit data items. For example, one set of inputs A may consist of four bits a3, a2, a1, a0, and another set of inputs B may also consist of four bits b3, b2, b1, b0. We want to multiplex those inputs to a four-bit output C, con-

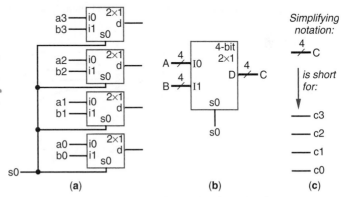

Figure 2.69 4-bit 2x1 mux: (a) internal design using four 2x1 muxes for selecting among 4-bit data items A or B, and (b) block diagram of a 4-bit 2x1 mux component. (c) The block diagram uses a common simplifying notation, using one thick wire with a slanted line and the number 4 to represent 4 single wires.

sisting of c3, c2, c1, c0. Figure 2.69(a) shows how to accomplish such multiplexing using four 2x1 muxes.

Because muxing data is so common, another common building block is that of an *N*-bit-wide *M*x1 multiplexer. So in our example, we would use a 4-bit 2x1 mux. Don't get confused, though—an *N*-bit *M*x1 multiplexer is really just the same as *N* separate *M*x1 multiplexers, with all those muxes sharing the same select inputs. Figure 2.69(b) provides the symbol for a 4-bit 2x1 mux.

Example 2.33 Multiplexed automobile above-mirror display

Some cars come with a display above the rearview mirror, as shown in Figure 2.70. The car's driver can press a button to select among displaying the outside temperature, the average miles per gallon of the car, the instantaneous miles per gallon, and the approximate miles remaining until the car runs out of gasoline. Assume the car's central computer sends the data to the display as four 8-bit binary numbers, T (the temperature), A (average mpg), I (instantaneous mpg), and M (miles remaining). T consists of 8 bits: t7, t6, t5, t4, t3, t2, t1, t0. Likewise for A, I, and M. Assume the display system has two additional inputs x and y, which

Figure 2.70 Above-mirror display.

always change according to the following sequence—00, 01, 10, 11—whenever the button is pressed (we'll see in a later chapter how to create such a sequence). When xy=00, we want to display T. When xy=01, we want to display A. When xy=10, we want to display I, and when xy=11, we want to display M. Assume the outputs D go to a display that knows how to convert the 8-bit binary number on D to a human-readable displayed number like that in Figure 2.70.

We can design the display system using eight 4x1 multiplexers. A simpler representation of that same design uses an 8-bit 4x1 multiplexer, as shown in Figure 2.71.

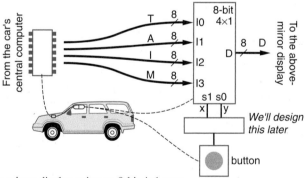

Figure 2.71 Above-mirror display using an 8-bit 4x1 mux.

Notice how many wires must be run from the car's central computer, which may be under the hood, to the above-mirror display—8*4=32 wires. That's a lot of wires. We'll see in a later chapter how to reduce the number of wires.

Notice in the previous example how simple a design can be when we can utilize higher-level building blocks. If we had to use regular 4x1 muxes, we would have 8 of them, and lots of wires drawn. If we had to use gates, we would have 40 of them. Of course, underlying our simple design in Figure 2.71 are in fact eight 4x1 muxes, and underlying those are 40 gates. And underlying those gates are lots more transistors. We see that the higher-level building blocks make our design task much more managable.

▶ 2.10 ADDITIONAL CONSIDERATIONS

Nonideal Gate Behavior—Delay

Ideally, a logic gate's output would change immediately in response to changes on the gate's inputs. The timing diagrams earlier in this chapter assumed such ideal zero-delay gates, as shown in Figure 2.72(a) for an OR gate. Unfortunately, real gate outputs don't change immediately, but rather after some short time delay. As an analogy, even the fastest automobiles can't go from 0 to 60 miles per hour in 0 seconds. A gate's delay is due in part to the fact that transistors don't switch from nonconducting to conducting (or vice versa) immediately—it takes some time for electrons to accumulate in the channel of an nMOS transistor, for example. Furthermore, electric current travels at the speed of light, which, while extremely fast, is still not infinitely fast. Additionally, wires aren't perfect and can slow down electric current because of "parasitic" characteristics like capacitance and inductance.

For example, the timing diagram in Figure 2.72(a) shows how an OR gate's output would ideally change from 0 to 1 when an input becomes 1. Figure 2.72(b) depicts how the output would actually rise slowly from 0 Volts, representing logic 0, to its higher voltage of 1.8 Volts, representing logic 1.

The maximum time for a gate's output to change (from 0 to 1 or 1 to 0) in response to an input change is the gate's *delay*. Delays for modern CMOS gates can be less than 1 nanosecond, which is extremely fast, but still not zero. Similarly, wires also have delays.

The delay of a circuit, known as ***circuit delay***, is the delay of the longest path from input to output, known as the circuit's ***critical path***. Figure 2.73 shows a circuit with sample delays shown. Each wire has a delay of 1 nanosecond. The delay of the AND gate, OR gate, and NOT gate is 1 ns, 1 ns, and 0.5 ns, respectively. Three paths through the circuit are shown, one from t to w, one from s to w, and one from k to w (the path

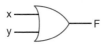

Figure 2.72 OR gate timing diagram: (a) ideal behavior without gate delay, (b) a more realistic depiction of F changing from lower to higher voltage, (c) F's value shown with logic 0 and 1 values but incorporating the delay.

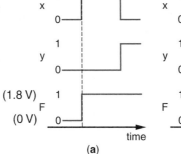

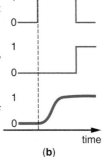

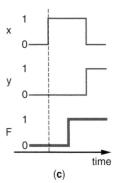

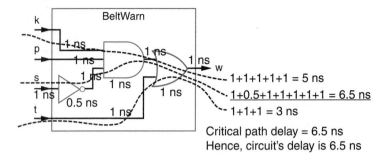

Figure 2.73 Computing the delay of the *BeltWarn* circuit from Example 2.8.

from p to w is the same length and thus not shown). The path from k to w passes through a wire (1 ns), the AND gate (1 ns), another wire (1 ns), the OR gate (1 ns), and finally the wire to the output (1 ns), for a total path delay of 5 ns. The path from s to w passes through a wire (1 ns), the NOT gate (0.5 ns), a wire (1 ns), the AND gate (1 ns), a wire (1 ns), the OR gate (1 ns), and finally the wire to the output (1 ns), for a path delay of 6.5 ns. Finally, the path from t to w passes through a wire (1 ns), the OR gate (1 ns), and a wire (1 ns), for a path delay of 3 ns. The path from s to w is thus the critical path, and hence the circuit's delay is said to be 6.5 ns. Even though the output would change in less than 6.5 ns in response to t's input changing, such information is not usually considered by digital designers; a designer using this circuit should expect to have to wait 6.5 ns for the output to change in response to *any* change on the inputs.

Active Low Inputs

Component inputs can generally be divided into two types. **Control inputs** influence the behavior of the component, such as the two select inputs of a 4x1 mux, or the enable input of a 3x8 decoder. In contrast, **data inputs** flow through the component, such as the 4 data inputs of a 4x1 mux, the 3 data inputs of a 3x8 decoder, or the inputs of any logic gate. Some control inputs involve the notion of being *active*—when the input is at one of its two levels, the input is carrying out its purpose; at the other level, the input is inactive.

For example, the enable input of a decoder is *active* when its value is set to enable the decoder. Normally the active value of a control input is 1, in which case the control input is said to be *active high*. However, sometimes the active value of a control input is 0, in which case the control input is said to be *active low*. For example, an active low decoder enable input would enable the decoder when 0, and disable the decoder when 1, as in Figure 2.74. Active low control inputs are typically denoted using an inversion bubble, as in the figure.

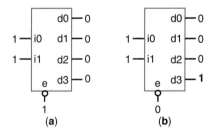

Figure 2.74 Decoder with active low enable input: (a) e=1: disabled, all outputs 0, (b) e=0: enabled, normal output.

Sometimes the input's name will also be modified to suggest the input's active low nature, such as e_L, /e, or ē. The reason for the existence of active low inputs is typically related to the efficiency of the components's internal circuit design.

When discussing the behavior of a component, designers will often use the term *assert* to mean setting a control input to the value that activates the associated operation. Thus, we might say that one must "assert" the enable input of a decoder to enable the decoder's outputs to be active. Using the term *assert* avoids possible confusion that could occur when some control inputs are active-high and others are active-low.

Demultiplexers and Encoders

Two additional components, demultiplexers and encoders, can also be considered combinational building blocks. However, those components are far less commonly used than their counterparts of multiplexers and decoders. Nevertheless, for completeness, we'll briefly introduce those additional components here. You may notice throughout this book that demultiplexers and encoders don't appear in many examples, if in any examples at all.

Demultiplexer

A demultiplexer has roughly the opposite functionality of a multiplexer. Specifically, a 1x*M* **demultiplexer** has one data input, and based on the values of $\log_2(M)$ select lines, passes that input through to one of *M* outputs. The other outputs stay 0.

Encoder

An **encoder** has the opposite functionality of a decoder. Specifically, an n x log2(n) encoder has n inputs and $\log_2(n)$ outputs. Of the n inputs, exactly one is assumed to be 1 at any given time (such would be the case if the input consisted of a sliding or rotating switch with n possible positions, for example). The encoder outputs a binary value over the $\log_2(n)$ outputs, indicating which of the n inputs was a 1. For example, a 4x2 encoder would have four inputs d3, d2, d1, d0, and two outputs e1, e0. For an input 0001, the output is 00. 0010 yields 01, 0100 yields 10, and 1000 yields 11. In other words, d0=1 results in an output of 0 in binary, d1=1 results in an output of 1 in binary, d2=1 results in an output of 2 in binary, and d3=1 results in an output of 3 in binary.

A *priority encoder* has similar behavior, but handles situations where more than one input is 1 at the same time. A priority encoder gives priority to the highest input that is a 1, and outputs the binary value of that input. For example, if a 4x2 priority encoder has inputs d3 and d1 both equal to 1 (so the inputs are 1010), the priority encoder gives priority to d3, and hence outputs 11 .

Schematic Capture and Simulation

How do designers know whether they designed a circuit correctly? Perhaps they created the truth table wrong, putting a 0 in an output column where they should have put a 1. Or perhaps they wrote down the wrong minterm, writing xyz when they should have written xyz'. For example, consider the number-of-ones counter in Example 2.25. That example involved creating a truth table, then equations, and finally a circuit. Is the circuit correct?

One method of checking a circuit is to reverse engineer the function from the circuit—starting with the circuit, we could convert the circuit to equations, and then the equations to a truth table. If the result is the same original truth table, then the circuit is likely to be correct. However, sometimes designers start with an equation rather than a truth table, as in Example 2.24. A designer can reverse engineer the circuit to an equation, but that equation may be different than the original equation, especially if the designer algebraically manipulated the original equation when designing the circuit. Furthermore, checking that two equations are equivalent may require converting to canonical form (sum-of-minterms), which may result in huge equations if the function has a large number of inputs.

In fact, even if a designer didn't make any mistakes in converting a mental under-standing of the desired function into a truth table or equation, how does the designer know that the original understanding was correct?

A commonly used method for checking that a circuit works as expected is called simulation. *Simulation* of a circuit is the process of providing sample inputs to the circuit and running a computer program that computes the circuit's output for the given inputs. A designer can then check that the output matches what is expected. The computer program that performs simulation is called a *simulator*.

To use simulation to check a circuit, a designer must describe the circuit using a method that enables computer programs to read the circuit. One method of describing a circuit is to draw the circuit using a schematic capture tool. A *schematic capture tool*

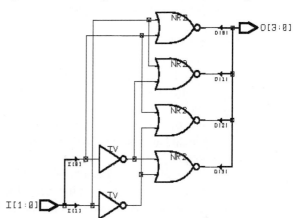

Figure 2.75 Display snapshot of a commercial schematic capture tool.

allows a user to place logic gates on a computer screen and to draw wires connecting those gates. The tool allows users to save their circuit drawings as computer files. All the circuit drawings in this chapter have represented examples of schematics—for example, the circuit drawing in Figure 2.62(b), which showed a 2x4 decoder, was an example of a schematic. Figure 2.75 shows a schematic for the same design, drawn using a popular commercial schematic capture tool. Schematic capture is used not only to capture circuits for simulator tools, but also for tools that map our circuits to physical implementations, which will be discussed in Chapter 7.

Once a designer has created a circuit using schematic capture, the designer must provide the simulator with a set of inputs that will be used to check for proper output. One way of providing the inputs is by drawing waveforms for the circuit's inputs. An input's *waveform* is a line that goes from left to right, representing the value of the input as time proceeds to the right. The line is drawn high to represent 1 and low to represent 0

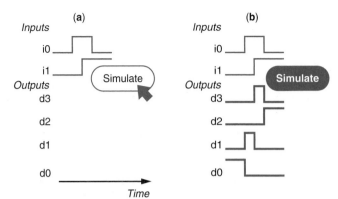

Figure 2.76 Simulation: (a) begins with us defining the inputs signal over time, (b) automatically generates the output waveforms when we ask the simulator to simulate the circuit.

for periods of time, as shown in Figure 2.76(a). After a designer is satisfied with the input waveforms, the designer instructs the simulator to simulate the circuit for the given input waveforms. The simulator determines what the circuit outputs would be for each unique combination of inputs, and generates waveforms for the outputs, as illustrated in Figure 2.76(b). The designer can then check that the output waveforms match the output values that are expected. Such checking can be done visually, or by providing certain checking statements (often called *assertions*) to the simulator.

Simulation still does not guarantee that a circuit is correct, but rather increases a designer's *confidence* that the circuit is correct.

▷ 2.11 COMBINATIONAL LOGIC OPTIMIZATIONS AND TRADEOFFS (SEE SECTION 6.2)

The earlier sections in this chapter described how to create basic combinational circuits. This section physically appears in this book as Section 6.2, and describes how to make those circuits better (smaller, faster, etc.)—namely, how to make optimizations and tradeoffs. One use of this book involves studying combinational logic optimizations and tradeoffs immediately after studying basic combinational logic design, meaning covering that section now (as Section 2.11). An alternative use of the book studies that section later (as Section 6.2), after also studying basic sequential design, datapath components, and register-transfer level design—namely, after Chapters 3, 4, and 5.

▷ 2.12 COMBINATIONAL LOGIC DESCRIPTION USING HARDWARE DESCRIPTION LANGUAGES (SEE SECTION 9.2)

Hardware description languages (HDLs) allow designers to describe their circuits using a textual language rather than as circuit drawings. This section introduces the use of HDLs to describe combinational logic. The section physically appears in the book as Section 9.2. One use of this book studies HDLs now (as Section 2.12), immediately after studying basic combinational logic. An alternative use of the book studies HDLs later (as Section 9.2), after mastery of basic combinational, sequential, and register-transfer level design.

▷ 2.13 CHAPTER SUMMARY

Section 2.1 introduced the idea of using a custom digital circuit to implement a system's desired functionality and defined combinational logic as a digital circuit whose outputs are a function of the circuit's present inputs. Section 2.2 provided a brief history of digital switches, starting from relays in the 1930s to today's CMOS transistors, with the main trend being the amazing pace at which switch size and delay have continued to shrink for the past several decades, leading to ICs capable of containing a billion transistors or more. Section 2.3 described the basic behavior of a CMOS transistor, just enough information to remove the mystery of how transistors work.

Section 2.4 introduced three fundamental building blocks for building digital circuits—AND gates, OR gates, and NOT gates (inverters), which are far easier to work with than transistors. Section 2.5 showed how Boolean algebra could be used to represent circuits built from AND, OR, and NOT gates, enabling us to build and manipulate circuits by using math—an extremely powerful concept. Section 2.6 introduced several different representations of Boolean functions, namely equations, circuits, and truth tables.

Section 2.7 described a straightforward three-step process for designing combinational circuits, and gave several examples of building real circuits using the three-step process.

Section 2.8 described why NAND and NOR gates are actually more commonly used than AND and OR gates in CMOS technology, and showed that any circuit built from AND, OR, and NOT gates could be built with NAND gates alone or NOR gates alone. That section also introduced two other commonly used gates, XOR and XNOR. Section 2.9 introduced two additional commonly used combinational building blocks, decoders and multiplexers.

Section 2.10 discussed how real gates actually have a small delay between the time that inputs change and the time that the gate's output changes. The section introduced active low inputs, and it also introduced some less commonly used combinational building blocks, demultiplexers and encoders. The section introduced schematic capture tools, which allow designers to draw circuits such that computer programs can read those circuits. The section also introduced simulation, which generates the output waveforms for designer-provided input waveforms, to help a designer verify that a circuit is correct.

▷ 2.14 EXERCISES

An asterisk (*) indicates an especially challenging problem.

SECTION 2.2: SWITCHES

2.1 A microprocessor in 1980 used about 10,000 transistors. How many of those microprocessors would fit in a modern chip having 3 billion transistors?

2.2 The first Pentium microprocessor had about 3 million transistors. How many of those microprocessors would fit in a modern chip having 3 billion transistors?

2.3 Describe the concept known as Moore's Law.

2.4 Assume for a particular year that a particular size chip using state-of-the-art technology can contain 1 billion transistors. Assuming Moore's Law holds, how many transistors will the same size chip be able to contain in ten years?

2.5 Assume a cell phone contains 50 million transistors. How big would such a cell phone be if the phone used vacuum tubes instead of transistors, assuming a vacuum tube has a volume of 1 cubic inch?

2.6 A modern desktop processor may contain 1 billion transistors in a chip area of 100 mm². If Moore's Law continues to apply, what would be the chip area for those 1 billion transistors after 9 years? What percentage is that area of the original area? Name a product into which the smaller chip might fit whereas the original chip would have been too big.

SECTION 2.3: THE CMOS TRANSISTOR

2.7 Describe the behavior of the CMOS transistor circuit shown in Figure 2.77, clearly indicating when the transistor circuit conducts.

2.8 If we apply a voltage to the gate of a CMOS transistor, why wouldn't the current flow from the gate to the transistor's source or drain?

Figure 2.77 Circuit combining two CMOS transistors.

2.9 Why does applying a positive voltage to the gate of a CMOS transistor cause the transistor to conduct between source and drain?

SECTION 2.4: BOOLEAN LOGIC GATES—BUILDING BLOCKS FOR DIGITAL CIRCUITS

2.10 Which Boolean operation—AND, OR, or NOT—is appropriate for each of the following:
   (a) Detecting motion in any motion sensor surrounding a house (each motion sensor outputs 1 when motion is detected).
   (b) Detecting that three buttons are being pressed simultaneously (each button outputs 1 when a button is being pressed).
   (c) Detecting the absence of light from a light sensor (the light sensor outputs 1 when light is sensed).

2.11 Convert the following English problem statements to Boolean equations. Introduce Boolean variables as needed.
   (a) A flood detector should turn on a pump if water is detected and the system is set to enabled.
   (b) A house energy monitor should sound an alarm if it is night and light is detected inside a room but motion is not detected.
   (c) An irrigation system should open the sprinkler's water valve if the system is enabled and neither rain nor freezing temperatures are detected.

2.12 Evaluate the Boolean equation F = (a AND b) OR c OR d for the given values of variables a, b, c, and d:
   (a) a=1, b=1, c=1, d=0
   (b) a=0, b=1, c=1, d=0
   (c) a=1, b=1, c=0, d=0
   (d) a=1, b=0, c=0, d=0

2.13 Evaluate the Boolean equation F = a AND (b OR c) AND d for the given values of variables a, b, c, and d:
   (a) a=1, b=1, c=0, d=1
   (b) a=0, b=0, c=0, d=1
   (c) a=1, b=0, c=0, d=0
   (d) a=1, b=0, c=1, d=1

2.14 Evaluate the Boolean equation F = a AND (b OR (c AND d)) for the given values of variables a, b, c, and d:
- (a) a=1, b=1, c=0, d=1
- (b) a=0, b=0, c=0, d=1
- (c) a=1, b=0, c=0, d=0
- (d) a=1, b=0, c=1, d=1

2.15 Show the conduction paths and output value of the OR gate transistor circuit in Figure 2.12 when: (a) x = 1 and y = 0, (b) x = 1 and y = 1.

2.16 Show the conduction paths and output value of the AND gate transistor circuit in Figure 2.14 when: (a) x = 1 and y = 0, (b) x = 1 and y = 1.

2.17 Convert each of the following equations directly to gate-level circuits:
- (a) F = ab' + bc + c'
- (b) F = ab + b'c'd'
- (c) F = ((a + b') * (c' + d)) + (c + d + e')

2.18 Convert each of the following equations directly to gate-level circuits:
- (a) F = a'b' + b'c
- (b) F = ab + bc + cd + de
- (c) F = ((ab)' + (c)) + (d + ef)'

2.19 Convert each of the following equations directly to gate-level circuits:
- (a) F = abc + a'bc
- (b) F = a + bcd' + ae + f'
- (c) F = (a + b) + (c' * (d + e + fg))

2.20 Design a system that sounds a buzzer inside a home whenever motion outside is detected at night. Assume a motion sensor has an output M that indicates whether motion is detected (M=1 means motion detected) and a light sensor with output L that indicates whether light is detected (L=1 means light is detected). The buzzer inside the home has a single input B that when 1 sounds the buzzer. Capture the desired system behavior using an equation, and then convert the equation to a circuit using AND, OR, and NOT gates.

2.21 A DJ ("disc jockey," meaning someone who plays music at a party) would like a system to automatically control a strobe light and disco ball in a dance hall depending on whether music is playing and people are dancing. A sound sensor has output S that when 1 indicates that music is playing, and a motion sensor has output M that when 1 indicates that people are dancing. The strobe light has an input L that when 1 turns the light on, and the disco ball has an input B that when 1 turns the ball on. The DJ wants the disco ball to turn on only when music is playing and nobody is dancing, and wants the strobe light to turn on only when music is playing and people are dancing. Create equations describing the desired behavior for B and for L, and then convert each to a circuit using AND, OR, and NOT gates,

2.22 Concisely describe the following situation using a Boolean equation. We want to fire a football coach (by setting F=1) if he is mean (represented by M=1). If he is not mean but has a losing season (represented by the Boolean variable L=1), we want to fire him anyway. Write an equation that translates the situation directly to a Boolean equation for F, without any simplification.

SECTION 2.5: BOOLEAN ALGEBRA

2.23 For the function F = a + a'b + acd + c':
- (a) List all the variables.
- (b) List all the literals.
- (c) List all the product terms.

2.24 For the function F = a'd' + a'c + b'cd' + cd:
  (a) List all the variables.
  (b) List all the literals.
  (c) List all the product terms.

2.25 Let variables T represent being tall, H being heavy, and F being fast. Let's consider anyone who is not tall as short, not heavy as light, and not fast as slow. Write a Boolean equation to represent each of the following:
  (a) You may ride a particular amusement park ride only if you are either tall and light, or short and heavy.
  (b) You may NOT ride an amusement park ride if you are either tall and light, or short and heavy. Use algebra to simplify the equation to sum of products.
  (c) You are eligible to play on a particular basketball team if you are tall and fast, or tall and slow. Simplify this equation.
  (d) You are NOT eligible to play on a particular football team if you are short and slow, or if you are light. Simplify to sum-of-products form.
  (e) You are eligible to play on both the basketball and football teams above, based on the above criteria. Hint: combine the two equations into one equation by ANDing them.

2.26 Let variables S represent a package being small, H being heavy, and E being expensive. Let's consider a package that is not small as big, not heavy as light, and not expensive as inexpensive. Write a Boolean equation to represent each of the following:
  (a) Your company specializes in delivering packages that are both small and inexpensive (a package must be small AND inexpensive for us to deliver it); you'll also deliver packages that are big but only if they are expensive.
  (b) A particular truck can be loaded with packages only if the packages are small and light, small and heavy, or big and light. Simplify the equation.
  (c) Your above-mentioned company buys the above-mentioned truck. Write an equation that describes the packages your company can deliver. Hint: Appropriately combine the equations from the above two parts.

2.27 Use algebraic manipulation to convert the following equation to sum-of-products form:
  F = a(b + c)(d') + ac'(b + d)

2.28 Use algebraic manipulation to convert the following equation to sum-of-products form:
  F = a'b(c + d') + a(b' + c) + a(b + d)c

2.29 Use DeMorgan's Law to find the inverse of the following equation: F = abc + a'b. Reduce to sum-of-products form. Hint: Start with F' = (abc + a'b)'

2.30 Use DeMorgan's Law to find the inverse of the following equation: F = ac' + abd' + acd. Reduce to sum-of-products form.

SECTION 2.6: REPRESENTATIONS OF BOOLEAN FUNCTIONS

2.31 Convert the following Boolean equations to a digital circuit:
  (a) F(a,b,c) = a'bc + ab
  (b) F(a,b,c) = a'b
  (c) F(a,b,c) = abc + ab + a + b + c
  (d) F(a,b,c) = c'

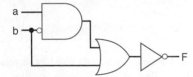

Figure 2.78 Combinational circuit for *F*.

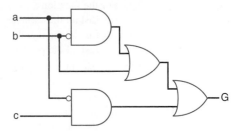

Figure 2.79 Combinational circuit for *G*.

2.32 Create a Boolean equation representation of the digital circuit in Figure 2.78.

2.33 Create a Boolean equation representation for the digital circuit in Figure 2.79.

2.34 Convert each of the Boolean equations in Exercise 2.31 to a truth table.

2.35 Convert each of the following Boolean equations to a truth table:
(a) $F(a,b,c) = a' + bc'$
(b) $F(a,b,c) = (ab)' + ac' + bc$
(c) $F(a,b,c) = ab + ac + ab'c' + c'$
(d) $F(a,b,c,d) = a'bc + d'$

TABLE 2.9 Truth table.

a	b	c	F
0	0	0	0
0	0	1	1
0	1	0	1
0	1	1	1
1	0	0	0
1	0	1	1
1	1	0	1
1	1	1	1

TABLE 2.10 Truth table.

a	b	c	F
0	0	0	1
0	0	1	0
0	1	0	1
0	1	1	0
1	0	0	1
1	0	1	1
1	1	0	1
1	1	1	0

TABLE 2.11 Truth table.

a	b	c	F
0	0	0	0
0	0	1	1
0	1	0	0
0	1	1	0
1	0	0	0
1	0	1	0
1	1	0	1
1	1	1	1

2.36 Fill in Table 2.8's columns for the equation: $F = ab + b'$

2.37 Convert the function F shown in the truth table in Table 2.9 to an equation. Don't minimize the equation.

2.38 Use algebraic manipulation to minimize the equation obtained in Exercise 2.37.

2.39 Convert the function F shown in the truth table in Table 2.10 to an equation. Don't minimize the equation.

2.40 Use algebraic manipulation to minimize the equation obtained in Exercise 2.39.

2.41 Convert the function F shown in the truth table in Table 2.11 to an equation. Don't minimize the equation.

2.42 Use algebraic manipulation to minimize the equation obtained in Exercise 2.41.

2.43 Create a truth table for the circuit of Figure 2.78.

2.44 Create a truth table for the circuit of Figure 2.79.

2.45 Convert the function F shown in the truth table in Table 2.9 to a digital circuit.

2.46 Convert the function F shown in the truth table in Table 2.10 to a digital circuit.

2.47 Convert the function F shown in the truth table in Table 2.11 to a digital circuit.

2.48 Convert the following Boolean equations to canonical sum-of-minterms form:
(a) $F(a,b,c) = a'bc + ab$
(b) $F(a,b,c) = a'b$
(c) $F(a,b,c) = abc + ab + a + b + c$
(d) $F(a,b,c) = c'$

TABLE 2.8 Truth table.

Inputs					Output
a	b	ab	b'	ab+b'	F
0	0				
0	1				
1	0				
1	1				

2.49 Determine whether the Boolean functions F = (a + b)'*a and G = a + b' are equivalent, using (a) algebraic manipulation and (b) truth tables.

2.50 Determine whether the Boolean functions F = ab' and G = (a' + ab)' are equivalent, using (a) algebraic manipulation and (b) truth tables.

2.51 Determine whether the Boolean function G = a'b'c + ab'c + abc' + abc is equivalent to the function represented by the circuit in Figure 2.80.

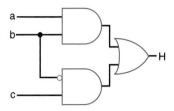

Figure 2.80 Combinational circuit for *H*.

2.52 Determine whether the two circuits in Figure 2.81 are equivalent circuits, using (a) algebraic manipulation and (b) truth tables.

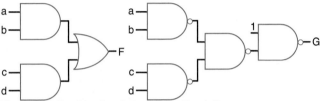

Figure 2.81 Combinational circuits for *F* and *G*.

2.53 * Figure 2.82 shows two circuits whose inputs are unlabeled.
   (a) Determine whether the two circuits are equivalent. Hint: Try all possible labelings of the inputs for both circuits.
   (b) How many circuit comparisons would need to be performed to determine whether two circuits with 10 unlabeled inputs are equivalent?

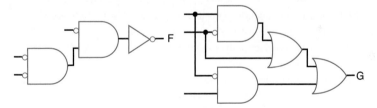

Figure 2.82 Combinational circuits for *F* and *G*.

SECTION 2.7: COMBINATIONAL LOGIC DESIGN PROCESS

2.54 A museum has three rooms, each with a motion sensor (m0, m1, and m2) that outputs 1 when motion is detected. At night, the only person in the museum is one security guard who walks from room to room. Create a circuit that sounds an alarm (by setting an output A to 1) if motion is ever detected in more than one room at a time (i.e., in two or three rooms), meaning there must be one or more intruders in the museum. Start with a truth table.

2.55 Create a circuit for the museum of Exercise 2.54 that detects whether the guard is properly patrolling the museum, detected by *exactly* one motion sensor being 1. (If no motion sensor is 1, the guard may be sitting, sleeping, or absent.)

2.56 Consider the museum security alarm function of Exercise 2.54, but for a museum with 10 rooms. A truth table is not a good starting point (too many rows), nor is an equation describing when the alarm should sound (too many terms). However, the inverse of the alarm function can be straightforwardly captured as an equation. Design the circuit for the 10-room security system by designing the inverse of the function, and then just adding an inverter before the circuit's output.

2.57 A network router connects multiple computers together and allows them to send messages to each other. If two or more computers send messages simultaneously, the messages "collide" and must be re-sent. Using the combinational design process of Table 2.5, create a collision detection circuit for a router that connects 4 computers. The circuit has 4 inputs labeled M0 through M3 that are 1 when the corresponding computer is sending a message and 0 otherwise. The circuit has one output labeled C that is 1 when a collision is detected and 0 otherwise.

2.58 Using the combinational design process of Table 2.5, create a 4-bit prime number detector. The circuit has four inputs—N3, N2, N1, and N0—that correspond to a 4-bit number (N3 is the most significant bit) and one output P that is 1 when the input is a prime number and that is 0 otherwise.

2.59 A car has a fuel-level detector that outputs the current fuel-level as a 3-bit binary number, with 000 meaning empty and 111 meaning full. Create a circuit that illuminates a "low fuel" indicator light (by setting an output L to 1) when the fuel level drops below level 3.

2.60 A car has a low-tire-pressure sensor that outputs the current tire pressure as a 5-bit binary number. Create a circuit that illuminates a "low tire pressure" indicator light (by setting an output T to 1) when the tire pressure drops below 16. Hint: you might find it easier to create a circuit that detects the inverse function. You can then just append an inverter to the output of that circuit.

SECTION 2.8: MORE GATES

2.61 Show the conduction paths and output value of the NAND gate transistor circuit in Figure 2.54 when: (a) $x = 1$ and $y = 0$, (b) $x = 1$ and $y = 1$.

2.62 Show the conduction paths and output value of the NOR gate transistor circuit in Figure 2.54 when: (a) $x = 1$ and $y = 0$, (b) $x = 0$ and $y = 0$.

2.63 Show the conduction paths and output value of the AND gate transistor circuit in Figure 2.55 when: (a) $x = 1$ and $y = 1$, (b) $x = 0$ and $y = 1$.

2.64 Two people, denoted using variables A and B, want to ride with you on your motorcycle. Write a Boolean equation that indicates that exactly one of the two people can come ($A=1$ means A can come; $A=0$ means A can't come). Then use XOR to simplify your equation.

2.65 Simplify the following equation by using XOR wherever possible: $F = a'b + ab' + cd' + c'd + ac$.

2.66 Use 2-input XOR gates to create a circuit that outputs a 1 when the number of 1s on inputs a, b, c, d is odd.

2.67 Use 2-input XOR or XNOR gates to create a circuit that detects whether an even number of the inputs a, b, c, d are 1s.

SECTION 2.9: DECODERS AND MUXES

2.68 Design a 3x8 decoder using AND, OR, and NOT gates.

2.69 Design a 4x16 decoder using AND, OR, and NOT gates.

2.70 Design a 3x8 decoder with enable using AND, OR, and NOT gates.

2.71 Design an 8x1 multiplexer using AND, OR, and NOT gates.

2.72 Design a 16x1 multiplexer using AND, OR, and NOT gates.

2.73 Design a 4-bit 4x1 multiplexer using four 4x1 multiplexers.

2.74 A house has four external doors, each with a sensor that outputs 1 if its door is open. Inside the house is a single LED that a homeowner wishes to use to indicate whether a door is open or closed. Because the LED can only show the status of one sensor, the homeowner buys a switch that can be set to 0, 1, 2, or 3 and that has a 2-bit output representing the switch position in binary. Create a circuit to connect the four sensors, the switch, and the LED. Use at least one mux (a single mux or an N-bit mux) or decoder. Use block symbols, each with a clearly defined function, such as "2x1 mux," "8-bit 2x1 mux," or "3x8 decoder"; do not show the internal design of a mux or decoder.

2.75 A video system can accept video from one of two video sources, but can only display one source at a given time. Each source outputs a stream of digitized video on its own 8-bit output. A switch with a single-bit output chooses which of the two 8-bit streams will be passed on a display's single 8-bit input. Create a circuit to connect the two video sources, the switch, and the display. Use at least one mux (a single mux or an N-bit mux) or decoder. Use block symbols, each with a clearly defined function, such as "2x1 mux," "8-bit 2x1 mux," or "3x8 decoder"; do not show the internal design of a mux or decoder.

2.76 A store owner wishes to be able to indicate to customers that the items in one of the store's eight aisles are temporarily discounted ("on sale"). The store owner thus mounts a light above each aisle, and each light has a single-bit input that turns on the light when 1. The store owner has a switch that can be set to 0, 1, 2, 3, 4, 5, 6, or 7, and that has a 3-bit output representing the switch position in binary. A second switch can be set up or down and has a single-bit output that is 1 when the switch is up; the store owner can set this switch down if no aisles are currently discounted. Use at least one mux (a single mux or an N-bit mux) or decoder. Use block symbols, each with a clearly defined function, such as "2x1 mux," "8-bit 2x1 mux," or "3x8 decoder"; do not show the internal design of a mux or decoder.

SECTION 2.10: ADDITIONAL CONSIDERATIONS

2.77 Determine the critical path of the following specified circuits. Assume that each AND and OR gate has a delay of 1 ns, each NOT gate has a delay of 0.75 ns, and each wire has a delay of 0.5 ns.
  (a) The circuit of Figure 2.37.
  (b) The circuit of Figure 2.41.

2.78 Design a 1x4 demultiplexer using AND, OR, and NOT gates.

2.79 Design an 8x3 encoder using AND, OR, and NOT gates. Assume that only one input will be 1 at any given time.

2.80 Design a 4x2 priority encoder using AND, OR, and NOT gates. If every input is 0, the encoder output should be 00.

Samson enjoyed physics and math in college, and focused his advanced studies on integrated circuit (IC) design, believing the industry to have a great future. Years later, he realizes his belief was true: "Looking back 20 years in high tech, we have experienced four major revolutions: the PC revolution, digital revolution, communication revolution, and Internet revolution—all four enabled by the IC industry. The impact of these revolutions to our daily life is profound."

He has found his job to be "very challenging, interesting, and exciting. I continually learn new skills to keep up, and to do my job more efficiently."

One of Samson's key design projects was for digital television, namely, high-definition TV (HDTV), involving companies like Zenith, Philips, and Intel. In particular, he led the 12-person design team that built Intel's first liquid crystal on silicon (LCoS) chip for rear-projection HDTV. "Traditional LCoS chips are analog. They apply different analog voltages on each pixel of the display chip so it can produce an image. But analog LCoS is very sensitive to noise and temperature variation. We used digital signals to do pulse width modulation on each pixel." Samson is quite proud of his team's accomplishments: "Our HDTV picture quality was much better."

Samson also worked on the 200-member design team for Intel's Pentium II processor. That was a very different experience. "For the smaller team project, each person had more responsibility, and overall efficiency was high. For the large team project, each person worked on a specific part of the project—the chip was divided into clusters, each cluster into units, and each unit had a leader. We relied heavily on design flows and methodologies."

Samson has seen the industry's peaks and valleys during the past two decades: "Like any industry, the IC job market has its ups and downs." He believes the industry survives the low points in large part due to innovation. "Brand names sell products, but without innovation, markets go elsewhere. So we have to be very innovative, creating new products so that we are always ahead in the global competition."

But "innovation doesn't grow on trees," Samson points out. "There are two kinds of innovations. The first is invention, which requires a good understanding of the physics behind technology. For example, to make an analog TV into a digital TV, we must know how human eyes perceive video images, which parts can be digitized, how digital images can be produced on a silicon chip, etc. The second kind of innovation reuses existing technology for a new application. For example, we can reuse advanced space technologies in a new non-space product serving a bigger market. e-Bay is another example—it reused Internet technology for online auctions. Innovations lead to new products, and thus new jobs for many years."

Thus, Samson points out that "The industry is counting on new engineers from college to be innovative, so they can continue to drive the high-tech industry forward. When you graduate from college, it's up to *you* to make things better."

CHAPTER 3

Sequential Logic Design: Controllers

▶ 3.1 INTRODUCTION

The output of a combinational circuit is a function of the circuit's present inputs. A combinational circuit has no *memory*—the feature of a circuit storing new bits and retaining those bits over time for later use. Combinational circuits alone are of limited usefulness. Designers typically use combinational circuits as part of larger circuits called sequential circuits—circuits that have memory. A *sequential circuit* is a circuit whose output depends not only on the circuit's present inputs, but also on the circuit's present *state*, which is all the bits currently stored in the circuit. The circuit's state in turn depends on the past *sequence* of the circuit's input values.

An everyday sequential system example is a lamp that toggles (changes from off to on, or from on to off) when its button is pressed, as was shown in Figure 2.1(c). After plugging in the lamp, push the lamp's button (the input) a first time, and the lamp turns on. Push the button a second time, and the lamp turns off. Push the button a third time, and the lamp turns on again. The system's output (whether the lamp is on or off) depends on the input and on whether the system is currently in the *state* of the lamp being on or off. That state in turn depends on the past sequence of input values since the system was initially powered on. In contrast, an everyday combinational system example is a basic doorbell, as was shown in Figure 2.1(a). Push the button (the input) now, and the bell (the output) rings. Push the button again, and the bell rings again. Push the button tomorrow and the bell rings the same each time. A basic doorbell has no state—its output value (whether the bell rings or not) depends solely on its present input value (whether the button is pressed or not).

Most digital systems with which you are likely familiar involve sequential circuits. A calculator contains a sequential circuit to store the numbers you enter, in order to operate on those numbers. A digital camera stores pictures. A traffic light controller stores information indicating which light is presently green. A kitchen timer that counts down from a set time to zero stores the present count value, to know what the next value should be.

This chapter describes sequential circuit building blocks called flips-flops and registers, which can store bits. It then introduces a sequential circuit design process in which a designer first captures desired behavior, and then converts that behavior to a type of sequential circuit known as a controller, comprised of a register and combinational logic.

▶ 3.2 STORING ONE BIT—FLIP-FLOPS

Sequential circuit design is aided by a building block that enables storing of a bit, much like combinational circuit design was aided by the AND, OR, and NOT gate building blocks. Storing a bit means that we can save either a 0 or a 1 in the block and later come back to see what was saved. For example, consider designing the flight attendant call-button system in Figure 3.1. An airline passenger can push the *Call* button to turn on a small blue light above the passenger's seat, indicating to a flight attendant that the passenger needs service. The light stays on even after the call button is released. The light can be turned off by pressing the *Cancel* button. Because the light must stay on even after the call button is released, a mechanism is needed to "remember" that the call button was pressed. That mechanism can be a bit storage block, in which a 1 will be stored when the call button is pressed, and a 0 stored when the cancel button is pressed. The inputs of this bit storage block will be connected to the call and cancel buttons, and the output to the blue light, as in Figure 3.1. The light illuminates when the block's output is 1.

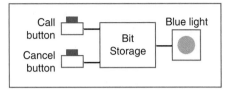

Figure 3.1 Flight attendant call-button system. Pressing *Call* turns on the light, which stays on after *Call* is released. Pressing *Cancel* turns off the light.

This section introduces the internal design of such a bit storage block by introducing several increasingly complex circuits able to store a bit—a basic SR latch, a level-sensitive SR latch, a level-sensitive D latch, and an edge-triggered D flip-flop. The D flip-flop will then be used to create a block capable of storing multiple bits, known as a register, which will serve as the main bit storage block in the rest of the book. Each successive circuit eliminates some problem of the previous one. Be aware that designers today rarely use bit storage blocks other than D flip-flops. We introduce the other blocks to provide the reader with an underlying intuition of the D flip-flop's internal design.

Feedback—The Basic Storage Method

The basic method used to store a bit in a digital circuit is *feedback*. You've surely experienced feedback in the form of audio feedback, when someone talking into a microphone stood in front of the speaker, causing a loud continuous humming sound to come out of the speakers (in turn causing everyone to cover their ears and snicker). The talker generated a sound that was picked up by the microphone, came out of the speakers (amplified), was picked up *again* by the microphone, came out the speakers again (amplified even more), etc. That's feedback.

Feedback in audio systems is annoying, but in digital systems is extremely useful. Intuitively, we know that somehow the output of a logic gate must feed back into the gate itself, so that the stored bit ends up looping around and around, like a dog chasing its own tail. We might try the circuit in Figure 3.2.

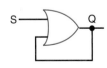

Figure 3.2 First (failed) attempt at using feedback to store a bit.

Suppose initially Q is 0 and S is 0. At some point, suppose we set S to 1. That causes Q to become 1, and that 1 feeds back into the OR gate, causing Q to be 1, etc. So even when S returns

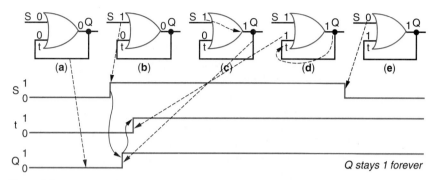

Figure 3.3 Tracing the behavior of our first attempt at bit storage.

to 0, Q stays 1. Unfortunately, Q stays 1 from then on, and we have no way of resetting Q to 0. But hopefully you understand the basic idea of feedback now—we did successfully store a 1 using feedback, but we couldn't store a 0 again.

Figure 3.3 shows the timing diagram for the feedback circuit of Figure 3.2. Initially, we set both OR gate inputs to 0 (Figure 3.3(a)). Then we set S to 1 (Figure 3.3(b)), which causes Q to become 1 slightly later (Figure 3.3(c)), assuming the OR gate has a small delay as discussed in Section 2.10. Q becoming 1 causes t to become 1 slightly later (Figure 3.3(d)), assuming the wire has a small delay too. Q will stay at 1. Finally, when we change S back to 0 (Figure 3.3(e)), Q will continue to stay 1 because t is 1. The first curved line with an arrow indicates that the event of S changing from 0 to 1 causes the event of Q changing from 0 to 1. An *event* is any change on a bit signal from 0 to 1 or from 1 to 0. The second curved line with an arrow indicates that the event of Q changing from 0 to 1 in turn causes the event of t changing from 0 to 1. That 1 then continues to loop around, forever, with no way for S to reset Q to 0.

Basic SR Latch

It turns out that the simple circuit in Figure 3.4, called a *basic SR latch*, implements the bit storage building block that we seek. The circuit consists of a pair of cross-coupled NOR gates. Making the circuit's S input equal to 1 causes Q to become 1, while making R equal to 1 causes Q to become 0. Making both S and R equal to 0 causes Q's current value to keep looping around. In other words, S "sets" the latch to 1, and R "resets" the latch to 0—hence the letters S (for *set*) and R (for *reset*).

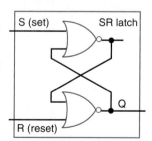

Figure 3.4 Basic SR latch.

Let's see why the basic SR latch works as it does. Recall that a NOR gate outputs 1 only when all the gate's inputs equal 0, as shown in Figure 3.5; if at least one input equals 1, the NOR gate outputs 0.

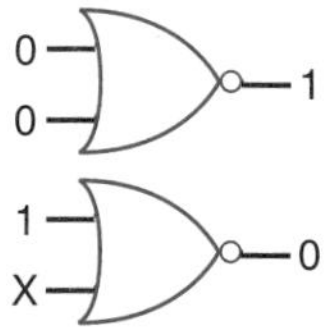

Figure 3.5 NOR behavior.

Suppose we make S=0 and R=1, as in the SR latch circuit of Figure 3.6, and that the values of Q and t are initially unknown. Because the bottom gate of the circuit has at least one input equal to 1 (R), the gate outputs 0—in the timing diagram, R becoming 1 causes Q to become 0. In the circuit, Q's 0 feeds back to the top NOR gate, which will have both its inputs equal to 0, and thus its output will be 1. In the timing diagram, Q becoming 0 causes t to become 1. In the circuit, that 1 feeds back to the bottom NOR gate, which has at least one input (actually, both) equal to 1, so the bottom gate continues to output 0. Thus the output Q equals 0, and all values are **_stable_,** meaning the values won't change as long as no external input changes.

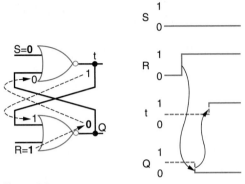

Figure 3.6 SR latch when S=0 and R=1.

Now suppose we keep S=0 and change R from 1 back to 0, as in Figure 3.7. The bottom gate still has at least one input equal to 1 (the input coming from the top gate), so the bottom gate continues to output 0. The top gate continues to have both inputs equal to 0 and continues to output 1. The output Q will thus still be 0. Therefore, the earlier R=1 *stored* a 0 into the SR latch, also known as *resetting* the latch, and that 0 remains stored even when R is changed back to 0. Note that R=1 will reset the latch regardless of the initial value of Q.

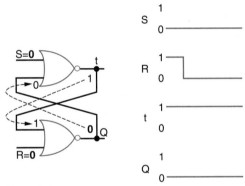

Figure 3.7 SR latch when S=0 and R=0, after R was previously 1.

Consider making S=1 and R=0, as in Figure 3.8. The top gate in the circuit now has one input equal to 1, so the top gate outputs a 0—the timing diagram shows the change of S from 0 to 1, causing t to change from 1 to 0. The top gate's 0 output feeds back to the bottom gate, which now has both inputs equal to 0 and thus outputs 1—the timing diagram shows the change of t from 1 to 0, causing Q to change from 0 to 1. The bottom gate's 1 output (Q) feeds back to the top gate, which has at least one input (actually, both of its inputs) equal to 1, so the top gate continues to output 0. The output Q therefore equals 1, and all values are stable.

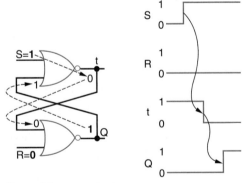

Figure 3.8 SR latch when S=1 and R=0.

Next, consider making S=0 and R=0 again, as in Figure 3.9. The top gate still has at least one input equal to 1 (the input coming from the bottom gate), so the top gate continues to output 0. The bottom gate continues to have both inputs equal to 0 and continues to output 1. The output Q is still 1. Thus, the earlier S=1 *stored* a 1 into the SR latch, also known as *setting* the latch, and that 1 remains stored even when we return S to 0. Note that S=1 will set the latch regardless of the initial value of Q.

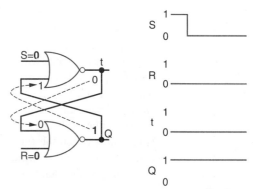

Figure 3.9 SR latch when S=0 and R=0, after S was previously 1.

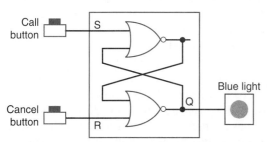

Figure 3.10 Flight attendant call-button system using a basic SR latch.

The basic SR latch can be used to implement the flight attendant call-button system as shown in Figure 3.10, by connecting the call button to S, the cancel button to R, and Q to the light. Pressing the call button sets Q to 1, thus turning on the light. Q stays 1 even when the call button is released. Pressing the cancel button resets Q to 0, thus turning off the light. Q stays 0 even when the cancel button is released.

Problem when SR=11 in a Basic SR latch

A problem with the basic SR latch is that if S and R are both 1, undefined behavior results—the latch might store a 1, it might store a 0, or its output might oscillate, changing from 1 to 0 to 1 to 0, and so on. In particular, if S = 1 and R = 1 (written as "SR=11" for short), both the NOR gates have at least one input equal to 1, and thus both gates output 0, as in Figure 3.11(a). A problem occurs when S and R are made 0 again. Suppose S and R return to 0 at the same time. Then both gates will have 0s at all their inputs, so each gate's output will change from 0 to 1, as in Figure 3.11(b). Those 1s feed back to the gates' inputs, causing the gates to output 0s, as in Figure 3.11(c). Those 0s feed back to the gate inputs again, causing the gates to output 1s. And so on. Going from 1 to 0 to 1 to 0 repeatedly is called ***oscillation***. Oscillation is not a desirable feature of a bit storage block.

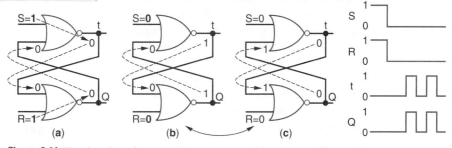

Figure 3.11 The situation of S=1 and R=1 causes problems—Q oscillates when SR return to 00.

In a real circuit, the delays of the upper and lower gates and wires would be slightly different from one another. So after some time of oscillation, one of the gates will get ahead of the other, outputting a 1 before the other does, then a 0 before the other does, until it gets far enough ahead to cause the circuit to enter a stable situation of either Q=0 or Q=1. Which situation will happen is unknown beforehand. A situation in which the final output of a sequential circuit depends on the delays of gates and wires is a ***race condition***. Figure 3.12 shows a race condition involving oscillation but ending with a stable situation of Q=1.

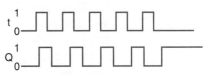

Figure 3.12 Q eventually settles to either 0 or 1, due to race condition.

Therefore, S and R must *never* be allowed to simultaneously equal 1 in an SR latch. A designer using an SR latch should add a circuit external to the SR latch that strives to ensure that S and R never simultaneously equal 1. For example, in the flight attendant call-button system of Figure 3.10, a passenger pushing both buttons at the same time might result in oscillation in the SR latch and hence a blinking light. The SR latch will eventually settle to 1 or 0, and thus the light will end up either on or off. A designer might therefore decide that if both buttons are pressed then the call button should take priority so that SR won't both be 1. Such behavior can be achieved using a combinational circuit in front of S and R, as shown in Figure 3.13. S should be 1 if the call button (denoted as Call) is pressed and either the cancel button (Cncl) is pressed or not pressed, so S = Call*Cncl + Call*Cncl' = Call. R should be 1 only if the cancel button is pressed *and* the call button is *not* pressed, meaning R = Cncl * Call'. The circuit in Figure 3.13 is derived directly from these equations.

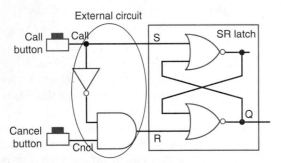

Figure 3.13 Circuit added external to SR latch striving to prevent SR=11 when both buttons are pressed.

Even with such an external circuit, S and R could still inadvertently both become 1 due to the delay of real gates (see Section 2.10). Assume the AND and NOT gates in Figure 3.13 have delays of 1 ns each (ignore wire delays for now). Suppose the cancel button is being pressed and hence SR=01, as in Figure 3.14, and then the call button is also pressed. S will change from 0 to 1 almost immediately, but R will remain at 1 for 2 ns longer, due to the AND and NOT gate delays, before changing to 0. SR would therefore be 11 for 2 ns. A temporary unintended signal value caused by circuit delays is called a ***glitch***.

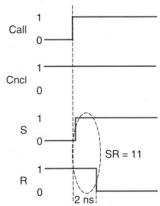

Figure 3.14 Gate delays can cause SR=11.

Significantly, glitches can also cause an unintended latch set or reset. Assume that the wire connecting the cancel button to the AND gate in Figure 3.13 has a delay of 4 ns (perhaps the wire is very long), in addition to the 1 ns AND and NOT gate delays. Suppose both buttons are pressed, so SR=10, and then the buttons are both released—SR should become 00. S will indeed change to 0 almost immediately. The top input of the AND gate will become 1 after the 1 ns delay of the NOT gate. The bottom input of that AND gate will remain 1 for 3 ns more, due to the 4 ns wire delay, thus causing R to change 1. After that bottom input finally changes to 0, yet another 1 ns will pass due to the AND gate delay before R returns to 0. Thus, R experienced a 4 ns glitch, which resets the latch to 0—yet a reset is clearly not what the designer intended.

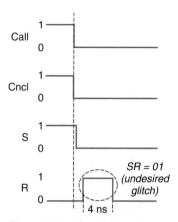

Figure 3.15 Wire delay leading to a glitch causing a reset.

Level -Sensitive SR Latch

A partial solution to the glitch problem is to extend the SR latch to have an *enable* input C as in Figure 3.16. When C=1, the S and R signals pass through the two AND gates to the S1 and R1 inputs of the basic SR latch, because S*1=S and R*1=R. The latch is enabled. But when C=0, the two AND gates cause S1 and R1 to be 0, regardless of the values of S and R. The latch is disabled. The enable input can be set to 0 when S and R might change so that glitches won't propagate through to S1 and R1, and then set to 1 only when S and R are stable. The question then remains of when to set the enable input to 1. That question will be answered in the upcoming sections.

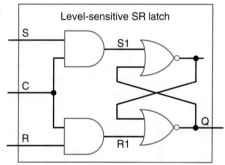

Figure 3.16 Level-sensitive SR latch—an SR latch with enable input C.

Figure 3.17 shows the call button system from Figure 3.13, this time using an SR latch with an enable input C. The timing diagram shows that if Cncl is 1 and then Call is changed to 1, a glitch of SR=11 occurs, as was already shown in Figure 3.14. However, because C=0, S1R1 stay at 00. When we later set the enable input to 1, the stable SR values propagate through to S1R1. An SR latch with an enable is called a ***level-sensitive SR latch***, because the latch is only sensitive to its S and R inputs when the level of the enable input is 1. It is also called a ***transparent SR latch***, because setting the enable input to 1 makes the internal SR latch transparent to the S and R inputs. It is also sometimes called a ***gated SR latch***.

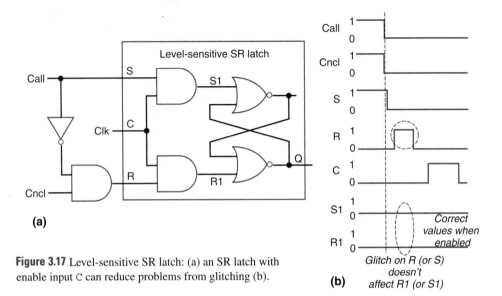

(a)

(b)

Figure 3.17 Level-sensitive SR latch: (a) an SR latch with enable input C can reduce problems from glitching (b).

Notice that the top NOR gate of an SR latch outputs the opposite value as the bottom NOR gate that outputs Q. Thus, an output Q' can be included on an SR latch almost for free, just by connecting the top gate to an output named Q'. Most latches come with both Q and Q' outputs. The symbol for a level-sensitive SR latch with such dual outputs is shown in Figure 3.18.

Figure 3.18 Symbol for dual-output level-sensitive SR latch.

Level-Sensitive D Latch—A Basic Bit Store

A designer using a level-sensitive SR latch has the burden of ensuring that S and R are never simultaneously 1 when the enable input is 1. One way to relieve designers of this burden is to introduce another type of latch, called a **level-sensitive D latch** (also known as a **transparent D latch** or **gated D latch**), shown in Figure 3.19. Internally, the latch's D input connects directly to the S input of a level-sensitive SR latch, and connects through an inverter to the R input of the SR latch. The D latch is thus either setting (when D=1) or resetting (when D=0) its internal basic SR latch when the enable input C is 1.

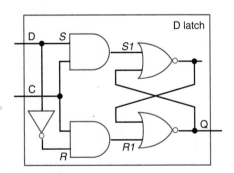

Figure 3.19 D latch internal circuit.

A level-sensitive D latch thus stores whatever value is present at the latch's D input when C = 1, and remembers that value when C = 0. Figure 3.20 shows a timing diagram of a D latch for sample input values on D and C; arrows indicate which signal changes cause other signals to change. When D is 1 and C is 1, the latch is set to 1, because S1 is 1 and R1 is 0. When D is 0 and C is 1, the latch is reset to 0, because R1 is 1 and S1 is 0. By making R the opposite of S, the D latch ensures that S and R won't both be 1 at the same time, as long as D is only changed when C is 0 (even if changed when C is 1, the inverter's delay could cause S and R to both be 1 briefly, but for too short of time to cause a problem).

The symbol for a D latch with dual-outputs (Q and Q') is shown in Figure 3.21.

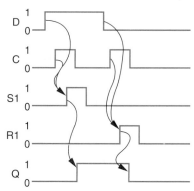

Figure 3.20 D latch timing diagram.

Figure 3.21 D latch symbol.

Edge-Triggered D Flip-Flop—A Robust Bit Store

The D latch still has a problem that can cause unpredictable circuit behavior—namely, signals can propagate from a latch output to another latch's input while the clock signal is 1. For example, consider the circuit in Figure 3.22 and the pulsing enable signals—a **pulse** is a change from 0 to 1 and back to 0, and a pulsing enable signal is called a **clock** signal. When Clk = 1, the value on Y will be loaded into the first latch and appear at that latch's output. If Clk still equals 1, then that value will also get loaded into the second latch. The value will keep propagating through the latches until Clk returns to 0. Through how many latches will the value propagate for a pulse on Clk? It's hard to say—we would have to know the precise timing delay information of each latch.

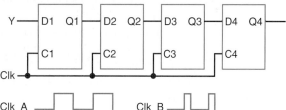

Figure 3.22 A problem with latches—through how many latches will Y propagate for each pulse of Clk_A? For Clk_B?

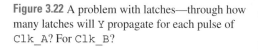

Figure 3.23 illustrates this propagation problem in more detail. Suppose D1 is initially 0 for a long time, changes to 1 long enough to be stable, and then Clk becomes 1. Q1 will thus change from 0 to 1 after about three gate delays, and thus D2 will also change from 0 to 1, as shown in the left timing diagram. If Clk is still 1, then that new value for D2 will propagate through the AND gates of the second latch, causing S2 to change from 0 to 1 and R2 from 1 to 0, thus changing Q2 from 0 to 1, as shown in the left timing diagram.

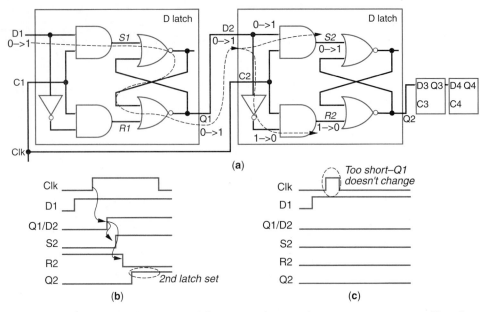

Figure 3.23 A problem with level-sensitive latches: (a) while C = 1, Q1's new value may propagate to D2, (b) such propagation can cause an unknown number of latches along a chain to get updated, (c) trying to shorten the clock's time at 1 to avoid propagation to the next latch, but long enough to allow a latch to reach a stable feedback situation, is hard because making the clock's high time too short prevents proper loading of the latch.

You might suggest making the clock signal such that the clock is 1 only for a short amount of time, so there's not enough time for the new output of a latch to propagate to the next latch's inputs. But how short is short enough? 50 ns? 10 ns? 1 ns? 0.1 ns? And if we make the clock's time at 1 too short, that time may not be long enough for the bit at a latch's D input to stabilize in the latch's feedback circuit, and we might therefore not successfully store the bit, as illustrated in Figure 3.23(c).

A good solution is to design a more robust block for storing a bit—a block that stores the bit at the D input at the *instant* that the clock rises from 0 to 1. Note that we didn't say that the block stores the bit instantly. Rather, the bit that will eventually get stored into the block is the bit that was stable at D at the instant that the clock rises from 0 to 1. Such a block is called an ***edge-triggered***

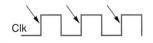

Figure 3.24 Rising clock edges.

D flip-flop. The word "edge" refers to the vertical part of the line representing the clock signal, when the signal transitions from 0 to 1. Figure 3.24 shows three cycles of a clock signal, and indicates the three rising clock edges of those cycles.

Edge-Triggered D Flip-Flop Using a Master-Servant Design. One way to design an edge-triggered D flip-flop is to use *two* D latches, as shown in Figure 3.25.

The first D latch, known as the ***master***, is enabled (can store new values on Dm) when Clk is 0 (due to the inverter), while the second D latch, known as the ***servant***, is enabled

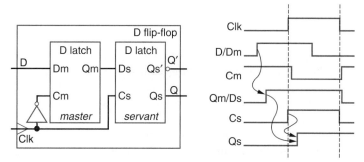

Figure 3.25 A D flip-flop implementing an edge-triggered bit storage block, internally using two D latches in a master-servant arrangement. The master D latch stores its Dm input while Clk = 0, but the new value appearing at Qm, and hence at Ds, does not get stored into the servant latch, because the servant latch is disabled when Clk = 0. When Clk becomes 1, the servant D latch becomes enabled and thus gets loaded with whatever value was in the master latch at the instant that Clk changed from 0 to 1.

when Clk is 1. Thus, while Clk is 0, the bit on D is stored into the master latch, and hence Qm and Ds are updated—but the servant latch does not store this new bit, because the servant latch is not enabled since Clk is not 1. When Clk becomes 1, the master latch becomes disabled, thus holding whatever bit was at the D input just before the clock changed from 0 to 1. Also, when Clk is 1, the servant latch becomes enabled, thus storing the bit that the master is storing, and that bit is the bit that was at the D input just before Clk changed from 0 to 1. The two latches thus implement an edge-triggered storage block—the bit that was at the input when Clk changed from 0 to 1 gets stored.

The edge-triggered block using two internal latches thus prevents the stored bit from propagating through more than one flip-flop when the clock is 1. Consider the chain of flip-flops in Figure 3.26, which is similar to the chain in Figure 3.22 but with D flip-flops in place of D latches.

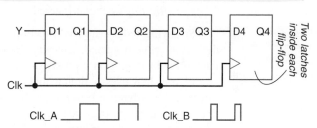

Figure 3.26 Using D flip-flops, we now know through how many flip-flops Y will propagate for Clk_A and for Clk_B—one flip-flop exactly per pulse, for either clock signal.

We know that Y will propagate through exactly one flip-flop on each clock cycle.

The drawback of a master-servant approach is that two D latches are needed to store one bit. Figure 3.26 shows four flip-flops, but there are two latches inside each flip-flop, for a total of eight latches.

Many alternative methods exist other than the master-servant method for designing an edge-triggered flip-flop. In fact, there are hundreds of different designs for latches and flip-flops beyond the designs shown above, with those designs differing in terms of their size, speed, power, etc. When using an edge-triggered flip-flop, a designer usually doesn't consider whether the flip-flop achieves edge-triggering using the master-servant method or using some other method. The designer need only know that the flip-flop is edge-trig-

The common name is actually "master-slave." Some choose instead to use the term "servant," due to many people finding the term "slave" offensive. Others use the terms "primary-secondary."

gered, meaning the data value present when the clock edge is rising is the value that gets loaded into the flip-flop and that will appear at the flip-flop's output some time later.

The above discussion is for what is known as **positive** or **rising** edge-triggered flip-flops, which are triggered by the clock signal changing from 0 to 1. There are also flip-flops known as **negative** or **falling** edge-triggered flip-flops, which are triggered by the clock changing from 1 to 0. A negative edge-triggered D flip-flop can be built using a master-servant design where the second flip-flop's clock input is inverted, rather than the first flip-flop's.

Positive edge-triggered flip-flops are drawn using a small triangle at the clock input, and negative edge-triggered flip-flops are drawn using a small triangle along with an inversion bubble, as shown in Figure 3.27. Because those symbols identify the clock input, those inputs typically are not given a name.

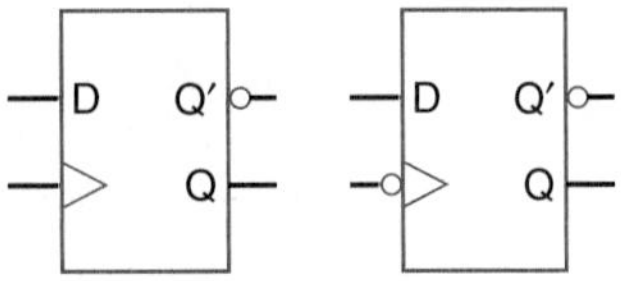

Bear in mind that although the master-servant design doesn't change the output until the falling clock edge, the flip-flop is still positive edgetriggered, because the flip-flop stored the value that was at the D input at the instant that the clock edge was *rising*.

Figure 3.27 Positive (shown on the left) and negative (right) edge-triggered D flip-flops. The sideways triangle input represents an edge-triggered clock input.

Latches versus Flip-Flops: Various textbooks define the terms latch and flip-flop differently. We'll use what seems to be the most common convention among designers, namely:

- A *latch* is level-sensitive, and

- A *flip-flop* is edge-triggered.

Designers commonly refer to flip-flops as just "flops."

So saying "edge-triggered flip-flop" would be redundant, since flip-flops are, by this definition, edge-triggered. Likewise, saying "level-sensitive latch" is redundant, since latches are by definition level-sensitive.

Figure 3.28 uses a timing diagram to illustrate the difference between level-sensitive (latch) and edge-triggered (flip-flop) bit storage blocks. The figure provides an example of a clock signal and a value on a signal D. The next signal trace is for the Q output of a D latch, which is level-sensitive. The latch ignores the first pulse on D (labeled as *3* in the figure) because Clk is low. However, when Clk becomes high (*1*), the latch output follows the D input, so when D changes from 0 to 1 (*4*), so does the latch output (*7*). The latch ignores the next changes on D when Clk is low (*5*), but then follows D again when Clk is high (*6, 8*).

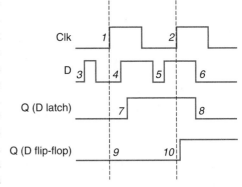

Figure 3.28 Latch versus flip-flop timing.

Compare the latch's signal trace with the next signal trace showing the behavior of a rising-edge-triggered D flip-flop. The value of D at the first rising clock edge (*1*) is 0, so the flip-flop stores and outputs a 0 (*9*). The value of D at the next rising clock edge (*2*) is 1, and thus the flip-flop stores and outputs a 1 (*10*). Notice that the flip-flop ignores all changes to D that occur between the rising clock edges (*3, 4, 5, 6*)—even ignoring changes on D when the clock is high (*4, 6*).

Clocks and Synchronous Circuits

The D flip-flop has an enable input that must be set to 1 for the block to store a bit. Most sequential circuits involving flip-flops use an enable signal that oscillates at a constant rate. For example, the enable signal could go high for 10 ns, then low for 10 ns, then high for 10 ns, then low for 10 ns, and so on, as in Figure 3.29. The time high and time low need not be the same, though in practice it usually is. (This book commonly shows the high time as shorter, to enhance figure readability).

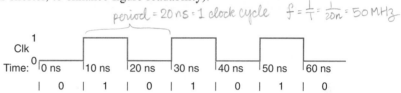

Figure 3.29 An example of a clock signal named Clk. Circuit inputs should only change while Clk = 0, such that latch inputs will be stable when Clk rises to 1.

An oscillating enable signal is called a **clock** signal, because the signal ticks (high, low, high, low) like a clock. A circuit whose storage elements can only change when a clock signal is active is known as a synchronous sequential circuit, or just **synchronous circuit** (the sequential aspect is implied—there is no such thing as a synchronous combinational circuit). A sequential circuit that does not use a clock is called an **asynchronous circuit.** We leave the important but challenging topic of asynchronous circuit design for a more advanced digital design textbook. Most sequential circuits designed and used today are synchronous.

Figure 3.30 Oscillator component.

Designers typically use an oscillator to generate a clock signal. An **oscillator** is a digital component that outputs a signal alternating between 1 and 0 at a constant frequency, like that in Figure 3.29. An oscillator component typically has no inputs (other than power) and has an output representing the clock signal as in Figure 3.30.

A clock signal's **period** is the time after which the signal repeats itself—or more simply, the time between successive 1s. The signal in Figure 3.29 has a period of 20 ns. A **clock cycle**, or just **cycle**, refers to one such segment of time, meaning one segment where the clock is 1 and then 0. Figure 3.29 shows three and a half clock cycles. A clock signal's **frequency** is the number of cycles per second, and is computed as 1/(the clock period). The signal in Figure 3.29 has a frequency of 1/20 ns = 50 MHz. The units of

---

▶ HOW DOES IT WORK?—QUARTZ OSCILLATORS.

Figure 3.31 Conceptual oscillator implementation.

Conceptually, an oscillator can be thought of as an inverter feeding back to itself, as in Figure 3.31. If C is initially 1, the value will feed back through the inverter, and so C will become 0, which feeds back through the inverter, causing C to become 1 again, and so on. The oscillation frequency would depend on the delay of the inverter. Real oscillators must regulate the oscillation frequency more precisely. A common type of oscillator uses *quartz*, a mineral consisting of silicon dioxide in crystal form. Quartz happens to vibrate if an electric current is applied

to it, and that vibration is at a precise frequency determined by the quartz size and shape. Furthermore, when quartz vibrates, it generates a voltage. So by making quartz a specific size and shape and then applying a current, we get a precise electronic oscillator. The oscillator can be attached to an IC's clock signal input, as in Figure 3.32. Some ICs come with a built-in oscillator.

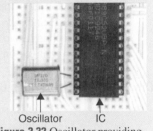

Figure 3.32 Oscillator providing a clock signal to an IC.

Freq.	Period
100 GHz	0.01 ns
10 GHz	0.1 ns
1 GHz	**1 ns**
100 MHz	10 ns
10 MHz	100 ns

Figure 3.33 Common frequency and period relationships.

frequency are Hertz, or Hz, where 1 Hz = 1 cycle per second. MHz is short for megahertz, meaning one million Hz.

A convenient way to mentally convert common clock periods to frequencies, and vice versa, is to remember that a 1 ns period equals a 1 GHz (gigahertz, meaning 1 billion Hz) frequency. Then, as shown in Figure 3.33, if one is slower (or faster) by a factor of 10, the other is slower (or faster) by a factor of 10 also—so a 10 ns period equals 100 MHz, while a 0.1 ns period equals 10 GHz.

Example 3.1 Flight attendant call-button using a D flip-flop

Let's now design the earlier-introduced flight attendant call-button system using a D flip-flop. If the call button is pressed, a 1 should be stored. If the cancel button is pressed, a 0 should be stored. If both buttons are pressed, we'll give priority to the call button, so a 1 should be stored. If neither button is pressed, the present value of Q should be stored back into the flip-flop. From this description, we see that a combinational circuit can be used to set the D flip-flop's input. The circuit's inputs will be Call, Cncl, and Q, and the output will be D, as shown in Figure 3.34(a).

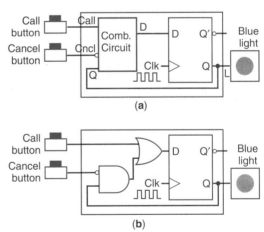

Figure 3.34 Flight attendant call-button system: (a) block diagram, and (b) implemented using a D flip-flop.

The circuit's desired behavior can be captured as the truth table in Table 3.1. If Call=0 and Cncl=0 (the first two rows), D equals Q's value. If Call=0 and Cncl=1 (the next two rows), D=0. If Call=1 and Cncl=0 (the next two rows), D=1. And if both Call=1 and Cncl=1 (the last two rows), the Call button gets priority, so D=1.

After some algebraic simplification, we obtain the following equation for D:

$$D = Cncl'Q + Call$$

We can then convert the equation to the circuit shown in Figure 3.34(b). That circuit is more robust than the earlier circuit using an SR latch in Figure 3.10. But it is still not as good as it could be; Section 3.5 will explain why we might want to add additional flip-flops at the Call and Cncl inputs. Furthermore, our design process in this example was ad hoc; the following two sections will introduce better methods for capturing desired behavior and converting to a circuit.

TABLE 3.1   D truth table for call-button system.

Call	Cncl	Q	D
0	0	0	0
0	0	1	1
0	1	0	0
0	1	1	0
1	0	0	1
1	0	1	1
1	1	0	1
1	1	1	1

The above sections went through several intermediate bit storage block designs before arriving at the robust D flip-flop design. Figure 3.35 summarizes those designs, including features and problems of each. Notice that the D flip-flop relies on an internal SR latch to maintain a stored bit *between* clock edges, and relies on the designer to introduce feedback outside the D flip-flop to maintain a stored bit *across* clock edges.

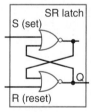 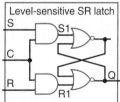 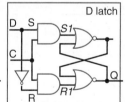 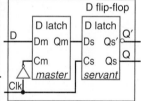

Feature: S=1 sets Q to 1, R=1 resets Q to 0. *Problem:* SR=11 yields undefined Q, other glitches may set/reset inadvertently.

Feature: S and R only have effect when C=1. An external circuit can prevent SR=11 when C=1. *Problem:* avoiding SR=11 can be a burden.

Feature: SR can't be 11. *Problem:* C=1 for too long will propagate new values through too many latches; for too short may not result in the bit being stored.

Feature: Only loads D value present at rising clock edge, so values can't propagate to other flip-flops during same clock cycle. *Tradeoff:* uses more gates internally, and requires more external gates than SR—but transistors today are more plentiful and cheaper.

Figure 3.35 Increasingly better bit storage blocks, leading to the D flip-flop.

▶ *A BIT OF HISTORY—RS, JK, T, AND D LATCHES AND FLIP-FLOPS.*

Many textbooks, especially those with origins in the 1970s and 1980s, introduce several types of latches and flip-flops and use many pages to describe how to design sequential circuits using those different types. In the 1980s, transistors on ICs were more costly and scarcer than today. The D flip-flop-based design for the call-button system in Figure 3.34(b) uses more transistors than the SR-latch-based design in Figure 3.10—not only does a D flip-flop contain more transistors internally, but it may require more external logic to set D to the appropriate value. Other flip-flop types included a JK flip-flop that acts like an SR flip-flop plus the behavior that the flip-flop toggles if both inputs are 1 (toggle

means to change from 0 to 1, or from 1 to 0), and a T flip-flop with a single input T that toggles the flip-flop when 1. For a given desired behavior, using a particular flip-flop type could save transistors. Designing sequential circuits for any flip-flop type was a challenging task, involving something called "excitation tables" and comparison of different designs, and was helpful for reducing circuit transistors. But today, in the era of billion-transistor ICs, the savings of such flip-flops are trivial. Nearly all modern sequential circuits use D flip-flops and hence are created using the more straightforward design process introduced in this chapter.

Basic Register—Storing Multiple Bits

A *register* is a sequential component that can store multiple bits. A basic register can be built simply by using multiple D flip-flops as shown in Figure 3.36. That register can hold four bits. When the clock rises, all four flip-flops get loaded with inputs I0, I1, I2, and I3 simultaneously.

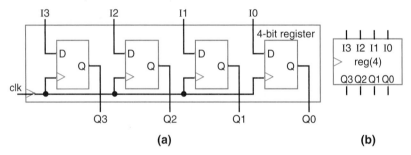

Figure 3.36 A basic 4-bit register: (a) internal design, (b) block symbol.

Such a register, made simply from multiple flip-flops, is the most basic form of a register—so basic that some companies refer to such a register simply as a "4-bit D flip-flop." Chapter 4 introduces more advanced registers having additional features and operations.

Example 3.2 Temperature history display using registers

We want to design a system that records the outside temperature every hour and displays the last three recorded temperatures, so that an observer can see the temperature trend. An architecture of the system is shown in Figure 3.37.

A timer generates a pulse on signal C every hour. A temperature sensor outputs the present temperature as a 5-bit binary number ranging from 0 to 31, corresponding to those temperatures in Celsius. Three displays convert their 5-bit binary inputs into a numerical display.

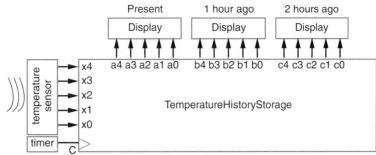

Figure 3.37 Temperature history display system.

(In practice, we would actually avoid connecting the timer output C to a clock input, instead only connecting an oscillator output to a clock input.)

We can implement the *TemperatureHistoryStorage* component using three 5-bit registers, as shown in Figure 3.38. Each pulse on signal C loads Ra with the present temperature on inputs x4..x0 (by loading the 5 flip-flops inside Ra with the 5 input bits). At the same time that register Ra gets loaded with that present temperature, register Rb gets loaded with the value that was in Ra. Likewise, Rc gets loaded with Rb's value. All three loads happen at the same time, namely, on the rising edge of C. The effect is that the values that were in Ra and Rb just before the clock edge are shifted into Rb and Rc, respectively.

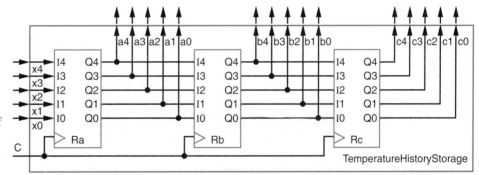

Figure 3.38 Internal design of the *Temperature History Storage* component.

Figure 3.39 shows sample values in the registers for several clock cycles, assuming all the registers initially held 0s, and assuming that as time proceeds the inputs x4..x0 have the values shown at the top of the timing diagram.

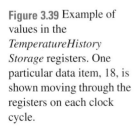

Figure 3.39 Example of values in the *TemperatureHistory Storage* registers. One particular data item, 18, is shown moving through the registers on each clock cycle.

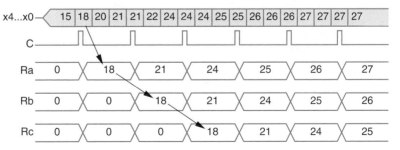

This example demonstrates one of the desirable aspects of synchronous circuits built from edge-triggered flip-flops—many things happen at once, yet we need not be concerned about signals propagating too fast through a register to another register. The reason we need not be concerned is because registers *only get loaded on the rising clock edge*, which effectively is an infinitely small period of time, so by the time signals propagate through a register to a second register, it's too late—that second register is no longer paying attention to its data inputs.

In practice, designers avoid connecting anything but an oscillator's output to the clock input of a register. A key reason is so that automated tools that analyze a circuit's timing characteristics can work properly; such tools are beyond the scope of this book. We connected a timer's output, which pulsed once per hour, in the above example for the purpose of an intuitive introduction to registers. A better implementation would instead have an oscillator connected to the clock input, and then use the "load" input of a register when the timer output pulsed. The load input of a register will be introduced in Chapter 4.

▶ 3.3 FINITE-STATE MACHINES (FSMS)

Registers store bits in a digital circuit. Stored bits mean the circuit has *memory* resulting in sequential circuits. A circuit's *state* is the value of all a circuit's stored bits. While a register storing bits happens to result in a circuit with state, state can be intentionally used to design circuits that have a specific behavior over time. For example, we can specifically design a circuit that outputs a 1 for exactly three cycles whenever a button is pressed. We could design a circuit that blinks lights in a specific pattern. We could design a circuit that detects if three buttons get pushed in a particular sequence and then unlocks a door. All these cases make use of state to create specific time-ordered behavior for a circuit.

Example 3.3   Three-cycles-high laser timer—a poorly done first design

Consider the design of a part of a laser surgery system, such as a system for scar removal or corrective vision. Such systems work by turning on a laser for a precise amount of time (see "How does it work?—Laser surgery" on page 123). A general architecture of such a system is shown in Figure 3.40.

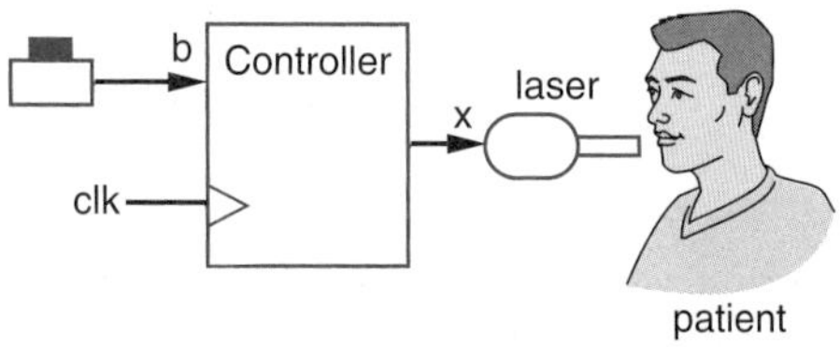

Figure 3.40 Laser timer system.

A surgeon activates the laser by pressing the button. Assume that the laser should then stay on for exactly 30 ns. Assume that the system's clock period is 10 ns, so that 3 clock cycles last 30 ns. Assume that b from the button is synchronized with the clock and stays high for exactly 1 clock cycle. We need to design a controller component that, once detecting that b = 1, holds x high for exactly 3 clock cycles, thus turning on the laser for 30 ns.

This is one example for which a microprocessor solution may not work. Using a microprocessor's programming statements that read input ports and write output ports may not provide a way to hold an output port high for exactly 30 ns—for example, when the microprocessor clock frequency is not fast enough.

Let's try to create a sequential circuit implementation for the system. After thinking about the problem for a while, we might come up with the (bad) implementation in Figure 3.41.

Knowing the output should be held high for three clock cycles, we used three flip-flops, with the idea being that we'll shift a 1 through those three flip-flops, taking three clock cycles for the bit to move through all three flip-flops. We ORed the flip-flop outputs to generate signal x, so that if any flip-flop contains a 1, the laser will be on. We made b the input to the first flip-

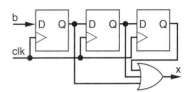

Figure 3.41 First (bad) attempt to implement the laser timer system.

flop, so when b=1, the first flip-flop stores a 1 on the next rising clock edge. One clock cycle later, the second flip-flop will get loaded with 1, and assuming b has now returned to 0, the first flip-flop will get loaded with 0. One clock cycle later, the third flip-flop will get loaded with 1, and the second flip-flop with 0. One clock cycle later, the third flip-flop will get loaded with 0. Thus, the circuit held the output x at 1 for three clock cycles after the button was pressed.

We did a poor job implementing this system. First, what happens if the surgeon presses the button a second time before the three cycles are completed? Such a situation could cause the laser to stay on too long. Is there a simple way to fix our circuit to account for that behavior? Second, we didn't use any orderly process for designing the circuit—we came up with the ORing of flip-flop outputs, but how did we come up with that? Will that method work for all time-ordered behavior that needs to be designed?

Two things are required to do a better job at designing circuits having time-ordered behavior: (1) a way to explicitly *capture* the desired time-ordered behavior, and (2) a technique for *converting* such behavior to a sequential circuit.

▶ *HOW DOES IT WORK?—LASER SURGERY.*

Laser surgery has become very popular in the past two decades, and has been enabled due to digital systems. Lasers, invented in the early 1960s, generate an intense narrow beam of coherent light, with photons having a single wavelength and being in phase (like being in rhythm) with one another. In contrast, a regular light's photons fly out in all directions, with a diversity of wavelengths. Think of a laser as a platoon of soldiers marching in synch, while a regular light is more like kids running out of school at the end-of-the-day bell. A laser's light can be so intense as to even cut steel. The ability of a digital circuit to carefully control the location, intensity, and duration of the laser is what makes lasers so useful for surgery.

One popular use of lasers for surgery is for scar removal. The laser is focused on the damaged cells slightly below the surface, causing those cells to be vaporized. The laser can also be used to vaporize skin cells that form bumps on the skin, due to scars or moles. Similarly, lasers can reduce wrinkles by smoothing the skin around the wrinkle to make the crevices more gradual and hence less obvious, or by stimulating tissue under the skin to stimulate new collagen growth.

Another popular use of lasers for surgery is for correcting vision. In one popular laser eye surgery method, the surgeon uses a laser to cut open a flap on the surface of the cornea, and then uses a laser to reshape the cornea by thinning the cornea in a particular pattern, with such thinning accomplished through vaporizing cells.

A digital system controls the laser's location, energy, and duration, based on programmed information of the desired procedure. The availability of lasers, combined with low-cost high-speed digital circuits, makes such precise and useful surgery now possible.

Mathematical Formalism for Sequential Behavior—FSMs

Chapter 2 introduced a process for designing a combinational circuit that involved first capturing the desired combinational behavior using a mathematical formalism known as a Boolean equation (or a truth table, which could be converted to an equation), and then converting the equation to a circuit. For sequential behavior, a Boolean equation is not sufficient—a more powerful mathematical formalism is needed that can describe time-ordered behavior.

Finite-state machines (FSMs) are one such formalism. The name is awkward, but the concept is straightforward. The main part of an FSM is a set of states representing every possible system "mode" or "situation." An FSM is "in" exactly one state at any time, that state being known as the FSM's current or present state.

My daughter's hamster can serve as an intuitive example. After having a hamster as a family pet, I've learned that hamsters basically have four states that can be named *Sleeping*, *Eating*, *RunningOnTheWheel*, and *TryingToEscape*. Hamsters spend most of their day sleeping (being nocturnal), a bit of time eating or running on the wheel, and the rest of their time desperately trying to escape from their cage. At any given time, the hamster is in exactly one of those four states.

The "TryingToEscape" state.

A digital example is a system that repeatedly sets an output x to 0 for one clock cycle and to 1 for one clock cycle, so the output over time will be 0 1 0 1 0 1 ... The system clearly has only two states, which might be named *Lo* and *Hi*. In state *Lo*, x = 0; in state *Hi*, x = 1. Those states and the transitions between them can be drawn as the state diagram in Figure 3.42(a). A **state diagram** is a graphical drawing of an FSM.

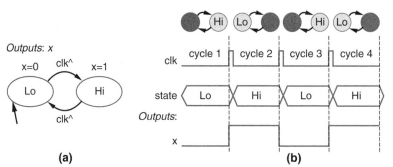

(a) **(b)**

Figure 3.42 A two-state FSM: (a) state diagram, (b) timing diagram describing the state diagram's behavior. Above the timing diagram, an animation of the state diagram highlights the current state in each clock cycle. "clk^" represents the rising edge of the clock signal.

Each state in the state diagram is drawn as an oval. Assume the system starts in state *Lo*, as indicated by the arrow pointing from nothing to state *Lo*. The diagram shows that state *Lo* sets x to 0 by having "x=0" drawn near or in the state. The diagram also shows that on the next rising edge of the clock signal, *clk^*, the system transitions to state *Hi*. Such transitions are drawn as directed edges, meaning a line with an arrow at one end. The diagram also shows that state *Hi* sets x to 1. On the next rising edge of the clock, the diagram shows that the system transitions back to state *Lo* again. State diagrams are a popular method for representing FSMs. FSMs can also be represented as a table or using various textual methods.

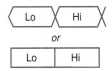

Figure 3.43
Displaying multi-bit or other values in a timing diagram.

Figure 3.42(b) provides a timing diagram showing the system's behavior. Above the timing diagram are state diagrams that show the current state colored in. The current state is also shown in the timing diagram itself using the graphical notation shown in Figure 3.43. A timing diagram easily shows a single bit's value by drawing the bit's line at the top or the bottom. But to represent something other than a single bit, like a current state or an integer value, the notation just lists the value as shown. A vertical line (or a pair of crossed lines) shows when the values change.

Note that an FSM only moves along a single transition for a single rising clock edge. In particular, when in state *Lo*, a rising clock edge causes a move along the transition to state *Hi*, but then the system must wait for *another* rising clock edge to move along the transition from *Hi* back to *Lo*.

Example 3.3 sought to build a system that held its output high for three cycles. Toward that end, the state diagram of Figure 3.42 can be extended to have four states, three of which set the output to 1, as in Figure 3.44(a). The output x will be 0 for one cycle and then 1 for three cycles, as shown in the timing diagram of Figure 3.44(b). The state diagram uses state names *Off*, *On1*, *On2*, and *On3*. State names are arbitrary; the only requirement is that an FSM's state names must each be unique. The state names in Figure 3.44 could have been *S0*, *S1*, *S2*, and *S3*, but names that describe a state's purpose in the FSM are preferable.

Figure 3.44 Three-cycles-high system: (a) state diagram, (b) timing diagram.

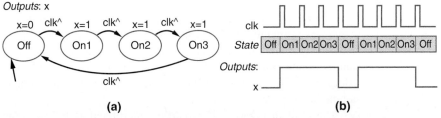

Boolean expressions can be associated with the transitions to extend the behavior. Figure 3.45(a) extends the state diagram by associating an expression with the transition from state *Off* to state *On1* such that the expression requires not just a rising clock, but also that b=1 (written just as b) in order for the transition to be taken. Another transition can be added from *Off* back to *Off*, with the expression of a rising clock and b=0 (written as b'). The timing diagram in Figure 3.45(b) shows the state and output behavior for the given input values on b. The initial state is *Off*. While b is 0, the FSM stays in *Off* (it keeps transitioning back to *Off* at each rising clock). When b becomes 1, the FSM transitions to *On1* at the next rising clock, then to *On2*, then *On3*, then back to *Off*.

Figure 3.45 Three-cycles-high system with button input: (a) state diagram, (b) timing diagram.

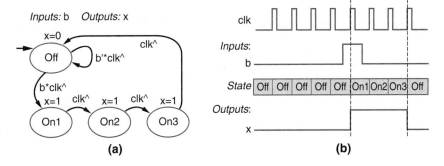

The above examples illustrate that a *finite-state machine* or *FSM* is a mathematical formalism consisting of several items:

- A set of states. The above example had four states: {*On1, On2, On3, Off*}.

- A set of inputs and a set of outputs. The example had one input: {b}, and one output: {x}.

- An *initial state*: the state in which to start when the system is first powered on. An FSM's initial state can be shown graphically by a directed edge (an edge with an arrow at one end) starting from no state and pointing to the initial state. An FSM can only have one initial state. The example's initial state was the state named *Off*. Note that *Off* is just a name, and does not suggest that the system's power is off (rather, it suggests that the laser is off).

- A set of transitions: An indication of the next state based on the current state and the current values of the inputs. The example used directed edges with associated input *conditions*, which is a Boolean expression of input variables, to indicate the next state. Those edges with conditions are called *transitions*. The example had several transitions, such as the edge with condition b*clk^.

- A description of what output values to assign in each state. The example assigns a value to x in every state. Assigning an output in an FSM is known as an *action*.

After being defined, an FSM can then be executed (even if just mentally)—what computer programmers might call "running" the FSM. The FSM starts with the current state being the initial state and then transitions to a different state based on the current state and input values, continuing as time proceeds. In each state, the FSM sets output values. Mentally executing an FSM is akin to mentally evaluating a Boolean equation for sample input values.

The FSM in Figure 3.45 would be interpreted as follows. The system starts in the initial state *Off*. The system stays in state *Off* until one of the state's two outgoing transitions has a true condition. One of those transitions has the condition of b'*clk^—in that case, the system transitions right back to state *Off*. The other transition has the condition of b*clk^—in that case, the system transitions to state *On1*. The system stays in state *On1* until its only outgoing transition's condition clk^ becomes true—in which case the system transitions to state *On2*. Likewise, the system stays in ·*On2* until the next rising clock edge, transitioning to *On3*. The system stays in *On3* until the next rising clock edge, transitioning back to state *Off*. State *Off* has associated the action of setting x=0, while the states *On1*, *On2*, and *On3* each set x=1.

▶ *"STATE" I UNDERSTAND, BUT WHY THE TERMS "FINITE" AND "MACHINE?"*

Finite-state machines, or FSMs, have a rather awkward name that sometimes causes confusion. The term "finite" is there to contrast FSMs with a similar representation used in mathematics that can have an infinite number of states; that representation is not very useful in digital design. FSMs, in contrast, have a limited, or finite, number of states. The term "machine" is used in its mathematical or computer science sense, being a *conceptual* object that can execute an abstract language—specifically, that sense of machine is *not* hardware. Finite-state machines are also known as *finite-state automata*. FSMs are used for many things other than just digital design.

The FSM in Figure 3.45 precisely describes the desired time-ordered behavior of the laser timer system from Example 3.3.

It is interesting to examine the behavior of this FSM if the button is pressed a second time while the laser is on. Notice that the transitions among the *On* states are independent of the value of *b*. So this system will always turn the laser on for exactly three cycles and then return to the *Off* state to await another press of the button.

Simplifying FSM Notation: Making the Rising Clock Implicit

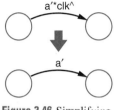

Figure 3.46 Simplifying notation: implicit rising clock edge on every transition.

Thus far the rising clock edge (clk^) has appeared in the condition of every FSM transition, because this book only considers the design of sequential circuits that are synchronous and that use rising edge-triggered flip-flops to store bits. Synchronous circuits with edge-triggered flip-flops make up the majority of sequential circuits in modern practice. As such, to make state diagrams more readable, most textbooks and designers follow the convention shown in Figure 3.46 wherein every FSM transition is *implicitly ANDed* with a rising clock edge. For example, a transition labeled "a'" actually means "a'*clk^." Subsequent state diagrams will not include the rising clock edge in transition conditions, instead following the convention that *every* transition is implicitly ANDed with a rising clock edge. Figure 3.47 illustrates the laser timer state diagram from Figure 3.45, redrawn using implicit rising clock edges.

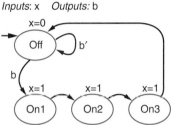

Figure 3.47 Laser timer state diagram assuming every transition is ANDed with a rising clock.

Figure 3.48 Transition is taken on next rising clock edge.

A transition with no associated condition as in Figure 3.48 simply transitions on the next rising clock edge, because of the implicit rising clock edge.

Following are more examples showing how FSMs can describe time-ordered behavior.

Example 3.4   Secure car key

Have you noticed that the keys for many new automobiles have a thicker plastic head than in the past (see Figure 3.49)? The reason is that, believe it or not, there is a computer chip inside the head of the key, implementing a secure car key. In a basic version of such a secure car key, when the driver turns the key in the ignition, the car's computer (which is under the hood and communicates using what's called the *basestation*) sends out a radio signal asking the car key's chip to respond by sending an identifier via a radio signal. The chip in the key then responds by sending the identifier

Figure 3.49 Why are the heads of car keys getting thicker? Note that the key on the right is thicker than the key on the left. The key on the right has a computer chip inside that sends an identifier to the car's computer, thus helping to reduce car thefts.

(ID), using what's known as a *transponder* (a transponder "transmits" in "response" to a request). If the basestation does not receive a response or the key's response has an ID different than the ID programmed into the car's computer, the computer shuts down and the car won't start.

Let's design the controller for such a key, having an ID of 1011 (real IDs are typically 32 bits long or more, not just 4 bits). Assume the controller has an input a that is 1 when the car's computer requests the key's ID. Thus the controller initially waits for the input a to become 1. The key should then send its ID (1011) serially, starting with the rightmost bit, on an output r; the key sends 1 on the first clock cycle, 1 on the second cycle, 0 on the third cycle, and finally 1 on the fourth cycle. The FSM for the controller is shown in Figure 3.50. Note that the FSM

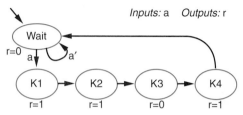

Figure 3.50 Secure car key FSM. Recall that each edge's condition includes an implicit rising clock edge.

sends the bits starting from the bit on the right, which is known as the *least significant bit* (LSB). The computer chip in the car key has circuitry that converts radio signals to bits and vice versa.

Figure 3.51 provides a timing diagram for the FSM for a particular situation. When we set a = 1, the FSM enters state *K1* and outputs r = 1. The FSM then proceeds through *K2*, *K3*, and *K4*, outputting r = 1, 0, and 1, respectively, even though we returned input a to 0.

Timing diagrams represent a particular situation defined by how we set the inputs. What would have happened if we had held a = 1 for many more clock cycles? The timing diagram in Figure 3.52 illustrates that situation. Notice how in that case the FSM, after returning to state *Wait*, proceeds to state *K1* again on the next cycle.

"So my car key may someday need its batteries replaced?" you might ask. Actually, no—those chips in keys draw their power, as well as their clock, from the magnetic component of the radio-frequency field generated from the computer basestation, as in RFID chips. The extremely low power requirement makes custom digital circuitry, rather than instructions on a microprocessor, a preferred implementation.

Computer chip keys make stealing cars a lot harder—no more "hot-wiring" to start a car, since the car's computer won't work unless it also receives the correct identifier. And the method above is actually an overly simplistic method—many cars have more sophisticated communication between the computer and the key, involving several communications in both directions, even using encrypted communication—making fooling the car's computer even harder. A drawback of secure car keys is that you

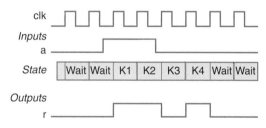

Figure 3.51 Secure car key timing diagram.

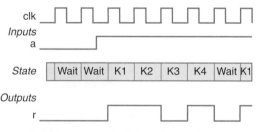

Figure 3.52 Secure car key timing diagram for a different sequence of values on input a.

can't just run down to the local hardware store and copy those keys for $5 any longer—copying keys requires special tools that today can run $50-$100. A common problem while computer chip keys were becoming popular was that low-cost locksmiths didn't realize the keys had chips in them, so copies were made and the car owners went home and later couldn't figure out why their car wouldn't start, even though the key fit in the ignition slot and turned.

Example 3.5 Flight-attendant call button

This example uses an FSM to describe the desired behavior of the flight-attendant call button system from Figure 3.1. The FSM has inputs `Call` and `Cncl` for the call and cancel buttons, and output `L` to control the light. `Call` will be given priority if both buttons are pressed. The FSM has two states, *LightOff,* which sets `L` to `0`, and *LightOn,* which sets `L` to `1`, as shown in Figure 3.53. *Light-Off* is the initial state. The FSM stays in that state until `Call` is `1`, which causes a transition to *LightOn.* If `Call` is `0`, the FSM stays in *LightOff.* In state *LightOn,* the only way to transition back to *LightOff* is if `Cncl` is `1` and `Call` is `0` (because the call button has priority), meaning `Cncl*Call'`. If that condition is false, i.e., `(Cncl*Call')'` is true, the FSM stays in *LightOn.*

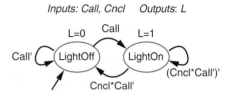

Figure 3.53 FSM for flight-attendant call button system.

Notice how clearly the FSM captures the behavior of the flight-attendant call button system. Once you understand FSMs, an FSM description is likely to be more concise and precise than an English description.

How to Capture Desired System Behavior as an FSM

The previous section showed FSM examples, but how were those FSMs originally created? Creating an FSM that captures desired system behavior can be a challenging task for a designer. Using the following method can help:

- List states: First list all possible states of the system, giving each a meaningful name, and denoting the initial state. Optionally add some transitions if they help indicate the purpose of each state.
- Create transitions: For each state, define all possible transitions leaving that state.
- Refine the FSM: Execute the FSM mentally and make any needed improvements.

The method described above is just a guide. Capturing behavior as an FSM may require some creativity and trial-and-error, as is the case in some other engineering tasks, like computer programming. For a complex system, a designer may at first list a few states, and then upon defining transitions the designer may decide that more states are required. While creating an FSM, the preciseness of the FSM may cause the designer to realize that the system's behavior should be different than originally anticipated. Note also that many different FSMs could be created that describe the same desired behavior; one FSM may be easier to understand while another FSM may have fewer states, for example. Experience can help greatly in creating correct and easy-to-understand FSMs that capture desired system behavior.

Example 3.6   Code detector

You've probably seen keypad-protected doors in airports or hospitals that require a person to press a sequence of buttons (i.e., a code) to unlock the door. A door may have three buttons, colored red, green, and blue, and a fourth button for starting the code. Pressing the start button followed by the sequence—red, blue, green, red—unlocks the door. Any other sequence would not unlock the door. An extra output a from the buttons compo-nent is 1 when *any* button is pressed; a is 1 for exactly one clock cycle no matter how long a button is pressed. Figure 3.54 shows a system block diagram. Our goal is to create an FSM that describes the *CodeDetector* block.

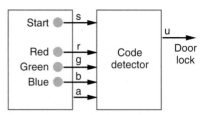

Figure 3.54 Code detector architecture.

List states: We first list the possible states of the code detector FSM, shown in Figure 3.55. A state is needed to wait for the start button to be pressed; we name that state *Wait*, and add transitions showing that the FSM stays in that state while s is 0. After the start button is pressed, a state is needed to wait for the first button to be pressed; we name that state *Start*. While in *Start*, if a button is pressed (a=1) and it is the red

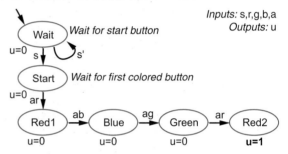

Figure 3.55 Code detector's possible states.

button (r=1), then the FSM should enter a state that indicates that the first colored button pressed was the correct one; we name that state *Red1*, and add a transition from *Start* to *Red1* with condi-tion ar (for a=1 AND r=1) to make clear that *Red1* is entered if the red button is pressed. While in *Red1*, if the blue button is pressed, the FSM should enter another state indicating that the second colored button pressed was correct; we name that state *Blue*, and add a transition from *Red1* to *Blue* also. Likewise, we add states *Green* and *Red2* for the last two of the four required button presses. If the FSM reaches the *Red2* state, then all four pressed buttons were the correct ones, and thus the door should be unlocked. Hence, state *Red2* has associated the action of u=1, while all the other states set u=0. At this point, the FSM is incomplete, but lists all the states and a few key tran-sitions to capture the main behavior of detecting the correct sequence of pressed colored buttons.

Create transitions: The next step is to create transitions for each state. State *Wait* already has a com-plete set of transitions: when s is 0, the FSM stays in *Wait*; when s is 1, the FSM goes to *Start*. State *Start*'s transitions should include waiting for a colored button to be pressed, so we add a transition with condition a' pointing back to *Start*, shown in Figure 3.56. If a button is pressed and that button is the red button, then

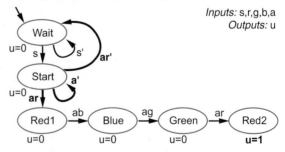

Figure 3.56 Code detector FSM with more transitions.

the FSM should go to state *Red1*; we'd already added that transition (ar). If a button is pressed and that button is not the red button (ar'), then the FSM should somehow enter a "fail" mode and not unlock the door. At this point, we might consider adding another state called *Fail*. Instead, we decide that the FSM should go back to the *Wait* state and just wait for the start button to be pressed again, so we add such a transition with condition ar' as shown.

The pattern of three transitions for state *Start* can be replicated for states *Red1*, *Blue*, and *Green*, modified to detect the correct colored button press as shown in Figure 3.57. Finally, we must decide what the FSM should do after the FSM reaches state *Red2* and unlocks the door. For simplicity of this example, we decide to have the FSM just return to state *Wait*, which locks the door again; a real system would keep the door unlocked for a fixed period of time before locking it again.

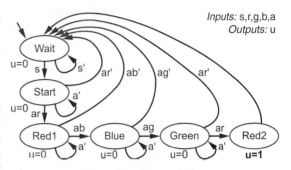

Figure 3.57 Code detector FSM with complete transitions.

Refine the FSM: We can now mentally execute the FSM to see if it behaves as desired:

- The FSM begins in the *Wait* state. As long as the start button is not pressed (s'), the FSM stays in *Wait*; when the start button s is pressed (and a rising clock edge arrives, of course), the FSM goes to the *Start* state.

- Being in the *Start* state means the FSM is now ready to detect the sequence red, blue, green, red. If no button is pressed (a'), the FSM stays in *Start*. If a button is pressed AND that button is the red button (ar), the FSM goes to state *Red1*. Instead, if a button is pressed AND that button is not the red button (ar'), the FSM returns to the Wait state—note that when in the *Wait* state, further presses of the colored buttons would be ignored, until the start button is pressed again.

- The FSM stays in state *Red1* as long as no button is pressed (a'). If a button is pressed AND that button is blue (ab), the FSM goes to state *Blue*; if that button is not blue (ab'), the FSM returns to state *Wait*. At this point, we detect a potential problem—what if the red button is still being pressed as part of the first button press when the next rising clock edge arrives? The FSM would go to state *Wait*, which is not what we want. One solution is to add another state, *Red1_Release*, that the FSM transitions to after *Red1*, and in which the FSM stays until a=0. For simplicity, we'll instead assume that each button has a special circuit that synchronizes the button with the clock signal. That circuit sets its output to 1 for exactly one clock cycle for each unique press of the button. This is necessary to ensure that the current state doesn't inadvertently change to another state if a button press lasts longer than a single clock cycle. We'll design such a synchronization circuit in Example 3.9.

- Likewise, the FSM stays in state *Blue* as long as no button is pressed (a'), and goes to state *Green* on condition ag, and state *Wait* on condition ag'.

- Finally, the FSM stays in *Green* if no button is pressed, and goes to state *Red2* on condition ar, and to state *Wait* on condition ar'.

- If the FSM makes it to state *Red2*, that means that the user pressed the buttons in the correct sequence—*Red2* will set u=1, thus unlocking the door. Note that all other states set u=0. The FSM then returns to state *Wait*.

The FSM works well for normal button presses, but let's mentally execute the FSM for unusual cases. What happens if the user presses the start button and then presses *all three colored buttons simultaneously*, four times in a row? The way the FSM is defined, the door would unlock! A solution to this undesired situation is to modify the transitions between the states that detect correct colored button presses, to detect not only the

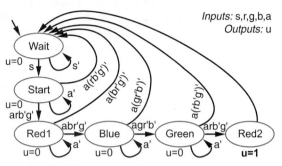

Inputs: s,r,g,b,a
Outputs: u

Figure 3.58 Improved code detector FSM.

correct colored button press, but also that the other colored buttons are *not* pressed. For example, for the transition leaving state *Start* with condition `ar`, the condition should instead be `a(rb'g')`. That change also means that the transition going back to state *Wait* should have the condition `a(rb'g')'`. The intuitive meaning of that condition is that a button was pressed, but it was not just the red button. Similar changes can be made to the other transition conditions too, resulting in the improved FSM of Figure 3.58.

▶ 3.4 CONTROLLER DESIGN

Standard Controller Architecture for Implementing an FSM as a Sequential Circuit

The previous section provided examples of capturing sequential behavior using FSMs. This section defines a process to convert an FSM to a sequential circuit. The sequential circuit that implements an FSM is commonly called a ***controller***. Converting an FSM to a controller is quite straightforward when a standard pattern, commonly called a standard architecture, is used for the controller. Other ways exist for implementing an FSM, but using the standard architecture results in a straightforward design process.

A standard controller architecture for an FSM consists of a register and combinational logic. For example, the standard controller architecture for the laser timer FSM of Figure 3.45 is shown in Figure 3.59. The controller's register stores the current FSM state and is thus called a ***state register***. Each state is represented as a unique bit encoding. For example, the laser timer's *Off* state could be encoded as 00, *On1* as 01, *On2* as 10, and *On3* as 11, the four states thus requiring a 2-bit state register.

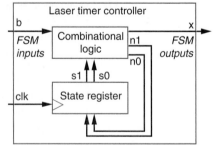

Figure 3.59 Standard controller architecture for the laser timer.

The combinational logic computes the output values for the present state, and also computes the next state based on the current state and current input values. Its inputs are thus the state register bits (s1 and s0 in the example of Figure 3.59) and the FSM's external inputs (b for the example). The combinational logic's outputs are the outputs of the FSM (x for the example), as well as the next state bits to be loaded into the state register (n1 and n0).

The details of the combinational logic determine the behavior of the circuit. The process for creating those details will be covered in the next section. A more general view of the standard controller architecture appears in Figure 3.60. That figure shows a state register that is *m* bits wide.

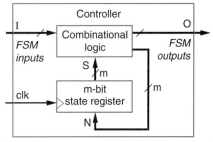

Figure 3.60 Standard controller architecture.

Controller (Sequential Logic) Design Process

As in the combinational logic design process in Chapter 2, the sequential logic design process (which we'll call the controller design process) consists of two steps shown in Table 3.2. The first step is to **capture** the behavior, and the second step is to **convert** that captured behavior into a circuit. Combinational logic was captured as equations or truth tables, but those formalisms are insufficient for the time-ordered behavior of a controller, so capturing a controller's behavior is done with an FSM. The second step of converting the captured behavior to a circuit requires several substeps as shown in Table 3.2. Each substep is a straightforward task—while the design process' first step of capturing the behavior as an FSM may require some trial-and-error, the second step of converting the FSM to a circuit is a straightforward "mechanical" activity even though it consists of several substeps. Examples will introduce and illustrate the controller design process.

TABLE 3.2 Controller design process.

	Step		Description
Step 1: Capture behavior	**Capture** *the FSM*		Create an FSM that describes the desired behavior of the controller.
Step 2: Convert to circuit	2A	**Set up** *the architecture*	Set up the standard architecture by using a state register of appropriate width and combinational logic. The logic's inputs are the state register bits and the FSM inputs; the logic's outputs are the next state bits and the FSM outputs.
	2B	**Encode** *the states*	Assign a unique binary number, known as an **encoding,** to each state. Any encoding is sufficient as long as each state has a unique encoding. Usually a minimum number of bits is used and an encoding is assigned to each state by counting up in binary.
	2C	**Fill in** *the truth table*	Translate the FSM into a truth table for the combinational logic such that the logic will generate the outputs and next state signals for the given FSM. Ordering the inputs with state bits first makes the correspondence between the table and the FSM clear.
	2D	**Implement** *the combinational logic*	Implement the combinational logic using any method.

Example 3.7   Three-cycles-high laser timer controller (continued)

The earlier-introduced laser timer can be implemented using the controller design process.

Step 1:   Capture the FSM. The FSM was already created in Figure 3.47.

Step 2A: Set up the architecture.   The standard controller architecture for the laser timer FSM was shown in Figure 3.59. The state register has two bits to represent each of the four states. The combinational logic has external input b and inputs s1 and s0 coming from the state register, and has external output x and outputs n1 and n0 going to the state register.

Step 2B: Encode the states.   A valid state encoding is: *Off*: 00, *On1*: 01, *On2*: 10, *On3*: 11. Any non-redundant encoding is fine. The state diagram with encoded states is in Figure 3.61.

Step 2C: Fill in the truth table.   Given the implementation architecture and the binary encoding of each state, the FSM can be translated into the truth table for the combinational logic, as shown in Table 3.3. Placing the inputs coming from the state register in the table's leftmost input columns allows us to easily see which rows correspond to which states. We fill all combinations of inputs on the left, as usual for a truth table. For each row, we look at the state diagram in Figure 3.61 to determine the appropriate outputs. For the two rows starting with s1s0 = 00 (state *Off*), x should be 0. If b = 0, the controller should stay in state *Off*, so n1n0 should be 00. If b = 1, the controller should go to state *On1*, so n1n0 should be 01.

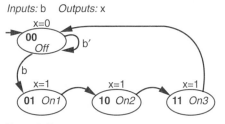

Figure 3.61 Laser timer state diagram with encoded states.

Likewise, for the two rows starting with s1s0 = 01 (state *On1*), x should be 1 and the next state should be *On2* (regardless of b's value), so n1n0 should be 10. We complete the last four rows similarly.

Note the difference between the FSM inputs and outputs of Figure 3.61, and the combinational logic inputs and outputs of Figure 3.62—the latter include the bits from and to the state register.

Step 2D: Implement the combinational logic.   The design can be completed using the combinational logic design process from Chapter 2. The following equations for the three combinational outputs come from the truth table:

$$x = s1 + s0 \text{ (note from the table that } x = 1 \text{ if } s1 = 1 \text{ or } s0 = 1)$$

$$n1 = s1's0b' + s1's0b + s1s0'b' + s1s0'b$$
$$n1 = s1's0 + s1s0'$$

$$n0 = s1's0'b + s1s0'b' + s1s0'b$$
$$n0 = s1's0'b + s1s0'$$

TABLE 3.3   Truth table for laser timer controller's combinational logic.

	Inputs			Outputs		
	s1	s0	b	x	n1	n0
Off	0	0	0	0	0	0
	0	0	1	0	0	1
On1	0	1	0	1	1	0
	0	1	1	1	1	0
On2	1	0	0	1	1	1
	1	0	1	1	1	1
On3	1	1	0	1	0	0
	1	1	1	1	0	0

We then obtain the sequential circuit in Figure 3.62, implementing the FSM.

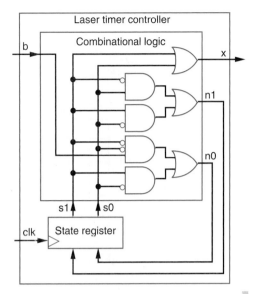

Figure 3.62 Final implementation of the three-cycles-high laser timer controller.

Many textbooks use different table organizations from that in Table 3.3. However, we intentionally organized the table so that it serves both as a *state table*, which is a tabular representation of an FSM, and as a truth table that can be used to design the combinational logic of the controller.

Example 3.8 Understanding the laser timer controller's behavior

To aid in understanding how a controller implements an FSM, this example traces through the behavior of the three-cycles-high laser timer controller. Assume the system is initially in state 00 (s1s0=00), b is 0, and the clock is currently low. As shown in Figure 3.63(a), based on the combinational logic, x will be 0 (the desired output in state 00), n1 will be 0, and n0 will be 0, meaning the value 00 will be waiting at the state register's inputs. Thus, on the *next* clock edge, 00 will be loaded into the state register, meaning the system stays in state 00—which is correct.

Now suppose b becomes 1. As shown in Figure 3.63(b), x will still be 0, as desired. n1 will be 0, but n0 will be 1, meaning the value 01 will be waiting at the state register's inputs. Thus, on the *next* clock edge, 01 will be loaded into the state register, as desired.

As in Figure 3.63(c), soon after 01 is loaded into the state register, x will become 1 (after the register is loaded, there's a slight delay as the new values for s1 and s0 propagate through the combinational logic gates). That output is correct—the system should output x=1 when in state 01. Also, n1 will become v and n0 will equal 0, meaning the value 10 will be waiting at the state register inputs. Thus, on the next clock edge, 10 will be loaded into the state register, as desired.

After 10 is loaded into the state register, x will stay 1, and n1n0 becomes 11. When another clock edge comes, 11 will be loaded into the register, x will stay 1, and n1n0 becomes 00.

When another clock edge comes, 00 will be loaded into the register. Soon after, x will become 0, and if b is 0, n1n0 will stay 00; if b is 1, n1n0 will become 01. Notice that the system is back in the state where it started.

Understanding how a state register and combinational logic implement a state machine can take a while, since in a particular state (indicated by the value presently in the state register), we generate

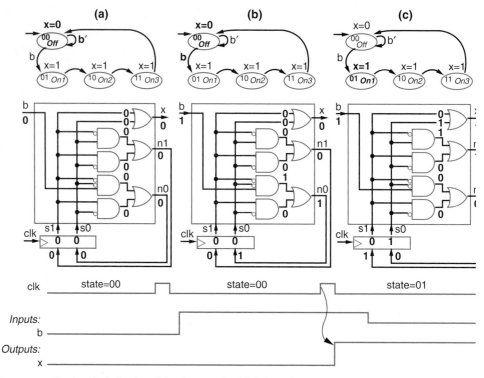

Figure 3.63 Tracing the behavior of the three-cycles-high laser timer controller.

the external output for that state, and we generate the signals for the *next* state—but we don't transition to that next state (i.e., we don't load the state register) until the next clock edge.

Example 3.9   Button press synchronizer

This example develops a circuit that synchronizes a button press to a clock signal, such that when the button is pressed, the result is a signal that is 1 for exactly one clock cycle. Such a synchronized signal is useful to prevent a single button press that lasts multiple cycles from being interpreted as multiple button presses. Figure 3.64 uses a timing diagram to illustrate the desired behavior.

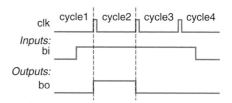

Figure 3.64 Desired timing diagram of the button press synchronizer.

The circuit's input will be a signal bi, and the output a signal bo. When bi becomes 1, representing the button being pressed, the system should set bo to 1 for exactly one cycle. The system waits for bi to return to 0 again, and then waits for bi to become 1 again, which would represent the next pressing of the button.

Step 1:   Capture the FSM.   Figure 3.65(a) shows an FSM describing the circuit's behavior. The FSM waits in state *A*, outputting bo=0, until bi is 1. The FSM then transitions to state *B*, outputting bo=1. The FSM will then transition to either state *A* or *C*, which both set bo=0 again, so that bo was 1 for just one cycle, as desired. The FSM goes from *B* to *A* if bi returned to 0. If bi is still 1, the FSM goes to state *C*, where the FSM waits for bi to return 0, causing a transition back to state *A*.

Step 2A: Set up the architecture. Because the FSM has three states, the architecture has a two-bit state register, as in Figure 3.65(b).

Step 2B: Encode the states. The three states can be straightforwardly encoded as 00, 01, and 10, as in Figure 3.65(c).

Step 2C: Fill in the truth table. We convert the FSM with encoded states to a truth table for the controller's combinational logic, as shown in Figure 3.65(d). For the unused state 11, we have chosen to output bo=0 and return to state 00.

Step 2D: Implement the combinational logic. We derive the equations for each combinational logic output, as shown in Figure 3.65(e), and then create the final circuit as shown.

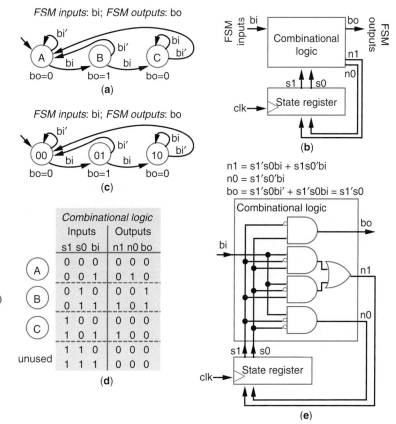

Figure 3.65 Button press synchronizer design steps: (a) initial FSM, (b) controller architecture, (c) FSM with encoded states, (d) truth table for the combinational logic, (e) final controller with implemented combinational logic.

Example 3.10 Sequence generator

This example designs a sequential circuit with four outputs: w, x, y, and z. The circuit should generate the following sequence of output patterns: 0001, 0011, 1100, and 1000, one per clock cycle. After 1000, the circuit should repeat the sequence. Sequence generators are common in a variety of systems, such as a system that blinks a set of four lights in a particular pattern for a festive lights display. Another example is a system that rotates an electric motor a fixed number of degrees each clock cycle by powering magnets around the motor in a specific sequence to attract the magnetized motor to the next position in the rotation—known as a ***stepper motor***, because the motor rotates in steps.

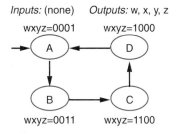

Figure 3.66 Sequence generator FSM.

The sequence generator controller can be designed using the controller design process:

Step 1: **Capture the FSM.** Figure 3.66 shows an FSM having four states labeled *A*, *B*, *C*, and *D* (though any other four unique names would do just fine) to generate the desired sequence.

Step 2A: **Set up the architecture.** The standard controller architecture for the sequence generator will have a 2-bit state register to represent the four possible states, no inputs to the logic, and outputs w, x, y, z from the logic, along with outputs n1 and n0, as shown in Figure 3.67.

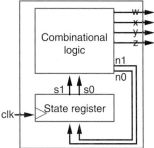

Figure 3.67 Sequence generator controller architecture.

Step 2B: **Encode the states.** The states can be encoded as follows—*A*: 00, *B*: 01, *C*: 10, *D*: 11. Any other encoding with a unique code for each state would also be fine.

Step 2C: **Fill in the truth table.** Table 3.4 shows the table for the FSM with encoded states.

Step 2D: **Implement the combinational logic.** An equation can be derived for each output of the combinational logic directly from the truth table. After some algebraic simplification, the equations are those shown below. The final circuit is shown in Figure 3.68.

TABLE 3.4 **State table for sequence generator controller.**

	Inputs		Outputs					
	s1	s0	w	x	y	z	n1	n0
A	0	0	0	0	0	1	0	1
B	0	1	0	0	1	1	1	0
C	1	0	1	1	0	0	1	1
D	1	1	1	0	0	0	0	0

$$w = s1$$
$$x = s1s0'$$
$$y = s1's0$$
$$z = s1'$$
$$n1 = s1 \text{ xor } s0$$
$$n0 = s0'$$

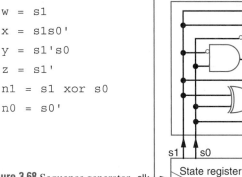

Figure 3.68 Sequence generator controller with implemented combinational logic.

Example 3.11 Secure car key controller (continued)

Let's complete the design for the secure car key controller from Example 3.4. We already carried out **Step 1: Capture the FSM**, shown in Figure 3.50. The remaining steps are as follows.

Step 2A: Set up the architecture. The FSM has five states, and thus requires a 3-bit state register, which can represent eight states; three states will be unused. The inputs to the combinational logic are a and the three state bits s2, s1, and s0, while the outputs are signal r and next state outputs n2, n1, and n0. The architecture is shown in Figure 3.69.

Step 2B: Encode the states. Let's encode the states using a straightforward binary encoding of 000 through 100. The FSM with state encodings is shown in Figure 3.70.

Step 2C: Fill in the truth table. The FSM converted to a truth table for the logic is shown in Table 3.5. For the unused states, we have chosen to set r = 0 and the next state to 000.

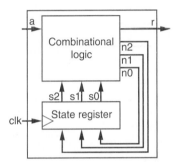

Figure 3.69 Secure car key controller architecture.

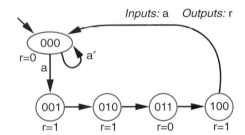

Figure 3.70 Secure car key FSM with encoded states.

Step 2D: Implement the combinational logic. We can design four circuits, one for each output, to implement the combinational logic. We leave this step as an exercise for the reader.

TABLE 3.5 Truth table for secure car key controller's combinational logic.

	s2	s1	s0	a	r	n2	n1	n0
			Inputs				**Outputs**	
Wait	0	0	0	0	0	0	0	0
	0	0	0	1	0	0	0	1
K1	0	0	1	0	1	0	1	0
	0	0	1	1	1	0	1	0
K2	0	1	0	0	1	0	1	1
	0	1	0	1	1	0	1	1
K3	0	1	1	0	0	1	0	0
	0	1	1	1	0	1	0	0
K4	1	0	0	0	1	0	0	0
	1	0	0	1	1	0	0	0
Unused	1	0	1	0	0	0	0	0
	1	0	1	1	0	0	0	0
	1	1	0	0	0	0	0	0
	1	1	0	1	0	0	0	0
	1	1	1	0	0	0	0	0
	1	1	1	1	0	0	0	0

Converting a Circuit to an FSM (Reverse Engineering)

We showed in Section 2.6 that a circuit, truth table, and equation were all forms able to represent the same combinational function. Similarly, a circuit, state table, and FSM are all forms able to represent the same sequential function.

The process in Table 3.2 for converting an FSM to a circuit can be applied in reverse to convert a circuit to an FSM. In general, converting a circuit to an equation or FSM is known as *reverse engineering* the behavior of the circuit. Not only is reverse engineering useful to help develop a better understanding of sequential circuit design, but it can also be used to understand the behavior of a previously-designed circuit such as a circuit created by a designer who is no longer at a company, and also to check that a circuit we designed has the correct behavior.

Example 3.12 Converting a sequential circuit to an FSM

Given the sequential circuit in Figure 3.71, find an equivalent FSM. We start from step 2D in Table 3.2. The combinational circuit already exists. Step 2C fills in a truth table. The combinational logic in the controller architecture has three inputs: two inputs s0 and s1 represent the contents of the state register, and x is an external input. Thus the truth table will have 8 rows because there are $2^3 = 8$ possible combinations of inputs. After listing the truth table and enumerating all combinations of inputs (e.g., s1s0x = 000, ..., s1s0x = 111), the techniques in Section 2.6 can be used to fill in the values of the outputs. Consider the output y. The combinational circuit shows that y = s1'. Knowing this, we place a 1 in the v column of the truth table in every row where s1 = 0, and place a 0 in the remaining spaces in the y column. Consider n0, which the circuit shows as having the Boolean equation n0 = s1's0'x. Accordingly, we set n0 to 1 when s1 = 0 and s0 = 0 and x = 1. We fill in the columns for z and n1 using a similar analysis and move on to the next step.

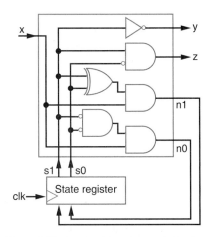

Figure 3.71 Circuit with unknown behavior.

Step 2B encodes the states. The states have already been encoded, so this step in reverse assigns a name to encoded state. We arbitrarily choose the names *A*, *B*, *C*, and *D*, seen in Table 3.6.

Step 2A sets up the standard controller architecture. This step requires no work since the controller architecture was already defined.

Finally, step 1 captures the FSM. Initially, we can set up an FSM diagram with the four states whose names were given in step 2A, shown in Figure 3.72(a). Next, we list the values of the FSM outputs y and z next to each state as defined by the truth table

TABLE 3.6 Truth table for circuit.

	Inputs			Outputs			
	s1	s0	x	n1	n0	y	z
A	0	0	0	0	0	1	0
	0	0	1	0	1	1	0
B	0	1	0	0	0	1	0
	0	1	1	1	0	1	0
C	1	0	0	0	0	0	1
	1	0	1	1	0	0	1
D	1	1	0	0	0	0	0
	1	1	1	0	0	0	0

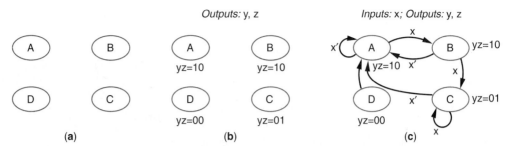

Figure 3.72 Converting a truth table to an FSM diagram: (a) initial FSM, (b) FSM with outputs specified, and (c) FSM with outputs and transitions specified.

in Table 3.6. For example, in state A (s1s0 = 00), the outputs y and z are 1 and 0, respectively, so we list "yz = 10" with state A in the FSM.

After listing the outputs for states B, C, and D, shown in Figure 3.72(b), we examine the state transitions specified in the truth table by n1 and n0. Consider the first row of the truth table, which says that n1n0 = 00 when s1s0x = 000. In other words, when in state A (s1s0 = 00), the next state is state A (n1n0 = 00) if x is 0. We can represent this in the FSM diagram by drawing an arrow from state A back to state A and labeling the new transition "x'." Now consider the second row of the truth table, which indicates that from state A, we transition to state B when x = 1. We add a transition arrow from state A to B and label it "x." After labeling all the transitions, we are left with the FSM in Figure 3.72(c).

Notice that state D cannot be reached from any other state and transitions to state A on any input. We can reasonably infer that the original FSM had only three states and state D is an extra, unused state. For completeness, it is preferable to leave state D in the final diagram, however.

Given any synchronous circuit consisting of logic gates and flip-flops, we can always redraw the circuit as consisting of a state register and logic—the standard controller architecture—just by grouping all the flip-flops together. Thus, the approach described above works for any synchronous circuit, not just a circuit already drawn in the form of the standard controller architecture.

Example 3.13 Reverse engineering the D-flip-flop-based flight-attendant call button system

Figure 3.34 showed a sequential circuit designed in an ad hoc manner rather than using this chapter's controller design process. Reverse engineering that circuit proceeds as follows. Treating the D flip-flop as a one-bit state register with input D and output Q, step 2D obtains the equation for the controller's output to the light as L = Q, and for the controller's next state as D = Cncl'Q + Call. Step 2C creates a truth table. The inputs to the combinational logic are Q, Call, and Cncl, while the outputs are D and L. The table is shown in Table 3.7, filling the output values based on the above equations for L and D. For step 2B in reverse, we give the name *LightOff* to the state Q=0, and *LightOn* to Q=1.

TABLE 3.7 Truth table for circuit.

	Inputs			Outputs	
	Q	Call	Cncl	D	L
Light Off	0	0	0	0	0
	0	0	1	0	0
	0	1	0	1	0
	0	1	1	1	0
Light On	1	0	0	1	1
	1	0	1	0	1
	1	1	0	1	1
	1	1	1	1	1

Step 2A requires no action. Finally, step 1 in reverse creates the FSM from the truth table. The FSM goes from *LightOff* (Q=0) to *LightOn* (Q=1) if `Call*Cncl'` + `Call*Cncl` is true, which simplified is just `Call`. It stays in *LightOff* if `Call'Cncl'` + `Call'Cncl` is true, which simplifies to `Call'`. The truth table also shows that the FSM goes from state *LightOn* to *LightOff* when `Call'*Cncl`

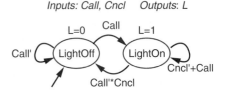

Figure 3.73 Reverse-engineered FSM for flight-attendant call button system.

is true. It stays in *LightOn* if the condition `Call'Cncl'` + `Call*Cncl'` + `Call*Cncl` is true, which simplifies to `Call'Cncl'` + `Call`, which further simplifies to `Cncl'` + `Call`.

Note that this FSM is equivalent to the FSM in Figure 3.53 created directly to describe the flight-attendant call button system's desired behavior; the conditions that look different can be manipulated to be the same. Thus, the circuit built using the ad hoc approach seems to be correct in this case.

Common Mistakes when Capturing FSMs

Some mistakes are commonly made when capturing an FSM, relating to properties regarding the transitions leaving a state. In short, *one and only one* transition condition should ever evaluate to true during any rising clock edge. The common mistakes involve:

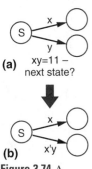

Figure 3.74 A state's transitions should be exclusive.

1. **Non-exclusive transitions**—For a given state, when a rising clock comes, all the state's transitions should be **exclusive**, meaning no more than one transition condition should be true. Consider an FSM with inputs x and y, and a state S with the two outgoing transitions shown in Figure 3.74(a). What happens when x = 1 and y = 1—which transition should the FSM take? An FSM should be **deterministic**, meaning the transition to take can always be uniquely determined. The FSM creator might label the transitions "x" and "x'y" as shown in Figure 3.74(b) to solve the problem. Actually, a particular type of FSM known as a **nondeterministic FSM** does allow more than one condition to be true and chooses among them randomly. But we want deterministic FSMs when designing circuits, so we won't consider nondeterministic FSMs further.

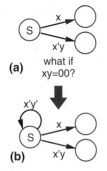

Figure 3.75 A state's transitions must be complete.

2. **Incomplete transitions**—For a given state, when a rising clock edge comes, the state's transitions must be **complete**, meaning *one* of the transitions from that state must have a true condition. In other words, every input combination should be accounted for in every state. Designers sometimes forget to ensure this. For example, consider an FSM with inputs x and y, and a state S with the outgoing transitions shown in Figure 3.75(a). What happens if the FSM is in S, and x = 0 and y = 0? Neither of the two transitions from the state has a true condition. The FSM is incompletely specified. An FSM creator can add a third transition, indicating what state to go to if x'y' is true, as in Figure 3.75(b). The three transitions now cover all possible values of x and y. A commonly forgotten transition is a transition pointing from a state back to itself. Sometimes making a transition the complement of another transition is a simple way to ensure completeness; e.g., if one of two transitions has the condition xy, then the other transition can be given the condition (xy)' (avoid trying to write that other condition as x'+y' as that commonly leads to mistakes).

A designer can verify the above two properties using Boolean algebra. The exclusive transitions property can be verified by ensuring that the *AND of every pair of conditions on a state's transitions always results in 0*. For example, if a state has two transitions, one with condition x and the other with condition x'y, transformations of Boolean algebra can be used as follows:

```
x * x'y
= (x * x') * y
= 0 * y
= 0
```

If a state has three transitions with conditions *C1*, *C2*, and *C3*, the designer can verify that $C1*C2=0$, $C1*C3=0$, and finally that $C2*C3=0$, thus verifying that every pair yields 0. Note that verifying that $C1*C2*C3=0$ does *not* verify that the transitions are exclusive; for example, if *C1* and *C2* were exclusive but *C2* and *C3* were not, $C1*C2*C3$ would still equal 0 because $0*C3=0$.

The second property of complete transitions can be verified by checking that the *OR of all the conditions on a state's transitions results in 1*. Considering the same example of a state that has two transitions, one with condition x and the other with condition x'y, transformations of Boolean algebra can be applied as follows:

```
x + x'y
= x*(1+y) + x'y
= x + xy + x'y
= x + (x+x')y
= x + y
```

The OR of those two conditions is not 1 but rather x+y. If x and y were both 0, neither condition would be true, and so the next state would not be specified in the FSM. Figure 3.75(b) fixed this problem by adding another transition, x'y'. Checking these transitions yields:

```
x + x'y + x'y'
= x + x'(y+y')
= x + x'*1
= x + x'
= 1
```

If a state has three transitions with conditions *C1*, *C2*, and *C3*, the designer can verify that $C1+C2+C3=1$.

Proving the properties for the transitions of every state can be time-consuming. A good FSM capture tool will verify the above two properties automatically and inform the designer of any problems.

Example 3.14 Verifying transition properties for the code detector FSM

Recall the code detector from Example 3.6. Suppose a designer instead captured the behavior as shown in Figure 3.76, using different conditions for the transitions leaving the states *Start*, *Red1*, *Blue*, and *Green*. We want to verify the exclusive transition property for the transitions leaving state *Start*. There are three conditions: ar, a', and a(r'+b+g). We thus have three pairs of conditions. We AND each pair and prove that each equals 0 as follows:

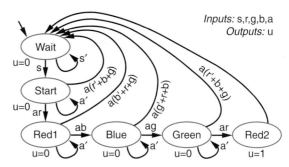

Figure 3.76 Problematic code detector FSM.

```
ar * a'         a' * a(r'+b+g)          ar * a(r'+b+g)
= (a*a')r       = (a'*a)*(r'+b+g)       = (a*a)*r*(r'+b+g)
= 0*r           = 0*(r'+b+g)            = a*r*(r'+b+g)
= 0             = 0                     = arr'+arb+arg
                                        = 0 + arb+arg
                                        = arb + arg
                                        = ar(b+g)
```

It appears the FSM has non-exclusive transitions, because the AND of the third pair of conditions does not result in 0, which in turn means both conditions could be true at the same time—resulting in a nondeterministic FSM (if both conditions are true, what is the next state?). Recall from the code detector problem description that we want to transition from the *Start* state to the *Red1* state when a button is pressed (a=1) and that button is the red button and no other colored button is pressed. The FSM in Figure 3.76 has the condition ar. The mistake is under-specifying this condition; it should instead be arb'g'—in other words, a button has been pressed (a) and it is the red button (r) and the blue button has not been pressed (b') and the green button has not been pressed (g'). The transition from *Start1* back to the *Wait* state could then be written as a(rb'g')' (which is the same as in Figure 3.76 after applying DeMorgan's Law). After this change, we can again try to verify the "only one condition is true" property for all pairs of the three conditions arb'g', a', and a(rb'g')':

As evidence that this "pitfall" is indeed common, we admit that the hypothetical mistake in this example was in fact a mistake made in an early edition of this book. A reviewer of the book caught it. We added this example and this note to stress the point that the mistake is common.

```
arb'g' * a'       a'*a(rb'g')'       arb'g' * a(rb'g')'
= aa'*rb'g'       = 0*(rb'g')'       = a*a*(rb'g')*(rb'g')'
= 0*rb'g'         = 0                write rb'g' as Y for clarity...
= 0                                  = a*a*Y*Y'
                                     = a*a*0
                                     = 0
```

We would need to change the transition conditions of the other states similarly (as was done in Figure 3.58), and then check the pairs of conditions for those states' transitions too.

To verify the completeness property for state *Start*, we OR the three conditions and prove they equal 1:

```
  arb'g' + a'' + a(rb'g')'
= a' + arb'g' + a(rb'g')' (write rb'g' as Y for clarity)
= a' + aY + aY'
= a' + a(Y+Y') = a' + a(1)
= a' + a
= 1
```

We would need to check the property for all other states too.

FSM and Controller Conventions

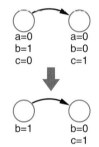

Figure 3.77
Unassigned outputs implicitly set to 0.

Simplifying FSM Notations: Unassigned Outputs

We already introduced the simplified FSM notation wherein every transition is implicitly ANDed with a rising clock edge. Another commonly used simplification involves assigning outputs. If an FSM has many outputs, listing the assignment of every output in every state can become cumbersome, and make the relevant behavior of the FSM hard to discern. A common simplifying notation is shown in Figure 3.77—if an output is not explicitly assigned in a state, the output is *implicitly* assigned a 0. If the assignment of an output to 0 in a state is fundamental to understanding that state's behavior, then the output should still be explicitly assigned to 0 in order to aid someone trying to understand the behavior of the FSM.

Simplifying Circuit Drawings: Implicit Clock Connections

Most sequential circuits have a single clock signal connected to all sequential components. A component is known to be sequential because of the small triangle input drawn on the component's block symbol. Many circuit drawings therefore use a simplification wherein the clock signal is assumed to be connected to all sequential components, as in Figure 3.78. This simplification leads to less cluttered wiring in the drawing.

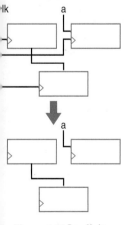

Figure 3.78 Implicit clock connections.

Mathematical Formalisms in Combinational and Sequential Circuit Design

This book has thus far described two mathematical formalisms, Boolean functions and FSMs, for designing combinational and sequential circuits, respectively. Note that those formalisms aren't *necessary* to design circuits. Recall that the first attempt at building a three-cycles-high laser timer in Figure 3.41 just involved connecting components together in the hopes of creating a correctly working circuit. However, using those formalisms provides for a structured method of designing circuits. Those formalisms also provide the basis for powerful automated tools to assist with design, such as a tool that would automatically check for the common pitfalls described earlier in this section, tools that automatically convert Boolean equations or FSMs into circuits, tools that verify that two circuits are equivalent, or tools that simulate systems. The chapter scarcely touched on all the benefits of those mathematical formalisms relating to automating the various aspects of designing circuits and of verifying that the circuits behave properly. The importance of using sound mathematical formalisms to guide design cannot be overstated.

▶ 3.5 MORE ON FLIP-FLOPS AND CONTROLLERS

Non-Ideal Flip-Flop Behavior

When first learning digital design we assume ideal behavior for logic gates and flip-flops, just like when first learning physics of motion we assume there's no friction or wind resistance. However, there is a non-ideal behavior of flip-flops—metastability—that is such a common problem in the practice of real digital design, we feel obliged to discuss the issue briefly here. Digital designers in practice should study metastability and possible solutions quite thoroughly before doing serious designs. Metastability comes from failing to meet flip-flop setup or hold times, which are now introduced.

Setup Times and Hold Times

Flip-flops are built from wires and logic gates, and wires and logic gates have delays. Thus, a real flip-flop imposes some restrictions on when the flip-flop's inputs can change relative to the clock edge, in order to ensure correct operation despite those delays. Two important restrictions are:

* *Setup time:* The inputs of a flip-flop (e.g., the D input) must be stable for a minimum amount of time, known as the *setup time*, *before* a clock edge arrives. This intuitively makes sense—the input values must have time to propagate through any flip-flop internal logic and be waiting at the internal gates' inputs before the clock pulse arrives.

* *Hold time:* The inputs of a flip-flop must remain stable for a minimum amount of time, known as the *hold time*, *after* a clock edge arrives. This also makes intuitive sense—the clock signal must have time to propagate through the internal gates to create a stable feedback situation.

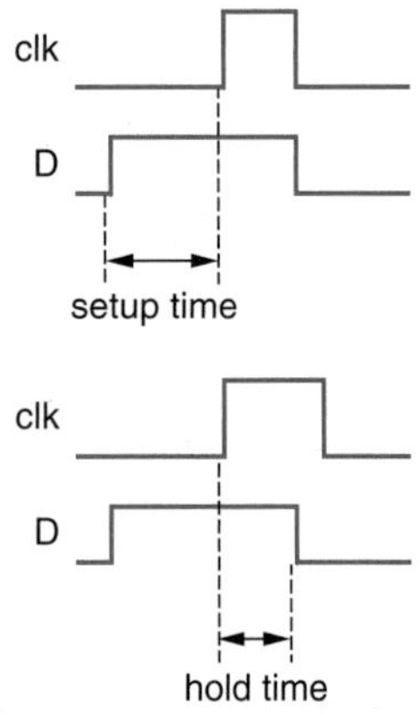

Figure 3.79 Flip-flop setup and hold time restrictions.

A related restriction is on the minimum clock pulse width—the pulse must be wide enough to ensure that the correct values propagate through the internal logic and create a stable feedback situation.

A flip-flop typically comes with a datasheet describing setup times, hold times, and minimum clock pulse widths. A *datasheet* is a document that tells a designer what a component does and how to properly use that component.

Figure 3.80 illustrates an example of a setup time violation. D changed to 0 too close to the rising clock. The result is that R was not 1 long enough to create a stable feedback situation in the cross-coupled NOR gates with Q being 0. Instead, Q glitches to 0 briefly. That glitch feeds back to the top NOR gate, causing Q' to glitch to 1 briefly. That glitch feeds back to the bottom NOR gate, and so on. The oscillation would likely continue until a race condition caused the circuit to settle into a stable situation of Q = 0 or Q = 1—or the circuit could enter a metastable state, which we now describe.

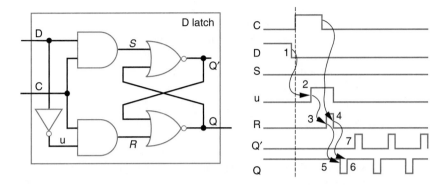

Figure 3.80 Setup time violation: D changed to 0 (1) too close to the rising clock. u changed to 1 after the inverter delay (2), and then R changed to 1 after the AND gate delay (3). But then the clock pulse was over, causing R to change back to 0 (4) before a stable feedback situation with Q=0 occurred in the cross-coupled NOR gates. R's change to 1 did cause Q to change to 0 after the NOR gate delay (5), but R's change back to 0 caused Q to change right back to 1 (6). The glitch of a 0 on Q fed back into the top NOR gate, causing Q' to glitch to 1 (7). That glitch of a 1 fed back to the bottom NOR gate, causing another glitch of a 0 on Q. That glitch runs around the cross-coupled NOR gate circuit (oscillation)—a race condition would eventually cause Q to settle to 1 or 0, or possibly enter a metastable state (to be discussed).

Metastability

If a designer fails to ensure that a circuit obeys the setup and hold times of a flip-flop, the result could be that the flip-flop enters a metastable state. A flip-flop in a *metastable state* is in a state other than a stable 0 or a stable 1. Metastable in general means that a system is only marginally stable—the system has other states that are far more stable. A flip-flop in a metastable state may have an output with a value that is not a 0 or a 1, instead outputting a voltage somewhere between that of a 0 and that of a 1. That voltage may also oscillate. Such an output is clearly a problem. Since a flip-flop's output is connected to other components like logic gates and other flip-flops, that strange voltage value may cause other components to output strange values, and soon the values throughout an entire circuit can be in bad shape.

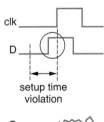

setup time violation

metastable state

Figure 3.81 Metastable flip-flop state caused by a setup time violation.

Why would we ever violate setup and hold times? After all, within a circuit we design, we can measure the longest possible path from any flip-flop output to any flip-flop input. As long as we make the clock period sufficiently longer than that longest path, we can ensure the circuit obeys setup times. Likewise, we can ensure that hold times are satisfied too.

The problem is that our circuit likely has to interface to external inputs, and we can't control when those inputs change, meaning those inputs may violate setup and hold times when connected to flip-flop inputs. For example, an input may be connected from a button being pressed by a user—the user can't be told to press the button so many nanoseconds before a clock edge and to be sure to hold the button so many nanoseconds after the clock edge so that setup and hold times are satisfied. So metastability is a problem primarily when a flip-flop has inputs that are not synchronized with the circuit's clock—in other words, metastability is a problem when dealing with **asynchronous inputs**.

Designers typically try to synchronize a circuit's asynchronous input to the circuit's clock before propagating that input to components in the circuit. A common way to synchronize an asynchronous input is to first *feed the asynchronous input into a D flip-flop*, and then use the output of that flip-flop wherever the input is needed, as shown for the asynchronous input `ai` in Figure 3.82.

"Hold on now!" you might say. Doesn't that synchronizing flip-flop experience the setup and hold time problem, and hence the same metastability issue? Yes, that's true. But at least the asynchronous input directly affects only *one* flip-flop, rather than perhaps several or dozens of flip-flops and other components. And that synchronizer flip-flop is specifically introduced for synchronization purposes and has no other purpose, whereas other flip-flops are being used to store bits for other purposes.

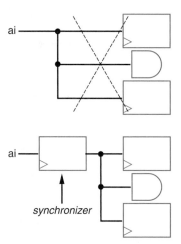

Figure 3.82 Feeding an asynchronous external input into a single flip-flop can reduce metastability problems.

We can therefore choose a flip-flop for the synchronizer that minimizes the metastability problem—we can choose an extremely fast flip-flop, and/or one with very small setup and hold times, and/or one with special circuitry to minimize metastability. That flip-flop may be bigger than normal or consume more power than normal, but there's only one such flip-flop per asynchronous input, so those issues aren't a problem. Bear in mind that no matter what we do, though, the synchronizer flip-flop could still become metastable, but at least we can minimize the odds of a metastable state happening by choosing a good flip-flop.

Another thing to consider is that a flip-flop will typically not stay metastable for very long. Eventually, the flip-flop will "topple" over to a stable `0` or a stable `1`, like how a coin tossed onto the ground may spin for a while (a metastable state) but will eventually topple over to a very stable head or tail. What many designers therefore do is introduce two or more flip-flops in series for synchronization purposes, as shown in Figure 3.83. So even if the first flip-flop becomes metastable, that flip-flop will likely reach a stable state before the next clock cycle, and thus the second flip-flop is even less likely to go metastable. Thus the odds of a

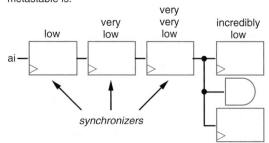

Figure 3.83 Synchronizer flip-flops reduce probability of metastability in a circuit's regular flip-flops.

metastable signal actually making it to our circuit's normal flip-flops are very low. This approach has the obvious drawback of delaying changes on the input signal by several cycles—in Figure 3.83, the rest of the circuit won't see a change on the input `ai` for three cycles.

As clock periods become shorter and shorter, the odds of the first flip-flop stabilizing before the next clock cycle decreases, so metastability is becoming a more challenging issue as clock periods shrink. Many advanced methods have been proposed to deal with the issue.

Nevertheless, no matter how hard we try, metastability will always be a possibility, meaning our circuit *may fail*. We can minimize the likelihood of failure, but we can't completely eliminate failures due to metastability. Designers often rate their designs using a measure called ***mean time between failures***, or ***MTBF***. Designers typically aim for MTBFs of many years. Many students find this concept—that we can't design fail-proof circuits—somewhat disconcerting. Yet, that concept is the real situation in design.

Designers of serious high-speed digital circuits should study the problem of metastability, and modern solutions to the problem, thoroughly.

Example 3.15   Adding a flip-flop to an asynchronous input to reduce the metastability problem

Figure 3.69 showed the controller circuit for a secure car key controller. Assuming the input a is asynchronous, then changes on input a could propagate through the controller's combinational logic to the state register's flip-flops such that flip-flop setup or hold times would be violated, resulting in metastable values. A synchronizer flip-flop could be added to the circuit's input to reduce the likelihood of metastability problems, as shown in Figure 3.84.

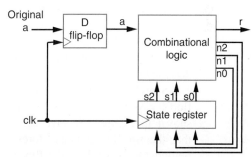

Figure 3.84 Secure car key controller extended with D flip-flop on asynchronous input to reduce chances of metastability problems.

Flip-Flop Reset and Set Inputs

Some D flip-flops (as well as other flip-flop types) come with extra inputs that can force the flip-flop to 0 or 1, independently of the D input. One such input is a *clear*, or *reset*, input that forces the flip-flop to 0. Another such input is a *set* input that forces the flip-flop to 1. Reset and set inputs are very useful for initializing flip-flops to an initial value (e.g., initializing all flip-flops to 0s) when powering up or resetting a system. These reset and set inputs should not be confused with the R and S inputs of an RS latch or flip-flop—the reset and set inputs are special control inputs to any type of flip-flop (D, RS, T, JK) that take priority over the normal data inputs of a flip-flop.

The reset and set inputs of a flip-flop may be either synchronous or asynchronous. A ***synchronous reset*** input forces the flip-flop to 0, regardless of the value on the D input, during a rising clock edge. For the flip-flop in Figure 3.85(a), setting R to 1 forces the flip-flop to 0 on the next clock edge. Likewise, a ***synchronous set*** input forces the flip-flop to 1 on a rising clock edge. The reset and set inputs thus have priority over the D

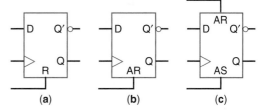

Figure 3.85 D flip-flops with: (a) synchronous reset R, (b) asynchronous reset AR, and (c) asynchronous reset and set.

input. If a flip-flop has both a synchronous reset and a synchronous set input, the flip-flop datasheet must inform the flip-flop user which has priority if both inputs are set to 1.

An ***asynchronous reset*** clears the flip-flop to 0 independently of the clock signal—the clock does not need to be rising, or even be 1, for the asynchronous reset to occur—hence the term "asynchronous." Likewise, an ***asynchronous set***, also known as ***preset***, can be used to asynchronously set the flip-flop to 1. A flip-flop's datasheet must indicate how long such inputs take to have effect, usually at least 1 clock cycle.

For brevity, we omit discussion of how synchronous/asynchronous reset/set inputs would be internally designed in a flip-flop.

Sample behavior of a D flip-flop's asynchronous reset input is shown in Figure 3.86. We assume that the flip-flop initially stores 1. Setting AR to 1 forces the flip-flop to 0, independent of any clock edge. When the next clock edge appears, AR is still 1, so the flip-flop stays 0 even though the input D is 1. When AR returns to 0, the flip-flop follows the D input on successive clock edges, as shown.

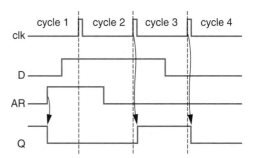

Figure 3.86 Asynchronous reset forces the flip-flop output Q to 0, independent of clk or D input

Initial State of a Controller

Particularly observant readers may have come up with a question when an earlier section implemented FSMs as controllers: what happened to the indication of the initial state of an FSM when we designed the controller implementing the FSM? The initial state of an FSM is the state that the FSM starts in when the FSM is first activated—or in controller terms, when the controller is first powered on. For example, the laser timer controller FSM in Figure 3.47 has an initial state of *Off*. When we converted graphical FSMs to truth tables, we ignored the initial state information. Thus, all of the controller circuits designed earlier in this chapter start in some random state based on whatever values happen to appear in the state register when the circuit is first powered on. Not knowing the initial state of a circuit could pose a problem—for example, we don't want our laser timer controller to start in a state that immediately turns on the laser.

One solution is to add an additional input, `reset`, to every controller. Setting `reset` to 1 should cause a load of the initial state into the state register. This initial state should be forced into the state register. The reset and set inputs of a flip-flop come in very handy in this situation. We can simply connect the controller's `reset` input to the reset and set inputs of the state register's flip-flops in a way that sets the flip-flops to the initial state when `reset` is 1. For example, if the initial state of a 2-bit state register should be 01, then we could connect the controller's reset input to reset and set inputs of the two flip-flops as shown in Figure 3.87.

Of course, for this reset functionality to work as desired, the designer must ensure that the controller's reset input is 1 when the system is first powered up. Ensuring that the reset input is 1 during power up can be handled using an appropriate electronic circuit connected to the on/off switch, the description of which is beyond the scope of this book.

Note that, if the synchronous reset or set inputs of a flip-flop are used, then the earlier-discussed setup and hold times, and associated metastability issues, apply to those reset and set inputs.

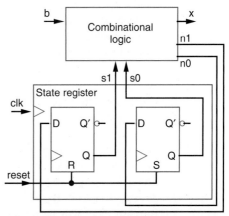

Figure 3.87 Three-cycles-high laser timer controller with a reset input that loads the state register with the initial state 01.

Non-Ideal Controller Behavior: Output Glitches

Glitching is the presence of temporary values on a wire typically caused by different delays of different logic paths leading to that wire. We saw an example of glitching in Figure 3.15. Glitching will also often occur when a controller changes states, due to different path lengths from each of the controller's state register flip-flops to the controller's outputs. Consider the three-cycles-high laser timer design in Figure 3.62. The laser should be off (output x=0) in state s1s0=00 and on (x=1) in states s1s0=01, s1s0=10, and s1s0=11. However, the delay of the wire from s1 to x's OR gate in the figure could be longer than the delay of the wire from s0 to that OR gate, perhaps due to different wire lengths. The result could be that when the state register changes state from s1s0=01 to s1s0=10, the OR gate's inputs could momentarily become 00. The OR gate would thus output 0 momentarily (a glitch). In the laser timer example, that glitch could momentarily shut off the laser—an undesired situation. Even worse would be glitches that momentarily turn *on* a laser.

A simple solution to controller output glitching is to add a flip-flop to the output. Figure 3.88 shows the laser-timer controller with a a flip-flop added to the x output. The flip-flop shifts the x output later by 1 clock cycle, which still results in three cycles high, but eliminates glitches from propagating to the x output—only the stable value appearing at the output would be loaded into the flip-flop on a rising clock edge. An output with a flip-flop added is called a **registered output** (think of the flip-flop as a one-bit register). Registered outputs are very common and should be used whenever there is any concern of glitches causing problems and when the shifting of the output later by one clock cycle is acceptable.

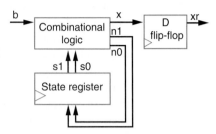

Figure 3.88 Laser timer controller with registered output to prevent glitches.

If the one cycle shift is not acceptable, an alternative registered output solution is to widen the state register such that each controller output Xj has its own bit Nj in the state register, and to encode each state Sk such that Nj is 1 whenever Xj is assigned 1 in that state, and such that Nj is 0 otherwise. Then, the output Xj should be connected directly from bit Nj of the state register. Because there will be no logic between the flip-flop for Nj and the output Xj, Xj will not experience glitches.

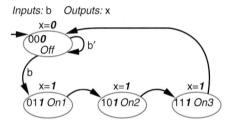

Figure 3.89 Laser timer state encoding with an extra bit corresponding to output x.

Figure 3.89 shows an encoding for the laser timer FSM where a bit has been added to the encoding corresponding to output x. The state encoding for state *Off* (which sets x to 0) has a 0 in that bit location, and has a 1 in the other three states (which set x to 1). Figure 3.90 shows how the controller would then connect x directly with its corresponding state register bit.

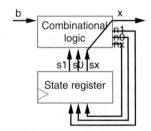

Figure 3.90 Laser timer controller with x connected to its state register bit.

Each of the above approaches has a drawback. The first approach shifts the outputs by one clock cycle and uses extra flip-flops. The second approach uses a wider state register and more combinational logic to compute the next state. Registered outputs therefore should be used when glitches should be avoided, like when the output controls a laser. In other cases, like in Chapter 5's use of controllers, the glitches don't cause problems and thus registered outputs aren't needed.

▷ 3.6 SEQUENTIAL LOGIC OPTIMIZATIONS AND TRADEOFFS (SEE SECTION 6.3)

The earlier sections described how to design basic sequential logic. This section, which physically appears in this book as Section 6.3, describes how to create *better* sequential logic (smaller, faster, etc.) using optimizations and tradeoffs. One use of this book involves studying sequential logic design optimizations and tradeoffs immediately after studying basic sequential logic design, meaning now. An alternative use studies sequential logic design optimizations and tradeoffs later, after studying the introduction of basic datapath components and RTL design (Chapters 4 and 5).

▷ 3.7 SEQUENTIAL LOGIC DESCRIPTION USING HARDWARE DESCRIPTION LANGUAGES (SEE SECTION 9.3)

This section, which physically appears in this book as Section 9.3, introduces HDLs for describing sequential logic. One use of this book studies HDLs for sequential logic immediately after studying basic sequential logic design, meaning now. An alternative use studies HDLs for sequential logic later.

▷ 3.8 PRODUCT PROFILE—PACEMAKER

A pacemaker is an electronic device that provides electrical stimulation to the heart to help regulate the heart's beating, steadying a heart whose body's natural "intrinsic" pacemaker is not working properly, perhaps due to disease. Implantable pacemakers, which are surgically placed under the skin as shown in Figure 3.91, are worn by over 1/2 million Americans. They are powered by a battery that lasts ten years or more. Pacemakers have improved the quality of life as well as lengthened the lives of many millions of people.

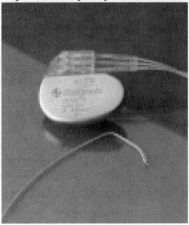 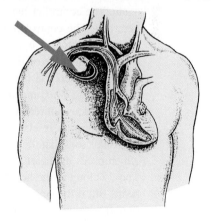

Figure 3.91 Pacemaker with leads (left), and pacemaker's location under the skin (right). Courtesy of Medtronic, Inc.

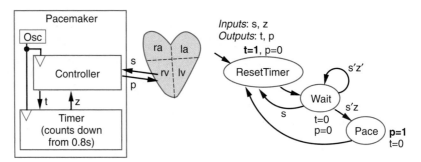

Figure 3.92 A basic pacemaker's controller FSM.

A heart has two atria (left and right) and two ventricles (left and right). The ventricles push the blood out to the arteries, while the atria receive the blood from the veins. A very simple pacemaker has one sensor to detect a natural contraction in the heart's right ventricle, and one output wire to deliver electrical stimulation to that right ventricle if the natural contraction doesn't occur within a specified time period—typically just under one second. Such electrical stimulation causes a contraction, not only in the right ventricle, but also the left ventricle.

We can describe the behavior of a simple pacemaker's controller using the FSM in Figure 3.92. The left side of the figure shows the pacemaker, consisting of a controller and a timer. The timer has an input t, which resets the timer when t=1. Upon being reset, the timer begins counting down from 0.8 seconds. If the timer counts down to 0, the timer sets its output z to 1. The timer could be reset before reaching 0, in which case the timer does not set z to 1, and instead the timer starts counting down from 0.8 seconds again. The controller has an input s, which is 1 when a contraction is sensed in the right ventricle. The controller has an output p, which the controller sets to 1 when the controller wants to cause a paced contraction.

The right side of the figure shows the controller's behavior as an FSM. Initially, the controller resets the timer in state *ResetTimer* by setting t = 1. Normally, the controller waits in state *Wait*, and stays in that state as long as a contraction is not detected (s') and the timer does not reach 0 (z'). If the controller detects a natural contraction (s), then the controller again resets the timer and returns to waiting again. On the other hand, if the controller sees that the timer has reached 0 (z = 1), then the controller goes to state *Pace*, which paces the heart by setting p=1, after which the controller returns to waiting again. Thus, as long as the heart contracts naturally, the pacemaker applies no stimulation to the heart. But if the heart doesn't contract naturally within 0.8 seconds of the last contraction (natural or paced), the pacemaker forces a contraction.

The atria receive blood from the veins, and contract to push the blood into the ventricles. The atrial contractions occur just before the ventricular contractions. Therefore, many pacemakers, known as "atrioventricular" pacemakers, sense and pace not just the ventricular contractions, but also the atrial contractions. Such pacemakers thus have two

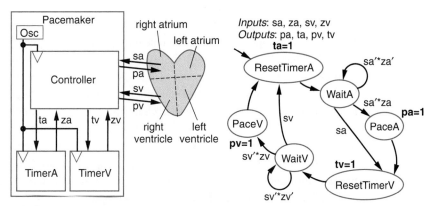

Figure 3.93 An atrioventricular pacemaker's controller FSM, using the convention that FSM outputs not explicitly set in a state are implicitly set to 0.

sensors, and two output wires for electrical stimulation, and may provide better cardiac output, with the desirable result being higher blood pressure (Figure 3.93).

The pacemaker has two timers, one for the right atrium (*TimerA*) and one for the right ventricle (*TimerV*). The controller initially resets *TimerA* in state *ResetTimerA*, and then waits for a natural atrial contraction, or for the timer to reach 0. If the controller detects a natural atrial contraction (sa), then the controller skips its pacing of the atrium. On the other hand, if *TimerA* reaches 0 first, then the controller goes to state *PaceA*, which causes a contraction in the atrium by setting pa=1. After an atrial contraction (either natural or paced), the controller resets *TimerV* in state *ResetTimerV*, and then waits for a natural ventricular contraction, or for the timer to reach 0. If a natural ventricular contraction occurs, the controller skips pacing of the ventricle. On the other hand, if *TimerV* reaches 0 first, then the controller goes to state *PaceV*, which causes a contraction in the ventricle by setting pv=1. The controller then returns to the atrial states.

Most modern pacemakers can have the timer parameters programmed wirelessly through radio signals so that doctors can try different treatments without having to surgically remove, program, and reimplant the pacemaker.

This example demonstrates the usefulness of FSMs in describing a controller's behavior. Real pacemakers have controllers with tens or even hundreds of states to deal with various details that we left out of the example for simplicity.

With the advent of low-power microprocessors, a trend in pacemaker design is that of implementing the FSM on a microprocessor rather than with a custom sequential circuit. Microprocessor implementation yields the advantage of easy reprogramming of the FSM, expanding the range of treatments with which a doctor can experiment.

▶ 3.9 CHAPTER SUMMARY

Section 3.1 introduced the concept of sequential circuits, namely circuits that store bits, Such circuits thus have memory, and the current values in such memory is known as state. Section 3.2 developed a series of increasingly robust bit storage blocks, including the SR latch, D latch, D flip-flop, and finally a register, which can store multiple bits. The section also introduced the concept of a clock, which synchronizes the loads of registers. Section 3.3 introduced finite-state machines (FSMs) for capturing the desired behavior of a sequential circuit, and a standard architecture able to implement FSMs, with an FSM implemented using the architecture known as a controller. Section 3.4 then described a process for converting an FSM to a controller implementation. Section 3.5 described several timing issues related to the use of flip-flops, including setup time, hold time, and metastability, and the use of synchronizer flip-flops to reduce metastability problems. The section introduced asynchronous clear and set inputs to flip-flops, and described their use for initializing an FSM to its initial state. The section described the problem of output glitches and the use of registered outputs to eliminate the problem. Section 3.8 highlighted a cardiac pacemaker and illustrated the use of an FSM to describe the pacemaker's behavior.

Designing a combinational circuit begins by capturing the desired circuit behavior using either an equation or a truth table, and then following a several step process to convert the behavior to a combinational circuit. Designing a sequential circuit begins by capturing the desired circuit behavior as an FSM, and then following a several-step process to convert the behavior to a circuit consisting of a register and a combinational circuit, which together are known as a controller. Thus, conceptually, the knowledge in Chapters 2 and 3 can be used to build any digital circuit. However, many digital circuits deal with input data that are many bits wide, such as two 32-bit inputs representing two binary numbers. Imagine how complex the equations, truth tables, or FSMs would be if they involved two 32-bit inputs. Fortunately, components have been developed specifically to deal with data inputs and that therefore simplify the design process—components that will be described in the next chapter.

▶ 3.10 EXERCISES

An asterisk (*) indicates an especially challenging problem.

SECTION 3.2: STORING ONE BIT—FLIP-FLOPS

3.1 Compute the clock period for the following clock frequencies.
    (a) 50 kHz (early computers)
    (b) 300 MHz (Sony Playstation 2 processor)
    (c) 3.4 GHz (Intel Pentium 4 processor)
    (d) 10 GHz (PCs of the early 2010s)
    (e) 1 THz (1 terahertz) (PC of the future?)

3.2 Compute the clock period for the following clock frequencies.
    (a) 32.768 kHz
    (b) 100 MHz
    (c) 1.5 GHz
    (d) 2.4 GHz

3.3 Compute the clock frequency for the following clock periods.
    (a) 1 s
    (b) 1 ms
    (c) 20 ns
    (d) 1 ns
    (e) 1.5 ps

3.4 Compute the clock frequency for the following clock periods.
    (a) 500 ms
    (b) 400 ns
    (c) 4 ns
    (d) 20 ps

3.5 Trace the behavior of an SR latch for the following situation: Q, S, and R have been 0 for a long time, then S changes to 1 and stays 1 for a long time, then S changes back to 0. Using a timing diagram, show the values that appear on wires S, R, t, and Q. Assume logic gates have a tiny nonzero delay.

3.6 Repeat Exercise 3.5, but assume that S was changed to 1 just long enough for the signal to propagate through one logic gate, after which S was changed back to 0—in other words, S did not satisfy the hold time of the latch.

3.7 Trace the behavior of a level-sensitive SR latch (see Figure 3.16) for the input pattern in Figure 3.94. Assume S1, R1, and Q are initially 0. Complete the timing diagram, assuming logic gates have a tiny but nonzero delay.

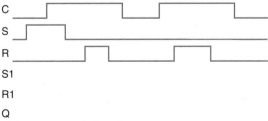

Figure 3.94 SR latch input pattern timing diagram.

3.8 Trace the behavior of a level-sensitive SR latch (see Figure 3.16) for the input pattern in Figure 3.95. Assume S1, R1, and Q are initially 0. Complete the timing diagram, assuming logic gates have a tiny but nonzero delay..

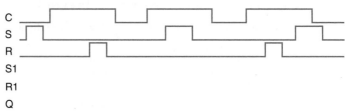

Figure 3.95 SR latch input pattern timing diagram.

3.9 Trace the behavior of a level-sensitive SR latch (see Figure 3.16) for the input pattern in Figure 3.96. Assume S1, R1, and Q are initially 0. Complete the timing diagram, assuming logic gates have a tiny but nonzero delay.

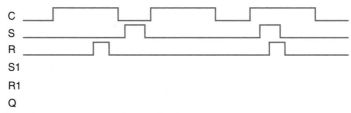

Figure 3.96 SR latch input pattern timing diagram.

3.10 Trace the behavior of a D latch (see Figure 3.19) for the input pattern in Figure 3.97. Assume Q is initially 0. Complete the timing diagram, assuming logic gates have a tiny but nonzero delay.

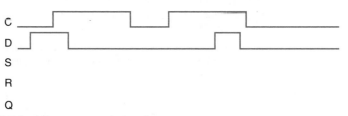

Figure 3.97 D latch input pattern timing diagram.

3.11 Trace the behavior of a D latch (see Figure 3.19) for the input pattern in Figure 3.98. Assume Q is initially 0. Complete the timing diagram, assuming logic gates have a tiny but nonzero delay.

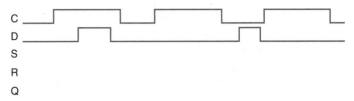

C
D
S
R
Q

Figure 3.98 D latch input pattern timing diagram.

3.12 Trace the behavior of an edge-triggered D flip-flop using a master-servant design (see Figure 3.25) for the input pattern in Figure 3.99. Assume each internal latch initially stores a 0. Complete the timing diagram, assuming logic gates have a tiny but nonzero delay.

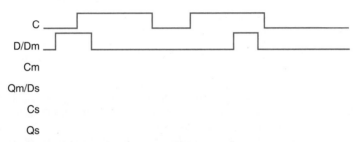

C
D/Dm
Cm
Qm/Ds
Cs
Qs

Figure 3.99 Edge-triggered D flip-flop input pattern timing diagram.

3.13 Trace the behavior of an edge-triggered D flip-flop using the master-servant design (see Figure 3.25) for the input pattern in Figure 3.100. Assume each internal latch initially stores a 0. Complete the timing diagram, assuming logic gates have a tiny but nonzero delay.

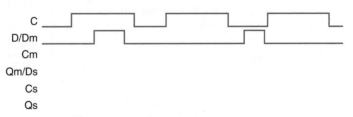

C
D/Dm
Cm
Qm/Ds
Cs
Qs

Figure 3.100 Edge-triggered D flip-flop input pattern timing diagram.

3.14 Compare the behavior of D latch and D flip-flop devices by completing the timing diagram in Figure 3.101. Assume each device initially stores a 0. Provide a brief explanation of the behavior of each device.

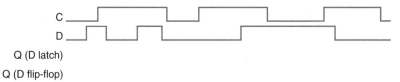

Q (D latch)

Q (D flip-flop)

Figure 3.101 D latch and D flip-flop input pattern timing diagram.

3.15 Compare the behavior of D latch and D flip-flop devices by completing the timing diagram in Figure 3.102. Assume each device initially stores a 0. Provide a brief explanation of the behavior of each device.

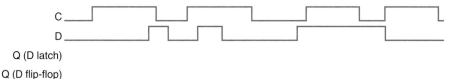

Q (D latch)

Q (D flip-flop)

Figure 3.102 D latch and D flip-flop input pattern timing diagram.

3.16 Create a circuit of three level-sensitive D latches connected in series (the output of one is connected to the input of the next). Use a timing diagram to show how a clock with a long high-time can cause the value at the input of the first D latch to trickle through more than one latch during the same clock cycle.

3.17 Repeat Exercise 3.16 using edge-triggered D flip-flops, and use a timing diagram to show how the input of the first D flip-flop does not trickle through to the next flip-flop, no matter how long the clock signal is high.

3.18 A circuit has an input X that is connected to the input of a D flip-flop. Using additional D flip-flops, complete the circuit so that an output Y equals the output of X's flip-flop but delayed by two clock cycles.

 3.19 Using four registers, design a circuit that stores the four values present at an 8-bit input D during the previous four clock cycles. The circuit should have a single 8-bit output that can be configured using two inputs s1 and s0 to output any one of the four registers. (Hint: use an 8-bit 4x1 mux.)

3.20 Consider three 4-bit registers connected as in Figure 3.103. Assume the initial values in the registers are unknown. Trace the behavior of the registers by completing the timing diagram of Figure 3.104.

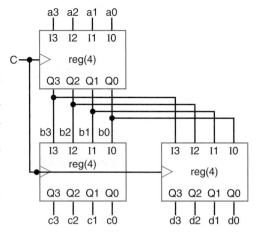

Figure 3.103 Register configuration.

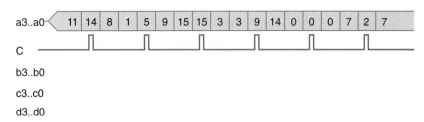

Figure 3.104 4-bit register input pattern timing diagram.

3.21 Consider three 4-bit registers connected as in Figure 3.105. Assume the initial values in the registers are unknown. Trace the behavior of the registers by completing the timing diagram of Figure 3.106.

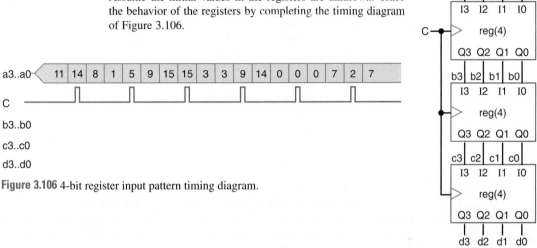

Figure 3.106 4-bit register input pattern timing diagram.

Figure 3.105 Register configuration.

SECTION 3.3: FINITE-STATE MACHINES (FSMS)

3.22 Draw a timing diagram (showing inputs, state, and outputs) for the flight-attendant call-button FSM of Figure 3.53 for the following scenario. Both inputs Call and Cncl are initially 0. Call becomes 1 for 2 cycles. Both inputs are 0 for 2 more cycles, then Cncl becomes 1 for 1 cycle. Both inputs are 0 for 2 more cycles, then both inputs Call and Cncl become 1 for 2 cycles. Both inputs become 0 for one last cycle. Assume any input changes occur halfway between two clock edges.

3.23 Draw a timing diagram (showing inputs, state, and outputs) for the code-detector FSM of Figure 3.58 for the following scenario. Recall that when a button (or buttons) is pressed, a becomes 1 for exactly 1 clock cycle, no matter how long the button (or buttons) is pressed. Initially no button is pressed. The user then presses buttons in the following order: red, green, blue, red. Noticing the final state of the system, can you suggest an improvement to the system to better handle such incorrect code sequences?

3.24 Draw a state diagram for an FSM that has an input X and an output Y. Whenever X changes from 0 to 1, Y should become 1 for two clock cycles and then return to 0—even if X is still 1. (Assume for this problem and all other FSM problems that an implicit rising clock is ANDed with every FSM transition condition.)

note: Y should only become 1 on a 0→1 transition

3.25 Draw a state diagram for an FSM with no inputs and three outputs x, y, and z. xyz should always exhibit the following sequence: 000, 001, 010, 100, repeat. The output should change only on a rising clock edge. Make 000 the initial state.

3.26 Do Exercise 3.25, but add an input I that can stop the sequence when set to 0. When input I returns to 1, the sequence resumes from where it left off.

3.27 Do Exercise 3.25, but add an input I that can stop the sequence when set to 0. When I returns to 1, the sequence starts from 000 again.

3.28 A wristwatch display can show one of four items: the time, the alarm, the stopwatch, or the date, controlled by two signals s1 and s0 (00 displays the time, 01 the alarm, 10 the stopwatch, and 11 the date—assume s1 and s0 control an *N*-bit mux that passes through the appropriate register). Pressing a button B (which sets B = 1) sequences the display to the next item. For example, if the presently displayed item is the date, the next item is the current time. Create a state diagram for an FSM describing this sequencing behavior, having an input bit B, and two output bits s1 and s0. Be sure to only sequence forward by one item each time the button is pressed, regardless of how long the button is pressed—in other words, be sure to wait for the button to be released after sequencing forward one item. Use short but descriptive names for each state. Make displaying the time be the initial state.

3.29 Extend the state diagram created in Exercise 3.28 by adding an input R. R=1 forces the FSM to return to the state that displays the time.

3.30 Draw a state diagram for an FSM with an input gcnt and three outputs x, y, and z. The xyz outputs generate a sequence called a Gray code in which exactly one of the three outputs changes from 0 to 1 or from 1 to 0. The Gray code sequence that the FSM should output is 000, 010, 011, 001, 101, 111, 110, 100, repeat. The output should change only on a rising clock edge when the input gcnt = 1. Make the initial state 000.

3.31 Trace through the execution of the FSM created in Exercise 3.30 by completing the timing diagram in Figure 3.107, where C is the clock input. Assume the initial state is the state that sets xyz to 000.

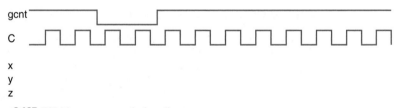

Figure 3.107 FSM input pattern timing diagram.

3.32 Draw a timing diagram for the FSM in Figure 3.108 with the FSM starting in state *Wait*. Choose input values such that the FSM reaches state *EN*, and returns to *Wait*..

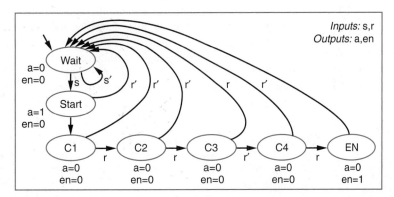

Figure 3.108 FSM.

3.33 For FSMs with the following numbers of states, indicate the smallest possible number of bits for a state register representing those states:
   (a) 4
   (b) 8
   (c) 9
   (d) 23
   (e) 900

3.34 How many possible states can be represented by a 16-bit register?

3.35 If an FSM has N states, what is the maximum number of possible transitions that could exist in the FSM? Assume that no pair of states has more than one transition in the same direction, and that no state has a transition point back to itself. Assuming there are a large number of inputs, meaning the number of transitions is not limited by the number of inputs? Hint: try for small N, and then generalize.

3.36 *Assuming one input and one output, how many possible four-state FSMs exist?

3.37 *Suppose you are given two FSMs that execute concurrently. Describe an approach for merging those two FSMs into a single FSM with identical functionality as the two separate FSMs, and provide an example. If the first FSM has N states and the second has M states, how many states will the merged FSM have?

3.38 *Sometimes dividing a large FSM into two smaller FSMs results in simpler circuitry. Divide the FSM shown in Figure 3.111 into two FSMs, one containing *G0–G3*, the other containing *G4–G7*. You may add additional states, transitions, and inputs or outputs between the two FSMs, as required. Hint: you will need to introduce signals between the FSMs for one FSM to tell the other FSM to go to some state.

SECTION 3.4: CONTROLLER DESIGN

3.39 Using the process for designing a controller, convert the FSM of Figure 3.109 to a controller, implementing the controller using a state register and logic gates.

3.40 Using the process for designing a controller, convert the FSM of Figure 3.110 to a controller, implementing the controller using a state register and logic gates.

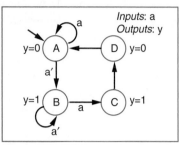

Figure 3.109 FSM example.

3.41 Using the process for designing a controller, convert the FSM you created for Exercise 3.24 to a controller, implementing the controller using a state register and logic gates.

3.42 Using the process for designing a controller, convert the FSM you created for Exercise 3.28 to a controller, implementing the controller using a state register and logic gates.

3.43 Using the process for designing a controller, convert the FSM you created for Exercise 3.30 to a controller, implementing the controller using a state register and logic gates.

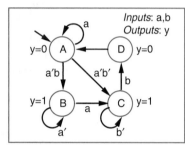

Figure 3.110 FSM example.

3.44 Using the process for designing a controller, convert the FSM in Figure 3.111 to a controller, stopping once you have created the truth table. Note: your truth table will be quite large, having 32 rows—you might therefore want to use a computer tool, like a word processor or spreadsheet, to draw the table.

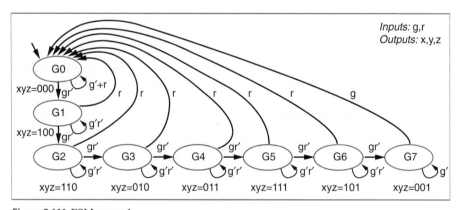

Figure 3.111 FSM example.

3.45 Create an FSM that has an input X and an output Y. Whenever X changes from 0 to 1, Y should become 1 for five clock cycles and then return to 0—even if X is still 1. Using the process for designing a controller, convert the FSM to a controller, stopping once you have created the truth table.

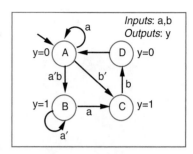

3.46 The FSM in Figure 3.112 has two problems: one state has non-exclusive transitions, and another state has incomplete transitions. By ORing and ANDing the conditions for each state's transitions, prove that these problems exist. Then fix these problems by refining the FSM, taking your best guess as to what was the FSM creator's intent.

Figure 3.112 FSM example.

3.47 Reverse engineer the poorly designed three-cycles-high circuit in Figure 3.41 to an FSM. Explain why the behavior of the circuit, as described by the FSM, is undesirable.

3.48 Reverse engineer the behavior of the sequential circuit shown in Figure 3.113.

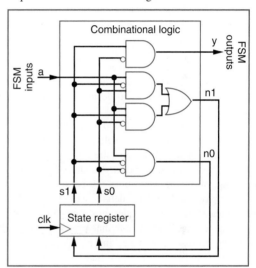

Figure 3.113 A sequential circuit to be reverse engineered.

SECTION 3.5: MORE ON FLIP-FLOPS AND CONTROLLERS

3.49 Use a timing diagram to illustrate how metastability can yield incorrect output for the secure car key controller of Figure 3.69. Use a second timing diagram to show how the synchronizer flip-flop introduced in Figure 3.84 may reduce the likelihood of such incorrect output.

3.50 Design a controller with a 4-bit state register that gets synchronously initialized to state 1010 when an input *reset* is set to 1.

3.51 Redraw the laser-timer controller timing diagram of Figure 3.63 for the case of the output being registered as in Figure 3.88.

3.52 Draw a timing diagram for three clock cycles of the sequence generator controller of Figure 3.68, assuming that AND gates have a delay of 2 ns and inverters (including inversion bubbles) have a delay of 1 ns. The timing diagram should show the incorrect outputs that appear temporarily due to glitching. Then introduce registered outputs to the controller using flip-flops at the outputs, and show a new timing diagram, which should no longer have glitches (but the output may be shifted in time).

▶ *DESIGNER PROFILE*

Brian got his bachelor's degree in electrical engineering and then worked for several years. Realizing the future demand for digital design targeting an increasingly popular type of digital chip known as FPGAs (see Chapter 7), he returned to school to obtain a master's degree in electrical engineering, with a thesis topic targeting digital design for FPGAs. He has been employed at two different companies, and is now working as an independent digital design consultant.

He has worked on a number of projects, including a system that prevents house fires by tripping a circuit breaker when electrical arcing is detected, a microprocessor architecture for speeding up the processing of digitized video, and a mammography machine for precise location detection of tumors in humans.

One of the projects he has found most interesting was a baggage scanner for detecting explosives. "In that system, there is a lot of data being acquired as well as motors running, x-rays being beamed, and other things happening, all at the same time. To be successful, you have to pay attention to detail, and you have to communicate with the other design teams so everyone is on the same page." He found that project particularly interesting because "I was working on a small part of a very large, complex machine. We had to stay focused on our part of the design, while at the same time being mindful of how all the parts were going to fit together in the end." Thus, being able to work alone as well as in large groups was important, requiring good communication and team skills. And being able to understand not only a part of the system, but also important aspects of the other parts was also necessary, requiring knowledge of diverse topics.

Brian is now an independent digital design consultant, something that many electrical engineers, computer engineers, and computer scientists choose to do after getting experience in their field. "I like the flexibility that being a consultant offers. On the plus side, I get to work on a wide variety of projects. The drawback is that sometimes I only get to work on a small part of a project, rather than seeing a product through from start to finish. And of course being an independent consultant means there's less stability than a regular position at a company, but I don't mind that."

Brian has taken advantage of the flexibility provided by consulting by taking a part-time job teaching an undergraduate digital design course and an embedded systems course at a university. "I really enjoy teaching, and I have learned a lot through teaching. And I enjoy introducing students to the field of embedded systems."

Asked what he likes most about the field of digital design, he says, "I like building products that make people's lives easier, or safer, or more fun. That's satisfying."

Asked to give advice to students, he says that one important thing is "to ask questions. Don't be afraid of looking dumb when you ask questions at a new job. People don't expect you to know everything, but they do expect you to ask questions when you are unsure. Besides, asking questions is an important part of learning."

4

Datapath Components

▶ 4.1 INTRODUCTION

Chapters 2 and 3 introduced increasingly complex building blocks with which to build digital circuits. Those blocks included logic gates, multiplexors, decoders, basic registers, and controllers. Controllers are good for implementing systems having *control* inputs. This chapter instead focuses on creating building blocks for systems having *data* inputs. Control and data inputs differ as follows:

- **Control:** A control input is usually one bit and represents a particular event or command that influences or directs the system's mode of operation.

- **Data:** A data input is usually multiple bits that collectively represent a single entity, like a 32-bit number from a temperature sensor or an 8-bit ASCII character, and that are operated on or transformed by the system.

As an analogy, a television has control inputs coming from the remote control; those inputs control the TV's mode of operation, such as turning the volume up or changing the channel. A television also has data inputs coming from a video cable; those data inputs are operated on to create the video seen on the TV display. Another example is a hand-held calculator; a user inputs numbers (data input) and issues commands like add or multiply (control inputs) to operate on that data.

Not all inputs are just control or just data—some inputs have features of both, just as humans can't be strictly divided into "tall" and "short" categories.

While a controller is a good building block for systems having control inputs and outputs, new building blocks are needed for systems that operate on data. Such blocks are *datapath components*. A circuit of datapath components is known as a *datapath*.

Datapaths can become quite complex, and therefore it is crucial to build datapaths from datapath components that each encapsulates an appropriately high level of functionality. For example, if you had to build a bicycle, you would probably build it by combining tires, a frame, a seat, handlebars, and so on. Each of those components encapsulates a high-level function of part of a bicycle. You started with a tire and not with rubber and glue. Rubber and glue make up the design of a tire, not the design of a bicycle. Likewise, when we design datapaths, we must have appropriately high-level datapath components—logic gates are too low-level. This chapter defines such datapath components and builds some simple datapaths. Chapter 5 will show how to combine datapaths and controllers to build even more capable digital systems.

▶ 4.2 REGISTERS

An *N-bit register* is a sequential component that can store *N* bits. *N* is called the register *width*. Typical register widths are 8, 16, and 32 bits, but can be as small as 1 or can be arbitrarily large. The bits in a register commonly represent data, such as 8 bits representing temperature data in binary.

The common name for storing data into a register is *loading*; the names *writing* and *storing* are also used. The opposite action of loading a register is known as *reading* a register's contents. Reading consists merely of observing a register's outputs and is therefore is not synchronized with the clock. Furthermore, reading a register does not change the bits inside the register, just like reading this book does not change the words inside the book.

Registers come in a variety of styles. The upcoming sections introduce some of the most common styles. Registers are the most fundamental datapath component, so several examples will be presented.

Parallel-Load Register

The most basic type of register, shown in Figure 3.36 in Chapter 3, consists of a set of flip-flops that are loaded on every clock cycle. That basic register is useful as the state register in a controller, because a controller's state register should be loaded on every clock cycle. However, most other uses of registers require some way to control whether or not a register is loaded on a particular clock cycle—on some cycles the register should be loaded, whereas on other cycles the register should keep its previous value.

Control of the loading of a register can be achieved by adding a 2x1 multiplexor in front of each flip-flop of a basic register as shown for the 4-bit register in Figure 4.1(a). When the register's load control input is 0 and the clock signal rises, each flip-flop stores its own Q value, as shown in Figure 4.1(b). Because Q is a flip-flop's present content, the contents of the flip-flops, and hence the register's contents, do not change when load is 0. In contrast, when the load input is 1 and the clock signal rises, each flip-flop is loaded with a data input I0, I1, I2, or I3—thus, the register is loaded with the data inputs when load is 1.

A register with a load line that controls whether the register is loaded with external inputs, with those inputs loaded in parallel, is called a *parallel-load register*. Figure 4.1(c) provides a block symbol for a 4-bit parallel-load register. A *block symbol* of a component shows a component's inputs and outputs without showing the component's internal details.

▶ WHY THE NAME "REGISTER"?

Historically, the term "register" referred to a sign or chalkboard onto which people could temporarily write out cash transactions, and later perform bookkeeping using those transactions. The term generally refers to a device for storing data. In this context, since a collection of flip-flops stores data, the name "register" seems quite appropriate.

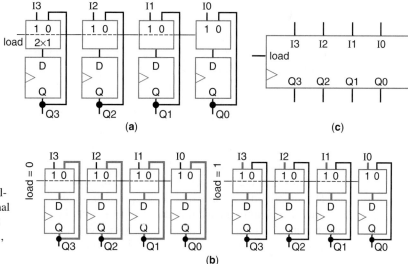

Figure 4.1 4-bit parallel-load register: (a) internal design, (b) paths when `load=0` and `load=1`, (c) block symbol.

Example 4.1 Weight sampler

Consider a scale used to weigh fruit at a grocery store . The scale may have a display that shows the present weight. We want to add a second display and a button that the user can press to remember the present weight (sometimes called "sampling"), so that when the fruit is removed, the remembered weight continues to be displayed on the second display. A block diagram of the system is shown in Figure 4.2.

Assume that the scale outputs the present weight as a 4-bit binary number, and the "Present weight" and "Saved weight" displays automatically convert their input binary number to the proper displayed value. We can design the *WeightSampler* block using a 4-bit parallel-load reg-

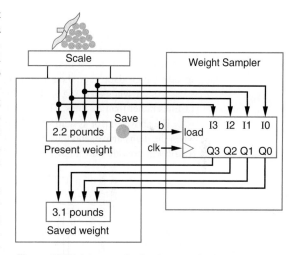

Figure 4.2 Weight sampler implemented using a 4-bit parallel-load register.

ister. We connect the button signal b to the load input of the register. The output connects to the "Saved weight" display. Whenever b is 1, the weight value gets loaded into the register, and thus appears on the second display. When b returns to 0, the register keeps its value, so the second display continues to show the same weight even if other items are placed on the scale and the first display changes. This example involved a control input b, and also two 4-bit data inputs and outputs.

Figure 4.3 Multibit wire shorthand notation for representing a bus.

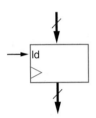

Figure 4.4 Simplified register symbol.

Buses. Data items consist of numerous bits. Building circuits operating on data items could therefore involve large numbers of wires to carry those bits. A group of N wires in a circuit that transport a data item is called a ***data bus*** or just ***bus***. N is the *width* of the bus. Figure 4.2 has a 4-bit bus connecting the scale to the register, and a 4-bit bus connecting the register to the saved-weight display.

Drawing each bus wire of a circuit can result in a cluttered and hard-to-read drawing; even the very simple circuit drawing of Figure 4.2 shows signs of such clutter. Thus, buses are typically drawn using the shorthand notation in Figure 4.3. The bus is drawn as a single bolded line with a small angled line drawn through the bolded line to denote multiple bits. When the number of bits is unclear, the number can be written next to that small angled line. Example 4.2 will use this shorthand notation for buses. The notation is just for drawings; the actual number of wires in the circuit is unchanged.

The simplified register component symbol in Figure 4.4 uses the shorthand notation for a bus. The simplified symbol also does not label the data inputs and outputs, and the component itself is not even labeled as a register—the fact that the component is a register is suggested by the bus input, bus output, and the clock input symbol (the triangle).

A common use of registers is to help reduce the actual number of wires in a circuit. Registers help by enabling multiplexing of M different data items over a single bus, with each data item stored in its own register, as will be illustrated in Example 4.2.

Example 4.2 Automobile above-mirror display using parallel-load registers

Chapter 2 described an example of a system that could display one of four 8-bit inputs, T, A, I, and M above a car's rearview mirror. The car's central computer was connected to the system using 32 wires (4*8), which is a lot of wires to connect from the computer to the mirror. Instead, assume the computer connects to the mirror as in Figure 4.5, using an 8-bit bus (C), 2 control lines a1a0 that specify which data item should presently appear on C (displaying T when a1a0=00, A when a1a0=01, I when a1a0=10, and M when a1a0=11), and a load control line load, for a total of 11 lines rather than 32 lines. The computer can send the data items in any order and at any time.

The above-mirror system should store data items in the appropriate register according to a1a0 when the items arrive, and thus the system needs four parallel-load registers to store each data item. a1a0 will provide the "address" that indicates which register to load, much like the address on an

Figure 4.5 Above-mirror display design. a1a0, set by the car's central computer, determines which register to load with C, while load=1 enables such loading. xy, which are independent of a1a0 and are set by the user pressing a mode button, determine which register to output to the display D.

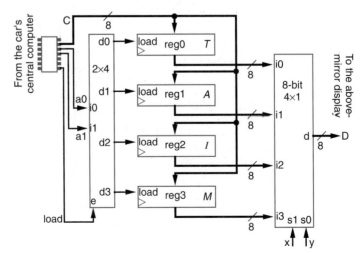

envelope indicates which house should receive the envelope. As in the earlier example, inputs xy determine which value to pass through to the 8-bit display output D, with xy sequenced by the user pressing the a button named *mode*, which is not shown in the figure.

The decoder decodes a1a0 to enable one of the four registers. The load line enables the decoder—if load is 0, no decoder output is 1 and so no register gets loaded. The multiplexer part of the system is the same as in the earlier example.

Let's consider a sample sequence of inputs. Suppose initially that all registers are storing 0s and xy=00. Thus, the display will show 0. If the user presses the *mode* button four times, the inputs xy will sequence through 01, 10, 11, and back to 00, still displaying 0 for each press (because all registers contain 0s). Now suppose that during some clock cycle, the car's computer sets a1a0=01, load=1, and C=00001010. Then register *reg1* will be loaded with 00001010. Because xy=00, the display will still show the contents of *reg0*, and thus the display will show 0. Now, if the user presses the *mode* button, xy will become 01, and the display will show the decimal value of *reg1*'s 00001010 value, which is ten in decimal. Pressing *mode* again will change xy to 10, so the display will show the contents of *reg2*, which is 0. At any time in the future, the car's computer can load the other registers or reload *reg1* with new values, in any order. Note that the loading of the registers is independent from the displaying of those registers.

This example involved control inputs a0, a1, load, x, and y, data input C, and data output D.

Example 4.3 Computerized checkerboard

Checkers (known in some countries as "draughts") is one of the world's most popular board games. A checkerboard consists of 64 squares, formed from 8 columns and 8 rows. Each player starts with 12 checkers (pieces) on the board. A computerized checkerboard may replace the checkers by using an LED (light-emitting diode) in each square. An on LED represents a checker in a square; an off LED represents no checker. For simplicity of the example, ignore the issue of each player having his own color of checkers. An example board is shown in Figure 4.6(a).

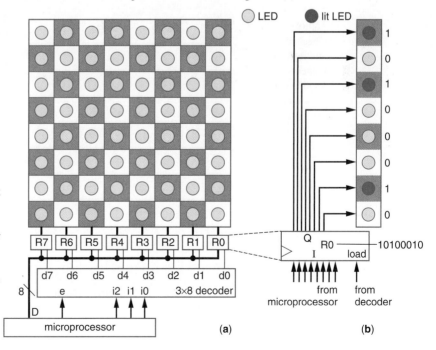

Figure 4.6 An electronic checkerboard: (a) eight 8-bit registers (*R7* through *R0*) can be used to drive the 64 LEDs, using one register per column, (b) detail of how one register connects to a column's LEDs and how the value 10100010 stored in that register would light three LEDs.

A computerized checkerboard typically has a microprocessor that keeps track of where each piece is located, moves pieces according to user commands or according to a checker-playing program (when playing against the computer), and keeps score.

Notice that the microprocessor must set values for 64 bits, one bit for each square. However, the inexpensive type of microprocessor used in such a device typically does not have 64 pins. The microprocessor needs external registers to store those bits that drive the LEDs. The microprocessor will write to those registers one at a time. The sequence of writes to the registers is so fast that an observer would see all the LEDs change at the same time, unable to notice that some LEDs are changing microseconds earlier than others.

Let's use one register per column, meaning eight 8-bit registers will be used in total as shown below the checkerboard in Figure 4.6(a). We named the registers *R7* through *R0*. Each register's 8 bits of data correspond to a particular row in the register's column, indicating whether the respective LED is on or off, as shown in Figure 4.6(b). The eight registers are connected to the microprocessor. The microprocessor uses eight pins (D) for data, three pins (i2, i1, i0) for addressing the appropriate register (which is decoded into a load line for each of the 8 registers), and one pin (e) for the register load line (connected to the decoder's enable), for a total of 12 pins—far fewer than 64 pins if registers were not used. To configure the checkerboard for the beginning of a game, the microprocessor would perform the sequence of register writes shown in Figure 4.7.

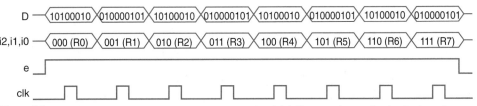

Figure 4.7 Timing diagram showing an input sequence that initializes an electronic checkerboard.

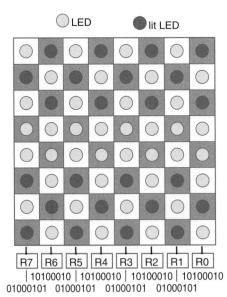

Figure 4.8
Checkerboard and register contents after loading registers for initial checker positions.

On the first rising clock edge, *R0* gets loaded with 10100010. On the second rising clock edge, *R1* gets loaded with 01000101. And so on. After eight clock cycles, the registers would contain the desired values, and the board's LEDs would be lit as shown in Figure 4.8.

▶ *HOW DOES IT WORK? COMPUTERIZED BOARD GAMES.*

Many of you have played a computerized board game, like checkers, backgammon, or chess, either using boards with small displays to represent pieces, or perhaps using a graphics program on a personal computer or website. The main method the computer uses for choosing among possible next moves is called **lookahead**. For the current configuration of pieces on the board, the computer considers all possible single moves that it might make. For each such move, it might also consider all possible single moves by the opponent. For each new configuration resulting from possible moves, the computer evaluates the configuration's goodness, or quality, and picks a move that may lead to the best configuration. The number of moves that the computer looks ahead (one computer move, one opponent move, another computer move, another opponent move) is called the *lookahead amount*. Good programs might lookahead three, four, five moves, or more. Looking ahead is costly in terms of compute time and memory—if each player has 10 possible moves per turn, then looking ahead two moves results in 10*10 =100 configurations to evaluate; three moves results in 10*10*10=1000 configurations, four moves in 10,000 configurations, and so on. Good game-playing programs will "prune"

configurations that appear to be very bad and thus unlikely to be chosen by an opponent, just as humans do, to reduce the configurations to be considered. Computers can examine millions of configurations, whereas humans can only mentally examine perhaps a few dozen. Chess, being perhaps the most complex of popular board games, has attracted extensive attention since the early days of computing. Alan Turing, considered one of the fathers of Computer Science, wrote much about using computers for chess, and is credited as having written the first computer chess program in 1950. However, humans proved better than computer chess programs until 1997, when IBM's Deep Blue computer defeated the reigning world champion in a classic chess match. Deep Blue had 30 IBM RS-6000 SP processors connected to 480 special purpose chess chips, and could evaluate 200 million moves per second, and hence many billions of moves in a few minutes. Today, chess tournaments not only match humans against computer programs, but also programs against programs, many such tournaments hosted by the International Computer Games Association.

(Source: *Computer Chess History*, by Bill Wall).

Shift Register

One thing a designer might want to do with a register is to shift the register's contents to the left or to the right. **Shifting** to the right means moving each stored bit one position to the right. If a 4-bit register originally stores `1101`, shifting right would result in `0110`, as shown in Figure 4.9(a). The rightmost bit (in this case a `1`) was "dropped," and a `0` was "shifted into" the leftmost bit. To build a register capable of shifting to the right, the register's flip-flops need to include connections similar to those shown in Figure 4.9(b).

A register capable of shifting its own contents is called a *shift register*. The design of a right shift register appears in Figure 4.10. The register has two control inputs, `shr` and `shr_in`. `shr=1` causes a right shift on a rising clock edge, while `shr=0` causes the register to maintain its present value. `shr_in` is the bit that should be shifted into the leftmost register bit during a shift operation.

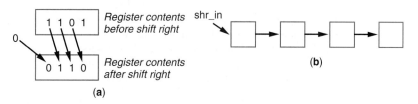

(a)

Figure 4.9 Right shift example: (a) sample contents before and after a right shift, (b) bit-by-bit view of the shift.

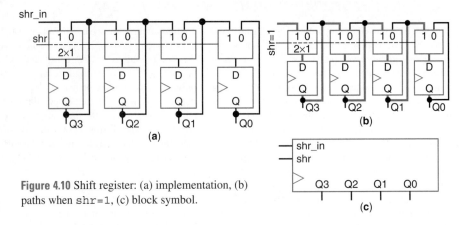

Figure 4.10 Shift register: (a) implementation, (b) paths when `shr=1`, (c) block symbol.

A **rotate register** is a slight variation of a shift register in which the outgoing bit gets shifted back in as the incoming bit. So on a right rotate, the rightmost bit gets shifted into the leftmost bit, as shown in Figure 4.11. The design for a rotate register is a slight modification of the design of Figure 4.10. The rightmost flip-flop output, rather than the `shr_in` input, would be connected to the leftmost mux's `i1` input. A rotate register also needs some way to get values into the register—either via a shift, or via parallel load.

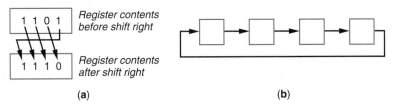

Figure 4.11 Right rotate example: (a) register contents before and after the rotate, (b) bit-by-bit view of the rotate operation.

Example 4.4 Above-mirror display using shift registers

Example 4.2 redesigned the connection between a car's central computer and an above-mirror display system to reduce the number of wires from 32 down to 8+2+1=11 by using an 8-bit data bus. However, even 11 wires is a lot of wires to have to run from the computer to the mirror. Let's reduce the wires even further by using shift registers in the above-mirror display system. The inputs to the above-mirror system from the car's computer will be one data bit `c`, two address lines `a1a0`, and a shift line `shift`, for a total of only 4 wires. When the computer is

This bundle should be thin—just a few wires, not eleven wires.

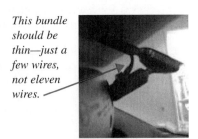

Figure 4.1 Serial communication enables thin cables.

Figure 4.12 Above-mirror display design using shift registers to reduce the number of lines coming from the car's computer. The computer sets `a1a0` to the desired register to load, and then holds `shift=1` for eight clock cycles. During those cycles, it sets `c` to the desired register contents bit-by-bit, one bit per clock cycle. The result is that the desired register is loaded with the sent 8-bit value.

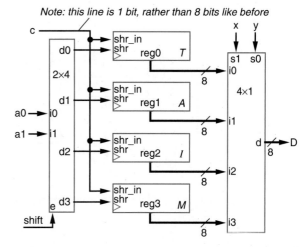

to write to one of the above-mirror system's registers, the computer sets `a1a0` appropriately and then sets `shift` to 1 for exactly eight clock cycles.

For each of those eight clock cycles, the computer will set `c` to one bit of the 8-bit data to be loaded, starting with the least-significant (rightmost) bit on the first clock cycle, and ending with the most-significant (leftmost) bit on the eighth clock cycle. The above-mirror system can thus be designed as shown in Figure 4.12.

When `shift=1`, the appropriate register gets a new value shifted in during the next eight clock cycles. This method achieves the same results as parallel loading but with fewer wires.

This example demonstrates a form of communication between digital circuits known as ***serial communication***, in which the circuits communicate data by sending the data one bit at a time.

Multifunction Registers

Some registers perform a variety of *operations*, also called *functions*, like load, shift right, shift left, rotate right, rotate left, etc. The desired operation can be achieved by setting the register's control inputs. The following section introduces several such ***multifunction registers***.

Register with Parallel Load and Shift Right

A popular combination of operations on a register is parallel load and shift. We can design a 4-bit register capable of parallel load and shift right as shown in Figure 4.13(a). Figure 4.13(b) shows a block symbol of the register.

> ### ▶ COMPUTER COMMUNICATIONS IN AN AUTOMOBILE USING SERIAL DATA TRANSFER.

Modern automobiles contain dozens of computers distributed throughout the car—some under the hood, some in the dashboard, some above the mirror, some in the door, some in the trunk, etc. Running wires throughout the car so those computers can communicate is a challenge. Most automobile computers communicate *serially*, meaning one bit at a time, like the communication in Example 4.4. Serial communication reduces the number of wires. A popular serial communication scheme in automobiles is known as the "CAN bus," short for Controller Area Network, which is an international standard defined by ISO (International Standards Organization) standard number 11898.

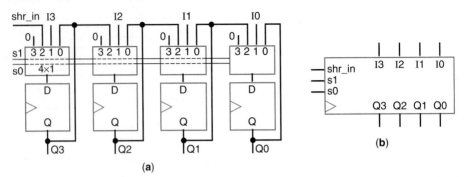

Figure 4.13 4-bit register with parallel load and shift right operations: (a) internal design, (b) block symbol.

The design uses a 4x1 mux rather than a 2x1 mux in front of each flip-flop, because each flip-flop can receive its next bit from one of three locations. The fourth mux input is unused. The table in Figure 4.14 describes the register's behavior. Such a table listing the operation for each combination of a component's control inputs is called an *operation table*.

Let's examine the mux and flip-flop of the rightmost bit. When s1s0=00, the mux passes the current flip-flop value back to the flip-flop,

s1	s0	Operation
0	0	Maintain present value
0	1	Parallel load
1	0	Shift right
1	1	(Unused)

Figure 4.14 Operation table of a 4-bit register with parallel load and shift right operations.

causing the flip-flop to get reloaded with its current value on the next rising clock, thus maintaining the current value. When s1s0=01, the mux passes the external I0 input to the flip-flop, causing the flip-flop to get loaded. When s1s0=10, the mux passes the present value of the flip-flop output from the left, Q1, thus causing a right shift. s1s0=11 is not a legal input to the register and thus should never occur; the mux passes 0s in this case, thus clearing the flip-flop.

▶ **UNUSED INPUTS**

The circuit in Figure 4.13 included a mux with 4 inputs, of which only 3 inputs were needed. Notice that we actually set the unused input to a particular value, rather than simply leaving the input unconnected. Remember that the input is controlling transistors inside the component—if we don't assign a value to the input, will the internal transistors conduct or not conduct? We don't really know, and so we could get undesired behavior from the mux. Leaving inputs unconnected should not be done. On the other hand, leaving outputs unconnected is no problem—an unconnected output may have a 1 or a 0 that simply doesn't control anything else.

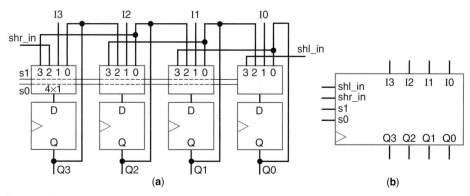

Figure 4.15 4-bit register with parallel load, shift left, and shift right operations: (a) internal design, (b) block symbol.

Register with Parallel Load, Shift Left, and Shift Right

Adding a shift left operation to the above 4-bit register is straightforward and is shown in Figure 4.15. Instead of connecting 0s to the I3 input of each 4x1 mux, we instead connect the output from the flip-flop to the right. The rightmost mux's I3 input would be connected to an additional input shl_in.

The register has the operations shown in Figure 4.16.

Load/Shift Register with Separate Control Inputs for Each Operation

Registers typically don't come with control inputs that encode the operation into the minimum number of bits like the control inputs on the registers designed above. Instead, each operation usually has its own control input.

For example, a register with the operations of load, shift left, and shift right might have the control inputs and the operation table shown in Figure 4.17. The four possible operations (maintain, shift left, shift right, and load) require at least two control inputs; the figure shows that the register has three control inputs—ld, shr, and shl.

Notice that the register designer must decide how the

s1	s0	Operation
0	0	Maintain present value
0	1	Parallel load
1	0	Shift right
1	1	Shift left

Figure 4.16 Operation table of a 4-bit register with parallel load, shift left, and shift right operations.

ld	shr	shl	Operation
0	0	0	Maintain present value
0	0	1	Shift left
0	1	0	Shift right
0	1	1	Shift right – shr has priority over shl
1	0	0	Parallel load
1	0	1	Parallel load – ld has priority
1	1	0	Parallel load – ld has priority
1	1	1	Parallel load – ld has priority

Figure 4.17 Operation table of a 4-bit register with separate control inputs for parallel load, shift left, and shift right.

Figure 4.18 Truth tables describing operations of a register with left/right shift and parallel load, along with the mapping of the register control inputs to the internal 4x1 mux select lines: (a) complete operation table defining the mapping of ld, shr, and shl to s1 and s0, and (b) a compact version of the operation table.

Inputs			Outputs		Note
ld	shr	shl	s1	s0	Operation
0	0	0	0	0	Maintain value
0	0	1	1	1	Shift left
0	1	0	1	0	Shift right
0	1	1	1	0	Shift right
1	0	0	0	1	Parallel load
1	0	1	0	1	Parallel load
1	1	0	0	1	Parallel load
1	1	1	0	1	Parallel load

(a)

ld	shr	shl	Operation
0	0	0	Maintain value
0	0	1	Shift left
0	1	X	Shift right
1	X	X	Parallel load

(b)

register will respond if more than one control input is 1. The operation table shows that if the user sets both shr and shl, shr gets priority. ld has priority over shr and shl.

The internal design of such a register is similar to the load/shift register designed above, except that the three control inputs of ld, shl, and shr need to be mapped to the two control inputs s1 and s0 of the earlier register. A simple combinational circuit can be used to perform such mapping, as shown in Figure 4.19.

We can design that combinational circuit starting from a simple truth table shown in Figure 4.18(a). From the table, we derive the following equations for the register's combinational circuit:

```
s1 = ld'*shr'*shl + ld'*shr*shl' + ld'*shr*shl
s0 = ld'*shr'*shl + ld
```

Replacing the combinational circuit box in Figure 4.19 by the gates described by the above equations would complete the register's design.

Register datasheets typically show the register operation table in a compact form, taking advantage of the priorities among the control inputs, as in Figure 4.18(b). A single X in a row means that row is actually two rows in the complete table, with one row having 0 in the position of the X, the other row having 1. Two Xs in a row means that row is actually four rows in the complete table, one row having 00 in the positions of those Xs, another row having 01, another 10, and another 11. And so on for three Xs, representing

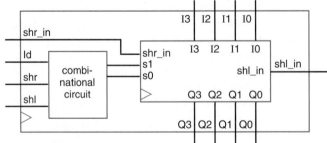

Figure 4.19 A combinational circuit maps the control inputs ld, shr, and shl to the mux select inputs s1 and s0.

▶ *SERIAL COMMUNICATION IN DESKTOP COMPUTERS.*

A desktop PC must communicate data with other devices like printers, displays, keyboards, and cameras. In the past, communicating large amounts of data, like sending a file to a printer, could be done faster using parallel wires as supported by a PC's parallel port—shown in Figure 4.20. That parallel port has 8 output data lines (plus 4 output control lines, 5 input lines, and 8 grounded lines). But parallel ports and plugs are big, cables with numerous internal wires are costly, and crosstalk problems (electromagnetic fields generated by a changing signal on one wire interfering with the signal on a nearby wire) exist. As higher-speed circuits could be designed over the years, communication clock frequencies could be made faster too. But transmitting data in parallel at high frequencies creates even more crosstalk problems. Transmitting data serially became more appealing, involving smaller ports and plugs, cheaper wires, and

fewer crosstalk problems that in turn enabled higher power and hence longer wires. The reduced crosstalk problems also enabled higher frequencies and hence faster communication. The popular USB interface is a serial communication scheme (*USB* is short for *universal serial bus*) used to connect personal computers and other devices together by wire. Furthermore, nearly all wireless communication schemes, such as WiFi and BlueTooth, use serial communication, sending one bit at a time over a radio frequency. While data communication between devices may be serial, computations inside devices are typically done in parallel. Thus, shift registers are commonly used inside circuits to convert internal parallel data into serial data to be sent to another device, and to receive serial data and convert that data into parallel data for internal device use.

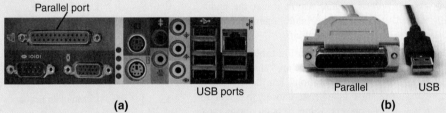

Figure 4.20 Parallel versus serial communication in desktop computers: (a) a PC having a parallel port and six serial USB ports, (b) parallel and USB plugs/cables.

8 rows. Note that putting higher-priority control inputs to the left in the table keeps the table's operations nicely organized.

Register Design Process

Table 4.1 describes a general process for designing a register with any number of functions.

TABLE 4.1 Four-step process for designing a multifunction register.

	Step	Description
1.	*Determine mux size*	Count the number of operations (don't forget the maintain present value operation) and add in front of each flip-flop a mux with at least that number of inputs.
2.	*Create mux operation table*	Create an operation table defining the desired operation for each possible value of the mux select lines.

TABLE 4.1 Four-step process for designing a multifunction register.

3.	*Connect mux inputs*	For each operation, connect the corresponding mux data input to the appropriate external input or flip-flop output (possibly passing through some logic) to achieve the desired operation.
4.	*Map control lines*	Create a truth table that maps external control lines to the internal mux select lines, with appropriate priorities, and then design the logic to achieve that mapping

We'll illustrate the register design process with an example.

Example 4.5 Register with load, shift, and synchronous clear and set

We want to design a register with the following operations: load, shift left, synchronous clear, and synchronous set, with unique control inputs for each operation (ld, shl, clr, set). The ***synchronous clear*** operation loads all 0s into the register on the next rising clock edge. The ***synchronous set*** operation loads all 1s into the register on the next rising clock edge. The term "synchronous" is included because some registers come with *asynchronous* clear or set operations (see Section 3.5). Following the register design method of Table 4.1, we perform the following steps:

Step 1: **Determine mux size.** There are 5 operations—load, shift left, synchronous clear, synchronous set, and *maintain present value*. Don't forget the maintain present value operation; that operation is implicit.

s2	s1	s0	Operation
0	0	0	Maintain present value
0	0	1	Parallel load
0	1	0	Shift left
0	1	1	Synchronous clear
1	0	0	Synchronous set
1	0	1	Maintain present value
1	1	0	Maintain present value
1	1	1	Maintain present value

Step 2: **Create mux operation table.** We'll use the first 5 inputs of an 8x1 mux for the desired 5 operations. For the remaining 3 mux inputs, we choose to maintain the present value, though those mux inputs should never be utilized. The table is shown in Figure 4.20.

Figure 4.20 Operation table for a register with load, shift, and synchronous clear and set.

Step 3: **Connect mux inputs.** We connect the mux inputs as shown in Figure 4.21, which for simplicity shows only the *n*th flip-flop and mux of the register.

Step 4: **Map control lines.** We'll give clr highest priority, followed by set, ld, and shl, so the register control inputs would be mapped to the 8x1 mux select lines as shown in Figure 4.22.

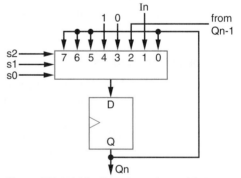

Figure 4.21 *N*th bit-slice of a register with the following operations: maintain present value, parallel load, shift left, synchronous clear, and synchronous set.

Figure 4.22 Truth table for the control lines of a register with the *N*th bit-slice shown in Figure 4.21.

Inputs				Outputs			
clr	set	ld	shl	s2	s1	s0	Operation
0	0	0	0	0	0	0	Maintain present value
0	0	0	1	0	1	0	Shift left
0	0	1	X	0	0	1	Parallel load
0	1	X	X	1	0	0	Set to all 1s
1	X	X	X	0	1	1	Clear to all 0s

Looking at each output in Figure 4.22, we derive the equations describing the circuit that maps the external control inputs to the mux select lines as follows:

```
s2 = clr'*set
s1 = clr'*set'*ld'*shl + clr
s0 = clr'*set'*ld + clr
```

We could then create a combinational circuit implementing those equations to map the external register control inputs to the mux select lines and hence to complete the register's design.

Some registers come with asynchronous clear and/or asynchronous set control inputs. Those inputs could be implemented by connecting them to asynchronous clear or asynchronous set inputs that exist on the flip-flops themselves (see Section 3.5).

▷ 4.3 ADDERS

Adding two binary numbers is perhaps the most common operation performed on data in a digital system. An *N-bit adder* is a combinational component that adds two *N*-bit data inputs A and B representing binary numbers, and generates an *N*-bit data output S representing the sum and a 1-bit output C representing the carry-out. A 4-bit adder adds two 4-bit numbers and outputs a 4-bit sum and a carry bit. For example, 1111 + 0001 would result in a carry of 1 and a sum of 0000—or 10000 if you treat the carry bit and sum bits as one 5-bit result. *N* is the *width* of the adder. Designing fast yet size-efficient adders is a subject that has received considerable attention for many decades.

Although it appears that an *N*-bit adder could be designed by following the combinational logic design process of Table 2.5, building an *N*-bit adder following that process is not practical when *N* is much larger than 8. To understand why, consider using that process to build a 2-bit adder, which adds two 2-bit numbers. The desired behavior can be captured as the truth table in Figure 4.23. Each output could then be converted to a sum-of-products equation and implemented as a two-level gate-based circuit.

The problem is that the approach results in excessively large truth tables and too many gates for wider adders. A 16-bit adder has 16 + 16 = 32 inputs, meaning the truth table would have over *four billion rows*. A two-level gate-based implementation of that table would likely require millions of gates. To illustrate this point, we performed an experiment that used the standard combinational logic design process to create adders of increasing width, starting with 1-bit adders on up. We used an advanced commercial logic

Inputs				Outputs			Inputs				Outputs		
a1	a0	b1	b0	c	s1	s0	a1	a0	b1	b0	c	s1	s0
0	0	0	0	0	0	0	1	0	0	0	0	1	0
0	0	0	1	0	0	1	1	0	0	1	0	1	1
0	0	1	0	0	1	0	1	0	1	0	1	0	0
0	0	1	1	0	1	1	1	0	1	1	1	0	1
0	1	0	0	0	0	1	1	1	0	0	0	1	1
0	1	0	1	0	1	0	1	1	0	1	1	0	0
0	1	1	0	0	1	1	1	1	1	0	1	0	1
0	1	1	1	1	0	0	1	1	1	1	1	1	0

Figure 4.23 Truth table for a 2-bit adder.

design tool, and asked the tool to create a design using two levels of logic (one level of AND gates feeding into an OR gate for each output) and using the minimum number of transistors.

The plot in Figure 4.24 summarizes results. A 6-bit adder (N=6) required about 2,000 transistors, a 7-bit adder required 4,000 transistors, and an 8-bit adder required 8,000 transistors. Notice how fast the number of transistors grows as the adder width is increased. This fast growth is an effect of exponential growth—for an adder width of N, the number of truth table rows is proportional to 2^N (more precisely, to 2^{N+N}). We could not complete our experiments for adders larger than 8 bits—the tool simply could not complete the design in a reasonable

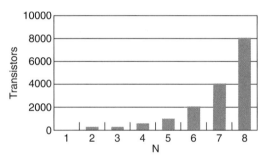

Figure 4.24 Why large adders aren't built using standard two-level combinational logic—notice the exponential growth. How many transistors would a 32-bit adder require?

amount of time. The tool needed 3 seconds to build the 6-bit adder, 40 seconds to build the 7-bit adder, and 30 minutes for the 8-bit adder. The 9-bit adder didn't finish after one full day. Clearly, this exponential growth prohibits using the standard design process for adders wider than perhaps 8 to 10 bits. Looking at this data, can you predict the number of transistors required by a 16-bit adder or a 32-bit adder using two levels of gates? From the figure, it looks like the number of transistors is doubling for each increase in N. Assuming the doubling trend continues for larger adders, then a 16-bit adder would have 8 more doublings beyond the 8-bit adder, meaning multiplying the size of the 8-bit adder by 2^8=256. So a 16-bit adder would require 8000 * 256 = about two million transistors. A 32-bit adder would require an additional 2^{16}= 65,536 doublings, meaning about 2 million * 65,536 = over *100 billion transistors*. That's a ridiculous number of transistors just to add two numbers. We clearly need another approach for designing larger adders.

Figure 4.25 Adding two binary numbers by hand, column by column: (a) rightmost column sums to 1, with no carry (0) to the next column, (b) second column sums to 0 with a 1 carried to the next column because 0+1+1 = 10 in base two, (c) third column is 1+1+1 = 11, so the sum is 1 and a 1 is carried to the next column, (d) leftmost column sums to 0 with a final carry of 1.

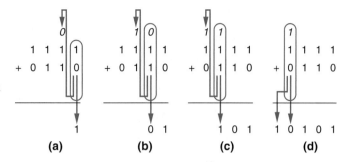

(a)   (b)   (c)   (d)

Adder—Carry-Ripple Style

An alternative approach to the standard combinational logic design process for adding two binary numbers is to instead create a circuit that mimics how people add binary numbers by hand—namely one column at a time. Consider the addition of the binary number A=1111 (15 in base ten) with B=0110 (6 in base ten), column by column, shown in Figure 4.25.

For each column, three bits are added, resulting in a sum bit for the present column and a carry bit for the next column. The first column is an exception in that only two bits are added, but that column still results in a sum bit and a carry bit. The carry bit of the last column becomes the fifth bit of the sum. The sum for the above numbers is 10101 (21 in base ten).

We can create a combinational component to perform the required addition for a single column, and then use four of those components to add the two 4-bit numbers. The inputs and outputs of such a component for a column are shown in Figure 4.26. Bear in mind that this method of creating an adder is intended to enable efficient design of wide adders such as a 32-bit adder. We illustrate the method using a 4-bit adder because that size adder keeps our figures small and readable, but if all we really needed was a 4-bit adder, the standard combinational logic design process for two-level logic might be sufficient.

We'll now design the components in each column of Figure 4.26.

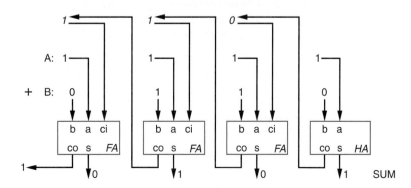

Figure 4.26 Using combinational components to add two binary numbers column by column.

Inputs		Outputs	
a	b	co	s
0	0	0	0
0	1	0	1
1	0	0	1
1	1	1	0

Figure 4.27 Truth table for a half-adder.

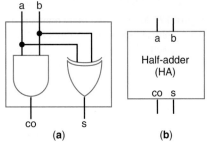

Figure 4.28 Half-adder: (a) circuit, (b) block symbol.

Half-Adder

A *half-adder* is a combinational component that adds two bits (a and b), and outputs a sum bit (s) and carry-out bit (co). (Note that we did *not* say that a half-adder adds *two 2-bit numbers*—a half-adder merely adds *two bits*.) The component labeled *HA* in Figure 4.26 is a half-adder. A half-adder can be designed using the straightforward combinational logic design process from Chapter 2 as follows:

Step 1: Capture the function. A truth table easily captures the function. The truth table is shown in Figure 4.27.

Step 2A: Create equations. The equations for each truth table output are co = ab and s = a'b + ab', which is the same as s = a xor b.

Step 2B: Implement as a circuit. The circuit for a half-adder implementing the equations is shown in Figure 4.28(a). Figure 4.28(b) shows a block symbol of a half-adder.

Full-Adder

A *full-adder* is a combinational component that adds three bits (a, b, and ci) and outputs a sum bit (s) and a carry-out bit (co). (A full-adder does *not* add *two 3-bit numbers*—it merely adds *three bits*.) The three components labeled *FA* in Figure 4.26 are full-adders. A full-adder can be designed using the combinational logic design process as follows:

Step 1: Capture the function. A truth table captures the function easily, shown in Figure 4.29.

Step 2A: Create equations. Equations for co and s can be derived from the truth table. For simplicity, we write ci as c. Algebraic methods can simplify the equations.

Inputs			Outputs	
a	b	ci	co	s
0	0	0	0	0
0	0	1	0	1
0	1	0	0	1
0	1	1	1	0
1	0	0	0	1
1	0	1	1	0
1	1	0	1	0
1	1	1	1	1

```
co = a'bc + ab'c + abc' + abc
co = a'bc + abc + ab'c + abc + abc' +
     abc
co = (a'+a)bc + (b'+b)ac + (c'+c)ab
co = bc + ac + ab

s  = a'b'c + a'bc' + ab'c' + abc
s  = a'(b'c + bc') + a(b'c' + bc)
s  = a'(b xor c) + a(b xor c)'
s  = a xor b xor c
```

Figure 4.29 Truth table for a full-adder.

During algebraic simplification for co, each of the first three terms could be combined with the last term abc, because each of the first three terms differed from the last term in just one literal. We thus created three instances of the last term abc (which doesn't change the function) and combined them with each of the first three terms. Don't worry if you can't come up with that simplification on your own yet—Section 6.2 introduces methods to make such simplification straightforward. If you have read that section, you might try using a K-map (introduced in that section) to simplify the equations.

Step 2B: Implement as a circuit.

The circuit for a full-adder is shown in Figure 4.30(a). The full-adder's block symbol is shown in Figure 4.30(b).

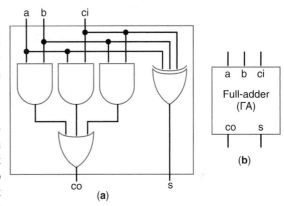

Figure 4.30 Full-adder: (a) circuit, (b) block symbol.

4-Bit Carry-Ripple Adder

Three full-adders and one half-adder can be connected as in Figure 4.31 to implement a 4-bit *carry-ripple adder*, which adds two 4-bit numbers and generates a 4-bit sum. The 4-bit carry-ripple adder also generates a carry-out bit.

A carry-in bit can be included on the 4-bit adder, which enables connecting 4-bit adders together to build larger adders. The carry-in bit is included by replacing the half-adder (which was in the rightmost bit position) by a full-adder, as in Figure 4.32.

Let's analyze the behavior of this adder. Suppose that all inputs have been 0s for a long time, meaning that S will be 0000, co will be 0, and all ci values of the full adders will also be 0. Now suppose that A becomes 0111 and B becomes 0001 at the same time (whose sum we know should be 01000). Those new values of A and B will propagate through the full-adders. Suppose the delay of a full-adder is 2 ns. So 2 ns after A and B change, the sum outputs of all the full-adders will change, as shown in Figure 4.33(a). So s3 will become 0+0+0=0 (with co3=0), s2 will become 1+0+0=1 (with co2=0), s1 will become 1+0+0=1 (with co1=0), and s0 will become 1+1=0 (with co0=1). But, 1111 + 0110 should *not* be 00110—instead, the sum should be 01000. What went wrong?

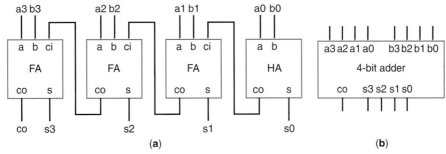

Figure 4.31 4-bit adder: (a) carry-ripple design with 3 full-adders and 1 half-adder, (b) block symbol.

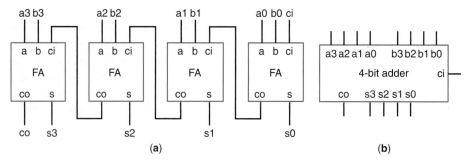

Figure 4.32 4-bit adder: (a) carry-ripple implementation with 4 full-adders and a carry-in input, (b) block symbol.

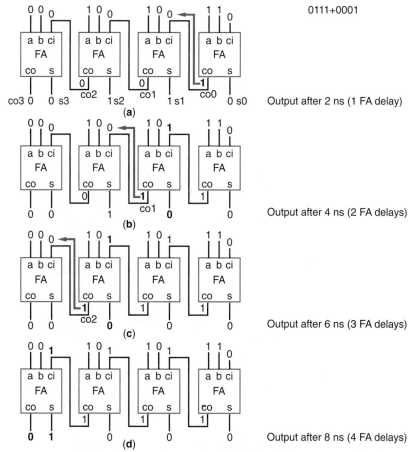

Figure 4.33 Example of adding `0111+0001` using a 4-bit carry-ripple adder. The output will exhibit temporarily incorrect ("spurious") results until the carry bit from the rightmost bit has had a chance to "ripple" all the way through to the leftmost bit.

Nothing went wrong—the carry-ripple adder simply isn't done yet after just 2 ns. After 2 ns, $co0$ changed from 0 to 1. We must allow time for that *new* value of $co0$ to proceed through the next full-adder. Thus, after another 2 ns, $s1$ will equal $1+0+1=0$ and $co2$ will become 1. So after 4 ns the output will be 00100 as shown in Figure 4.33(b).

Keep waiting. After a third full-adder delay, the new value of $co2$ will have propagated through the next full-adder, resulting in $s2$ becoming $1+0+1=0$ and $co2$ becoming 1. So after 6 ns, the output will be 00000 as shown in Figure 4.33(c).

A little more patience. After a fourth full-adder delay, $co2$ has had time to propagate through the last full-adder, resulting in $s3$ becoming $0+0+1=1$ and $co3$ staying 0. Thus, after 8 ns the output will be 01000 as in Figure 4.33(d)—01000 is the correct result.

To recap, until the carry bits had time to ripple through all the adders, from right to left, the output was not correct. The intermediate output values are known as **spurious values**. The **delay** of a component is the time required for the outputs to be the stable correct value after any change on the inputs. The delay of a 4-bit carry-ripple adder is equal to the delay of four full-adders, which is the time for the carry bits to ripple through all the adders—hence, the term *carry-ripple adder.*

The term "ripple-carry" adder is actually more common. I prefer the term "carry-ripple" for consistent naming with other adder types, like carry-select and carry-lookahead, which Chapter 6 describes.

People often initially confuse full-adders and *N*-bit adders. A full-adder adds 3 bits. In contrast, a 3-bit adder adds two 3-bit numbers. A full-adder produces one sum bit and one carry bit. In contrast, a 3-bit adder produces three sum bits and one carry bit. A full-adder is usually used to add only *one column* of two binary numbers, whereas an *N*-bit adder is used to add two *N*-bit numbers.

An *N*-bit adder often comes with a carry-in bit, so that the adder can be cascaded with other *N*-bit adders to form larger adders. Figure 4.34(a) shows an 8-bit adder built from two 4-bit adders. The carry-in bit (ci) on the right would be set to 0 when adding two 8-bit numbers. Figure 4.34(b) shows a block symbol of that 8-bit adder, and Figure 4.34(c) shows a simplified block symbol that is commonly used.

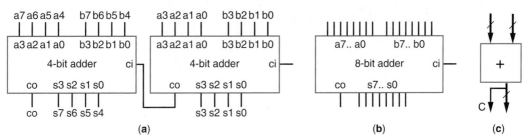

Figure 4.34 8-bit adder: (a) carry-ripple implementation built from two 4-bit carry-ripple adders, (b) block symbol, (c) simplified block symbol.

Example 4.6 DIP-switch-based adding calculator

This example designs a simple calculator that can add two 8-bit binary numbers and produce an 8-bit result. The input binary numbers come from two 8-switch DIP switches and the output will be displayed using 8 LEDs, as illustrated in Figure 4.35. An 8-bit **DIP (dual inline package)** switch is a simple digital component having switches that a user can move up or down by hand; the up position outputs a 1 on the corresponding pin and down outputs a 0. An **LED** (light-emitting diode) is a small light that illuminates when the LED's input is 1, and is dark when the input is 0.

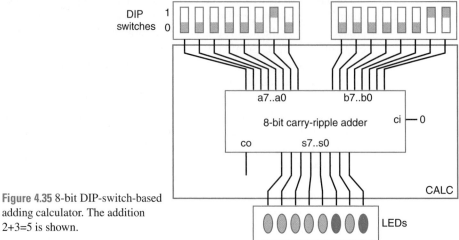

Figure 4.35 8-bit DIP-switch-based adding calculator. The addition 2+3=5 is shown.

The calculator can be implemented using an 8-bit carry-ripple adder for the CALC block, as in Figure 4.35. When a user moves the switches on a DIP switch, the new binary values propagate through the carry-ripple adder's gates, generating spurious values until the carry bits have finally propagated through the entire circuit, at which point the output stabilizes and the LEDs display the correct new sum. The spurious values are likely too fast to be visible on the LEDs by humans.

To avoid the LEDs changing while the user is moving switches, we can introduce a button e (for "equals") that indicates when the result should be displayed. The user presses e after configuring both DIP switches as the new inputs to be summed. We can connect the e input to the load input of a parallel load register as in Figure 4.36. When a user moves switches on the DIP switches, intermittent values appear at the adder outputs, but are blocked at the register's inputs, as the register holds its previous value and hence the LEDs display that value. When the e button is pressed, then on the next clock edge the register will be loaded, and the LEDs will display the new result.

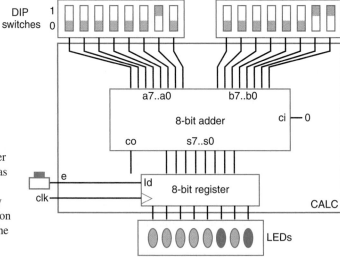

Figure 4.36 8-bit DIP-switch-based adding calculator, using a register to block output changes as the user configures the switches. The LEDs only get updated after the button is pressed, which loads the output register.

Notice that the displayed value will be correct only if the sum is 255 or less. We could connect co to a ninth LED to display sums between 256 and 511.

Delay and Size of a 32-Bit Carry-Ripple Adder

Assuming full-adders are implemented using two levels of gates (ANDs followed by an OR) and that every gate has a delay of "1 gate-delay," let's compute the total delay of a 32-bit carry-ripple adder, and also compute the size of such an adder.

To determine the delay, note that the carry must ripple from the first full-adder to the 32nd full-adder (referring to the adder in Figure 4.33 may help). The delay of the first full-adder is 2 gate-delays. The new carry must then ripple through the second full-adder, resulting in another 2 gate-delays. And so on. Thus, the total delay of the 32-bit carry-ripple adder is 64 gate-delays. Supposing a gate-delay is 1 ns, then the total delay would be 64 ns.

To determine the size, note that the full-adder in Figure 4.30 would require about 30 transistors: about 12 transistors for the three 2-input AND gates (4 transistors each), 6 transistors for the 3-input OR gate, and 12 for the 3-input XOR gate. Because the 32-bit adder uses 32 full-adders, the total size of the 32-bit carry-ripple adder is (12 transistors/full-adder)*(32 full-adders)=384 transistors. That's a lot less than the 100 billion transistors predicted from the data in Figure 4.24.

The 32-bit carry-ripple adder has a long delay but a reasonable number of transistors. Section 6.4 shows to build faster adders at the expense of using some more transistors.

trade-off: delay ⟷ # of transistors

Example 4.7 Compensating weight scale using an adder

A scale, such as a bathroom scale, uses a sensor to determine the weight of an object (e.g., a person) on the scale. The sensor's readings for the same object may change over time due to wear and tear on the sensing system (such as a spring losing elasticity), resulting perhaps in reporting a weight that is a few pounds too low. Thus, the scale may have a knob that the user can turn to compensate for the low reported weight. The knob indicates the amount to add to a given weight before displaying the weight. Suppose that a knob can be set to change an input compensation amount by a value of 0, 1, 2, ..., or 7, as shown in Figure 4.37.

We can implement the system using an 8-bit carry-ripple adder as shown in the figure. On every rising clock edge, the display register will be loaded with the sum of the currently sensed weight plus the compensation amount.

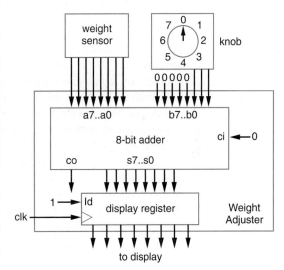

Figure 4.37 Compensating scale: the dial outputs a number from 0 to 7 (000 to 111), which gets added to the sensed weight and then displayed.

Incrementer

Sometimes a designer needs to just add a constant "1" to a number, rather than adding two general numbers. A *constant* is a number that does not change in a circuit. For example, a designer may want a register to count up from 0 to 255, which involves adding 1 to the register's current value and loading the result back into the register. The designer could use a carry-ripple adder to perform the addition, but an adder is designed to add any two numbers and thus has more gates than necessary to just add 1. A common component is thus an adder specifically designed just to add 1 to a number, known as an *incrementer*.

An incrementer can be designed using the combinational logic design process from Chapter 2. Design starts with the truth table shown in Figure 4.38. Each output row's values can be obtained simply by adding 1 to the corresponding input row binary number. We would then derive an equation for each output. It is easy to see from the table that the equation for c0 is c0=a3a2a1a0. It is also easy to see that s0=a0'. We would derive equations for the remaining outputs. Finally, the equations would be converted to circuits. The resulting incrementer would have a total delay of only two gate-delays. However, as we saw for *N*-bit adders, larger numbers of inputs can lead to very large truth tables that result in unreasonably large circuits.

Inputs				Outputs				
a3	a2	a1	a0	c0	s3	s2	s1	s0
0	0	0	0	0	0	0	0	1
0	0	0	1	0	0	0	1	0
0	0	1	0	0	0	0	1	1
0	0	1	1	0	0	1	0	0
0	1	0	0	0	0	1	0	1
0	1	0	1	0	0	1	1	0
0	1	1	0	0	0	1	1	1
0	1	1	1	0	1	0	0	0
1	0	0	0	0	1	0	0	1
1	0	0	1	0	1	0	1	0
1	0	1	0	0	1	0	1	1
1	0	1	1	0	1	1	0	0
1	1	0	0	0	1	1	0	1
1	1	0	1	0	1	1	1	0
1	1	1	0	0	1	1	1	1
1	1	1	1	1	0	0	0	0

Figure 4.38 Truth table for four-bit incrementer.

As was the case for *N*-bit adders, we could design a more size-efficient incrementer by mimicking the way humans do addition by hand, as in Figure 4.39. However, note in the figure that adding 1 to a binary number involves only two bits per column, not three bits per column like when adding two general binary numbers. Recall that a half-adder adds two bits (see Section 4.3). Thus, a simple incrementer could be built using half-adders, as in Figure 4.40.

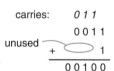

Figure 4.39 Adding 1 to a binary number requires only 2 bits per column.

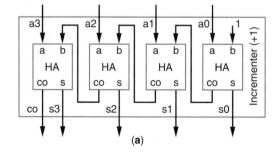

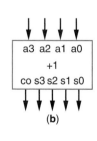

Figure 4.40 4-bit incrementer: (a) internal design, (b) block symbol.

▶ 4.4 COMPARATORS

Designs often need their circuit to compare two binary numbers to determine if the numbers are equal or if one number is greater than the other. For example, a system might sound an alarm if a thermometer measuring human body temperature reports a temperature greater than 103 degrees Fahrenheit (39.4 degrees Celsius). Comparator components perform such comparison of binary numbers.

Equality (Identity) Comparator

An *N-bit equality comparator* (sometimes called an *identity comparator*) is a combinational component that compares two *N*-bit data inputs A and B, and sets an output control bit eq to 1 if those two data inputs are equal. Two *N*-bit inputs, such as two 4-bit inputs A:a3a2a1a0 and B:b3b2b1b0, are equal if each of their corresponding bit pairs are equal. So A equals B if a3=b3, a2=b2, a1=b1, and a0=b0. For example if A is 1011 and B is 1011, then A equals B.

Following the combinational logic design process of Table 2.5, a 4-bit equality comparator can be designed by first capturing the function as an equation:

$$eq = (a3b3+a3'b3') * (a2b2+a2'b2') *$$
$$(a1b1+a1'b1') * (a0b0+a0'b0')$$

Each term detects if the corresponding bits are equal, namely if both bits are 1 or both bits are 0. The expressions inside each of the parentheses describe the behavior of an XNOR gate (recall from Chapter 2 that an XNOR gate outputs 1 if the gate's two input bits are equal), so the above equation can be replaced by the equivalent equation:

$$eq = (a3 \text{ xnor } b3) * (a2 \text{ xnor } b2) * (a1 \text{ xnor } b1) * (a0 \text{ xnor } b0)$$

The equation can be converted to the circuit in Figure 4.41(a).

Of course, a comparator could be designed starting with a truth table, but that would be cumbersome for a large comparator, with too many rows in the truth table to easily work with by hand. A truth table approach enumerates all the possible situations for which all the bits are equal, since only those situations would have a 1 in the column for the output eq. For two 4-bit numbers, one such situation will be 0000=0000. Another will be 0001=0001. Clearly, there will be as many situations as there are 4-bit binary

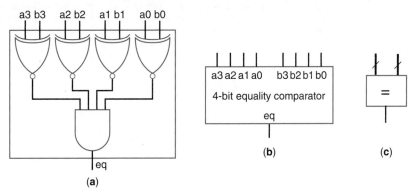

Figure 4.41 Equality comparator: (a) internal design, (b) block symbol, (c) simplified symbol.

numbers—meaning there will be $2^4=16$ situations where both numbers are equal. For two 8-bit numbers, there will be 256 equal situations. For two 32-bit numbers, there will be four billion equal situations. A comparator built with such an approach will be large if we don't minimize the equation, and that minimization will be hard with such large numbers of terms. The XNOR-based design is simpler and scales to wider inputs easily—widening the inputs from four bits to five bits involves merely adding one more XNOR gate to Figure 4.41(a).

Magnitude Comparator—Carry-Ripple Style

An ***N-bit magnitude comparator*** is a combinational component that compares two N-bit data inputs A and B representing binary numbers, and outputs whether A>B, A=B, or A<B using three control signals AgtB, AeqB, and AltB.

We have already seen several times that designing certain datapath components by starting with a truth table involves too large of a truth table. Let's instead design a magnitude comparator by considering how humans compare numbers by hand. Consider comparing two 4-bit numbers A:a3a2a1a0=1011, B:b3b2b1b0=1001. We start by looking at the high-order bits of A and B, namely, a3 and b3. Since they are equal (both are 1), we look at the next pair of bits, a2 and b2. Again, since they are equal (both are 0), we look at the next pair of bits, a1 and b1. Since a1>b1 (1>0), we conclude that A>B.

Thus, comparing two binary numbers takes place by comparing from the high bit-pairs down to the low bit-pairs. As long as bit-pairs are equal, comparison continues with the next lower bit-pair. As soon as a bit-pair is different, a conclusion can be made that A>B if ai=1 and bi=0, or that A<B if bi=1 and ai=0. Based on this comparison concept, we can design a magnitude comparator using the structure shown in Figure 4.42(a).

Each stage works as follows. If in_gt=1 (meaning a higher stage determined A>B), this stage need not compare bits and instead just sets out_gt=1. Likewise, if in_lt=1 (meaning a higher stage determined A<B), this stage just sets out_lt=1. If in_eq=1 (meaning higher stages were all equal), this stage must compare bits, setting the output out_gt=1 if a=1 and b=0, setting out_lt=1 if a=0 and b=1, and setting out_eq=1 if a and b both equal 1 or both equal 0.

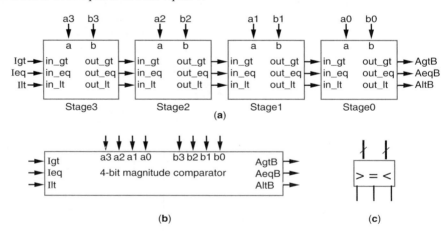

Figure 4.42 4-bit magnitude comparator: (a) internal design using identical components in each stage, (b) block symbol, (c) simplified symbol without ripple inputs.

We could capture the function of a stage's block using a truth table with 5 inputs. A simpler way is to capture the function as the following equations derived from the above explanation of how each stage works; the circuit for each stage would follow directly from these equations:

```
out_gt = in_gt + (in_eq * a * b')
out_lt = in_lt + (in_eq * a' * b)
out_eq = in_eq * (a XNOR b)
```

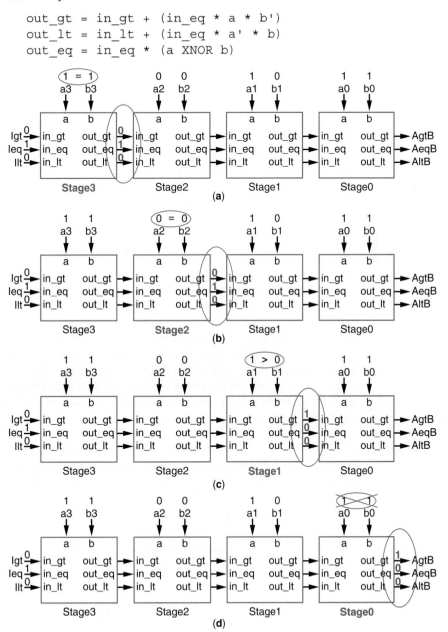

Figure 4.43 The "rippling" within a magnitude comparator.

Figure 4.43 shows how this comparator works for an input of A=1011 and B=1001. We can view the comparator's behavior as consisting of four stages:

- In *Stage3* shown in Figure 4.43(a), we start by setting the external input Ieq=1, to force the comparator to actually do the comparison. *Stage3* has in_eq=1, and since a3=1 and b3=1, then out_eq will become 1, while out_gt and out_lt will become 0.

- In *Stage2* shown in Figure 4.43(b), we see that since out_eq of *Stage3* connects to in_eq of *Stage2*, then *Stage2*'s in_eq will be 1. Since a2=0 and b2=0, then out_eq will become 1, while out_gt and out_lt will be 0.

- In *Stage1* shown in Figure 4.43(c), we see that since *Stage2*'s out_eq is connected to *Stage1*'s in_eq, *Stage1*'s in_eq will be 1. Since a1=1 and b1=0, out_gt will become 1, while out_eq and out_lt will be 0.

- In *Stage0* shown in Figure 4.43(d), we see that the outputs of *Stage1* cause *Stage0*'s in_gt to become 1, which directly causes *Stage0*'s out_gt to become 1, and causes out_eq and out_lt to be 0. Notice that the values of a0 and b0 are irrelevant. Since *Stage0*'s outputs connect to the comparator's external outputs, AgtB will be 1, while AeqB and AltB will be 0.

Because of the way the result ripples through the stages in a manner similar to a carry-ripple adder, a magnitude comparator built this way is often referred to as having a *carry-ripple* style implementation, even though what's rippling is not really a "carry" bit.

The 4-bit magnitude comparator can be connected straightforwardly with another 4-bit magnitude comparator to build an 8-bit magnitude comparator, and likewise to build any size comparator, simply by connecting the comparison outputs of one comparator (AgtB, AeqB, AltB) with the comparison inputs of the next comparator (Igt, Ieq, Ilt).

If each stage is built from two levels of logic, and a gate has a delay of "1 gate-delay"), then each stage will have a delay of 2 gate-delays. So the delay of a carry-ripple style 4-bit magnitude comparator is (4 stages)*(2 gate-delays/stage)=8 gate-delays. A 32-bit comparator built with this style will have a delay of (32 stages)*(2 gate-delays/stage)=64 gate-delays.

Example 4.8 Computing the minimum of two numbers using a comparator

We want to design a combinational component that takes two 8-bit inputs A and B, and outputs an 8-bit output C that is the minimum of A and B. We can use a magnitude comparator and an 8-bit 2x1 multiplexor to implement this component, as shown in Figure 4.44.

Figure 4.44 A combinational component to compute the minimum of two numbers: (a) internal design using a magnitude comparator, (b) block symbol.

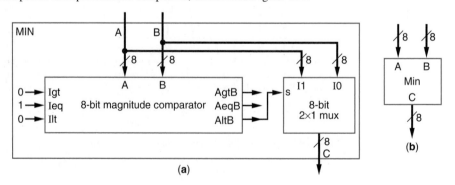

If A<B, the comparator's AltB output will be 1. In this case, we want to pass A through the mux, so we connect AltB to the 8-bit 2x1 mux select input, and A to the mux's I1 input. If AltB is 0, then either AgtB=1 or AeqB=1. If AgtB=1, we want to pass B. If AeqB=1, we can pass either A or B (since they are identical), and so let's pass B. We thus simply connect B to the I0 input of the 8-bit 2x1 mux. In other words, if A<B, we'll pass A, and if A is not less than B, we'll pass B.

Notice that we set the comparator's Ieq control input to 1, and the Igt and Ilt inputs to 0. These values force the comparator to compare its data inputs.

▶ 4.5 MULTIPLIER—ARRAY-STYLE

An *NxN multiplier* is a component that multiplies two *N*-bit input binary numbers A (the multiplicand) and B (the multiplier), and outputs an (*N+N*)-bit result. For example, an 8x8 multiplier multiplies two 8-bit binary numbers and outputs a 16-bit result. Designing an *NxN* multiplier in two levels of logic using the standard combinational design process will result in too complex of a design, as we've already seen for previous operations like addition and comparison. For multipliers with *N* greater than about 4, we need a more efficient method.

We can create a reasonably sized multiplier by mimicking how humans perform multiplication by hand. Consider multiplying two 4-bit binary numbers 0110 and 0011 by hand:

```
      0110   (the top number is called the multiplicand)
      0011   (the bottom number is called the multiplier)
      ----   (each row below is called a partial product)
      0110   (because the rightmost bit of the multiplier is 1, and 0110*1=0110)
     0110    (because the second bit of the multiplier is 1, and 0110*1=0110)
    0000     (because the third bit of the multiplier is 0, and 0110*0=0000)
  +0000      (because the leftmost bit of the multiplier is 0, and 0110*0=0000)
  --------
  00010010   (the product is the sum of all the partial products: 18, which is 6*3)
```

Each partial product is easily obtained by ANDing the present multiplier bit with the multiplicand. Thus, multiplication of two 4-bit numbers A (a3a2a1a0) and B (b3b2b1b0) can be represented as follows:

```
                  a3    a2    a1    a0
              x   b3    b2    b1    b0
  -----------------------------------------
                 b0a3  b0a2  b0a1  b0a0        (pp1)
  +           b1a3  b1a2  b1a1  b1a0    0      (pp2)
  +        b2a3  b2a2  b2a1  b2a0    0     0   (pp3)
  +  b3a3  b3a2  b3a1  b3a0    0     0     0   (pp4)
  -----------------------------------------
  p7  p6   p5    p4    p3    p2    p1    p0
```

Note that b0a0 means b0 AND a0. After generating the partial products (*pp1*, *pp2*, *pp3*, and *pp4*) by ANDing the present multiplier bit with each multiplicand bit, we merely

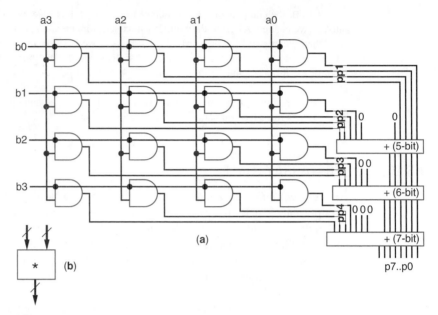

Figure 4.45 4-bit by 4-bit array-style multiplier: (a) internal design, (b) simplified block symbol.

need to sum those partial products together. We can use three adders of varying widths for computing that sum. The resulting design is shown in Figure 4.45(a).

This design for this 4-bit multiplier has a reasonable size, being about three times bigger than a 4-bit carry-ripple adder. The design has reasonable speed. The delay consists of 1 gate-delay for generating the partial products, plus the delay of the adders. If each adder is a carry-ripple adder, then the 5-bit adder delay will be 5*2=10 gate-delays, the 6-bit adder delay will be 6*2=12 gate-delays, and the 7-bit adder delay will be 7*2=14 gate-delays. If we assume that the total delay of the adders is simply the sum of the adder delays, then the total delay would thus be 1+10+12+14=37 gate-delays. However, the total delay of carry-ripple adders when chained together is actually a little less than the sum of delays—see Exercise 4.15.

Delays for larger multipliers, which will have an even longer chain of adders, will be even slower. Faster multiplier designs are possible at the expense of more gates.

▶ 4.6 SUBTRACTORS AND SIGNED NUMBERS

An *N*-bit **subtractor** is a combinational component that takes two *N*-bit data inputs A and B, representing binary numbers, and outputs an *N*-bit result S equaling A–B.

Subtractor for Positive Numbers Only

For now, let's assume we are only dealing with positive numbers, so the subtractor's inputs are positive, and the result is always positive. Subtraction gets slightly more complex when negative results are considered, like 5–7= –2, and thus far we haven't discussed representation of negative numbers. The result of subtraction always being positive could be the case, for example, when a system only subtracts smaller numbers from larger numbers, such as when compensating a sampled temperature that will always be greater than 80 using a small compensation value that will always be less than 10.

Designing an *N*-bit subtractor using the standard combinational logic design process suffers from the same exponential size growth problem as an *N*-bit adder, as discussed in Section 4.3. Instead, we can again build an efficient component by mimicking subtraction by hand.

Figure 4.46(a) shows subtraction of 4-bit binary numbers "by hand." Starting with the first column, a is less than b (0 < 1), necessitating a borrow from the previous column. The first column result is then 10−1=1 (stated in base ten: two minus one equals one). The second column has a 0 for a because of the borrow by the first column, making a < b (0 < 1), generating a borrow from the third column—which must itself borrow from the fourth column. The result of the second column is then 10−1=1. The third column, because of the borrow generated by the second column, has an a of 1, which is not less than b, so the result of the third column is 1−1=0. The fourth column has a=0 due to the borrow from the third column, and since b is also 0, the result is 0−0=0.

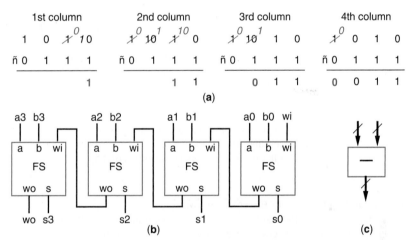

Figure 4.46 Design of a 4-bit subtractor: (a) subtraction "by hand", (b) borrow-ripple implementation with four full-subtractors with a borrow-in input wi, (c) simplified block symbol.

Based on the above-described behavior, we could connect four "full-subtractors" in a ripple manner as shown in Figure 4.46(b), similar to a carry-ripple adder. A *full-subtractor* has input wi representing a borrow by the previous column, an output wo representing a borrow from the next column, and of course inputs a and b and output s. We use w's for the borrows rather than b's because b is already used for the input; the w comes from the end of the word "borrow." We leave the design of a full-subtractor as an exercise for the reader.

Example 4.9 DIP-switch-based adding/subtracting calculator

In Example 4.6, we designed a simple calculator that could add two 8-bit binary numbers and produce an 8-bit result, using DIP switches for inputs, and a register plus LEDs for output. Let's extend that calculator to allow the user to choose among addition and subtraction operations. We'll

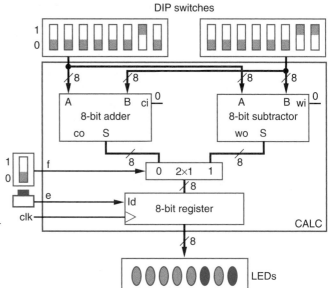

DIP switches

Figure 4.47 8-bit DIP-switch-based adding/subtracting calculator. Control input f selects between addition and subtraction.

introduce a single-switch DIP switch that sets a signal f (for "function") as another system control input. When f=0, the calculator should add; when f=1, the calculator should subtract.

One implementation of this calculator would use an adder, a subtractor, and a multiplexor, comprising a simple *datapath* as shown in Figure 4.47. The f input chooses whether to pass the output from the adder or subtractor through the mux to the register inputs. When the user presses e, either the addition or subtraction result gets loaded into the register and displayed at the LEDs.

This example assumes the result of a subtraction is always a positive number, never negative. It also assumes that the result is always between 0 and 255.

Example 4.10 Color space converter—RGB to CMYK

Computer monitors, digital cameras, scanners, printers, and other electronic devices deal with color images. Those devices treat an image as millions of tiny *pixels* (short for "picture elements"), which are indivisible dots representing a tiny part of the image. Each pixel has a color, so an image is just a collection of colored pixels. A good computer monitor may support over 10 million unique colors for each pixel. How does a monitor create each unique color for a pixel? In a method used in what are known as RGB monitors, the monitor has three light sources inside—red, green, and blue. Any color of light can be created by adding specific intensities of each of the three colors. Thus, for each pixel, the monitor shines a specific intensity of red, of green, and of blue at that pixel's location on the monitor's screen, so that the three colors add together to create the desired pixel color. Each subcolor (red, green, or blue) is typically represented as an 8-bit binary number (thus each ranging from 0 to 255), meaning a color is represented by 8+8+8=24 bits. An (R, G, B) value of (0, 0, 0) represents black. (10, 10, 10) represents a very dark gray, while (200, 200, 200) represents a light gray. (255, 0, 0) represents red, while (100, 0, 0) represents a darker (nonintense) red. (255, 255, 255) represents white. (109, 35, 201) represents some mixture of the three base colors. Representing color using intensity values for red, green, and blue is known as an ***RGB color space.***

RGB color space is great for computer monitors and certain other devices, but not the best for some other devices like printers. Mixing red, green, and blue ink on paper will not result in white, but rather in black. Why? Because ink is not light; rather, ink reflects light. So red ink reflects red light, absorbing green and blue light. Likewise, green ink absorbs red and blue light. Blue ink absorbs red and green light. Mix all three inks together on paper, and the mixture absorbs all light, reflecting none, thus yielding black. Printers therefore use a different color space based on the complementary colors of red/green/blue, namely, cyan/magenta/yellow, known as a ***CMY color space***. Cyan ink *absorbs* red, reflecting green and blue (the mixture of which is cyan). Magenta ink *absorbs* green light, reflecting red and blue (which is magenta). Yellow ink *absorbs* blue, reflecting red and green (which is yellow).

A color printer commonly has three color ink cartridges, one cyan, one magenta, and one yellow. Figure 4.48 shows the ink cartridges for a particular color printer. Some printers have a single cartridge for color instead of three, with that single cartridge internally containing separated fluid compartments for the three colors.

A printer must convert a received RGB image into CMY. Let's design a fast circuit to perform that conversion. Given three 8-bit values for R, G, and B for a given pixel, the equations for C, M, and Y are simply:

```
C = 255 - R
M = 255 - G
Y = 255 - B
```

255 is the maximum value of an 8-bit number. A circuit for such conversion can be built with subtractors as in Figure 4.49.

Actually, the conversion needs to be slightly more complex. Ink isn't perfect, meaning that mixing cyan, magenta, and yellow yields a black that doesn't look as black as you might expect. Furthermore,

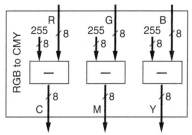

Figure 4.48 A color printer mixes cyan, magenta, and yellow inks to create any color. The picture shows inside a color printer having those three colors' cartridges on the right, labeled C, M, and Y. Such printers may use black ink directly (the big cartridge on the left), rather than mixing the three colors, to make grays and blacks, in order to create a better-looking black and to conserve the more expensive color inks.

colored inks are expensive compared to black ink. Therefore, color printers use black ink whenever possible. One way to maximize use of black ink is to factor out the black from the C, M, and Y values. In other words, a (C, M, Y) value of (250, 200, 200) can be thought of as (200, 200, 200) plus (50, 0, 0).

The (200, 200, 200), which is a light gray, can be generated using black ink. The remaining (50, 0, 0) can be generated using a small amount of cyan, and using no magenta or yellow ink at all, thus saving precious color ink. A CMY color space extended with black is known as a ***CMYK color space*** (the "K" comes from the last letter in the word "black." "K" is used instead of "B" to avoid confusion with the "B" from "blue").

An RGB to CMYK converter can thus be described as:

```
K = Minimum (C, M, Y)
C2 = C - K
M2 = M - K
Y2 = Y - K
```

Figure 4.49 RGB to CMY converter.

C, M, and Y are defined as earlier. We thus create the *datapath* circuit in Figure 4.50 for converting an RGB color space to a CMYK color space. We've used the *RGBtoCMY* component from Figure 4.49. We've also used two instances of the MIN component that we created in Example 4.8 to compute the minimum of two numbers; using two such components computes the minimum of three numbers. Finally, we use three more subtractors to remove the K value from the C, M, and Y values. In a real printer, the imperfections of ink and paper require even more adjustments. A more realistic color space converter multiplies the R, G, and B values by a series of constants, which can be described using matrices:

$$
\begin{vmatrix} C \\ M \\ Y \end{vmatrix} = \begin{vmatrix} m00 & m01 & m02 \\ m10 & m11 & m12 \\ m20 & m21 & m22 \end{vmatrix} * \begin{vmatrix} R \\ G \\ B \end{vmatrix}
$$

Further discussion of such a matrix-based converter is beyond the scope of this example.

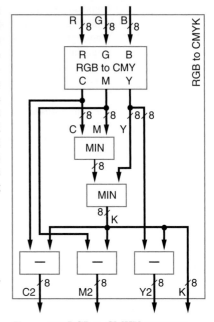

Figure 4.50 RGB to CMKY converter.

Representing Negative Numbers: Two's Complement Representation

The subtractor design in the previous section assumed positive input numbers and positive results. But in many systems, results may be negative, and in fact the input values may even be negative numbers. We thus need a way to represent negative numbers using bits.

One obvious but not very effective representation is known as ***signed-magnitude representation***. In this representation, the highest-order bit is used only to represent the number's sign, with 0 meaning positive and 1 meaning negative. The remaining low-order bits represent the magnitude of the number. In this representation, and using 4-bit numbers, 0111 would represent +7, while 1111 would represent –7. Thus, four bits could represent –7 to 7. (Notice, by the way, that both 0000 and 1000 would represent 0, the former representing 0, the latter –0.) Signed-magnitude is easy for humans to understand, but doesn't lend itself easily to the design of simple arithmetic components like adders and subtractors. For example, if an adder's inputs use signed-magnitude representation, the adder would have to look at the highest-order bit and then internally perform either an addition or a subtraction, using different circuits for each.

We are introducing ten's complement just for intuition purposes—we'll actually be using two's complement.

Instead, the most common method of representing negative numbers and performing subtraction in a digital system actually uses a trick that allows us to *use an adder to perform subtraction*. The key to performing subtraction using addition lies in what are known as *complements*. We'll first introduce complements in the base ten number system just so you can familiarize yourself with the concept, but bear in mind that the intention is to use complements in base two, not base ten.

Consider subtraction involving two single-digit base ten numbers, say 7–4. The result should be 3. Let's define the ***complement*** of a single-digit base ten number A as *the number that when added to A results in a sum of ten*. So the complement of 1 is 9, of 2 is 8, and so on. Figure 4.51 provides the complements for the numbers 1 through 9.

The wonderful thing about a complement is that you can use it to perform subtraction using addition, by replacing the number being subtracted with its complement, then by adding, and then by finally throwing away the carry. For example:

$$7 - 4 \longrightarrow 7 + 6 = 13 \longrightarrow \cancel{1}3 = 3$$

We replaced 4 by its complement 6, and then added 6 to 7 to obtain 13. Finally, we threw away the carry, leaving 3, which is the correct result. Thus, *we performed subtraction using addition*.

1 ⟶ 9
2 ⟶ 8
3 ⟶ 7
4 ⟶ 6
5 ⟶ 5
6 ⟶ 4
7 ⟶ 3
8 ⟶ 2
9 ⟶ 1

Figure 4.51 Complements in base ten.

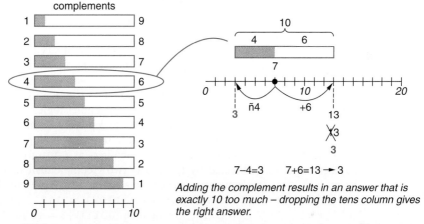

7–4=3   7+6=13 ⟶ 3

Adding the complement results in an answer that is exactly 10 too much – dropping the tens column gives the right answer.

Figure 4.52 Subtracting by adding—subtracting a number (4) is the same as adding the number's complement (6) and then dropping the carry, since by definition of the complement, the result will be exactly 10 too much. After all, that's how the complement was defined—the number plus its complement equals 10.

A number line helps us visualize why complements work, as shown in Figure 4.52. Complements work for any number of digits. Say we want to perform subtraction using two two-digit base ten numbers, perhaps 55–30. The complement of 30 would be the number that when added to 30 results in 100, so the complement of 30 is 70. 55+70 is 125. Throwing away the carry yields 25, which is the correct result for 55–30.

So using complements achieves subtraction using addition.

"Not so fast!" you might say. In order to determine the complement, don't we have to perform subtraction? We know that 6 is the complement of 4 by computing 10–4=6. We know that 70 is the complement of 30 by computing 100–30=70. So haven't we just moved the subtraction to another step—the step of computing the complement?

Yes. Except, it turns out that *in base two, we can compute the complement in a much simpler way—just by inverting all the bits and adding 1*. For example, consider com-

Two's complement can be computed simply by inverting the bits and adding 1—thus avoiding the need for subtraction when computing a complement.

puting the complement of the 3-bit base-two number 001. The complement would be the number that when added to 001 yields 1000–you can probably see that the complement should be 111. To check, we can use the same method for computing the complement as in base ten, computing the two's complement of 001 as 1000–001=111. So 111 is the complement of 001. However, it just so happens that if we invert all the bits of 001 and add 1, we get the same result! Inverting the bits of 001 yields 110; adding 1 yields 110+1=111, which is the correct complement.

Thus, to perform a subtraction, say 011–001, we would perform the following:

```
011 - 001
—-> 011 + ((001)'+1)
  = 011 + (110+1)
  = 011 + 111
  = 1010                    (throw away the carry)
—-> 010
```

That's the correct answer, and the method didn't involve subtraction—only an invert and additions.

We omit discussion as to why one can compute the complement in base two by inverting the bits and adding 1—for our purposes, we just need to know that the trick works for binary numbers.

There are actually two types of complements of a binary number. The type described above is known as the ***two's complement***, obtained by inverting all the bits of the binary number and adding 1. Another type is known as the ***one's complement***, which is obtained simply by inverting all the bits, without adding a 1. The two's complement is much more commonly used in digital circuits and results in simpler logic.

Two's complement leads to a simple way to represent negative numbers. Say we have four bits to represent numbers, and we want to represent both positive and negative numbers. We can choose to represent positive numbers as 0000 to 0111 (0 to 7). Negative numbers would be obtained by taking the two's complement of the positive numbers, because a – b is the same as a + (–b). So –1 would be represented by taking the two's complement of 0001, or (0001)'+1 = 1110+1 = 1111. Likewise, –2 would be (0010)'+1 = 1101+1 = 1110. –3 would be (0011)'+1 = 1100+1 = 1101. And so on. –7 would be (0111)'+1 = 1000+1 = 1001. Notice that the two's complement of 0000 is 1111+1 = 0000. Two's complement representation has only one representation of 0, namely, 0000 (unlike signed-magnitude representation, which had two representations of 0). Also notice that we can represent –8 as 1000. So two's complement is slightly asymmetric, representing one more negative number than positive numbers. A 4-bit two's-complement number can represent any number from –8 to +7.

Say you have 4-bit numbers and want to store –5. –5 would be (0101)'+1 = 1010+1 = 1011. Now you want to add –5 to 4 (or 0100). So you simply add 1011 + 0100 = 1111, which is the correct answer of –1.

The highest-order bit in two's complement acts as a sign bit: 0 means positive, 1 means negative.

Note that negative numbers all have a 1 in the highest-order (leftmost) bit; thus, the highest-order bit in two's complement is often referred to as the ***sign bit***, 0 indicating a positive number, 1 a negative number. An N-bit binary number that only represents positive numbers is called an ***unsigned number*** and can represent numbers from 0 to 2^N-1. For example, an 8-bit unsigned number can represent numbers from 0 to 255. An N-bit binary number that can represent positive or negative numbers is called a ***signed number*** (more specifically, a signed two's-complement number, which is the most common form and the only form this book uses). A signed number can represent numbers from -2^{N-1} to $+2^{N-1}$-1. For example, an 8-bit signed number can represent numbers -128 to +127. You can't tell whether a number like 1011 is a signed or unsigned number (or even a number at all) just by looking at it; somebody has to tell you what the bits represent.

If you want to know the magnitude of a two's complement negative number, you can obtain the magnitude by taking the two's complement again. So to determine what number 1111 represents, we can take the two's complement of 1111: (1111)'+1 = 0000+1 = 0001. We put a negative sign in front to yield −0001, or −1.

This is a helpful and commonly-used method when learning two's complement; remember it.

A quick method for humans to mentally figure out the magnitude of a negative number in 4-bit two's complement (having a 1 in the high order bit) is to subtract the magnitude of the three lower bits from 8. So for 1111, the low three bits are 111 or 7, so the magnitude is 8−7=1, which in turn means that 1111 represents −1. For an 8-bit two's complement number, we would subtract the magnitude of the lower 7 bits from 128. So 10000111 would be −(128−7) = −121.

To summarize, we can represent negative numbers using two's complement representation. Addition of two's complement numbers proceeds unmodified—we just add the numbers. Even if one or both numbers are negative, we simply add the numbers. We perform subtraction of A − B by taking the two's complement of B and then adding that two's complement to A, resulting in A + (−B). We compute the two's complement of B by simply inverting the bits of B and then adding 1. B could have originally been positive or negative; the two's complement correctly negates B in either case.

Building a Subtractor Using an Adder and Two's Complement

Knowledge of the two's complement representation leads to a technique to subtract using an adder. To compute A − B, we compute A + (−B), which is the same as A + B' + 1 because −B can be computed as B' + 1 in two's complement. Thus, to perform subtraction we invert B and input a 1 to the carry-in of an adder, as shown in Figure 4.53.

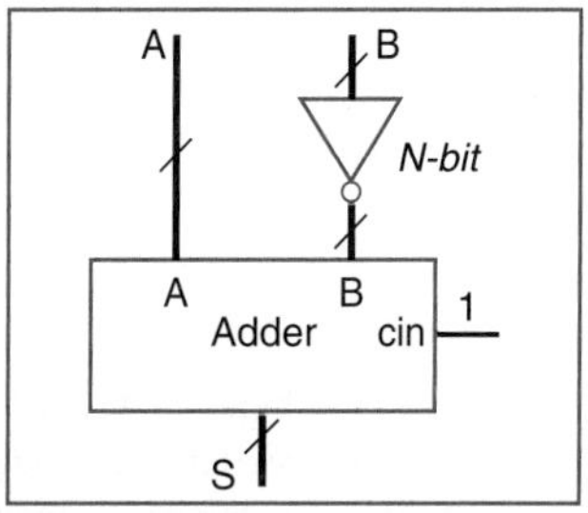

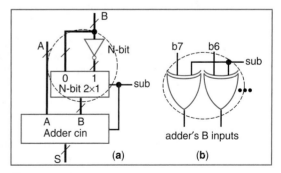

Figure 4.53 Two's complement subtractor built with an adder.

Adder/Subtractor

An adder/subtractor component can be straightforwardly designed, having a control input sub. When sub=1 the component subtracts, but when sub=0 the component adds. The design is shown in Figure 4.54(a). The *N*-bit 2x1 multiplexor passes B when sub=0, and passes B' when sub=1. sub is connected to cin also, so that cin is 1 when subtracting. Actually, XORs can be used instead of the inverters and mux, as shown in Figure 4.54(b). When sub=0, the

Figure 4.54 Two's complement adder/subtractor using a mux, (b) alternative circuit for B using XOR gates.

output of XOR equals the other input's value. When sub=1, the output of the XOR is the inverse of the other input's value.

Example 4.11 DIP-switch-based adding/subtracting calculator (continued)

Let's revisit our DIP-switch-based adding/subtracting calculator of Example 4.9. Observe that at any given time, the output displays the results of either the adder or subtractor, but never both simultaneously. Thus, we really don't need both an adder and a subtractor operating in parallel; instead, we can use a single adder/subtractor component. Assuming DIP switches have been set, setting f=0 (add) versus f=1 (subtract) should result in the following computations:

```
00001111 + 00000001 (f=0)  =  00010000
00001111 - 00000001 (f=1)  =  00001111 + 11111110 + 1 =
    00001110
```

We achieve this simply by connecting f to the sub input of the adder/subtractor, as shown in Figure 4.55.

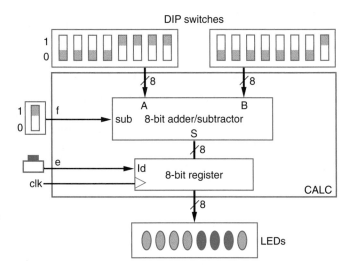

Figure 4.55 8-bit DIP-switch-based adding/subtracting calculator, using an adder/subtractor and two's comlement number representation.

Let's consider signed numbers using two's complement. If the user is unaware that two's complement representation is being used and the user will only be inputting positive numbers using the DIP switches, then the user should only use the low-order 7 switches of the 8-switch DIP inputs, leaving the eighth switch in the 0 position, meaning the user can only input numbers ranging from 0 (00000000) to 127 (01111111). The reason the user can't use the eighth bit is that in two's complement representation, making the highest-order bit a 1 causes the number to represent a negative number.

If the user is aware of two's complement, then the user could use the DIP switches to represent negative numbers too, from –1 (11111111) down to –128 (10000000). Of course, the user will need to check the leftmost LED to determine whether the output represents a positive number or a negative number in two's complement form.

► WHY SUCH CHEAP CALCULATORS? ECONOMY OF SCALE

Several earlier examples dealt with designing simple calculators. Cheap calculators, costing less than a dollar, are easy to find. Calculators are even given away for free by many companies selling something else. But a calculator internally contains a chip implementing a digital circuit, and chips normally aren't cheap. Why are some calculators such a bargain?

The reason is known as *economy of scale*, which means that products are often cheaper when produced in large volumes. Why? Because the design and setup costs can be amortized over larger numbers. Suppose it costs $1,000,000 to design a custom calculator chip and to setup the chip's manufacturing (not so unreasonable a number)—design and setup costs are often called *nonrecurring engineering*, or *NRE*, costs. If you plan to produce and sell one such chip,

then you need to add $1,000,000 to the selling price of that chip if you want to break even (meaning to recover your design and setup costs) when you sell the chip. If you plan to produce and sell 10 such chips, then you need to add $1,000,000/10 = $100,000 to the selling price of each chip. If you plan to produce and sell 1,000,000 such chips, then you need to add only $1,000,000/1,000,000 = $1 to the selling price of each chip. And if you plan to produce and sell 10,000,000, you need to add a mere $1,000,000/10,000,000 = $0.10 = 10 cents to the selling price of each chip. If the actual raw materials only cost 20 cents per chip, and you add another 10 cents per chip for profit, then I can buy the chip from you for a mere 40 cents. And I can then give away such a calculator for free, as many companies do, as an incentive for people to buy something else.

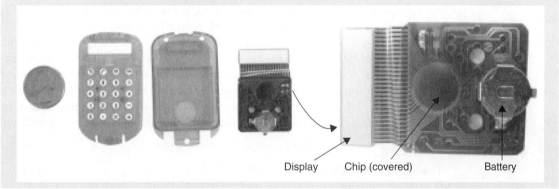

Display   Chip (covered)   Battery

Detecting Overflow

When performing arithmetic using fixed-width binary numbers, sometimes the result is wider than the fixed bitwidth, a situation known as *overflow*. For example, consider adding two 4-bit binary numbers (just regular binary numbers for now, not two's complement numbers) and storing the result as another 4-bit number. Adding 1111 + 0001 yields 10000—a 5-bit number, which is bigger than the 4 bits available to store the result. In other words, 15+1=16, and 16 requires 5 bits in binary. We can easily detect overflow when adding two binary numbers simply by looking at the carry-out bit of the adder—a carry-out of 1 indicates overflow. So a 4-bit adder adding 1111 + 0001 would output 1 + 0000, where the 1 is the carry-out—indicating overflow.

When using two's complement numbers, detecting overflow is more complicated. Suppose we have 4-bit numbers in two's complement form. Consider the addition of two positive numbers, such as 0111 and 0001 in Figure 4.56(a). A 4-bit adder would output 1000, but that is incorrect—the result of 7+1 should be 8, but 1000 represents –8 in two's complement.

The problem is that the largest positive number that a 4-bit two's complement number can represent is 7. So when adding two positive numbers, overflow can be detected by checking whether the result's most significant bit is 1.

Likewise, consider adding two negative numbers, such as 1111 and 1000 in Figure 4.56(b). An adder would output a sum of 0111 (and a carry-out of 1), which is incorrect: $-1 + -8$ should be -9, but 0111 is +7.

sign bits

overflow   *overflow*   *no overflow*
(a)   (b)   (c)

If the numbers' sign bits have the same value, which differs from the result's sign bit, overflow has occurred.

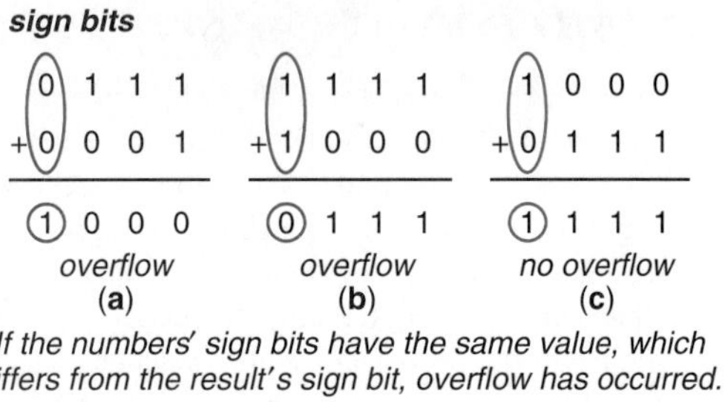

Figure 4.56 Two's complement overflow detection comparing sign bits: (a) when adding two positive numbers, (b) when adding two negative numbers, (c) no overflow.

The problem is that the most negative number that a 4-bit two's complement can represent is -8. Thus, when adding two negative numbers, overflow can be detected by checking whether the most significant bit is a 0 in the result.

Adding a positive with a negative, or a negative with a positive, can never result in overflow. The result will always be less negative than the most negative number or less positive than the most positive number. The extreme is the addition of $-8+7$, which is -1. Increasing -8 or decreasing 7 in that addition still results in a number between -8 and 7.

Thus, detecting overflow in two's complement involves detecting that both input numbers were positive but yielded a negative result, or that both input numbers were negative but yielded a positive result. Restated, detecting overflow in two's complement involves detecting that the sign bits of both inputs are the same but differ from the result's sign bit. If the sign bit of one input is a and the sign bit of the other input is b, and the sign bit of the result is r, then the following equation outputs 1 when there is overflow:

```
overflow = abr' + a'b'r
```

Though the circuit implementing the overflow detection equation is simple and intuitive, we can create an even simpler circuit if the adder generates a carry-out. The simpler method merely compares the carry into the sign bit column with the carry-out of the sign bit column—if the carry-in and carry-out differ, overflow has occurred. Figure 4.57 illustrates this method for several cases. In Figure 4.57(a), the carry into the sign bit is 1, whereas the carry-out is 0. Because the carry-in and carry-out differ, overflow has occurred. A circuit detecting whether two

overflow   *overflow*   *no overflow*
(a)   (b)   (c)

If the carry into the sign bit column differs from the carry-out of that column, overflow has occurred.

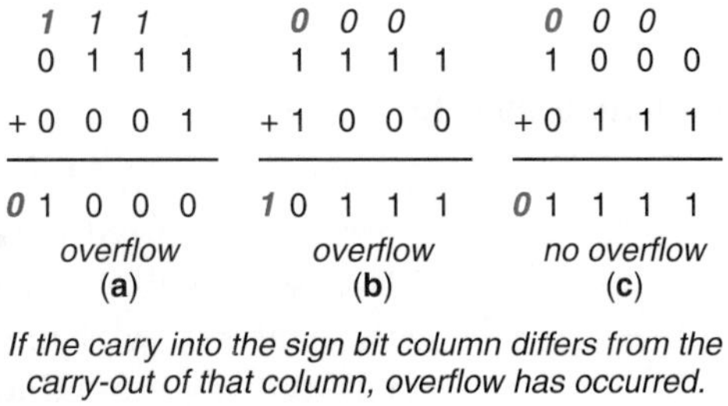

Figure 4.57 Two's complement overflow detection comparing carry into and out of the sign bit column: (a) when adding two positive numbers, (b) when adding two negative numbers, (c) no overflow.

bits differ is just an XOR gate, which is slightly simpler than the circuit of the previous method. We omit discussion as to why this method works, but looking at the cases in Figure 4.57 should help provide the intuition.

▶ 4.7 ARITHMETIC-LOGIC UNITS—ALUS

An *N-bit arithmetic-logic unit (ALU)* is a combinational datapath component able to perform a variety of arithmetic and logic operations on two *N*-bit wide data inputs, generating an *N*-bit data output. Example arithmetic operations include addition and subtraction. Example logic operations include AND, OR, XOR, etc. Control inputs to the ALU indicate which particular operation to perform. To understand the need for an ALU component, consider the following example.

Example 4.12 Multi-function calculator without using an ALU

Let's extend the earlier DIP-switch-based calculator to support eight operations, determined by a three-switch DIP switch that provides three inputs x, y, and z to the system, as shown in Figure 4.58. For each combination of the three switches, we want to perform the operations shown in Table 4.2 on the 8-bit data inputs A and B, generating the 8-bit output on S.

TABLE 4.2 Desired calculator operations

Inputs			Operation	Sample output if A=00001111, B=00000101
x	y	z		
0	0	0	S = A + B	S=00010100
0	0	1	S = A - B	S=00001010
0	1	0	S = A + 1	S=00010000
0	1	1	S = A	S=00001111
1	0	0	S = A AND B (bitwise AND)	S=00000101
1	0	1	S = A OR B (bitwise OR)	S=00001111
1	1	0	S = A XOR B (bitwise XOR)	S=00001010
1	1	1	S = NOT A (bitwise complement)	S=11110000

The table includes several bitwise operations (AND, OR, XOR, and complement). A *bitwise operation* applies to each corresponding pair of bits of A and B separately.

We can design a datapath circuit for the calculator as shown in Figure 4.58, using a separate datapath component to compute each operation: an adder computes the addition, a subtractor computes the subtraction, an incrementer computes the increment, and so on. However, that datapath is very inefficient with respect to the number of wires, power consumption, or delay. There are too many wires that must be routed to all those components, and especially to the mux, which will have 8*8 = 64 inputs. Furthermore, every operation is computed all the time, and that wastes power. Such a design is akin to a restaurant cooking every meal that a customer might order and then serving the customer just the one meal that the customer actually orders.

Furthermore, imagine that the calculator deals not with 8-bit numbers, but instead with 32-bit numbers, and supports not just 8 operations but 32 operations. Then the design would have even

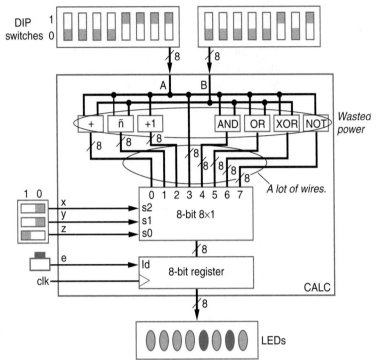

Figure 4.58 8-bit DIP-switch-based multifunction calculator, using separate components for each function.

more wires (32*32 = 1024 wires at the mux inputs), and even more power consumption. Furthermore, a 32x1 mux will require several levels of gates, because due to practical reasons, a 32-input logic gate (inside the mux) will likely need to be implemented using several levels of smaller logic gates.

We saw in the above example that using separate components for each operation is not efficient. To solve the problem, note that the calculator can only be configured to do one operation at a time, so there is no need to compute all the operations in parallel, as was done in the example. Instead, we can create a single component (an ALU) that can compute any of the eight operations. Such a component would be more area- and power-efficient, and would have less delay because a large mux would not be needed.

Let's start with an adder as the base internal ALU design. To avoid confusion, the inputs to the internal adder are named IA and IB, short for "internal A" and "internal B," to distinguish those inputs from the external ALU inputs A and B. We start with the design shown in Figure 4.59(a). The ALU consists of an adder and some logic in front of the adder's inputs, called an arithmetic/logic extender, or *AL-extender*. The purpose of the

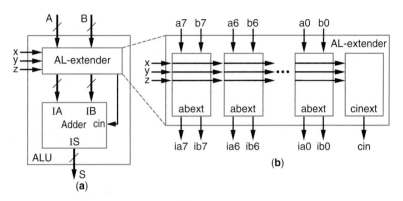

Figure 4.59 Arithmetic-logic unit: (a) ALU design based on a single adder, with an arithmetic/logic extender, (b) arithmetic/logic extender detail.

AL-extender is to set the adder's inputs based on the values of the ALU's control inputs x, y, and z, such that the desired arithmetic or logic result appears at the adder's output. The *AL-extender* actually consists of eight identical components labeled *abext*, one for each pair of bits ai and bi, as shown in Figure 4.59(b). It also has a component *cinext* to compute the cin bit.

Thus, we need to design the *abext* and *cinext* components to complete the ALU design. Consider the first four calculator operations from Table 4.2, which are all arithmetic operations:

- When xyz=000, S=A+B. So in that case, we want IA=A, IB=B, and cin=0.
- When xyz=001, S=A-B. So we want IA=A, IB=B', and cin=1.
- When xyz=010, S=A+1. So we want IA=A, IB=0, and cin=1.
- When xyz=011, S=A. So we want IA=A, IB=0, and cin=0. Notice that A will pass through the adder, because A+0+0=A.

The last four ALU operations are all logical operations. We can compute the desired operation in the *abext* component, and input the result to IA. We then set IB to 0 and cin to 0, so that the value on IA passes through the adder unchanged.

One possible design of *abext* places an 8x1 mux in front of each output of the *abext* and *cinext* components, with x, y, and z as the select inputs, in which case we would set each mux data input as described above. A more efficient and faster design would create a custom circuit for each component output. We leave the completion of the internal design of the *abext* and *cinext* components as an exercise for the reader.

Example 4.13 redesigns the multifunction calculator of Example 4.12, this time utilizing an ALU.

Example 4.13 Multi-function calculator using an ALU

Example 4.12 built an eight-function calculator without an ALU. The result was wasted area and power, complex wiring, and long delay. Using the above-designed ALU, the calculator could instead be built as the datapath in Figure 4.60. Notice the simple and efficient design.

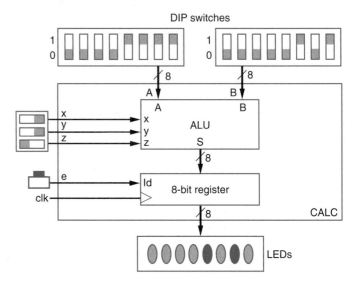

Figure 4.60 8-bit DIP-switch-based multi-function calculator using an ALU.

▷ 4.8 SHIFTERS

Shifting is a common operation applied to data. Shifting can be used to rearrange bits of data. Shifting is useful for communicating data serially as was done in Example 4.4. Shifting is also useful for multiplying or dividing an *unsigned* binary number by a factor of 2. In base ten, you are familiar with the idea that multiplying by 10 can be done by simply appending a 0 to a number. For example, 53 times 10 is 530. Appending a 0 is the same as shifting left one position (and shifting in a 0). Likewise, in base two, multiplying an unsigned binary number by 2 can be done by appending a 0, meaning shifting left one position. So 0101 times 2 is 1010. Furthermore, in base ten, multiplying by 100 can be done by appending two 0s, meaning shifting left twice. So in base two, multiplying by 4 can be done by shifting left twice. Shifting left three times in base two multiplies by 8. And so on. Because shifting an unsigned binary number left is the same as multiplying by 2, shifting an unsigned binary number right is the same as dividing by 2. So 1010 divided by 2 is 0101.

Although shifting can be done using a shift register, sometimes we find the need to use a separate combinational component that performs the shift and that can also shift by different numbers of positions and in either direction.

Simple Shifters

An *N-bit shifter* is a combinational component that can shift an *N*-bit data input by a fixed amount to generate an *N*-bit data output. The simplest shifter shifts one position in one direction. A simple 4-bit shifter that shifts left one position has a straightforward design consisting of just wires as shown in Figure 4.61(a). Note that the shifter has an additional input that is the value to shift into the rightmost bit. The notation "<<1" indicates a left shift ("<<") by 1 position; a right shift would use ">>."

Figure 4.61
Combinational shifters: (a) left shifter design, with block symbol shown at bottom, (b) left shift or pass component, (c) left/right shift or pass component.

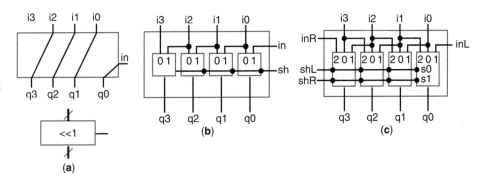

A more capable simple shifter can either shift one position when an additional input sh is 1 or can pass the inputs through to the outputs unshifted when sh is 0. The design of such a shifter uses 2x1 muxes as shown in Figure 4.61(b). An even more capable simple shifter shown in Figure 4.61(c) can shift left or right one position. When both shift control inputs are 0, the inputs pass through unchanged. shL=1 causes a left shift, and shR=1 causes a right shift. When both those control inputs are 1, the shifter could be designed to pass the inputs through unchanged (not shown in the figure). A simple shifter's shift amount could be something other than 1; for example, a shifter component might shift right by two places, denoted as ">>2."

Example 4.14 Temperature averager

Consider a system that reads the unsigned binary output T of a sensor such as a speed or temperature sensor in an aircraft. The system may sample the sensor several times a second and average recent samples (called a *sliding* average) to help compensate for sensor imperfections that cause occasional spurious sensor readings; e.g., a speed sensor's last four readings may be 202, 203, 235, 202—that 235 reading is probably incorrect.

Let's design a system that computes the average of four registers Ra, Rb, Rc, and Rd, storing the result in a register Ravg and outputting the result on output Tavg. The average is computed as (Ra+Rb+Rc+Rd) / 4. Dividing by 4 is the same as shifting right by two. Thus, we can design the system as a

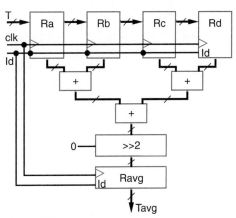

Figure 4.62 Temperature averager using a right-shift-by-2 simple shifter component to divide by 4.

datapath having three adders, a simple right shifter that shifts by two places (with a shift in value of 0), and registers, as shown in Figure 4.62.

This section stated that shifting was the same as multiplication or division by factors of 2 for *unsigned* numbers. Simple shifting would not accomplish such multiplication or division for *signed* numbers. For example, consider the signed 4-bit number 1010, meaning –6. Right shifting to try to divide by 2 would result in 0101 or +5, which is not the correct result of –1, or 1111. Likewise, left shifting to try to multiply by 2 would result in 0100, or 4, rather than –4, or 1100. Solutions exist but are beyond the scope of this book.

Strength Reduction.   Multiplication by a constant number that is a power of 2 (2, 4, 8, 16, etc.) can be done using left shifts, but systems commonly multiply by other constant numbers, such as by 5 or by 10. While a designer could use a multiplier component (described in Section 4.5), multipliers use more transistors than shifters or adders. Thus, designers sometimes replace multiplications by a series of shifts and adds that compute the same result, because shifter components and adder components are small and fast compared to multipliers. Replacing costly operations by a series of less costly operations is known as ***strength reduction*** and is common in digital design as well as in software compilation. For example, a system may require computing 5*C. A designer might rewrite that computation as 4*C + C, thus requiring a left-shift-by-2 component (for 4*C) and an adder, which together are still smaller and faster than a multiplier.

Division is slightly harder to do precisely using shifts and adds but can still be done using a similar strength reduction approach. For example, C/5 is C*(1/5), and 1/5 = 0.20. 1/5 could be approximated by converting to a fraction that is close to 0.20 and that has a denominator that is a power of 2, such as 102/512 (0.199). Then the numerator could be computed as the sum of powers of two, i.e., 102/512 is (64+32+4+2)/512. Therefore, C/5 nearly equals C*(64+32+4+2)/512, or (C*64 + C*32 + C*4+C*2)/512. All the multiplications and divisions in that equation can be achieved using left shifts or right shifts, i.e., ((C<<6) + (C<<5) + (C<<2) + (C<<1)) >> 9. For even more accuracy, a larger denominator (and hence numerator) could be used to get closer to 0.20. At some point, though, the number of shifts and adds may exceed the cost of a divider component.

Example 4.15 Celsius to Fahrenheit converter

We are given a digital thermometer that digitizes a temperature into an 8-bit unsigned binary number C representing the temperature in Celsius. For example, 30 degrees Celsius would be digitized as 00011110. We want to convert that temperature to Fahrenheit, again using 8 unsigned bits. The equation for converting is:

    F = C*9/5 + 32

We can rewrite the equation as:

    F = C + C*4/5 + 32

C*4/5 is 4*(C/5). We saw above that C/5 can be closely approximated as:

    (C*64+C*32+C*4+C*2)/512

The multiplication of the above equation by 4 to obtain 4*(C/5) changes the denominator to 128. Thus, the equation for converting can be rewritten as:

    F = C+(C*64+C*32+C*4+C*2)/128+32

The equation for F has been rewritten such that any multiplications or divisions are by a constant power of 2 and are thus replaceable by shifts.

The datapath circuit implementing the rewritten equation is shown in Figure 4.63. Consider an input C=00011110 representing 30 degrees Celsius, which is 86 degrees according to the first conversion equation above. The circuit's "<<6" shifter shifts the input 6 places to the left; shifting 00011110 6 places left yields 10000000, which loses information (30*64 is not just 128). To avoid information loss, we can increase the number of internal wires—let's increase them to 16 bits. All wires and components in the figure are thus 16 bits wide. The input would be padded on the left with 0s—*padding* means to fill values for the bits introduced when widening multibit data. The input C left-padded to 16 bits would be 0000 0000 0001 1110 (we added spaces just for readability). The top four shifters and the top three adders of Figure 4.63 would thus compute:

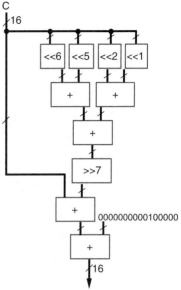

$$
\begin{array}{ll}
  & 0000\ 0111\ 1000\ 0000 & (C\ \text{<<}6) \\
+ & 0000\ 0011\ 1100\ 0000 & (C\ \text{<<}5) \\
+ & 0000\ 0000\ 0111\ 1000 & (C\ \text{<<}2) \\
+ & \underline{0000\ 0000\ 0011\ 1100} & (C\ \text{<<}1) \\
= & 0000\ 1011\ 1111\ 0100 &
\end{array}
$$

F = C +(C*64+C*32+C*4+C*2)/128 + 32

Figure 4.63 Celsius to Fahrenheit converter datapath using shifts and adds.

The shift right by 7 would output 0000 0000 0001 0111. The adder that adds this result to the input C of 0000 0000 0001 1110 would output 0000 0000 0011 0101. The bottom-most adder adds this result to the constant 32 (0000 0000 0010 0000) to yield the final output of 0000 0000 0101 0101. The leftmost 8 bits can be dropped to yield the 8-bit output for F of 01010101, which is 85 in binary—slightly off from the correct value of 86 due to the shift and add approximation approach, but close. A larger denominator (and hence numerator) in the approximation approach would yield higher accuracy at the expense of more shifts and adds.

▶ Fahrenheit versus Celsius—The U.S. and the Metric System

The U.S. usually represents temperature using Fahrenheit, whereas most of the world uses the metric system's Celsius. Presidents and other U.S. leaders have desired to switch to the metric system for almost as long as the U.S. has existed, and several acts have been passed over the centuries, the most recent being the Metric Conversion Act of 1975 (amended several times since). The Act designates the metric system as the preferred system of weights and measures for U.S. trade and commerce. Yet switching to metric has been slow, and few Americans today are comfortable with metric. The problem with such a slow transition was poignantly demonstrated in 1999 when the Mars Climate Orbiter, costing several hundred million dollars, was destroyed when entering the Mars atmosphere too quickly. The reason: "a navigation error resulted from some spacecraft commands being sent in English units instead of being converted to metric units." (Source: www.nasa.gov). I was an elementary school student in the 1970s when the U.S. had a big push to switch. Unfortunately, teaching of the metric system often focused not on the elegant metric system itself, but rather on converting from existing U.S. units to metric units, e.g., 1 mile equals 1.609 kilometers, and 1 gallon equals 3.785 liters. Many Americans thus found the metric system "difficult." No wonder.

Choosing Bitwidths. As alluded to in previous examples, operating on N-bit numbers requires that some attention be paid to the bitwidths of internal wires and components. If two N-bit numbers are added together, the resulting value could require $N+1$ bits. If two N-bit numbers are multiplied, the resulting value could require $2N$ bits. When multiplication is performed using left shifts, bits may be dropped off of the left (meaning overflow); when division is performed using right shifts, bits may be dropped off of the right (meaning that rounding is occurring). For expected input value ranges, determining the minimum width of all internal wires and components requires mathematical analysis that is beyond the scope of this book. Instead, we describe a few introductory guidelines here.

First, a designer can determine the maximum data value that would occur during computation and then make all the internal wires and components wide enough to support that maximum value. For example, the system described in Example 4.15 involved computing C*64+C*32+C*4+C*2 for a C possibly as large as 255, meaning the maximum data value could be 18,137, which would require 15 bits. In the example, we set all the internal wires and components to 16 bits.

Second, if division will be done, it may be a good idea to do the division as late as possible to minimize the rounding that might occur with each division. For example, if a is 0010 and b is 0010 and if right shifts are used for division, then (a+b)/4 is 0100 shifted right twice, or 0001; instead, a/4 + b/4 would yield 0010 shifted right twice plus 0010 shifted right twice, or 0000 + 0000 = 0000; the rounding errors of the earlier divisions caused a poor result. Example 4.15 multiplied the input by four different amounts, added the products, and then divided, i.e., (C*64+C*32+C*4+C*2)/128. The division could have instead been applied to each product first followed by addition, i.e., C*64/128+C*32/128+C*4/128+C*2/128), which in fact would reduce to C/2+C/4+C/32+C/64. While this equation looks simpler and would even use one less shifter, the result would have more rounding error. Of course, doing the division as late as possible must be balanced with the need to prevent the intermediate sums from getting very large, which could result in very wide components and sets of wires. For example, adding 800 numbers and then dividing by 2 might be better accomplished by adding perhaps 8 numbers at a time and dividing each such sum by 2, then finally adding all the results.

Barrel Shifter

An *N-bit barrel shifter* is a general purpose N-bit shifter component that can shift any number of positions. For simplicity, consider only left shifts for the moment. An 8-bit barrel shifter can shift left by 1, 2, 3, 4, 5, 6, or 7 positions (and of course by 0 positions, meaning no shift is done). An 8-bit barrel shifter therefore requires 3 control inputs, say x, y, and z, to specify the distance of the shift. xyz=000 may mean no shift, xyz=001 means shift by 1 position, xyz=010 means shift by 2 positions, etc. A barrel shifter could be useful to replace several shift components (such as the five shifters in Figure 4.63) by a single component to save transistors or wires (later chapters will show how to do that), or when the shift-amount is not known while the circuit is being designed.

We could design such a barrel shifter using 8 distinct shifters: a 1-place left shifter, a 2-place left shifter, and so on. The 8 shifters' outputs would be connected to an 8-bit 8x1 mux having xyz connected to its select lines, and the mux output would be the barrel shifter's output. While conceptually straightforward, such a design has problems similar to building a multifunction ALU using a distinct component for each operation—too many wires, excessive power consumption, and potentially long delay.

A more elegant design for an 8-bit barrel shifter consists of 3 cascaded simple shifters, as shown in Figure 4.64. The first simple shifter can shift left four positions (or none), the second can shift left by two positions (or none), and the third by one position (or none). Notice that the shifts "add" to one another—shifting left by 2, then by 1, results in a total shift of 3 positions. Thus, configuring each shifter appropriately yields a total shift of any amount between zero and seven. Connecting the control inputs xyz to the shifters is easy—just think of xyz as a binary number representing the amount of the shift: x represents shifting by four, y shifting by two, and z shifting by one. So we just connect x to the left-by-four shifter, y to the left-by-two shifter, and z to the left-by-one shifter, as shown in Figure 4.64.

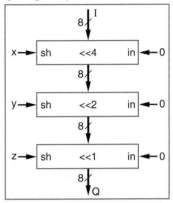

Figure 4.64 8-bit barrel shifter (left shift only).

The above design considered a barrel shifter that could only shift left. The design could easily be extended to support both left and right shifts. The extension involves replacing the internal left shifters by shifters that could shift left or right, each shifter having a control input indicating the direction. The barrel shifter would also have a direction control input, connected to each internal shifter's direction control input.

Finally, the barrel shifter can easily be extended to support rotates as well as shifts. The extension would replace the internal shifters by rotators that could either shift or rotate, each having a control input indicating whether to shift or rotate. The barrel shifter would also have a shift-or-rotate control input, connected to each internal shifter's shift-or-rotate control input.

▶ 4.9 COUNTERS AND TIMERS

An *N-bit counter* is a sequential component that can increment or decrement its own value on each clock cycle when a count enable control input is 1. *Increment* means to add 1, and *decrement* means to subtract 1. A counter that can increment its value is known as an *up-counter*, while a *down-counter* decrements its value. A 4-bit up-counter would thus count the following sequence: 0000, 0001, 0010, 0011, 0100, 0101, 0110, 0111, 1000, 1001, 1010, 1011, 1100, 1101, 1110, 1111, 0000, 0001, etc. Notice that a counter *wraps around* (also known as *rolling over*) from the highest value (1111) to 0. Likewise, a down-counter would wrap around from 0 to the highest value. A control output on the counter, often called *terminal count* or tc, becomes 1 during the clock cycle that the counter has reached its terminal (meaning "last" or "end") count value, after which the counter will wrap around.

Figure 4.65 shows the block symbol of a 4-bit up-counter. When `clr=1`, the counter's value is synchronously cleared to 0. When `cnt=1`, the counter increments its value on every clock cycle. When `cnt=0`, the counter maintains its present value. `clr` has priority over `cnt`. On the cycle that the counter wraps around from `1111` to `0000`, the counter sets `tc=1` for that cycle, returning `tc` to `0` on the next cycle.

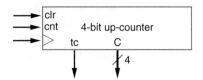

Figure 4.65 4-bit up-counter block symbol.

Up-Counter

An up-counter design is shown in Figure 4.66, using a parallel-load register to store the current count value and using an incrementer component to add 1 to the current value. When `clr=1`, the register will be cleared to 0. When `cnt=0`, the register will maintain its present value due to `ld` being 0. When `cnt=1`, the register will be loaded with its present value plus 1. Note that the 4-input AND gate causes terminal count `tc` to become 1 when the counter reaches `1111`.

A down-counter can be designed similarly to an up-counter. The incrementer would be replaced by a decrementer. The terminal count `tc` should become 1 when the down-counter reaches `0000` and would thus be implemented using a NOR gate rather than the AND gate in the up-counter—recall that NOR outputs 1 when all its inputs are 0s. The reason the down-counter detects `0000` for `tc` rather than `1111` like the up-counter is because a down-counter wraps around after `0000`, as in the following count sequence: `0100, 0011, 0010, 0001, 0000, 1111, 1110, ....`

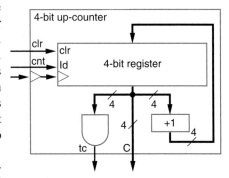

Figure 4.66 4-bit up-counter internal design.

Example 4.16 *Turnstile with display*

This example designs a system that displays the number of people who have passed through a turnstile. Turnstiles are commonly found at entrances of amusement parks, sports stadiums, and other facilities with controlled entrances. We'll assume the turnstile outputs a pulse on a signal P whenever a person passes through. The system should output in binary the number of people that have passed through, and that output is connected to a display that will output that number in decimal. The system should also have a button to reset the display to 0.

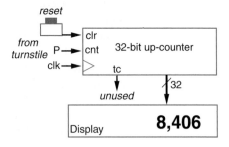

Figure 4.67 Turnstile display using an up-counter.

The system can be straightforwardly designed using an up-counter as shown in Figure 4.67. The reset button connects to the up-counter's clear input. Assuming the pulse on P is one clock cycle in duration (see Chapter 3), then P can be connected to the up-counter's cnt input. We must have some idea of the maximum number of people that might pass through the turnstile between resets of the display, because we don't want the counter to wrap around. We might choose to use a 32-bit counter to be safe, which can count up to about 4 billion people. The display would also have to be able to accept a 32-bit input and display that number in decimal.

Note that a pulse on P must be only one clock cycle in duration for this design to work as desired. If a pulse on P for one person passing through the turnstile were longer than one clock cycle, the system would count up once for every clock cycle that the pulse was 1.

Up/Down-Counter

An up/down-counter can count either up or down. It requires a control input dir to indicate the count direction, in addition to the count enable control input cnt. dir=0 will mean to count up and dir=1 to count down. Figure 4.68 shows the design of such a 4-bit up/down-counter. A 4-bit-wide 2x1 mux passes either the decremented or incremented value, with dir selecting among the two—dir=0 (count up) passes the incremented value, and dir=1 (count down) passes the decremented value. The passed value gets loaded into the 4-bit register if cnt=1. dir also selects whether to pass the NOR or AND output to the terminal count tc external output—dir=0 (count up) selects the AND, while dir=1 (count down) selects the NOR.

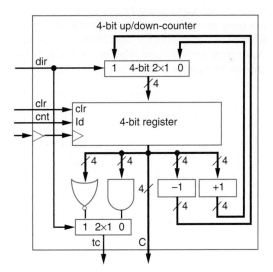

Figure 4.68 4-bit up/down-counter design.

Counter with Load

A well-known counter with load is the "program counter" used in a microprocessor. It holds the address of the current program instruction, normally counting up to go to the next instruction's address, but sometimes being loaded to an entirely new address due to a branch instruction.

Counters often come with the ability to start counting from a particular value, achieved by loading the counter's register with an input value. Figure 4.69 shows the design of a 4-bit up-counter with load. When control input ld is 1, the 2x1 mux passes the input L to the register; when ld is 0, the mux passes the incremented value. The design ORs the counter's ld and cnt signals to generate the load signal for the register. When cnt is 1, the incremented value will be loaded. When ld is 1, the load data will be loaded. Even if cnt is 0, ld=1 causes the register to be loaded. A synchronous clear input is also provided, which has priority over load and count inputs because the register's clear input has priority over the register's load input. A down-counter or up/down-counter could similarly be extended to have a parallel load.

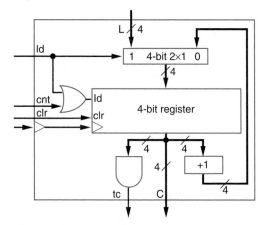

Figure 4.69 Internal design of a 4-bit up-counter with parallel load.

Example 4.17 New Year's Eve countdown display

Example 2.30 utilized a microprocessor to output the numbers 59 down to 0, and a decoder to illuminate one of 60 lights based on that output. This example replaces the microprocessor by a down-counter with load to output 59 down to 0. Suppose we have an 8-bit down-counter available, which can count from 255 down to 0. We need to load 59 and then count down. Assume the user can press a button called restart to load 59 into the counter, and then the user can move a switch countdown from the 0 position (don't count) to the 1 position (count) to begin the countdown. The system implementation is shown in Figure 4.70.

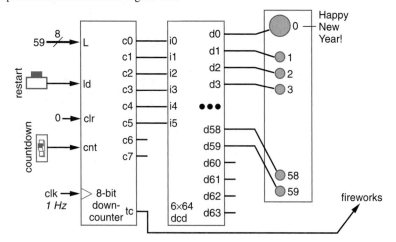

Figure 4.70 Happy New Year countdown system using a down-counter with load.

Some people mistakenly assume that the decoder could be eliminated by using a 60-bit counter instead of an 8-bit counter because there are 60 lights. However, a 60-bit counter would count the following sequence 59 (000...000111011), 58 (000...000111010), and so on. Those binary outputs connected directly to the lights would illuminate the lights differently than desired; rather than illuminating one light at a time, the approach would light multiple lights at a time.

The tc signal Figure 4.70 will be 1 at the same time as the decoder's d0 output. We've connected tc to an output called fireworks, which we'll assume activates a device that ignites fireworks. Note that after reaching 0 the counter will wrap around and continue counting from 255, 254, and so on, until the countdown switch is set to the "don't count" position again.

Clock Divider. One use of a counter is to convert one clock frequency into a lower frequency; a component that performs such conversion is known as a ***clock divider***. Suppose we have a 512 MHz input clock (the fast clock), but want a 2 MHz clock signal (the slow clock). The fast clock frequency should thus be divided by 256. We can convert the fast clock into a desired slow clock signal p by

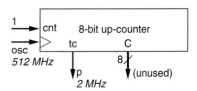

Figure 4.71 Clock divider.

using an 8-bit counter. The 8-bit counter wraps around every 256 cycles, at which time its terminal count output becomes 1 for one fast-clock cycle, so we simply connect the fast clock oscillator signal to the counter's clock input, set the counter's load input to 1, and then use the counter's tc output as the slow-clock signal, as shown in Figure 4.71.

A *clock multiplier* does the opposite of a clock divider, converting an input clock frequency into a higher frequency. Its design is more complex than a clock divider, involving something called a phased-lock loop, and is beyond our scope here.

Sometimes the amount by which to divide the fast clock frequency is not a power of 2. Such clock division can be accomplished using a counter with parallel load, or with some external logic, as shown in the next example.

Example 4.18 1 Hz pulse generator using a 60 Hz oscillator

In the U.S., electricity to the home operates as an alternating current with a frequency of 60 Hz. Some appliances convert this signal to a 60 Hz digital signal, and then divide the 60 Hz digital signal to a 1 Hz signal, to drive a clock or other device needing to keep track of time at the granularity of seconds. Unlike Example 4.1, we can't simply use a counter of a particular bitwidth, since no basic up-counter wraps around after 60 cycles—a 5-bit counter wraps around every 32 cycles, while a 6-bit counter wraps every 64 cycles.

Assume we have a 6-bit down-counter with parallel load. The desired clock divider can be designed by setting the counter's load input to the constant 59 (111011) and using the tc output to reload the register, as in Figure 4.72(a). When the counter counts down to 0, the circuit automatically reloads with 59. Two mistakes are common when considering this circuit. The first mistake is to believe 60 should be loaded rather than 59. We load 59 because the 0 value is counted too. Think of a smaller count example like wanting to reach the terminal count every 3 cycles; you'd load 2 (not 3) so that the counter would count 2, 1, 0, then 2, 1, 0, etc. The second mistake is to believe that this counter would skip the value 0 because of tc being 1 during that clock cycle. Take a moment to understand the timing behavior. When the counter value is 1 and the next rising clock edge arrives, then slightly *after* that clock edge the counter value changes to 0 and tc becomes 1.

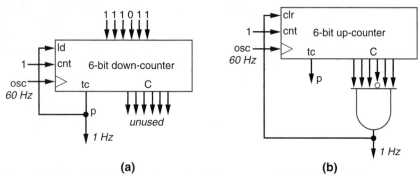

Figure 4.72 Clock divider for a factor other than a power of 2: (a) using a 6-bit up-counter with synchronous clear, (b) using a 6-bit down-counter with parallel load.

Thus, the counter stays at 0 until the *next* rising clock edge, at which time the 1 on tc causes a load of 59 back into the counter.

An up-counter could be used instead, again with tc connected to load. To obtain 60 cycles between counter wrap arounds, we need to set the counter's load input to 63–59 = 4. People sometimes mistakenly think that 63–60 = 3 should be loaded, but remember that the first value is counted too. Think of a smaller count example like wanting to reach the terminal count every 3 cycles. You'd load 61 (not 60) so that the counter would count 61, 62, 63, then 61, 62, 63, etc.

Alternatively, suppose we only have an up-counter with a synchronous clear input but without parallel load (counters without parallel load exist because they have fewer inputs, which may result in fewer wires or fewer pins). In this case, we could use external logic to generate a signal that will be 1 when the counter's value is 59, and connect that signal to the counter's synchronous clear input so that the value after 59 will be 0, as shown in Figure 4.72(b). Alternatively, a down-counter with synchronous clear could be used, in which case the external logic should detect 63–59=4.

Using a Counter to Measure Time. A designer can use an up-counter to measure the time between events, such as the time between a first press of a button and a second press. The designer can create a circuit that initially clears the counter to 0. When the first event occurs, the circuit should set the counter's control input cnt to 1. When the second event occurs, then the circuit should set cnt to 0. The final value in the counter thus indicates the number of clock cycles that transpired between the first and second event. Multiplying this number by the clock period driving the counter yields the time that transpired. Suppose the counter's clock frequency is 1 kHz, meaning each cycle lasts 1 millisecond. If the final value in the counter is 526, then 526 milliseconds passed between events. Care must be taken to use a counter that is wide enough and/or a clock that is slow enough to ensure that the counter will not wrap around while measuring the time interval of interest.

Example 4.19 Highway speed measuring system

Many highways and freeways have systems that measure the speed of cars at various parts of the highway and upload that speed information to a central computer. Such information is used by law enforcement, traffic planners, and radio and Internet traffic reports.

One technique for measuring the speed of a car uses two sensors embedded under the road, as illustrated in Figure 4.74. When a car is over a sensor, the sensor outputs a 1; otherwise, the sensor outputs a 0. A sensor's output travels on underground wires to a speed-measuring computer box, some of which are above the ground and others of which are underground. The speed measurer determines speed by dividing the distance between the sensors (which is fixed and known) by the time taken by a vehicle to travel from the first sensor to the second sensor. If the distance between the sensors is 0.01 miles, and a vehicle takes 0.5 seconds to travel from the first to the second sensor, then the vehicle's speed is 0.01 miles / (0.5 seconds * (1 hour / 3600 seconds)) = 72 miles per hour.

To measure the time between the two sensors separated by 0.01 miles, we can construct a simple FSM that controls a 16-bit up-counter clocked at 1 kHz, as shown in Figure 4.74. State *S0* clears the counter to 0. The FSM transitions to state *S1* when a car passes over the first sensor. *S1* starts the counter counting up. The FSM stays in *S1* until the car passes over the second sensor, causing a transition to state *S2*. *S2* stops the counting and computes the time using the counter's output C. The counter's 1 kHz clock means that each cycle is 0.001 seconds, so the measured time would be C * 0.001 s. That result would then be multiplied by (0.01 miles) / (3600 seconds/hour) to

---

▶ *HOW DOES IT WORK? CAR SENSORS IN ROADS.*

How does a highway speed sensor or a traffic light car sensor know that a car is present in a particular lane? The main method today uses what's called an *inductive loop*. A loop of wire is placed just under the pavement—you can usually see the cuts, as in Figure 4.73(a). That loop of wire has a particular "inductance," which is an electronics term describing the wire's opposition to a change in electric current—higher inductance means the wire has higher opposition to changes in current. It turns out that placing a big hunk of metal (like a car) near the loop of wire changes the wire's inductance. (Why? Because the metal disrupts the magnetic field created by a changing current in the wire—but that's getting beyond our scope.) The traffic light control circuit keeps checking the wire's inductance (perhaps by trying to change the current and seeing how much the current really changes in a certain time period), and if inductance is more than normal, the circuit assumes a car is above the loop of wire.

Many people think that the loops seen in the pavement are scales that measure weight—I've seen bicyclists jumping up and down on the loops trying to get a light to change. That doesn't work, but it sure is entertaining to watch.

Many others believe that small cylinders attached to a traffic light's support arms, like that in Figure 4.73(b), detect vehicles. Those instead are typically devices that detect a special encoded radio or infrared-light signal from emergency vehicles, causing the traffic light to turn green for the emergency vehicle (e.g., 3M's "Opticom" system). Such systems are another example of digital systems, reducing the time needed by emergency vehicles to reach the scene of an emergency as well as reducing accidents involving the emergency vehicle itself proceeding through a traffic light, thus often saving lives.

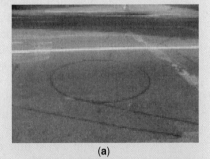

(a)

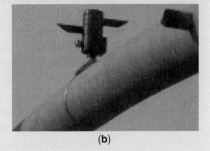

(b)

Figure 4.73 (a) Inductive loop for detecting a vehicle on a road, (b) emergency vehicle signal sensor for changing an intersection's traffic light to green for the approaching emergency vehicle.

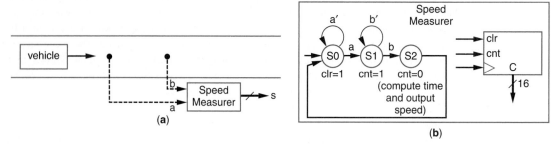

Figure 4.74 Measuring vehicle speeds in a highway speed measuring system: (a) sensors in road feeding into the speed measuring system, (b) state machine controlling an up-counter.

determine a car's speed in miles per hour. We omit the implementation details of the speed computation.

Timers

A *timer* is a sequential component that can be programmed to repeatedly generate a short pulse at a user-specified time interval such as every 300 milliseconds. The component is sometimes called a *programmable interval timer.* A timer has a base time unit such as 1 microsecond. A designer programs the timer to a desired time interval by loading a binary number representing the desired multiplication of the base time unit. If a timer's base time unit is 1 microsecond and the designer wants the timer to pulse every 50 microseconds, the designer would load 50 into the timer. If the designer wants a pulse every 300 milliseconds, which means 300,000 microseconds, the designer would load the number 300,000 into the timer. A timer's *width* is the bitwidth of the number than can be loaded; the width defines the maximum time interval of the timer. For example, a 32-bit timer with a base time of 1 microsecond has a maximum interval of $2^{32}*1$ microseconds, or about 4,000 seconds. A timer has an enable control input that activates the timing function.

A timer can be designed using a parallel-load down-counter and a register as in Figure 4.75(a), which shows the design for a 32-bit timer with a 1 microsecond base time unit. The register holds the multiplier number decremented by 1 to compensate for the fact that a down-counter includes 0 in its count; thus, a designer should only load a value greater than 1 (note: most timers actually require the user to subtract 1 from the number before loading; we include the −1 inside the timer to make subsequent designs easier to understand). An input `load` set to `1` causes the register to be loaded with input M, and also loads the down-counter with input M. The down-counter is clocked by a 1 microsecond oscillator, which could be a standalone oscillator that is internal to the timer, or which could be derived by dividing the clock input of the timer. When `enable` is `1`, the counter counts down once per microsecond until reaching 0, at which time the counter's `tc` output becomes `1`, causing the output Q to become `1` for one microsecond. The `tc=1` also causes the counter to be loaded again with the value held in the register.

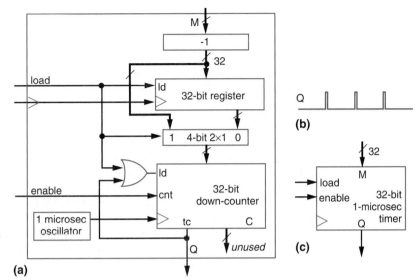

Figure 4.75 Timer:
(a) internal design,
(b) example timer output
when enabled, (c) block
symbol.

A timer "ticks" like a clock when enabled as shown in Figure 4.75(b). The period is M times the base time unit. The block symbol for a timer is shown in Figure 4.75(c).

A timer is similar to an oscillator. One distinction is that a timer is typically programmable while an oscillator is not, but the distinction is not very rigid and sometimes a timer is called a "programmable timer/oscillator." In terms of usage, designers typically use an oscillator as the clock input of sequential components, whereas designers use a timer to generate events that are detected by an FSM's transition conditions and thus serve as inputs to a controller.

Some variations of timers are commonplace. One variation is a timer with an additional control input once; if that input is 1, the timer stops when it reaches the end of its first interval, thus holding its Q output at 1 rather than pulsing Q and repeating. Such a timer is referred to as a one-shot timer or simply a ***one-shot***. Another variation is a timer having a second register that can be loaded with the time for which each pulse should be held high. For example, if a timer has a base unit of 1 microsecond, a multiplier register loaded with 500, and a time-high register loaded with 200, then the timer's output would be 1 for 200 microseconds, then 0 for 300 microseconds, then 1 for 200 microseconds again, and so on. This timer variation is known as a ***pulse-width modulator*** or ***PWM***. The percentage of time spent high during each interval is known as the PWM's *duty cycle*; the above example's duty cycle is 200/500 = 40%.

Digital circuits are commonly used in systems that must sample inputs or generate outputs at specified time intervals. For example, an audio recording system (see Chapter 1) may sample an input audio signal 44,000 times per second, a traffic light controller system may keep a green light on for 30 seconds, a laser surgery system may turn on a laser for 500 microseconds, or a video display system may write a new value to a point on the display (a pixel) every 0.1 microseconds. The circuits can use timer components to generate events that indicate when specific time intervals have passed.

Example 4.20 Laser surgery system using a timer

Chapter 3 introduced an example of a laser surgery system, illustrated again in Figure 4.76(a), that turned on a laser for a specific time interval. In that example, the desired time interval of 30 ns was achieved by introducing three states into an FSM that was clocked at 10 ns. What if the desired time interval was instead 300 ms? Introducing states for this interval and a 10 ns clock would require introducing 30 million states, which is clearly not practical for an FSM. Instead, we can use a timer. We connect a controller to a 32-bit 1-microsecond timer as in Figure 4.76(b). We capture the behavior of the controller as the FSM in Figure 4.76(c); the timing behavior of this FSM is shown in Figure 4.76(d). The *Off* state loads the timer with 300,000. When the button is pressed, the FSM enters state *Strt*, which starts the timer; the timer will actually start on the next clock cycle. On that next clock cycle, the FSM enters state *On* and turns on the laser. 300 ms later, the timer's output Q will become 1. On the next clock (10 ns later), the FSM enters state *Off*, which turns off the laser and also disables the timer. The next time the button is pressed, the process starts over again.

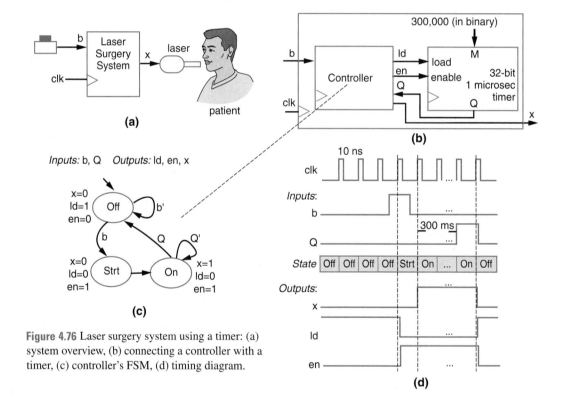

Figure 4.76 Laser surgery system using a timer: (a) system overview, (b) connecting a controller with a timer, (c) controller's FSM, (d) timing diagram.

Note that the system actually keeps the laser on for 300 ms plus 10 ns; this is an effect of using the external timer, and is not likely to be significant for this particular system's desired time interval.

▶ 4.10 REGISTER FILES

An *MxN register file* is a datapath memory component that provides efficient access to a collection of *M* registers, where each register is *N* bits wide. To understand the need for a register file component in building good datapaths, rather than just using *M* separate registers, consider Example 4.13.

Example 4.21 Above-mirror display system using 16 32-bit registers

Recall the above-mirror display system from Example 4.2. Four 8-bit registers were multiplexed to an 8-bit output. Suppose instead that the system required sixteen 32-bit registers, to display more values, each of more precision. We would therefore need a 32-bit-wide 16x1 multiplexor, as shown in Figure 4.77. From a purely digital logic perspective, the design is just fine. But in practice, that multiplexor is very inefficient. Count the number of wires that would be fed into that multiplexor—16x32 = 512 wires. That's a lot of wires to try to route from the registers to the muxes—try plugging 512 wires into the back of one stereo system for a hands-on demonstration. Having too many wires in a small area is known as *routing congestion*.

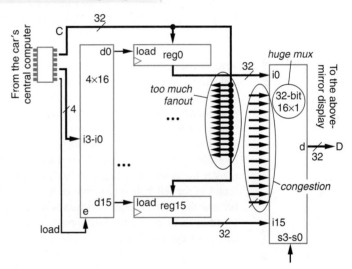

Figure 4.77 Above-mirror display design, assuming sixteen 32-bit registers. The mux has too many input wires, resulting in congestion. Also, the data lines C are fanned out to too many registers, resulting in weak current.

Likewise, consider routing the data input to all sixteen registers. Each data input wire is being branched into sixteen subwires. Imagine electric current being like a river of water—branching a main river into sixteen smaller rivers will yield much less water flow in each smaller river than in the main river. Likewise, branching a wire, known as *fanout*, can only be done so many times before the branched wires' currents are too small to sufficiently control transistors. Furthermore, low-current wires may be very slow, so fanout can create long delays over wires too.

The fanout and routing congestion problems illustrated in the previous example can be solved by observing that the system never needs to load more than one register at a time, nor read more than one register at a time either. An *MxN* register file solves the fanout and congestion problems by grouping the *M* registers into a single component, with that component having a single *N*-bit-wide data input, and a single *N*-bit-wide data output. The wiring inside the component is done carefully to handle fanout and congestion. Figure 4.78 shows a block symbol of a 16x32 register file (16 registers, each 32-bits wide).

Consider writing a value to a register in a register file. We would place the data to be written on the input W_data. We then need a way to indicate which register to write this data into. Since there are 16 registers, four bits are needed to specify a particular register. Those four bits are called the register's *address*. We would thus set input W_addr to the desired register's address. For example, to write to register 7, we would set W_addr=0111. To indicate that we actually want to write on a particular clock cycle (we won't want to write on every cycle), we would set the input W_en to 1. The collection of inputs W_data, W_addr, and W_en is known as a register file's *write port*.

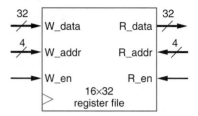

Figure 4.78 16x32 register file symbol.

Reading is similar. We would specify the register to read on input R_addr, and set R_en=1. Those values cause the register file to output the addressed register's contents onto output R_data. R_data, R_addr, and R_en are known as a register file's *read port*.

The read and write ports are independent of one another. During one clock cycle, we can write to one register and read from another (or the same) register. Such simultaneous reading and writing works as follows. When the addresses appear at the register file's inputs, the register file will shortly afterwards (due to internal wire/gate delays) output the data corresponding to the read address. When the next rising clock edge arrives, the register file will shortly afterwards (due to internal delays) load the write data into the register corresponding to the write address.

Let's consider how to internally design a register file. For simplicity, consider a 4x32 register file, rather than the 16x32 register file described above. One internal design of a 4x32 register file is shown in Figure 4.79. Let's consider the circuitry for writing to this register file, found in the left half of the figure. If W_en=0, the register file won't write to any register, because the write decoder's outputs will be all 0s. If W_en=1, then the write decoder decodes W_addr and sets to 1 the load input of exactly one register. That register will be written on the next clock cycle with the value on W_data.

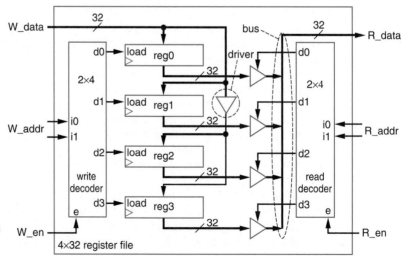

Figure 4.79 One possible internal design of a 4x32 register file.

Notice the circled triangular one-input one-output component placed on the W_data line (there would actually be 32 such components since W_data is 32 bits wide). That component is known as a ***driver***, sometimes called a ***buffer***, illustrated in Figure 4.80(a). A driver's output value equals its input, but the output is a stronger (higher current) signal. Remember the fanout problem described in Example 4.21? A driver reduces the fanout problem. In Figure 4.79, the W_data lines only fanout to two registers before they go through the driver. The driver's output then fans out to only two more registers. Thus, instead of a fanout of four, the W_data lines have a fanout of only two (actually three if you count the driver itself). The insertion of drivers is beyond the scope of this book, and is instead a subject for a VLSI design book or an advanced digital design book. But seeing at least one example of the use of a driver hopefully gives you an idea of one reason why a register file is a useful component—the component hides the complexity of fanout from a designer.

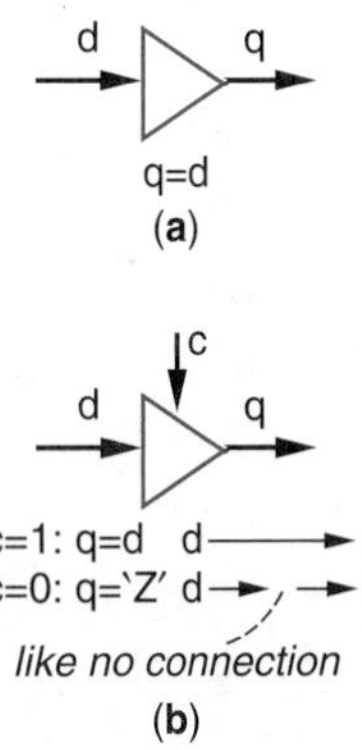

To understand the read circuitry, you must first understand the behavior of another new component in Figure 4.79—the triangular component having two inputs and one output. That component is known as a ***three-state driver*** or ***three-state buffer***, illustrated in Figure 4.80(b). When the control input c is 1, the component acts like a regular driver—the component's output equals its input. However, when the control input c is 0, the driver's output is neither 0 nor 1, but instead what is known as high-impedance, written as "Z." High-impedance can be thought of as no connection at all between the driver's input and output. "Three-state" means the driver has three possible output states—0, 1, and Z.

Consider the circuitry for reading from the register file, found in the right half of Figure 4.79. If R_en=0, the register file won't read from any register, since the read decoder's outputs will be all 0s, meaning all the three-state drivers will output Zs, and thus the output R_data will be high-impedance. If R_en=1, then the read decoder decodes R_addr and sets to 1 the control input of exactly one three-state driver, which will pass its register value through to the R_data output.

Such components are more commonly known as "tri-state" drivers rather than "three-state." But "tri-state" is a registered trademark of National Semiconductor Corp., so rather than putting the required trademark symbol after every use of the term "tri-state," many documents use the term "three-state."

Be aware that each shown three-state driver actually represents a set of 32 three-state drivers, one for each of the 32 wires coming from the 32-bit registers and going to the 32-bit R_data output. All 32 drivers in a set are controlled by the same control input.

The wires fed by the various three-state drivers are known as a ***shared bus***, as indicated in Figure 4.79 and detailed in Figure 4.81. A shared bus is a popular alternative to a multiplexor when each mux data input is many bits wide and/or when there are many mux data inputs, because a shared bus results in less congestion.

Notice that the register file design scales well to larger numbers of registers. The write data lines can be

d ▷ q

q=d

(a)

d ▷ q

c=1: q=d   d──────▶ q
c=0: q='Z' d─▶╱, ─▶ q

like no connection

(b)

Figure 4.80 (a) driver, (b) three-state driver.

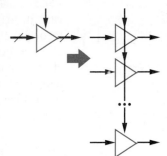

Figure 4.81 Each driver in Figure 4.79 is actually 32 drivers.

driven by more drivers if necessary. The read data lines are fed from three-state drivers, and thus there is no congestion at a single multiplexor. The reader may wish to compare the register file design in Figure 4.79 with the design in Figure 4.5, which was essentially a poor design of a register file.

Figure 4.82 provides example timing diagrams describing writing and reading of a register file. During *cycle1*, the contents of the register file are unknown, so the register file's contents are shown as "?." During *cycle1*, we set W_data=9 (in binary, of course), W_addr=3, and W_en=1. Those values cause a write of 9 to register file location 3 on the first clock edge. Notice that we had set R_en=0, so the register file outputs nothing ("z"), and the value we put on R_addr does not matter (the value is a "don't care," written as "x").

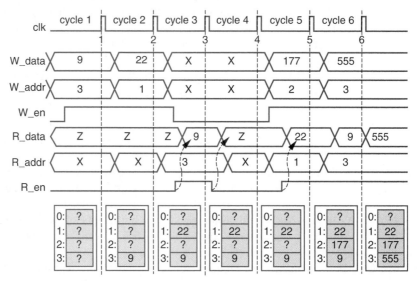

Figure 4.82 Writing and reading a register file.

During *cycle2*, we set W_data=22, W_addr=1, and W_en=1. These values cause a write of 22 to register file location 1 on clock edge 2.

During *cycle3*, we set W_en=0, so then it doesn't matter to what values we set W_data and W_addr. We also set R_addr=3 and R_en=1. Those values cause the register file to read out the contents of register file location 3 onto R_data, causing R_data to output 9. Notice that the reading is not synchronized to clock edge 3—R_data changes soon after R_en becomes 1. Examining the design of Figure 4.79 should make clear why reading is not synchronous—setting R_en to 1 simply enables the output decoder to turn on one set of the three-state buffers.

During *cycle4*, we return R_en to 0. Note that this causes R_data to become "z" again.

During *cycle5*, we want to simultaneously write and read the register file. We read location 1 (which causes R_data to become 22) while simultaneously writing location 2 with the value 177.

Finally, during *cycle6*, we want to simultaneously read and write the same register file location. We set R_addr=3 and R_en=1, causing location 3's contents of 9 to appear on R_data shortly after setting those values. We also set W_addr=3, W_data=555, and

`W_en=1`. On clock edge 6, 555 thus gets stored into location 3. Notice that soon after that clock edge, `R_data` also changes to 555.

The ability to simultaneously read and write locations of a register file, even the same location, is a widely used feature of register files. The next example makes use of that feature.

Example 4.22 Above-mirror display system using a 16x32 register file

Example 4.2 used four 8-bit registers for an above-mirror display system. Example 4.21 extended the system to use sixteen 32-bit registers, resulting in fanout and congestion problems. We can redo that example using a register file. The design is shown in Figure 4.83. Since the system always outputs one of the register values to the display, we tied the `R_en` input to 1. Notice that the writing and reading of particular registers are independent of one another.

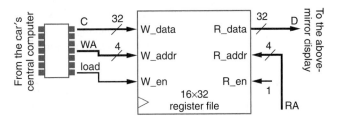

Figure 4.83 Above-mirror display design, using a register file.

A register file having one read port and one write port is sometimes referred to as a **dual-ported register file**. To make clear that the two ports consist of one read port and one write port, such a register file may be referred to as follows: *dual-ported (1 read, 1 write) register file*.

A register file may actually have just one port, which would be used for both reading and writing. Such a register file has only one set of data lines that can serve as inputs or outputs, one set of address inputs, an enable input, and one more input indicating whether we wish to write or read the register file. Such a register file is known as a **single-ported register file**.

Multiported (2 Read, 1 Write) Register File. Many register files have three ports: one write port, and two read ports. Thus, in the same clock cycle, two registers can be read simultaneously, and another register written. Such a register file is especially useful in a microprocessor, since a typical microprocessor instruction operates on two registers and stores the result in a third register, like in the instruction "R0 <— R1 + R2."

We can create a second read port in a register file by adding another set of lines, `Rb_data`, `Rb_addr`, and `Rb_en`. We would introduce a second read decoder with inputs `Rb_addr` and enable input `Rb_en`, a second set of three-state drivers, and a second bus connected to the `Rb_data` output.

Other Register File Variations. Register files come in all sorts of configurations. Typical numbers of registers in a register file range from 4 to 1024, and typical register widths range from 8 bits to 64 bits per register, but sizes may vary beyond those ranges. Register files may have one port, two ports, three ports, or even more, but increasing to many more than three ports can slow down the register file's performance and increase its size significantly, due to the difficulty of routing all those wires around inside the register file. Nevertheless, you'll occasionally run across register files with perhaps 3 write ports and 3 read ports, when concurrent access is critical.

▷ 4.11 DATAPATH COMPONENT TRADEOFFS (SEE SECTION 6.4)

For each datapath component introduced in previous sections, we created the most basic and easy-to-understand implementation. This section, which physically appears in the book as Section 6.4, describes alternative implementations of several datapath components. Each alternative trades off one design criteria for another—most of those alternatives trade off larger size in exchange for less delay. One approach to using this book involves studying those alternative implementations immediately after studying the basic implementations (meaning now). Another approach studies those alternative implementations later, after studying how to use datapath components during register-transfer level design.

▷ 4.12 DATAPATH COMPONENT DESCRIPTION USING HARDWARE DESCRIPTION LANGUAGES (SEE SECTION 9.4)

This section, which physically appears in the book as Section 9.4, shows how to use HDLs to describe several datapath components. One approach to using this book studies such HDL use now, while another approach studies such HDL use later.

▷ 4.13 PRODUCT PROFILE: AN ULTRASOUND MACHINE

If you or someone you know has ever had a baby, then you may have seen ultrasound images of that baby before he/she was born, like the images of a fetus' head in Figure 4.84(a).

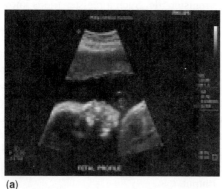

(a)

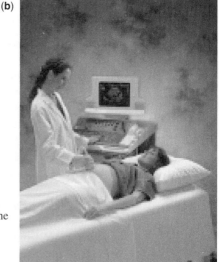

(b)

Figure 4.84 (a) Ultrasound image of a fetus, created using an ultrasound device that is simply placed on the mother's abdomen (b) and that forms the image by generating sound waves and listening to the echoes. Photos courtesy of Philips Medical Systems.

That image wasn't taken by a camera somehow inserted into the uterus, but rather by an ultrasound machine pressed against the mother's skin and pointed toward the fetus. Ultrasound imaging is now common practice in obstetrics—mainly helping doctors to track the fetus' progress and correct potential problems early, but also giving parents a huge thrill when they get their first glimpse of their baby's head, hands, and little feet!

Functional Overview

This section briefly describes the key functional ideas of how ultrasound imaging works. Digital designers don't typically work in a vacuum—instead, they apply their skills to particular applications, and thus designers typically learn the key functional ideas underlying those applications. We therefore introduce you to the basic ideas of ultrasound applications. Ultrasound imaging works by sending sound waves into the body and listening to the echoes that return. Objects like bones yield different echoes than objects like skin or fluids, so an ultrasound machine processes the different echoes to generate images like those in Figure 4.84(a)—strong echoes might be displayed as white, weak ones as black. Today's ultrasound machines rely heavily on fast digital circuits to generate the sounds waves, listen to the echoes, and process the echo data to generate good quality images in real time.

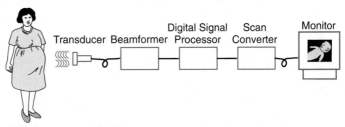

Figure 4.85 Basic components of an ultrasound machine.

Figure 4.85 illustrates the basic parts of an ultrasound machine. Let's discuss each part individually.

Transducer

A *transducer* converts energy from one form to another. You're certainly familiar with one type of transducer, a stereo speaker, which converts electrical energy into sound by changing the current in a wire, which causes a nearby magnet to move back and forth, which pushes the air and hence creates sound. Another familiar transducer is a dynamic microphone, which converts sound into electrical energy by letting sound waves move a magnet, which induces current changes in a nearby wire. In an ultrasound machine, the transducer converts electrical pulses into sound pulses, and sound pulses (the echoes) into electrical pulses, but the transducer uses piezoelectric crystals instead of magnets. Applying electric current to such a crystal causes the crystal to change shape rapidly, or vibrate, thus generating sound waves—typically in the 1 to 30 Megahertz frequency range. Humans can't hear much above 30 kilohertz—the term "ultrasound" refers to the fact that the frequency is beyond human hearing. Inversely, sound waves (echoes) hitting the crystal create electric current. An ultrasound machine's transducer component may contain hundreds of such crystals, which we can think of as hundreds of transducers. Each such transducer is considered to form a *channel*.

Beamformer

A *beamformer electronically* "focuses" and "steers" the sound beam of an array of transducers to or from particular focal points, without actually moving any hardware like a dish to obtain such focusing and steering.

To understand the idea of beamforming, we must first understand the idea of additive sound. Consider two loud fireworks exploding at the same time, one 1 mile away from you, and the other 2 miles away. You'll hear the closer firework after about 5 seconds—assuming sound travels 0.2 miles/second (or 1 mile every 5 seconds)—a reasonable approximation. You'll hear the farther firework after about 10 seconds. So you'll hear "boom ... (five seconds pass) ... boom." However, suppose instead that the closer firework exploded 5 seconds later than the farther one. Then you'll hear both at the same time—one big "BOOM!" That's because the two sounds add together. Now suppose there are 100 fireworks spread throughout a city, and you want all the sound from those fireworks to reach one particular house (perhaps somebody you don't like very much) at the same time. You can do this by exploding the closer fireworks later than the farther fireworks. If you time everything just right, that particular house will hear a tremendously loud single "BOOOOOM!!!!" probably rattling the house's walls pretty well, as if one huge firework had exploded. Other houses throughout the city will instead hear a series of quieter booms, since the timing of the explosions don't result in all the sounds adding at those other houses.

Now you understand a basic principle of beamforming: If you have multiple sound sources (fireworks in our example, transducers in an ultrasound machine) in different locations, you can cause the sound to add together at any desired point in space, by carefully timing the generation of sound from each source such that all the sound waves arrive at the desired point at the same time. In other words, you can *electronically* focus and steer the sound beam by introducing appropriate delays. Focusing and steering the sound to a particular point is useful because then *that point will produce a much louder echo than all other points*, so we can easily hear the echo from that point over all the echoes from other points.

Figure 4.86 illustrates the concept of electronic focusing and steering, using two sound sources to focus and steer a beam to a desired point *X*.

At the first time step (Figure 4.86(a)), the bottom source has begun transmitting its sound wave. After two time steps (Figure 4.86(b)), the top source has begun transmitting its sound wave. After three time steps (Figure 4.86(c)), the waves from both sensors reach the focal point, adding together. They'll continue adding as long as the waves from both sources are in phase with one another. We can simplify the drawing by showing only the lines from the sources to the focal point, as shown in Figure 4.86(d).

An ultrasound machine uses this ability to electronically focus and steer sound, in order to scan, point by point, the entire region in front of the transducers. The machine scans each point tens of times per second.

For each focal point, the machine needs to listen to the echo that comes back from whatever object is located at the focal point, to determine if that object is bone, skin, blood, etc., utilizing the fact that each such object generates a different echo. Remember, the echo from the focal point will be louder than echoes from other points, because the sound adds at that point. We can use beamforming to also focus in on a particular point in space that we want to *listen* to. In the same way that we generated sound pulses with par-

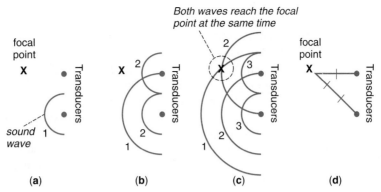

Figure 4.86 Focusing sound at a particular point using beamforming: (a) first time step—only the bottom transducer generates sound, (b) second time step—the top transducer now generates sound too, (c) third time step—the two sound waves add at the focal point, (d) an illustration showing that the top transducer is two time steps away from the focal point, while the bottom transducer is three time steps away, meaning the top transducer should generate sound one time step later than the bottom transducer.

ticular delays to focus the sound on a particular point, likewise, to "listen" to the sounds from a particular point, we also want to introduce delays to the signals received by the transducers. That's because the sounds will arrive at the closer transducers sooner than at the farther transducers, so by using appropriate delays, we can "line up" the signals from each transducer so that the sounds coming from the focal point all add together. This concept is shown in Figure 4.87.

Note that there will certainly be echoes from other points in the region, but those coming from the focal point will be much stronger—hence, the weaker echoes can be filtered out.

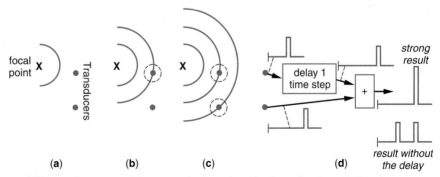

Figure 4.87 Listening to sound from a particular point using beamforming: (a) first time step, (b) second time step—the top transducer has heard the sound first, (c) third time step—the bottom transducer hears the sound at this time, (d) delaying the top transducer by one time step results in the waves from the focal point adding, amplifying the sound.

Notice that beamforming can be used to listen to a particular point even if the sounds coming from that point are not echoes coming back from our own sound pulses—the sound could be coming from the object at the point itself, such as a car engine or a person talking. Beamforming is the electronic equivalent to pointing a big parabolic dish in a particular direction, but beamforming requires no moving parts.

Beamforming is tremendously common in a wide variety of sonar applications, such as observing a fetus, observing a human heart, searching for oil underground, monitoring the surroundings of a submarine, spying, etc. Beamforming is used in some hearing aids having multiple microphones, to focus in on the source of detected speech—in that case, the beamforming must be adaptive. Beamforming can be used in multimicrophone cell phones to focus in on the user's voice, and can even be used in cellular telephone base stations (using radio signals, though, not sound waves) to focus a signal going to or coming from a cell phone.

Sound waves are vibrations of air, water, or some other medium, traveling at nearly a thousand miles per hour through air. Radio waves are electromagnetic waves, requiring no such medium (they can travel through space), and traveling at nearly a billion miles per hour (the speed of light in a vacuum).

Signal Processor, Scan Converter, and Monitor

The signal processor analyzes the echo data of every point in the scanned region, by filtering out noise (see Section 5.13 for a discussion on filtering), interpolating between points, assigning a level of gray to each point depending on the echoes heard (echoes corresponding to bones might be shaded as white, liquid as black, and skin as gray, for example), and other tasks. The result is a gray-scale image of the region. The scan converter steps through this image to generate the necessary signals for a black-and-white monitor, and the monitor displays the image.

Digital Circuits in an Ultrasound Machine's Beamformer

Much of the control and signal processing tasks in an ultrasound machine are carried out using software running on one or more microprocessors, typically special microprocessors specifically designed for digital signal processing, known as digital signal processors, or DSPs. But certain tasks are much more amenable to custom digital circuitry, such as those in the beamformer.

Sound Generation and Echo Delay Circuits

Beamforming during the sound generation step consists of providing appropriate delays to hundreds of transducers. Those delays vary depending on the focal point, so they can't be built into the transducers themselves. Instead, we can place a delay circuit in front of each transducer, as shown in Figure 4.88. For a given focal point, the DSP writes the appropriate delay value into each delay circuit, by writing the delay value on the bus labeled `delay_out`, writing the "address" on the lines labeled `addr`, and enabling the decoder. The decoder will thus set the load line of one of the *OutDelay* components.

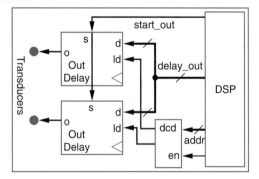

Figure 4.88 Transducer output delay circuits for two channels.

After writing to every such component, the DSP starts all of them simultaneously by setting `start_out` to `1`. Each *OutDelay* component will, after the specified delay, pulse its o output, which we'll assume causes the transducer to generate sound. The DSP would then set `start_out` to `0`, and then listen for the echo.

We can implement the *OutDelay* component using a down-counter with parallel load, as shown in Figure 4.89. The parallel load inputs L and ld load the down-counter with its count value. The cnt input commences the down-counting—when the counter reaches zero, the counter pulses tc. The data output of the counter is unused in this implementation.

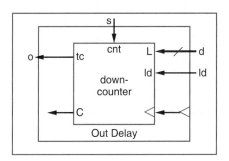

Figure 4.89 OutDelay circuit.

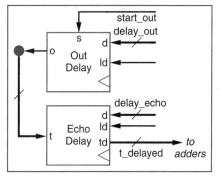

Figure 4.90 Tranducer output and echo delay circuits for one channel.

After the ultrasound machine sends out sound waves focused on a particular focal point, the machine must listen to the echo coming back from that focal point. This listening requires appropriate delays for each transducer to account for the differing distances of each transducer from the focal point. Thus, each transducer needs another delay circuit for delaying the received echo signal, as shown in Figure 4.90. The *EchoDelay* component receives on input t the signal from the transducer, which we'll assume has been digitized into a stream of *N*-bit values. The component should output that signal on output t_delayed, delayed by the appropriate amount. The delay amount can be written by the DSP using the component's d and ld inputs.

We can implement the *EchoDelay* component using a series of registers, as shown in Figure 4.91. That implementation can delay the output signal by 0, 1, 2, or 3 clock cycles, simply using the appropriate select line values for the 4x1 mux. A longer register chain, along with a larger mux, would support longer delays. The DSP configures the delay amount by writing to the top register, which sets the 4x1 mux select lines. A more flexible implementation of the *EchoDelay* component would instead use a timer component.

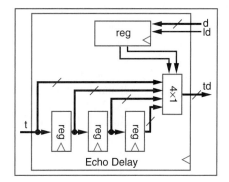

Figure 4.91 EchoDelay circuit.

Summation Circuits—Adder Tree

The output of each transducer, appropriately delayed, should be summed to create a single echo signal from the focal point, as was illustrated in Figure 4.87. That illustration had only two transducers, and thus only one adder. What if we have 256 transducers, as would be more likely in a real ultrasound machine? How do we add 256 values? We could add the values in a linear way, as illustrated on the left side of Figure 4.92(a) for eight values. The delay of that circuit is roughly equal to the delay of seven adders. For 256 values, the delay would roughly be that of 255 adders. That's a very long delay.

We can do better by reorganizing how we compute the sum, using a configuration of adders known as an **adder tree**. In other words, rather than computing $(((((((A+B)+C)+D)+E)+F)+G)+H$, depicted in Figure 4.92(a), we could instead compute $((A+B)+(C+D))$ + $((E+F)+(G+H))$, as shown in Figure 4.92(b). The answer comes out the same, and uses the same number of adders, but the latter method computes four additions in parallel, then two additions in parallel, and then performs a last addition. The delay is thus only that of three adders. For 256 values, the tree's first level would compute 128 additions in parallel, the second level would compute

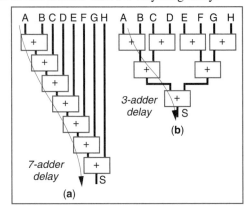

Figure 4.92 Adding many numbers: (a) linearly, (b) using an adder tree. Note that both methods use seven adders.

64 additions, then 32, then 16, then 8, then 4, then 2, and finally 1 last addition. Thus, that adder tree would have eight levels, meaning a total delay equal to eight adder delays. That's a lot faster than 256 adder delays—*32 times faster*, in fact.

The output of the adder tree can be fed into a memory to keep track of the results for the DSP, which may access the results sometime after they are generated.

Multipliers

We presented a greatly simplified version of beamforming above. In reality, many other factors must be considered during beamforming. Several of those considerations can be accounted for by multiplying each channel with specific constant values, which the DSP again sets individually for each channel. For example, focusing on a point close to the handheld device may require us to more heavily weigh the incoming signals of transducers near the center of the device. A channel may therefore actually include a multiplier, as shown in Figure 4.93. The DSP

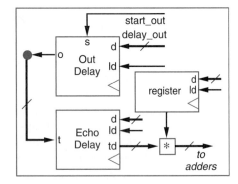

Figure 4.93 Channel extended with a multiplier.

could write to the register shown, which would represent a constant by which the transducer signal would be multiplied.

Our introduction of the ultrasound machine is greatly simplified from a real machine, yet even in this simplified introduction, you can see many of this chapter's datapath components in use. We used a down-counter to implement the *OutDelay* component, and several registers along with muxes for the *EchoDelay* component. We used many adders to sum the incoming transducer signals. And we used a multiplier to weigh those incoming signals.

Future Challenges in Ultrasound

Over the past two decades, ultrasound machines have moved from mostly analog machines to mostly digital machines. The digital systems consist of both custom digital circuits and software on DSPs and microprocessors, working together to create real-time images.

One of the main trends in ultrasound machines involves creating three-dimensional (3-D) images in real time. Most ultrasound machines of the 1990s and 2000s generated two-dimensional images, with the quality of those images (e.g., more focal points per image) improving during those decades. In contrast to two-dimensional ultrasound, generating 3-D images requires viewing the region of interest from different perspectives, just like people view things from their two eyes. Such generation also requires extensive computations to create a 3-D image from the two (or more) perspectives. The result is a picture like that in Figure 4.94.

That's a fetus' face. Impressive, isn't it? Keep in mind that image is made solely from sound waves bouncing into a woman's womb. Color can also be added to distinguish among different fluids and tissues. Those computations take time, but faster processors, coupled with clever custom digital circuits, are bringing real-time 3-D ultrasound closer to reality.

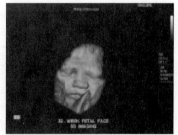

Figure 4.94 3-D ultrasound image of a fetus's face. Photo courtesy of Philips Medical Systems.

Another trend is toward making ultrasound machines smaller and lighter, so that they can be used in a wider variety of health care situations. Early machines were big and heavy, with more recent ones coming on rollable carts. Some recent versions are handheld. A related trend is making ultrasound machines cheaper, so that perhaps every doctor could have a machine in every examination room, every ambulance could carry a machine to help emergency personnel ascertain the extent of certain wounds, and so on.

Ultrasound is used for numerous other medical applications, such as imaging of the heart to detect artery or valve problems. Ultrasound is also used in various other applications, like submarine region monitoring.

▶ 4.14 CHAPTER SUMMARY

This chapter began (Section 4.1) by introducing the idea of new building blocks intended for common operations on multibit data, with those blocks known as datapath components. The chapter then introduced a number of datapath components, including registers, adders, comparators, multipliers, subtractors, arithmetic-logic units, shifters, counters, timers, and register files. For each component, the chapter examined two aspects: the internal design of the component, and the use of the component as part of a datapath to implement a desired system.

The chapter ended (Section 4.13) by describing some basic principles underlying the operation of an ultrasound machine, and showing how several of the datapath components might be used to implement parts of such a machine. One thing you might notice is how designing a real ultrasound machine would require some knowledge of the domain of ultrasound. The requirement that a software programmer or digital designer have some understanding of an application domain is quite common.

In the coming chapter, you will apply your knowledge of combinational logic design, sequential logic design (controller design), and datapath components, to build digital circuits that can implement general and powerful computations.

▶ 4.15 EXERCISES

An asterisk (*) indicates an especially challenging problem.

For exercises relating to datapath components, each problem may indicate whether the problem emphasizes the component's internal design or the component's use.

SECTION 4.2: REGISTERS

4.1 Trace the behavior of an 8-bit parallel-load register with 8-bit input I, 8-bit output Q, and load control input ld by completing the timing diagram in Figure 4.95.

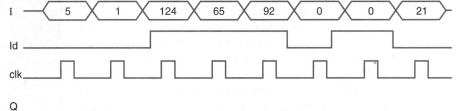

Figure 4.95 Timing diagram.

4.2 Trace the behavior of an 8-bit parallel-load register with 8-bit input I, 8-bit output Q, load control input ld, and synchronous clear input clr by completing the timing diagram in Figure 4.96.

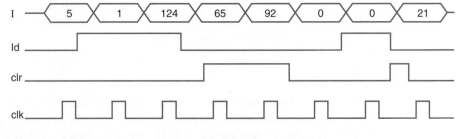

Figure 4.96 Timing diagram.

4.3 Design a 4-bit register with 2 control inputs s1 and s0; 4 data inputs I3, I2, I1, and I0; and 4 data outputs Q3, Q2, Q1, and Q0. When s1s0=00, the register maintains its value. When s1s0=01, the register loads I3...I0. When s1s0=10, the register clears itself to 0000. When s1s0=11, the register complements itself, so for example, 0000 would become 1111, and 1010 would become 0101. (*Component design problem.*)

4.4 Repeat the previous problem, but when s1s0=11, the register reverses its bits, so 1110 would become 0111, and 1010 would become 0101. (*Component design problem.*)

4.5 Design an 8-bit register with 2 control inputs s1 and s0, 8 data inputs I7...I0, and 8 data outputs Q7...Q0. s1s0=00 means maintain the present value, s1s0=01 means load, and s1s0=10 means clear. s1s0=11 means to swap the high nibble with the low nibble (a nibble is 4 bits), so 11110000 would become 00001111, and 11000101 would become 01011100. (*Component design problem.*)

4.6 The radar gun used by a police officer outputs a radar signal and measures the speed of cars as they pass. However, when an officer wants to ticket an individual for speeding, he must save the measured speed of the car on the radar unit. Build a system to implement a speed save feature for the radar gun. The system has an 8-bit speed input S, an input B from the save button on the radar gun, and an 8-bit output D that will be sent to the radar's gun speed display. (*Component use problem.*)

4.7 Design a system with an 8-bit input I that can be stored in 8-bit registers A, B, and/or C when input La, Lb, and/or Lc is 1, respectively. So if inputs La and Lb are 1, then registers A and B will be loaded with input I, but register C will keep its current value. Furthermore, if input R is 1, then the register values swap such that $A=B$, $B=C$, and $C=A$. Input R has priority over the L inputs. The system has one clock input also. (*Component use problem.*)

SECTION 4.3: ADDERS

4.8 Trace the values appearing at the outputs of a 3-bit carry-ripple adder for every one full-adder-delay time period when adding 111 with 011. Assume all inputs were previously 0 for a long time.

4.9 Assuming all gates have a delay of 1 ns, compute the longest time required to add two numbers using an 8-bit carry-ripple adder.

4.10 Assuming AND gates have a delay of 2 ns, OR gates have a delay of 1 ns, and XOR gates have a delay of 3 ns, compute the longest time required to add two numbers using an 8-bit carry-ripple adder.

4.11 Design a 10-bit carry-ripple adder using 4-bit carry-ripple adders. (*Component use problem.*)

4.12 Design a system that computes the sum of three 8-bit numbers, using 8-bit carry-ripple adders. (*Component use problem.*)

4.13 Design an adder that computes the sum of four 8-bit numbers, using 8-bit carry-ripple adders. (*Component use problem.*)

4.14 Design a digital thermometer system that can compensate for errors in the temperature sensing device's output T, which is an 8-bit input to the system. The compensation amount can be positive only and comes to the system as a 3-bit binary number c, b, and a (a is the least significant bit), which come from a 3-pin DIP switch. The system should output the compensated temperature on an 8-bit output U. (*Component use problem.*)

4.15 We can add three 8-bit numbers by chaining one 8-bit carry-ripple adder to the output of another 8-bit carry-ripple adder. Assuming every gate has a delay of 1 time-unit, compute the longest delay of this three 8-bit number adder. Hint: you may have to look carefully inside the carry-ripple adders, even inside the full-adders, to correctly compute the longest delay from any input to any output. (*Component use problem.*)

SECTION 4.4: COMPARATORS

4.16 Trace through the execution of the 4-bit magnitude comparator shown in Figure 4.43 when $a=15$ and $b=12$. Be sure to show how the comparisons propagate thought the individual comparators.

4.17 Design a system that determines if three 4-bit numbers are equal, by connecting 4-bit magnitude comparators together and using additional components if necessary. *(Component use problem.)*

4.18 Design a 4-bit carry-ripple-style magnitude comparator that has two outputs, a greater-than or equal-to output gte, and a less-than or equal-to output lte. Be sure to clearly show the equations used in developing the individual 1-bit comparators and how they are connected to form the 4-bit circuit. *(Component design problem.)*

4.19 Design a circuit that outputs 1 if the circuit's 8-bit input equals 99:
   (a) using an equality comparator,
   (b) using gates only.
   Hint: In the case of (b), you need only 1 AND gate and some inverters. *(Component use problem.)*

4.20 Use magnitude comparators and logic to design a circuit that computes the minimum of three 8-bit numbers. *(Component use problem.)*

4.21 Use magnitude comparators and logic to design a circuit that computes the maximum of two 16-bit numbers. *(Component use problem.)*

4.22 Use magnitude comparators and logic to design a circuit that outputs 1 when an 8-bit input a is between 75 and 100, inclusive. *(Component use problem.)*

4.23 Design a human body temperature indicator system for a hospital bed. Your system takes an 8-bit input representing a person's body temperature, which can range from 0 to 255. If the measured temperature is 95 or less, set output A to 1. If the temperature is 96 to 104, set output B to 1. If the temperature is 105 or above, set output C to 1. Use 8-bit magnitude comparators and additional logic as required. *(Component use problem.)*

4.24 You are working as a weight guesser in an amusement park. Your job is to try to guess the weight of an individual before they step on a scale. If your guess is not within ten pounds of the individual's actual weight (higher or lower), the individual wins a prize. So if you guess 85 and the actual weight is 95, the person does not win; if you'd guessed 84, the person wins. Build a weight guess analyzer system that outputs whether the guess was within ten pounds. The weight guess analyzer has an 8-bit guess input G, an 8-bit input from the scale W with the correct weight, and a bit output C that is 1 if the guessed weight was within the defined limits of the game. Use 8-bit magnitude comparators and additional logic or components as required. *(Component use problem.)*

SECTION 4.5: MULTIPLIER—ARRAY-STYLE

4.25 Assuming all gates have a delay of 1 time-unit, which of the following designs will compute the 8-bit multiplication $A*9$ faster:
   (a) a circuit as designed in Exercise 4.45, or
   (b) an 8-bit array style multiplier with one input connected to a constant value of nine.

4.26 Design an 8-bit array-style multiplier. *(Component design problem.)*

4.27 Design a circuit to compute $F=(A*B*C)+3*D+12$. A, B, C, and D are 16-bit inputs, and F is a 16-bit output. Use 16-bit multiplier and adder components, and ignore overflow issues.

SECTION 4.6: SUBTRACTORS AND SIGNED NUMBERS

4.28 Convert the following two's complement binary numbers to decimal numbers:
(a) 00001111
(b) 10000000
(c) 10000001
(d) 11111111
(e) 10010101

4.29 Convert the following two's complement binary numbers to decimal numbers:
(a) 01001101
(b) 00011010
(c) 11101001
(d) 10101010
(e) 11111100

4.30 Convert the following two's complement binary numbers to decimal numbers:
(a) 11100000
(b) 01111111
(c) 11110000
(d) 11000000
(e) 11100000

4.31 Convert the following 9-bit two's complement binary numbers to decimal numbers:
(a) 011111111
(b) 111111111
(c) 100000000
(d) 110000000
(e) 111111110

4.32 Convert the following decimal numbers to 8-bit two's complement binary form:
(a) 2
(b) −1
(c) −23
(d) −128
(e) 126
(f) 127
(g) 0

4.33 Convert the following decimal numbers to 8-bit two's complement binary form:
(a) 29
(b) 100
(c) 125
(d) −29
(e) −100
(f) −125
(g) −2

4.34 Convert the following decimal numbers to 8-bit two's complement binary form:
(a) 6
(b) 26
(c) −8
(d) −30
(e) −60
(f) −90

4.35 Convert the following decimal numbers to 9-bit two's complement binary form:
  (a) 1
  (b) −1
  (c) −256
  (d) −255
  (e) 255
  (f) −8
  (g) −128

4.36 Repeat Exercise 4.14 except that the compensation amount can be positive or negative, coming to the system via four inputs d, c, b, and a from a 4-pin DIP switch (d is the most significant bit). The compensation amount is in two's complement form (so the person setting the DIP switch must know that). Design the circuit. What is the range by which the input temperature can be compensated? *(Component use problem.)*

4.37 Create the internal design of a full-subtractor. *(Component design problem.)*

4.38 Create an absolute value component *abs* with an 8-bit input A that is a signed binary number, and an 8-bit output Q that is unsigned and that is the absolute value of A. So if the input is 00001111 (+15) then the output is also 00001111 (+15), but if the input is 11111111 (−1) then the output is 00000001 (+1).

4.39 Using 4-bit subtractors, build a circuit that has three 8-bit inputs A, B, and C, and a single 8-bit output F, where $F=(A–B)–C$. *(Component use problem.)*

SECTION 4.7: ARITHMETIC-LOGIC UNITS—ALUS

4.40 Design an ALU with two 8-bit inputs A and B, and control inputs x, y, and z. The ALU should support the operations described in Table 4.3. Use an 8-bit adder and an arithmetic/logic extender. *(Component design problem.)*

TABLE 4.3 Desired ALU operations.

Inputs			Operation
x	y	z	
0	0	0	S = A − B
0	0	1	S = A + B
0	1	0	S = A * 8
0	1	1	S = A / 8
1	0	0	S = A NAND B (bitwise NAND)
1	0	1	S = A XOR B (bitwise XOR)
1	1	0	S = Reverse A (bit reversal)
1	1	1	S = NOT A (bitwise complement)

4.41 Design an ALU with two 8-bit inputs A and B, and control inputs x, y, and z. The ALU should support the operations described in Table 4.4. Use an 8-bit adder and an arithmetic/logic extender. *(Component design problem.)*

TABLE 4.4 Desired ALU operations.

Inputs			Operation
x	y	z	
0	0	0	S = A + B
0	0	1	S = A AND B (bitwise AND)
0	1	0	S = A NAND B (bitwise NAND)
0	1	1	S = A OR B (bitwise OR)
1	0	0	S = A NOR B (bitwise NOR)
1	0	1	S = A XOR B (bitwise XOR)
1	1	0	S = A XNOR B (bitwise XNOR)
1	1	1	S = NOT A (bitwise complement)

4.42 An instructor teaching Boolean algebra wants to help her students learn and understand basic Boolean operators by providing the students with a calculator capable of performing bitwise AND, NAND, OR, NOR, XOR, XNOR, and NOT operations. Using the ALU specified in Exercise 4.41, build a simple logic calculator using DIP switches for input and LEDs for output. The logic calculator should have three DIP switch inputs to select which logic operation to perform. *(Component use problem.)*

SECTION 4.8: SHIFTERS

4.43 Design an 8-bit shifter that shifts its inputs two bits to the right (shifting in 0s) when the shifter's shift control input is 1. *(Component design problem.)*

4.44 Design a circuit that outputs the average of four 8-bit unsigned binary inputs
   (a) ignoring overflow issues,
   (b) using wider internal components or wires to avoid losing information due to overflow.
   (Component use problem.)

4.45 Design a circuit whose 16-bit output is nine times its 16-bit input D representing an unsigned binary number. Ignore overflow issues. *(Component use problem.)*

4.46 Design a special multiplier circuit that can multiply its 16-bit input by 2, 4, 8, 16, or 32, specified by three inputs a, b, c (abc=000 means no multiply, abc=001 means multiply by 2, abc=010 means by 4, abc=011 means by 8, abc=100 means by 16, abc=101 means by 32). *Hint:* A simple solution consists entirely of just one copy of a component from this chapter. *(Component use problem.)*

4.47 Use strength reduction to create a circuit that computes $P=27*Q$ using only shifts and adds. P is a 12-bit output and Q is a 12-bit input. Estimate the transistors in the circuit and compare to the estimated transistors in a circuit using a multiplier.

4.48 Use strength reduction to create a circuit that approximately computes $P=(1/3)*Q$ using only shifters and adders. Strive for accuracy to the hundredths place (0.33). P is a 12-bit output and Q is a 12-bit input. Use wider internal components and wires as necessary to prevent internal overflow.

4.49 Show the internal values of the barrel shifter of Figure 4.64, when I=01100101, x=1, y=0, and z=1. Be sure to show how the input I is shifted after each internal shifter stage. *(Component design problem.)*

4.50 Using the barrel shifter shown in Figure 4.64, what settings of the inputs x, y, and z are required to shift the input *I* left by six positions?

SECTION 4.9: COUNTERS AND TIMERS

4.51 Design a 4-bit up-counter that has two control inputs: cnt enables counting up, while clear synchronously resets the counter to all 0s:
(a) using a parallel load register as a building block,
(b) using flip-flops and muxes by following the register design process of Section 4.2.
(Component design problem.)

4.52 Design a 4-bit down-counter that has three control inputs: cnt enables counting up, clear synchronously resets the counter to all 0s, and set synchronously sets the counter to all 1s:
(a) using a parallel load register as a building block,
(b) using flip-flops and muxes by following the register design process of Section 4.2.
(Component design problem.)

4.53 Design a 4-bit up-counter with an additional output upper. upper outputs a 1 whenever the counter is within the upper half of the counter's range, 8 to 15. Use a basic 4-bit up-counter as a building block. *(Component design problem.)*

4.54 Design a 4-bit up/down-counter that has four control inputs: cnt_up enables counting up, cnt_down enables counting down, clear synchronously resets the counter to all 0s, and set synchronously sets the counter to all 1s. If two or more control inputs are 1, the counter retains its current count value. Use a parallel-load register as a building block. *(Component design problem.)*

4.55 Design a circuit for a 4-bit decrementer. *(Component design problem.)*

4.56 Assume an electronic turnstile internally uses a 64-bit counter that counts up once for each person that passes through the turnstile. Knowing that California's Disneyland park attracts about 15,000 visitors per day, and assuming they all pass that one turnstile, how many days would pass before the counter would roll over? *(Component use problem.)*

4.57 Design a circuit that outputs a 1 every 99 clock cycles:
(a) Using an up-counter with a synchronous clear control input, and using extra logic,
(b) Using a down-counter with parallel load, and using extra logic.
(c) What are the tradeoffs between the two designs from parts (a) and (b)?
(Component use problem.)

4.58 Give the count range for the following sized up-counters:
(a) 8-bits, 12-bits, 16-bits, 20-bits, 32-bits, 40-bits, 64-bits, and 128-bits.
(b) For each size of counter in part (a), assuming a 1 Hz clock, indicate how much time would pass before the counter wraps around; use the most appropriate units for each answer (seconds, minutes, hours, days, weeks, months, or years).
(Component use problem.)

4.59 Create a clock divider that converts a 14 MHz clock into a 1 MHz clock. Use a down-counter with parallel load. Clearly indicate the width of the down-counter and the counter's load value. *(Component use problem.)*

4.60 Assuming a 32-bit microsecond timer is available to a controller, and a controller clock frequency of 100 MHz, create a controller FSM that blinks an LED by setting an output L to 1 for 5 ms and then to 0 for 13 ms, and then repeats. Use the timer to achieve the desired timing (i.e., do not use a clock divider). For this example, the blinking rate can vary by a few clock cycles. *(Component use problem.)*

SECTION 4.10: REGISTER FILES

4.61 Design an 8x32 two-port (1 read, 1 write) register file. *(Component design problem.)*

4.62 Design a 4x4 three-port (2 read, 1 write) register file. *(Component design problem.)*

4.63 Design a 10x14 register file (one read port, one write port). *(Component design problem.)*

4.64 A 4x4 register file's four registers initially each contain 0101.

(a) Show the input values necessary to read register 3 and to simultaneously write register 3 with the value 1110.

(b) With these values, show the register file's register values and output values before the next rising clock edge, and after the next rising clock edge.

▶ *DESIGNER PROFILE*

Roman began studying Computer Science in college due to his interest in software development. During his undergraduate studies, his interests expanded to also include the fields of digital design and embedded systems, which eventually led him to become involved in research developing new methods to help designers quickly build large integrated circuits (ICs). Roman continued his education through graduate studies and received his MS in Computer Science, after which Roman worked for both a large company designing ICs for consumer electronics, as well as a start-up company focusing on high-performance processing.

Roman enjoys working as both a software developer and hardware engineer and believes that "fundamentally software and hardware design are very similar, both relying on efficiently solving difficult problems. While good problem solving skills are important, good learning skills are also important." Contrary to what many students may believe, he points out that "learning is a fundamental activity and skill that does not end when you receive your degree. In order to solve problems, you often are required to learn new skills, adopt new programming languages and tools, and determine if existing solutions will help you solve the problems you face as an engineer." Roman points out that digital design has changed at a rapid pace over the last few decades, requiring engineers to learn new design techniques, learn new programming languages, such as VHDL or SystemC, and be able to adopt new technologies to stay successful. "As the industry continues to advance at such a rapid pace, companies do not only hire engineers for what they already know, but more so on how well those engineers can continue to expand their knowledge and learn new skills." He points out that "college provides students with an excellent opportunity to not only learn the essential information and skills from their course work but also to learn additional information on their own, possibly by learning different programming languages, getting involved in research, or working on larger design projects."

Roman is motivated by his enjoyment of the work he does as well being able to work with other engineers who share his interests. "Motivation is one of the keys to success in an engineering career. While motivation can come from many different sources, finding a career that you are truly interested in and enjoy really helps. Co-workers are also a great source of motivation as well as knowledge and technical advice. Working as a member of a team that communicates well is very rewarding. You are able to motivate each other and use your strengths along with the strengths of your co-workers to achieve goals far beyond that which you could achieve on your own."

5

Register-Transfer Level (RTL) Design

▷ 5.1 INTRODUCTION

Previous chapters introduced methods to capture behavior and to implement that behavior as a digital circuit. Chapter 2 introduced a method to capture basic combinational behavior using equations or truth tables, and to implement that behavior as a circuit of two or more levels of gates. Chapter 3 introduced a method to capture basic sequential behavior using finite-state machines (FSMs), and to implement that behavior as a circuit having a register and combinational logic, which together are known as a controller. This chapter will focus on capturing even higher-level sequential behavior, using a high-level state machine (HLSM) whose inputs, outputs, state actions, and transition conditions can all involve higher-level data types like binary numbers or integers rather than just the Boolean type used in FSMs. To implement such behavior, this chapter will introduce a method to convert a high-level state machine into a circuit consisting of a controller connected to a datapath, which together are known as a ***processor***. The datapath is composed of datapath components defined in Chapter 4, including registers, adders, comparators, etc., custom connected such that the datapath can perform the specific operations defined by the high-level state machine. The controller sets the datapath's signals in each state such that the state's actions and transition conditions are carried out.

The above discussion uses the term "higher-level," which should be explained. Digital designers commonly distinguish among the different levels shown in Figure 5.1. The more complex the building blocks, the higher the level of *abstraction* that the designer deals with. Connecting transistors into circuits to build gates or other components is called ***transistor-level design***. Designing combinational or sequential circuits as in Chapters 2 and 3 involves circuits whose building blocks are primarily logic gates, and is thus called ***logic-level design***. Designing processors involves circuits whose building blocks are registers and other datapath components, and involves transferring data from registers, through other datapath components like adders, and back to registers. Such design is thus called *register-transfer level design* or ***RTL design***—which is the focus of this chapter. In the 1970s and 1980s, most digital design practice occurred at the logic level. Today, most practice is at the register-transfer level. Improving tools continue to move design practice to higher levels. Higher levels deal with fewer and higher-

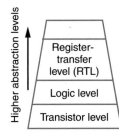

Higher abstraction levels

Register-transfer level (RTL)

Logic level

Transistor level

Figure 5.1 Levels of digital design.

complexity building blocks, and thus can enable design of higher-complexity circuits with less time and effort.

The term "microprocessor" became popular in the 1980s when programmable processors shrank from occupying many boards or chips down to occupying just a single chip. "Micro" refers to being small.

The name *processor* is best known from its use in the name *microprocessor*. A microprocessor is a *programmable* processor, which is a general predesigned processor created to carry out any desired computation (see Chapter 8). This chapter instead focuses on designing *custom processors*, which are processors each of whose design is special-ized to implement one specific computation, like converting a Celsius number to Fahrenheit. As such, custom processors can be extremely small, low-power, and fast com-pared to programmable processors. Custom processors and programmable processors often coexist in digital systems. For example, a TV set-top box may use a programmable processor to carry out most of the functions related to changing channels, controlling volume, etc., but may use custom processors to very quickly decompress the video data that is streaming into the system and to quickly display that data on the TV screen.

RTL design begins by capturing desired behavior. A formalism for capturing RTL behavior is a high-level state machine.

▶ 5.2 HIGH-LEVEL STATE MACHINES

Some behaviors are too complex to capture using just an equation, truth table, or FSM. Consider capturing the behavior of a custom processor for a soda machine dispenser that dispenses a soda when enough money has been depos-ited into the machine. A block diagram of the processor system is shown in Figure 5.2. A coin detector provides the processor with a 1-bit input c that becomes 1 for one clock cycle when a coin is detected, and an 8-bit input a indicates the value in cents of the inserted coin, such as 25 cents (00011001) or 10 cents (00001010). Another 8-bit input s

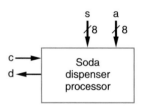

Figure 5.2 Soda dispenser block symbol.

indicates the cost of a soda, such as 60 cents (00111100), which can be set by the machine owner. When the processor has detected that the total value of deposited coins equals or exceeds the cost of a soda (e.g., 25 + 25 + 10 >= 60), the processor should set an output bit d to 1 for one clock cycle, causing a soda to be dispensed (this machine has only one type of soda, and does not give change). Assume that the value a persists until the next coin is deposited, and that many clock cycles (e.g., thousands) occur between successive coins being deposited.

An FSM is not sufficient for capturing the data aspects of this system's behavior. An FSM can only have Boolean (i.e., single-bit) inputs, not an 8-bit data input representing a binary number. An FSM has no convenient way of keeping track of the total data value of coins deposited so far. An FSM can only perform Boolean operations, not the data addi-tion operation (e.g., 25 + 10) required to keep track of the total value of coins deposited.

A *high-level state machine* (*HLSM*) extends FSMs with the data features needed to capture more complex behaviors, including:

- *multibit data inputs and outputs* rather than just single bits,
- *local storage*, and
- *arithmetic operations* like add and compare, rather than just Boolean operations.

This chapter will use HLSMs whose local storage is loaded on rising clock edges. Also, each local storage item and multibit input or output is assumed to be unsigned, unless specifically denoted as "signed" (see Section 4.6).

Figure 5.3 shows an HLSM describing the behavior of the soda dispenser processor. The HLSM initially sets output d to 0 and sets a local storage item *tot* to 0. The HLSM then waits in state *Wait* to detect a coin being deposited. When detected, the HLSM goes to state *Add*, which adds the coin's value *a* to *tot*, after which the HLSM returns to *Wait*. If *tot*'s value is less than the cost *s* of a soda (*tot* < *s*), the HLSM continues to wait for more coins. Otherwise, the HLSM goes to state *Disp*, which sets d to 1 to dispense a soda, after which the HLSM returns to state *Init* to clear *tot* back to 0 and start over again.

As a reminder, this book usually uses a Courier *font for names and constants representing a bit, and italics for other names. So* "d" *and* "0" *represent bit values, while* "tot" *and* "0" *represent normal data items.*

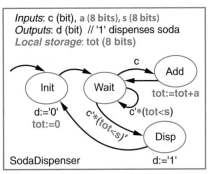

Figure 5.3 Soda dispenser high-level state machine with non-FSM constructs highlighted.

The state machine is *not* an FSM, because of reasons highlighted in the figure. One reason is because the state machine has inputs that are 8-bit types, whereas FSMs only allow inputs and outputs of Boolean types (a single bit each). Another reason is because the state machine declares local storage *tot* to store intermediate data, whereas FSMs don't allow local data storage—the only "stored" item in an FSM is the state itself. A third reason is because the state actions and transition conditions involve data operations like *tot* := 0 (remember that *tot* is 8-bits wide), *tot* < *s*, and *tot* := *tot* + *a* (where the "+" is addition, not OR), whereas an FSM allows only Boolean operations like AND or OR.

This chapter will use the following conventions for HLSMs, also used for FSMs:

• Each transition is implicitly ANDed with a rising clock edge.

• Any *bit* output not explicitly assigned a value in a state is implicitly assigned a 0. Note: this convention does not apply for multibit outputs.

This chapter will also use the following conventions for HLSMs:

• To distinguish between a bit 0 or 1 and a binary number 0 or 1, HLSMs will surround bit values with single quotes as in '0' and '1'. In Figure 5.3, note that the bit output d is assigned the bit '0' while the multibit storage *tot* is assigned 0 (without quotes), which is the integer representation of the 8-bit binary number 00000000. Being 8 bits wide, *tot* could be assigned the number 0, 1, 2, 3, ..., up to 255. In contrast, being a bit, d can only be assigned '0' or '1'. To assign a multibit item with a multibit constant, double quotes will be used, e.g., *tot* = "00000000".

• To avoid confusion between arithmetic comparison and assignment, HLSMs will use "==" for comparison and ":=" for assignment. "=" will not be used for either. In Figure 5.3, note that assigning d is written as d := '0' rather than as d = 0, and assigning *tot* is written as *tot* := 0. If *tot* had to be compared to *s* for equality on a transition, such comparison would be written as *tot* == *s*, making clear that *tot* is being compared with *s* and not being assigned the value of *s*. Comparing for less than or equal to would be written as *tot <= s*.

- Every HLSM multibit output is registered (see Chapter 3). As such, every HLSM multibit output *X* must have a storage item *Xreg* declared that is the same width as *X*. Writing to *X* is accomplished by writing to *Xreg*; writes directly to *X* are not allowed. *Xreg* can be read; *X* cannot. If desired, a single-bit output B can be registered by declaring a local storage item `Breg`.

To aid in understanding, an HLSM can include text that describes some aspect of the HLSM. Such text is preceded by "//" and is known as a ***comment***. One comment appears in Figure 5.3 to describe the behavior of output d.

As was true for FSMs, capturing behavior as an HLSM can be challenging. As in Chapter 3 for FSMs, the capture process for HLSMs can be aided by first listing all possible states (with some transitions included if helpful), then creating all possible transitions leaving each state, and finally by mentally executing the HLSM and refining it if necessary. The following example illustrates creation of an HLSM for a simple system.

Example 5.1 Cycles-high counter

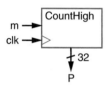

Figure 5.4 Cycles-high counter block diagram.

This example captures an HLSM for a system having a bit input m and a 32-bit output P. The system should output the total number of clock cycles for which the input m is 1. For example, after powering on the system, if m is 0 for 20 cycles, then 1 for 15 cycles, then 0 for 12 cycles, and then 1 for 3 cycles, the system output at that point should be 18 (15 + 3). P connects to a display that converts the 32-bit number into a displayed integer. Such a cycles-high counter system might be useful to determine the total time that a car's brakes are applied, that a laser has been turned on, etc.

Figure 5.5(a) shows the first HLSM state *S_Clr* that initializes the output *P* to 0 by setting its storage item *Preg* to 0. *Preg* accomplishes the storage of the cycles-high count, and thus declaring another local storage item is not necessary. Figure 5.5(b) introduces a second state *S_Wt* that waits for m to be 1; transitions are shown for this state. Finally, Figure 5.5(c) introduces a third state *S_Inc* that increments *Preg* once for each clock cycle that m is 1; transitions are also shown for this state. The HLSM now has all possible transitions. Mentally executing the HLSM seems to validate that it correctly captures the desired behavior.

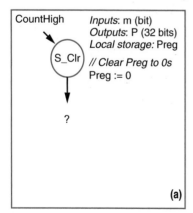
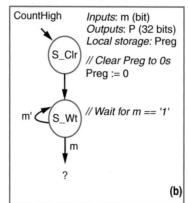
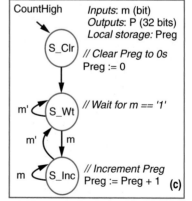

Figure 5.5 HLSM for cycles-high counter: (a) initial state, (b) waiting for m to be 1, (c) incrementing *Preg* when m is 1.

Example 5.2 Laser-based distance measurer

Many applications require accurately measuring the distance of an object from a known point. For example, road builders need to accurately determine the length of a stretch of road. Map makers need to accurately determine the locations and heights of hills and mountains and the sizes of lakes. A giant crane for constructing skyrise buildings needs to accurately determine the distance of the sliding crane arm from the base. In all of these applications, stringing out a tape measure to measure the distance is not very practical. A better method involves laser-based distance measurement.

In laser-based distance measurement, a laser is pointed at the object of interest. The laser is briefly turned on and a timer is started. The laser light, traveling at the speed of light, travels to the object and reflects back. A sensor detects the reflection of the laser light, causing the timer to stop. Knowing the time T taken by the light to travel to the object and back, and knowing that the speed of light is 3×10^8 meters/second, the distance D can be computed easily by the equation: $2D = T$ seconds $* 3 \times 10^8$ meters/second. Laser-based distance measurement is illustrated in Figure 5.6.

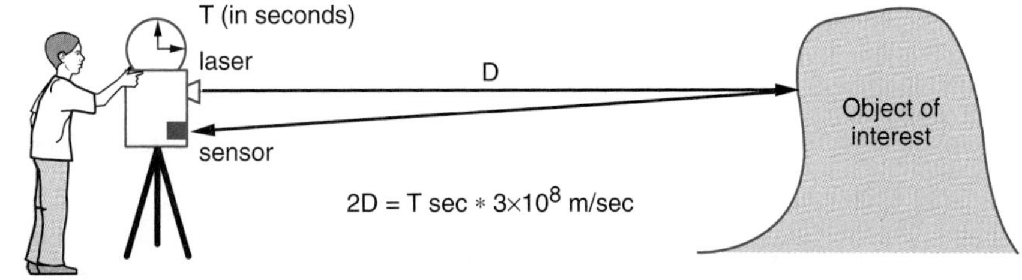

Figure 5.6
Laser-based distance measurement.

This example captures an HLSM to describe the behavior of a processor that controls a laser to compute distances up to 2000 meters. A block diagram of the system is shown in Figure 5.7. The system has a bit input B, which equals 1 when the user presses a button to start the measurement. Another bit input S comes from the sensor and is 1 when the reflected laser is detected. A bit output L controls the laser, turning the laser on when L is 1. Finally, an N-bit output D indicates the distance in binary, in units of meters—a display converts that binary number into a decimal number and displays the results on an LCD for the user to read. D will have to be at least 11 bits, since 11 bits can represent the numbers 0 to 2047, and the system should measure distances up to 2000 meters. To be safe, we'll make D 16 bits.

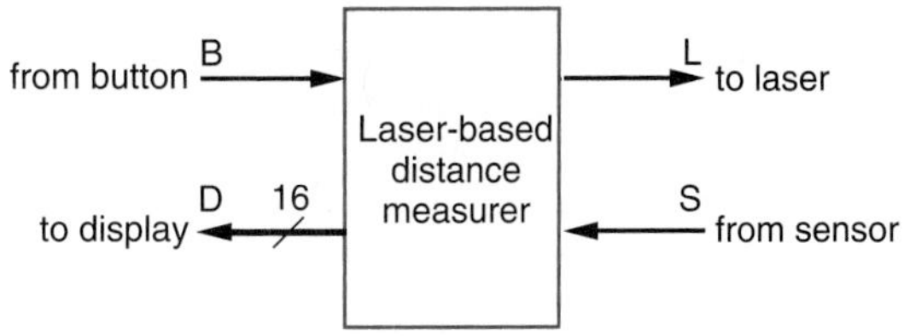

Figure 5.7 Block diagram of the laser-based distance measurer.

To facilitate the creation of the state machine, we first enumerate the sequence of events that would typically occur in the measurement system:

- The system powers on. Initially, the system's laser is off and the system outputs a distance of 0 meters.
- The system waits for the user to press button B to initiate measurement.
- After the button is pressed, the system should turn the laser on. We'll choose to leave the laser on for one clock cycle.

- After the laser is turned on, the system should wait for the sensor to detect the laser's reflection. Meanwhile, the system should count how many clock cycles occur from the time the laser was turned on until the reflection is sensed.

- After the reflection is sensed, the system should use the number of cycles that occurred since the laser was pulsed to compute the distance to the object of interest. The system should then return to waiting for the user to press the button again so that a new measurement can be taken.

The above sequence guides our construction of an HLSM. We begin with an initial state named *S0* as shown in Figure 5.8. *S0's* task is to ensure that when the system powers on, the system does not output an incorrect distance, and the system does not turn the laser on. Note that output *D* is not written directly, but rather the output's local storage *Dreg* is written instead. Recall that the assignment L := '0' assigns the bit 0 to the one-bit output L, whereas the assignment *Dreg* := 0 assigns the 16-bit binary number 0 (which is actually 0000000000000000) to the 16-bit storage *Dreg*.

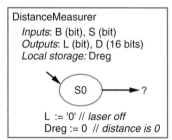

Figure 5.8 Partial HLSM for the distance measurer: Initialization.

After initialization, the measurement system waits for the user to press the button to initiate the measurement process. To perform the waiting, we add a state named *S1* as shown in Figure 5.9. The shown transitions cause the state machine to remain in state *S1* while B is 0 (i.e., while B' is true). Be aware that the L is implicitly assigned 0 in this state, because of the convention that any single-bit output not explicitly assigned in a state is implicitly assigned 0. On the other hand, *Dreg*, corresponding to a local storage item, is unchanged in this state.

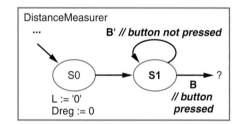

Figure 5.9 Distance measurer HLSM (cont.): Waiting for a button press.

When B becomes 1, the laser should be turned on for one cycle. The HLSM should transition to a state that turns the laser on, followed by a state that turns the laser off. We'll call the laser-on state *S2* and the laser-off state *S3*. Figure 5.10 shows how *S2* and *S3* are introduced into the HLSM.

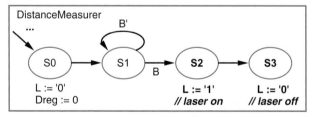

Figure 5.10 Distance measurer HLSM (cont.): Turning the laser on for one cycle.

In state *S3*, the HLSM should wait until the sensor detects the laser's reflection (S). The state machine remains in *S3* while S is 0. The HLSM should meanwhile count the clock cycles between the laser being turned on and the laser's reflection being sensed. We can measure time by counting the number of clock cycles and multiplying that number by the clock period (T = cycles counted * clock period). Thus, we introduce a *local storage* item named *Dctr* to keep track of the cycles counted. The HLSM increments *Dctr* as long as the HLSM is waiting for the laser's reflection. (For simplicity, we ignore the possibility that no reflection is detected.) The HLSM must also initialize *Dctr* to 0 before

Figure 5.11
Distance
measurer HLSM
(cont.): Waiting
for the laser
reflection and
counting clock
cycles.

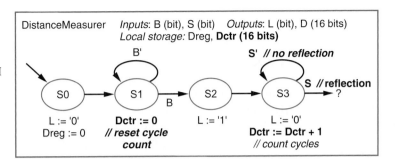

counting; such initialization can be added to state *S1*. With these modifications, the HLSM is seen in Figure 5.11.

Once the reflection is detected (S=1), the HLSM should compute the distance D that is being measured. Figure 5.6 shows that $2*D = T * 3\times10^8$ m/sec. We know that the time T in seconds is $Dctr$ * *clock period*. To simplify the calculation of D, assume the clock frequency is 3×10^8 Hz (which is 300 MHz), so the clock period is $1 / (3\times10^8)$ sec. Thus, $2*D = (Dctr / 3\times10^8)$ sec * 3×10^8 meters/sec = $Dctr$ meters, and so $D = (Dctr / 2)$ meters. We'll perform this calculation in a state named *S4*. The final HLSM is shown in Figure 5.12. All possible transitions from each state have already been included. A mental execution seems to confirm that the HLSM behaves as desired.

Figure 5.12
Completed
HLSM for
the distance
measurer,
including
calculation
of *D*.

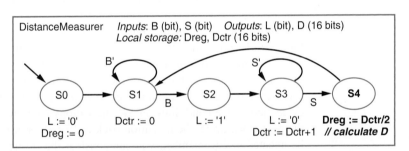

A laser-based distance measurer could use a faster clock frequency to measure distance with a greater precision than 1 meter.

The HLSM described above is just one type of FSM extension. Dozens of extended FSM varieties exist. The particular variety of HLSM described above and used throughout this chapter is sometimes called an **FSM with data** or **FSMD**. A different state machine variation that was previously popular was called **algorithmic state machines**, or **ASMs**. ASMs are similar to flowcharts, except that ASMs include a notion of a clock that enables transitions from one state to another (a traditional flowchart does not have an explicit clock concept). ASMs contain more "structure" than a state machine. A state machine can transition from any state to any other state, whereas an ASM restricts transitions in a way that causes the computation to look more like an algorithm—an ordered sequence of instructions. An ASM uses several types of boxes, including state boxes, condition boxes, and output boxes. ASMs typically also allowed local data storage and data operations. The advent of hardware description languages (see Chapter 9) seems to have largely replaced the use of ASMs, because hardware description languages

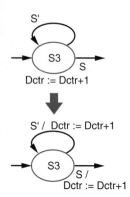

Figure 5.13 A storage update can be thought of as occuring on outgoing transitions.

contain the constructs supporting algorithmic structure, and much more. We do not describe ASMs further.

In the HLSMs of this chapter, all writes to storage items in a state's actions are to storage items that are loaded on rising clock edges only. As such, writing a value to a storage item in a state's actions does not actually cause the storage item to be updated until the *next rising clock* edge. So the update occurs at the *end* of the state when the next rising clock edge causes a transition. For example, consider the state action "*Dctr* := *Dctr* + 1" in state *S3* of the distance measurer HLSM in Figure 5.12. When a clock edge causes a transition from *S2* to *S3*, *Dctr* will initially be 0. While in *S3* during that clock cycle, *Dctr* will still be 0. When the *next* clock edge arrives, *Dctr* will be updated to 1 (i.e., to *Dctr* + 1, meaning 0 + 1 = 1), and the HLSM will transition back to *S3* if s is 0. *Dctr* will remain 1 until the next clock edge, when it will become *Dctr* + 1 = 1 + 1 = 2. A simple way to visualize a state's local storage updates is to consider those updates as occuring on each outgoing transition instead of in the state, as in Figure 5.13. Because local storage item updates occur at the end of a state when the next rising clock edge occurs, and because transitions are taken on that same clock edge, then a transition whose condition uses the storage item uses the non-updated value. A common mistake is to assume the transition uses the updated value.

For example, suppose a system waits for an input control bit B to become 1 and then sets an output P to 1 for 50 cycles. Rather than using 50 states to set P high, an HLSM can use a local storage item. Figure 5.14(a) shows an HLSM using local storage *Jreg*, for the case of setting the output P to 1 for 2 cycles rather than 50 so that the example is easier to understand. The diagram for that HLSM in Figure 5.14(b) shows that *S0*'s action of *Jreg* := 1 occurs at the same time as the transition to *S1* during the next clock edge. Then, even though *S1*'s action is *Jreg* := *Jreg* +1, *J* remains 1 for the duration of the clock cycle, and so the conditions on *S1*'s transitions with *Jreg*<2 will be comparing 1<2. On the next clock cycle, the transition back to *S1* will be taken and *Jreg* will simultaneously be updated to 2 (remember, you can consider the storage update as occuring on the outgoing transitions). During that second cycle in *S1*, the transition comparison will be 2<2, so on the next clock edge the transition to *S0* will be taken and *Jreg* will simultaneously be updated with 3 (that value of 3 will never be used, and at the end of state *S0*, *Jreg* will become 1 again).

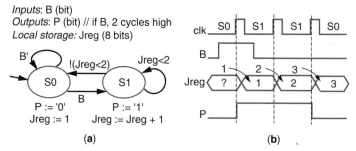

Figure 5.14 HLSM clocked storage update behavior: (a) HLSM with storage *Jreg*, (b) *S0*'s setting *Jreg* to *1* doesn't occur until the next clock edge, which is also when *S1* is entered. *S1*'s setting of *Jreg*:=*Jreg*+1 will set *Jreg* to 2, but not until the next edge, meaning *Jreg*<2 is false for the first *S1* state.

Because the updates of a state's actions occur at the next clock edge, the order in which local storage item actions are listed in a state does not matter—all the updates occur simultaneously at the end of the state. For example, swapping two storage items *A* and *B* in a state could be achieved by "*A* := *B*" followed by "*B* := *A*", or by "*B* := *A*" followed by "*A* := *B*." The results are identical in either listing of the actions—at the end of the state, *A* and *B* get updated with the previous values of *B* and *A*, respectively. Think of the updates being prepared in the state, but not actually occuring until the next clock. Figure 5.14(b) shows the updates that are prepared in each state, with arrows indicating when the updates actually occur.

▶ 5.3 RTL DESIGN PROCESS

RTL design follows a two-step process, as was the case for combinational design in Chapter 2 and for sequential design in Chapter 3. The first step is to *capture* the desired behavior, and the second step is to *convert* that behavior as a circuit. This chapter captures behavior using an HLSM; designers sometimes use other formalisms too. Converting an HLSM to a circuit is aided by the use of a standard processor architecture, similar to how converting an FSM to a circuit in Chapter 3 was aided by the use of a standard con-troller architecture consisting of a state register and combinational logic. A stan-

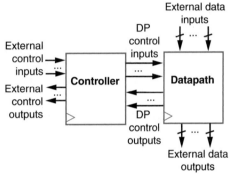

Figure 5.15 Standard processor architecture: controller/datapath pair.

dard processor architecture is shown in Figure 5.15, consisting of a controller connected with a datapath. The datapath will have the ability to carry out each particular data oper-ation present in the HLSM, by having the necessary datapath components (e.g., if the HLSM requires an addition and a comparison, then the datapath will include an adder and a comparator). The controller will set the control input signals of the various datapath components (e.g., the load control input of a register) to carry out the specific actions of each particular state and to transition to appropriate next states based on the control output signals of those datapath components.

To help understand the controller/datapath pair in the standard processor architecture, consider the cycles-high counter from Example 5.1, which is revisited in Figure 5.16. Figure 5.16(a) shows the system block diagram and describes the system's desired behavior. As this chapter's convention is to always register data outputs, the figure already shows a register *Preg* connected to data output *P*. Figure 5.16(b) shows the desired behavior captured as an HLSM created in the earlier example. The behavior requires that the computation "*Preg* := *Preg* + 1" be performed. As such, Figure 5.16(c) shows an adder whose two inputs are *Preg* and a constant 1, and whose output is con-nected to *Preg*. Thus, computing "*Preg* := *Preg* + 1" can be achieved simply by setting *Preg*'s ld control input to 1. Furthermore, the required computation "*Preg* := 0" can be achieved by setting *Preg*'s clr control input to 1. Thus, the circuit of the adder and register form a datapath that is capable of performing the data computation required for the system's behavior.

What is still needed is a component, denoted as "?" in the figure, to control that datapath to carry out the right computation at the right time to achieve the desired cycles-high count behavior. That component is a controller as shown in Figure 5.16(d). The controller's behavior is described as an FSM (as in Chapter 3) and is similar to the HLSM's behavior in Figure 5.16(b), except that each desired data operation is replaced by control actions that use the datapath to carry out the desired data operation. Rather than "*Preg* := 0," the controller's FSM executes the action "Preg_clr = 1," which clears the register. Rather than "*Preg* := *Preg* + 1," the controller's FSM executes the action "Preg_ld = 1," which loads *Preg* with *Preg* + 1 because that is how the datapath is set up. The controller thus uses the datapath to implement the overall desired system behavior. Using methods from Chapter 3, the FSM in Figure 5.16(d) could be converted to a circuit, thus completing the design of the cycles-high count processor circuit.

As seen in Figure 5.16, converting an HLSM to a controller and datapath circuit requires creating a datapath capable of carrying out the required data operations, connecting the datapath to a controller block, and converting the HLSM into an FSM that describes the controller's behavior.

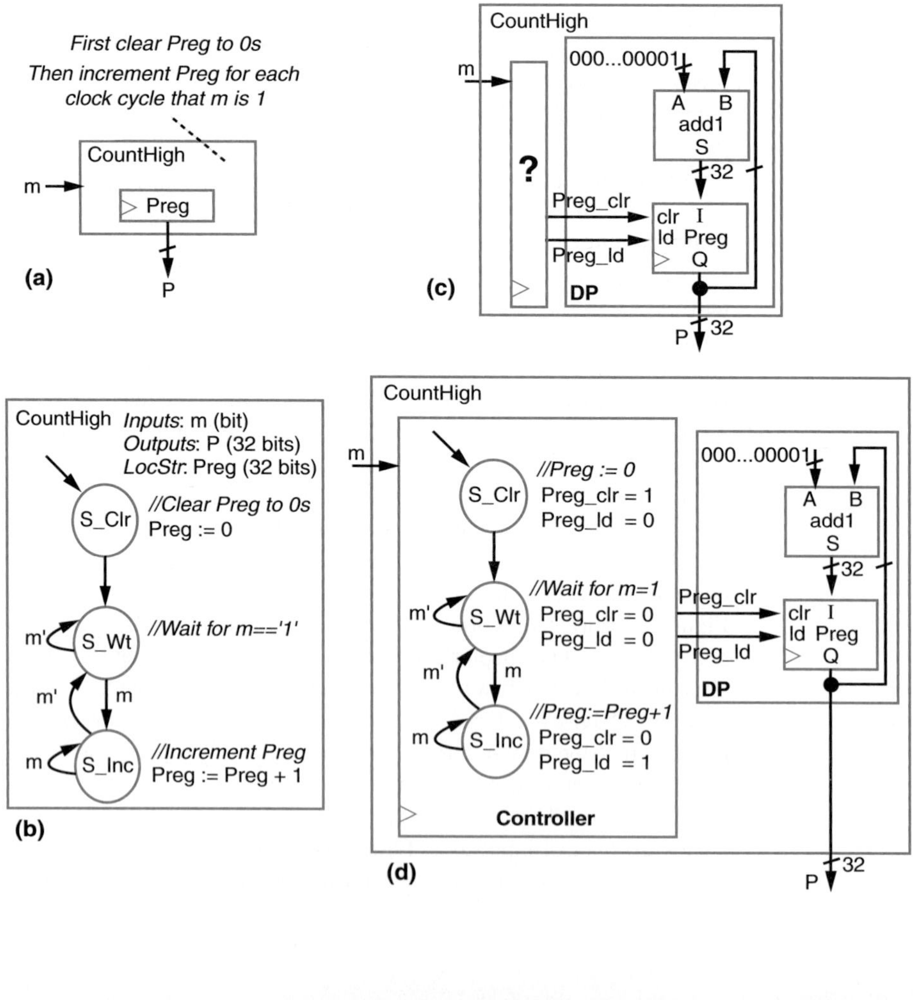

Figure 5.16
Example requiring a controller and datapath pair: (a) desired behavior, (b) HLSM description of desired behavior (*LocStr* means Local storage), (c) datapath with potential to implement behavior, but requiring time-varying setting of the datapath's control signals, (d) FSM showing datapath control signal values that should be set in each state to achieve behavior.

Thus, an RTL design process consisting of first capturing desired behavior and then converting the behavior to a circuit is summarized in Table 5.1.

Table 5.1   RTL design method.

	Step	Description
Step 1: Capture behavior	*Capture a high-level state machine*	Describe the system's desired behavior as a high-level state machine. The state machine consists of states and transitions. The state machine is "high-level" because the transition conditions and the state actions are more than just Boolean operations on single-bit inputs and outputs.
Step 2: Convert to circuit	**2A** *Create a datapath*	Create a datapath to carry out the data operations of the high-level state machine.
	2B *Connect the datapath to a controller*	Connect the datapath to a controller block. Connect external control inputs and outputs to the controller block.
	2C *Derive the controller's FSM*	Convert the high-level state machine to a finite-state machine (FSM) for the controller, by replacing data operations with setting and reading of control signals to and from the datapath.

Another substep may be necessary, in which one selects a clock frequency. Designers seeking high performance may choose a clock frequency that is the fastest possible based on the longest register-to-register delay in the final circuit. Implementing the controller's FSM as a sequential circuit as in Chapter 3 would then complete the design.

We'll provide a simple example of the RTL design process before defining each step in more detail.

Example 5.3 Soda dispenser

This example completes the design of the soda dispenser whose HLSM was captured in Figure 5.3, which thus completed **Step 1** of the RTL design process.

Step 2A is to create a datapath. The datapath needs a register for the storage item *tot*, an adder connected to *tot* and *a* to compute *tot* + *a*, and a comparator connected to *tot* and *s* to compute *tot*<*s*. The resulting datapath appears in Figure 5.17.

Step 2B is to connect the datapath to a controller, as in Figure 5.18. Notice that the controller's inputs and outputs are all just one-bit signals.

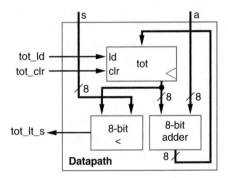

Figure 5.17 Soda dispenser datapath.

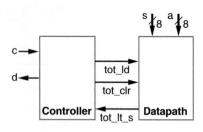

Figure 5.18 Soda dispenser controller/datapath pair.

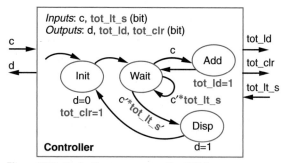

Figure 5.19 Soda dispenser controller FSM.

While an HLSM diagram uses ":=" and "==" to distinguish assignment and equality, and uses "'1'" and "1" to distinguish a bit 1 from an integer 1, an FSM diagram has no need for such distinctions (equality is never checked, and everything is a bit) and thus for FSM diagrams we still use the style defined in Chapter 3.

Step 2C is to derive the controller's FSM from the HLSM. The FSM has the same states and transitions as the HLSM, but utilizes the datapath to perform any data operations. Figure 5.19 shows the FSM for the controller. In the HLSM, state *Init* had a data operation of "*tot := 0*" (*tot* is 8 bits wide, so that assignment of 0 is a data operation). We replace that assignment by setting `tot_clr=1`, which clears the *tot* register to 0. State *Wait*'s transitions had data operations comparing "*tot < s*." Now that a comparator exists to compute that comparison for the controller, then the controller need only look at the result of that comparison by using the signal `tot_lt_s`. State *Add* had a data operation of *tot = tot + a*. The datapath computes that addition for the controller using the adder, so the controller merely needs to set `tot_ld=1` to cause the addition result to be loaded into the *tot* register.

To complete the design, we would implement the controller's FSM as a state register and combinational logic. Figure 5.20 shows a partial state table for the controller, with the states encoded as *Init*: 00, *Wait*: 01, *Add*: 10, and *Disp*: 11. To complete the controller design, we would complete the state table, create a 2-bit state register, and create a circuit for each of the five outputs from the table, as discussed in Chapter 3. Appendix C provides details of completing the controller's design. That appendix also traces through the functioning of the controller and datapath with one another.

	s1	s0	c	tot_lt_s	n1	n0	d	tot_ld	tot_clr
Init	0	0	0	0	0	1	0	0	1
	0	0	0	1	0	1	0	0	1
	0	0	1	0	0	1	0	0	1
	0	0	1	1	0	1	0	0	1
Wait	0	1	0	0	1	1	0	0	0
	0	1	0	1	0	1	0	0	0
	0	1	1	0	1	0	0	0	0
	0	1	1	1	1	0	0	0	0
Add	1	0	0	0	0	1	0	1	0
			• • •				• • •		
Disp	1	1	0	0	0	0	1	0	0
			• • •				• • •		

Figure 5.20 Soda dispenser controller state table (partial).

We now discuss each RTL design method step in more detail, while illustrating each step with another example.

Step 2A—Creating a Datapath using Components from a Library

Given a high-level state machine, the RTL design process requires creating a datapath that can implement all the data storage and computations on data items present in the HLSM. Doing so will enable replacing the HLSM by an FSM that merely controls the datapath. The task of "creating a datapath" can be decomposed into several subtasks.

Step 2A: Create a datapath

(a) Make all *data* inputs and outputs to be datapath inputs and outputs.

(b) Instantiate a register component into the datapath for every declared local storage item in the HLSM.

(c) Methodically examine each state action and each transition condition for data computations. Instantiate and connect datapath components to implement each data computation. Instantiate multiplexors in front of component inputs when muxes become necessary to share a component input among computations in different states.

Instantiate means to add a new component into a circuit. Using the term "instantiate" rather than "add" helps avoid possible confusion with the use of the term "add" to mean arithmetic addition (e.g., saying "we add two registers" could otherwise be confusing). An instantiated component is called an ***instance***. A new component instance should be given a name that is unique from any other datapath component instance's name. So a new register instance might be named "*Reg1*." Another register instantiated later might be named "*Reg2*." Actually, meaningful names should be used whenever possible. One register might be "*TemperatureReg*" and another register "*HumidityReg*."

A set of known components is needed to indicate what types of components can be instantiated. Such a set of allowable components is called a ***library***. Chapter 4 described the design and behavior of several datapath components. Figure 5.21 shows a small library consisting of several such components, indicating the inputs and outputs of each component and a brief summary of each component's behavior.

The first component in the library is an N-bit register with clear and parallel load functions. If the clock is rising (denoted as $clk^\wedge$), then clr=1 clears the register, while ld=1 loads the register (if both are 1, clear has priority). The second component is an N-bit adder (without a carry output). The third component is an N-bit comparator with less-than, equals, and greater-than control outputs; that comparator assumes unsigned inputs. The fourth component is a shifter that can be instantiated as a left shifter or as a right

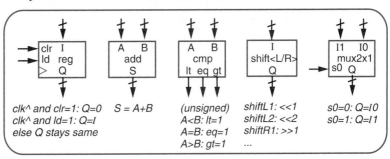

Figure 5.21 A basic datapath component library.

shifter, and that can be instantiated to shift a fixed number of places. The fifth component is an N-bit 2x1 multiplexor. Each component can be instantiated as any bitwidth N; e.g., an 8-bit register or a 32-bit register can be instantiated. Note that the concept of a library of datapath components differs from the familiar concept of a library as a collection of books. In a library of books, checking out a book means removing the book from the library, meaning nobody else can then check out that same book; only one instance of the book exists. A library of datapath components, in contrast, is more like a library of electronic books that can be printed out. Instantiating a component means creating a *new* occurrence of that component, much like one might print out a new copy of an electronic book—instantiating the component or printing a new copy of a book does not change the library of components or of electronic books.

Figure 5.22 provides several examples of converting (always occuring) actions into datapaths. Figure 5.22(a) indicates that the datapath should always compute "*Preg* := $X +$ $Y + Z$." The corresponding datapath uses two adder instances and a register instance, connected such that the input to the register is $X + Y + Z$. The register's load control input is hardwired to 1, meaning the register will be loaded on every clock cycle (for these examples, the actions always occur on every clock cycle so the control inputs are hardwired to constants; for HLSMs, the control inputs will be set on a state-by-state basis depending on the actions of the state).

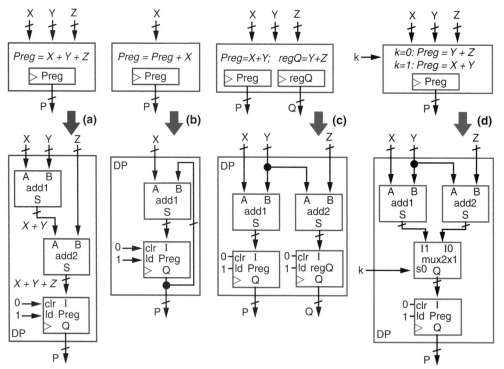

Figure 5.22 Simple examples using a datapath to perform computations on input data, with the desired behavior on top and the datapath (DP) on the bottom: (a) adding three values using two adders, (b) accumulating values using a register, (c) a two-output example, (d) an example requiring a mux.

Figure 5.22(b) indicates that the desired datapath behavior is adding the input *X* to register *Preg* on every clock cycle; the corresponding datapath thus connects *X* and the output of *Preg* to an adder, and connects the adder's output to *Preg*. Figure 5.22(c) indicates that the desired datapath behavior involves two distinct additions "*X+Y*" and "*Y+Z*" being computed for two distinct data outputs on each clock cycle; the datapath uses two adders and the shown connections. Finally, Figure 5.22(d) lists the desired behavior as loading *Preg* with *Y+Z* when the datapath control input k is 0, and instead loading *Preg* with *X+Y* when k is 1; the datapath uses two adders and uses a 2x1 mux to route the appropriate adder output to *Preg*'s input depending on the value of k. (In fact, an alternative datapath could use just one adder, with a mux in front of each adder input to route the appropriate inputs to the adder depending on k.)

When instantiating a new component for an HLSM's datapath, datapath control inputs must be introduced corresponding to the component's control inputs. For example, instantiating a register requires introducing two datapath control inputs corresponding to the register's load and clear control inputs. Unique names should be given to each new datapath control input, ideally describing which component the input controls and the control operation performed. For example, if a register named *Reg1* is instantiated, two new datapath control inputs must be added, possibly being named *Reg1_ld* and *Reg1_clr*. Likewise, control outputs of a component may be needed by the controller, like the output of a comparator, in which case those datapath control outputs should be given meaningful unique names too.

Example 5.4 Laser-based distance measurer—Creating a datapath

We continue Example 5.2 by first creating a datapath for the HLSM of Figure 5.12.

Step 2A—Create a datapath. We follow the subtasks of the create-a-datapath task to create the datapath shown in Figure 5.23:

(a) Output *D* is a data output (16 bits), so *D* becomes an output of the datapath, as shown in Figure 5.23.

(b) By convention of this chapter, every data output is registered, and thus a 16-bit register *Dreg* was declared as local storage. *Dreg* is now instantiated and connected to output *D*. A 16-bit register is also instantiated for the 16-bit local storage *Dctr*. Datapath control inputs are added for each register, with each input having a unique name: *Dreg_clr* and *Dreg_ld* for *Dreg*'s control inputs, and *Dctr_clr* and *Dctr_ld* for *Dctr*'s control inputs.

(c) Because state *S3* has the action "*Dctr := Dctr + 1*," a 16-bit adder is instantiated, whose inputs are *Dctr*'s data output and a constant 1, and whose output is connected to *Dctr*'s data input. Because state *S4* writes *D* with *Dctr* divided by 2, a 16-bit right-shift-by-1

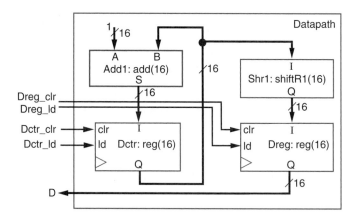

Figure 5.23 Datapath for the laser-based distance measurer.

component (which achieves division by 2 as discussed in Chapter 4) is instantiated between *Dctr* and *Dreg* to implement the divide by 2.

Step 2B—Connecting the Datapath to a Controller

Step 2B of the RTL design process is straightforward. This step simply involves creating a controller component having the system's control inputs and outputs, and then connecting the controller component with the datapath control inputs and outputs.

Example 5.5 Laser-based distance measurer—Connecting the datapath to a controller

Continuing the RTL design process for the previous example proceeds as follows.

Step 2B—Connect the datapath to a controller. We connect the datapath to a controller as shown in Figure 5.24. We connect the control inputs and outputs B, L, and S to the controller, and the data output *D* to the datapath. We also connect the controller to the datapath control inputs *Dreg_clr*, *Dreg_ld*, *Dctr_clr*, and *Dctr_ld*. Normally we don't draw the clock generator component, but we've explicitly shown the clock generator in the figure to make clear that the generator must be exactly 300 MHz for this particular circuit.

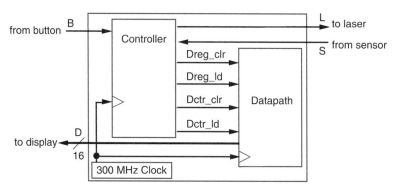

Figure 5.24 Controller/ datapath (processor) design for the laser-based distance measurer.

Step 2C—Deriving the Controller's FSM

If the datapath was created correctly, then deriving an FSM for the controller is straight-forward. The FSM will have the same states and transitions as the HLSM. We merely define the controllers inputs and outputs to be the FSM's inputs and outputs (all will now be single bits), and replace any data computations in the HLSM's actions and conditions by the appropriate datapath control signal values. Remember, the datapath was created specifically to carry out those computations, and therefore we should only need to appropriately configure the datapath control signals to implement each particular computation at the right time.

Example 5.6 Laser-based distance measurer—Deriving the controller's FSM

Continuing the RTL design process for the previous example proceeds as follows.

Step 4—Derive the controller's FSM. This step defines the behavior of the controller. The controller's behavior is defined by converting the HLSM from Figure 5.12 into an FSM, replacing the data operations, like "*Dctr* := 0," by controller input and output signal assignments and conditions, like "*Dctr_clr* = 1," as shown in Figure 5.25. Notice that the FSM does not directly indicate the computations that are happening in the datapath. For example, *S4* loads *Dreg* with *Dctr/2*, but the FSM itself only shows *Dreg*'s load signal being activated. Thus, the overall system behavior can be determined by looking at both the controller's FSM and the datapath.

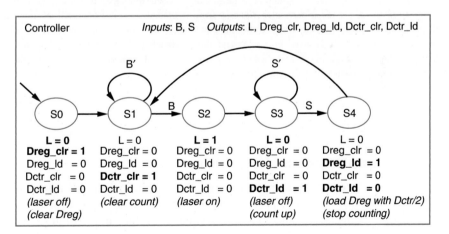

Figure 5.25 FSM description of the controller for the laser-based distance measurer. The desired action in each state is shown in italics in the bottom row; the corresponding bit signal assignment that achieves that action is shown in bold.

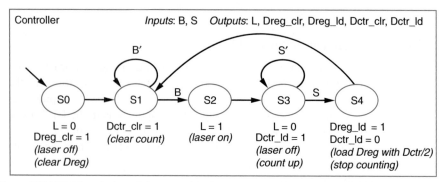

Figure 5.26 FSM description of the controller for the laser-based distance measurer, using the convention that FSM outputs not explicitly assigned a value in a state are implicitly assigned 0.

Recall from Chapter 3 that we typically follow the convention that FSM output signals not explicitly assigned in a state are implicitly assigned 0. Following that convention, the FSM would look as in Figure 5.26. We may still choose to explictly show the assignment of 0 (e.g., L = 0 in state *S3*) when that assignment is a key action of a state. The key actions of each state were bolded in Figure 5.25.

We would complete the design by implementing this FSM, using a 3-bit state register and combinational logic to describe the next state and output logic, as was described in Chapter 3.

▶ *HOW DOES IT WORK?—AUTOMOTIVE ADAPTIVE CRUISE CONTROL*

The early 2000s saw the advent of automobile cruise control systems that not only maintained a particular speed, but also maintained a particular *distance* from the car in front—thus slowing the automobile down when necessary. Such "adaptive" cruise control thus adapts to changing highway traffic. Adaptive cruise controllers must measure the distance to the car in front. One way to measure that distance uses a laser-based distance measurer, with the laser and sensor placed in the front grill of the car, connected to a circuit and/or microprocessor that computes the distance. The distance is then input to the cruise control system, which determines when to increase or decrease the automobile's speed.

▶ 5.4 MORE RTL DESIGN

Additional Datapath Components for the Library

The datapath component library of Figure 5.21 included a few components. Chapter 4 defined other components that are also commonly found in datapath component libraries. Figure 5.27 includes more such components that may exist in a library. One component is a subtractor; this particular subtractor used signed input and output numbers (a subtractor dealing with unsigned numbers is also possible). Another component is a multiplier; this multiplier deals with unsigned numbers (a multiplier for signed numbers is also possible). An absolute value component (designed in a Chapter 4 exercise) uses a signed number as input and outputs the number's magnitude as an unsigned number. An up-counter component is shown with synchronous clear and increment inputs; clear has priority. A down-

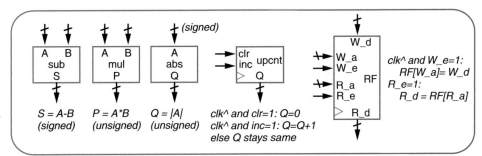

Figure 5.27
More datapath
components for
the library of
Figure 5.21.

counter component could be similarly included. Each component can be instantiated with
an arbitrary width of *N*. The last component is a register file with one write port and one
read port. The component can be instantiated with a width of *N* and with a number of
words *M*; the width of the address inputs *W_a* and *R_a* will be $\log_2(M)$, while *W_d* and
R_d will have widths of *N*.

RTL Design Involving Register Files or Memories

RTL designs commonly involve register file or memory components. Register files were
introduced in Chapter 4. Memory will be discussed in Section 5.7; for now, consider a
memory to be a register file with just one port. Register file and memory components are
especially useful for storing arrays.

An ***array*** in an HLSM is an ordered list of items, such as a list named *A* of four 8-bit
numbers. Such a list might be defined in an HLSM as "Local storage: *A*[4](8-bit)." List
items can be accessed using the notation "*A*[*i*]" where *i* is known as the ***index***. The
indices start with 0. For example, *A*[0] reads item 0, and *A*[3] reads item 3 (which is actually the fourth and last item), while "*A*[1] := 8" writes 8 into item 1. Indices must be
within the allowed range; e.g., *A*[–1] or *A*[4] are not allowed for array *A* above. If an
HLSM executes the actions "*A*[0] := 9; *A*[1] := 8; *A*[2] := 7; *A*[3] := 22", then the array
will consist of the numbers <9, 8, 7, 22>, and "*X* := *A*[1]" would set *X* to 8. An HLSM's
inputs, outputs, or local storage items can be declared as arrays, which can lead to more
readable HLSM descriptions for behaviors that deal with lists of items.

During the RTL design process, an array can be mapped to an instantiated register
file or memory component. The following provides a basic example.

Example 5.7 Array example using a register file

Create an HLSM that declares an array *A* with four 11-bit words. Initialize *A*[0] to 9, and *A*[1] to
12. Then, if *A*[0] is 8, output *A*[1] on an 11-bit output *P*; otherwise, repeat the initialization. Note
that this HLSM is not particularly useful and is used for example purposes only.

Figure 5.28(a) shows an HLSM for the desired behavior. The array *A* is declared as local
storage, and the array's items such as *A*[0] and *A*[1] can then be read and written like other local
storage items. Note that the first state initializes the output *Preg*—good practice involves always initializing outputs.

Figure 5.28(b) shows a datapath for the HLSM. The datapath has a register file of the same
dimensions as the array. It has 11-bit constants 12 (which is actually 00000001100), 9, and 8.
Because the register file write input *W_d* at one time should get 9 and at another time should get 12,

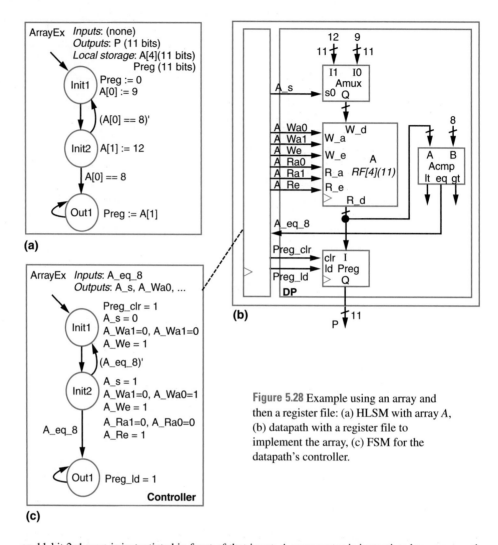

Figure 5.28 Example using an array and then a register file: (a) HLSM with array *A*, (b) datapath with a register file to implement the array, (c) FSM for the datapath's controller.

an 11-bit 2x1 mux is instantiated in front of that input. A comparator is instantiated to compare the register file output to a constant 8. *Preg* is also instantiated for the output *P*. Control lines are included for all the components and given unique names, like *A_s* for the select control input of the mux in front of the register file. Note that the lt and gt control outputs of the comparator are unused. A controller is shown connected with the datapath.

Figure 5.28(c) shows the FSM for the controller. The controller has a single input, *A_eq_8*. It has numerous outputs, *A_s*, *A_Wa0*, ..., *Preg_ld* (for space reasons, the figure lists only the first few; the outputs can be seen in Figure 5.28(b)). State *Init1* clears *Preg* to 0 simply by setting Preg_clr to 1. The state then needs to get the constant 9 at the input of the register file; the state does so by setting *AMux*'s A_s input to 0 so that the constant 9 will pass through the mux and to the register file's *W_d* input. The state also sets the register file write address to "00" by setting A_Wa1 to 0 and A_Wa0 to 0, and enables a register file write by setting A_We to 1. Thus, at the end of state *Init1*, register 0 (which corresponds to *A[0]*) inside the register file will be loaded with the constant 9, and *Preg* will be cleared to 0.

State *Init2* similarly sets up the register file for a write, but this time sets A_s to 1 so that the constant 12 passes through, and sets the write address to "01" so that register 1 (*A*[1]) will be written. Furthermore, this state must set up the register file to read *A*[0] because the result is needed in the state's transition conditions. Thus, the state sets the read address lines to "00" and enables a read by setting A_Re to 1. Recall that reading a register file is not a synchronous operation, but rather the read data appears at the output shortly after the read enable is set to 1. That read data will propagate through the comparator, causing the control line A_eq_8 to become 1 or 0, and that value will be ready to be used by state *Init2*'s transitions when the next clock edge arrives.

State *Out1* sets up the register file to read address 0, and sets Preg_ld to 1. Thus, at the end of the state, *Preg* will be loaded with the value in register 0 (*A*[0]) of the register file. (Notice that the HLSM as defined would never actually reach state *Out1* during execution; the HLSM is for example purposes only.)

We could have created the HLSM with the first state having both the actions *A*[0] := 9 and *A*[1] := 12. However, during implementation as a controller and datapath, we would have noticed that the only register file available has only one write port, and thus we would have had to introduce a second initialization state so that each state has no more than one write to the register file.

The previous example demonstrated basic use of a register file. The following example provides a more interesting use that illustrates the benefit of being able to index an array. The example also uses register files that exist external to the processor being designed.

Example 5.8 Video compression—sum of absolute differences

After a 2004 natural disaster in Indonesia, a TV news reporter broadcast from the scene by "camera phone." The video was smooth as long as the scene wasn't changing significantly. When the scene changed (like panning across the landscape), the video became very jerky—the camera phone had to transmit complete pictures rather than just differences, resulting in fewer frames transmitted over the limited bandwidth of the camera phone.

Digitized video is becoming increasingly commonplace, like in the case of DVDs (see Section 6.7 for further information on DVDs). A straightforward digitized video consists of a sequence of digitized pictures, where each picture is known as a ***frame***. However, such digitized video results in huge data files. Each pixel of a frame is stored as several bytes, and a frame may contain about a million pixels. Assume then that each frame requires about 1 Mbyte, and video is played at approximately 30 frames per second (a normal rate for a TV), so that's 1 Mbyte/frame * 30 frames/sec = 30 Mbytes/sec. One minute of video would require 60 sec * 30 Mbytes/sec = 1.8 Gbytes, and 60 minutes would require 108 Gbytes. A 2-hour movie would require over 200 Gbytes. That's a lot of data, more than can be downloaded quickly over the Internet, or stored on a DVD, which can only hold between 5 Gbytes and 15 Gbytes. In order to make practical use of digitized video with web pages, digital camcorders, cellular telephones, or even DVDs, we need to compress those files into much smaller files. A key technique in compressing video is to recognize that successive frames often have much similarity, so instead of sending a sequence of digitized pictures, we can send one digitized picture frame (a "base" frame), followed by data describing just the difference between the base frame and the next frame. We can send just the difference data for numerous frames, before sending another base frame. Such a method results in some loss of quality, but as long as we send base frames frequently enough, the quality may be acceptable.

Of course, if there is much change from one frame to the next (like for a change of scene, or lots of activity), we can't use the difference method. Video compression devices therefore need to quickly estimate the similarity between two successive digitized frames to determine whether frames can be sent using the difference method. A common way to determine the similarity of two frames is to compute what is known as the ***sum of absolute differences (SAD***, pronounced "ess-aye-dee"). For each pixel in frame 1, SAD involves computing difference between that pixel and the corresponding pixel in frame 2. Each pixel is represented by a number, so difference means the difference in numbers. Suppose a pixel is represented with a byte (real pixels are usually represented

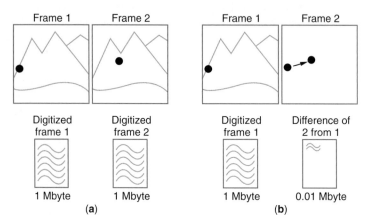

Figure 5.29 A key principle of video compression recognizes that successive frames have much similarity: (a) sending every frame as a distinct digitized picture, (b) instead, sending a base frame and then difference data, from which the original frames can later be reconstructed. If we could do this for 10 frames, (a) would require 1 Mbyte * 10 = 10 Mbytes, while (b) (compressed) would require only 1 Mbyte + 9 * 0.01 Mbyte = 1.09 Mbytes, an almost 10x size reduction.

by at least three bytes), and the pixels at the upper left of frames 1 and 2 in Figure 5.29(a) are being compared. Say frame 1's upper-left pixel has a value of 255. Frame 2's pixel is clearly the same, so would have a value of 255 also. Thus, the difference of these two pixels is $255 - 255 = 0$. SAD would compare the next pixels of both frames in that row, finding the difference to be 0 again. And so on for all the pixels in that row for both frames, as well as the next several rows. However, when computing the difference of the leftmost pixel of the middle row, where that black circle is located, we see that frame 1's pixel will be black, say with a value of 0. On the other hand, frame 2's corresponding pixel will be white, say with a value of 255. So the difference is $255 - 0 = 255$. Likewise, somewhere in the middle of that row, we'll find another difference, this time with frame 1's pixel white (255) and frame 2's pixel black (0)—the difference is again $255 - 0 = 255$. Note that only the difference matters to SAD, not which is bigger or smaller, so we are actually looking at the absolute value of the difference between frame 1 and frame 2 pixels. Summing the absolute value of the differences for every pair of pixels results in a number that represents the similarity of the two frames—0 means identical, and bigger numbers means less similar. If the resulting sum is below some threshold (e.g., below 1,000), the video compression method might apply the method of sending the difference data, as in Figure 5.29(b)—we don't explain how to compute the difference data here, as that is beyond the scope of this example. If the sum is above the threshold, then the difference between the blocks is too great, so the compression method might instead send the full digitized frame for frame 2. Thus, video with similarity among frames will achieve a higher compression than video with many differences.

Actually, most video compression methods compute similarity not between two entire frames, but rather between corresponding 16x16 pixel blocks—yet the idea is the same.

Computing the sum of absolute differences is slow on a microprocessor, so that task may be done using a custom digital circuit, while other tasks may remain on a microprocessor. For example, you might find an SAD circuit inside a digital camcorder, or inside a cellular telephone that supports video. Let's design such a circuit. A block diagram is shown in Figure 5.30(a). The circuit's inputs will be a 256-byte register file A, holding the contents of a 16x16 block of pixels of frame 1, and another 256-byte register file B, holding the corresponding block of frame 2. Another

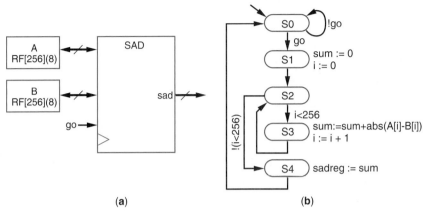

Inputs: A, B [256](8 bits); go (bit)
Outputs: sad (32 bits)
Local storage: sum, sadreg (32 bits); i (9 bits)

(a) **(b)**

Figure 5.30 Sum-of-absolute-differences (SAD) component: (a) block diagram, and (b) HLSM.

circuit input go tells the circuit when to begin computing. An output *sad* will present the result after some number of clock cycles.

Step 1 of the RTL design process is to capture behavior with an HLSM. We can describe the behavior of the SAD component using the HLSM shown in Figure 5.30(b). We declare the inputs, outputs, and local registers *sum* and *i*. The *sum* register will hold the running sum of differences; we make this register 32 bits wide. The *i* register will be used to index into the current pixel in the block memories; *i* will range from 0 to 256, and therefore we'll make it 9 bits wide. We also must declare the 32-bit storage item *sadreg* that registers the *sad* output. The HLSM initially waits for the input go to become 1. The HLSM then initializes registers *sum* and *i* to 0. The HLSM next enters a loop: if *i* is less than 256, the HLSM computes the absolute value of the difference of the two blocks' pixels indexed by *i* (the notation *A[i]* refers to register *i* of register file *A*), updates the running sum, increments *i*, and repeats. Otherwise if *i* is not less than 256, the HLSM loads *sadreg* with the sum, which now represents the final sum, and returns to the first state to wait for the go signal to become 1 again. (The reader may notice that HLSM did not follow good design practice by not initializing *sadreg*; a better HLSM would include a state before S0 that initializes *sadreg* to 0).

We re-emphasize that the order of storage update actions in a state does not impact the results, because all those actions occur simultaneously at the end of the state. For the state inside the loop, arranging the actions as "*sum := sum + abs(A[i]-B[i]); i := i + 1*" or as "*i := i + 1; sum := sum + abs(A[i]-B[i])*" does not impact the results. Either arrangement uses the old value of *i*.

Step 2A of the RTL design process is to create a datapath. We see from the HLSM that we need a subtractor, an absolute-value component, an adder, and a comparison of i to 256. We build the datapath shown in Figure 5.31. The adder will be 32 bits wide, so the 8-bit input coming from the *abs* component will need to have 0s appended as its high 24 bits. We have also introduced interfaces to the external register files. Data inputs *A_data* and *B_data* come from each register file. Because both register files always have the same address read at the same time, we use data output *AB_addr* as the address for both register files. We also use a control output AB_rd as the read enable for both register files.

Step 2B is to connect the datapath to a controller block, as shown in Figure 5.31.

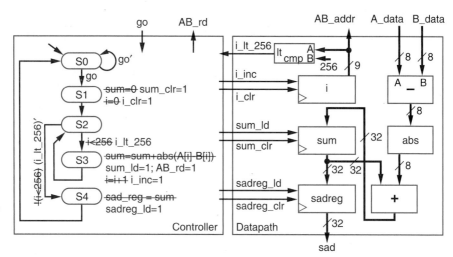

Figure 5.31 SAD datapath and controller FSM.

Step 2C is to convert the HLSM to an FSM. The FSM appears on the left side of Figure 5.31. For convenience, the FSM shows the original high-level actions (crossed out), and the replacement by the FSM actions.

To complete the design, we would convert the FSM to a controller implementation (a state register and combinational logic) as described in Chapter 3.

Comparing Microprocessor and Custom Circuit Implementations

Example 5.8 stated that output *sad* will present the result some number of clock cycles after go becomes 1. Let's determine that number of cycles. After go becomes 1, the HLSM will spend one cycle initializing registers in *S1*, then will spend two cycles in each of the 256 loop iterations (states *S2* and *S3*), and finally one more cycle to update the output register in state *S4*, for a total of $1 + 2*256 + 1 = 514$ cycles.

If the SAD algorithm ran on a microprocessor, the algorithm would likely need more than two clock cycles per loop iteration. It would need two cycles to load internal registers, then a cycle for subtract, perhaps two cycles for absolute value, and a cycle for sum, for a total of six cycles per iteration. The custom circuit built in the above example, at two cycles per iteration, is thus about three times faster for computing SAD, assuming equal clock frequencies. Section 6.5 will show how to build a SAD circuit that is *much* faster.

▶ DIGITAL VIDEO—IMAGINING THE FUTURE.

People seem to have an insatiable appetite for good-quality video, and thus much attention is placed on developing fast and/or power-efficient encoders and decoders for digital video devices, like DVD players and recorders, digital video cameras, cell phones supporting digital video, video conferencing units, TVs, TV set-top boxes, etc. It's interesting to think toward the future—assuming video encoding/decoding becomes even more powerful and digital communication speeds increase, we might imagine video displays (with audio) on our walls at home or work that continually display what's happening at another home (perhaps our mom's house) or at a partner office on the other side of the country—like a virtual window to another place. Or we might imagine portable devices that enable us to continually see what someone else wearing a tiny camera—perhaps our child or spouse—sees. Those items could significantly change our living patterns.

RTL Design Pitfall Involving Storage Updates

A common mistake in creating an HLSM is assuming that a clocked storage item is updated in the state in which the item is written. Such an assumption is incorrect, and can lead to unexpected behavior when the HLSM reads the storage item in the same state, and likewise when the HLSM reads the storage item in a transition leaving that state. For example, Figure 5.32(a) shows a simple HLSM. Examine the HLSM and then answer the following two questions:

- What will be the value of Q after state A?
- What will be the final state: C or D?

The answers may surprise you. The value of Q will not be 99; Q's value will actually be unknown. The reason is illustrated by the timing diagram in Figure 5.32(b). State A prepares to load a 99 into R on the next clock edge, and prepares to load the value of storage item R into storage item Q on the next clock edge. When the next clock edge occurs, both those loads occur *simultaneously*. Q therefore gets whatever value was in R just before the next clock edge, which is unknown to us.

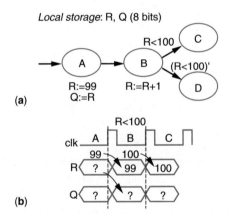

(a)

(b)

Figure 5.32 High-level state machine that behaves differently than some people may expect, due to reads of a clocked storage item in the same state as writes to that item: (a) HLSM, (b) timing diagram.

Furthermore, the final state will not be D, but will rather be C. The reason is illustrated by the timing diagram in Figure 5.32(b). State B prepares to load 100 into R on the next clock cycle, and prepares to load the next state based on the transition condition. R is 99, and therefore the transition condition $R<100$ is true, meaning the HLSM is prepared to make state C the next state, not state D. On the next clock edge, R becomes 100, and the next state becomes C.

The key is to always remember that *a state's actions* **prepare** *the values that will occur on the next rising clock edge—but those values* **don't actually get loaded into** **storage items** *until that next clock edge.* Thus, any expressions in a state's actions or outgoing transition conditions will be using the previous values of storage items, not the values being assigned in that state itself. By the same reasoning, all the actions of a state occur simultaneously on the next clock edge, and thus could be listed in any order.

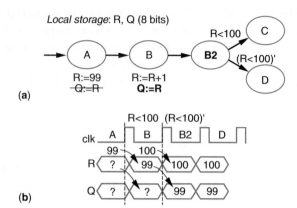

(a)

(b)

Figure 5.33 HLSM that ensures storage item reads occur at least one state after writes: (a) HLSM, (b) timing diagram.

Assuming that the designer actually wants Q to equal 99 and the final state to be D, then a solution is to insure that local storage writes occur at least one state before reads that rely on those writes. Figure 5.33(a) shows a new HLSM in which the assignment of $Q:=R$ has been moved to state B, after $R=99$ has taken effect. Furthermore, the HLSM has a new state $B2$ that simply waits for R to be updated with the new value before that value is read in the transition conditions. The timing diagram in Figure 5.33(b) shows the behavior that the designer expected.

An alternative solution for the transition issue in this case would be to utilize comparison values that take into account that the old value is being used. So instead of comparing R to 100, the comparisons might instead be to 99.

RTL Design Involving a Timer

RTL design commonly requires capturing behavior that uses explicit time intervals. For example, a design may have to repeatedly blink an LED off for 1 second and on for 1 second. Determining when a time interval like 1 second has passed can be achieved by pre-instantiating a 32-bit 1-microsecond timer component T as in Figure 5.34(a). Then, an HLSM as shown in Figure 5.34(b) can declare a special item T as a timer, which can be loaded like a local storage item but which also has an enable input T_en and a rollover output T_Q implicitly associated with the item. The HLSM can make use of the declared timer to detect 1-second intervals. The HLSM loads 1 second (1,000,000 microseconds) into the timer in state *Init* by writing $T := 1000000$. The HLSM then enables the timer in state *Off* by setting T_en to 1, and also sets output L to 0 to turn the LED off. The HLSM waits in that state until the timer's T_Q output becomes 1, which will happen after 1 second. The HLSM then transitions to state *On*, which turns on the LED, and stays in that state until T_Q becomes 1 again, which will happen after another 1 second. The HLSM returns to state *Off* , staying there for 1 second again, and so on. (Note that this HLSM

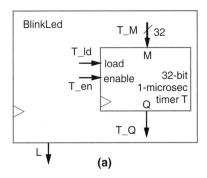 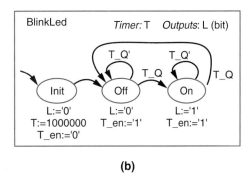

Figure 5.34 Blinking LED example: (a) pre-instantiated timer, (b) HLSM making use of the timer to turn the LED off for 1 second (1,000,000 microseconds), then off for 1 second, and repeating.

assumes that the timer output T_Q stays 1 for only one clock cycle, which indeed is how the timer compnent was designed in Chapter 4.)

The HLSM can be straighforwardly converted to a controller and datapath. The datapath would consist of just the timer component with the constant "1000000" at the timer's data input. The controller would connect with the timer's control signals, and the controller's FSM would be identical to the HLSM except that the assignment $T := 1000000$ would be replaced with T_ld = 1.

The above example required only one time interval to be repeatedly measured throughout the HLSM, namely 1 second; as such, the timer component was initialized once and then enabled for the rest of the HLSM's execution. However, a timer can also be used to measure different intervals in the same HLSM. For example, an alternative blinking LED example stays off for 1 second but then stays on for 2 seconds. Such behavior can be captured by repeatedly re-initializing the timer as shown in Figure 5.35(b). The HLSM stays in state *OffWait* for 1 second, by loading 1 second (1,000,000 microseconds) into the timer in state *OffInit*, and then by enabling the timer in state *OffWait* and staying in that state until the timer's output T_Q becomes 1. Likewise, state *OnInit* loads 2 seconds into the timer, and state *OnWait* enables the timer and waits for the timer's output to become 1. Converting this HLSM to a processor would thus have the timer *T* in the datapath. *T_M* would have a 2x1 mux to route either 1000000 or 2000000 to the timer's data input, thus completing the datapath. The controller would connect with the timer and mux control signals. Converting the HLSM to an FSM for the controller would consist merely of replacing the *T* assignments by the appropriate 2x1 mux select line assignment and by setting T_ld to 1. (Notice that each initialization state adds an extra clock cycle, which is likely not a problem for a blinking LED system but would need to be compensated for if a precise 3 second blinking period was required.) An alternative solution could use two timers, one to compute the 1-second interval, and the other for the 2-second interval.

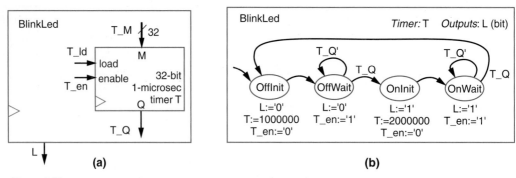

Figure 5.35 Blinking LED example: (a) pre-instantiated timer, (b) HLSM making use of the timer to turn the LED on for 1 second (1,000,000 microseconds), then off for 2 seconds, and repeating.

Button Debouncing

Button debouncing is a typical task in RTL design that also illustrates the use of a timer. A button is an common input device to a digital circuit. Ideally, a button outputs 1 when pressed, and outputs 0 when not pressed. Actually, though, a real button may output some spurious 0s just after being pressed. The reason is because the button is a mechanical device, and pressing the button down down results in a small amount of *bounce* as the button settles in the down position. An analogy is dropping a hard ball such as a billiard ball or a bowling ball onto the floor—the ball will bounce slightly before coming to rest onto the floor. The bounce of a button is illustrated in Figure 5.36. Instead of

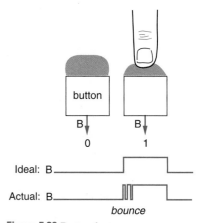

Figure 5.36 Button bounce.

B becoming 1 and staying 1 when initially pressed down, B changes to 1, then briefly changes back to 0, then to 1, then 0 again, and finally settles at 1. Typical buttons may exhibit bounce for a few milliseconds after being pressed down. Bounce is a problem because the bouncing signal appears to be several distinct rapid button presses rather than just one press—the actual B signal in Figure 5.36 suggests that the button was pressed three times. A simple solution is to create a circuit that converts the actual B signal into the ideal B signal, a process known as *button debouncing*.

Example 5.9 Button debouncer

A button debouncer converts a signal like the actual B signal shown in Figure 5.36 into the ideal B signal of that figure. One approach to designing a debouncer first notes that typical buttons bounce for only a few milliseconds. Thus, a debouncer could, upon detecting the change from 0 to 1 on an input Bin, set an output Bout to 1 and then hold that output 1 for at least, say, 20 milliseconds; the bouncing should complete well before those 20 milliseconds. This approach assumes that a button press will always last for at least 20 milliseconds, which is a reasonable assumption for buttons pressed by humans (otherwise, this approach extends a shorter press into a longer 20-millisecond press).

The desired behavior can be captured as the HLSM in Figure 5.37. Measuring 20 milliseconds in the HLSM is achieved by pre-instantiating a 32-bit microsecond timer component, and then using that component in the HLSM. State *Init* loads the timer component with the value 20 milliseconds (20,000 microseconds). State *WaitBin* waits for the button input Bin to become 1, after which state *Wait20* sets Bout to 1, enables the

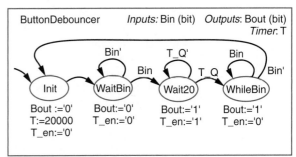

Figure 5.37 Button debouncer.

timer, and waits until the timer output T_Q becomes 1, thus waiting for 20 milliseconds regardless of the value of Bin. After the 20 milliseconds have passed, the HLSM enters state *WhileBin*, which continues to set Bout to 1 as long as Bin is still 1. When Bin returns to 0 (meaning the button is released), the HLSM starts over again.

A Data-Dominated RTL Design Example

Some systems have an extensive datapath and a relatively simple controller. Such a system is known as **data-dominated system**. In contrast, a system with a simple datapath and relatively complex controller is known as a **control-dominated system**. A data-dominated system may have only a few states, and in fact may have only one state. Within those few states, however, may be extensive computations. Nevertheless, the RTL design process can proceed as before. The following example illustrates the design of a data-dominated system.

Example 5.10 FIR filter

A **digital filter** takes a stream of digital inputs and generates a stream of digital outputs with some feature of the input stream removed or modified. A **stream** is a sequence of values separated by a fixed amount of time. Figure 5.38 shows a block diagram of a popular digital filter known as an FIR filter. Input *X* and output *Y* are *N* bits wide each, such as 12 bits each. As a filtering example,

Figure 5.38 FIR filter block diagram.

consider the following stream of digital temperature values on X coming from a car engine temperature sensor sampled every second: 180, 180, 181, *240*, 180, 181. That 240 is probably not an accurate measurement, as a car engine's temperature cannot jump 60 degrees in one second. A digital filter would remove such "noise" from the input stream, generating perhaps an output stream on Y like: 180, 180, 181, *181*, 180, 181.

An finite impulse response filter, or FIR filter (commonly pronounced by saying the letters "F" "I" "R"), is a popular general digital filter design that can be used for a variety of filtering goals. Figure 5.38 shows a block diagram of an FIR filter. The basic idea of an FIR filter is simple: the present output is obtained by multiplying the present input value by a constant, and adding that result to the previous input value times a constant, and adding that result to the next-earlier input value times a constant, and so on. In a sense, adding to previous values in this manner results in a weighted average. Section 5.13 describes digital filtering and FIR filters in more detail. For the purpose of this example, we merely need to know that an FIR filter can be described by an equation with the following form:

$$y(t) = c0 \times x(t) + c1 \times x(t-1) + c2 \times x(t-2)$$

An FIR filter with three terms as in the above equation is known as a *3-tap* FIR filter. Real FIR filters typically have many tens of taps—we use only three taps for the purpose of illustration. A filter designer using an FIR filter achieves a particular filtering goal *simply by choosing the FIR filter's constants*; i.e., by selecting values for *c0, c1, c2*, etc.

Figure 5.39 shows an HLSM for an FIR filter with a 12-bit input and output, thus fulfilling **Step 1** of the RTL design process. Note the simplicity of the HLSM, which has only two states, and which actually spends all its time in just the second state *FC* (standing for "FIR Compute"). In addition to declaring the input *X* and output *Y*, the HLSM declares 12-bit local storage items *xt0*, *xt1*, and *xt2* for the three most recent input values; *xt0* will be for the current value, *xt1* for the value from time *t-1* (the previous clock cycle), and *xt2* for the value from time *t-2*. It also declares

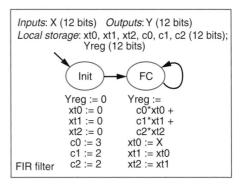

Figure 5.39 FIR filter HLSM.

12-bit local storage items for the three filter constants *c0, c1*, and *c2*, and for the storage item *Yreg* associated with output Y. State *Init* initializes the output by setting the output's storage item *Yreg* to 0. The state also initializes the *xt* registers to 0s. The state sets the *c* registers to hold the constants for this particular FIR filter, which for this filter are 3, 2, and 2. State *FC* computes the FIR equation for the current values in the *xt* registers and sets *Yreg* to the computed value. That state also updates the *xt* registers, setting *xt0* to the current value on input X, *xt1* to *xt0*, and *xt2* to *xt1*. Recall that all those updates occur at the end of the state when the next rising clock edge arrives, and that all those updates occur simultaneously.

Step 2A is to create a datapath. Substep (a) involves making *X* a datapath input and *Y* a datapath output. Substep (b) involves instantiating the seven local storage registers. Substep (c) involves examining state *Init* and then instantiating constants 3, 2, and 2 at the inputs of the *c* registers. Examining state *FC* reveals the need to instantiate 3 multipliers and two adders, and to connect them as shown in the figure. That state also requires that the inputs of each *xt* register be connected as shown.

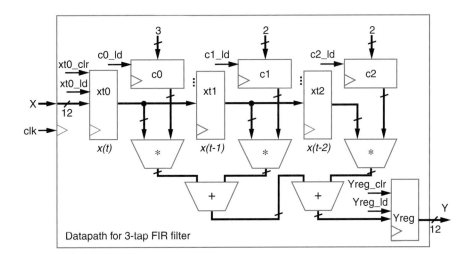

Figure 5.40 FIR filter datapath.

Datapath for 3-tap FIR filter

Step 2B connects the datapath to a controller, which the figure does not show but which follows similarly from previous examples. Figure 5.40 does show the control inputs to the registers that will be needed by the controller (the control inputs for *xt1* and *xt2* are shown as "..." to save space in the figure).

Finally, **Step 2C** would convert the HLSM of Figure 5.39 into an FSM for the controller. State *Init* would set the clear line for *Yreg* and each *xt* reg to 1, and would set the load line for each *c* register to 1. State *FC* would simply set the load line for *Yreg* and for each *xt* reg to 1.

Commonly an FIR filter should sample the input at a specified rate, such as once every 10 microseconds. A timer can be used for this purpose. The HLSM would be extended to configure, enable, and then monitor the timer as in earlier examples.

Comparing Microprocessor and Custom Circuit Implementations

It is interesting to compare the performance of the circuit implementation of a 3-tap FIR filter with a microprocessor implementation. The datapath's critical path goes from the *xt* and *c* registers, through one multiplier, and through two adders, before reaching *Yreg*. For the circuit implementation, assume that the adder has a 2 ns delay. Also assume that chaining the adders together results in the delays adding, so that two adders chained together have a delay of 4 ns (detailed analysis of the internal gates of the adders could show the delay to actually be slightly less). Assume the multiplier has a 20 ns delay. Then the critical path, or longest register-to-register delay (to be discussed further in Section 5.5) would be from *c0* to *Yreg*, going through the multiplier and two adders as shown in Figure 5.40. That path's length would be 20 + 4 = 24 ns. Note that the path from *c1* to *Yreg* would be equally long, but not longer. A critical path of 24 ns means the datapath could be clocked at a frequency of 1 / 24 ns = 42 MHz. In other words, a new sample could appear at *X* every 24 ns, and new outputs would appear at *Y* every 24 ns.

Now consider the circuit performance of a larger-sized filter: a 100-tap FIR filter rather than a 3-tap filter. Assume that 100 multipliers are available—then the 100 multiplications could occur simultaneously in 100 multipliers just as the 3 multiplications occurred simultaneously. Thus, the main performance difference is that the circuit must add 100 values rather than just 3. Recall from Section 4.13 that an adder tree is a fast way to add many values. One hundred values will require a tree with 7 levels—50 additions, then 25, then 13 (roughly), then 7, then 4, then 2, then 1. So the total delay would be 20 ns (for the multiplier) plus seven adder-delays (7*2ns = 14 ns), for a total delay of 34 ns.

For a microprocessor implementation, assume 10 ns per instruction. Assume that each multiplication or addition would require two instructions. A 100-tap filter would need approximately 100 multiplications and 100 additions, so the total time would be (100 multiplications * 2 instr/mult + 100 additions * 2 instr/add) * 10 ns per instruction = 4000 ns. In other words, the circuit implementation would be over 100 times faster (4000 ns / 34 ns) than the microprocessor implementation. A circuit could therefore process 100 times more data than a microprocessor implementation, resulting in better filtering.

▶ 5.5 DETERMINING CLOCK FREQUENCY

RTL design produces a processor circuit consisting of a datapath and a controller. Inside the datapath and controller are registers that require a clock signal. A clock signal has a particular **clock frequency**, which is the number of clock cycles per second, also known as Hertz (Hz). The frequency impacts how fast the circuit executes its specified task. Obviously, a lower frequency will result in slower execution, while a higher frequency will result in a faster execution. Conversely stated, a larger clock period (the duration of a clock cycle, which is the inverse of frequency) is slower, while a smaller period is faster.

Designers of digital circuits often want their circuits to execute as fast as possible. However, a designer cannot choose an arbitrarily high clock frequency (meaning an arbitrarily small period). Consider, for example, the simple circuit in Figure 5.41, in which registers *a* and *b* feed through an adder into register *c*. The adder has a delay of 2 ns, meaning that when the adder's inputs change, the adder's outputs will not be stable until after 2 ns—before 2 ns, the adder's outputs will have spurious values (see Section 4.3). If the designer chooses a clock period of 10 ns, the circuit should work fine. Shortening the period to 5 ns will speed the execution. But shortening the period to 1 ns will result in incorrect circuit behavior. One clock

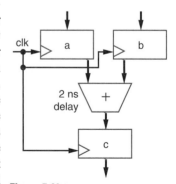

Figure 5.41 Longest path is 2 ns.

cycle might load new values into registers *a* and *b*. The next clock cycle will load register *c* 1 ns later (as well as loading *a* and *b* again), but the output of the adder won't be stable until 2 ns have passed. The value loaded into register *c* will thus be some spurious value that has no useful meaning, and will not be the sum of *a* and *b*.

Thus, a designer must be careful not to set the clock frequency too high. To determine the highest possible frequency, a designer must analyze the entire circuit and find the *longest* path delay from *any* register to *any* other register, or from any circuit input to any register. The longest register-to-register or input-to-register delay in a circuit is known as the circuit's **critical path.** A designer can then choose a clock whose period is *longer* than the circuit's critical path.

Figure 5.42 illustrates a circuit with four possible paths from any register to any other register:

- One path starts at register *a*, goes through the adder, and ends at register *c*. That path's delay is 2 ns.

- Another path starts at register *a*, goes through the adder, then through the multiplier, and ends at register *d*. That path's delay is 2 ns + 5 ns = 7 ns.

- Another path starts at register *b*, goes through the adder, through the multiplier, and ends at register *d*. That path's delay is also 2 ns + 5 ns = 7 ns.

- The last path starts at register *b*, goes through the multiplier, and ends at register *d*. That path's delay is 5 ns.

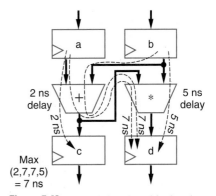

Figure 5.42 Determining the critical path.

The longest path is thus 7 ns (there are two paths with that delay). Thus, the clock period must be at least 7 ns.

The above analysis assumes that the only delay between registers is caused by logic delays. In reality, *wires* also have a delay. In the 1980s and 1990s, the delay of logic dominated over the delay of wires—wire delays were often negligible. But in modern chip technologies, the delay of wires may equal or even exceed the delay of logic, and thus wire delays cannot be ignored. Wire delays add to a path's length just as logic delays do. Figure 5.43 illustrates a path length calculation with wire delays included.

Furthermore, the above analysis does not consider setup times for the registers. Recall from Section 3.5 that flip-flop inputs (and hence register inputs) must be stable for a specified amount of time *before* a clock edge. The setup time also adds to the path length.

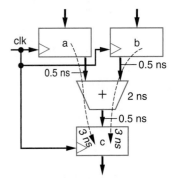

Figure 5.43 Longest path is 3 ns, considering wire delays.

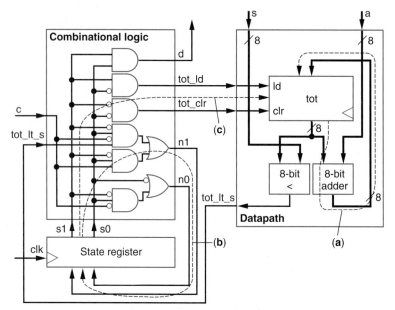

Figure 5.44 Critical paths throughout a circuit: (a) within a datapath, (b) within a controller, (c) between a controller and datapath.

Even considering wire delays and setup times, designers typically choose a clock period that is still *longer* than the critical path by an amount depending on how conservative the designer wants to be with respect to ensuring that the circuit works under a variety of operating conditions. Certain conditions can change the delay of circuit components, such as very high temperature, very low temperature, age, electrical interference, etc. Generally, the longer the period beyond the critical path, the more conservative the design. For example, a designer might determine that the critical path is 7 ns, but might choose a clock period of 10 ns or even 15 ns, the latter being very conservative.

If desiring low power, a designer might choose an even lower frequency to reduce circuit power. Section 6.6 describes why reducing the clock frequency reduces power.

When analyzing a processor (controller and datapath) to find the critical path, a designer must be aware that register-to-register paths exist not just within the datapath as in Figure 5.43(a), but also within the controller as in Figure 5.43(b), and between the controller and datapath as in Figure 5.43(c), and even between the processor and external components.

▶ CONSERVATIVE CHIP MAKERS, AND PC OVERCLOCKING.

Chip makers usually publish their chips' maximum clocking frequency somewhat lower than the real maximum—perhaps 10%, 20%, or even 30% lower. Such conservatism reduces the chances that the chip will fail in unanticipated situations, such as extremes of hot or cold weather, or slight variations in the chip manufacturing process. Many personal computer enthusiasts have taken advantage of such conservatism by "overclocking" their PCs, meaning setting the clock frequency higher than a chip's published maximum, by changing the PC's BIOS (basic input/output system) settings. Numerous websites post statistics on the successes and failures of people trying to overclock nearly every PC processor—it seems the norm is about 10%–40% higher than the published maximum. We don't recommend overclocking (for one, you may damage the microprocessor due to overheating), but it's interesting to see the common presence of conservative design.

The number of possible paths in a circuit can be quite large. Consider a circuit with N registers that has paths from every register to every other register. Then there are $N*N$, or N^2 possible register-to-register paths. For example, if N is 3 and the three registers are named A, B, and C, then the possible paths are: A—>A, A—>B, A—>C, B—>A, B—>B, B—>C, C—>A, C—>B, C—>C, for $3*3 = 9$ possible paths. For $N=50$, there may be up to 2500 possible paths. Because of the large number of possible paths, automated tools can be of great assistance. ***Timing analysis*** tools automatically analyze all paths to determine the longest path, and may also ensure that setup and hold times are satisfied throughout the circuit.

▷ 5.6 BEHAVIORAL-LEVEL DESIGN: C TO GATES (OPTIONAL)

As transistors per chip continue to increase and hence designers build more complex digital systems that use those additional transistors, digital system behavior becomes harder to understand. A designer building a new digital system may find it useful to first describe the desired system behavior using a programming language, like C, C++, or Java, in order to capture desired behavior correctly. Alternatively, the designer may use the high-level programming constructs in a hardware description language, like the VHDL or Verilog languages, to first capture the desired behavior correctly. Then, the designer converts that programming language description to an RTL design by first converting the description to an HLSM RTL description, and then proceeding with RTL design. Converting a system's programming language description to an RTL description is known as ***behavioral-level design***. We'll introduce behavioral-level design using an example.

Example 5.11 Sum of absolute differences in C for video compression

Recall Example 5.8, which created a sum-of-absolute-differences component. That example started with an HLSM—but that HLSM wasn't very easy to understand. We can more easily describe the computation of the sum of absolute differences using C code as shown in Figure 5.45.

That code is much easier to understand for most people than the HLSM in Figure 5.30. Thus, for some designs, C code (or something similar) is the most natural starting point.

To begin the RTL design process, a designer can convert the C code to an HLSM like that in Figure 5.30, and then proceed to complete the RTL design process and hence design the circuit.

Figure 5.45 C program description of a sum-of-absolute-differences computation—the C program may be easier to develop and easier to understand than an HLSM.

```
int SAD (byte A [256], byte B [256]) / / not quite C syntax
{
    uint sum; short uint i;
    sum = 0;
    i = 0;
    while (i < 256) {
        sum = sum + abs (A[i] – B[i]);
        i = i + 1;
    }
    return (sum);
}
```

It is instructive to define a structured method for converting C code to an HLSM. Defining such a method makes it clear that C code can be *automatically translated* to either software on a programmable processor (such translation known as *compilation*), or *to a custom digital circuit* (such translation known as *synthesis*). We point out that most designers that start with C code and then continue with RTL design do *not* necessarily follow a particular method in performing such conversion. However, automated tools *do* follow a method having some similarities to the one described below.

We also point out that the conversion method will sometimes result in "extra" states that you might notice could be combined with other states—these extra states would be combined by a later optimization step, though we'll combine some of them as the method proceeds.

Consider three basic types of statements in C code—assignment statements, while loops, and condition statements (if-then-else). Equivalent HLSM templates exist for each such statement.

Figure 5.46 HLSM template for assignment statement.

An assignment statement in C translates into one HLSM state. The state's actions execute the assignment as in Figure 5.46.

An *if-then* statement in C translates into the HLSM structure of Figure 5.47. A state checks the condition of the *if* statement and has two transitions, one for the statement's condition being true, and the other for false. The true one points to the states for the *then* part of the statement. The false one points past those states to an end state.

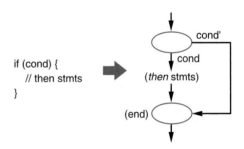

Figure 5.47 Template for *if-then* statement.

An *if-then-else* statement in C similarly translates to a state that checks the condition of the *if* statement, but this time pointing to states for the *else* part if the condition is false, as shown in Figure 5.48.

The *else* part commonly contains another *if* statement because C programmers may have multiple *else if* parts in a region of code. That if statement is translated as described earlier.

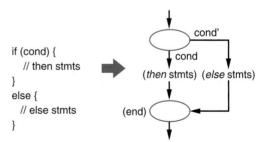

Figure 5.48 Template for *if-then-else* statement.

Finally, a *while* loop statement in C translates into states similar to an *if-then* statement, except that after executing the *while*'s statements, if the *while* condition is true, the state machine branches back to the condition check state rather than to the end state. The template appears in Figure 5.49. Only when the condition is false is the end state reached.

Given these simple templates, a wide variety of C programs can be converted to HLSMs, and the RTL design process can then be used to convert those HLSMs to digital circuits.

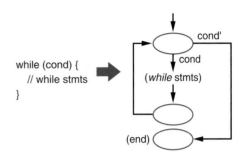

Figure 5.49 Template for *while* loop statement.

Example 5.12 Converting an if-then-else statement to a state machine

We are given the C-like code shown in Figure 5.50(a), which computes the maximum of two unsigned data inputs *X* and *Y*. We can translate that code to an HLSM by first translating the *if-then-else* statement to states using the method of Figure 5.48, as shown in Figure 5.50(b). We then translate the *then* statements to states, and then the *else* statements, yielding the final state machine in Figure 5.50(c).

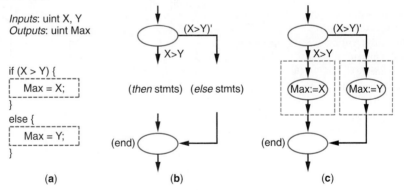

Figure 5.50 Behavioral-level design starting from C code: (a) C code for computing the max of two numbers, (b) translating the if-then-else statement to a high-level state machine, (c) translating the *then* and *else* statements to states. From the state machine in (c), we could use our RTL design method to complete the design. Note: max can be implemented more efficiently; we use max here to provide an easy-to-understand example.

Example 5.13 SAD C code to high-level state machine conversion

We wish to convert the C program description of the sum-of-absolute-differences behavior in Figure 5.45 to an HLSM. The code is shown in Figure 5.51(a), written as an infinite loop rather than a procedure call, and using an input go to indicate when the system should compute the SAD. The "while (1)" statement, after some optimization, translates just to a transition from the last state back to the first state, so we'll hold off on adding that transition until we have formed the rest of the state machine. We begin with the statement "while (!go)," which, based on the template approach, translates to the states shown in Figure 5.51(b). Since the loop has no statements in the loop body, we can simplify the loop's states as shown in Figure 5.51(c). Figure 5.51(c) also shows the states for the next two statements, which are assignment statements. Since those two assignments could be done simultaneously, we merge the two states into one, as shown in Figure 5.51(d). We then translate the next *while* loop, using the *while* loop template, to the states shown in Figure 5.51(e). We fill in the states for the *while* loop's statements in Figure 5.51(f), merging the two assignment statement states into one state since the assignments can be done simultaneously. Figure 5.51(f) also

Figure 5.51 Behavioral-level design of the sum-of-absolute-differences code: (a) original C code, written as an infinite loop, (b) translating the statement "while (!go);" to a state machine, (c) simplified states for "while (!go);" and states for the assignment statements that follow, (d) merging the two assignment states into one, (e) inserting the template for the next while loop, (f) inserting the states for that while loop, merging two assignment statements into one, (g) the final high-level state machine, with the "while (1)" included by transitioning from the last state back to the first state, and with obviously unnecessary states removed.

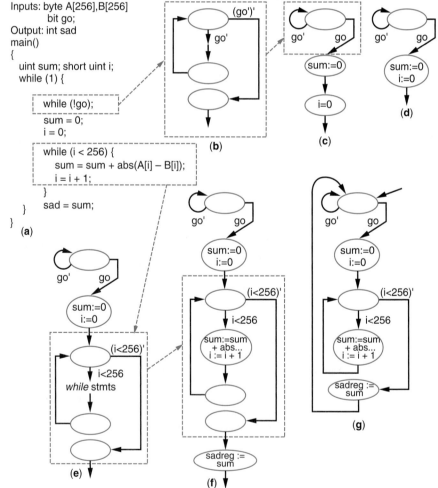

shows the state for the last statement of the C code, which assigns *sad=sum*. Finally, we eliminate obviously unnecessary empty states, and add a transition from the last state to the first state to account for the entire code being enclosed in a "while (1)" loop.

Notice the similarity between the HLSM in Figure 5.51(g) and the HLSM designed from scratch in Figure 5.30.

We will need to map the C data types to bits at some point. For example, the C code declares *i* to be a short unsigned integer, which means 16 bits. So we could declare *i* to be 16 bits in the HLSM. Or, knowing the range of *i* to be 0 to 256, we could instead define *i* to be 9 bits (C doesn't have a 9-bit-wide data type).

We could then proceed to design a controller and datapath from this HLSM, as was done in Figure 5.31. Thus, we can translate C code to a circuit by using a straightforward automatable method.

The previous example shows how C code can be converted to a custom digital circuit using methods that are fully automatable. General C code can contain additional types of statements, some of which can be easily translated to states. For example, a *for* loop can be translated to states by first transforming the *for* loop into a *while* loop. A *switch* statement can be translated by first translating the *switch* statement to *if-then-else* statements.

Some C constructs pose problems for converting to a circuit, though. For example, pointers and recursion are not easy to translate. Thus, tools that automate behavioral design from C code typically impose restrictions on the allowable C code that can be handled by the tool. Such restrictions are known as **subsetting** the language.

While we have emphasized C code in this section, obviously any similar language, such as C++, Java, VHDL, Verilog, etc., can be converted to custom digital circuits—with appropriate language subsetting.

▶ 5.7 MEMORY COMPONENTS

RTL design involves instantiating and connecting datapath components to form datapaths that are controlled by controllers. RTL design often utilizes some additional components outside the datapath and controller.

One such component is a memory. An **MxN memory** is a memory component able to store *M* data items of *N* bits each. Each data item in a memory is known as a **word**. Figure 5.52 depicts the storage available in an *MxN* memory.

Memory can be categorized into two groups: RAM memory, which can be written to and read from, and ROM memory, which can only be read from. However, as shall be discussed, the distinction between the two categories is blurring due to new technologies.

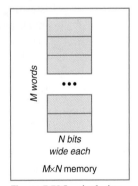

M words

*N bits
wide each*

MxN memory

Figure 5.52 Logical view of a memory.

Random Access Memory (RAM)

A random-access memory (RAM) is logically the same as a register file (see Section 4.10)—both are memory components whose words (each of which can be thought of as a register) can be individually read and written using address inputs. The differences between a RAM and a register file are:

- The size of *M*—We typically refer to smaller memories (from 4 to 512 or perhaps even 1024 words or so) as register files, and larger memories as RAMs.
- The bit storage implementation—For large numbers of words, a compact implementation becomes increasingly important. Thus, a RAM typically uses a very compact implementation for bit storage that will be described below, rather than using a faster but larger flip-flop.
- The memory's physical shape—For large numbers of words, the physical shape of the memory's implementation becomes important. A tall rectangular shape will have some short wires and some long wires, whereas a square shape will have all medium-length wires. A RAM therefore typically has a square shape to reduce the memory's critical path. Reads are performed by first reading out an entire row of words from the RAM, and then selecting the appropriate word (column) out of that row.

There is no clear-cut border between what defines a register file and what defines a RAM. Smaller memories (typically) tend to be called register files, and larger memories tend to be called RAMs. But you'll often see the terms used quite interchangeably.

A typical RAM is single-ported, with that port having both read and write capability (one at a time). Some RAMs are dual-ported. In contrast, register files are almost never single-ported. Furthermore, RAMs with more ports are much less common than for register files, because a RAM's larger size makes the delay and size overhead of extra ports much more costly. Nevertheless, conceptually, a RAM can have an arbitrary number of read ports and write ports, just like a register file.

Figure 5.53 shows a block diagram for a 1024x32 single-port RAM (*M* = 1024, *N* = 32). *data* is a 32-bit-wide set of data lines that can serve either as input lines during writes or as output lines during reads. *addr* is a 10-bit input serving as the address lines during reads or writes. rw is a 1-bit control input that indicates whether the present operation should be a read or a write (e.g., rw = 0 means read, rw = 1 means write). en is a 1-bit control input that enables the RAM for reading or writing—if we don't want to read or write during a particular clock cycle, we set en to 0 to prevent a read or write (regardless of the value of rw).

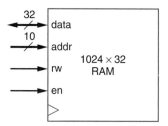

Figure 5.53 1024x32 RAM block symbol.

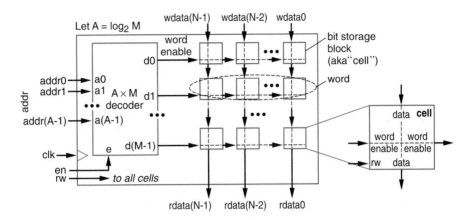

Figure 5.54 Logical internal structure of a RAM.

Figure 5.54 shows the logical internal structure of an *MxN* RAM. "Logical" structure means that we can think of the structure being implemented in that way, although a real physical implementation may possess a different actual structure. (As an analogy, a logical structure of a telephone includes a microphone and a speaker connected to a phone line, although real physical telephones vary tremendously in their implementations, including handheld devices, headsets, wireless connections, built-in answering machines, etc.) The main part of the RAM structure is the grid of bit storage blocks, also known as *cells*. A collection of *N* cells forms a word, and there are *M* words. The address inputs feed into a decoder, each output of which enables all the cells in one word corresponding to the present address values. The enable input en can disable the decoder and prevent any word from being enabled. The read/write control input rw also connects to every cell to control whether the cell will be written with wdata, or read out to rdata. The data lines are connected through one word's cell to the next word's cell, so each cell must be designed to only output its contents when enabled and thus output nothing when disabled, to avoid interfering with another cell's output.

▶ WHY IS IT CALLED "RANDOM ACCESS" MEMORY?

In the early days of digital design, RAMs did not exist. If you had information you wanted your digital circuit to store, you stored it on a magnetic drum, or a magnetic tape. Tape drives (and drum drives too) had to spin the tape to get the head, which could read or write onto the tape, above the desired memory location. If the head was currently above location 900, and you wanted to write to location 999, the tape would have to spin past 901, 902, ..., 998, until location 999 was under the head. In other words, the tape was accessed *sequentially*. When RAM was first released, its most appealing feature was that any "random" address could be accessed in the same amount of time as any other address—regardless of the previously read address. That's because there is no "head" used to access a RAM, and no spinning of tapes or drums. Thus, the term "random access" memory was used, and has stuck to this day.

Notice that the RAM in Figure 5.54 has the same inputs and outputs as the RAM block diagram in Figure 5.53, except that the RAM in Figure 5.54 has separate write and read data lines whereas Figure 5.53 has a single set of data lines (a single port). Figure 5.55 shows how the separate lines might be combined inside a RAM having just a single set of data lines.

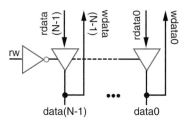

Figure 5.55 RAM data input/output for a single port.

Bit Storage in a RAM

The key feature distinguishing RAM from a register file is the RAM's compactness. Recall that Chapter 3 implemented a bit storage block using a D flip-flop. Because RAMs store large numbers of bits, RAMs utilize a bit storage block that is more compact, but slower, than a flip-flop. This section briefly describes the internal design of the bit storage blocks inside two popular types of RAM—static RAM and dynamic RAM. However, be forewarned that the internal design of those blocks involves electronics issues beyond the scope of this book, and instead is within the scope of textbooks on VLSI or advanced digital design. Fortunately, a RAM component hides the complexity of its internal electronics by using a memory controller, and thus a digital designer's interaction with a RAM remains as discussed in the previous section.

Static RAM

Static RAM (SRAM) uses a bit storage block having two inverters connected in a loop as shown in Figure 5.56. A bit d will pass through the bottom inverter to become d', then through the top inverter to become d again—thus, the bit is stored in the inverter loop. Notice that this bit storage block has an extra line data' passing through it, compared with the logical RAM structure in Figure 5.54.

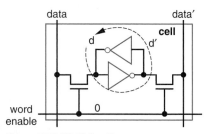

Figure 5.56 SRAM cell.

Writing a bit into this inverter loop is accomplished by setting the data line to the value of the desired bit, and data' to the complement. To store a 1, the memory controller sets data to 1 and data' to 0 as in Figure 5.57. To store a 0, the controller sets data to 0 and data' to 1. The controller then sets enable to 1 so both shown transistors will conduct. The data and data' values will appear in the inverter loop as shown, overwriting any previous value.

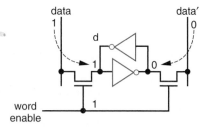

Figure 5.57 Writing a 1 to an SRAM cell.

Reading the stored bit can be done by first setting the data and data' lines *both* to 1, which is an act known as ***precharging***), and then setting enable to 1. One of the enabled transistors will have a 0 at one end, causing the precharged 1 on the data or data' to drop to a voltage slightly less than a regular logic 1. Both the data and data' lines connect to a special circuit called a *sense amplifier* that detects whether the voltage on data is slightly higher than data', meaning logic 1 is stored, or whether the voltage on data' is slightly higher than on data, meaning logic 0 is stored. Details of the electronics are beyond our scope.

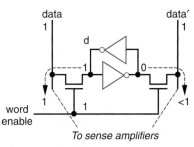

Figure 5.58 Reading an SRAM.

Notice that the bit storage block of Figure 5.58 utilizes six transistors—two inside each of the two inverters, and two transistors outside the inverters. Six transistors are fewer than needed inside a D flip-flop. A tradeoff is that special circuitry must be used to read a bit stored in this bit storage block, whereas a D flip-flop outputs regular logic values directly. Such special circuitry slows the access time of the stored bits.

SRAM maintains the stored bit as long as power is supplied to the transistors. The stored bit (except when written) does *not change*—it is *static* (not changing).

Dynamic RAM

An alternative bit storage block used in RAM and popular for its compactness has only a single transistor per block. Such a block utilizes a relatively large capacitor at the output of the transistor, as shown in Figure 5.59(a). The block is known as dynamic RAM (DRAM) because the stored bit *changes* as will be seen—the bit is *dynamic* (changing).

Writing can occur when enable is 1. When enabled, data=1 will charge the top plate of the capacitor to a 1, while data=0 will make the plate 0. When enable is returned to 0, a 1 on the top plate will begin to discharge across to the bottom plate of the capacitor and on to ground. Such discharging is the nature of a capacitor. However, the capacitor is intentionally designed to be relatively large, so that the discharge takes a long time, during which time the bit d is effectively considered as stored in the capacitor. Figure 5.59(b) provides a timing diagram illustrating the charge and discharge of the capacitor.

Reading can be done by first setting data to a voltage midway between 0 and 1, and then setting enable to 1. The value stored in

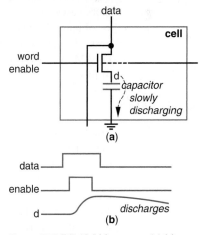

Figure 5.59 DRAM bit storage (a) bit storage block, (b) discharge.

the capacitor will alter the voltage on the data line, and that altered voltage can be sensed by special circuits connected to the data line that amplify the sensed value to either a logic 1 or a logic 0.

It turns out that reading the charge stored in the capacitor discharges the capacitor. Thus, a DRAM must immediately write the read bit back to the bit storage block after reading the block. A DRAM therefore contains a memory controller that automatically performs such a write back.

Because a bit stored in the capacitor gradually discharges to ground, the RAM must *refresh* every bit storage block before the bits completely discharge and hence the stored bit is lost. To refresh a bit storage block, the RAM must read the block and then write the read bit back to the block. Such refreshing may be done every few microseconds. The RAM must include a built-in memory controller that automatically performs these refreshes.

DRAM chips first appeared in the early 1970s, and could hold only a few thousand bits. Modern DRAMs can hold many billions of bits.

Note that the RAM may be busy refreshing itself at a time that we wish to read the RAM. Furthermore, every read must be followed by an automatic write. Thus, RAM based on one-transistor plus capacitor technology may be slower to access.

Compared to SRAM, DRAM is even more compact, requiring only one transistor per bit storage block rather than six transistors. The tradeoff is that DRAM requires refreshing, which ultimately slows the access time. Another tradeoff is that creating the relatively large capacitor in a DRAM requires a special chip fabrication process, and thus incorporating DRAM with regular logic can be costly. In the 1990s, incorporating DRAM with regular logic on the same chip was nearly unheard of. Technology advancements, however, have led to DRAM and logic appearing on the same chip in more cases.

Figure 5.60 graphically depicts the compactness advantages of SRAM over register files, and DRAM over SRAM, for storing the *same* number of bits.

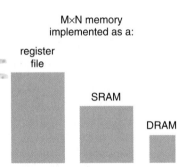

Figure 5.60 Depiction of compactness benefits of SRAM and DRAM (not to scale).

Using a RAM

Figure 5.61 shows timing diagrams describing how to write and read the RAM of Figure 5.53. The timing diagram shows how to write a 9 and a 13 into locations 500 and 999 during clock edges 1 and 2, respectively. The diagram shows how to read location 9 of the RAM in the next cycle, by setting *addr*=9, *data*=Z, and rw=0 (meaning read). Shortly after rw becomes 0, *data* becomes 500 (the value we had previously stored in location 9). Notice that we had to first disable the setting of *data* by setting it to Z (which can be accomplished using a three-state buffer) so as not to interfere with the data being read from the RAM. Also notice that this RAM's read functionality is asynchronous.

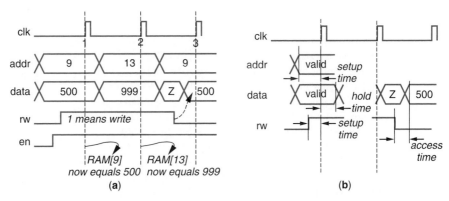

Figure 5.61 Reading and writing a RAM: (a) timing diagrams, (b) setup, hold, and access times.

The delay between our setting the `rw` line to read and the read data stabilizing at the *data* output is known as the RAM's ***access time*** or ***read time***.

The next example uses a RAM during RTL design.

Example 5.14 Digital sound recorder using a RAM

This example designs a system that can record sound digitally and that can play back that recorded sound. Such a recorder is found in various toys, in telephone answering machines, in cell phone outgoing announcements, and numerous other devices. An analog-to-digital converter is needed to digitize the sound, a RAM to store the digitized sound, a digital-to-analog converter to output the digitized sound, a three-state buffer to disable the data line going into the RAM, and a processor (to be designed) to control both converters and the RAM. Figure 5.62 shows a block diagram of the system.

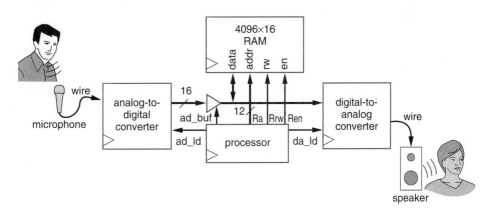

Figure 5.62 Utilizing a RAM in a digital sound recorder system.

To store digitized sound, the processor block can implement the HLSM segment shown in Figure 5.63. The HLSM first intializes its internal address storage item *a* to 0 in state *S*. Next, in state *T* the HLSM loads a value into the analog-to-digital converter to cause a new analog sample to be digitized, and sets the three-state buffer to pass that digitized value to the RAM's *data* lines. That state also writes *a* to the local storage *Rareg* that exists for the RAM address *Ra*, and sets the RAM control lines to enable writing. The HLSM then transitions to state *U* whose transitions check the value of *a* against 4095. That state also increments *a*. The HLSM returns to state *T* and hence continues writing samples into sequential memory addresses as long as the

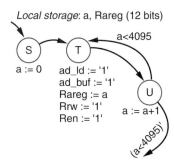

Figure 5.63 HLSM for storing digitized sound in RAM.

memory is not yet filled, meaning as long as $a < 4095$. Notice that the comparison is with 4095 rather than with 4096. This is because the action in state *U* of $a := a + 1$ does not cause an update until the next clock edge, so the comparison $a < 4095$ on state *U*'s outgoing transition uses the old value of *a*, not the incremented value (see Section 5.4 for further discussion).

To playback the stored digitized sound, the processor can implement the HLSM segment shown in Figure 5.64. After initializing the local storage item *a* in state *V*, the HLSM enters state *W*. State *W* disables the three-state buffer to avoid interfering with the RAM's output data that will appear during RAM reads. State *W* also sets the RAM address lines, and sets the RAM control lines to enable reading. The read data will thus appear on the *data* lines. The next state *X* loads a value into the digital-to-analog converter to convert the data just read from RAM to the analog signal. That state also increments *a*. The HLSM returns to state *W* to continue reading, until the entire memory has been read.

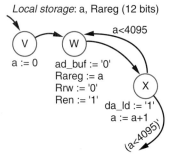

Figure 5.64 HLSM for playing sound from RAM.

Read-Only Memory (ROM)

A read-only memory (ROM) is a memory that can be read from but not written to. Because of being read-only, the bit-storage mechanism in a ROM can be made to have several advantages over a RAM, including:

- *Compactness*—A ROM's bit storage may be even smaller than that of a RAM.
- *Nonvolatility*—A ROM's bit storage maintains its contents even after the power supply to the ROM is shut off. When power is turned back on, the ROM's contents can be read again. In contrast, a RAM loses its contents when power is shut off. A memory that loses its contents when power is shut off is known as **volatile**, while a memory that maintains its contents without power is known as **nonvolatile**.

- *Speed*—A ROM may be faster to read than a RAM, especially compared to a DRAM.

- *Low-power*—A ROM does not consume power to maintain its contents, in contrast to a RAM. Thus, a ROM consumes less power than a RAM.

Therefore, when the data stored in a memory will not change, a designer may choose to store that data in a ROM to gain the above advantages.

Figure 5.65 shows a block symbol of a 1024x32 ROM. The logical internal structure of an *MxN* ROM is shown in Figure 5.66. Notice that the internal structure is very similar to the internal structure of a RAM shown in Figure 5.54. Bit storage blocks forming a word are enabled by a decoder output, with the decoder input being the address. However, because a ROM can only be read and cannot be written, there is no need for an `rw` input control to specify read versus write, nor for *wdata* inputs to provide data being written. Also, because no synchro-

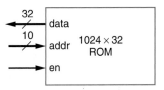

Figure 5.65 1024x32 ROM block symbol.

nous writes occur in a ROM, the ROM does not have a clock input. In fact, not only is a ROM an asynchronous component, but in fact a ROM can be thought of as a *combinational* component (when we only read from the ROM; we'll see variations later).

Some readers might at this point be wondering how a designer can write the initial contents of a ROM that will later be read. After all, if a designer can't write the contents of a ROM at all, then the ROM is really of no use. Obviously, there must be a way to write the contents of a ROM, but in ROM terminology, the writing of the initial contents of a ROM is known as ***ROM programming***. ROM types differ in their bit storage block implementations, which in turn causes differences in the methods used for ROM programming. We now describe several popular bit storage block implementations for ROM.

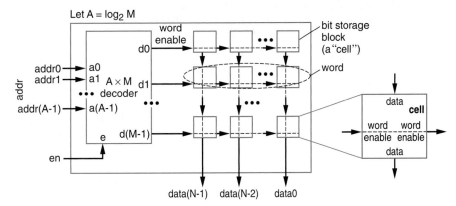

Figure 5.66 Logical internal structure of a ROM.

ROM Types

Mask-programmed ROM

Figure 5.67 illustrates the bit storage cell for a mask-programmed ROM. A *mask-programmed ROM* has its contents programmed when the chip is manufactured, by directly *wiring* 1s to cells that should store a 1, and 0s to cells that should store a 0. Recall that a "1" is actually a higher-than-zero voltage coming from one of several power input pins to a chip—thus, wiring a 1 means wiring the power input pin directly to the cell. Likewise, wiring a 0 to a cell means wiring the ground pin directly to the cell. Be aware that

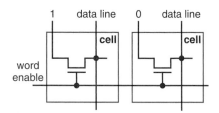

Figure 5.67 Mask-programmed ROM cells: left cell programmed with 1, right cell with 0.

Figure 5.67 presents a *logical* view of a mask-programmed ROM cell—the actual physical design of such cells may be somewhat different. For example, a common design strings several vertical cells together to form a large NOR-like logic gate. We leave details for more advanced textbooks on CMOS circuit design.

Wires are placed onto chips during manufacturing by using a combination of light-sensitive chemicals and light passed through lenses and "masks" that block the light from reaching regions of the chemicals. (See Chapter 7 for further details.) Hence the term "mask" in mask-programmed ROM.

Mask-programmed ROM has the best compactness of any ROM type, but the contents of the ROM must be known during chip manufacturing. This ROM type is best suited for high-volume well-established products in which compactness or very low cost is critical, and in which programming of the ROM will never be done after the ROM's chip is manufactured.

Fuse-Based Programmable ROM—One-Time Programmable (OTP) ROM

Figure 5.68 illustrates the bit storage cell for a fuse-based ROM. A *fuse-based ROM* uses a fuse in each cell. A fuse is an electrical component that initially conducts from one end to the other just like a wire, but whose connection from one end to the other can be destroyed ("blown") by passing a higher-than-normal current through the fuse. A blown fuse does not conduct and is instead an open circuit (no connection). In the figure, the cell on the left has its fuse intact, so when the cell is enabled, a 1 appears on the data line. The cell on the right has its fuse blown, so when the cell is enabled, nothing appears on the data line (special electronics will be necessary to convert that nothing to a logic 0).

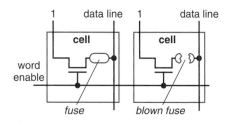

Figure 5.68 Fuse-based ROM cells: left cell programmed with 1, right cell with 0.

A fuse-based ROM is manufactured with all fuses intact, so the initially stored contents are all 1s. A user of this ROM can program the contents by connecting the ROM to a special device known as a ***programmer***, that provides higher-than-normal currents to only those fuses in cells that should store 0s. Because a user can program the contents of this ROM, the ROM is known as a programmable ROM, or ***PROM***.

A blown fuse cannot be changed back to its initial conducting form. Thus, a fuse-based ROM can only be programmed once. Fuse-based ROM are therefore also known as ***one-time programmable (OTP) ROM***.

Erasable PROM—EPROM

Figure 5.69 depicts a logical view of an erasable PROM cell. An ***erasable PROM***, or ***EPROM***, cell uses a special type of transistor, having what is known as a floating gate, in each cell. The details of a floating gate transistor are beyond the scope of this section, but briefly—a floating gate transistor has a special gate in which electrons can be "trapped." A transistor with electrons trapped in its gate stays in the nonconducting situation, and thus is programmed to store a 0. Otherwise, the cell is considered to store a 1. Special electronic circuitry converts sensed currents on the data lines as logic 1 or 0.

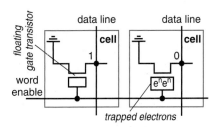

Figure 5.69 EPROM cells: left cell programmed with 1, right cell with 0.

An EPROM cell initially has no electrons trapped in any floating gate transistors, so the initially stored contents are all 1s. A programmer device applies higher-than-normal voltages to those transistors in cells that should store 0s. That high voltage causes electrons to *tunnel* through a small insulator into the floating gate region. When the voltage is removed, the electrons do not have enough energy to tunnel back, and thus are trapped as shown in the right cell of Figure 5.69.

The electrons can be freed by exposing the electrons to ultraviolet (UV) light of a particular wavelength. The UV light energizes the electrons such that they tunnel back through the small insulator, thus escaping the floating gate region. Exposing an EPROM chip to UV light therefore "erases" all the stored 0s, restoring the chip to having all 1s as contents, after which it can be programmed again. Hence the term "erasable" PROM. Such a chip can typically be erased and reprogrammed about ten thousand times or more, and can retain its contents without power for ten years or more. Because a chip usually appears inside a black package that doesn't pass light, a chip with an EPROM requires a window in that package through which UV light can pass, as shown in Figure 5.70.

Figure 5.70 The "window" in the package of a microprocessor that uses an EPROM to store programs.

EEPROM and Flash Memory

An *electrically erasable PROM*, or *EEPROM*, utilizes the EPROM programming method of using high voltage to trap electrons in a floating gate transistor. However, unlike an EPROM that requires UV light to free the electrons and hence erase the PROM, an EEPROM uses another high voltage to free the electrons, thus avoiding the need for placing the chip under UV light.

Because EEPROMs use voltages for erasing, those voltages can be applied to specific cells only. Thus, while EPROMs must be erased in their entirety, EEPROMs can be erased one word at a time. Thus, we can erase and reprogram certain words in an EEPROM without changing the contents of other words.

Some EEPROMs require a special programmer device for programming, but most modern EEPROMs do not require special voltages to be applied to the pins, and also include internal memory controllers that manage the programming process. Thus, we can reprogram an EEPROM device's contents (or part of its contents) without ever removing the chip from its system—such a device is known as being *in-system programmable*. Most such devices can therefore be read and written in a manner very similar to a RAM.

Figure 5.71 shows a block diagram of an EEPROM. Notice that the data lines are bidirectional, just as was the case for RAM. The EEPROM has a control input write. write=0 indicates a read operation (when en=1), while write=1 indicates that the data on the data lines should be programmed into the word at the address specified by the address lines. Programming a word into an EEPROM takes time, though, perhaps several dozens, hundreds, or even thousands of clock cycles. Therefore, EEPROMs may have a control output busy to indicate that programming is not yet complete. While the

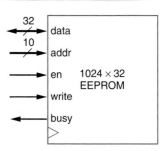

Figure 5.71 1024x32 EEPROM block symbol.

device is busy, a circuit that writes to the EEPROM should not try writing to a different word; that write will likely be ignored. Most EEPROMs will load the data to be programmed and the address into internal registers, freeing the circuit that is writing the EEPROM from having to hold these values constant during programming.

Modern EEPROMs can be programmed hundreds of thousands to millions of times or more, and can retain their contents for several decades to one hundred years or more without power.

While erasing one word at a time is fine for some applications that utilize EEPROM, other applications need to erase large blocks of memory quickly—for example, a digital camera application would need to erase a block of memory corresponding to an entire picture. *Flash memory* is a type of EEPROM in which all the words within a large block of memory can be erased very quickly, typically simultaneously, rather than one word at a time. A flash memory may be completely erased by setting an erase control input to 1. Many flash memories also allow only a specific region, known as a *block* or *sector*, to be erased while other regions are left untouched.

Using a ROM

Below are examples of using a ROM during RTL design.

Example 5.15 Talking doll using a ROM

We wish to design a doll that speaks the message "Nice to meet you" whenever the doll's right arm is moved. A block diagram of the system is shown in Figure 5.72. A vibration sensor in the doll's right arm has an output v that is 1 when vibration is sensed. A processor detects the vibration and should then output a digitized version of the "Nice to meet you" message to a digital-to-analog converter attached to a speaker. The "Nice to meet you" message will be the prerecorded voice of a professional actress. Because that message will not change for the lifetime of the doll product, we can store that message in a ROM.

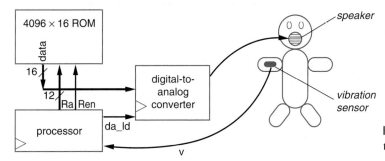

Figure 5.72 Utilizing a ROM in a talking doll system.

Figure 5.73 shows an HLSM segment that plays the message after detecting vibration. The machine starts in state *S*, initializing the ROM address counter *a* to *0*, and waiting for vibration to be sensed. When vibration is sensed, the machine proceeds to state *T*, which reads the current ROM location. The machine moves on to state *U,* which loads the digital-to-analog converter with the read value from ROM, increments *a*, and proceeds back to *T* as long as *a* hasn't reached 4095 (remember that the transition from *U* uses the value of *a* before the increment, so should compare to 4095, not to 4096).

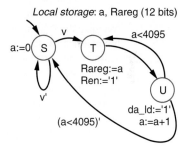

Figure 5.73 HLSM for reading the ROM.

Because this doll's message will never change, we might choose to use a mask-programmed ROM or an OTP ROM. We might utilize OTP ROM during prototyping or during initial sales of the doll, and then produce mask-programmed ROM versions during high-volume production of the doll.

Example 5.16 Digital telephone answering machine using a flash memory

This example designs the outgoing announcement part of a telephone answering machine (e.g., "We're not home right now, leave a message"). That announcement should be stored digitally, should be recordable by the machine owner any number of times, and should be saved even if power is removed from the answering machine. Recording begins immediately after the owner presses a record button, which sets a signal rec to 1.

Because we must be able to record the announcement, we thus cannot use a mask-programmed ROM or OTP ROM. Because removing power should not cause the announcement to be lost, we cannot use a RAM. Thus, we might choose an EEPROM or a flash memory. We'll use a flash memory as shown in Figure 5.74. Notice that the flash memory has the same interface as a RAM,

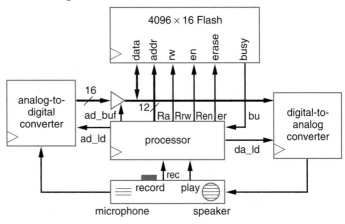

Figure 5.74 Utilizing a flash memory in a digital answering machine.

except that the flash memory has an extra input named erase, which on this particular flash memory clears the contents of the entire flash. While the flash memory is erasing itself, the flash sets an output busy to 1, during which time we cannot write to the flash memory.

Figure 5.75 shows an HLSM segment for recording the announcement. The HLSM segment begins when the record button is pressed. State *S* activates the erase of the flash memory (er=1), and then state *T* waits for the erasing to complete (bu'). Such erasing should occur in just a few milliseconds, so that the start of the spoken announcement isn't missed. The HLSM then transitions to state *U*, which copies a digitized sample from the analog-digital converter to the flash memory, writing to the current address *a*. State *U* also increments *a*. The next state *V* checks to see if the memory is filled with samples by checking if *a* < 4096, returning to state *U* until the memory is filled.

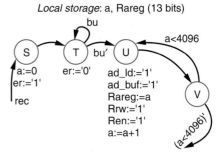

Figure 5.75 HLSM for storing digitized sound in a flash memory.

Notice that, unlike previous examples, this HLSM increments *a* before the state that checks for the last address (state *V*), so *V*'s transitions use 4096, not 4095. We show this version just for variety. The earlier examples may be slightly better because they require that *a* and the comparator only be 12 bits wide (to represent 0 to 4095) rather than 13 bits wide (to represent 0 to 4096).

This HLSM assumes that writes to the flash occur in one clock cycle. Some flash memories require more time for writes, asserting their busy output until the write has completed. For such a flash, we would need to add a state between states U and V, similar to the state T between S and U.

To prevent missing sound samples while waiting, we might want to first save the entire sound sample in a 4096x16 RAM, and then copy the entire RAM contents to the flash.

The Blurring of the Distinction between RAM and ROM

Notice that EEPROM and flash ROM blur the distinction between RAM and ROM. Many modern EEPROM devices are writable just like a RAM, having nearly the same interface, with the only difference being longer write times to an EEPROM than to a RAM. However, the difference between those times is shrinking each year.

Further blurring the distinction are ***nonvolatile RAM*** (***NVRAM***) devices, which are RAM devices that retain their contents even without power. Unlike ROM, NVRAM write times are just as fast as regular RAM—typically one clock cycle. One type of NVRAM simply includes an SRAM with a built-in battery, with the battery able to supply power to the SRAM for perhaps ten years or more. Another type of NVRAM includes both an SRAM and an EEPROM—the NVRAM controller automatically backs up the SRAM's contents into the EEPROM, typically just at the time when power is being removed. Furthermore, extensive research and development into new bit storage technologies are leading to NVRAMs that are even closer to RAM in terms of performance and density while being nonvolatile. One such technology is known as MAGRAM, short for magnetic RAM, which uses magnetism to store charge, having access times similar to DRAM, but without the need for refreshing, and with nonvolatility.

Thus, digital designers have a tremendous variety of memory types available to them, with those types differing in their cost, performance, size, nonvolatility, ease of use, write time, duration of data retention, and other factors.

▶ 5.8 QUEUES (FIFOs)

Sometimes a designer's data storage needs specifically require reading items in the same order that the items were written. For example, a busy restaurant may maintain a waiting list of customers—the host writes customer names to the *rear* of the list, but when a table becomes available, the host reads the next customer's name from the *front* of the list and removes that name from the list. Thus, the first customer written to the list is the first customer read from the list. A *queue* is a list that is written at the rear of the list but read from the beginning of the list, with a read also removing the read item from the list, as illustrated in Figure 5.76. The common term for a queue in American English is a "line"—for example, you stand in a line at the grocery store, with people entering the rear of the line, and being served from

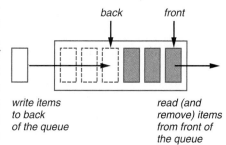

write items to back of the queue

read (and remove) items from front of the queue

Figure 5.76 Conceptual view of a queue.

the front of the line. In British English, the word "queue" is used directly in everyday language (which sometimes confuses Americans who visit other English-speaking countries). Because the first item written into the list will be the first item read out of the list, a queue is known as being *first-in first-out* (FIFO). As such, sometimes queues are called *FIFO queues*, although that term is redundant because a queue is by definition first-in first-out. The term *FIFO* itself is often used to refer to a queue. The term *buffer* is also sometimes used. A write to a queue is sometimes called a *push* or *enqueue*, and a read is sometimes called *pop* or *dequeue*.

A queue can be implemented using a memory—either a register file or a RAM, depending on the queue size needed. When using a memory, the front and rear will move to different memory locations as the queue is written and read, as illustrated in Figure 5.77. The figure shows an initially empty eight-word queue with front and rear both set to memory address 0. The first sample action on the queue is a write of item A, which goes to the rear (address 0), and the rear increments to address 1. The next sample action is a write of item B, which goes to the rear (address 1), and the rear increments to 2. The next action is a read, which comes from the front (address 0) and thus reads out item A, and the front increments to 1.

Subsequent reads and writes continue likewise, except that when the rear or front reaches 7, its next value should be 0, not 8. In other words, the memory can be thought of as a circle, as shown in Figure 5.78.

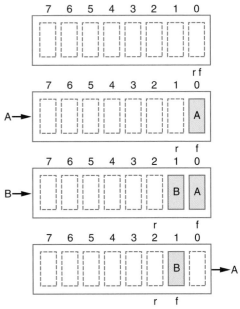

Figure 5.77 Writing and reading a queue implemented in a memory causes the front (*f*) and rear (*r*) to move.

Two queue conditions of interest:

- *Empty*: no items are in the queue. This condition can be detected as *front = rear*, as seen in the topmost queue of Figure 5.77.

- *Full*: there is no room to add items to the queue, meaning there are N items in a queue of size N. This comes about when the rear wraps around and catches back up to the front, meaning *front = rear*.

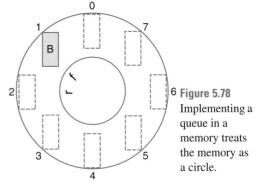

Figure 5.78 Implementing a queue in a memory treats the memory as a circle.

Unfortunately, notice that the conditions for detecting the queue being empty and the queue being full are the same—the front address equals the rear address. One way to tell the two conditions apart is to keep track of whether a write or a read preceded the front and rear addresses becoming equal.

In many uses of a queue, the circuit writing the queue operates independently from the circuit reading the queue. Thus, a queue implemented with a memory may use a two-port memory having separate read and write ports.

An 8-word queue can be implemented using an 8-word two-port register file and additional components, as depicted in Figure 5.79. A 3-bit up-counter maintains the front address while another 3-bit up-counter maintains the rear address. Notice that these counters will naturally wrap around from 7 to 0, or from 0 to 7, as desired when treating the memory as a circle. An equality comparator detects whether the front counter equals the rear counter. A controller writes the write data to the register file and increments the rear counter during a write, reads the read data from the register file and increments the front counter during a read, and determines whether the queue is full or empty based on the equality comparison

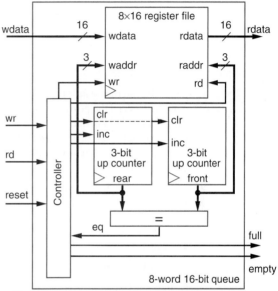

Figure 5.79 Architecture of an 8-word 16-bit queue.

as well as whether the previous operation was a write or a read. We omit further description of the queue's controller, but it can be built by starting with an FSM.

A circuit that uses a queue should never read an empty queue or write a full queue—depending on the controller design, such an action might just be ignored or might put the queue into a misleading internal state (e.g., the front and rear addresses may cross over).

Many queues come with one or more additional control outputs that indicate whether the queue is half full or perhaps 80% full.

Queues are commonplace in digital systems. Some examples include:

- A computer keyboard writes the pressed keys into a queue and meanwhile requests that the computer read the queued keys. You might at some time have typed faster than your computer was reading the keys, in which case your additional keystrokes were ignored—and you may have even heard beeps each time you pressed additional keys, indicating the queue was full.

- A digital video camera may write recently captured video frames into a queue, and concurrently may read those frames from the queue, compress them, and store them on tape or another medium.

- A computer printer may store print jobs in a queue while those jobs are waiting to be printed.

- A modem stores incoming data in a queue and requests a computer to read that data. Likewise, the modem writes outgoing data received from the computer into a queue and then sends that data out over the modem's outgoing medium.

- A computer network router receives data packets from an input port and writes those packets into a queue. Meanwhile, the router reads the packets from the queue, analyzes the address information in the packet, and then sends the packet along one of several output ports.

Example 5.17 Using a queue

Show the internal state of an 8-word queue, and the popped data values, after each of the following sequences of pushes and pops, assuming an initially empty queue:

1. Push 9, 5, 8, 5, 7, 2, and 3.

2. Pop

3. Push 6

4. Push 3

5. Push 4

6. Pop

Figure 5.80 shows the queue's internal states. After the first sequence of seven pushes (step 1), we see that the rear address points to address 7. The pop (step 2) reads from the front address of 0, returning data of 9. The front address increments to 1. Note that although the queue might still contain the value of 9 in address 0, that 9 is no longer accessible during proper queue operation, and thus is essentially gone. The push of 6 (step 3) increments the rear address, which wraps around from 7 to 0. The push of 3 (step 4) increments the rear address to 1, which now equals the front address, meaning the queue is now full. If a pop were to occur now, it would read the value 5. But instead, a push of 4 occurs (step 5)—this push should not have been performed, because the queue is full. Thus, this push puts the queue into an erroneous state, and we cannot predict the behavior of any subsequent pushes or pops.

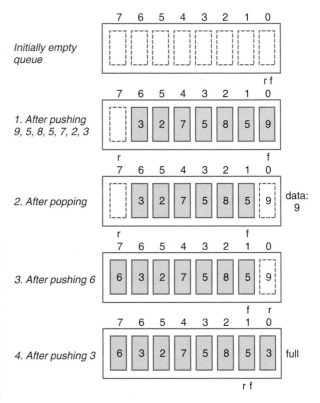

Initially empty queue

1. After pushing 9, 5, 8, 5, 7, 2, 3

2. After popping — data: 9

3. After pushing 6

4. After pushing 3 — full

5. After pushing 4 — ERROR! Pushing a full queue results in unknown state

Figure 5.80 Example pushes and pops of a queue.

A queue could of course come with some error-tolerance behavior built in, perhaps ignoring pushes when full, or perhaps returning some particular value (like 0) if popped when empty.

▶ 5.9 MULTIPLE PROCESSORS

RTL design can be aided by capturing behavior using multiple concurrently-executing HLSMs and converting those HLSMs to multiple processors. For example, consider the laser-based distance measurer from Example 5.13. The system has an input B from a button. Section 5.4 explained that button inputs may need to be

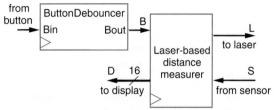

Figure 5.81 A system with two concurrently-executing processors.

debounced. Rather than attempting to modify the laser-based distance measurer's HLSM of Figure 5.12 to also perform button debouncing, a simpler approach is to build the system using two processors as shown in Figure 5.81. The button debouncer is a processor having a controller and datapath. Likewise, the laser-based distance measurer is another processor having its own controller and datapath. The first processor's output serves as the second processor's input, representing a debounced button input.

As another example, recall the code detector of Example 3.6. The example assumed that the inputs from the buttons were each synchronized to the clock such that each unique press would result in the corresponding signal being 1 for exactly one clock cycle. Such synchronization was achieved by designing a button press synchronizer in Example

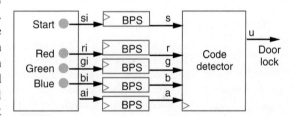

Figure 5.82 A system with multiple concurrently-executing processors.

3.9. The system could then be built as shown in Figure 5.82, with a button press synchronizer (BPS) processor instantiated for each input. The system thus consists of 5 BPS processors and one code detector processor (each of those processors happen to consist of just a controller and no datapath, but each is a processor nevertheless).

Many different interfaces between processors are possible through the use of global items. A signal, register, or other component that is not inside a processor is called a *global* signal, a global register, or global component, respectively. Possible interfaces between processors include:

- Control signal: The above examples represent the simplest interface between processors involving one processor writing a control output that another processor reads. The processors are said to share a global control signal.

- Data signal: Another interface involves a processor writing a data output that the other processor reads. The processors share a global data signal.

- Register: One processor may write to a global register that another processor reads.

- Register file: One processor may connect to the write port of a global two-port (one-read one-write port) register file while another processor connects to the read port.

- Queue: One processor may connect to the write lines of a global queue, while another processor connects to the read lines. A processor should not write if the queue is full, and the other processor should not read if the queue is empty. A common version of this interface uses a one-word queue, effectively representing a register whose written contents must be read before the register can be written again.

Even though the multiple processors (and global components) execute concurrently, they all use the same clock signal, and thus the processors are **synchronized**. Such synchronization avoids metastability issues in the interfaces between the processors (unsynchronized processors are also possible but are not considered in this book).

Note that if a multiple processor system has an unregistered output of one processor connecting to an input of another processor, the system's critical path could be from a register of one processor to a register of another processor.

Example 5.18 Temperature statistics system using multiple processors

Design a system with a 16-bit unsigned input *T* from a temperature sensor, and a 16-bit output *A*. The system should sample *T* every 1 second. Output *A* should be computed every minute and should equal the average of the most recent 64 samples.

We could try to capture the behavior using a single HLSM, but that approach may lead to a complicated HLSM. Instead, we'll use two HLSMs that will be interfaced using a one-write-port one-read-port 64x16 register file. The first HLSM, *Tsample*, will write the sampled value into successive register file addresses. The second HLSM, *Avg*, will compute

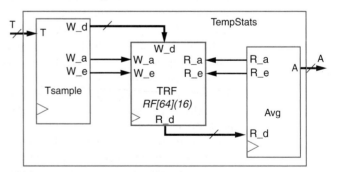

Figure 5.83 A temperature statistics system.

the average of the register file's contents. Figure 5.83 shows a block diagram of the system.

The procedure of defining the HLSMs would follow from previous examples and is not shown. There would be three top-level objects: a 64x16 register file *TRF*, an HLSM *Tsample*, and an HLSM *Avg*. HLSM *Tsample* would declare a timer and a 6-bit local storage item *addr*, initialize the timer with 1 second, and then write input *T* to *TRF[addr]* every 1 second and increment *addr* (note that *addr* would wrap around from 63 to 0). HLSM *Avg* would declare a timer and a local storage item *sum*, initialize the timer with 60 seconds, and then compute the average every 60 seconds. Computing the average would be achieved by reading each word 0 to 63 of the register file TRF one at a time, adding each to *sum*. To avoid overflow, *sum* might be made 32 bits wide. Then, the HLSM would divide the sum by 64 to compute the average, and would output the result on *A*. Recall that a one-read-port one-write-port register file can support both a read and a write operation in the same clock cycle, which is what allows the two HLSMs to access the register file independently.

Notice how simple the design is when the sampling and averaging behaviors are kept separate.

Example 5.19 Digital camera with multiple processors and queues

Section 1.3 introduced a digital camera example that consisted of three tasks: reading picture elements from an image sensor, compressing those elements, and storing the results into a memory. Figure 5.84 shows processors for the three tasks along with interfaces between them. Consider the interface between the *Read* and *Compress* processors. Assume *Compress* sometimes runs faster and sometimes runs slower depending on what item is being compressed. A queue is a good interface for such a situation. In this case, an 8-bit 8-word queue is used. When *Read* runs faster than *Compress*, *Read* can push more items onto the queue (until the queue is full, at which point *Read* must wait until the queue is not full). When *Compress* runs faster than *Read*, *Compress* can pop more items (until the queue is empty, at which point *Compress* must wait for the queue to be not empty). The queue thus improves overall performance, while also ensuring that items are accessed by *Compress* before being overwritten by *Read*. Similarly, a queue exists between *Compress* and *Store*.

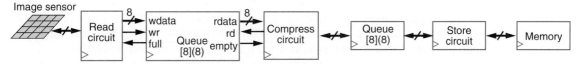

Figure 5.84 Three processor circuits and two queues in a digital camera system.

▶ 5.10 HIERARCHY—A KEY DESIGN CONCEPT

Managing Complexity

Throughout this book, we have been utilizing a powerful design concept known as hierarchy. **Hierarchy** in general is defined as an organization with a few "things" at the top, and each thing possibly consisting of several other things. Perhaps the most widely known example of a hierarchy is a country. At the top is a country, which consists of many states or provinces, each of which in turn consists of many cities. A three-level hierarchy involving a country, provinces, and cities is shown in Figure 5.85.

Figure 5.86 shows the same country, but this time showing only the top two levels of hierarchy—countries and provinces. Indeed, most maps of a country only show these top two levels (possibly showing key cities in each province/state, but certainly not all the cities)—showing all the cities makes the map far too detailed and cluttered. A map of a province/state, however, might then show all the cities within that state. Thus, we see that hierarchy plays an important role in understanding countries (or at least their maps).

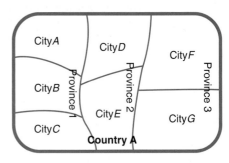

Figure 5.85 Three-level hierarchy example: a country, made up of provinces, each made up of cities.

Likewise, hierarchy plays an important role in digital design. In Chapter 2, we introduced the most fundamental component in digital systems—the transistor. In Chapters 2 and 3, we introduced several basic components composed from transistors, like AND gates, OR gates, and NOT gates, and then some slightly more complex components composed from gates: multiplexers, decoders, flip-flops, etc. In Chapter 4, we composed the basic components into a higher level of components, like registers, adders, ALUs, multipliers, etc. In Chapter 5, we composed earlier components into datapaths, composed controllers and datapaths, into processors, and created memories and queues from earlier components too.

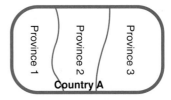

Figure 5.86 Hierarchy showing just the top two levels.

Use of hierarchy enables us to manage complex designs. Imagine trying to comprehend the design of Figure 5.40 at the level of logic gates—that design likely consists of several thousand logic gates. Humans can't comprehend several thousand things at once. But they can comprehend a few dozen things. As the number of things grows beyond a few dozen, we therefore group those things into a new thing, to manage the complexity. However, hierarchy alone is not sufficient—we must also associate an understandable meaning to the higher-level things we create, a task known as abstraction.

Abstraction

Hierarchy may not only involve grouping things into a larger thing, but may also involve associating a higher-level behavior to that larger thing. So when we grouped transistors to form an AND gate, we didn't just say that an AND gate was a group of transistors—rather, we associated a specific behavior with the AND gate, with that behavior describing the behavior of the group of transistors in an easily understandable way. Likewise, when we grouped logic gates into a 32-bit adder, we didn't just say that an adder was a group of logic gates—rather, we associated a specific understandable behavior with the adder: a 32-bit adder adds two 32-bit numbers.

Associating higher-level behavior with a component to hide the complex inner details of that component is a process known as *abstraction*.

Abstraction frees a designer from having to remember, or even understand, the low-level details of a component. Knowing that an adder adds two numbers, a designer can use an adder in a design. The designer need not worry about whether the adder internally is implemented using a carry-ripple design, or using some complicated design that is perhaps faster but larger. Instead, the designer just needs to know the delay of the adder and the size of the adder, which are further abstractions.

Composing a Larger Component from Smaller Versions of the Same Component

A common design task is to *compose* a larger version of a component from smaller versions of the same component. For example, suppose 3-input AND gates are available in a library, but a 9-input AND gate is needed in a design. A designer can compose several 3-input AND gates to form a 9-input AND gate as shown in Figure 5.87. A designer could compose OR gates into a larger OR gate, and XOR gates into larger XOR gates, similarly. Some compositions might require more than two levels—composing an 8-bit AND from 2-input ANDs requires four 2-input ANDs in the first level, two 2-input ANDs in the second level, and a 2-input AND in the third level. Some compositions might end up with

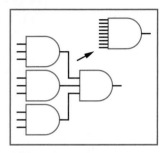

Figure 5.87 Composing a 9-input AND gate from 3-input AND gates.

extra inputs that must be hardwired to 0 or 1—an 8-input AND built from 3-input ANDs would look similar to Figure 5.87, but with the bottom input of the bottom AND gate hardwired to 1.

A general rule to compose any size AND gate from any sizes of smaller AND gates is as follows: fill the first level with (the largest available) AND gates until the sum of the number of inputs equals the desired number of inputs, then fill the second level similarly (feeding first-level outputs to the second-level gates), until the last level has just one gate. Connect any unused AND gate inputs to 1. Composing NAND, NOR, or XNOR gates into larger gates of the same kind would require a few more gates to maintain the same behavior.

Multiplexers can also be composed together to form a larger multiplexer. For example, suppose 4x1 and 2x1 muxes were available in a library, but an 8x1 mux was needed. A designer could compose the smaller muxes into an 8x1 mux as shown in Figure 5.88. Notice that s2 selects among group i0-i3 and i4-i7, while s1 and s0 select one input from the group. The select line

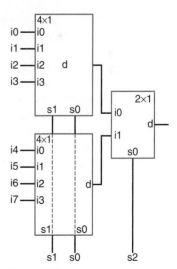

Figure 5.88 An 8x1 mux composed from 4x1 and 2x1 muxes.

values pass the appropriate input through to the output. For example, `s2s1s0 = 000` passes `i0` through, `s2s1s0 = 100` passes `i4`, and `s2s1s0 = 111` passes `i7`.

A common composition problem is that of creating a larger memory from smaller ones. The larger memory may have wider words, may have more words, or both.

As an example of needing wider words, suppose 1024x8 ROMs are available in a library, but a 1024x32 ROM is needed. Composing the smaller ROMs into the larger one is straightforward, as shown in Figure 5.89. Four 1024x8 ROMs are needed to obtain 32 bits per word. The 10 address inputs are connected to all four ROMs. Likewise, the enable input is connected to all four ROMs. The four 8-bit outputs are grouped into the desired 32-bit output. Thus, each ROM stores one byte of the 32-bit word. Reading a location such as location 99 results in four simultaneous reads of the byte at location 99 of each ROM.

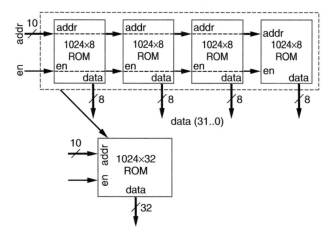

Figure 5.89 Composing a 1024x32 ROM from 1024x8 ROMs.

As an example of needing more words, suppose again that 1024x8 ROMs are available in a library, but this time a 2048x8 ROM is needed. The larger ROM has an extra address line because it has twice as many words to address as the smaller ROMs. Figure 5.90 shows how to use two 1024x8 ROMs to create a 2048x8 ROM. The top ROM represents the top half of the memory (1024 words), and the bottom ROM represents the bottom half of the memory (1024 words). The 11th address line (`a10`) enables either the top ROM or the bottom ROM—the other 10 bits represent the offset into the ROM. That 11th bit feeds into a 1x2 decoder, whose outputs feed into the ROM enables. Figure 5.91 uses a table of addresses to show how the 11th bit selects among the two smaller ROMs.

Finally, since only one ROM will be active at any time, the output data lines can be tied together to form the 8-bit output, as shown in Figure 5.90.

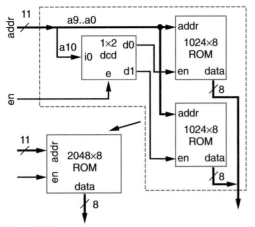

Figure 5.90 Composing a 2048x8 ROM from 1024x8 ROMs.

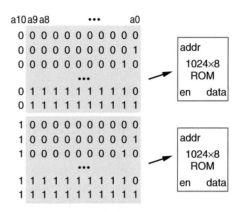

Figure 5.91 When composing a 2048x8 ROM from two 1024x8 ROMs, we can use the highest address bit to choose among the two ROMs; the remaining address bits offset into the chosen ROM.

Note that any bit could be used to select between the top ROM and bottom ROM. Designers sometimes use the lowest-order bit (a0) to select. The top ROM would thus represent all even addresses, and the bottom ROM would represent all odd addresses.

If the desired ROM is four times larger than the available ROM, then two address lines would select from four ROMs via a 2x4 decoder. If the desired ROM is eight times larger, then three address lines and a 3x8 decoder would be used. Other sizes follow similarly.

The approaches for creating a ROM with wider words and with more words can be used together. Suppose a 4096x32 ROM is needed, but only 1024x8 ROMs are available. A designer can first create a 4096x8 ROM by using four ROMs one on top of the other and by feeding the top two address lines to a 2x4 decoder to select the appropriate ROM. The designer can then widen the ROM by adding 3 more ROMs to each row.

Most of the datapath components in Chapter 4 can be composed into larger versions of the same type of component.

▷ 5.11 RTL DESIGN OPTIMIZATIONS AND TRADEOFFS (SEE SECTION 6.5)

Previous sections in this chapter described how to perform register-transfer level design to create processors consisting of a controller and a datapath. This section, which physically appears in the book as Section 6.5, describes how to create processors that are better optimized, or that trade off one feature for another (e.g., size for performance). One use of this book studies such RTL optimizations and tradeoffs immediately after introducing RTL design, meaning now. Another use studies them later.

▶ 5.12 RTL DESIGN USING HARDWARE DESCRIPTION LANGUAGES (SEE SECTION 9.5)

This section, which physically appears in the book as Section 9.5, describes use of HDLs during RTL design. One use of this book studies such HDL use immediately after introducing RTL design (meaning now). Another use studies use of HDLs later.

▶ 5.13 PRODUCT PROFILE: CELL PHONE

A cell phone, short for "cellular telephone" and also known as a mobile phone, is a portable wireless telephone that can be used to make phone calls while moving about a city. Cell phones have made it possible to communicate with distant people nearly anytime and anywhere. Before cell phones, most telephones were tied to physical places like a home or an office. Some cities supported a radio-based mobile telephone system using a powerful central antenna somewhere in the city, perhaps atop a tall building. Because radio frequencies are scarce and thus carefully doled out by governments, such a radio telephone system could only use perhaps tens or a hundred different radio frequencies, and thus could not support large numbers of users. Those few users therefore paid a very high fee for the service, limiting such mobile telephone use to a few wealthy individuals and to key government officials. Those users had to be within a certain radius of the main antenna, measured in tens of miles, to receive service, and that service typically didn't work in another city.

Cells and Basestations

Cell phone popularity exploded in the 1990s, growing from a few million users to hundreds of millions of users in that decade (even though the first cell phone call was made way back in 1973, by Martin Cooper of Motorola, the inventor of the cell phone), and today it is hard for many people to remember life before cell phones. The basic technical idea behind cell phones divides a city into numerous smaller regions, known as *cells* (hence the term "cell phone"). Figure 5.92 shows a city divided into three cells. A typical city might actually be divided into dozens, hundreds, or even thousands of cells. Each cell has its own radio antenna and equipment in the

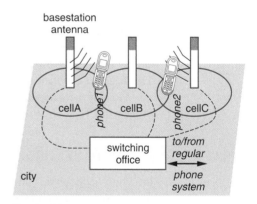

Figure 5.92 *Phone1* in cell *A* can use the same radio frequency as *phone2* in cell *C*, increasing the number of possible mobile phone users in a city.

center, known as a ***basestation***. Each basestation can use dozens or hundreds of different radio frequencies. Each basestation antenna only needs to transmit radio signals powerful enough to reach the basestation's cell area. Thus, nonadjacent cells can actually *reuse* the same frequencies, so the limited number of radio frequencies allowed for mobile phones can thus be shared by more than one phone at one time. Hence, far more users can be supported, leading to reduced costs per user. Figure 5.92 illustrates that *phone1* in cell *A* can use the same radio frequency as *phone2* in cell *C*, because the radio signals from cell *A* don't reach cell *C*. Supporting more users means greatly reduced cost per user, and more basestations means service in more areas than just major cities.

Figure 5.93(a) shows a typical basestation antenna. The basestation's equipment may be in a small building or commonly in a small box near the base of the antenna. The antenna shown actually supports antennas from two different cellular service providers—one set on the top, one set just under, on the same pole. Land for the poles is expensive, which is why providers share, or sometimes find existing tall structures on which to mount the antennas, like buildings, park light posts, and other interesting places (e.g., Figure 5.93(b)). Some providers try to disguise their antennas to make them more soothing to the eye, as in Figure 5.93(c)—the entire tree in the picture is artificial.

Figure 5.93 Basestations found in various locations.

All the basestations of a service provider connect to a central switching office of a city. The switching office not only links the cellular phone system to the regular "landline" phone system, but also assigns phone calls to specific radio frequencies, and handles switching among cells of a phone moving between cells.

How Cellular Phone Calls Work

Suppose you are holding *phone1* in *cell A* of Figure 5.91. When you turn on the cell phone, the phone listens for a signal from a basestation on a control frequency, which is a special radio frequency used for communicating commands (rather than voice data) between the basestation and cell phone. If the phone finds no such signal, the phone reports a "No Service" error. If the phone finds the signal from basestation *A*, the phone then transmits its own identification (ID) number to basestation *A*. Every cell phone has its own unique ID number. (Actually, there is a nonvolatile memory card inside each phone that has that ID number—a phone user can potentially switch cards among phones, or have multiple cards for the same phone, switching cards to change phone numbers.) Basestation *A* communicates this ID number to the central switching office's computer, and thus the service provider computer database now records that your phone is in *cell A*. Your phone intermittently sends a control signal to remind the switching office of the phone's presence.

If somebody then calls your cell phone's number, the call may come in over the regular phone system, which goes to the switching office. The switching office computer database indicates that your phone is in *cell A*. In one type of cell phone technology, the switching office computer assigns a specific radio frequency supported by basestation *A* to the call. Actually, the computer assigns two frequencies, one for talking, one for listening, so that talking and listening can occur simultaneously on a cell phone—let's call that frequency pair a channel. The computer then tells your phone to carry out the call over the assigned channel, and your phone rings. Of course, it could happen that there are so many phones already involved with calls in *cell A* that basestation *A* has no available frequencies—in that case, the caller may hear a message indicating that user is unavailable.

Placing a call proceeds similarly, but your cell phone initiates the call, ultimately resulting in assigned radio frequencies again (or a "system busy" message if no frequencies are presently available).

Suppose that your phone is presently carrying out a call with basestation *A*, and that you are moving through *cell A* toward *cell B* in Figure 5.92. Basestation *A* will see your signal weakening, while basestation *B* will see your signal strengthening, and the two basestations transmit this information to the switching office. At some point, the switching office computer will decide to switch your call from basestation *A* to basestation *B*. The computer assigns a new channel for the call in *cell B* (remember, adjacent cells use different sets of frequencies to avoid interference), and sends your phone a command (through basestation *A*, of course) to switch to a new channel. Your phone switches to the new channel and thus begins communicating with basestation *B*. Such switching may occur dozens of times while a car drives through a city during a phone call, and is transparent to the phone user. Sometimes the switching fails, perhaps if the new cell has no available frequencies, resulting in a "dropped" call.

Inside a Cell Phone

Basic Components

A cell phone requires sophisticated digital circuitry to carry out calls. Figure 5.94 shows the insides of a typical basic cell phone. The printed-circuit boards include several chips implementing digital circuits. One of those circuits performs analog-to-digital conversion of a voice (or other sound) to a signal stream of 0s and 1s, and another performs digital-to-analog conversion of a received digital stream back to an analog signal. Some of the circuits, typically software on a microprocessor, execute tasks that manage the various features of the phone, such as the menu system, address book, games, etc. Note that any data that you save on your cell phone (e.g., an address book, customized ring tones, game high score information, etc.) will likely be stored on a flash memory, whose nonvolatility ensures the data stays saved in memory even if the battery dies or is removed. Another important task involves responding to commands from the switching office. Another task carried out by the digital circuits is filtering. One type of filtering removes the carrier radio signal from the incoming radio frequency. Another type of filtering removes noise

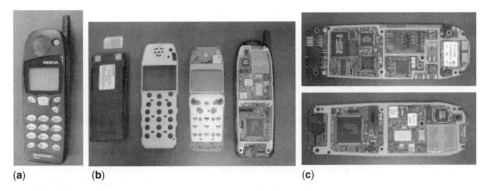

(a) (b) (c)

Figure 5.94 Inside a cell phone: (a) handset, (b) battery and ID card on left, keypad and display in center, digital circuitry on a printed-circuit board on right, (c) the two sides of the printed-circuit board, showing several digital chip packages mounted on the board.

from the digitized audio stream coming from the microphone, before transmitting that stream on the outgoing radio frequency. Let's examine filtering in more detail.

Filtering and FIR Filters

Filtering is perhaps the most common task performed in digital signal processing. Digital signal processing operates on a stream of digital data that comes from digitizing an input signal, such as an audio, video, or radio signal. Such streams of data are found in countless electronic devices, such as CD players, cell phones, heart monitors, ultrasound machines, radios, engine controllers, etc. *Filtering* a data stream is the task of removing particular aspects of the input signal, and outputting a new signal without those aspects.

A common filtering goal is to remove *noise* from a signal. You've certainly heard noise in audio signals—it's that hissing sound that's so annoying on your stereo, cell phone, or cordless phone. You've also likely adjusted a filter to reduce that noise, when you adjusted the "treble" control of your stereo (though that filter may have been implemented using analog methods rather than digital). Noise can appear in any type of signal, not just audio. Noise might come from an imperfect transmitting device, an imperfect listening device (e.g., a cheap microphone), background noise (e.g., freeway sounds coming into your cell phone), electrical interference from other electric appliances, etc. Noise typically appears in a signal as random jumps from a smooth signal.

Another common filtering goal is to remove a *carrier frequency* from a signal. A carrier frequency is a signal added to a main signal for the purpose of transmitting that main signal. For example, a radio station might broadcast a radio signal at 102.7 MHz. 102.7 MHz is the carrier frequency. The carrier signal may be a sine wave of a particular frequency (e.g., 102.7 MHz) that is added to the main signal, where the main signal is the music signal itself. A receiving device locks on to the carrier frequency, and then filters out the carrier signal, leaving the main signal.

An FIR filter (usually pronounced by saying the letters "F" "I" "R"), short for "finite impulse response," is a very general filter design that can be used for a huge variety of filtering goals. The basic idea of an FIR filter is very simple: multiply the present input value by a constant, and add that result to the previous input value times a constant, and add that result to the next-earlier input value times a constant, and so on. A designer using an FIR filter achieves a particular filtering goal *simply by choosing the FIR filter's constants*.

Mathematically, an FIR filter can be described as follows:

$$y(t) = c0 \times x(t) \ + \ c1 \times x(t-1) \ + \ c2 \times x(t-2) \ + \ c3 \times x(t-3) \ + \ c4 \times x(t-4) \ + \ldots$$

t is the present time step. *x* is the input signal, and *y* is the output signal. Each term (e.g., *c0*x(t)*) is called a **tap**. So the above equation represents a 5-tap FIR filter.

Let's see some examples of the versatility of an FIR filter. Assume we have a 5-tap FIR filter. For starters, to simply pass a signal through the filter unchanged, we set *c0* to 1, and we set *c1=c2=c3=c4*=0. To amplify an input signal, we can set *c0* to a number larger than 1, perhaps setting *c0* to 2. To create a smoothing filter that outputs the average of the present value and the past four input values, we can simply set all the constants to equivalent values that add to 1, namely, *c1=c2=c3=c4=c5*=0.2. The results of such a filter applied to a noisy input signal are shown in Figure 5.95. To smooth and amplify, we can set all constants to equivalent values that add to something greater than 1, for example, *c1=c2=c3=c4=c5*=1, resulting in 5x amplification. To create a smoothing filter that only includes the previous two rather than four input values, we simply set *c3* and *c4* to 0. We see that we can build all the above different filters just by changing the constant values of an FIR filter. The FIR filter is indeed quite versatile.

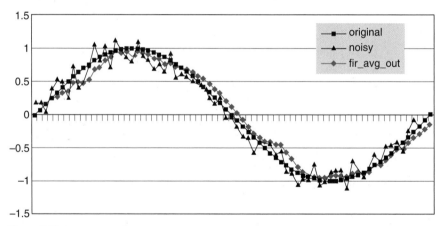

Figure 5.95 Results of a 5-tap FIR filter with *c0=c1=c2=c3=c4*=0.2 applied to a noisy signal. The original signal is a sine wave. The noisy signal has random jumps . The FIR output (fir_avg_out) is much smoother than the noisy signal, approaching the original signal. Notice that the FIR output is slightly shifted to the right, meaning the output is slightly delayed in time (probably a tiny fraction of a second delayed). Such slight shifting is usually not important to a particular application.

That versatility extends even further. We can actually filter out a carrier frequency using an FIR filter, by setting the coefficients to different values, carefully chosen to filter out a particular frequency. Figure 5.96 shows a main signal, *in1*, that we want to transmit. We can add that to a carrier signal, *in2*, to obtain the composite signal, *in_total*. The signal *in_total* is the signal that would be the signal that is transmitted by a radio station, for example, with *in1* being the signal of the music, and *in2* the carrier frequency.

Now say a stereo receiver receives that composite signal, and needs to filter out the carrier signal, so the music signal can be sent to the stereo speakers. To determine how to filter out the carrier signal, look carefully at the samples (the small filled squares in Figure 5.96) of that carrier signal. Notice that the sampling rate is such that if we take any sample, and add it to a sample from three time steps back, we get 0. That's because for a positive point, three samples earlier was a negative point of the same magnitude. For a negative point, three samples earlier was a positive point of the same magnitude. And for a zero point, three samples earlier was also a zero point. Likewise, adding a carrier signal

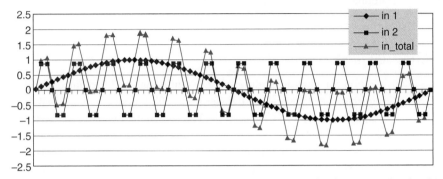

Figure 5.96 Adding a main signal *in1* to a carrier signal *in2*, resulting in a composite signal *in_total*.

sample to a sample three steps later also adds to zero. So to filter out the carrier signal, we can add each sample to a sample three time steps back. Or we can add each sample to 1/2 times a sample three steps back, plus 1/2 times a sample three steps ahead. We can achieve this using a 7-tap FIR filter with the following seven coefficients: 0.5, 0, 0, 1, 0, 0, 0.5. Since that sums to 2, we can scale the coefficients to add to 1, as follows: 0.25, 0, 0, 0.5, 0, 0, 0.25. Applying such a 7-tap FIR filter to the composite signal results in the FIR output shown in Figure 5.97. The main signal is restored. We should point out that we chose the main signal such that this example would come out very nicely—other signals might not be restored so perfectly. But the example demonstrates the basic idea.

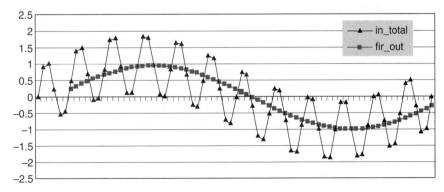

Figure 5.97 Filtering out the carrier signal using a 7-tap FIR filter with constants 0.25, 0, 0, 0.5, 0, 0, 0.25. The slight delay in the output signal typically poses no problem.

While 5-tap and 7-tap FIR filters can certainly be found in practice, many FIR filters may contain tens or hundreds of taps. FIR filters can certainly be implemented using software (and often are), but many applications require that the hundreds of multiplications and additions for every sample be executed faster than is possible in software, leading to custom digital circuit implementations. Example 5.10 illustrated the design of a circuit for an FIR filter.

Many types of filters exist other than FIR filters. Digital signal filtering is part of a larger field known as digital signal processing, or DSP. DSP has a rich mathematical foundation and is a field of study in itself. Advanced filtering methods are what make cell phone conversations as clear as they are today.

▶ 5.14 CHAPTER SUMMARY

Section 5.1 introduced different levels of design and explained that digital design today is mostly done at the register-transfer level (RTL). Like combinational design in Chapter 2 and sequential design in Chapter 3, RTL design starts by capturing behavior and then involves converting that behavior to a circuit. Section 5.2 introduced the high-level state machine (HLSM) formalism for capturing RTL behavior. Section 5.3 introduced a procedure for converting an HLSM to a circuit consisting of a controller and datapath, which together are known as a processor. The datapaths used components defined in Chapter 4 capable of executing the HLSM's data operations, and the controller was built using methods from Chapter 3. Section 5.4 showed how RTL design could make use of register files and of timers, and also showed a data-oriented example. Section 5.5 showed how to set a circuit's clock frequency based on the circuit's critical path. Section 5.6 demonstrated how a sequential program like a C program can be converted to gates using straightforward transformations that convert the C program into RTL behavior. Such conversion makes it clear that a digital system's functionality can be implemented as either software on a microprocessor or as a custom digital circuit (or even as both). The differences between microprocessor and custom circuit implementations relate to design metrics like system performance, power consumption, size, cost, and design time. Modern digital designers must be comfortable migrating functionality between software on a microprocessor and custom digital circuits, in order to obtain the best overall implementation with respect to constraints on design metrics. Section 5.7 introduced several memory components commonly used in RTL design, including RAM and ROM components. Section 5.8 introduced a queue component that can be useful during RTL design. Section 5.9 provided a basic introduction to creating circuits consisting of multiple processor circuits interacting with one another. Section 5.10 discussed the concepts of hierarchy and abstraction, and provided examples of composing a component from smaller components of the same kind.

Chapters 1 through 5 emphasized straightforward design processes for increasingly complex systems, but did not emphasiz how to design *optimized* systems. Optimization is the focus of the next chapter.

▶ 5.15 EXERCISES

For each exercise, unless otherwise indicated, assume that the clock frequency is much faster than any input events of interest, and that any inputs have already been debounced. An asterisk (*) indicates an especially challenging problem.

SECTION 5.2: HIGH-LEVEL STATE MACHINES

5.1 Draw a timing diagram to trace the behavior of the soda dispenser HLSM of Figure 5.3 for the case of a soda costing 50 cents and for the following coins being deposited: a dime (10 cents), then a quarter (25 cents), and then another quarter. The timing diagram should show values for all system inputs, outputs, and local storage items, and for the systems' current state.

5.2 Capture the following system behavior as an HLSM. The system counts the number of events on a single-bit input B and always outputs that number unsigned on a 16-bit output C, which is initially 0. An event is a change from 0 to 1 or from 1 to 0. Assume the system count rolls over when the maximum value of C is reached.

5.3 Capture the following system behavior as an HLSM. The system has two single-bit inputs U and D each coming from a button, and a 16-bit output C, which is initially 0. For each press of U, the system increments C. For each press of D, the system decrements C. If both buttons are pressed, the system does not change C. The system does not roll over; it goes no higher than than the largest C and no lower than C=0. A press is detected as a change from 0 to 1; the duration of that 1 does not matter.

5.4 Capture the following system behavior as an HLSM. A soda machine dispenser system has a 2-bit control input C1 C0 indicating the value of a deposited coin. C1C0 = 00 means no coin, 01 means nickel (5 cents), 10 means dime (10 cents), and 11 means quarter (25 cents); when a coin is deposited, the input changes to indicate the value of the coin (for possibly more than one clock cycle) and then changes back to 00. A soda costs 80 cents. The system displays the deposited amount on a 12-bit output D. The system has a single-bit input S coming from a button. If the deposited amount is less than the cost of a soda, S is ignored. Otherwise, if the button is pressed, the system releases a single soda by setting a single-bit output R to 1 for exactly one clock cycle, and the system deducts the soda cost from the deposited amount.

5.5 Create a high-level state machine that initializes a 16x32 register file's contents to 0s, beginning the initialization when an input rst becomes 1. The register file does *not* have a clear input; each register must be individually written with a 0. Do not define 16 states; instead, declare a local storage item so that only a few states need to be defined.

5.6 Create a high-level state machine for a simple data encryption/decryption device. If a single-bit input b is 1, the device stores the data from a 32-bit signed input I, referring to this as an *offset* value. If b is 0 and another single-bit input e is 1, then the device "encrypts" its input I by adding the stored offset value to I, and outputs this encrypted value over a 32-bit signed output J. If instead another single-bit input d is 1, the device "decrypts" the data on I by subtracting the offset value before outputting the decrypted value over J. Be sure to explicitly handle all possible combinations of the three input bits.

SECTION 5.3: RTL DESIGN PROCESS

For problems in this section, unless otherwise stated, when converting an HLSM to a controller and datapath, derive the controller's FSM as was done in Figure 5.16 (i.e., don't implement the FSM further), and only use datapath components from the datapath component library of Figure 5.21.

5.7 Create a datapath for the HLSM in Figure 5.98.

5.8 Create a datapath for the HLSM in Figure 5.63.

5.9 For the HLSM in Figure 5.14, complete the RTL design process:
(a) Create a datapath.
(b) Connect the datapath to a controller.
(c) Derive the controller's FSM.

Inputs: A, B, C (16 bits); go, rst (bit)
Outputs: S (16 bits), P (bit)
Local registers: sum, Sreg

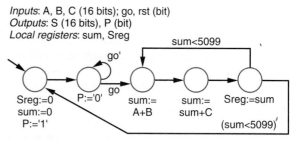

Figure 5.98 Sample high-level state machine.

5.10 Given the HLSM in Figure 5.99, complete the RTL design process to achieve a controller (FSM) connected with a datapath.

5.11 Given the partial HLSM in Figure 5.75 for the system of Figure 5.74, proceed with the RTL design process to achieve a controller (partial FSM) connected with a datapath.

5.12 Use the RTL design process to create a 4-bit up-counter with input cnt (1 means count up), clear input clr, a terminal count output tc, and a 4-bit output Q indicating the present count. Only use datapath components from Figure 5.21. After deriving the controller's FSM, implement the controller as a state register and combinational logic.

Inputs: start(bit), data(8 bits), addr(8 bits), w_wait(bit)
Outputs: w_data(8 bits), w_addr(8 bits), w_wr(bit)
Local storage: w_datareg(8 bits), w_addrreg(8 bits)

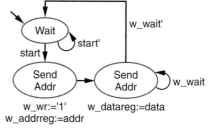

Figure 5.99 HLSM.

5.13 Use the RTL design process to design a system that outputs the average of the most recent two data input samples. The system has an 8-bit unsigned data input I, and an 8-bit unsigned output *avg*. The data input is sampled when a single-bit input S changes from 0 to 1. Choose internal bitwidths that prevent overflow.

5.14 Use the RTL design process to create an alarm system that sets a single-bit output `alarm` to 1 when the average temperature of four consecutive samples meets or exceeds a user-defined threshold value. A 32-bit unsigned input CT indicates the current temperature, and a 32-bit unsigned input WT indicates the warning threshhold. Samples should be taken every few clock cycles. A single-bit input `clr` when 1 disables the alarm and the sampling process. Start by capturing the desired system behavior as an HLSM, and then convert to a controller/datapath.

5.15 Use the RTL design process to design a reaction timer system that measures the time elapsed between the illumination of a light and the pressing of a button by a user. The reaction timer has three inputs, a clock input *clk*, a reset input *rst,* and a button input B. It has three outputs, a light enable output *len*, a 10-bit reaction time output *rtime,* and a *slow* output indicating that the user was not fast enough. The reaction timer works as follows. On reset, the reaction timer waits for 10 seconds before illuminating the light by setting *len* to 1. The reaction timer then measures the length of time in milliseconds before the user presses the button B, outputting the time as a 12-bit binary number on *rtime*. If the user did not press the button within 2 seconds (2000 milliseconds), the reaction timer will set the output *slow* to 1 and output 2000 on *rtime*. Assume that the clock input has a frequency of 1 kHz. Do not use a timer component in the datapath.

SECTION 5.4: MORE RTL DESIGN

For problems in this section, unless otherwise indicated, allowable datapath components are from Figure 5.21 and Figure 5.27, and controller design can end after deriving the FSM. Use the RTL design process for problems that state the need to "design" a system.

5.16 Create an FSM that interfaces with the datapath in Figure 5.100. The FSM should use the datapath to compute the average value of the 16 32-bit elements of any array *A*. Array *A* is stored in a memory, with the first element at address 25, the second at address 26, and so on. Assume that putting a new value onto the address lines *M_addr* causes the memory to almost immediately output the read data on the *M_data* lines. Ignore overflow issues.

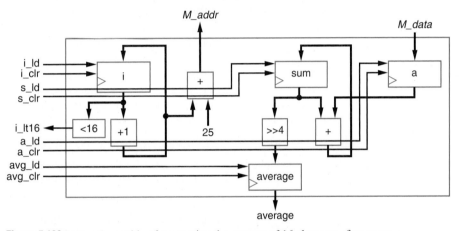

Figure 5.100 Datapath capable of computing the average of 16 elements of an array.

5.17 Design a system that repeatedly computes and outputs the sum of all *positive* numbers within a 512-word register file *A* consisting of 32-bit signed numbers.

5.18 Design a system that repeatedly computes and outputs the *maximum* value found within a register file *A* consisting of 64 32-bit unsigned numbers.

5.19 Using a timer, design a system with single-bit inputs U and D corresponding to two buttons, and a 16-bit output *Q* which is initially 0. Pressing the button for U causes *Q* to increment, while D causes a decrement; pressing both buttons causes *Q* to stay the same. If a single button is held down, *Q* should then continue to increment or decrement at a rate of once per second as long as the button is held. Assume the buttons are already debounced. Assume Q simply rolls over if its upper or lower value is reached.

5.20 Using a timer, design a display system that reads the ASCII characters from a 64-word 8-bit register file *RF* and writes each word to a 2-row LED-based display having 32 characters per row, doing so 100 times per second. The display has an 8-bit input *A* for the ASCII character to be displayed, a single-bit input row where 0 or 1 denotes the top or bottom row respectively, a 5-bit input *col* that indicates a column in the row, and an enable input en whose change from 0 to 1 causes the character to be displayed in the given row and column. The system should write *RF*[0] through *RF*[15] to row 0's columns 0 to 15 respectively, and *RF*[16] to *RF*[31] to row 1.

5.21 Design a data-dominated system that computes and outputs the sum of the absolute values of 16 separate 32-bit registers (*not* in a register file) storing signed numbers (do not consider how those numbers get stored). The computation of the sum should be done using a single equation in one state. The computation should be performed once when a single-bit input go changes from 0 to 1, and the computed result should be held at the output until the next time go changes from 0 to 1.

SECTION 5.5: DETERMINING CLOCK FREQUENCY

5.22 Assuming an inverter has a delay of 1 ns, all other gates have a delay of 2 ns, and wires have a delay of 1 ns, determine the critical path for the full-adder circuit in Figure 4.30.

5.23 Assuming an inverter has a delay of 1 ns, all other gates have a delay of 2 ns, and wires have a delay of 1 ns, determine the critical path for the 3x8 decoder of Figure 2.62.

5.24 Assuming an inverter has a delay of 1 ns, all other gates have a delay of 2 ns, and wires have a delay of 1 ns, determine the critical path for the 4x1 multiplexer of Figure 2.67.

5.25 Assuming an inverter has a delay of 1 ns, and all other gates have a delay of 2 ns, determine the critical path for the 8-bit carry-ripple adder, assuming a design following Figure 4.31 and Figure 4.30, and: (a) assuming wires have no delay, (b) assuming wires have a delay of 1 ns.

5.26 (a) Convert the laser-based distance measurer's FSM in Figure 5.26 to a state register and logic. (b) Assuming all gates have a delay of 2 ns and the 16-bit up-counter has a delay of 5 ns, and wires have no delay, determine the critical path for the laser-based distance measurer. (c) Calculate the corresponding maximum clock frequency for the circuit.

SECTION 5.6: BEHAVIORAL-LEVEL DESIGN: C TO GATES (OPTIONAL)

5.27 Convert the following C-like code, which calculates the greatest common divisor (GCD) of the two 8-bit numbers *a* and *b*, into a high-level state machine.

```
Inputs: byte a, byte b, bit go
Outputs: byte gcd, bit done
GCD:
while(1) {
   while(!go);
   done = 0;
   while ( a != b ) {
     if( a > b ) {
       a = a - b;
     }
     else {
       b = b - a;
     }
   }
   gcd = a;
   done = 1;
}
```

5.28 Use the RTL design process to convert the high-level state machine created in Exercise 5.27 to a controller and a datapath. Design the datapath to structure, but design the controller to an FSM and then stop.

5.29 Convert the following C-like code, which calculates the maximum difference between any two numbers within an array *A* consisting of 256 8-bit values, into a high-level state machine.

```
Inputs: byte a[256], bit go
Outputs: byte max_diff, bit done
MAX_DIFF:
while(1) {
  while(!go);
  done = 0;
  i = 0;
  max = 0;
  min = 255; // largest 8-bit value
  while( i < 256 ) {
    if( a[i] < min ) {
      min = a[i];
    }
    if( a[i] > max ) {
      max = a[i];
    }
    i = i + 1;
  }
  max_diff = max - min;
  done = 1;
}
```

5.30 Use the RTL design process to convert the high-level state machine created in Exercise 5.30 to a controller and a datapath. Design the datapath to structure, but design the controller to tan FSM and then stop.

5.31 Convert the following C-like code, which calculates the number of times the value *b* is found within an array *A* consisting of 256 8-bit values, into a high-level state machine.

```
Inputs: byte a[256], byte b, bit go
Outputs: byte freq, bit done
FREQUENCY:
while(1) {
  while(!go);
  done = 0;
  i = 0;
  freq = 0;
  while( i < 256 ) {
    if( a[i] == b ) {
      freq = freq + 1;
    }

  }
  done = 1;
}
```

5.32 Use the RTL design process to convert the high-level state machine you created in Exercise 5.31 to a controller and a datapath. Design the datapath to structure, but design the controller to the point of an FSM only.

5.33 Develop a template for converting a do{ }while loop of the following form to a high-level state machine.

```
do {
    // do while statements
} while (cond);
```

5.34 Develop a template for converting a for() loop of the following form to a high-level state machine.

```
for(i=start; i<cond; i++)
{
    // for statements
}
```

5.35 Compare the time required to execute the following computation using a custom circuit versus using a microprocessor. Assume a gate has a delay of 1 ns. Assume a microprocessor executes one instruction every 5 ns. Assume that $n=10$ and $m=5$. Estimates are acceptable; you need not design the circuit, or determine exactly how many software instructions will execute.

```
for (i = 0; i<n, i++) {
    s = 0;
    for (j = 0; j < m, j++) {
        s = s + c[i]*x[i + j];
    }
    y[i] = s;
}
```

SECTION 5.7: MEMORY COMPONENTS

5.36 Calculate the approximate number of DRAM bit storage cells that will fit on an IC with a capacity of 10 million transistors.

5.37 Calculate the approximate number of SRAM bit storage cells that will fit on an IC with a capacity of 10 million transistors.

5.38 Summarize the main differences between DRAM and SRAM memories.

5.39 Draw a circuit of transistors showing the internal structure for all the storage cells for a 4x2 DRAM (four words, 2 bits each), clearly labeling all internal components and connections.

5.40 Draw a circuit of transistors showing the internal structure for all the storage cells for a 4x2 SRAM (four words, 2 bits each), clearly labeling all internal components and connections.

5.41 Summarize the main differences between EPROM and EEPROM memories.

5.42 Summarize the main differences between EEPROM and flash memories.

5.43 Use an HLSM to capture the design of a system that can save data samples and then play them back. The system has an 8-bit input D where data appears. A single-bit input S changing from 0 to 1 requests that the current value on D (i.e., a sample) be saved in a nonvolatile memory. Sample requests will not arrive faster than once per 10 clock cycles. Up to 10,000 samples can be saved, after which sampling requests are ignored. A single-bit input P changing from 0 to 1 causes all recorded samples to be played back—i.e., to be written to an output Q one sample at a time in the order they were saved at a rate of one sample per clock cycle. A single-bit input R resets the system, clearing all recorded samples. During playback, any sample or reset request is ignored. At other times, reset has priority over a sample request. Choose an appropriate size and type of memory, and declare and use that memory in your HLSM.

SECTION 5.8: QUEUES (FIFOS)

5.44 For an 8-word queue, show the queue's internal state and provide the value of popped data for the following sequences of pushes and pops: (1) push A, B, C, D, E, (2) pop, (3) pop, (4) push U, V, W, X, Y, (5) pop, (6) push Z, (7) pop, (8) pop, (9) pop.

5.45 Create an FSM describing the queue controller of Figure 5.79. Pay careful attention to correctly setting the `full` and `empty` outputs.

5.46 Create an FSM describing the queue controller of Figure 5.79, but with error-preventing behavior that ignores any pushes when the queue is full, and ignores pops of an empty queue (outputting 0).

SECTION 5.9: MULTIPLE PROCESSORS

5.47 A system S counts people that enter a store, incrementing the count value when a single-bit input P changes from 1 to 0. The value is reset when R is 1. The value is output on a 16-bit output C, which connects to a display. Furthermore, the system has a lighting system to indicate the approximate count value to the store manager, turning on a red LED (LR=1) for 0 to 99, else a blue LED (LB=1) for 100 to 199, else a green LED (LG=1) for 200 and above. Draw a block diagram of the system and its peripheral components, using *two* processors for the system S. Show the HLSM for each processor.

5.48 A system S counts the cycles high of the most recent pulse on a single-bit input P and displays the value on a 16-bit output D, holding the value there until the next pulse completes. The system also keeps track of the previous 8 values, and computes and outputs the average of those values on a 16-bit output A whenever an input C changes from 0 to 1. The system holds that output value until the next change of C from 0 to 1. Draw a block diagram of the system and its peripheral components, using two processors and a global register file for the system. Show the HLSM for each processor.

5.49 A keypad needs to be interfaced with a computer. The keypad has a 4-bit output K representing the encoding of the key that was pressed and a single-bit output E that changes from 0 to 1 when a key is pressed. The computer has a corresponding 4-bit input CK and single-bit input CE. However, sometimes the computer is busy with other tasks and takes some time to receive the key, so it has an output Crec that it sets to 1 for one clock cycle when the key value has been received. Design a systems S in between the keypad and computer that can buffer up to 32 key values while the computer is busy. Show a block diagram of S composed of two processors and a queue, along with interfaces to the keypad and computer, and show HLSMs for each processor.

SECTION 5.10: HIERARCHY—A KEY DESIGN CONCEPT

5.50 Compose a 20-input AND gate from 2-input AND gates.

5.51 Compose a 16x1 mux from 2x1 muxes.

5.52 Compose a 4x16 decoder with enable from 2x4 decoders with enable.

5.53 Compose a 1024x8 RAM using only 512x8 RAMs.

5.54 Compose a 512x8 RAM using only 512x4 RAMs.

5.55 Compose a 1024x8 ROM using only 512x4 ROMs.

5.56 Compose a 2048x8 ROM using only 256x8 ROMs.

5.57 Compose a 1024x16 RAM using only 512x8 RAMs.

5.58 Compose a 1024x12 RAM using 512x8 and 512x4 RAMs.

5.59 Compose a 640x12 RAM using only 128x4 RAMs.

5.60 *Write a program that takes a parameter *N*, and automatically builds an N-input AND gate from 2-input AND gates. Your program merely needs to indicate how many 2-input AND gates exist in each level, from which one could easily determine the connections.

▶ *DESIGNER PROFILE*

Chi-Kai started college as an engineering major, and became a Computer Science major due to his developing interests in algorithms and in networks. After graduating, he worked for a Silicon Valley startup company that made chips for computer networking. His first task was to help simulate those chips before the chips were built. For over 10 years now, he has worked on multiple generations of networking devices that buffer, schedule, and switch ATM network cells and Internet Protocol packets. "The chips required to implement networking devices are complex components that must all work together almost perfectly to provide the building blocks of telecommunication and data networks. Each generation of devices becomes successively more complex."

When asked what skills are necessary for his job, Chi-Kai says "More and more, breadth of one's skill set matters more than depth. Being an effective chip engineer requires the ability to understand chip architecture (the big picture), to design logic, to verify logic, and to bring up the silicon in the lab. All these parts of the design cycle interplay more and more. To be truly effective at one particular area requires hands-on knowledge of the others as well. Also, each requires very different skills. For example, verification requires good software programming ability, while bring up requires knowing how to use a logic analyzer—good hardware skills."

High-end chips, like those involved in networking, are quite costly, and require careful design. "The software design process and the chip design process are fundamentally different. Software can afford to have bugs because patches can be applied. Silicon is a different story. The one-time expenses to spin a chip are on the order of $500,000. If there is a show-stopping bug, you may need to spend another $500,000. This constraint means the verification approach taken is quite different—effectively: there can be no bugs." At the same time, these chips must be designed quickly to beat competitors to the market, making the job "extremely challenging and exciting."

One of the biggest surprises Chi-Kai encountered in his job is the "incredible importance of good communication skills." Chi-Kai has worked in teams ranging from 10 people to 30 people, and some chips require teams of over 100 people. "Technically outstanding engineers are useless unless they know how to collaborate with others and disseminate their knowledge. Chips are only getting more complex—individual blocks of code in a given chip have the same complexity as an entire chip only a few years ago. To architect, design, and implement logic in hardware requires the ability to convey complexity." Furthermore, Chi-Kai points out that "just like any social entity, there are politics involved. For example, people are worried about aspirations for promotion, financial gain, and job security. In this greater context, the team still must work together to deliver a chip." So, contrary to the conceptions many people have of engineers, engineers must have excellent people skills, in addition to strong technical skills. Engineering is a social discipline.

6

Optimizations and Tradeoffs

▶ 6.1 INTRODUCTION

The previous chapters described how to design digital circuits using straightforward techniques. This chapter will describe how to design *better* circuits. For our purposes, *better* means circuits that are smaller, faster, or consume less power. Real-world design may involve additional criteria.

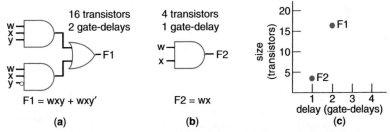

Figure 6.1 A circuit transformation that improves both size and delay, called an *optimization*: (a) original circuit, (b) optimized circuit, (c) plot of size and delay of each circuit.

Consider the circuit for the equation involving F1 shown in Figure 6.1(a). The circuit's size, assuming two transistors per gate input and ignoring inverters for simplicity, is $8 * 2 = 16$ transistors. The circuit's delay, which is the longest path from any input to the output, is 2 gate-delays. We could algebraically transform the equation into that for F2 shown in Figure 6.1(b). F2 represents the same function as F1, but requires only 4 transistors instead of 16, and has a delay of only 1 gate-delay instead of 2. The transformation improved both size and delay, as shown in Figure 6.1(c). A transformation that improves all criteria of interest is called an *optimization*.

Now consider the circuit for a different function in Figure 6.2(a), implementing the equation for G1. The circuit's size (assuming 2 transistors per gate input) is 14 transistors, and the circuit's delay is 2 gate-delays. We could algebraically transform the equation into that shown for G2 in Figure 6.2(b), which results in a circuit having only 12 transistors. However, the reduction in transistors comes at the expense of a longer delay of 3 gate-delays, as shown in Figure 6.2(c). Which circuit is better, the circuit for G1 or for

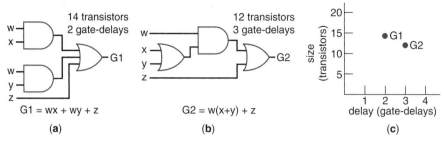

Figure 6.2 A circuit transformation that improves size but worsens delay, called a *tradeoff:*
(a) original circuit, (b) transformed circuit, (c) plot of size and delay of each circuit.

*A **tradeoff**
improves some
criteria at the
expense of other
criteria of interest.
An **optimization**
improves all
criteria of interest,
or improves some
of those criteria
without worsening
the others.*

G2? The answer depends on whether the size or delay criteria is more important. A transformation that improves one criteria at the expense of another criteria is called a ***tradeoff***.

You likely perform optimizations and tradeoffs every day. Perhaps you regularly commute by car from one city to another via a particular route. You might be interested in two criteria: commute time and safety. Other criteria, such as scenery along the route, may not be of interest. If you choose a new route that improves both commute time and safety, you have *optimized* your commute. If you instead choose a route that improves safety (e.g., avoiding a dangerous intersection) at the expense of increased commute time, you have made a *tradeoff* (and perhaps wisely so).

Figure 6.3 illustrates optimizations versus tradeoffs for three different starting designs, involving the criteria of delay and size, smaller being better for each criteria. Obviously, optimizations are preferred over tradeoffs, since optimizations improve both criteria, or at least improve one criteria without worsening another criteria, as shown by the horizontal and vertical arrows in Figure 6.3(a). But sometimes one criteria can't

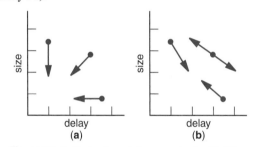

Figure 6.3 Optimizations (a), versus tradeoffs (b).

be improved without worsening another criteria. For example, if a car designer wants to improve a car's fuel efficiency, the designer may have to make the car smaller—a tradeoff between the criteria of fuel efficiency and comfort.

Some criteria commonly of interest to digital system designers include:

- ***Performance***: a measure of execution time for a computation on the system.
- ***Size***: a measure of the number of transistors, or silicon area, of a digital system.
- ***Power***: a measure of the energy consumed by the system per second, directly relating to both the heat generated by the system and to the battery energy consumed by computations.

Dozens of other criteria exist.

Optimizations and tradeoffs can be made throughout nearly all stages of digital design. This chapter describes some common optimizations and tradeoffs for typical criteria, at various levels of design.

▷ 6.2 COMBINATIONAL LOGIC OPTIMIZATIONS AND TRADEOFFS

Chapter 2 described how to design combinational logic, namely how to convert desired combinational behavior into a circuit of gates. Optimization and tradeoff methods can be applied to make those circuits better.

Two-Level Size Optimization Using Algebraic Methods

Implementing a Boolean function using only two levels of gates—a level of AND gates followed by one OR gate—usually results in a circuit having minimum delay. Recall from Chapter 2 that any Boolean equation can be written in sum-of-products form, simply by "multiplying out" the equation—for example, $xy(w+z) = xyw + xyz$. Thus, any Boolean function can be implemented using two levels of gates, simply by converting its equation to sum-of-products form and then using AND gates for the products followed by an OR gate for the sum.

A popular optimization is to *minimize the number of transistors* of a two-level logic circuit implementation of a Boolean function. Such optimization is traditionally called *two-level logic optimization*, or sometimes *two-level logic minimization*. We'll refer to it as ***two-level logic size optimization***, to distinguish such optimization from the increasingly popular optimizations of *performance* and *power*, as well as from other possible digital design optimizations.

In the 1970s/ 1980s, when transistors were costly (e.g., cents each), logic optimization was synonymous with size minimization, which dominated digital design. Today's cheaper transistors (e.g., 0.0001 cents each) make optimizations of other criteria equally or more critical.

Optimizing size requires a method to determine the number of transistors for a given circuit. A common method for quickly estimating the number of transistors:

- Assumes that every logic gate input requires two transistors. So a 3-input logic gate (whether an AND, OR, NAND, or NOR) would require $3 * 2 = 6$ transistors. The circuits inside logic gates shown in Section 2.4 reveal why two transistors per gate input is a common assumption.

- Ignores inverters when determining the number of transistors, for simplicity.

The problem of two-level logic size optimization can be viewed algebraically as the problem of *minimizing the number of literals and terms of a Boolean equation that is in sum-of-products form*. The reason the problem can be viewed algebraically is because, as shown in Chapter 2, a sum-of-products Boolean equation can be translated directly to a circuit using a level of AND gates followed by an OR gate. For example, the equation $F = wxy + wxy'$ from Figure 6.1(a) has six literals, w, x, y, w, x, and y', and two terms, wxy and wxy', for a total of $6 + 2 = 8$ literals and terms. Each literal and each term translates approximately to a gate input in a circuit, as shown in Figure 6.1(a)—the literals translate to AND gate inputs, and the terms translate to OR gate inputs. The circuit thus has $3 + 3 + 2 = 8$ gate inputs. With two transistors per gate input, the circuit has $8 * 2 = 16$ transistors. The number of literals and terms can be minimized algebraically: $F = wxy + wxy' = wx(y+y') = wx$. That equation has two literals, w and x, resulting in 2 gate inputs, or $2 * 2 = 4$ transistors, as shown in Figure 6.1(b). Note that a one-term equation does not require an OR gate, so the term is not counted for the transistor estimate. Likewise, a one-literal term would not require an AND gate and so that literal would not be counted.

Example 6.1 Two-level logic size optimization using algebraic methods

Minimize the number of literals and terms in a two-level implementation of the equation

$$F = xyz + xyz' + x'y'z' + x'y'z$$

Minimization can be done using algebraic transformations:

$$F = xy(z + z') + x'y'(z + z')$$
$$F = xy*1 + x'y'*1$$
$$F = xy + x'y'$$

There doesn't seem to be any further minimization possible. Thus, the equation has been transformed from having 12 literals and 4 terms (meaning 12 + 4 = 16 gate inputs, or 32 transistors), down to having only 4 literals and 2 terms (meaning 4 + 2 = 6 gate inputs, or 12 transistors).

The previous example showed the most common algebraic transformation used to simplify a Boolean equation in sum-of-products form, a transformation that can be written as:

$$ab + ab' = a(b+b') = a*1 = a$$

The transformation is sometimes called ***combining terms to eliminate a variable***, and is known formally as the ***uniting theorem***. The previous example applied the transformation twice, once with xy being a and with z being b, and a second time with x'y' being a and with z being b.

Sometimes a term must be duplicated to increase opportunities for combining terms to eliminate a variable, as illustrated in the next example.

Example 6.2 Reusing a term during two-level logic size optimization

Minimize the number of literals and terms in a two-level implementation of the equation

$$F = x'y'z' + x'y'z + x'yz$$

You might notice two opportunities to combine terms to eliminate a variable:

$$1: x'y'z' + x'y'z = x'y'$$
$$2: x'y'z + x'yz = x'z$$

Notice that the term x'y'z appears in both opportunities, but that term only appears once in the original equation. We'll therefore first replicate the term in the original equation (such replication doesn't change the function, because a = a + a) so that we can use the term twice when combining terms to eliminate a variable, as follows:

$$F = x'y'z' + x'y'z + x'yz$$
$$F = x'y'z' + x'y'z + x'y'z + x'yz$$
$$F = x'y'(z+z') + x'z(y'+y)$$
$$F = x'y' + x'z$$

After combining terms to eliminate a variable, the resulting term might also be combinable with other terms to eliminate a variable, as shown in the following example.

Example 6.3 Repeatedly combining terms to eliminate a variable

Minimize the number of literals and terms in a two-level implementation of the equation

$$G = xy'z' + xy'z + xyz + xyz'$$

We can combine the first two terms to eliminate a variable, and the last two terms also:

$$G = xy'(z'+z) + xy(z+z')$$
$$G = xy' + xy$$

We can combine the two remaining terms to eliminate a variable:

$$G = xy' + xy$$
$$G = x(y'+y)$$
$$G = x$$

In the previous examples, how did we "see" the opportunities to combine terms to eliminate a variable? The examples' original equations happened to be written in a way that made seeing the opportunities easy—terms that could be combined were side-by-side. Suppose instead the equation in Example 6.1 had been written as

$$F = x'y'z + xyz + xyz' + x'y'z'$$

That's the same function, but the terms appear in a different order. We might see that the middle two terms can be combined:

$$F = x'y'z + xyz + xyz' + x'y'z'$$
$$F = x'y'z + xy(z+z') + x'y'z'$$
$$F = x'y'z + xy + x'y'z'$$

But then we might not see that the left and right terms can be combined. We therefore might stop minimizing, thinking that we had obtained a fully minimized equation.

There is a visual method to help us *see* opportunities to combine terms to eliminate a variable, a method that the next section describes.

A Visual Method for Two-Level Size Optimization—K-Maps

Karnaugh Maps, or *K-maps* for short, are a visual method intended to assist humans to algebraically minimize Boolean equations having a few (two to four) variables. They actually are not commonly used any longer in design practice, but nevertheless, they are a very effective means for *understanding* the basic optimization methods underlying today's automated tools. A K-map is essentially a graphical representation of a truth table, meaning a K-map is yet another way to represent a function (other ways including an equation, truth table, and circuit). The idea underlying a K-map is to graphically place minterms adjacent to one another if those minterms differ in one variable only, so that we can actually "see" the opportunity for combining terms to eliminate a variable.

Three-Variable K-Maps

Figure 6.4 shows a K-map for the equation

$$F = x'y'z + xyz + xyz' + x'y'z'$$

which is the equation from Example 6.1 but with terms appearing in a different order. The map has eight cells, one for each possible combination of variable values. Let's examine the cells in the top row. The upper-left cell corresponds to $xyz=000$, meaning $x'y'z'$. The next cell to the right corresponds to $xyz=001$, meaning $x'y'z$. The next cell to the right corresponds to $xyz=011$, meaning $x'yz$. And the rightmost top cell corresponds to $xyz=010$, meaning $x'yz'$. Notice that the ordering of those top cells is *not* in increasing binary order. Instead, the order is 000, 001, 011, 010, rather than 000, 001, 010, 011. The

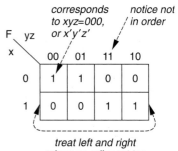

Figure 6.4 Three-variable K-map.

ordering is such that *adjacent cells differ in exactly one variable*. For example, the cells for $x'y'z$ (001) and $x'yz$ (011) are adjacent, and differ in exactly one variable, namely y. Likewise, the cells for $x'y'z'$ and xyz' are adjacent, and differ only in variable x. The map is also assumed to have its *left and right edges adjacent*, so the rightmost top cell (010) is adjacent to the leftmost top cell (000)—note that those cells too differ in exactly one variable. Adjacent means abutted either horizontally or vertically, but *not diagonally*, because diagonal cells differ in more than one variable. Adjacent bottom-row cells also differ in exactly one variable. And cells in a column also differ in exactly one variable.

A Boolean function can be represented as a K-map by placing 1s in the cells corresponding to the function's minterms. So for the equation F above, 1s are placed in cells corresponding to minterms $x'y'z$, xyz, xyz', and $x'y'z'$, as shown in Figure 6.4. 0s are placed in the remaining cells. Notice that a K-map is just another representation of a truth table. Rather than showing the output for every possible combination of inputs using a table, a K-map uses a graphical map. Therefore, a K-map is yet another representation of a Boolean function, and in fact is another standard representation.

The usefulness of a K-map for size minimization is that, because the map is designed such that adjacent cells differ in exactly one variable, then we know that *two adjacent 1s in a K-map indicate that we can combine the two minterms to eliminate a variable*. In other words, a K-map lets us easily see when two terms can be combined to eliminate a variable. Such combining is indicated by drawing a circle around two adjacent 1s, and then writing the term that results after the differing variable is removed. The following example illustrates.

In a K-map, adjacent cells differ in exactly one variable.

K-maps enable us to see opportunities to combine terms to eliminate a variable.

Example 6.4 Two-level logic size optimization using a K-map

Minimize the number of literals and terms in a two-level implementation of the equation

$$F = xyz + xyz' + x'y'z' + x'y'z$$

Note that this is the same equation as in Example 6.1. The K-map representing the function is shown in Figure 6.5. Adjacent 1s exist at the upper left of the map, so we circle those 1s to yield the term x'y'—in other words, *the circle is a shorthand notation* for x'y'z' + x'y'z = x'y'. Likewise, adjacent 1s exist at the bottom right cell of the map, so we draw a circle representing xyz + xyz' = xy. Thus, F = x'y' + xy.

The term "circle" is used even though the shape may be an oval or other shape.

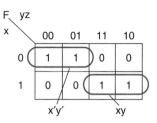

Figure 6.5 Minimizing a three-variable function using a K-map.

Recall from Example 6.3 that sometimes terms can be repeatedly combined to eliminate a variable, resulting in even fewer terms and literals. That example can be redone using a different order of simplifications as follows:

$$G = xy'z' + xy'z + xyz + xyz'$$
$$G = x(y'z' + y'z + yz + yz')$$
$$G = x(y'(z'+z) + y(z+z'))$$
$$G = x(y'+y)$$
$$G = x$$

Notice that the second line ANDs x with the OR of all possible combinations of variables y and z. Obviously, one of those combinations of y and z will be true for any values of y and z, and thus the subexpression in parentheses will always evaluate to 1, as was algebraically affirmed in the remaining lines above.

In addition to helping us see when two minterms can be combined to eliminate a variable, K-maps provide a graphical way to see when four minterms can be combined to eliminate two variables, as done above for G. We need to look for four 1s in adjacent cells, where the cells form either a rectangle or a square (but not a shape like an "L"). Those four cells will have one variable the same and all possible combinations of the other two variables. Figure 6.6 shows the above function G as a three-variable K-map. The K-map has

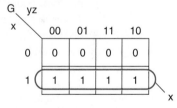

Figure 6.6 Four adjacent 1s.

four adjacent 1s in the bottom row. The four minterms corresponding to those 1s are xy'z', xy'z, xyz, and xyz'— note that x is the same in all four minterms, while all four combinations of y and z appear in those minterms. A circle drawn around the bottom four 1s represents the simplification of G shown in the equations above. The result is G = x. In other words, the circle is a shorthand notation for the algebraic simplification of G shown in the five equations above.

Note that circles could have been drawn around the left two 1s and the right two 1s of the K-map as shown in Figure 6.7, resulting in G = xy' + xy. Clearly, G can be further simplified to x(y'+y) =x. Thus, we should always draw the largest circle possible in order to best minimize the equation.

As another example of four adjacent 1s, consider the equation

$$H = x'y'z + x'yz + xy'z + xyz$$

Figure 6.8 shows the K-map for that equation's function. Circling the four adjacent 1s yields the minimized equation H = z.

Sometimes circles need to be drawn that include the same 1 twice. Consider the following equation:

$$I = x'y'z + xy'z' + xy'z$$
$$+ xyz + xyz'$$

Figure 6.9 shows the K-map for that equation's function. A circle can be drawn around the bottom four 1s to reduce those four minterms to just x. But that leaves the single 1 in the top row, corresponding to minterm x'y'z. That minterm must be somehow included in the minimized equation, since leaving that minterm out would change the function. The minterm could be ORed with the equation, yielding I = x + x'y'z, but that equation is not minimized because the original equation included minterm xy'z, and xy'z + x'y'z = (x+x')y'z = y'z. On the K-map, a circle can be drawn around the top 1 that also includes the 1 in the cell below. The minimized function is thus I = x + y'z.

Including a 1 twice in different circles doesn't change the function, because doing so is the same as duplicating a minterm. Duplicating a minterm doesn't change the function, because a = a + a. The algebraic equivalent of the twice-circled 1 of Figure 6.9 is:

$$I = x'y'z + xy'z' + xy'z + xyz + xyz'$$
$$I = x'y'z + xy'z + xy'z' + xy'z + xyz + xyz'$$
$$I = (x'y'z + xy'z) + (xy'z' + xy'z + xyz + xyz')$$
$$I = (y'z) + (x)$$

The duplicated minterm resulted in better optimization.

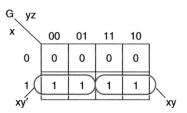

Figure 6.7 Non-optimal circles.

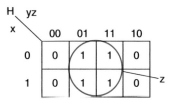

Figure 6.8 Four adjacent 1s.

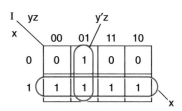

Figure 6.9 Circling a 1 twice.

On the other hand, there's no reason to circle 1s more than once if the 1s are already included in a minimized term. For example, the K-map for the equation

$$J = x'y'z' + x'y'z + xy'z + xyz$$

appears in Figure 6.10. There's no reason to draw the circle resulting in the term y'z. The other two circles cover all the 1s, meaning those two circles' terms cause the equation to output 1 for all the required input combinations. The third circle just results in an extra term without changing the function. Thus, not only should the largest possible circles be drawn to cover all the 1s, but the *fewest* circles should be drawn too.

Draw the fewest circles possible, to minimize the number of terms.

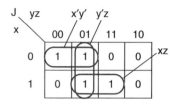

Figure 6.10 An unnecessary term.

As mentioned earlier, the left and right sides of a K-map are considered to be adjacent. Thus, circles can be drawn that wrap around the sides of a K-map. For example, the K-map for the equation

$$K = xy'z' + xyz' + x'y'z$$

appears in Figure 6.11. The two cells in the corners with 1s are adjacent since the left and right sides of the map are adjacent, and therefore one circle can be drawn that covers both, resulting in the term xz'.

Sometimes a 1 does not have any adjacent 1s. In that case, a circle is drawn around that single 1, resulting in a term that is also a minterm. The term x'y'z in Figure 6.11 is an example of such a term.

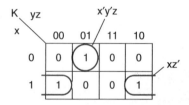

Figure 6.11 Sides are adjacent.

A circle in a three-variable K-map must involve one cell, two adjacent cells, four adjacent cells, or eight adjacent cells. A circle can *not* involve only three, five, six, or seven cells. The circle must represent algebraic transformations that eliminate variables appearing in all possible combinations, since those variables can be factored out and then combined to a 1. Three adjacent cells don't have all combinations of two variables—one combination is missing. Thus, the circle in Figure 6.12 would not be valid, since it corresponds to xy'z' + xy'z + xyz, which doesn't simplify down to one term. To cover that function, two circles are needed, one around the left pair of 1s, the other around the right pair.

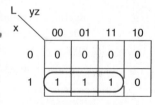

Figure 6.12 Invalid circle.

If all the cells in a K-map have 1s, like for the function E in Figure 6.13, then there are eight adjacent 1s. A circle can be drawn around those eight cells. Since that circle represents the ORing of all possible combinations of the function's three variables, and since obviously one of those combinations will be true for any combination of input values, the equation minimizes to just E = 1.

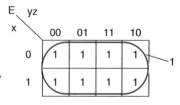

Figure 6.13 Four adjacent 1s.

Whenever in doubt as to whether a circle is valid, just remember that the circle represents a shorthand for algebraic transformations that combine terms to eliminate a variable. A circle must represent a set of terms for which all possible combinations of some variables appear while other variables are identical in all terms. The changing variables can be eliminated, resulting in a single term without those variables.

Four-Variable K-Maps

K-maps are also useful for minimizing four-variable Boolean functions. Figure 6.14 shows a four-variable K-map. Again, notice that every adjacent pair of cells in the K-map differs by exactly one variable. Also, the left and right sides of the map are considered adjacent, and the top and bottom edges of the map are also adjacent—note that the left and right cells differ by only one variable, as do the top and bottom cells.

The K-map in the figure has been filled in for the following equation:

$$F = w'xy'z' + w'xy'z + w'x'yz$$
$$+ w'xyz + wxyz + wx'yz$$

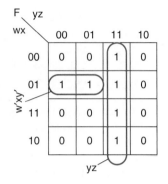

Figure 6.14 Four-variable K-map.

The 1s in the map can be covered with the two circles shown in Figure 6.14, resulting in the terms $w'xy'$ and yz. The resulting minimized equation is therefore $F = w'xy' + yz$.

A circle covering eight adjacent cells would represent all combinations of three variables, so algebraic manipulation would eliminate all three variables and yield one term. For example, the function in Figure 6.15 simplifies to the single term z as shown.

Legal-sized circles in a four-variable K-map are one, two, four, eight, or sixteen adjacent cells. Circling all sixteen cells results in a function that equals 1.

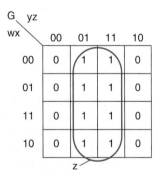

Figure 6.15 Eight adjacent cells.

Larger K-Maps

K-maps for five and six variables have been proposed, but are rather cumbersome to use effectively. We do not discuss them further.

A K-map can be drawn for a two-variable function, as shown in Figure 6.16. However, a two-variable K-map isn't particularly useful, because two-variable functions are easy to minimize algebraically.

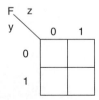

Figure 6.16 Two-variable K-map.

Using a K-Map

Given any Boolean function of three or four variables, the following method summarizes how to use a K-map to minimize the function:

1. *Convert* the function's equation into sum-of-minterms form.

2. *Place* a 1 in the appropriate K-map cell for each minterm.

3. *Cover* all the 1s by drawing the *minimum* number of *largest* circles such that every 1 is included at least once, and write the corresponding term.

4. *OR* all the resulting terms to create the minimized function.

The first step, converting to sum-of-minterms form, can be done algebraically as in Chapter 2. Alternatively, many people find it easier to combine steps 1 and 2, by converting the function's equation to sum-of-products form (where each term is not necessarily a minterm), and then filling in the 1s on the K-map corresponding to each term. For example, consider the four-variable function

$$F = w'xz + yz + w'xy'z'$$

The term w'xz corresponds to the two lightly shaded cells in Figure 6.17, so 1s are placed in those cells. The term yz corresponds to the entire dark-shaded column in the figure. The term w'xy'z' corresponds to the single unshaded cell shown on the left with a 1.

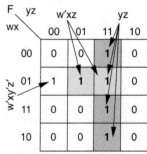

Figure 6.17 w'xz and yz terms.

Minimization would proceed by covering the 1s with circles and ORing all the terms. The function in Figure 6.17 is identical to the function in Figure 6.14, for which the obtained minimized equation was $F = w'xy' + yz$.

Example 6.5 Two-level logic size optimization using a three-variable K-map

Minimize the following equation:

$$G = a + a'b'c' + b(c' + bc')$$

Let's begin by converting the equation to sum-of-products:

$$G = a + a'b'c' + bc' + bc'$$

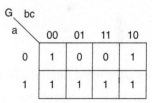

Figure 6.18 Terms on the K-map.

We place 1s in a three-variable K-map corresponding to each term as in Figure 6.18. The bottom row corresponds to the term a, the top left cell to term a'b'c', and the right column to the term bc' (which happens to appear twice in the equation).

We then cover the 1s using the two circles shown in Figure 6.19. ORing the resulting terms yields the minimized equation G = a + c'.

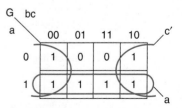

Figure 6.19 A cover.

Example 6.6 Two-level logic size optimization using a four-variable K-map

Minimize the following equation:

$$H = a'b'(cd' + c'd') + ab'c'd' + ab'cd' + a'bd + a'bcd'$$

Converting to sum-of-products form yields

$$H = a'b'cd' + a'b'c'd' + ab'c'd' + ab'cd' + a'bd + a'bcd'$$

We fill in the 1s corresponding to each term, resulting in the K-map shown in Figure 6.20. The term a'bd corresponds to the two cells whose 1s are in italics. All the other terms are minterms and thus correspond to one cell.

We cover the 1s using circles as shown. One "circle" covers the four corners, resulting in the term b'd'. That circle may look strange, but remember that the top and bottom cells are adjacent, and the left and right cells are adjacent. Another circle results in the term a'bd, and a third circle results in the term a'bc. The minimized two-level equation is therefore:

$$H = b'd' + a'bc + a'bd$$

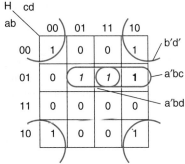

Figure 6.20 K-map example.

There can be many different minimized equations for the same function. For example, note the bolded 1 in Figure 6.20. We covered that 1 by drawing a circle that included the 1 to the left, yielding the term a'bc. Alternatively, we could have drawn a circle that included the 1 above, yielding the term a'cd', resulting in the minimized equation

$$H = b'd' + a'cd' + a'bd$$

Not only does that equation represent the same function as the previous equation, that equation would also require the same number of transistors as the previous equation. Thus, we see that there may be multiple minimized equations that are equally good.

Don't Care Input Combinations

Sometimes, certain input combinations, known as ***don't care*** combinations, of a Boolean function are guaranteed to never appear. For those combinations, we don't care whether the function outputs a 1 or a 0, because the function will never actually see those input values—the output for those inputs just doesn't matter. As an intuitive example, if you become ruler of the world, will you live in a palace or a castle? The output (your answer) doesn't matter, because the input (you becoming ruler of the world) is guaranteed to never happen.

Thus, when given a don't care input combination, we can choose whether to output a 1 or a 0 for each input combination, such that we obtain the best minimization possible. We can choose whatever output yields the best minimization, because the output for those don't care input combinations doesn't matter, as those combinations simply won't happen.

Algebraically, don't care terms can be introduced into an equation during algebraic minimization to create the opportunity to combine terms to eliminate a variable. As a simple example, consider a function $F = xy'z'$, for which it is also guaranteed that the terms $x'y'z'$ and $xy'z$ can each never evaluate to 1. Notice that introducing the first don't care term to the equation would result in $F = xy'z' + x'y'z' = (x+x')y'z' = y'z'$. Thus, introducing that don't care term $x'y'z'$ into the equation yields a minimization benefit. However, continuing by introducing the second don't care term does not yield such a benefit, so there is no need to introduce that term too.

In a K-map, don't care input combinations can be easily handled by placing an X in a K-map for each don't care minterm. The Xs don't *have* to be covered with circles, but some Xs *can* be covered if doing so enables drawing bigger circles while covering the 1s, meaning fewer literals will appear in the term corresponding to the circle. The above function F can be converted to the K-map shown in Figure 6.21, having a 1 corresponding to $xy'z'$ when the function *must* output 1, and having two Xs corresponding to

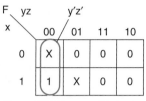

Figure 6.21 K-map with don't cares.

$x'y'z'$ and $xy'z$ when the function *may* output 1 if that helps minimize the function. Drawing a single circle results in the minimized equation $F = y'z'$. (Be careful in this discussion not to confuse the uppercase X, corresponding to a don't care, with the lowercase x, corresponding to a variable.)

Remember, don't cares don't *have* to be covered. The cover in Figure 6.22 gives an example of a wasteful use of don't cares. The circle covering the bottom X, yielding term xy', is not needed. That term is not wrong, because we don't care whether the output is 1 or 0 when $xy'z$ evaluates to 1. But that term yields a larger circuit because the resulting equation is $F = y'z' + xy'$. Since we don't care, it is better to make the output 0 when $xy'z$ is 1 to yield a smaller circuit.

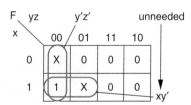

Figure 6.22 Wasteful use of Xs.

Example 6.7 Two-level logic size optimization with don't cares on a K-map

Minimize the following equation

$$F = a'bc' + abc' + a'b'c$$

given that terms $a'bc$ and abc are don't cares. Intuitively, those don't cares mean that bc can never be 11.

We begin by creating the 3-variable K-map in Figure 6.23. We place 1s in the three cells for the function's minterms. We then place Xs in the two cells for the don't cares. We can cover the upper-left 1 using a circle that includes an X. Likewise, including the two Xs in a circle covers the two 1s on the right with a bigger circle. The resulting minimized equation is $F = a'c + b$.

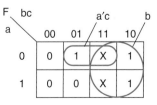

Figure 6.23 Using don't cares.

Without don't cares, the equation would have minimized to $F = a'b'c + bc'$. Assuming two transistors per gate input and ignoring inverters, the equation minimized without don't cares would require $(3+2+2) * 2 = 14$ transistors (3 gate inputs for the first AND gate, 2 for the second AND gate, and 2 for the OR gate, times 2 transistors per gate input). In contrast, the equation minimized with don't cares requires only $(2 + 0 + 2)*2 = 8$ transistors.

Example 6.8 Don't care input combinations in a sliding switch example

Consider a sliding switch shown in Figure 6.24 that can be in one of five positions, with three outputs x, y, and z indicating the position in binary. So xyz can take on the values of 001, 010, 011, 100, and 101. The other values for xyz are not possible, namely

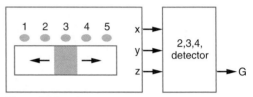

Figure 6.24 Sliding switch example.

the values 000, 110, and 111, meaning or $x'y'z'$, xyz', and xyz. We wish to design combinational logic, with x, y, and z inputs, that outputs 1 if the switch is in position 2, 3, or 4, corresponding to xyz values of 010, 011, or 100.

A Boolean equation describing the desired logic is: $G = x'yz' + x'yz + xy'z'$. We can minimize the equation using a K-map as shown in Figure 6.25. The minimized equation that results is: $G = xy'z' + x'y$.

However, if don't cares are considered, a simpler minimized equation can be obtained. In particular, we know that none of the three minterms $x'y'z'$, xyz', and xyz can ever be true, because the switch can only be in one of the above-stated five positions. So it doesn't matter whether a circuit outputs a 1 or a 0 for those three other minterms.

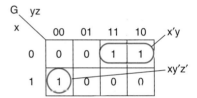

Figure 6.25 Without don't cares.

We can include these don't care input combinations as Xs on the K-map as shown in Figure 6.26. When covering the 1s in the top right, a larger circle can now be drawn, resulting in the term y. When covering the 1 at the bottom left, a larger circle can also be drawn, resulting in the term z'. Although all Xs were covered in this example, recall that not all Xs need be covered. The minimized equation that results is: $G = y + z'$.

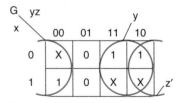

Figure 6.26 With don't cares.

That minimized equation using don't cares looks a lot different than the minimized equation without don't cares. But keep in mind the circuit still works the same. For example, if the switch is in position 1, then xyz will be 001, so $G = y + z'$ evaluates to 0 as desired.

Several common situations lead to don't cares. Sometimes don't cares come from physical limits on the inputs—a switch can't be in two positions at once, for example. If you've read Chapter 5, then you may realize that another common situation where don't cares arise is in the controller of a datapath. If the controller isn't reading or writing to a particular memory or register file in a given state, then it doesn't matter what address appears at the memory or register file during that state. Likewise, if a mux feeds into a register and the controller isn't loading the register in a given state, then the mux select value is a don't care in that state because it doesn't matter which mux data input passes through the mux during that state. If a controller isn't going to load the output of an ALU into a register in a given state, then it doesn't matter what function the ALU computes during that state.

Don't cares must be used with caution. The criteria of circuit size usually has to be balanced with other criteria, like reliable, error-tolerant, and safe circuits, when deciding whether to use don't cares. We must ask ourselves—is it *ever* possible that the input combination might occur, even in an error situation? And if it is possible, then should we care what the circuit outputs in that situation?

Automating Two-Level Logic Size Optimization

Visual Use of K-Maps Is Limited

Although the visual K-map method is helpful in two-level optimization of three- and four-variable functions, the visual method is unmanageable for functions with many more variables. One problem is that we can't effectively visualize maps beyond 5 or 6 variables. Another problem is that humans make mistakes, and might accidentally not draw the biggest circle possible on a K-map. Furthermore, the order in which a designer begins covering 1s may result in a function that has more terms than would have been obtained using a different order. For example, consider the function shown in the K-map of Figure 6.27(a). Starting from the left, a designer might first draw the circle yielding the term y'z', then the circle yielding x'y', then the circle yielding yz, and finally the circle yielding xy, for a total of four terms. The K-map in Figure 6.27(b) shows an alternative cover. After drawing the circle yielding the term y'z', the designer draws the circle yielding x'z, and then the circle yielding xy. The alternative cover uses only three terms instead of four.

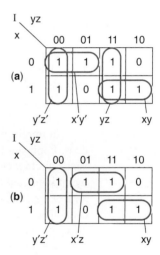

Figure 6.27 A cover is not necessarily optimal: (a) a four-term cover, and (b) a three-term cover of the same function.

Concepts Underlying Automated Two-Level Size Optimization

Because of the above-mentioned problems, two-level logic size optimization is done primarily using automated computer-based tools executing heuristics or exact algorithms. A *heuristic* is a problem solving method that *usually* yields a good solution, which is ideally close to the optimal, but *not necessarily* optimal. An *exact algorithm*, or just algorithm, is a problem solving method that yields the optimal solution. An **optimal solution** is as good as or better than any other possible solution with respect to the criteria of interest.

This section now defines some concepts underlying heuristics and exact algorithms for two-level logic size optimization. Those concepts will be illustrated graphically on K-maps, but such illustration is only intended to provide the reader with an intuition of the concepts—automated tools do *not* use K-maps.

Recall that a function can be written as a sum-of-minterms equation. A **minterm** is a product term that includes all the function's variables exactly once, in either true or complemented form. The **on-set** of a Boolean function is the set of minterms that define when the function should evaluate to 1 (i.e., when the function is "on"). Consider the function F = x'y'z + xyz' + xyz, whose K-map representation is shown in Figure 6.28. F's on-set is {x'y'z, xyz, xyz'}. The **off-set** of a Boolean function consists of all the minterms that define when the function should evaluate to 0. F's off-set

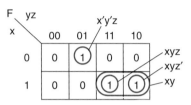

Figure 6.28 Minterms (the three smaller circles) and implicants (all the circles).

is {x'y'z', x'yz', x'yz, xy'z', xy'z}. Using compact minterms representation (see Section 2.6), the on-set is {1,6,7} and the off-set is {0,2,3,4,5}.

An **implicant** is a product term that may include fewer than all the function's variables, but is a term that only evaluates to 1 if the function should evaluate to 1. The function F above has four implicants: x'y'z, xyz', xyz, and xy. Graphically, an implicant is any legal (but not necessarily the biggest possible) circle on a K-map, as shown in Figure 6.28. All minterms are obviously implicants, but not all implicants are minterms.

An implicant **covers** a minterm if the implicant evaluates to 1 whenever the minterm does. Implicant xy covers minterms xyz' and xyz of function F. Graphically, an implicant's circle includes the 1s of the covered minterms. Replacing minterms in an equation by an implicant that covers those minterms does not change the function. For function F, xyz' + xyz can be replaced by xy because xy covers those two minterms. A set of implicants that covers the on-set of a function (and covers no other minterms) is known as a cover of the function or **function cover**. For the above function, one function cover is x'y'z + xyz + xyz'. Another cover is x'y'z + xy. Yet another cover is x'y'z + xyz + xyz' + xy.

Removing a variable from a term is known as **expanding** the term, which is the same as expanding the size of a circle on a K-map. For example, the term xyz can be expanded by removing z, leading to the term xy. If the original term is an implicant of a function, a new term obtained by expanding the original term may or may not be an implicant of the function. For example, for function F in Figure 6.28, expanding the term xyz to the term xy results in an implicant of the function. Expanding the term xyz' to xy also results in an implicant (the same one). But expanding xyz to xz (by eliminating y) does not result in an implicant—xz covers minterm xy'z, which is not in the function's on-set.

A **prime implicant** of a function is an implicant with the property that if any variable were eliminated from the implicant, the result would be a term covering a minterm not in the function's on-set; a prime implicant cannot be expanded into another implicant. Graphically, a prime implicant corresponds to circles that are the largest possible—enlarging the circle further would result in covering 0s, which changes the function. In Figure 6.28, x'y'z and xy are prime implicants. Removing any variable from implicant x'y'z would result in a term that covers a minterm that is not in the on-set. Removing any variable from implicant xy would also result in a term that covers minterms not in the on-set. On the other hand, xyz is not a prime implicant, because z can be removed from that implicant without changing the function; xy covers minterms xyz and xyz', both of which are in the on-set. Likewise, xyz' is not a prime implicant, because z' can be removed. There is usually no need to cover a function with anything other than prime implicants, because a prime implicant achieves the same function with fewer literals than non-prime implicants. This is equivalent to saying that we should always draw the biggest circles possible in K-maps.

An ***essential prime implicant*** is a prime implicant that is the *only* prime implicant that covers a particular minterm in a function's on-set. Graphically, an essential prime implicant is the only circle (the largest possible, of course, since the circle must represent a prime implicant) that covers a particular 1. A nonessential prime implicant is a prime implicant whose covered minterms are also covered by one or more other prime implicants. Figure 6.29 shows a function G that has four prime implicants, but only two of which are essential. x'y' is an essential prime implicant because it is the only prime implicant that covers minterm x'y'z'. xy is an essential prime implicant because it is the only prime impli-

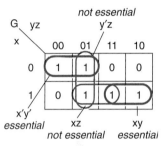

Figure 6.29 Essential prime implicants.

cant that covers minterm xyz'. y'z is a nonessential prime implicant because both of its covered minterms are covered by other implicants (those other prime implicants may or may not be essential prime implicants). Likewise, xz is not essential.

For the earlier function F in Figure 6.28, x'y'z is an essential prime implicant because it is the only prime implicant covering x'y'z. xy is also an essential prime implicant because it is the only prime implicant that covers xyz (and likewise the only prime implicant that covers xyz').

The significance of essential prime implicants is that each essential prime implicant *must* be included in a function's cover, otherwise there would be some required minterms that would not be covered by any prime implicant. On the other hand, each nonessential prime implicant may or may not be included in function's cover. In Figure 6.29, neither of the nonessential prime implicants, y'z and xz, must appear in the function's cover. Of course, in this case, one of them must appear in the function cover in order to cover minterm xy'z (the bottom left 1 in the K-map), but neither of them individually is essential.

The Tabular Method (Quine-McCluskey)

Given the notions of prime implicants and essential prime implicants, an automatable approach for two-level logic size optimization is shown in Table 6.1, known as the ***tabular method***. The method was originally developed by Quine and McCluskey and is commonly referred to as the ***Quine-McCluskey method***. The method begins with a function's minterms, which can be obtained algebraically from any equation describing the

TABLE 6.1 **Automatable tabular method for two-level logic size optimization.**

Step	Description
1 *Determine prime implicants*	Starting with minterm implicants, methodically compare all pairs (actually, all pairs whose numbers of uncomplemented literals differ by one) to find opportunities to combine terms to eliminate a variable, yielding new implicants with one less literal. Repeat for new implicants. Stop when no implicants can be combined. All implicants not covered by a new implicant are prime implicants.
2 *Add essential prime implicants to the function's cover*	Find every minterm covered by only one prime implicant, and denote that prime implicant as essential. Add essential prime implicants to the cover, and mark all minterms covered by those implicants as already covered.
3 *Cover remaining minterms with nonessential prime implicants*	Cover the remaining minterms using the minimal number of remaining prime implicants.

function as shown in Chapter 2. The first step of the tabular method is to determine all prime implicants of the function by methodically comparing all pairs of implicants (starting with minterms) to find opportunities to combine terms to eliminate a variable. The second step finds the essential prime implicants among those prime implicants and includes them in the function's cover (because by definition, essential prime implicants must be included in the cover), and notes all the minterms that are covered by those essential prime implicants. The last step covers remaining minterms using the fewest remaining prime implicants. The steps will be illustrated using the following function:

$$F = x'y'z' + x'y'z + x'yz + xy'z + xyz' + xyz$$

Step 1 finds all prime implicants. It begins by considering each minterm as an implicant; function F has 6 such implicants. The step compares every pair of implicants to detect opportunities to combine terms to eliminate a variable, as illustrated in Figure 6.30(a). For example, the first implicant x'y'z' is compared with each of the other implicants. When compared with the second implicant x'y'z, the result is x'y'z' + x'y'z = x'y'. On the other hand, when compared with the third implicant x'yz, no combining is possible (indicated by the word "No" in the figure); likewise, no combining is possible when compared with the other implicants ("No" is not shown for those). The second implicant is then compared with each of the third, fourth, fifth, and sixth implicants (it has already been compared with the first implicant). And so on for each of the remaining implicants.

In doing these comparisons, one may notice that combining terms to eliminate a variable is only possible if the number of uncomplemented literals in the two implicants differs by exactly one. For example, x'y'z' has 0 uncomplemented literals and x'y'z has 1 uncomplemented literal (z), so comparing those terms could possibly lead to them being combined. On the other hand, comparing x'y'z' with x'yz, which has 2 uncomplemented literals (y and z), makes no sense—those two terms can't possibly differ by only 1 literal and thus they could never be combined. Likewise, comparing implicants with the same number of uncomplemented literals makes no sense either because those implicants must have two (or more) variables whose complementing differs; e.g., x'yz and xy'z each has 2 uncomplemented literals and thus the two terms can't possibly be

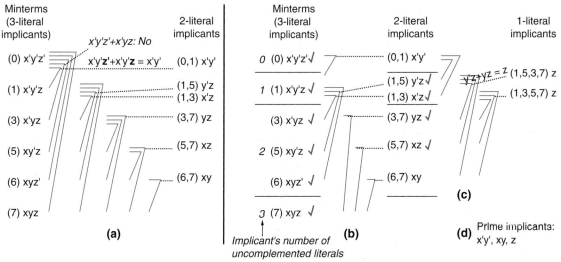

Figure 6.30 First step of tabular method for function F: (a) comparing all pairs of 3-literal implicants (minterms) for opportunities to combine terms to eliminate a variable, (b) comparison of two terms is actually only necessary if the number of uncomplemented literals in the terms differs by one, (c) repeating the comparisons for the new 2-literal implicants, (d) prime implicants are all implicants not covered by a lower-literal implicant.

*In digital design automation (and in computer algorithms in general), skipping items that cannot possibly lead to a good solution is known as **pruning**; think of all possible solutions as being the leaves of a tree's branches—skipping items is like pruning branches of the tree.*

combined. Thus, the minterms can be grouped according to their number of uncomplemented literals as shown in Figure 6.30(b), and then comparisons between items in groups whose number does not differ by exactly one can be skipped.

Comparing a pair may lead to a new implicant. The implicants in the pair cannot possibly be a prime implicants because each can be expanded into the new implicant. For example, x'y'z' and x'y'z cannot be prime implicants because each can be expanded into implicant x'y'. A check mark can be placed next to each such implicant as in Figure 6.30(b). Furthermore, keeping track of which minterms are covered by which implicants will be helpful, so each minterm's number (see compact sum-of-minterms representation in Chapter 2) is shown in parentheses next to the minterm, and each new implicant has in parentheses the list of minterms that the implicant covers.

The pairwise comparisons repeat for the new implicants; e.g., F's 2-literal implicants are compared as in Figure 6.30(c). Such comparisons again only compare implicants whose number of uncomplemented literals differs by exactly one. Furthermore, no comparison is necessary between implicants having a different number of literals, such as between the 3-literal and 2-literal implicants, because such comparisons couldn't possibly lead to terms being combined, due to the different numbers of literals.

The comparisons continue until no new implicants result. All unchecked implicants must be prime implicants, because those implicants could not be expanded into another implicant.

Step 2 determines all essential prime implicants and adds them to the function's cover. Determining essential prime implicants begins by creating a table as in Figure 6.31(a) with one column for each prime implicant (as determined in Step 1) and one row for each minterm. An "X" is placed in the table if the column's prime implicant covers

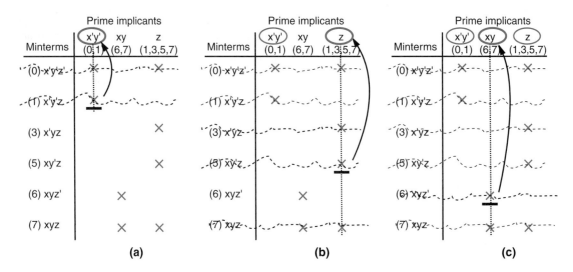

Figure 6.31 Second step of tabular method for function F: (a) the sole X (underlined) in the second row means that only prime implicant x'y' covers minterm x'y'z, so x'y' is an essential prime implicant. The prime implicant is circled to indicate it being added to F's cover, and all its covered minterms' rows are crossed out to indicate those minterms are now covered. (b) The fourth row also has a sole X, so prime implicant z is essential and thus added to the cover, and its covered minterms' rows are crossed out. (c) Prime implicant xy is also essential, so it is added and its rows crossed out. For F, the essential prime implicants cover all the minterms, and thus the method's third step is not needed. The final cover is F = x'y' + xy + z.

the row's minterm; keeping the list of minterm numbers with each prime implicant in Step 1 now makes it easy to determine which minterms are covered by a prime implicant.

Next, each row is examined to see if only one X exists in the row. Figure 6.31(a) shows that the second row has a sole X, which means that prime implicant x'y' is the only prime implicant that covers minterm x'y'z and is therefore an essential prime implicant. x'y' is thus added to the function's cover, indicated by being circled. Now that x'y' is part of the function's cover, both minterms covered by x'y' are covered (indicated by the vertical dotted line), and thus their rows can be crossed out of the table as shown, because those minterms no longer need to be considered.

The search for rows with a sole X continues. A sole X is found in the fourth row, and thus prime implicant z is essential and so is added to the function's cover, and its covered minterms' rows are crossed out. A sole X is then found in the fifth row, and thus prime implicant xy is essential and is similarly added to the cover and its row crossed out.

Step 3 is to use the fewest remaining prime implicants to cover any remaining minterms. However, all minterms were covered by Step 2; i.e., all rows have been crossed out. Thus, for this function, the essential prime implicants completely cover the function. The final minimized equation is therefore F = x'y' + xy + z.

The reader may find it useful to minimize F using a K-map to help understand the minimization achieved by the tabular method.

Don't care minterms can be introduced into the tabular method by including them as function minterms during Step 1, which finds all prime implicants. However, Step 2 would only include the function's on-set minterms and not the don't care minterms, because Step 2 finds essential prime implicants, which only relate to the on-set minterms. Of course, those essential prime implicants may have been more expanded thanks to the presence of the don't care minterms in Step 1. Likewise, Step 3 would only include on-set minterms because only those minterms must be covered to provide a cover of the function, but again, the prime implicants being used may have been more expanded thanks to don't care minterms in Step 1.

Methods that Enumerate All Minterms or Compute All Prime Implicants May Be Inefficient

The tabular method works reasonably for functions with perhaps tens of variables. However, for larger functions, just listing all the minterms could result in a huge amount of data. A function of 10 variables could have up to 2^{10} minterms—that's 1024 minterms, which is reasonable. But a function of 32 variables could have up to 2^{32} minterms, or up to about four billion minterms. Representing those minterms in a table requires prohibitive computer memory. And comparing those minterms with other minterms could require on the order of (four billion)^2 computations, or quadrillions of computations (a quadrillion is a thousand times a trillion). Even a computer performing 10 billion computations per second would require 100,000 seconds to perform all those computations, or 27 hours. And for 64 variables, the numbers go up to 2^{64} possible minterms, or quadrillions of minterms, and quadrillions^2 of computations, which could require a month of computation. Functions with 100 inputs, which are not uncommon, would require an absurd amount of memory, and many years of computations. Even computing all prime implicants, without first listing all minterms, is computationally prohibitive for many modern-sized functions.

Iterative Heuristic for Two-Level Logic Size Optimization

Because enumerating all minterms of a function, or even just all prime implicants, is prohibitive in terms of computer memory and computation time for functions with many variables, most automated tools use methods that instead iteratively transform the original function's equation in an attempt to find improvements to the equation. *Iterative improvement* means repeatedly making small changes to an existing solution until the decision is made to stop, perhaps because changes are no longer yielding improvements, or perhaps because the tool has run for enough time. As an example of making small changes to an existing solution, consider the equation

```
F = abcdefgh + abcdefgh'+ jklmnop
```

Clearly, this equation can be reduced simply by combining the first two terms and removing variable h, resulting in F = abcdefg + jklmnop. However, enumerating the minterms, as required in the earlier-described size optimization methods, would have resulted in roughly 1000 minterms and then millions of computations to find the prime implicants. Such enumeration and computation are obviously not necessary to minimize this equation. An iterative improvement approach is better suited to this problem.

A simple iterative improvement heuristic that is reasonably effective uses repeated application of the expand operation. The **expand** operation removes a literal from a term. Trying all possible expands of every term may take too much compute time, and thus the heuristic randomly chooses which term to expand and randomly chooses how to expand that term. For example, consider the function F = x'z + xy'z + xyz. A heuristic might try to expand the term x'z by removing x', or by removing z. Note that expanding a term *reduces* the number of literals—the concept that *expanding* a term *reduces* the number of literals in a term may take a while to get accustomed to. Thinking of K-map circles may help, as shown in Figure 6.32—the bigger the circle, the fewer the resulting literals. An expansion is **legal** if the new term covers only minterms in the function's on-set, or equivalently, does *not* cover a minterm in the function's off-set. In other words, an expansion is legal if the new term is still an implicant of the function. Figure 6.32(a) shows that expanding term x'z to z for the given function is legal because the expanded term covers only 1s, whereas expanding x'z to x' is not legal because the expanded term covers at least one 0. If an expansion is legal, the heuristic replaces the original term by the expanded term, and then *searches for and removes any other term covered by the expanded term.* In Figure 6.32(a), the expanded term z covers terms xy'z and xyz, so both those latter terms can be removed.

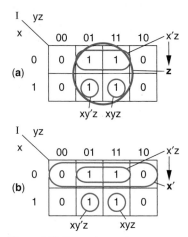

Figure 6.32 Expansions of term x'z in the function F = x'z + xy'z + xyz: (a) legal, (b) not legal (because the expanded term covers 0s).

The expand operation was illustrated on a K-map merely to aid in understanding the intuition of the operation—K-maps are nowhere to be found in heuristic two-level logic size optimization tools.

As another example, consider the earlier introduced function

$$F = abcdefgh + abcdefgh' + jklmnop$$

A heuristic might randomly choose to first try expanding the first term abcdefgh. It might randomly try expanding that term to bcdefgh (i.e., literal a has been removed). However, that term covers the term a'bcdefgh, which covers minterms that are not in the function's on-set, so that expansion is not legal. The heuristic might try other expansions, finding them not legal either, until the heuristic comes across the expansion to abcdefg (i.e., literal h was removed). That term covers only the minterms covered by abcdefgh and abcdefgh', both of which are clearly implicants because they appear in the original function, and thus the new term must also be an implicant. Therefore, the heuristic replaces the first term by the expanded term:

$$F = abcdefgh + abcdefgh' + jklmnop$$

The heuristic then searches for terms covered by the new expanded term, and removes such terms:

$$F = abcdefg\cancel{h} + \cancel{abcdefgh'} + jklmnop$$

$$F = abcdefg + jklmnop$$

Thus, using just the expand operation, the heuristic improved the equation. There is no guarantee that the heuristic will find the above expansion that yields the size reduction, but for a relatively small amount of compute time—far less than required for exact two-level logic size optimization—the heuristic's random search is very likely to find that expansion.

Example 6.9 Iterative heuristic for two-level logic size optimization using *expand*

Minimize the following equation, which was also minimized in Example 6.4, using repeated random application of the expand operation:

$$F = xyz + xyz' + x'y'z' + x'y'z$$

In other words, the on-set consists of the minterms {7, 6, 0, 1}, and so the off-set consists of the minterms {2, 3, 4, 5}.

Suppose the heuristic randomly chooses to expand term xyz. The heuristic may try to expand xyz to xy. Is that a legal expansion? xy covers minterms xyz' (minterm 6) and xyz (minterm 7), both in the on-set. Thus, the expansion is legal, so the heuristic replaces xyz by xy, yielding the new equation

$$F = xy\cancel{z} + xyz' + x'y'z' + x'y'z$$

The heuristic then looks for implicants covered by the new implicant xy. xyz' is covered by xy, so the heuristic eliminates xyz', yielding

$$F = xy + \cancel{xyz'} + x'y'z' + x'y'z$$

The heuristic may continue trying to expand that first term. It may try expanding the term from xy to x. The term x covers minterms $xy'z'$ (minterm 4), $xy'z$ (minterm 5), xyz' (minterm 6), and xyz (minterm 7). The term x thus covers minterms 4 and 5, which are not in the on-set but instead are in the off-set. That expansion is not legal. The heuristic may try expanding xy to y, but again finds that expansion is not legal.

The heuristic might then try to expand next term, $x'y'z'$, to $x'y'$. That expanded term covers minterms $x'y'z'$ (minterm 0) and $x'y'z$ (minterm 1), both in the on-set, so the expansion is legal. The heuristic thus replaces the original term by the expanded term

$$F = xy + x'y'\cancel{z'} + x'y'z$$

The heuristic searches for other terms covered by the expanded term, and finds that $x'y'z$ is covered by $x'y'$, so removes $x'y'z$ to leave

$$F = xy + x'y' + \cancel{x'y'z}$$

The heuristic may try expanding the term $x'y'$ further, but will find that neither possible expansion (x', or y') is legal. Thus, the above equation represents the minimized equation found by the heuristic. Notice that this happens to be the same result as obtained when minimizing the same initial equation in Example 6.4.

In the previous example, even though the heuristic generated the optimally minimized equation, there is no guarantee that the results from the heuristic will always be optimal.

More advanced heuristics utilize additional operations beyond just the expand operation. One such operation is the reduce operation, which can be thought of as the opposite of expand. The **reduce** operation adds a literal to a given term. A reduction is legal if the equation with the new term still covers the function. Adding a literal to a term is like reducing the size of a circle on a K-map. Adding a literal to a term reduces the number of minterms covered by the term, hence the name *reduce*. Another operation is **irredundant**, which removes a term entirely as long as the new equation still covers the function. If so, the removed term was "redundant," hence the name *irredundant*.

A heuristic may iterate among the expand, reduce, irredundant, and other operations, such as in the following heuristic: Try 10 random expansion operations, then 5 random reduce operations, then 2 irredundant operations, and then repeat (iterate) the whole sequence until no improvement occurs from one iteration to the next. Modern two-level size optimization tools differ mainly in their ordering of operations and number of iterations.

Recall that this section stated that modern heuristics don't enumerate all the minterms of a function's on-set, yet the previous example did enumerate all those minterms—actually, the on-set minterms were given in the initial equation. When the on-set minterms are not known, many advanced methods exist to efficiently represent a function's on-set and off-set without enumerating the minterms in those sets, and also to quickly check if a term covers terms in the off-set. Those methods are beyond the scope of the book, and are instead the subject of textbooks on digital design synthesis.

One of the original tools that performed automated heuristics as well as exact two-level logic optimization was called **Espresso**, developed at the University of California, Berkeley. The algorithms and heuristics in Espresso formed the basis of many modern commercial logic optimization tools.

Multilevel Logic Optimization—Performance and Size Tradeoffs

The previous sections discussed two-level logic size optimization. In practice, the speed of two levels of logic may not be necessary. Three, four, or more levels of logic may be acceptable if those additional levels reduce the amount of required logic. As a simple example, consider the equation

$$F1 = ab + acd + ace$$

This equation can't be minimized for two-level logic. The resulting two-level circuit is shown in Figure 6.33(a). However, algebraic manipulation can be done to yield

$$F2 = ab + ac(d + e) = a(b + c(d + e))$$

That equation can be implemented with the circuit shown in Figure 6.33(b). The multilevel logic implementation implements the same function but results in fewer transistors, at the expense of more gate-delays, as illustrated in Figure 6.33(c). The multilevel implementation thus represents a *tradeoff* when compared with the two-level implementation.

Automated heuristics for multilevel logic optimization iteratively transform the initial function's equation, similar to the iterative improvement used by automatic heuristics for two-level logic size optimization. The multilevel heuristics may optimize one of the criteria (size or delay), possibly at the expense of the other criteria.

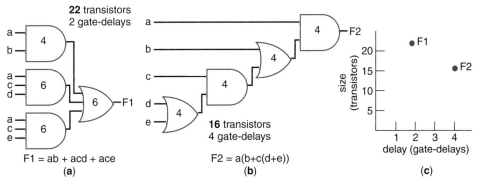

F1 = ab + acd + ace
(a)

F2 = a(b+c(d+e))
(b)

(c)

Figure 6.33 Using multilevel logic to tradeoff performance and size: (a) a two-level circuit, (b) multilevel circuit with fewer transistors but more delay, (c) illustration of the size versus delay tradeoff. Numbers inside gates represent transistor counts, estimated as 2 transistors per gate input.

Example 6.10 Multilevel logic optimization

Minimize the following function's circuit size, at the possible expense of increased delay, by algebraically manipulating the initial equation. Plot the tradeoff of the initial and size-optimized circuits with respect to size and delay.

        F1 = abcd + abcef

The circuit corresponding to the equation is shown in Figure 6.34(a). The circuit requires 22 transistors and has a delay of 2 gate-delays.

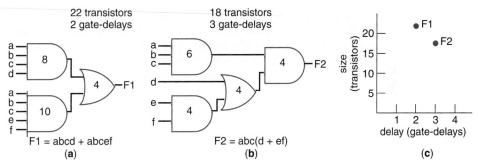

F1 = abcd + abcef
(a)

F2 = abc(d + ef)
(b)

(c)

Figure 6.34 Multilevel logic to trade off performance and size: (a) two-level circuit, (b) multilevel circuit with fewer transistors, (c) tradeoff of size versus delay. Numbers inside gates represent transistor counts.

We can algebraically manipulate the equation by factoring out the abc term from the two terms, as follows:

        F2 = abcd + abcef = abc(d + ef)

The circuit for that equation is shown in Figure 6.34(b). The circuit requires only 18 transistors, but has a longer delay of 3 gate-delays. The plot in Figure 6.34(c) shows the size and performance for each design.

If a circuit already has more than two levels, then sometimes multilevel logic optimization can reduce size without increasing delay, by modifying logic that exists off the circuit's critical path. A circuit's **critical path** is the longest path from any input to the circuit's output.

Example 6.11 Reducing noncritical path size with multilevel logic

Use multilevel logic to reduce the size of the circuit in Figure 6.35(a), without extending the circuit's delay. Note that the circuit initially has 26 transistors. Furthermore, the longest delay from any input to the output is three gate-delays. That delay occurs through the critical path shown by the dashed line in the figure.

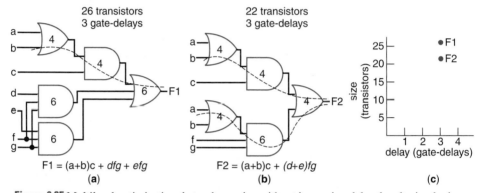

Figure 6.35 Multilevel optimization that reduces size without increasing delay, by altering logic on a noncritical path: (a) original circuit, (b) new circuit with fewer transistors but same delay, (c) illustration of the size optimization with no tradeoff of delay.

The other paths through the circuit are only two gate-delays. Thus, if we reduce the size of the logic for the noncritical paths and extend those paths to three gate-delays, the overall delay of the circuit would be unchanged. The noncritical parts of the equation for F1 in Figure 6.35(a) are italicized. We can algebraically modify the noncritical parts by factoring out the term fg, resulting in the new equation and circuit shown in Figure 6.35(b). One of the modified paths is now also three gate-delays, so the circuit now has two equally long critical paths, both having three gate-delays. The resulting circuit has only 22 transistors compared to 26 in the original circuit, yet still has the same delay of three gate-delays, as illustrated in Figure 6.35(c). So overall, we've performed a size optimization with no penalty in performance.

Generally, multilevel logic optimization makes use of **factoring**, such as abc + abd = ab(c+d), to reduce the number of gates.

Multilevel logic optimization is probably more commonly used by modern tools than two-level logic optimization. Multilevel logic optimization is also extensively used by automatic tools that map circuits to FPGAs. FPGAs are discussed in Chapter 7.

▶ 6.3 SEQUENTIAL LOGIC OPTIMIZATIONS AND TRADEOFFS

Chapter 3 described the design of sequential logic, namely of controllers. When creating an FSM and converting the FSM to a controller's state register and logic, some optimizations and tradeoffs can be applied.

State Reduction

State reduction, also known as *state minimization*, is an optimization that reduces an FSM's number of states without changing the FSM's behavior. Reducing the number of states may reduce the size of the state register and combinational logic that implement the FSM.

Reducing the number of states is possible when the FSM contains states that are equivalent to one another. Consider the FSM of Figure 6.36(a), having input x and output y. States A and D are equivalent. Regardless of whether the present state is A or D, the outputs will be identical for any sequence of inputs. For example, if the present state is A and the input sequence for four clock edges is 1, 0, 0, 1, the state sequence will be A, B, D, B, so the output sequence will be 0, 1, 0, 1. If instead execution starts in D, the same input sequence will result in a state sequence of D, B, D, B, so the

Inputs: x; Outputs: y

(a)

Inputs: x; Outputs: y

(b)

x → [ ] → y

if x = 1,0,0,1
then y = 0,1,0,1

(c)

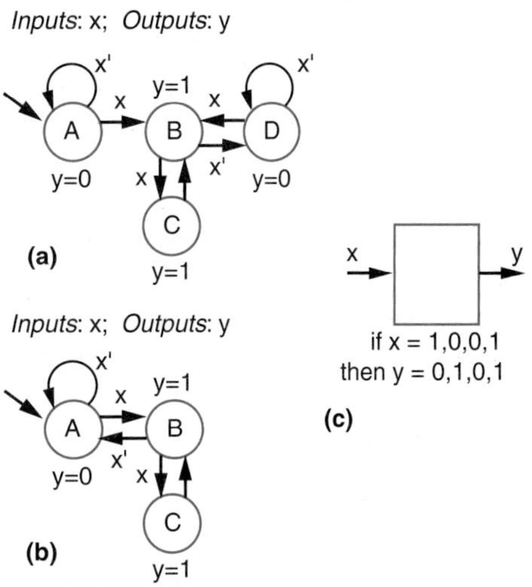

Figure 6.36 Equivalent FSMs: (a) original FSM, (b) equivalent FSM with fewer states, (c) the FSMs are indistinguishable from the outside, providing identical output behavior for *any* input sequence.

output sequence will again be 0, 1, 0, 1. In fact, for all possible input sequences, the output sequence starting from state A would be identical to the output sequence starting from state D. States A and D are thus equivalent. Thus, the FSM can be redrawn as in Figure 6.36(b). The FSMs in Figure 6.36(a) and (b) have exactly the same behavior—for any sequence of inputs, the two FSMs provide exactly the same sequence of outputs. If either FSM is encapsulated as a box as in Figure 6.36(c), the outside world cannot distinguish between the two FSMs based on the generated outputs.

Two states are equivalent if

1. both states assign the same values to outputs, AND
2. for all possible sequences of inputs, the FSM outputs will be the same starting from either state.

If two states are equivalent, then one of the states can be removed from the FSM, and any transitions pointing to that state can instead point to the other state.

For large FSMs, visual inspection to detect equivalent states is not feasible—a more systematic and automatable approach is needed.

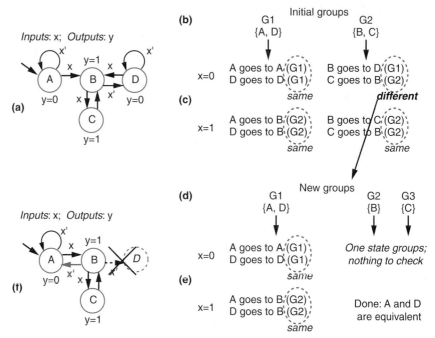

Figure 6.37 The partitioning method for state minimization: (a) original FSM, (b) initial groups based on output assignments, (c) checking next state's group for each input value; *B* and *C* go to states in different groups so cannot be equivalent, (d) new partition with *B* and *C* in different groups, (e) checking next state groups again yields no non-equivalent states within a group, so *A* and *D* are equivalent, (f) new FSM with *D* replaced by *A*.

State Reduction Using the Partitioning Method

A **partitioning method** can be used to find groups of equivalent states in an FSM. The method maintains a set of groups where states in different groups *cannot* be equivalent, whereas states in each group *might* be equivalent.

The first step of the method is to partition states into groups based on the values they assign to outputs—states assigning the same values are placed into the same group. For the FSM of Figure 6.37(a), the initial groups are *G1*: {*A, D*} (because *A* and *D* each outputs y = 0) and *G2*: {*B, C*} (because each outputs y = 1) as shown in Figure 6.37(b).

The next step involves checking next states. The states within a group are examined. For each possible input value, the next state is listed for each state. If for the same input value, two states in a group go to states in different groups, then those two states cannot possibly be equivalent. Figure 6.37(c) starts with group *G1* (having states *A* and *D*) and shows that for x = 0, *A* goes to a state in group *G1*, and *D* goes to a state in *G1*; both go to states in the same group, *G1*. For x = 1, *A* goes to a state in *G2*, and *D* goes to a state in *G2*; both go to states in the same group, *G2*. Thus, *A* and *D* might still be equivalent. Figure 6.37(c) proceeds to examine states in group *G2* (having states *B* and *C*) and shows that for x = 0, *B* goes to a state in *G1* whereas *C* goes to a state in *G2*. Thus, *B* and *C* cannot possibly be equivalent, because for the same input value, they transition to states that have already been determined to not be equivalent.

Upon detecting that two states in a group are not equivalent, the method partitions the group into subgroups so that states determined to be non-equivalent are in separate groups, as in Figure 6.37(d). The step of checking next states then repeats, as shown in Figure 6.37(e). This time, the step does not find any non-equivalent states in a group. After such a pass through the step, the states within a group are known to be equivalent.

For a group of equivalent states, one of the states can be selected to remain in the FSM. The other states and their outgoing transitions can be removed, Any transitions pointing to those removed states can be redirected to point to the remaining state. Figure 6.37(f) shows that the transition with condition x' pointing to state *D* is redirected to point to state *A*. Note that the transitions leaving a removed state need not be replaced; they are guaranteed to already exist on the remaining state, because state equivalence means that the remaining state has the same next state for each input value (i.e., the state has the same transitions) as did the removed state.

An alternative state reduction method known as an ***implication table*** method is commonly found in digital design textbooks. However, we have found the partitioning method to be more intuitive while also being automatable.

We now provide another example of state reduction.

Example 6.12 Minimizing states in an FSM using the partitioning method

This example minimizes the states in the FSM of Figure 6.38(a). The first step partitions the states according to their output assignments, yielding *G1*={*S3, S0, S4*} and *G2*={*S2, S1*}.

The next step examines next states for each group. Starting with states in group *G1*, for x=0, *S3* goes to *S3* (*G1*), *S0* goes to *S2* (*G2*), and *S4* goes to *S4* (*G1*). Clearly *S0* cannot be equivalent to *S3* or *S4*, because *S0* goes to a state in *G2*, while the *S3* and *S4* go to states in G1. Likewise, for x=1, *S3* goes to *S0* (*G1*), *S0* goes to *S1* (*G2*), and *S4* goes to *S0* (*G1*), again showing *S0* to be non-equivalent to *S3* and *S4*.

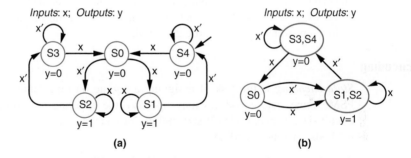

Figure 6.38 FSM state reduction example: (a) original FSM, (b) reduced FSM.

Thus, the method partitions *G1* to yield new groups: *G1*={*S3,S4*}, *G2*={*S2,S1*}, and *G3*={*S0*}. The method then repeats the step that examines next states. For group *G1*, for x=0, *S3* goes to *S3* (*G1*), and *S4* goes to *S4* (*G1*). For x=1, *S3* goes to *S0* (*G3*), and *S4* goes to *S0* (*G3*). Thus, *S3* and *S4* still might be equivalent. For group *G2*, for x=0, *S2* goes to *S3* (*G1*), and *S1* goes to *S4* (*G1*). For x=1, *S2* goes to *S2* (*G2*), and *S1* goes to *S1* (*G2*). Thus, *S1* and *S2* might still be equivalent. Group *G3* has only one state so there is nothing to examine. Thus, this pass through the next state step found no non-equivalent states. Therefore, states *S3* and *S4* (which are in group *G1*) are equivalent, and states *S2* and *S1* (which are in *G2*) are equivalent. The resulting FSM is shown in Figure 6.38(b).

Inputs: x; Outputs: z

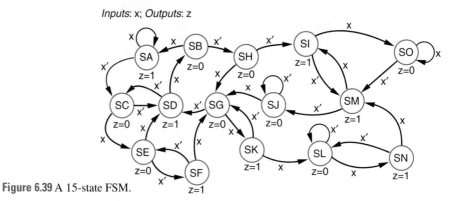

Figure 6.39 A 15-state FSM.

State reduction is typically performed using automated tools. For smaller FSMs, the tools may implement a method similar to the partitioning method. For larger FSMs, the tools may need to resort to heuristics to avoid inordinately large numbers of state comparisons.

Reducing the number of states does not guarantee a reduction of size of the resulting circuit. One reason is because reducing the states might not reduce the number of required state register bits—reducing the states from 15 down to 12 does not reduce the minimum state register size, which is four in either case. Another reason is because, even if the state reduction reduces the state register size, the combinational logic size could possibly *increase* with a smaller state register, due to the logic having to decode the state bits. Thus, automated state reduction tools may need to actually implement the combinational logic before and after state reduction, to determine if state reduction ultimately yields improvements for a particular FSM.

State Encoding

State encoding is the task of assigning a unique bit representation for each state in an FSM. Some state encodings may optimize the resulting controller circuit by reducing circuit size, or may trade off size and performance in the circuit. We now discuss several methods for state encoding.

Alternative Minimum-Bitwidth Binary Encodings

Previously, we assigned a unique binary encoding to each state in an FSM using the fewest number of bits possible, representing a *minimum-bitwidth binary encoding*. If there were four states, we used two bits. If there were five, six, seven, or eight states, we used three bits. The encoding represented the state in the controller's state register. There are many ways to map minimum-bitwidth binary encodings to a set of states. Say we are given four states, A, B, C, and D. One encoding is A:00, B:01, C:10, D:11. Another encoding is A:01, B:10, C:11, D:00. In fact, there are 4*3*2*1 = 4! (four factorial) = 24 possible encodings into two bits (4 encoding choices for the first state, 3 for the next state, 2 for the next, and 1 for the last state). For eight states, there are 8!, or over 40,000, possible encodings into three bits. For N states, there are N! (N factorial) possible encodings—a huge number for any N greater than 10 or so. One encoding may result in less combinational logic than another encoding. Automated tools may try several different encodings (but not all N! encodings) to reduce combinational logic in the controller.

Example 6.13 Alternative binary encoding for three-cycles-high laser timer

Example 3.7 encoded states using a straightforward binary encoding, starting with 00, then 01, then 10, and then 11. The resulting design had 15 gate inputs (ignoring inverters). We can try instead the alternative binary encoding shown in Figure 6.40.

Table 6.2 provides the truth table for the new encoding, bolding the differences from the original encoding.

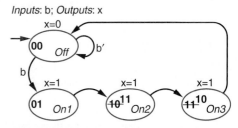

Inputs: b; Outputs: x

Figure 6.40 Laser timer state diagram with alternative binary state encoding.

The truth table yields the following equations for the three combinational logic outputs of a controller:

$$x = s1 + s0 \quad \text{(note from the table that}$$
$$x=1 \text{ if } s1=1 \text{ or } s0=1)$$

$$n1 = s1's0b' + s1's0b + s1s0b'$$
$$\quad + s1s0b$$
$$n1 = s1's0 + s1s0$$
$$n1 = s0$$

$$n0 = s1's0'b + s1's0b + s1's0b'$$
$$n0 = s1's0'b + s1's0b + s1's0b$$
$$\quad + s1's0b'$$
$$n0 = s1'b(s0' + s0) + s1's0(b+b')$$
$$n0 = s1'b + s1's0$$

The resulting circuit would have only 8 gate inputs: 2 for x, 0 for n1 (n1 is connected to s0 directly with a wire), and 4+2 for n0. The 8 gate inputs are significantly fewer than the 15 gate inputs needed for the binary encoding of Example 3.7. This encoding reduces size without any increase in delay, thus representing an optimization.

TABLE 6.2 Truth table for laser timer controller with alternative encoding.

	Inputs			Outputs		
	s1	s0	b	x	n1	n0
Off	0	0	0	0	0	0
	0	0	1	0	0	1
On1	0	1	0	1	1	**1**
	0	1	1	1	1	**1**
On2	1	1	0	1	1	0
	1	1	1	1	1	0
On3	1	0	0	1	0	0
	1	0	1	1	0	0

One-Hot Encoding

There is no requirement that a set of states be encoded using the fewest number of bits. For example, four states *A, B, C,* and *D* could be encoded using three bits instead of just two bits, such as *A:*000, *B:*011, *C:*110, *D:*111. Using more bits requires a larger state register, but possibly less logic. A popular encoding scheme is called ***one-hot encoding***, wherein the number of bits used for encoding equals the number of states, and each bit corresponds to exactly one state. For example, a one-hot encoding of four states *A, B, C,* and *D* uses four bits, such as *A:*0001, *B:*0010, *C:*0100, *D:*1000. The main advantage of one-hot encoding is speed—because the state can be detected from just one bit and thus need not be decoded using an AND gate, the controller's next state and output logic may involve fewer gates and/or gates with fewer inputs, resulting in a shorter delay.

Example 6.14 One-hot encoding example

Consider the simple FSM of Figure 6.41, which repeatedly generates the output sequence 0, 1, 1, 1, 0, 1, 1, 1, etc. A straightforward minimal binary encoding is shown, which is then crossed out and replaced with a one-hot encoding.

The binary encoding results in the truth table shown in Table 6.3. The resulting equations are:

    n1 = s1's0 + s1s0'

    n0 = s0'

    x = s1 + s0

The one-hot encoding results in the truth table shown in Table 6.4. The resulting equations are:

    n3 = s2

    n2 = s1

    n1 = s0

    n0 = s3

    x = s3 + s2 + s1

Inputs: none; Outputs: x

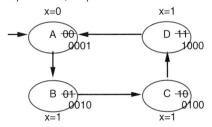

Figure 6.41 FSM for given sequence.

TABLE 6.3   Truth table using binary encoding.

	Inputs		Outputs		
	s1	s0	n1	n0	x
A	0	0	0	1	0
B	0	1	1	0	1
C	1	0	1	1	1
D	1	1	0	0	1

Figure 6.42 shows the resulting circuits for each encoding. The binary encoding yields more gates but, more importantly, requires two levels of logic. The one-hot encoding in this example requires only one level of logic. Notice that the logic to generate the next state is just wires in this example (other examples may require some logic). Figure 6.42(c) illustrates that the one-hot encoding has less delay, meaning a faster clock frequency could be used for that circuit.

TABLE 6.4   Truth table using one-hot encoding.

	Inputs				Outputs				
	s3	s2	s1	s0	n3	n2	n1	n0	x
A	0	0	0	1	0	0	1	0	0
B	0	0	1	0	0	1	0	0	1
C	0	1	0	0	1	0	0	0	1
D	1	0	0	0	0	0	0	1	1

Figure 6.42 One-hot encoding can reduce delay: (a) minimum binary encoding, (b) one-hot encoding, (c) though total sizes may be roughly equal (one-hot encoding uses fewer gates but more flip-flops), one-hot yields a shorter critical path.

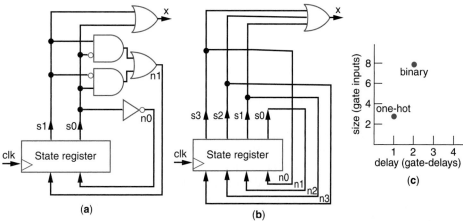

(a)

(b)

(c)

Example 6.15 Three-cycles-high laser timer using one-hot encoding

Example 3.7 encoded states using a straightforward binary encoding, starting with 00, then 01, then 10, and then 11. This example uses a one-hot encoding of the four states, requiring four bits as shown in Figure 6.43.

Table 6.6 shows a truth table for the FSM of Figure 6.43, using the one-hot encoding of the states. Not all rows are shown, since the table would then be too large.

The last step is to design the combinational logic. Deriving equations for each output directly from the table (assuming all other input combinations are don't cares), and minimizing those equations algebraically, results in the following:

$$x = s3 + s2 + s1$$
$$n3 = s2$$
$$n2 = s1$$
$$n1 = s0*b$$
$$n0 = s0*b' + s3$$

This circuit would require $3+0+0+2+(2+2) = 9$ gate inputs.

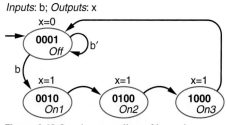

Inputs: b; *Outputs*: x

Figure 6.43 One-hot encoding of laser time.

TABLE 6.6 Truth table for laser timer controller with one-hot encoding.

	Inputs					Outputs				
	s3	s2	s1	s0	b	x	n3	n2	n1	n0
Off	0	0	0	1	0	0	0	0	0	1
	0	0	0	1	1	0	0	0	1	0
On1	0	0	1	0	0	1	0	1	0	0
	0	0	1	0	1	1	0	1	0	0
On2	0	1	0	0	0	1	1	0	0	0
	0	1	0	0	1	1	1	0	0	0
On3	1	0	0	0	0	1	0	0	0	1
	1	0	0	0	1	1	0	0	0	1

Thus, the circuit has fewer gate inputs than the original binary encoding's 15 gate inputs—but one must also consider that a one-hot encoding uses more flip-flops.

More importantly, the circuit with one-hot encoding is slightly faster. The critical path for that circuit is n0 = s0*b' + s3. The critical path for the circuit with regular binary encoding is n0 = s1's0'b + s1s0'. The regular binary encoded circuit requires a 3-input AND gate feeding into a 2-input OR gate, whereas the one-hot encoded circuit has a 2-input AND gate feeding in a 2-input OR gate. Because a 2-input AND actually has slightly less delay than a 3-input AND gate, the one-hot encoded circuit has a slightly shorter critical path.

For examples with more states, the critical path reductions from one-hot encoding may be even greater, and reductions in logic size may also be more pronounced. At some point, of course, one-hot encoding results in too large a state register—for example, an FSM with 1000 states would require a 10-bit state register for a binary encoding, but would require a 1000-bit state register for a one-hot encoding, which is probably too big to consider. In such cases, encodings may be considered that use a number of bits in between that for a binary encoding and that for a one-hot encoding.

Output Encoding

Output encoding uses the output values assigned in a state as the encoding for that state. For example, a problem might require repeatedly outputting the following sequence on a pair of outputs x and y: 00, 11, 10, 01. That behavior can be captured using an FSM with four states A, B, C, and D, as shown in Figure 6.44. A straightforward binary encoding for those states would be A:00, B:01, C:10, and D:11, as shown in Figure 6.44. A controller for this system will have a two-bit state register, logic to determine the next state, and logic to generate the output from the present state. In contrast, output encoding would simply use the output values of each state as the encoding of that state, meaning the encoding for the example would be A:00, B:11, C:10, and D:01. Such an encoding will still result in a two-bit state register and logic to generate the next state, but there won't be logic to generate the output from the present state.

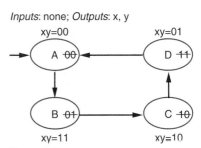

Inputs: none; Outputs: x, y

Figure 6.44 FSM for given sequence.

Output encoding may reduce the amount of logic by eliminating the logic that generates the outputs from the present state encoding—that logic is reduced to just wires.

Straightforward output encoding is possible if two conditions are satisfied:

1. The FSM has at least as many outputs as needed for a binary encoding of the states, and

2. The output values assigned by each state are unique.

For example, if the FSM in Figure 6.44 had only the one output x, then output encoding would not work because there are too few outputs, so condition 1 above is not satisfied. Or, if the four states had output values of 00, 11, 01, 11, output encoding would not work because two of the states have output values (i.e., 11) that are not unique.

If the number of outputs is less than the number needed for a binary encoding of the states, or if the same output values are assigned in different states, a variation of output encoding can be used in which "dummy" outputs are added as needed. For example, if four states have outputs 00, 11, 01, 11, a dummy output could be appended so that the four states have outputs 000, 110, 010, 111. That third output's value is set to ensure that each state has a unique output value and hence a unique encoding. The dummy output is only used for state encoding purposes and never appears at the system's output. The first two bits can be directly connected to the outputs.

In contrast, if the number of outputs exceeds the number needed for a binary encoding of the states, then a subset of outputs whose values are unique in each state could be used for the state encoding, thus reducing unnecessary state register bits. For example, if four states have output values 000011, 000110, 110000, and 011001, then the rightmost two bits could be used as the state encoding: 11, 10, 00, and 01.

Note that output encoding can be used to eliminate controller output glitching as was discussed in Section 3.5, due to there being no logic between the state register bits and the outputs.

Even if output encoding is not fully used, using output encoding for as many states as possible may still serve to reduce logic. For example, four states with outputs 00, 11, 01, 11 might encode states as 00, 11, 01, and 10—only the last state's encoding differs from the output.

Example 6.16 Sequence generator using output encoding

Example 3.10 involved design of a sequence generator for the sequence 0001, 0011, 1100, 1000 on a set of four outputs, as shown in Figure 6.45. That example encoded the states using a two-bit binary encoding of A:00, B:01, C:10, and D:11. This example instead uses output encoding. The four outputs are more than the minimum of two bits needed to encode the four states. Each state's output values are also unique. Thus, output encoding can be considered for this example.

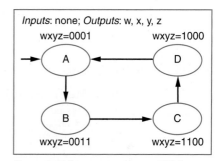

Figure 6.45 Sequence generator FSM.

Table 6.7 shows a partial truth table for the sequence generator using output encoding. Notice that the outputs themselves w, x, y, and z don't need to appear in the table, as they will be the same as s3, s2, s1, and s0. We use a partial table to avoid having to show all 16 rows, and we assume that all unspecified rows represent don't cares. The table leads to the following equations for each output:

$$n3 = s1 + s2$$
$$n2 = s1$$
$$n1 = s1's0$$
$$n0 = s1's0 + s3s2'$$

TABLE 6.7 Partial truth table for sequence generator controller using output encoding.

	Inputs				Outputs			
	s3	s2	s1	s0	n3	n2	n1	n0
A	0	0	0	1	0	0	1	1
B	0	0	1	1	1	1	0	0
C	1	1	0	0	1	0	0	0
D	1	0	0	0	0	0	0	1

We obtained those equations by looking at all the 1s for a particular output, and visually determining a minimal input equation that would generate those 1s and 0s for the other shown column entries (all other output values, not shown, are don't cares).

Figure 6.46 shows the final circuit. Notice that there is no output logic—the outputs w, x, y, and z connect directly to the state register.

Compared to the circuit obtained in Example 3.10 using binary encoding, the output encoded circuit in Figure 6.46 actually appears to use more transistors, due to using a wider state register. In other examples, an output encoded circuit might use fewer transistors.

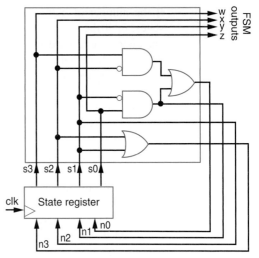

Figure 6.46 Sequence generator controller with output encoding.

Whether one-hot encoding, binary encoding, output encoding, or some variation thereof results in the fewest transistors or a shorter critical path depends on the example itself. Thus, modern tools may try a variety of different encodings for a given problem to determine which works best.

Moore versus Mealy FSMs

Basic Mealy Architecture

The FSMs described in this book have thus far all been a type of FSM known as a Moore FSM. A ***Moore FSM*** is an FSM whose outputs are a function of the FSM's state. An alternative type of FSM is a Mealy FSM. A ***Mealy FSM*** is an FSM whose outputs are a function of the FSM's states *and inputs*. Sometimes a Mealy FSM results in fewer states than a Moore FSM, representing an optimization. Sometimes those fewer states come at the expense of timing complexities that must be handled, representing a tradeoff.

Recall the standard controller architecture of Figure 3.60, reproduced in Figure 6.47. The architecture shows one block of combinational logic, responsible for converting the present state and external inputs into the next state and external outputs.

Because a Moore FSM's outputs are solely a function of the present state (and not of the external inputs), then the architecture can be refined to have two combinational logic blocks: the ***next-state***

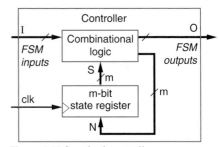

Figure 6.47 Standard controller architecture—general view.

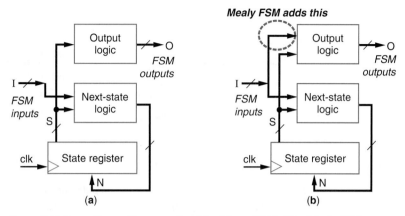

Figure 6.48 Controller architectures for: (a) a Moore FSM, (b) a Mealy FSM.

logic block converts the present state and external inputs into a next state, and the ***output logic*** block converts the present state (but *not* the external inputs) into external outputs, as shown in Figure 6.48(a).

In contrast, a Mealy FSM's outputs are a function of both the present state and the external inputs. Thus, the output logic block for a Mealy FSM takes both the present state *and* the external FSM inputs as input, rather than just the present state, as shown in Figure 6.48(b). The next-stage logic is the same as for a Moore FSM, taking as input both the present state and the external FSM inputs.

Graphically, the FSM output assignments of a Mealy FSM would be listed with each transition, rather than each state, because each transition represents a present state and a particular input value. Figure 6.49 shows a two-state Mealy FSM with an input b and an output x. When in state *S0* and b = 0, the FSM outputs x = 0 and stays in state *S0*, as indicated by the transition labeled "b'/x=0". When in state *S0* and b = 1, the FSM outputs x = 1 and goes to state *S1*. The "/" is used simply to separate the transition's input conditions from the output assignments—the "/" does not mean "divide" here. Because the transition from *S1* to *S0* is taken no matter what the input value, the transition is listed simply as "/x=0," meaning there is no input condition, but there is an output assignment.

Inputs: b; Outputs: x

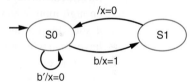

Figure 6.49 A Mealy FSM associates outputs with transitions, not with states.

Mealy FSMs May Have Fewer States

The seemingly minor difference between a Mealy and a Moore FSM, namely that a Mealy FSM's output is a function of the state *and* the current inputs, can lead to fewer states for some behaviors when captured as a Mealy FSM. For example, consider the simple soda dispenser controller FSM in Figure 6.50(a). Setting d = 1 dispenses a

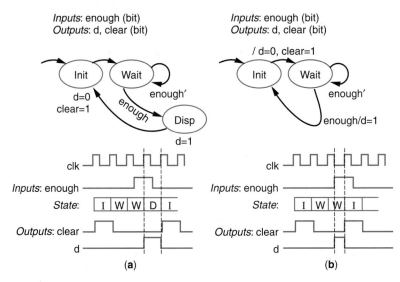

Figure 6.50 FSMs for the soda dispenser controller: (a) Moore FSM has actions in states, (b) Mealy FSM has actions on transitions, resulting in fewer states for this example.

soda. The FSM starts in state *Init*, which sets d = 0 and sets an output clear = 1 which clears a device keeping count of the amount of money deposited into the soda dispenser machine. The FSM transitions to state *Wait*, where the FSM waits to be informed, through the cnough input, that enough money has been deposited. Once enough money has been deposited, the FSM transitions to state *Disp*, which dispenses a soda by setting output d=1, and the FSM then returns to state *Init*. (Readers who have read Chapter 5 may notice this example is a simplified version of the soda machine example in Section 5.2; familiarity with that example is not required for the present discussion.).

Like with Moore FSMs, we follow the convention that unassigned outputs in a Mealy FSM state diagram are implicitly assigned 0.

Figure 6.50(b) shows a Mealy FSM for the same controller. The initial state *Init* has no actions itself, but rather has a conditionless transition to state *Wait* that has the initialization actions d = 0 and clear = 1. In state *Wait*, a transition with condition enough' returns to state *Wait* without any actions listed. Another transition with condition enough has the action d = 1, and takes the FSM back to the *Init* state. Notice that the Mealy FSM does not need the *Disp* state to set d = 1; that action occurs on a transition. Thus, the Mealy FSM has fewer states than the Moore FSM for this example.

The Mealy state diagram in Figure 6.50(b) uses a convention similar to the convention used for Moore FSMs in Section 3.4, namely that any outputs not explicitly assigned on a transition are implicitly assigned a 0. As with Moore FSMs, we still set an output to 0 explicitly if the assignment is key to the FSM's behavior (such as the assignment of d = 0 in Figure 6.50(b)).

Example 6.17 Beeping wristwatch FSM using a Mealy machine

Create an FSM for a wristwatch that can display one of four registers by setting two outputs s1 and s0, which control a 4x1 multiplexer that passes one of the four registers through. The four registers correspond to the watch's present time (s1s0=00), the alarm setting (01), the date (10), and a stopwatch (11). The FSM should sequence to the next register, in the order listed above, each time a button b is pressed (assume b is synchronized with the clock as to be high for only 1 clock cycle on each unique button press). The FSM should set an output p to 1 each time the button is pressed, causing an audible beep to sound.

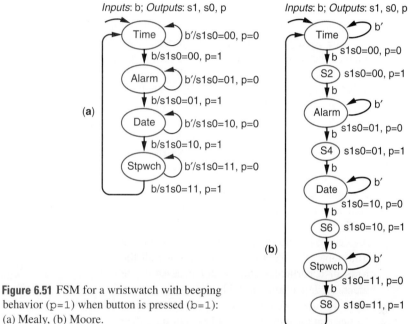

(a)

(b)

Figure 6.51 FSM for a wristwatch with beeping behavior (p=1) when button is pressed (b=1): (a) Mealy, (b) Moore.

Figure 6.51(a) shows a Mealy FSM describing the desired behavior. Notice that the Mealy FSM easily captures the beeping behavior, simply by setting p = 1 on the transitions that correspond to button presses. In the Moore FSM of Figure 6.51(b), we had to add an extra state in between each pair of states in Figure 6.51, with each extra state having the action p=1 and having a conditionless transition to the next state.

Notice that the Mealy FSM has fewer states than the Moore machine. A drawback is that we aren't guaranteed that a beep will last at least one clock cycle, due to timing issues that we will describe.

Timing Issues with Mealy FSMs

Mealy FSM outputs are not synchronized with clock edges, but rather can change in between clock edges if an input changes. For example, consider the timing diagram shown in Figure 6.50(a) for a soda dispenser's Moore FSM. Note that the output d becomes 1 *not right after* the input enough became 1, but rather *on the first clock edge after* enough became 1. In contrast, the timing diagram for the Mealy FSM in Figure

6.50(b) shows that the output d becomes 1 *right after* the input enough becomes 1. Moore outputs are synchronized with the clock; in particular, Moore outputs only change upon entering a new state, which means Moore outputs only change slightly after a rising clock edge loads a new state into the state register. In contrast, Mealy outputs can change not just upon entering a new state, but also at any time that an input changes, because Mealy outputs are a function of both the state and the inputs. We took advantage of this fact to eliminate the *Disp* state from the soda dispenser's Mealy FSM in Figure 6.50(b). Notice in the timing diagram, however, that the d output of the Mealy FSM *does not stay 1 for a complete clock cycle*. If we are unsure as to whether d's high time is long enough, we could include a *Disp* state in the Mealy FSM. That state would have a single transition, with no condition and with action d = 1, pointing back to state *Init*. In that case, d would be 1 for longer than one clock cycle (but less than two cycles).

The Mealy FSM feature of outputs being a function of states and inputs, which enables the reduction in number of states in some cases, also has an undesirable characteristic—the outputs may glitch if the inputs glitch in between clock cycles. A designer using a Mealy FSM should determine whether such glitching could pose a problem in a particular circuit. One solution to the glitching is to insert flip-flops between an asynchronous Mealy FSM's inputs and the FSM logic, or between the FSM logic and the outputs. Such flip-flops make the Mealy FSM synchronous, and the outputs will change at predictable intervals. Of course, such flip-flops introduce a one clock cycle delay.

Implementing a Mealy FSM

A controller to implement a Mealy FSM is created in a way nearly identical to that of a controller for Moore FSMs as described in Section 3.4. The only difference is that when creating a truth table, the FSM outputs' values for all the rows of a particular state won't necessarily be identical. For example, Table 6.8 shows a truth table for the Mealy FSM of Figure 6.50(b). Notice that the output d should be 0 in state *Wait* (s0 = 1) if enough = 0, but should be 1 if enough = 1. In contrast, in a Moore truth table, an output's values are identical within a given state. Given the truth table of Table 6.8, implementing the combinational logic would proceed in the same manner described in Section 3.4.

TABLE 6.8 Mealy truth table for soda dispenser

	Inputs		Outputs		
	s0	enough	n0	d	clear
Init	0	0	1	0	1
	0	1	1	0	1
Wait	1	0	1	0	0
	1	1	0	1	0

Combining Moore and Mealy FSMs

Designers often utilize FSMs that are a combination of Moore and Mealy types. Such a combination allows the designer to specify some actions in states, and others on transitions. Such a combination provides the reduced number of states advantage of a Mealy FSM, yet avoids having to replicate a state's actions on every outgoing transition of a state. This simplification is really just a convenience to a designer describing the FSM; the underlying implementation will be the same as for the Mealy FSM having replicated actions on a state's outgoing transitions.

Viewing the two "o's" in the word Moore as states may help you remember that a Moore FSM's actions occur in the states, while Mealy is on the transitions.

Example 6.18 Beeping wristwatch FSM using a combined Moore/Mealy machine

Figure 6.52 shows a combined Moore/Mealy FSM describing the beeping wristwatch of Example 6.17. The FSM has the same number of states as the Mealy FSM in Figure 6.51(a), because the FSM still associates the beep behavior p=1 with transitions, avoiding the need for extra states to describe the beep. But the combined FSM is easier to comprehend than the Mealy FSM, because the assignments to s1s0 are associated with each state rather than being duplicated on every outgoing transition.

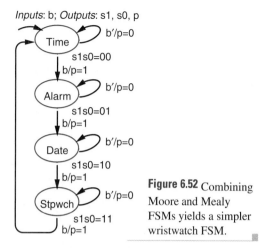

Inputs: b; *Outputs*: s1, s0, p

Figure 6.52 Combining Moore and Mealy FSMs yields a simpler wristwatch FSM.

▶ 6.4 DATAPATH COMPONENT TRADEOFFS

Chapter 4 created several components that are useful in datapaths. That chapter created the most basic, easy-to-understand versions of those components. This section describes methods to build faster or smaller versions of some of those components.

Faster Adders

Adding two numbers is an extremely common operation in digital circuits, so it makes sense to try to create an adder that is faster than a carry-ripple adder. Recall that a carry-ripple adder requires that the carry bits ripple through all the full-adders before all the outputs are correct. The longest path through the circuit, shown in Figure 6.53, is known as the circuit's **critical path**. Since each full-adder has a delay of two gate-delays, then a 4-bit carry-ripple adder has a delay of $4 * 2 = 8$ gate-delays. A 32-bit carry-ripple adder's delay is $32 * 2 = 64$ gate-delays. That's rather slow, but the nice thing about a carry-ripple adder is that it doesn't require very many gates. If a full-adder uses 5 gates, then a 4-bit carry-ripple adder requires only $4 * 5 = 20$ gates, and a 32-bit carry-ripple adder would only require $32 * 5 = 160$ gates.

Figure 6.53 4-bit carry-ripple adder, with the longest path (the critical path) shown.

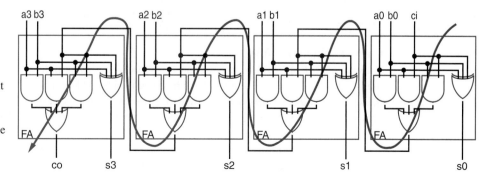

A useful adder would be an adder whose delay is much closer to the delay of just 5 or 6 gate-delays, at the possible expense of more total gates.

Two-Level Logic Adder

One obvious way to create a faster adder at the expense of more gates is to use the earlier-defined two-level combinational logic design process. An adder designed using two levels of logic has a delay of only two gate-delays. That's certainly fast. But recall from Figure 4.24 that building an N-bit adder using two levels of logic results in excessively large circuits as N increases beyond 8 or so. To be sure you get this point, let's restate the previous sentence slightly:

> Building an N-bit adder using two levels of logic results in *shockingly large circuits* as N increases beyond 8 or so.

For example, we estimated (in Chapter 4) that a two-level 16-bit adder would require about 2 million transistors, and that a two-level 32-bit adder would require about 100 billion transistors.

On the other hand, building a 4-bit adder using two levels of logic results in a big but reasonably sized adder—about 100 gates, as was shown in Figure 4.25. A larger adder could be built by cascading such fast 4-bit adders together. An 8-bit adder could

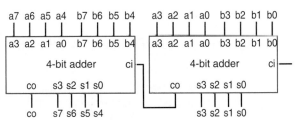

Figure 6.54 8-bit adder built from two fast 4-bit adders.

be built by cascading two fast 4-bit adders together, as shown in Figure 6.54. If each 4-bit adder is built from two levels of logic, then each 4-bit adder has a delay of 2 gate-delays. The 4-bit adder on the right takes 2 gate-delays to generate the sum and carry-out bits, after which the 4-bit adder on the left takes another 2 gate-delays to generate its outputs, resulting in a total delay of 2 + 2 = 4 gate-delays. For a 32-bit adder built from eight 4-bit adders, the delay would be 8 * 2 = 16 gate-delays, and the size would be about 8 * 100 gates = 800 gates. That's much better than the 32 * 2 = 64 gate-delays of a carry-ripple adder, though the improved speed comes at the expense of more gates than the 32 * 5 = 160 gates of the carry-ripple adder. Which design is better? The answer depends on a designer's requirements—the design using two-level logic 4-bit adders is better if the designer needs more speed and can afford the extra gates, whereas the design using carry-ripple 4-bit adders is better if the designer doesn't need the speed or can't afford the extra gates. The two options represent a tradeoff.

Carry-Lookahead Adder

A *carry-lookahead adder* improves on the speed of a carry-ripple adder without using as many gates as a two-level logic adder. The basic idea is to "look ahead" into lower stages to determine whether a carry will be created in the present stage. This lookahead concept is very elegant and generalizes to other problems. We will therefore spend some time introducing the intuition underlying lookahead.

Consider the addition of two 4-bit numbers shown in Figure 6.55(b), with the carries in each column labeled c0, c1, c2, c3, and c4.

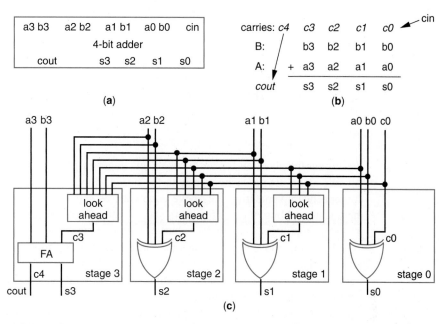

Figure 6.55 Adding two binary numbers by a naive inefficient carry-lookahead scheme—each stage looks at all earlier bits and computes whether the carry-in bit to that stage would be a 1. The longest delay is stage 3, which has 2 logic levels for the lookahead, and 2 logic levels for the full-adder, for a total delay of only four gate-delays.

A Naive Inefficient Carry-Lookahead Scheme. One simple but inefficient carry-lookahead approach is as follows. Recall that the output equations for a full-adder having inputs a, b, and c, and outputs co and s, are

```
s = a xor b xor c
co = bc + ac + ab
```

So we know that the equations for c1, c2, and c3 in a 4-bit adder will be

```
c1 = co0 = b0c0 + a0c0 + a0b0
c2 = co1 = b1c1 + a1c1 + a1b1
c3 = co2 = b2c2 + a2c2 + a2b2
```

In other words, the equation for the carry-in to a particular stage is the same as the equation for the carry-out of the previous stage.

We can substitute the equation for c1 into c2's equation, resulting in:

```
c2 = b1c1 + a1c1 + a1b1
c2 = b1(b0c0 + a0c0 + a0b0) + a1(b0c0 + a0c0 + a0b0) + a1b1
c2 = b1b0c0 + b1a0c0 + b1a0b0 + a1b0c0 + a1a0c0 +
     a1a0b0 + a1b1
```

We can then substitute the equation for $c2$ into $c3$'s equation, resulting in:

```
c3 = b2c2 + a2c2 + a2b2
c3 = b2(b1b0c0 + b1a0c0 + b1a0b0 + a1b0c0 + a1a0c0 +
     a1a0b0 + a1b1) + a2(b1b0c0 + b1a0c0 + b1a0b0
     + a1b0c0 + a1a0c0 + a1a0b0 + a1b1) + a2b2
c3 = b2b1b0c0 + b2b1a0c0 + b2b1a0b0 + b2a1b0c0 +
     b2a1a0c0 + b2a1a0b0 + b2a1b1 + a2b1b0c0
     + a2b1a0c0 + a2b1a0b0 + a2a1b0c0 + a2a1a0c0
     + a2a1a0b0 + a2a1b1 + a2b2
```

We'll omit the equation for $c4$ to save a few pages of paper.

We could create each stage with the needed inputs, and include a lookahead logic component implementing the above equations, as shown in Figure 6.55(c). Notice that there is no rippling of carry bits from stage to stage—each stage computes its own carry-in bit by "looking ahead" to the values of the previous stages.

While the above demonstrates the basic idea of carry-lookahead, the scheme is not very efficient. $c1$ requires 4 gates, $c2$ requires 8 gates, and $c3$ requires 16 gates, with each gate requiring more inputs in each stage. If we count gate inputs, $c1$ requires 9 gate inputs, $c2$ requires 27 gate inputs, and $c3$ requires 71 gate inputs. Building a larger adder, say an 8-bit adder, using this lookahead scheme would thus likely result in excessively large size. While the presented scheme is therefore not practical, it serves to introduce the basic idea of carry-lookahead: each stage looks ahead at the inputs to the previous stages and computes for itself whether that stage's carry-in bit should be 1, rather than waiting for the carry-in bit to ripple from previous stages, to yield a 4-bit adder with a delay of only 4 gate-delays.

An Efficient Carry-Lookahead Scheme. A more efficient carry-lookahead scheme is as follows. Consider again the addition of two 4-bit numbers A and B, shown in Figure 6.56(a). Suppose that we add each column's two operand bits (e.g., $a0 + b0$) using a half-adder, ignoring the carry-in bit of that column. The resulting half-adder outputs (carry-out and sum) provide useful information about the carry for the next stage. In particular:

- If the addition of $a0$ with $b0$ results in a carry-out of 1, then $c1$ will be 1 regardless of whether $c0$ is a 1 or 0. Why? If we add $a0+b0+c0$, then $1+1+0=10$, while $1+1+1=11$ (the "+" symbol represents add here, not OR)—both cases generate a carry-out of 1. Recall that a half-adder computes its carry-out as ab.
- If the addition of $a0$ with $b0$ results in a sum of 1, then $c1$ will be 1 only if $c0$ is 1. In particular, if we add $a0+b0+c0$, then $1+0+1=10$ and $0+1+1=10$. Recall that a half-adder computes its sum as a XOR b.

In other words, $c1$ will be 1 if $a0b0 = 1$, OR if $a0$ XOR $b0 = 1$ AND $c0 = 1$. The following equations describe the carry bits (the "+" symbol represents OR here, not add):

```
c1 = a0b0 + (a0 xor b0)c0
c2 = a1b1 + (a1 xor b1)c1
c3 = a2b2 + (a2 xor b2)c2
c4 = a3b3 + (a3 xor b3)c3
```

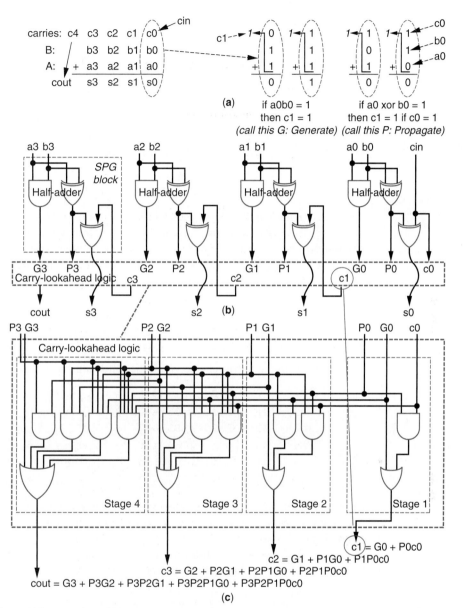

Figure 6.56 Adding two binary numbers using a fast carry-lookahead scheme: (a) idea of using propagate and generate terms, (b) computing the propagate and generate terms and providing them to the carry-lookahead logic, (c) using the propagate and generate terms to quickly compute the carries for each column. The correspondence between $c1$ in figures (c) and (b) is shown by two circles connected by the line; similar correspondences exist for $c2$ and $c3$.

A half-adder can be included in each stage to add the two operand bits for that column, as shown in Figure 6.56(b). Each half-adder outputs a carry-out bit (which is ab) and a sum bit (which is a XOR b). Note in the figure that for a given column, the half-adder's sum output merely needs to be XORed with the column's carry-in bit to compute that column's sum bit, because the sum bit for a column is just a XOR b XOR c (as described in Section 4.3).

Why those names?
When a0b0=1, we
know we should
***generate** a 1 for*
c1. When a0 XOR
b0 = 1, we know
we should
***propagate** the c0*
value as the value
of c1, meaning c1
should equal c0.

The carry-output of the half-adder can be named ***generate***, symbolized as G—so G0 means a0b0, G1 means a1b1, G2 means a2b2, and G3 means a3b3. The sum output of the half-adder can be named ***propagate***—so P0 means a0 XOR b0, P1 means a1 XOR b1, P2 means a2 XOR b2, and P3 means a3 XOR b3. In short:

$$Gi = aibi \ (generate)$$
$$Pi = ai \ XOR \ bi \ (propagate)$$

The computation of the carry-lookahead, rather than directly examining the operand bits of previous stages as in the naive lookahead scheme (e.g., stage 1 examining a0 and b0), instead examines the half-adder outputs of the previous stage (e.g., stage 1 examines G0 and P0). Why? Because the lookahead logic will be simpler than in the naive scheme.

The equations for each carry bit can be rewritten as follows:

$$c1 = G0 + P0c0$$
$$c2 = G1 + P1c1$$
$$c3 = G2 + P2c2$$
$$c4 = G3 + P3c3$$

Substituting as in the naive scheme yields the following carry-lookahead equations:

$$c1 = G0 + P0c0$$

$$c2 = G1 + P1c1 = G1 + P1(G0 + P0c0)$$
$$c2 = G1 + P1G0 + P1P0c0$$

$$c3 = G2 + P2c2 = G2 + P2(G1 + P1G0 + P1P0c0)$$
$$c3 = G2 + P2G1 + P2P1G0 + P2P1P0c0$$

$$c4 = G3 + P3G2 + P3P2G1 + P3P2P1G0 + P3P2P1P0c0$$

The P and G symbols represent simple terms: Gi = aibi, Pi = ai XOR bi.

Figure 6.56(c) shows the circuits implementing the carry-lookahead equations for computing each stage's carry.

Figure 6.57 shows a high-level view of the carry-lookahead adder's design from Figure 6.56(b) and (c). The four blocks on the top are responsible for generating the sum,

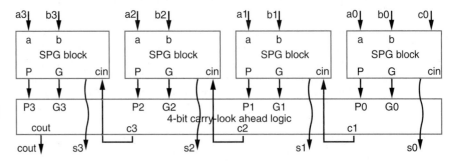

Figure 6.57 High-level view of a 4-bit carry-lookahead adder.

propagate, and generate bits—let's call those "*SPG blocks*." Recall from Figure 6.56(b) that each SPG block consists of just three gates. The 4-bit carry-lookahead logic uses the propagate and generate bits to precompute the carry bits for high-order stages, using only two levels of gates. The complete 4-bit carry-lookahead adder requires only 26 gates: 4*3=12 gates for the non-lookahead logic, and then 2+3+4+5=14 gates for the lookahead logic.

The delay of this 4-bit adder is only 4 gate-delays—1 gate through the half-adder, 2 gates through the carry-lookahead logic, and 1 gate to finally generate the sum bit. Those gates can be seen in Figure 6.56(b) and (c). An 8-bit adder built using the same carry-lookahead scheme would still have a delay of only 4 gate-delays, but would require 68 gates: 8*3=24 gates for the non-lookahead logic, and 2+3+4+5+6+7+8+9=44 gates for the lookahead logic. A 16-bit carry-lookahead adder would still have a delay of 4 gate-delays, but would require 200 gates: 16*3=48 gates for the non-lookahead logic, and 2+3+4+5+6+7+8+9+10+11+12+13+14+15+16+17=152 gates for the lookahead logic. A 32-bit carry-lookahead adder would have a delay of 4 gate-delays, but would require 656 gates: 32*3=96 gates for the non-lookahead logic, and 152+18+19+20+21+22+23+24+25 +26+27+28+29+30+31+32+33=560 gates.

Unfortunately, there are problems that make the size and delay of large carry-lookahead adders less attractive. First, the above analysis counts gates but not gate inputs; gate inputs would better indicate the number of transistors needed. Notice in Figure 6.56 that the gates are wider in higher stages. For example, stage 3 has a 4-input OR gate and 4-input AND gate, while stage 4 has a 5-input OR gate and 5-input AND gate as highlighted in Figure 6.58. Stage 32 of a 32-bit carry-lookahead adder would have 33-input OR and AND gates, along with other large gates. Since gates with more inputs need more transistors, then in terms of transistors, the carry-lookahead design is actually quite large. Furthermore, those huge gates would not have the same delay as a 2-input AND or OR gate. Such huge gates are typically built using a tree of smaller gates, leading to more gate-delays.

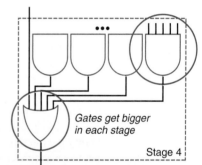

Gates get bigger in each stage

Stage 4

Figure 6.58 Gate size problem.

Hierarchical Carry-Lookahead Adders. Building a 4-bit or even 8-bit carry-lookahead adder using the previous section's method may be reasonable with respect to gate sizes, but larger carry-lookahead adders begin to involve gates with too many inputs.

A larger adder could instead be built by connecting smaller adders in a carry-ripple manner. For example, suppose 4-bit carry-lookahead adders are available. A16-bit adder can be built by connecting four 4-bit carry-lookahead adders, as shown in Figure 6.59. If each 4-bit carry-lookahead adder has a four gate delay, then the total delay of the 16-bit adder is 4+4+4+4=16 gate-delays. Compare this to the delay of a 16-bit carry-ripple adder—if each full-adder has a two gate-delay, then a 16-bit carry-ripple adder has a delay of 16*2=32 gate-delays. Thus, the 16-bit adder built from four carry-lookahead adders connected in a carry-ripple manner is twice as fast as the 16-bit carry-ripple adder. (Actually,

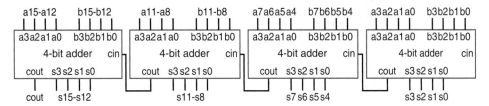

Figure 6.59 16-bit adder implemented using 4-bit adders connected in a carry-ripple manner. Can the delay of the rippling be avoided?

careful observation of Figure 6.53 reveals that the carry-out of a four-bit carry-lookahead adder would be generated in three gate-delays rather than four, resulting in even faster operation of the 16-bit adder built from four carry-lookahead adders—but for simplicity, let's not look inside the components for such detailed timing analysis.) Sixteen gate-delays is good, but can we do better? Can we avoid having to wait for the carries to ripple from the lower-order 4-bit adders to the higher-order adders?

In fact, avoiding the rippling is exactly what was done when developing the 4-bit carry-lookahead adder itself. Thus, we can *repeat the same carry-lookahead process outside* of the 4-bit adders, to quickly provide the carry-in values to the higher-order 4-bit adders. To accomplish this, we add another 4-bit carry-lookahead logic block outside the four 4-bit adders, as shown in Figure 6.60. The carry-lookahead logic block has exactly the same internal design as was shown in Figure 6.56(c). Notice that the lookahead logic needs propagate (P) and generate (G) signals from each adder block. Previously, each input block output the P and G signals just by ANDing and XORing the block's `ai` and `bi` input bits. However, in Figure 6.60, each block is a 4-bit carry-lookahead adder. We therefore must modify the internal design of a 4-bit carry-lookahead adder to output its P and G signals, so that those adders can be used with a second-level carry-lookahead generator.

Thus, let's extend the 4-bit carry-lookahead logic of Figure 6.56 to output P and G signals. The equations for the P and G outputs of a 4-bit carry-lookahead adder can be written as follows:

$$P = P3P2P1P0$$
$$G = G3 + P3G2 + P3P2G1 + P3P2P1G0$$

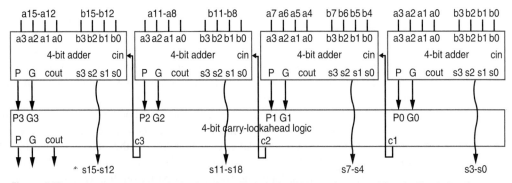

Figure 6.60 16-bit adder implemented using four CLA 4-bit adders and a second level of lookahead.

To understand these equations, recall that propagate meant that the output carry for a column should equal the input carry of the column (hence propagating the carry through the column). For that to be the case for the carry-in and carry-out of a 4-bit adder, the first stage of the 4-bit adder must propagate its input carry to its output carry, the second stage must propagate its input carry to its output carry, and so on for the third and fourth stages. In other words, each internal propagate signal must be 1, hence the equation P = P3P2P1P0.

Likewise, recall that generate meant that the output carry of a column should be a 1 (hence generating a carry of 1). Generate should thus be 1 if the first stage generates a carry (G0) and all the higher stages propagate the carry through (P3P2P1), yielding the term P3P2P1G0. Generate should also be a 1 if the second stage generates a carry and all higher stages propagate the carry through, yielding the term P3P2G1. Likewise for the third stage, whose term is P3G2. Finally, generate should be 1 if the fourth stage generates a carry, represented as G3. ORing all four of these terms yields the equation G = G3 + P3G2 + P3P2G1 + P3P2P1G0.

We would then revise the 4-bit carry-lookahead logic of Figure 6.56(c) to include two additional gates in stage four, one AND gate to compute P = P3P2P1P0, and one OR gate to compute G = G3 + P3G2 + P3P2G1 + P3P2P1G0 (note that stage four already has AND gates for each term, so we need only add an OR gate to OR the terms). For conciseness, we omit a figure showing these two new gates.

We can introduce additional levels of 4-bit carry-lookahead generators to create even larger adders. Figure 6.61 illustrates a high-level view of a 32-bit adder built using 32 SPG blocks and three levels of 4-bit carry-lookahead logic. Notice that the carry-looka-

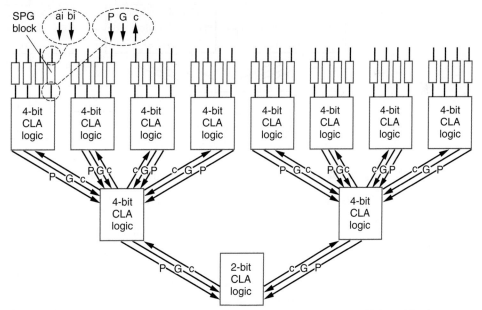

Figure 6.61 View of multilevel carry-lookahead showing the tree structure, which enables fast addition with reasonable numbers and sizes of gates. Each level adds only two gate-delays.

head logic forms a tree. Total delay for the 32-bit adder is only two gate-delays for the SPG blocks, and two gate-delays for each level of carry-lookahead (CLA) logic, for a total of 2+2+2+2 = 8 gate-delays. (Actually, closer examination of gate delays within each component would demonstrate that total delay of the 32-bit adder is actually less than 8 gate-delays.) Carry-lookahead adders built from multiple levels of carry-lookahead logic are known as **multilevel** or **hierarchical carry-lookahead adders**.

In summary, the carry-lookahead approach results in faster additions of large binary numbers (more than 8 bits or so) than a carry-ripple approach, at the expense of more gates. However, by clever hierarchical design, the carry-lookahead gate size is kept reasonable.

Carry-Select Adders

Another way to build a larger adder from smaller adders is known as carry-select. Consider building an 8-bit adder from 4-bit adders. A carry-select approach uses two 4-bit adders for the high-order four bits, labeled *HI4_1* and *HI4_0* in Figure 6.62. *HI4_1* *assumes* the carry-in will be 1, while *HI4_0* *assumes* the carry-in will be 0, so both generate stable output at the same time that *LO4* generates stable output—after 4 gate-delays (assuming the 4-bit adder has a delay of four gate-delays). The *LO4* carry-out value selects among *HI4_1* or *HI4_0*, using a 5-bit-wide 2x1 multiplexer—hence the term *carry-select adder*.

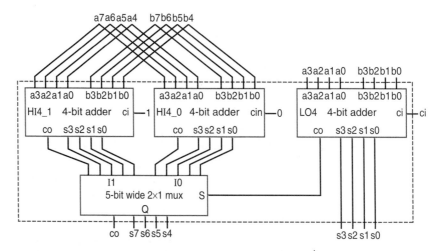

Figure 6.62 8-bit carry-select adder implemented using three 4-bit adders.

The delay of a 2x1 mux is 2 gate-delays, so the total delay of the 8-bit adder is 4 gate-delays for *HI4_1* and *HI4_0* to generate correct sum bits (*LO4* executes in parallel), plus 2 gate-delays for the mux (whose select line is ready after only 3 gate-delays), for a total of 6 gate-delays. Compared with a carry-lookahead implementation using two 4-bit adders, the carry-select adder reduced the total delay from 7 gate-delays down to 6 gate-delays. The cost is one extra 4-bit adder. If a 4-bit carry-lookahead adder requires 26 gates, then the design with two 4-bit adders requires 2*26 = 52 gates, while the carry-select adder requires 3*26 = 78 gates, plus the gates for the 5-bit 2x1 mux.

A 16-bit carry-select adder can built using 4-bit carry-lookahead adders by using multiple levels of multiplexing. Each nibble (four bits) has two 4-bit adders, one assuming a carry-in of 1, the other assuming 0. *Nibble0*'s carry-out selects, using a multiplexer, the appropriate adder for *Nibble1*. *Nibble1*'s selected carry-out selects the appropriate adder for *Nibble2*. *Nibble2*'s selected carry-out selects the appropriate adder for *Nibble3*. The delay of such an adder is 6 gate-delays for *Nibble1*, plus 2 gate-delays for *Nibble2*'s selection, plus 2 gate-delays for *Nibble3*'s selection—for a total of only 10 gate-delays. Cascading four 4-bit adders would yield $4+4+4+4 = 16$

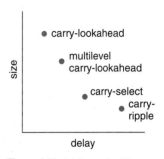

Figure 6.63 Adder tradeoffs.

gates-delays. The speedup of the carry-select version over the cascaded version would be 16 / 10 = 1.6. Total size would be $7*26 = 182$ gates, plus the gates for the three 5-bit 2x1 muxes. Carry-select adders provide good speed for reasonable size.

Figure 6.63 illustrates the tradeoffs among adder designs. Carry-ripple is the smallest but has the longest delay. Carry-lookahead is the fastest but has the largest size. Carry-select is a compromise between the two, involving some lookahead and some rippling. The choice of the most appropriate adder for a design depends on the speed and size constraints of the design.

Smaller Multiplier—Sequential (Shift-and-Add) Style

An array-style multiplier can be fast, but may require many gates for wide-bitwidth (e.g., 32-bit) multipliers. This section develops a sequential multiplier instead of a combinational one to reduce the size of the multiplier. The idea of a sequential multiplier is to keep a running sum of the partial products and compute each partial product one at a time, rather than computing all the partial products at once and summing them.

Figure 6.64 provides an example of 4-bit multiplication. Assume the running of sum is initialized to 0000. Each step corresponds to a bit in the multiplier (the second number). Step 1 computes the partial product as 0110, which is added to the running sum of 0000 to obtain 00110. Step 2 computes the partial product as 0110, which is added to the proper columns of the running sum of 00110 to obtain 010010. Step 3 computes the partial product as 0000, which are added to the proper columns of the running sum. Likewise for step 4. The final running sum is 00010010, which is the correct product of 0110 and 0011.

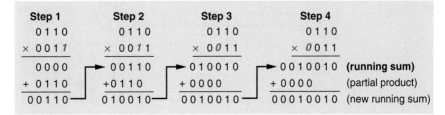

Figure 6.64 Multiplication done by generating a partial product for each bit in the multiplier (the number on the bottom), accumulating the partial products in a running sum.

Computing each partial product is easy, requiring just the ANDing of the current multiplicand bit with every bit in the multiplier to yield the partial product. So if the current multiplicand bit is 1, the AND creates a copy of the multiplier as the partial product. If the current multiplicand bit is 0, the AND creates 0 as the partial product.

The next thing to determine is how to add each partial product to the proper columns of the running sum. Notice that the partial product should be moved to the left by one bit relative to the running sum after each step. We can look at this another way—the running sum should be moved to the *right* by one bit after each step. Look at the multiplication illustration in Figure 6.64 until you "see" how the running sum moves one bit to the right relative to each partial product.

Therefore, the running sum can be computed by initializing an 8-bit register to 0. Each step adds the partial product for the current multiplicand bit to the leftmost four bits of the running sum, and shifts the running sum one bit to the right, shifting a 0 into the leftmost bit. So the running sum register should have a clear function, a parallel load function, and a shift right function. A circuit showing the running sum register and an adder to add each partial product to that register is shown in Figure 6.65.

The last thing to be determined is how to control the circuit so that the circuit does the right thing during each step, which is the purpose of controllers. Figure 6.66 shows an FSM describing the desired controller behavior of the sequential multiplier.

In terms of performance, the sequential multiplier requires two cycles per bit, plus 1 cycle for initialization. So a 4-bit multiplier would require 9 cycles, while a 32-bit multi-

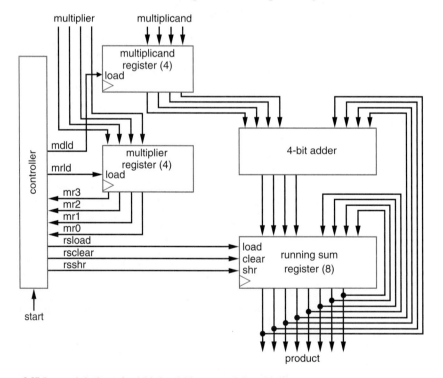

Figure 6.65 Internal design of a 4-bit by 4-bit sequential multiplier.

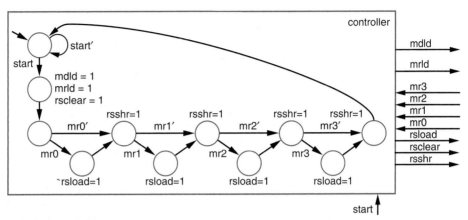

Figure 6.66 FSM describing the controller for the 4-bit multiplier.

plier would require 65 cycles. The longest register-to-register delay is from a register through the adder to a register. If the adder is a carry-lookahead adder having only 4 gate-delays, then the total delay for a 4-bit multiplication would be 9 cycles * 4 gate-delays/cycle = 36 gate-delays. The total delay for a 32-bit multiplication would be 65 cycles * 4 gate-delays/cycle = 260 gate-delays. While slow, notice that this multiplier's size is quite small, requiring only an adder, a few registers, and a state-register and some control logic for the controller. For a 32-bit multiplier, the size would be far smaller than an array-style multiplier requiring 31 adders.

The multiplier's design can be further improved by using a shifter in the datapath, but we omit details of that improved design.

▶ 6.5 RTL DESIGN OPTIMIZATIONS AND TRADEOFFS

Chapter 5 described the RTL design process. While creating the datapath during RTL design, several optimizations and tradeoffs can be used to create smaller or faster designs.

Pipelining

Microprocessors continue to become smaller, faster, and less expensive, and thus designers use microprocessors whenever possible to implement desired digital system behavior. But designers continue to choose to build their own digital circuits to implement desired behavior of many digital systems, with a key reason for that choice being *speed*. One method for obtaining speed from digital circuits is through the use of pipelining. *Pipelining* means breaking a large task down into a sequence of stages such that data moves through the stages like parts moving through a factory assembly line. Each stage produces output used by the next stage, and all stages operate

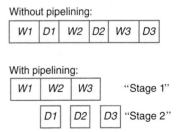

Figure 6.67 Applying pipelining to dishwashing: washing and drying dishes can be done concurrently.

concurrently, resulting in better performance than if data had to be fully processed by the task before new data could begin being processed. An example of pipelining is washing dishes with a friend, with you washing and your friend drying (Figure 6.67). You (the first stage) pick up a dish (dish 1) and wash it, then hand it to your friend (the second stage). You pick up the next dish (dish 2) and wash it *concurrently* to your friend drying dish 1. You then wash dish 3 while your friend dries dish 2. Dishwashing this way is nearly twice as fast as when washing and drying aren't done concurrently.

Consider a system with data inputs W, X, Y, and Z, that should repeatedly output the sum S = W + X + Y + Z. The system could be implemented using an adder tree as shown in Figure 6.68(a). The fastest clock for this design must not be faster than the longest path between any pair of registers, known as the critical path. There are four possible paths from any register output to any register input, and each path goes through two adders. If each adder has a delay of 2 ns, then each path is 2+2 = 4 ns long. Thus, the critical path is 4 ns, and so the fastest clock has a period of at least 4 ns, meaning a frequency of no more than 1 / 4 ns = 250 MHz.

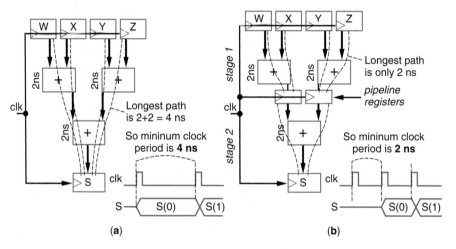

Figure 6.68 Non-pipelined versus pipelined datapaths: (a) four register-to-register paths of 4 ns each, so longest path is 4 ns, meaning minimum clock period is 4 ns, or 1/4 ns = 250 MHz, (b) six register-to-register paths of 2 ns each, so longest path is 2 ns, meaning minimum clock period of 2 ns, or 1/2 ns = 500 MHz.

Figure 6.68(b) shows a pipelined version of this design. We merely add registers between the first and second rows of adders. Since the purpose of these registers is solely related to pipelining, they are known as **pipeline registers**, though their internal design is the same as any other register. The computations between pipeline registers are known as **stages**. By inserting those registers and thus creating a two-stage pipeline, the critical path has been reduced from 4 ns down to only 2 ns, and so the fastest clock has a period of at least 2 ns, meaning a frequency of no more than 1/2 ns = 500 MHz. In other words, just by inserting those pipeline registers, we've *doubled the performance* of the design!

Latency versus Throughput

The term "performance" needs to be refined due to the pipelining concept. Notice in Figure 6.68(b) that the first result *S(0)* doesn't appear until after two cycles, whereas the design in Figure 6.68(a) outputs the first result after only one cycle, because data must now pass through an extra row of registers. The term *latency* refers to delay for new input data to result in new output data. Latency is one kind of performance. Both designs in the figure have a latency of 4 ns. Figure 6.68(b) also shows that a new value for *S* appears every 2 ns, versus every 4 ns for the design in Figure 6.68(a). The term *throughput* refers to the rate at which new data can be input to the system, and similarly, the rate at which new outputs appear from the system. The throughput of the design in Figure 6.68(a) is 1 sample every 4 ns, while the throughput of the design in Figure 6.68(b) is 1 sample every 2 ns. Thus, the performance improvement of the pipelined design can be more precisely described as having *doubled the throughput* of the design.

Example 6.19 Pipelined FIR filter

Recall the 100-tap FIR filter from Example 5.8. We estimated that implementation on a microprocessor would require 4000 ns, while a custom digital circuit implementation would require only 34 ns. That custom digital circuit utilized an adder tree, with seven levels of adders—50 additions, then 25, then 13 (roughly), then 7, then 4, then 2, then 1. The total delay was 20 ns (for the multiplier) plus seven adder-delays (7*2ns = 14ns), for a total delay of 34 ns. We can further improve the throughput of that filter using pipelining. Noticing that the multipliers' delay of 20 ns is roughly equal to the adder tree delay of 14 ns, we decide to insert pipeline registers (50 of them since there are 50 multipliers feeding into 50 adders at the top of the adder tree) between the multipliers and adder tree, thus dividing the computation task into two stages, as shown in Figure 6.69. Those pipeline registers shorten the critical path from 34 ns down to only 20 ns, meaning we can clock the circuit faster and hence improve the throughput. The throughput speedup of the unpipelined design compared to the

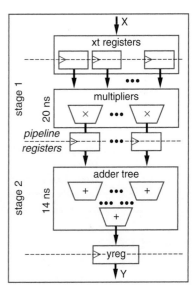

Figure 6.69 Pipelined FIR filter.

microprocessor implementation was 4000/34 = 117, while the throughput speedup of the pipelined design is 4000/20 = 200. The additional speedup is obtained mostly just by inserting some registers.

Although we could pipeline the adder tree also, that would not gain higher throughput, since the multiplier stage would still represent the critical path. We can't clock a pipelined system any faster than the longest stage, since otherwise that stage would fail to load correct values into the stage's output pipeline registers.

The latency of the non-pipelined design is one cycle of 34 ns, or 34 ns total. The latency of the pipelined design is two cycles of 20 ns, or 40 ns total. Thus, pipelining improves the throughput of this example at the expense of latency, representing a tradeoff.

Concurrency

A key reason for designing a custom digital circuit, rather than writing software that executes on a microprocessor, is to achieve improved performance. A common method of achieving performance in a custom digital circuit is through concurrency. **Concurrency** in digital design means to divide a task into several independent subparts, and then to execute those subparts simultaneously. As an analogy, if we have a stack of 200 dishes to wash, we might divide the stack into 10 sub-stacks of 20 dishes each, and then give 10 of our neighbors each a sub-stack. Those neighbors simultaneously go home, wash and dry their respective sub-stacks, and return to us their completed dishes. We would get a ten times speedup in dishwashing (ignoring the time to divide the stack and move sub-stacks from home to home).

Several previous examples used concurrency already. For example, the FIR filter datapath of Figure 5.38 had three multipliers executing concurrently.

The following example uses concurrency to create a faster version of an earlier example.

Example 6.20 Sum-of-absolute-difference component with concurrency

Example 5.8 designed a custom circuit for a sum-of-absolute-difference (SAD) component, and estimated that component to be three times faster than a software-on-microprocessor solution. Further improvement is possible. Notice that comparing one pair of corresponding pixels of two frames is independent of comparing another pair. Thus, such comparisons are an ideal candidate for concurrency.

We first need to be able to read the pixels concurrently. Concurrent reading can be achieved by changing the block memories A and B, which earlier were 256-byte memories. Instead, we can use 16-word memories where each word is 16 bytes (the total memory size is still 256 bytes). Thus, each memory read corresponds to reading an entire pixel row of a 16x16 block. We can then concurrently determine the differences among all 16 pairs of pixels from A and B. Figure 6.70 shows a new datapath and controller FSM for a more concurrent SAD component.

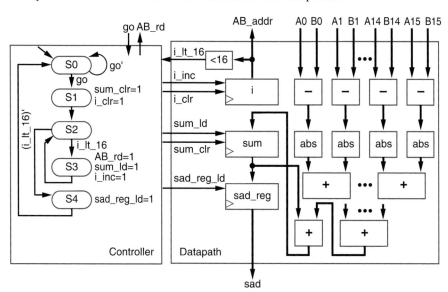

Figure 6.70 SAD datapath using concurrency for speed, along with the controller FSM.

The datapath consists of 16 subtractors operating concurrently on the 16 pixels of a row, followed by 16 absolute value components. The 16 resulting differences feed into an adder tree, whose result gets added with the present sum, for writing back into the sum register. The datapath compares its counter *i* with 16, since there are 16 rows in a block, and so the difference between rows must be computed 16 times. The controlling FSM loops 16 times to accumulate the differences of each row, and then loads the final result into the register *sad_reg*, which connects to the SAD component's output *sad*.

The analysis after Example 5.8 estimated that a software solution would require about six cycles per pixel pair comparison. Since there are 256 pixels in a 16x16 block, the software would require 256 * 6 = 1536 cycles to compare a pair of blocks. The SAD circuit with concurrency instead requires only 1 cycle to compare each row of 16 pixels, which the circuit must do 16 times for a block, resulting in only 16 * 1 = 16 cycles. Thus, the SAD circuit's speedup over software is 1536 / 16 = 96. In other words, the relatively simple SAD circuit using concurrency runs nearly 100 times faster than a software solution. That sort of speedup eventually translates to better-quality digitized video from whatever video appliance is being designed.

Pipelining and concurrency can be combined to achieve even greater performance improvements.

Component Allocation

When the same operation is used in two different states of a high-level state machine, a designer can choose to instantiate either two functional units with one for each state, or one functional unit that will be shared among the two states. For example, Figure 6.71 shows a portion of an HLSM with two states *A* and *B* that each have a multiplication operation. A designer can choose to use two distinct multipliers as shown in Figure 6.71(a) (assume the t variables represent registers). The figure also shows the control signals that would be set in each state of the FSM controlling that datapath, with the t1 register being loaded in the first state (t1ld=1), and the t4 register being loaded in the second state (t4ld=1).

However, because a state machine can't be in two states at the same time, the FSM will perform only one multiplication at a time, so the one multiplier can be shared among

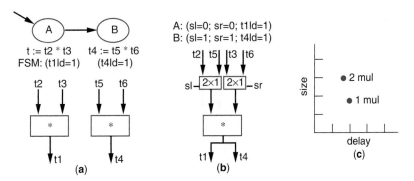

Figure 6.71 Two different component allocations: (a) two multipliers, (b) one multiplier, (c) the one-multiplier allocation represents a tradeoff of smaller size for slightly more delay.

the two states. Because fast multipliers are big, such sharing could save many gates. A datapath with only one multiplier appears in Figure 6.71(b). In each state, the controller FSM would configure the multiplexer select lines to pass the appropriate operands through to the multiplier, and to load the appropriate destination register. So in the first state *A*, the FSM would set the select line for the left multiplexer to 0 (sl=0) to let t2 pass through and would set the select line for the right multiplexer to 0 (sr=0) to let t3 pass through, in addition to setting t1ld=1 to load the result of the multiplication into the t1 register. Likewise, the FSM in state *B* sets the muxes to pass t5 and t6, and loads t4.

Figure 6.71(c) illustrates that the one-multiplier design would have smaller size at the expense of slightly more delay due to the multiplexers.

The terms "operator" and "operation" refer to behavior, like addition or multiplication. The terms "component" and "functional unit" refer to an item in a circuit, like an adder or a multiplier.

A component library might consist of numerous different functional units that could potentially implement a desired operation. For a multiplication, there may be several multiplier components: *MUL1* might be very fast but large, while *MUL2* might be very small but slow, and *MUL3* may be somewhere in between. There may also be fast but large adders, small but slow adders, and several choices in between. Furthermore, some components might support multiple operations, like an adder/subtractor component, or an ALU. Choosing a particular set of functional units to implement a set of operations is known as **component allocation**. Automated RTL design tools consider dozens or hundreds of possible component allocations to find the best ones that represent a good tradeoff between size and performance.

Operator Binding

Given an allocation of components, a designer must choose which operations to assign, or **bind**, to which components. For example, Figure 6.72 shows three multiplication operations, one in state *A*, one in state *B*, and one in state *C*. Figure 6.72(a) shows one possible mapping of multiplication operations to two multipliers, resulting in two multiplexers. Figure 6.72(b) shows an alternative mapping to two multipliers, which results in only one multiplexer, since the same operand (*t3*) is fed to the same multiplier *MULA* in two different states and thus that multiplier's input doesn't require a mux. Thus, the second mapping results in fewer gates, with no performance loss—an optimization, as shown in

Figure 6.72 Two different operator bindings: (a) *Binding 1* uses two muxes, (b) *Binding 2* uses only one mux, (c) *Binding 2* represents an optimization compared to *Binding 1*.

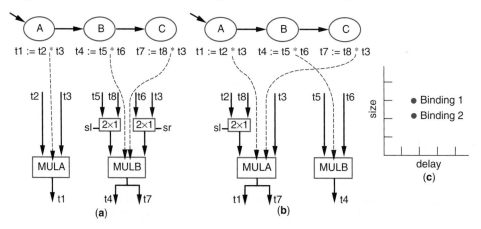

Figure 6.72(c). Note that binding not only maps operators to components, but also chooses which operand to map to which component input; if we had mapped t3 to the left operand of *MULA* in Figure 6.72(b), then *MULA* would have required two muxes rather than just one.

Mapping a given set of operations to a particular component allocation is known as *operator binding*. Automated tools typically explore hundreds of different bindings for a given component allocation.

Of course, the tasks of component allocation and operator binding are interdependent. If only one component is allocated, then all operators must be bound to that component. If two components are allocated, then there are some choices in binding. If many components are allocated, then many more choices for binding exist. Thus, some tools will perform allocation and binding simultaneously, and other tools will iterate between the two tasks. Together, component allocation and operator binding are sometimes referred to as *resource sharing*.

Operator Scheduling

Given a high-level state machine, additional states may be introduced to enable creating a smaller datapath. For example, consider the HLSM in Figure 6.73(a).The HLSM has three states, with state *B* having two multiplications. Since those two multiplications occur in the same state, and each will be a single clock cycle, then two multipliers (at least) are needed in the datapath to support the two simultaneous multiplications in state *B*. But what if enough gates exist for only one multiplier? In that case, the operations can be rescheduled so that there is at most only one multiplication performed in any one state, as in Figure 6.73(b). Thus, when components are being allocated, only one multiplier need be allocated as shown, and as was also done in Figure 6.71(b). The result is a smaller but slower design due to the extra state's clock cycle, as illustrated in Figure 6.73(c).

Converting a computation from occurring concurrently in one state to occurring across several states is known as *serializing* a computation.

Of course, the inverse rescheduling is also possible. Suppose we started with the HLSM of Figure 6.73(b). If plenty of gates and available and improved performance are

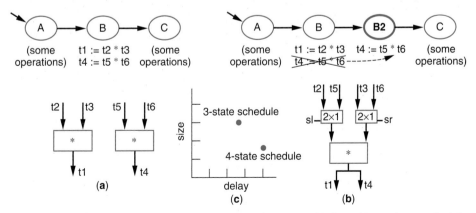

Figure 6.73 Scheduling: (a) initial 3-state schedule requires two multipliers, (b) new 4-state schedule requires only one multiplier, (c) new schedule trades off size for delay (extra state).

desired, the operations can be rescheduled such that the operations of states *B2* and *B* are merged into the one state *B*, as in Figure 6.73(a). The result is a faster but larger design requiring two multipliers instead of one.

Generally, introducing or merging states and assigning operations to those states are together a task known as ***operator scheduling***.

You may have noticed that operator scheduling is interdependent with component allocation, which you may recall was interdependent with operator binding. Thus, the tasks of scheduling, allocation, and binding are all interdependent. Modern tools may combine the tasks and/or may iterate among the tasks several times in search of good designs.

Example 6.21 Smaller FIR filter using operator scheduling

Consider the 3-tap FIR filter of Example 5.10. That design had one state containing the key datapath actions, as shown in Figure 6.74(a). We could reduce the size of the datapath by scheduling the operations across several states, such that at most one multiplication and one addition occurs per state, as shown in Figure 6.74(b). The first state loads the *x* registers with samples—note that the ordering of those actions next to the state doesn't matter, since all the actions occur simultaneously. That state also clears a new register named *sum*, which was introduced to keep track of the intermediate tap sums to be computed in the later states. The second state computes the first tap of the filter result, the next state computes the second tap, and the next state computes the third tap. The last state outputs the result, and then the HLSM returns to the first state again.

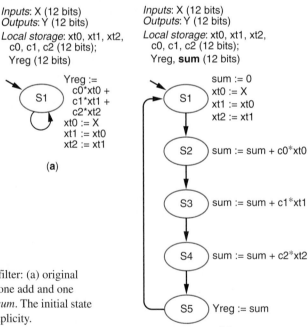

Figure 6.74 HLSM for 3-tap FIR filter: (a) original state, (b) five states with at most one add and one multiply per state, using register *sum*. The initial state is omitted from the figure for simplicity.

A new datapath for this HLSM is shown in Figure 6.75, which can be compared with the original datapath of Figure 5.40 (the new datapath figure only shows control lines that were added to the original datapath). The datapath requires only one multiplier and one adder, because there is at most one multiplication and one addition in any given state in Figure 6.74. The particular configuration of the multiplier, adder, and register in Figure 6.75 is extremely common in signal processing circuits and is known as a ***multiply-accumulate*** (***MAC***) unit. The datapath multiplexes the inputs to the MAC unit.

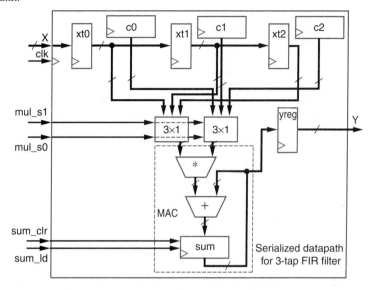

Figure 6.75 Serial FIR filter datapath. The components in the dashed box comprise what is known as a multiply-accumulate (MAC) component.

The performance of the concurrent design of Example 5.10 was estimated assuming 1 ns per gate, 2 ns per adder, and 20 ns per multiplier. The design had a critical path of 20 ns for the multiplier and then 4 ns for two adders in series, for a total of 24 ns. That was also the time between new results being taken in at the inputs and generated at the output: 24 ns. Using the more precise performance measures of latency and throughput defined in Section 6.5, the concurrent design has a latency of 24 ns (delay from input to output) and a throughput of 1 sample every 24 ns. The serial design has a critical path equal to the delay through a mux, multiplier, and adder. Assuming two gate-delays for the mux, we obtain a delay of 2 ns + 20 ns + 2 ns, or 24 ns. The latency from input to output is five states, meaning 5 * 24 ns = 120 ns. The throughput is 1 sample every 120 ns. Thus, the concurrent 3-tap FIR filter has 120/25 = 5 times faster latency, as well as 5 times faster throughput, compared to the serial FIR filter. Recall from Example 6.19 that a pipelined concurrent FIR filter has even faster throughput.

The performance difference between serial and concurrent becomes even more pronounced for an FIR filter with more taps. The latency of a concurrent 100-tap FIR filter was estimated in Section 5.4 to be 34 ns (the delay is greater than the concurrent 3-tap filter because the 100-tap filter needs an adder tree). The serial design would still have a 24 ns critical path, but would require 102 states (1 to initialize, 100 to compute the taps, and 1 to output), for a latency of 102 * 24 ns = 2448 ns. Thus, the latency speedup of the concurrent design would be 2448 / 34 = 72.

We should also consider the size difference between the serial and concurrent designs. Let's assume for illustrative purposes that an adder requires approximately 500 gates and a multiplier requires 5000 gates. The serial design's one multiplier and one adder would thus require only 5500 gates. For a 3-tap FIR filter, the concurrent design's 3 multipliers and 2 adders would require 5000*3 + 500*2 = 16,000 gates. For a 100-tap FIR filter, the concurrent design's 100 multipliers alone would require 100*5000 = 500,000 gates—100 times more gates than the serial design.

Intuitively, these numbers make sense. A concurrent design for 100 taps uses about 100 times more gates (due to using 100 multipliers instead of just 1) compared to a serial design, yet achieves about 100 times better performance (due to computing 100 multiplications concurrently rather than computing one multiplication at a time).

Depending on performance needs and size constraints, a designer might consider designs in between the two extremes of serial and concurrent. One such design would have two multipliers and would be roughly twice as big and twice as fast as the serial design. A design with ten multipliers would be roughly ten times as big and ten times as fast as the serial design. Figure 6.76 illustrates tradeoffs among serial and concurrent designs for an FIR filter. The above sections should have made it quite clear that RTL design presents an enormous range of possible solutions to the designer. A single high-level state machine can be implemented as any of a huge variety of possible implementations that differ tremendously in their sizes and performance.

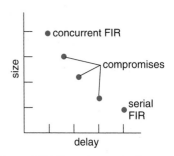

Figure 6.76 FIR design tradeoffs.

Moore versus Mealy High-Level State Machines

In the same way that either a Moore or a Mealy FSM can be created (see Section 6.3), we can create Moore or Mealy high-level state machines. In the case of a high-level state machine, a Moore type can only have actions associated with the states, while a Mealy type can have actions associated with the transitions. As was the case with FSMs, a Mealy type may result in fewer states. Mixing Moore and Mealy types is commonly done in HLSMs.

▶ 6.6 MORE ON OPTIMIZATIONS AND TRADEOFFS

Serial versus Concurrent Computation

Having seen in this chapter numerous examples of tradeoff techniques at various levels of design, we can detect a common theme underlying some of those tradeoffs. The common theme is that of serial versus concurrent computation. *Serial* means to perform tasks one at a time. *Concurrent* means to perform tasks at the same time.

For example, in combinational logic design, we can reduce logic size by factoring out terms. By factoring out terms, we are essentially serializing the computation, by computing the factored out terms first, and then combining the results with other terms. In datapath component design, we can improve an adder's speed by computing carries concurrently, rather than waiting for the carry to ripple serially. In RTL design, we can schedule operations across several states, serializing the operations to reduce size compared to concurrent operations in a single state. Example 6.20 and Example 6.21 both illustrated serial versus concurrent computation tradeoffs, for an SAD circuit and an FIR circuit, respectively.

Trading off between serial and concurrent computation is a fundamental concept spanning all levels of digital design. As a general rule, a concurrent design is faster but larger, while a serial design is smaller but slower.

Typically, numerous design options exist that span the range in between fully serial and fully concurrent designs.

Optimizations and Tradeoffs at Higher versus Lower Levels of Design

As a general rule, the optimizations and tradeoffs made at the higher levels of design may have a much greater impact on design criteria than the optimizations and tradeoffs made at lower levels of design. For example, imagine wanting to drive to a city on the other side of the country in as little time as possible. We could reduce time by reducing the number of stops we make to eat, meaning we carry our own food in the car. We could also reduce time by reducing stops for fuel, meaning we use a car with the longest driving capacity per gas tank. Some people (not you, of course) might even consider driving faster than the legal speed limit. But those are not the first things you typically think of when trying to reduce driving time for a cross-country trip. The most important decision is which route to take. One route might be 4000 miles long, while another route may be only 2000 miles. The high-level decision of which route to take has far more impact than all the lower-level decisions mentioned previously. Those lower-level decisions are only really useful to us if we made the right high-level decision, and then still want to reduce the time further.

In digital design, optimization/tradeoff decisions at the higher levels (e.g., RTL decisions) may have a much larger impact than decisions at the lower levels (e.g., datapath component decisions or multilevel logic decisions). For example, the RTL decision to build a serial or concurrent FIR filter (Example 6.21) will have a far greater impact on circuit size and performance than the datapath-component-level decision to use a carry-ripple or carry-lookahead adder, or the combinational-logic-level deci-

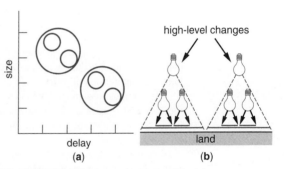

Figure 6.77 Higher- versus lower-level decisions: (a) higher-level decisions (denoted by the larger two circles) focus the design into a region, while lower-level decisions tune within the region, (b) spotlight analogy.

sion to use two-level or multilevel logic. Those lower-level decisions merely tune the size and performance of the higher-level decision. Figure 6.77(a) illustrates this concept. An analogy might be a spotlight shining down on land, illustrated in Figure 6.77(b)—moving the spotlight left or right at high altitude (higher-level decisions) has a larger impact on which land region (possible solutions) is illuminated than do lower-altitude movements (lower-level decisions).

Algorithm Selection

When attempting to implement a system as a digital circuit, perhaps the highest-level design decision, having therefore the most significant impact on design criteria like size, performance, power, etc., is the selection of an algorithm. An *algorithm* is a set of steps that solve a problem. The same problem can be solved by different algorithms. Algorithms for the same problem, when implemented as a digital circuit, may result in tremendously different performance and/or size. Some algorithms may simply be better than others (optimization without much tradeoff), while other algorithms may represent tradeoffs among performance, size, and other criteria. Selecting an algorithm for a digital design problem is perhaps the highest level of design, and can have the biggest impact on design criteria. For example, earlier examples showed various implementations of an FIR filter. But there are many other filtering algorithms that are very different from the algorithm used in FIR. Some algorithms may provide higher-quality filtering at the expense of more required computation; others may provide lower quality but need less computation.

The following example illustrates algorithm selection.

Example 6.22 Data compression using different table lookup algorithms

We wish to compress data being sent over a long-distance computer network in order to achieve faster communication by sending fewer bits. One method for such compression is to use short codes for frequently appearing data values. For example, suppose each data item is 32 bits long. We might analyze the data we expect to send and find the 256 most frequently appearing data values. We could then assign a unique 8-bit code to each of those 256 values. When sending data over the network, we first send a bit indicating whether we are about to send an encoded 8-bit data item or a raw 32-bit data item—if the first bit is 1, that might mean encoded, and a 0 might mean raw. If all the data items being sent happen to be among the top 256 most frequent ones, then we'd be sending 9 bits per data item (1 bit indicating whether encoded, plus 8 bits of encoded data) rather than 32 bits per data item—a compression of nearly 4x, which could translate to about 4 times faster communication.

We might design the encoder using a 256-word memory that stores the 256 most frequent values in sorted order, from smallest to largest in binary. The code would then be the address of that word in the memory. Figure 6.78 shows sample contents of such a memory, in hexadecimal. The contents vary depending on the communicating applications we are considering.

One algorithm for searching a list of values in a memory is known as *linear search*. Starting at address 0, we compare each memory word's contents with the data item we are looking for (known as the key), incrementing the address and repeating until we find a match, at which point we treat the address at which there was a match as the encoded value. If we get to address 255 and don't find a match, we will transmit the raw data. The linear search algorithm is a slow way to search a sorted list in memory. The algorithm requires 256 reads and compares for data items that aren't in the memory, which may translate to 256 cycles. For data items that are in the memory, we would require on average 128 reads.

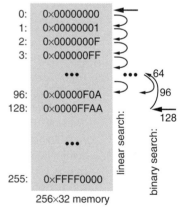

Figure 6.78 Searching a sorted memory for the key 0x00000F0A —linear search requires 97 reads/ compares, binary search only 3.

A faster algorithm for searching a list of items in a memory is known as **binary search**. We first sort the list and then store the list in the memory (we need only sort once). To look up an item, we start in the middle of the memory, meaning address 128, and compare that word's contents with the key. If the contents' value is less than 128, then we know that the key, if it exists in the memory, must be somewhere between 0 and 127. So we go to the middle of that range, meaning address 64, and again compare. If the value there is less than the key, we search 0 to 63; if greater, we search 65–127. So after each comparison, we decrease the remaining possible range of addresses in which the key lies by one half. Halving 256 repeatedly can only be done 8 times: 256, 128, 64, 32, 16, 8, 4, 2, 1. In other words, after at most 8 comparisons, we've either seen the key, or shrunk the range to 1, meaning the key can't be found in the memory. Binary search is 256/8 = 32 times faster than linear search when the key does not exist in the memory, and roughly that much faster when the key exists in the memory too. Yet binary search only requires a slightly smarter controller.

The choice of algorithm makes a big difference in performance for this example—a much bigger difference than is determined by, say, the speed of the comparator being used.

Power Optimization

Power is becoming an important design criteria, both in high-end computing as well as in embedded computing. The unit of power is **watts**, which represents the energy per second (i.e., joules per second). In high-end computing, like desktop PCs, servers, or video-game consoles, the chips inside a computer consume a lot of power, causing the chips to become very hot. For example, a typical chip inside a PC may consume 60 watts—think about touching a 60-watt light bulb (but don't actually touch one) to understand how hot that is. Designing low-power chips reduces the need for expensive chip cooling methods beyond simple fans in high-end computing, and also reduces the electricity costs, which can be quite significant for companies operating large numbers of computers.

In embedded computing, even simple cooling methods likes fans may not be available—a cell phone does not have a fan (if it did, people might find their tie or scarf getting stuck in that fan). Portable devices might have chips that run at only 1 watt or less.

Furthermore, portable devices typically get their energy from batteries, and thus low-power chips are necessary to extend battery life—especially considering the fact that batteries are not improving fast enough to keep pace with increasing power consumption. By some measures, energy demand per chip is doubling about every three years (going along with Moore's Law). Figure 6.79 plots such energy demands compared to battery energy densities improving at their present rate of only about 8% per year. The increasing gap shown translates to shorter battery lifetimes for a device like a cell phone, or translates to bigger batteries.

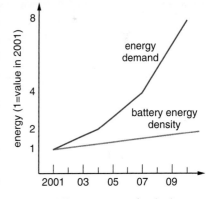

Figure 6.79 Battery energy density is improving more slowly than the increasing energy demands of digital chips.

The most popular IC technology today uses CMOS transistors, and the biggest contributor to power consumption in CMOS is the switching of values from 0 to 1. The reason for this is that wires aren't perfect, having capacitance (we don't put a capacitor there on purpose—it is simply a result of the fact that wires aren't perfect conductors of electricity). Switching the wire from 0 to 1 requires charging that capacitor. Switching from 1 back to 0 causes that charge to be discharged to ground. That switching results in power being consumed. This power is known as ***dynamic power***, since this power comes from the changing of signals ("dynamic" means "changing"). Dynamic power consumption of a CMOS wire is proportional to the size of the capacitance (C) of the wire, multiplied by the voltage (V) squared, multiplied by the frequency at which the wire switches (f), namely

$$P = k * CV^2 f \quad \text{(equation for CMOS dynamic power consumption)}$$

where k is some constant. Computing the dynamic power of a circuit is achieved by adding up the power computed by the above equation for every wire.

Looking at the above equation, one can clearly see that lowering the voltage will cause the greatest reduction in dynamic power, because of the voltage having a quadratic (squared) contribution to dynamic power. Low-level circuit designers seek to reduce power by creating transistors that operate at the lowest voltage possible, to reduce the V term, and that have the smallest wire capacitance possible, to reduce the C term. Digital designers can therefore choose to utilize gates that operate with a lower voltage.

Unfortunately, lower-voltage gates have a longer delay than higher-voltage gates, resulting in a tradeoff between power and performance.

Another way to reduce the dynamic power consumed by a circuit is to reduce the circuit's clock frequency, which obviously reduces the f term for all the clock wires in the circuit, as well as for the many other wires that change on each clock edge (like register wires and the logic connected to those registers' outputs). But again, reducing the clock frequency slows performance, resulting in a tradeoff between power and performance.

The chief technical officer at a major chip design company told me in 2004 that, for their company, "Power is enemy number one."

Contrary to digital design in the 1980s and 1990s, power is a key challenge today. The reason is that IC makers have scaled IC voltage down nearly as low as possible, yet are putting more transistors on each IC every year due to shrinking of transistor sizes, meaning more wires switching on the same IC. And capacitance isn't decreasing at the same rate as transistor sizes. The result is that an IC consumes more power as more transistors are put on the IC, which can result in problems due to too much heat and fast battery energy consumption.

Clock Gating (Advanced Technique)

Assuming the C and V terms have been reduced to the greatest extent possible using transistor-level design techniques, power can be reduced further by reducing f, the frequency at which wires switch. One method for reducing such power is known as clock gating. ***Clock gating*** is the disabling of the clock signal in regions of the chip that are not computing anything at a given time. Clock gating saves power because a significant percentage of the wires switching in a chip are the wires that distribute the clock to all the registers and flip-flops—perhaps 20%–30% of the power consumption is due to the clock signal switching throughout the chip. Clock gating reduces f without slowing the clock frequency itself.

In clock gating, the clock signal is disabled by ANDing the clock signal with an enable signal that is set in the state machine. Recall that a register with parallel load internally reloads the same value from the register's flip-flops back into the flip-flops on a rising clock edge. Preventing the clock edge from appearing keeps the same values in the flip-flops, yielding the same net result—the register's contents don't change.

Clock gating is not something that digital designers typically do themselves. Rather, modern synthesis tools may allow us to specify clock enable and disable using special commands in each state. However, adding a gate on a clock signal delays the clock signal, resulting in clock signals in different parts of the circuit being slightly different from one another, an effect known as ***clock skew***. The tools therefore automatically perform timing analysis to ensure that the clock skew does not change overall circuit behavior. Furthermore, putting gates on a clock signal can reduce the sharpness of the clock edges, and so tools may use special gates. Nevertheless, the technique is widely used by low-power tools in practice. The next example illustrates clock gating.

Example 6.23 Serial FIR filter with clock gating to reduce power

We designed a serial FIR filter in Example 6.21. A five-state FSM controlled the datapath. The state machine loaded the three *xt* registers only in the first state, state *S1*, and loaded the *yreg* register only in the last state, state *S5*. Yet, the design routed the clock signal to all four registers utilizing four wires, labeled n1–n4 in Figure 6.80(a). Notice from the timing diagram at the top of the figure that n1–n4 change identically as the clock signal changes, and remember that every such change consumes dynamic power.

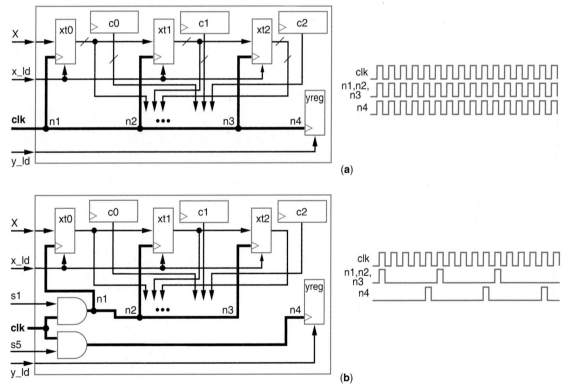

Figure 6.80 Clock gating: (a) the clock signal switches every cycle on all the heavily bolded wires, but the *xt* registers are only loaded in state *S1*, and the *yreg* in state *S5*—so most of the clock switching is wasted; (b) gating the clock reduces the switching on the clock wires.

Figure 6.80(b) shows a design using clock gating. The controller gates the clock to the *xt* registers by setting s1 to 0 in all states but *S1*. Likewise, the controller gates the clock to the *yreg* register by setting *s5* to 0 in all states but *s5*. Notice the significant decrease in signal switching on the clock's wires n1–n4, shown at the bottom of Figure 6.80.

Low-power gates on noncritical paths

Not all gates are equally fast. Engineers that build gates from transistors can make a gate faster by increasing the size of the gate's transistors, or by operating the gate at a higher voltage, or by other means. Thus, one two-input AND gate might have a 1 ns delay, while another two-input AND gate might have a 2 ns delay. The latter AND may consume less power, due to its smaller size or lower voltage.

To reduce the power consumed by a circuit, the entire circuit can use low-power gates, at the expense of slower performance, as illustrated in Figure 6.81.

Alternatively, low-power gates can be put only on noncritical paths, so those paths are lengthened but to no longer than the critical path, as in the next example.

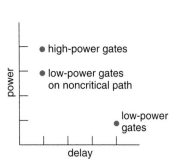

Figure 6.81 Using low-power gates can reduce some power without changing delay, or reduce more power at the expense of delay.

Example 6.24 Reducing noncritical path power with multilevel logic

Example 6.11 reduced the size of a noncritical path by using multilevel logic. In this example, we instead reduce the power consumed by the noncritical path by using low-power gates. Assume that normal gates have a delay of 1 ns and consume 1 nanowatt of power, and that low-power gates have a delay of 2 ns and consume 0.5 nanowatts of power.

The left side of Figure 6.82 shows the same circuit from Example 6.11, having a critical path of 3 gate-delays. Assume that all the gates are normal gates, meaning the critical path delay is 3 ns, and the total power consumption is 5 nanowatts.

The bottom two AND gates lie on two noncritical paths having delays of only 2 ns. We can thus replace those AND gates by low-power AND gates. The result is that the two paths' delays lengthen to 3 ns, so become equal to the critical path delay, but not longer. The result is also that the total power becomes only 4 nanowatts instead of 5 nanowatts (a 20% reduction).

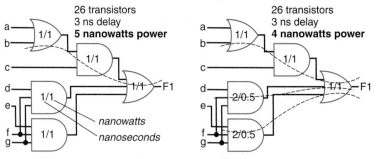

Figure 6.82 Using low-power gates on noncritical paths. Numbers inside a gate represent the gate's delay in nanoseconds and the gate's power consumption in nanowatts.

▶ 6.7 PRODUCT PROFILE: DIGITAL VIDEO PLAYER/RECORDER

Digital Video Overview

In the 1990s, the digitization of video became practical due to faster, smaller, and lower-power digital circuits. Previously, video was largely captured, stored, and played using analog methods. Digitized video works by sampling an analog video signal and transforming the samples to digital values. Such digitization is similar to the audio digitization example from Figure 1.1, but with some additional work.

A video is actually a series of quickly displayed still pictures, known as *frames*, as shown in Figure 6.83(a). One second of video might consist of about 30 frames—the human eyes and brain see such a rapid sequence of frames as a smooth, continuous video.

A digital display may be divided into several hundred thousand tiny "picture elements," or *pixels*. A typical size might be about 720 across and 480 down. For each frame, a digitized sample captures several values for each pixel, like the intensity of the red, blue, and green components of the light at that pixel, converting analog measurements of those intensities into digital numbers. The result is the representation of a digitized frame as a (large) series of 0s and 1s, and the representation of a digitized

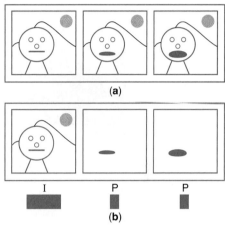

Figure 6.83 Video: (a) is a series of pictures, or frames, with much interframe redundancy, (b) can be constructed from I (intra) frames and P (predicted) frames, shown with relative bit encoding sizes.

video as a large series of digitized frames. Digitized video can be transmitted, stored, replayed, and copied with much higher-quality than analog video. Furthermore, digitized video can be compressed, resulting possibly in higher-quality video than analog video transmitted or stored using the same medium.

DVD—One Form of Digital Video Storage

Digital video discs (also known as digital versatile discs), or **DVDs**, store video in a digital format. First sold in 1997, DVDs replaced the analog video technology known as VHS tape. DVD players appear in home entertainment centers, personal computers, automobiles (especially family-oriented vehicles), and even as stand-alone portable units. In 2001, consumer electronics companies introduced the first DVD *recorder* to market, allowing individuals to record television shows to special recordable DVDs. The popularity of DVDs compared to the previously popular analog-based VHS technology stems from several advantages, including better-quality video, no deterioration in video quality over time, and the ability to jump directly to particular parts in a video without having to sequentially forward or rewind.

DVDs store large amounts of data on a thin reflective layer of metal. Although the metal layer within a DVD looks flat from our perspective, there are actually billions of tiny pits on the metal layer that store the data. These pits, or lack of pits (called *lands*), store the binary data on the DVD. Figure 6.84 shows how a DVD player reads the information off a DVD. Using a very precise laser, the laser's light is focused onto the metal layer within the DVD. The metal layer reflects the light onto an optical sensor that can detect whether the light is reflected off of a pit or a land. By detecting the different regions, the optical sensor creates a stream of binary values as it reads the DVD.

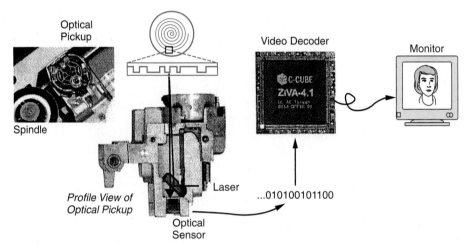

Figure 6.84 How a DVD player reads a DVD. The DVD player's optical pickup element shines a laser on the surface of the DVD. The DVD reflects the laser back to an optical sensor, and the optical sensor uses the intensity of the reflected laser to output the sequence of 0s and 1s stored on the DVD. A video decoder circuit converts the binary data to a sequence of frames that humans interpret as a moving picture.

The DVD's binary data is organized into a series of tracks that spiral outward from the center of the DVD. As the DVD player is reading the data, the laser and optical sensor must slowly move outward from the center of the DVD to the outer edge. If a DVD is dual-layered, the data on the disk's second layer is stored in a spiral that moves from the disk's outer to inner edge. The motivation for the second layer's reverse spiral is to prevent the laser and optical sensor from needing to reposition itself to the center of the disk after focusing on the second layer during a layer change. (You may have noticed a DVD pause momentarily at a certain point in a movie during a layer change.)

A single-layer single-sided DVD can store 4.7 gigabytes of data (meaning 37.6 gigabits), but that amount is not enough for a movie unless the data is compressed. Consider a video with a resolution of 720 pixels by 480 pixels, using 24 bits of information per pixel, and displayed at 30 frames per second. One frame would require 720*480*24 = 8,294,400 bits, or about 8 Mbits. One second of video, or 30 frames, would require 30*8,294,400 = 248,832,000 bits, or about 250 Mbits. A 100-minute movie would thus require about 250 Mbits/sec * 100 min * 60 sec/min = 1500 Gbits. But a DVD can only hold 37.6 Gbits. To store a movie, a DVD must store the video in a compressed format.

A DVD is only one of many different digital video storage media. Digitized video may be stored on any storage media capable of storing 0s and 1s in some form, such as on tape (used in many digital video cameras), on a flash memory (used in digital cameras and cell phones with video recording capability), on a CD, or on a computer hard drive. All such media are typically still quite limited and thus require compression methods.

MPEG-2 Video Encoding—Sending Frame Differences Using I-, P-, and B-Frames

MPEG-2 video compression was defined and standardized by the Motion Picture Expert Group in 1994 (as an improvement over the 1992 MPEG-1 standard), and is used in DVDs, digital television, and numerous other digital video devices. MPEG-2 compression ratios range from 30:1 to 100:1 or more. The compression ratio is determine by dividing the number of bits of the digitized video before compression, by the number of bits after compression. So if a digitized video requires 400 gigabytes uncompressed but only 4 gigabytes compressed, the compression ratio would be 400/4 = 100:1. Note that packing 1500 Gbits of a movie into 37.6 Gbits would require a compression ratio of 1500 Gbits/37.6 Gbits = 40:1.

The key observation leading to MPEG-2's compression method is that typically very little difference exists between two successive frames in a video—in other words, video typically has much interframe redundancy. For example, a frame may consist of a person standing in front of a mountain, as in Figure 6.83(a). The next frame (which represents perhaps 1/30th of a second later) may be almost identical to the previous frame, except that the person's mouth has opened slightly. The next frame may still be almost identical, with the person's mouth opened slightly more. And so on.

Therefore, MPEG-2 does not merely encode each frame as a distinct picture. Instead, to take advantage of the interframe redundancy, MPEG-2 may choose to encode each frame as one of the following:

- An *I-frame*, or intracoded frame, is a complete picture.
- A *P-frame*, or predicted frame, is a frame that merely describes the difference between the current frame and the previous frame. Thus, to derive the picture for this frame, one must combine the P-frame with the previous frame.

For example, Figure 6.83(b) shows P-frames that contain only the differences from the previous frame. A P-frame will obviously require fewer bits than an I-frame. Example frame sizes might be about 8 Mbits for an I-frame, but only 2 Mbits for a P-frame. Thus, instead of representing 30 frames as 30 complete pictures (30 I-frames), a compression method might represent those frames using the following sequence of frames: **I** P P P P P P P P P P P P P **I** P P P P P P P P P P P P P P P. The compression ratio in this example would thus be 8 Mbits * 30 / (2 * 8 Mbits + 28 * 2 Mbits) = 240 / 72 = 3.3:1. Obviously, a picture created by combined predicted frames with a previous frame won't be a perfect representation of the original picture, especially if there is a lot of motion in the video. MPEG-2 thus trades off some quality for compression.

To achieve even further reductions, MPEG-2 uses a third frame type:

- A *B-frame*, or bidirectional predicted frame, is a frame that can store differences from previous and *future* frames.

B-frames can thus be even smaller than P-frames. An example B-frame size might be just 1 Mbit.

Example 6.25 Computing compression ratios involving I-, P-, and B-frames

Assume a 30-frame MPEG-2 sequence has the following frame sequence: **I** B B P B B P B B P B B P B B **I** B B P B B P B B P B B P B B. Assume average frame sizes of 8 Mbits for I-frames, 2 Mbits for P-frames, and 1 Mbit for B-frames. Compute the compression ratio.

The compression ratio in this example would be 8 Mbits * 30 / (2 * 8 Mbits + 8 * 2 Mbits + 20 * 1 Mbits) = 240 / 52 = 4.6 : 1.

The example sequence of frames is in fact fairly typical for MPEG-2 video, with I-frames occurring about every 12–15 frames.

MPEG-2 video encoders may seek to create about 30 frames per second. With hundreds of thousands of pixels per frame that must be compared with another frame, MPEG-2 encoding requires a large amount of computation to determine which frames should be I, P, and B, and what should be the values for the P- and B-frames. Furthermore, much of that computation will consist of the *same* computation performed between corresponding regions of two frames. Thus, many MPEG-2 encoders utilize custom digital circuits to parallelize those computations at the expense of more hardware size. For instance, Example 6.20 built a sum-of-absolute-differences circuit using more parallelism than in Example 5.9, at the expense of a larger circuit size. Such a circuit would be useful in a video encoder needing to quickly determine whether a frame should be encoded as a P- or B-frame, or instead should be encoded as an I-frame. Additional circuits might compute the actual values of P- and B-frames.

Likewise, an MPEG-2 video decoder might use circuits to quickly recompose I-, P-, and B-frames back into full-picture frames—although decoding MPEG-2 video is easier than encoding because the actual determination of P- and B-frame contents is only done during encoding; decoding merely needs to combine P- and B-frames with their surrounding frames.

Transforming to the Frequency Domain for Further Compression

DCT—Discrete Cosine Transform

We saw in the previous section that sending a frame (P or B) that is just the difference from a previous or future frame can result in some compression. However, the compression ratios achieved were only about 4:1. Recall earlier that a DVD needs perhaps a 40:1 compression ratio to store a full-length movie. Thus, further compression is needed.

MPEG-2 therefore further compresses each I-, P- and B-frame individually. The compression method involves applying what is known as a discrete cosine transform to 8x8 blocks of pixel values within each frame. The discrete cosine transform is also used in the well-known JPEG standard for compressing still images, like those in a digital camera. The *discrete cosine transform*, or *DCT*, transforms information from the spatial domain to the frequency domain. (The DCT is similar to another popular technique known as the fast Fourier transform, or FFT, also used for translating to the frequency domain.)

Translating to the frequency domain is a powerful concept, which is widely used in digital signal processing. To understand this concept, consider wanting to digitally store the analog signal shown in Figure 6.85, using the fewest bits possible. The signal is a 1 Hz cosine wave with an amplitude of 10. To store the signal digitally, we could sample the signal at frequent intervals, perhaps every millisecond, and record the measured signal value as a binary number, perhaps 8 bits wide. One second would thus result in 1000 * 8 = 8000 bits. On the other hand, we could just store the fact that the signal is a cosine wave with a frequency of 1 Hz and an amplitude of 10. If we store each of those numbers as an 8-bit value, then we only need to store 8 + 8 = 16 bits. Sixteen bits is far less than 8000 bits.

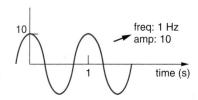

Figure 6.85 Digitizing signals by translating to the frequency domain.

Of course, not all signals that we want to digitize are simple cosine waves. But—and this is the key idea underlying frequency domain representation—*we can approximate any original signal as a sum of cosine waves of different frequencies and amplitudes*. If we break the original signal into small regions, we obtain even better approximation. For example, we might approximate one region as the sum of a 1 Hz cosine wave of amplitude 5 plus a 2 Hz cosine wave of amplitude 3. We might approximate another region as the sum of 50 different cosine waves of different frequencies and amplitudes. The smaller the region we consider, and the more different cosine wave frequencies we consider, the more accurate will be our approximation to the real signal.

Rather than storing the actual frequencies along with the amplitudes of the cosine waves, we could instead decide only to consider using particular frequencies, such as: 1 Hz, 2 Hz, 4 Hz, 8 Hz, 16 Hz, and so on. Then, we can simply send the amplitudes of those particular cosine waves: (5, 3, 0, 0, 0, ...). Let's refer to these amplitudes as coefficients.

The DCT in MPEG-2 converts an input 8x8 block, whose values represent pixel intensities, to an 8x8 block representing the coefficients of predetermined "frequencies." In the video domain, each frequency represents a different block pattern, with low frequency being an almost constant pattern and high frequency being a changing pattern (like a checkerboard). The DCT determines a set of coefficients such that adding the predetermined patterns together with each pattern multiplied by its coefficient yields one resulting pattern very similar to the original input block.

The equation for a two-dimensional DCT applied to an 8x8 block of numbers is:

$$F(u,\ v) = \frac{1}{4}C(u)C(v) \sum_{x=0}^{8}\sum_{y=0}^{8} D[x,\ y]\cos\left(\frac{\pi(2x+1)u}{16}\right)\cos\left(\frac{\pi(2y+1)v}{16}\right)$$

$$C(h) = \begin{cases} \dfrac{1}{\sqrt{2}}\ h = 0 \\ 1,\ otherwise \end{cases}$$

The input is an 8x8 block, $D[x,\ y]$. The output is another 8x8 block, with $F(u,v)$ computing the coefficient at row u, column v for the output block.

An MPEG-2 encoder may utilize custom digital circuits for fast DCT computation. Notice that computing each coefficient requires evaluating the rightmost term (let's call that term the inner term) 64 times, and that must be done for each of the 64 coefficients, meaning 64*64 = 4096 evaluations of the term. And that inner term itself requires several multiplications. Furthermore, the DCT operates on 8x8 blocks, but in a 720x480 I-frame there will be 5400 such blocks. Thus, the DCT for one I-frame could require 5400*4096 = 22 million computations of the inner term. And that encoding may have to occur at 30 frames per second. You can begin to see why an MPEG-2 encoder may need to use custom digital circuits to compute the DCT quickly, using extensive parallelism and pipelining to obtain the necessary performance.

The DCT computation can be sped up further by precomputing the cosine terms of the inner term. Notice that the DCT computes two cosines based on the input values of u and x and the input values of v and y. However, because the DCT operates on 8x8 blocks, the variables u, v, x, and y only range in value from 0 to 7. Therefore, we can precompute the 64 possible cosine values needed for the DCT computation and store those values in an 8x8 table, which may be programmed into a ROM. We can then rewrite the DCT transform as follows:

$$F(u,\ v) = \frac{1}{4}C(u)C(v)\sum_{x=0}^{8}\sum_{y=0}^{8}D[x,\ y]\cos[x,\ u]\cos[y,\ v]$$

Using a ROM to store the precomputed cosine values speeds up the computation of the inner term of the DCT.

Quantization

Translating to the frequency domain using the DCT does not directly perform compression—we merely converted an input 8x8 block to an output 8x8 block. That output 8x8 block represents amplitudes of particular cosine wave frequencies. We can achieve compression by rounding those amplitudes, such that we use fewer bits to represent the amplitudes. For example, suppose we use 8 bits to represent the amplitude, meaning we can represent amplitudes ranging from 0 to 255. Suppose we only represent even amplitudes, meaning 2, 4, ..., 254. In that case, we can drop the lowest-order bit, in the representation of the amplitude, resulting in only 7 bits. The decoder would merely append a 0 to the 7-bit number to obtain an 8-bit number again. For example, the 8-bit number 00001111 would be compressed to the 7-bit number 0000111 with an implicit **0** in the eighth bit. The decoder would expand that 7-bit number back to the 8-bit number 00001110—notice that the decoded number is slightly different than the original, being 14 rather than the original 15 (an example of why MPEG-2 compression loses some image quality). We could take this rounding concept further, only representing amplitudes that are multiples of 4 (thus dropping the two lowest-order bits, yielding a 6-bit representation), or are multiples of 8 (dropping the three lowest-order bits, yielding a 5-bit representation). 00001**111** might be represented as 00001 with three implicit 0s, thus decoded back to 00001**000**. The decoded number of 8 is different from the original number 15 due to the rounding.

The rounding described above, achieved by dropping low-order bits to achieve compression, is known as *quantization*. Notice the tradeoff—more rounding yields more compression, at the expense of accuracy. Fortunately, *humans don't notice such rounding in the high-frequency components of the picture*—our vision just isn't that precise. We also don't notice minor differences in the high-frequency components of sound—our hearing isn't that precise. Think of a very high-pitched sound, so high it could perhaps break glass. You probably couldn't tell the difference between two such high-pitched sounds of slightly different frequencies—they are both just high. Likewise, our eyes can't detect slight rounding of color values in a highly complex scene. So MPEG-2 applies quantization more aggressively on the DCT output block's high-frequency coefficients than on the low-frequency coefficients.

After quantization, the 64 values in the 8x8 block are treated as a list of 64 numbers. Those 64 numbers are then run-length encoded. *Run-length encoding* is a compression method that reduces consecutive occurrences of zeros by a number indicating the number of consecutive zeros rather than representing those zeros themselves. For example, consider wanting to represent the following 5 numbers: 0, 0, 0, 0, 24. If each value is 6 bits, the 5 numbers require 5*6 = 30 bits. On the other hand, we could just send a pair of numbers, the first indicating the number of leading zeros, the second indicating the nonzero number. So 0, 0, 0, 0, 24 would be encoded as (4, 24)—4 leading zeros, followed by the number 24. If each value is 6 bits, the run-length encoded version requires only 2*6=12 bits. Any sequence of numbers could similarly be replaced by a sequence of number pairs, each pair replacing a sequence of zeros and a number. The sequence 0, 0, 0, 0, 24, 0, 0, 8, 0, 0, 0, 0, 0, 0, 16 could thus be replaced by three pairs: (4, 24), (2, 8), (6, 16), reducing the number of bits from 15*6=90 down to 6*6=36 bits. Note that the number of zeros at the beginning of the sequence or in between nonzero numbers may be zero, and the last number may be zero. For example, the sequence 2, 0, 0, 63, 2, 0, 0, 0, 0, 0 could be encoded as (0,2), (2,63), (0,2), (4,0).

Run-length encoding achieves good compression only if there are many 0s in the sequence of numbers. Fortunately, the nature of the DCT leads to many 0 numbers (not all cosine frequencies are needed to approximate a signal region, so those frequencies will have 0 coefficients), especially after quantization (many coefficients are just small numbers, which become 0 during quantization). Thus, applying run-length encoding after quantization leads to further compression.

Example 6.26 Computing compression ratios involving quantization and run-length encoding

Continuing Example 6.25, assume that the 30-frame MPEG-2 sequence has the same frame sequence and average sizes as that example, but that each frame is further compressed by DCT conversion to the frequency domain followed by quantization and run-length encoding. Assume the DCT output block consists of 64 8-bit numbers, that quantization reduces the average number size to 5-bit numbers, and that run-length encoding reduces the resulting number sequence size to 30% of its original size.

The compression ratio would be 8 Mbits * 30 / 5/8 * 0.30 *(2 * 8 Mbits + 8 * 2 Mbits + 20 * 1 Mbits) = 240 / 9.7 = 25:1.

Huffman Coding

After run-length encoding, each block consists of a sequence of numbers. Some numbers will occur in that sequence more frequently than others. *Huffman coding* is a method of reducing the number of bits required to represent a set of values, by creating shorter encodings for the frequently occurring values, and longer encodings for the less frequent value.

Huffman coding, a form of encoding known as entropy encoding, is another powerful concept in digital data compression. Suppose you wish to represent an original sequence of 16 numbers 0, 3, 3, 31, 0, 3, 5, 8, 9, 7, 15, 14, 3, 0, 3, 0. Assuming 5 bits per number, a straightforward binary encoding would be: `00000` `00011` `00011` `11111` `00000` `00011` `00101`, and so on, for a total of 16*5 = **80 bits**. We can reduce this total by first observing that there are only 9 unique symbols: 0, 3, 5, 7, 8, 9, 14, 15, and 31. We really only need 4 bits to uniquely identify each symbol. We could thus assign the nine unique symbols to 4-bit encodings using the following definitions: 0=`0000`, 3=`0001`, 5=`0010`, 7=`0011`, ..., 31=`1001` (note that the encodings are no longer the binary number representations of the original numbers). Thus, the original sequence of numbers (0, 3, 3, 31, 0, 3, 5, ...) would be encoded as `0000` `0001` `0001` `1001` `0000` `0001` `0010` etc., for a total of 16*4 = **64 bits**. The key observation here is that we can encode numbers using any arbitrary unique bit patterns we desire, as long as the encoder and decoder are both aware of the encoding definitions.

We can take this definition concept a step further, by using encodings of different lengths. Observing that 3 and 0 occur more frequently than the other numbers, we might give 3 and 0 shorter encodings. So we might create the following encoding definitions: 0=`00`, 3=`10`, 5=`010`, 7=`0110`, 8=`0111`, 9=`1100`, 14=`1101`, 15=`1110`, 31=`1111`. How these definitions were created is just beyond the scope of this discussion, though it's really not hard to learn. Notice that the encodings are such that the shorter encodings do not appear at the left of any of the longer encodings. For example, `00` does not appear at the left of any of the longer encodings, like `010`, `0110`, `0111`, etc. This feature allows the decoder to know when it has reached the end of the code word—when the decoder has seen `00`, it knows it has found an encoded 0 (because no other encoding starts with `00`); when it sees `10`, it knows it has found a 3 (because no other encoding starts with `10`). But when the decoder sees `01`, it must look at the next bit, and if it sees `010`, it knows it has found a 5 (because no other encoding starts with `010`). Using this variable-length encoding scheme, the original sequence (0, 3, 3, 31, 0, 3, 5, ...) would be encoded as `00` `10` `10` `1111` `00` `10` `010` etc. We have inserted the spaces just for readability; the actual encoding would just be `00101011110010010` etc. The total number of bits would be 4 * 2 (for the four 0s, encoded with the two bits `00`) + 5 * 2 (for the five 3s, encoded with the two bits `10`) + 1*3 (for the one 5, encoded with the three bits `010`) plus 6*4 (for the six remaining numbers 31, 8, 9, 7, 15, and 14, each encoded as 4 bits), totaling **45 bits**—much reduced from the original 80 bits required by the straightforward binary encoding.

Huffman coding achieves good compression when some numbers occur much more frequently than other numbers in the sequence of numbers to be encoded. Fortunately, this is indeed the case after DCT, quantization, and run-length tasks are performed on a block of a frame. For example, there may be plenty of 0s, 1s, 2s, etc., and fewer occurrences of higher numbers.

Example 6.27 Computing compression ratios involving Huffman coding

Continuing Example 6.26, assume that pairs of numbers after quantization and run-length encoding are Huffman coded, and that such encoding reduces the number of bits by 50%.

The compression ratio would thus be 240 / 0.50* 9.7 = 50:1.

Summary

Summarizing MPEG-2 video encoding:

- The use of I-, P-, and B-frames achieves compression by not resending redundant information of successive frames, but rather just sending the differences.

- The DCT transforms 8x8 blocks of frames to the frequency domain, which doesn't achieve compression itself, but rather enables compression in the next steps.

- Quantization achieves further compression by reducing the number of bits needed to represent the DCT coefficients, through rounding.

- Run-length encoding achieves further compression by replacing sequences of zero coefficients by a number indicating the number of such zeros.

- Huffman coding achieves further compression by encoding frequently occurring coefficient numbers with shorter encodings than less frequently occurring coefficient numbers.

The sequence of steps is shown graphically in Figure 6.86.

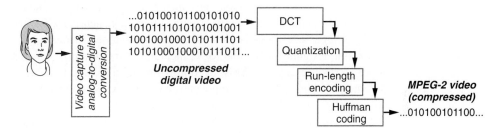

Figure 6.86 MPEG-2 video compression encoding overview.

Our example compression ratio calculations yielded a ratio of about 50:1. In fact, the compression ratio can be varied by varying each of the above steps. We can use fewer I-frames to achieve even higher compression at the cost of degraded video quality, or more I-frames for improved video quality at the cost of more bits. Likewise, we can vary the amount of quantization to trade off quality and compression ratio. Because a typical movie will have some slow-changing scenes and other rapidly changing scenes, and some complex colored frames and other simpler frames, the compression ratio for different parts of a video may actually vary. Notice the permeating presence of *tradeoffs* (primarily between quality and compression ratio) throughout MPEG-2 encoding.

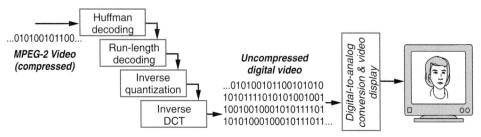

Figure 6.87 MPEG-2 video decoding overview.

An MPEG-2 decoder merely needs to apply the above steps in reverse, as illustrated in Figure 6.87, to convert an MPEG-2 stream of bits back into a series of pictures, or video.

Clearly, MPEG-2 encoding and decoding require a lot of computations performed at speeds fast enough to create smooth-looking, good-quality video. Custom digital circuits can help achieve those required speeds.

▷ 6.8 CHAPTER SUMMARY

Section 6.1 introduced the idea that sometimes a particular design criteria can be improved without hurting other criteria (optimization), but usually improving one criteria is done at the expense of another criteria (tradeoff). Section 6.2 discussed the problem of two-level logic size minimization, introducing K-maps as a visual method and an automatable tabular method, and then describing automatable heuristics for two-level as well as multilevel logic size minimization. Section 6.3 discussed methods for optimization and tradeoffs in designing sequential logic, including state minimization, state encoding, and Moore versus Mealy type FSMs. Section 6.4 highlighted several alternative methods for implementing some datapath components, including a faster adder using carry-lookahead, and a smaller multiplier using sequential multiplication. Section 6.5 described methods for RTL optimizations and tradeoffs, including the powerful concepts of pipelining and concurrency as means of achieving good performance, which is a key purpose of digital design. The section also described the RTL methods of component allocation, operator binding, and operator scheduling. Section 6.6 briefly surveyed some higher-level methods, including the general idea of serial versus concurrent computation, and the selection of efficient algorithms. The section also introduced some basic concepts of power reduction, including clock gating, and the use of low-power gates.

As can be seen from this chapter, there are many methods for improving designs. Yet, this chapter just scratched the surface of such methods. An entire multibillion-dollar-per-year industry exists that specializes in making automated tools for converting behavioral descriptions of desired system functionality into highly optimized circuit implementations—that industry is known as electronic design automation (EDA) or as computer-aided design (CAD). This chapter hopefully gave enough exposure at least to understand the basic idea behind circuit optimization at various levels of design abstraction, ranging from the gate level up to the RTL level and beyond.

▶ 6.9 EXERCISES

SECTION 6.1: INTRODUCTION

6.1 Define the terms "optimization" and "tradeoff."

6.2 A homeowner wishes to increase the amount of light inside the house during the day, with the only criteria of interest being the amount of light and the cost of electricity. Describe how to increase the light via: (a) an optimization, (b) a tradeoff.

SECTION 6.2: COMBINATIONAL LOGIC OPTIMIZATIONS AND TRADEOFFS

6.3 Perform two-level logic size optimization for $F(a,b,c) = ab'c + abc + a'bc + abc'$ using (a) algebraic methods, (b) a K-map. Express the answers in sum-of-products form.

6.4 Perform two-level logic size optimization for $F(a,b,c) = a + a'b'c + a'c$ using a K-map.

6.5 Perform two-level logic size optimization for $F(a,b,c,d) = a'bc' + abc'd' + abd$ using a K-map.

6.6 Perform two-level logic size optimization $F(a,b,c,d) = ab + a'b'd'$ using a K-map.

6.7 Perform two-level logic size optimization for $F(a,b,c) = a'b'c + abc$, assuming input combinations $a'bc$ and $ab'c$ can never occur (those two minterms represent don't cares).

6.8 Perform two-level logic size optimization for $F(a,b,c,d) = a'bc'd + ab'cd'$, assuming that a and b can never both be 1 at the same time, and that c and d can never both be 1 at the same time (i.e., there are don't cares).

6.9 Consider the function $F(a,b,c) = a'c + ac + a'b$. Using a K-map: (a) Determine which of the following terms are implicants (but not necessarily prime implicants) of the equation: $a'b'c'$, $a'b'$, $a'bc$, $a'c$, c, bc, $a'bc'$, $a'b$. (b) Determine which of those terms are prime implicants of the function.

6.10 For the function $F(a,b,c) = a'c + ac + a'b$, determine all prime implicants and all essential prime implicants: (a) using a K-map, (b) using the tabular method.

6.11 For the equation $F(a,b,c,d) = ab'c' + abc'd + abcd + a'bcd + a'bcd'$, determine all prime implicants and all essential prime implicants: (a) using a K-map, (b) using the tabular method.

6.12 Use repeated application of the expand operation to heuristically minimize the equation $F(a,b,c) = a'b'c + a'bc + abc$. (a) Try expanding each term for each variable. (b) Instead, determine a way to randomly choose an expand operation, and then apply 5 random expands.

6.13 Use repeated application of the expand operation to heuristically minimize the equation $F(a,b,c,d,e) = abcde + abcde' + abcd'e'$. (a) Try expanding each term for each variable. (b) Instead, determine a way to randomly choose an expand operation, and then apply 5 random expands.

6.14 Using algebraic methods, reduce the number of gate inputs for the following equation by creating a multilevel circuit: $F(a,b,c,d,e,f,g) = abcde + abcd'e'fg + abcd'e'f'g'$. Assume only AND, OR, and NOT gates will be used. Draw the circuit for the original equation and for the multilevel circuit, and clearly list the delay and number of gate inputs for each circuit.

SECTION 6.3: SEQUENTIAL LOGIC OPTIMIZATIONS AND TRADEOFFS

6.15 Reduce the number of states for the FSM in Figure 6.88 using the partitioning method.

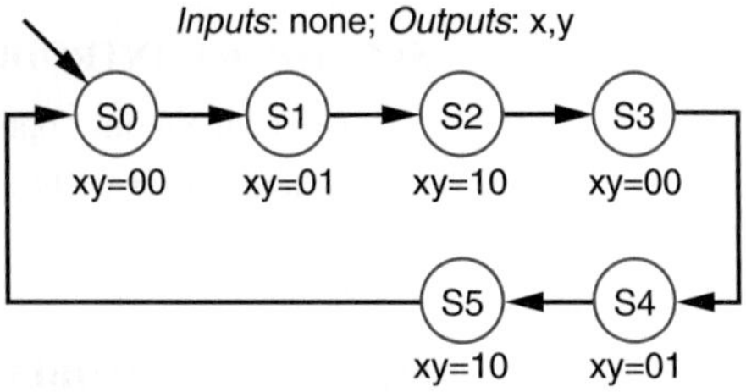

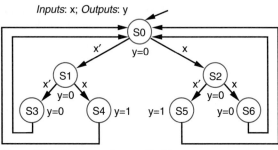

Figure 6.88 FSM example.

6.16 Reduce the number of states for the FSM in Figure 6.89 using the partitioning method.

6.17 Reduce the number of states for the FSM in Figure 6.90 using the partitioning method.

6.18 Compare the logic size (number of gate inputs) and the delay (number of gate-delays) of a straightforward 2-bit binary encoding of the FSM in Figure 6.91 using a 3-bit output encoding versus using a one-hot encoding.

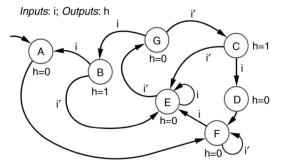

Figure 6.89 Sequence detector for bit patterns 01 and 10.

6.19 Compare the logic size (number of gate inputs) and the delay (number of gate-delays) of a minimal bitwidth state encoding versus an output encoding for the laser-based distance measurer FSM shown in Figure 5.26.

Figure 6.90 FSM example.

6.20 Compare the logic size (number of gate inputs) and the delay (number of gate-delays) of a minimum binary encoding, an output encoding (if it is possible; if not, indicate why not), and a one-hot encoding of the laser timer FSM in Figure 3.47.

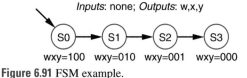

Figure 6.91 FSM example.

6.21 Convert the Moore FSM for the code detector circuit shown in Figure 3.58 to the nearest Mealy FSM equivalent.

6.22 Convert the Moore FSM in Figure 6.92 to the nearest Mealy FSM equivalent.

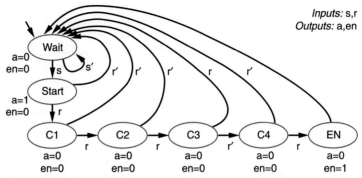

Figure 6.92 FSM example.

6.23 Convert the Mealy FSM in Figure 6.93 to the nearest Moore equivalent.

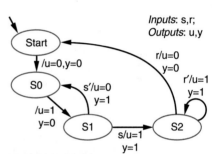

Figure 6.93 FSM example.

6.24 Convert the Mealy FSM in Figure 6.94 to the nearest Moore equivalent.

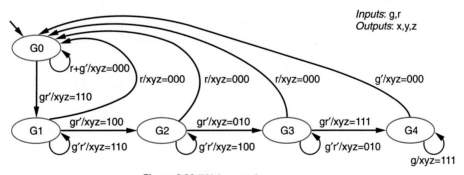

Figure 6.94 FSM example.

SECTION 6.4: DATAPATH COMPONENT TRADEOFFS

6.25 Trace the execution of the 4-bit carry-lookahead adder shown in Figure 6.57 when a = 11 (eleven) and b = 7. Show all the input and output values of the SPG blocks and of the carry-lookahead block initially and after each relevant number of gate delays.

6.26 Trace the execution of the 4-bit carry-lookahead adder shown in Figure 6.57 when a = 5 and b = 4. Show all the input and output values of the SPG blocks and of the carry-lookahead block initially and after each relevant number of gate delays.

6.27 Trace the execution of the 16-bit carry-lookahead adder built from 4-bit adders as shown in Figure 6.60 when a = 43690 and b = 21845. Do not trace internal behavior of the individual 4-bit carry-lookahead adders.

6.28 (a) Design a 64-bit hierarchical carry-lookahead adder using 4-bit carry-lookahead adders. (b) What is the total delay through the 64-bit adder? (c) What is the speedup of the carry-lookahead adder compared to a 64-bit carry-ripple adder; compute speedup as (slower time)/ (faster time).

6.29 Design a 24-bit hierarchical carry-lookahead adder using 4-bit carry-lookahead adders.

6.30 Design a 16-bit carry-select adder using 4-bit carry-ripple adders.

SECTION 6.5: RTL DESIGN OPTIMIZATIONS AND TRADEOFFS

6.31 The adder tree shown in Figure 6.95 is used to compute the sum of eight inputs on every clock cycle, where the sum is S = R + T + U + V + W + X + Y + Z. (a) Design a pipelined version of the adder tree to maximize the frequency at which the clock input can operate. (b) Create a timing diagram of the pipelined tree circuit showing the values of pipeline registers and the output register for the following input values: R=1, T=2, U=3, V=4, W=5, X=6, Y=7, and Z=8. (c) If the delay

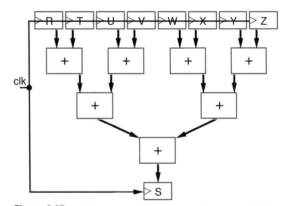

Figure 6.95 Adder tree used to compute the sum of eight inputs every clock cycle.

of an adder is 3 ns, compare the fastest clock frequency of the original circuit versus the pipelined circuit. (d) Again assuming 3 ns adders, compare the fastest latency and throughput values for the original circuit versus the pipelined circuit.

6.32 (a) Convert the C-like code of Figure 6.96 to a high-level state machine. Ignore overflow. (b) Use the RTL design process shown in Table 5.1 to convert the HLSM to a controller and a datapath. Design the datapath to structure, but design the controller to the point of an FSM only. (c) Redesign the datapath to allow for concurrency in which four multiplications and two additions can be performed concurrently. Assume memory ports can be introduced as needed. (d) Assuming a multiplier delay is 4 ns and an adder delay is 2 ns, list the fastest clock period, latency, and throughput for the original design and for the more concurrent design, assuming the critical path is in the datapath. (e) Introduce more multipliers or adders and pipeline registers as needed to further improve the speed of the design, and compare the clock period, throughput, and latency with the previous two designs.

```
Inputs: byte a[256], b[256]
Outputs: byte sum, byte c[256]
MULT:
int i=0;
int sum = 0;
while( i < 256 ) {
  c[i] = a[i] * b[i];
  sum = sum + c[i];
  i++;
}
```

Figure 6.96 C-like code.

6.33 (a)Convert the C-like code in Figure 6.97 to a high-level state machine. Ignore overflow. (b) Use the RTL design process shown in Table 5.1 to convert the HLSM to a controller and a datapath. Design the datapath to structure, but design the controller to the point of an FSM only. (c) Redesign your datapath to allow for concurrency in which three comparisons, three additions, and three multiplications can be performed concurrently.

```
Inputs: byte a[256], byte b[256], byte cy
Output: byte sumx, byte sumy, byte c[256]
MULT_OR_ADD:
int i=0;
int sumx = 0;
int sumy = 0;
while( i < 256 ) {
  if( a[i] > 128 ) {
    c[i] = a[i] * b[i];
    sumx = sumx + c[i];
  }
  else {
    c[i] = a[i] * (b[i] + cy);
    sumy = sumy + c[i];
  }
  i++;
}
```

Figure 6.97 C-like code.

6.34 Redesign the datapath and controller designed in Exercise 6.33 by allowing up to nine concurrent additions and inserting pipeline registers, updating the controller as necessary. Assuming a comparator has a delay of 4 ns, an adder has a delay of 3 ns, and a multiplier has a delay of 20 ns, how long will the circuit take to finish its computation?

6.35 Given the HLSM in Figure 6.98, create two different designs: one optimized for minimum circuit speed and the other optimized for minimum circuit size. Be sure to clearly indicate the component allocation, operator binding, and operator scheduling used to design the two circuits.

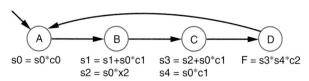

s0 = s0*c0 s1 = s1+s0*c1 s3 = s2+s0*c1 F = s3*s4*c2
          s2 = s0*x2   s4 = s0*c1

Figure 6.98 High-level state machine for Exercise 6.39.

SECTION 6.6: MORE ON OPTIMIZATIONS AND TRADEOFFS

6.36 Trace through the execution of the binary search algorithm when searching for the number 86 in the following sorted list of 15 numbers: 1, 10, 25, 62, 74, 75, 80, 84, 85, 86, 87, 100, 106, 111, 121. How many comparisons were required to find the number using the binary search and how many comparisons would have been required using a linear search?

6.37 Trace through the execution of the binary search algorithm when searching for the number 99 in the following list of 15 numbers: 1, 10, 25, 62, 74, 75, 80, 84, 85, 87, 99, 100, 106, 111, 121. How many comparisons were required to look for the number using the binary search and how many comparisons are required using a linear search?

6.38 Trace through the execution of the binary search algorithm when searching for the number 121 in the list of numbers from the previous example. How many comparisons were required to find the number using the binary search and how many comparisons are required using a linear search?

6.39 Using the list of 15 numbers from Exercise 6.37, how many numbers can be found faster using a linear search algorithm compared with the binary search algorithm?

6.40 Given the logic gate library in Figure 6.99, optimize the circuit in Figure 6.100 by reducing power consumption without increasing the circuit's delay.

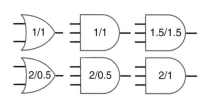

Figure 6.99 Logic gate library. 2/0.5 format means 2 ns delay/0.5 nw power.

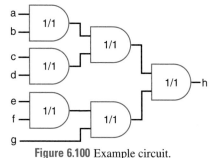

Figure 6.100 Example circuit.

6.41 Given the logic gates shown in Figure 6.99, optimize the circuit in Figure 6.101 by reducing power consumption without increasing the circuit's delay.

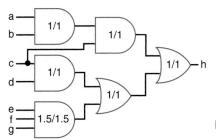

Figure 6.101 Example circuit.

6.42 Given the logic gates shown in Figure 6.99, optimize the circuit in Figure 6.102 by reducing power consumption without increasing the circuit's delay.

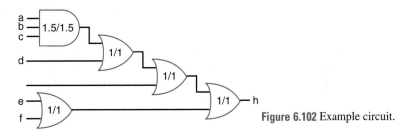

Figure 6.102 Example circuit.

6.43 Given the logic gates shown in Figure 6.99, optimize the circuit in Figure 6.103 by reducing power consumption without increasing the circuit's delay.

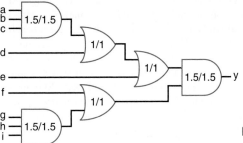

Figure 6.103 Example circuit.

Smita has degrees in Electronics Engineering and in Computer Science, and has worked in the digital design field for nearly a decade. She spent a lot of time thinking about the choice of a college major. "What major should I invest my focus, energy, heart, and soul for what will be some of the most productive years of my life?" She chose engineering, for several reasons. "First, engineering is a career in itself—unlike some other majors, jobs specifically for engineering majors are out there. With engineering, I would learn the most valuable and universal of skills: problem solving. Second, engineers have many options, because engineers are highly valued for their problem solving skills by other professions, such as management consulting, marketing, and investment banking. And electrical and computer engineers can choose from a range of industries in which to work: telecommunications, image processing, medical devices, IC fabrication, and even banking. This was a phenomenal discovery for me!"

Smita continued her education by doing graduate studies in Computer Science, researching methods for automatically designing integrated circuits (IC) or chips—"a fascinating field because it involves a mix of hardware and software skills and knowledge. I continued in this profession after school and worked for a company that develops computer-aided design (CAD) software used by hardware designers who work with a type of chip called an FPGA (field programmable gate array). FPGAs can be used for an amazing variety of applications all the way from high-speed telecommunication chips to low-speed and low-cost chips that go into electronic toys and games. Our software saves designers many months or even years of time. In fact, without our software, it would be absolutely impossible for people to design most chips even if they had a decade or more to do it."

Smita (shown mountain climbing above) loves her work. "My work is intellectually stimulating, and I have an opportunity to innovate, create, and actually build something really useful." She also enjoys the people-aspect of her work. "I work in teams of dynamic people because most projects, hardware or software, are done in teams of 3–8 people these days. The people on my team

are also my friends, and it's a lot of fun to work with them."

In her decade of work so far, Smita has taken on some management responsibilities. "As manager of one of the four products that my company develops, I play a variety of different roles. I work with my team of 7 software developers to determine what features to build in the product and how best to build those features. I work with the marketing and sales team to understand what the customers need and how best to message and position our product. Finally, I work with other groups that are involved in releasing a product — technical publications, application engineering, and product engineering. The diversity of my job makes it very interesting.

Smita enjoys the respect that engineers receive. "As an engineer, I am highly respected by customers, partner companies, and by our marketing and sales organizations because I have a deep understanding of our products. I really know my stuff since I built it, and I get recognized for it." And regarding the pay: "I get compensated very well for my skills." She also likes the lifestyle: "I get in to work around 10 a.m. and leave around 7 p.m. I don't have early morning meetings unlike the folks in marketing and sales, and I can work from home once a week or more often if I wish. This is also a great career for women—I can take time off and return to my job without much penalty when I have children. I can tailor my work hours as I need as my children are growing up. Lastly, I realize that I can move from engineering to other functions such as marketing and sales, but not the other way around! That's a great benefit of being an engineer—more options."

Smita recommends that engineering and computer science students focus on certain things while in college.

"First, get a good understanding of both hardware and software. Systems are highly integrated today, and there are very few companies that develop one without paying very close attention to the other. For instance, though I write software, I need to completely understand the hardware for which it will be used. My husband, on the other hand, designs telecommunication chips but works very closely with his software team, especially during the initial design stages when they decide what to implement in hardware versus software and how to design the hardware interface so that the software algorithms work efficiently.

"So, what do I mean by a good understanding of hardware and software? In software, I think it is most important to develop good software 'habits.' Treat your program like a well-landscaped garden—you want it to be beautiful and weed-free. Understand data structures well, and know when one is more appropriate than the other. Organize your code, be disciplined, cross the Ts and dot the Is, document diligently, have your code reviewed by friends, and finally, don't be afraid to throw away code and rewrite it if you discover a better way.

"In hardware, understand the basics of logic design and then make sure you also understand the capacitive, inductive, and resistive properties of circuits since these play a big role in designing the high-speed circuits of today.

"Other than these hardware and software skills, become adept at math and analysis. Learn to frame problems and break them down until you can solve them. Be experimental and try different tools and methods. Have a hypothesis and then go about proving or disproving it. If you haven't already, you will soon discover that engineering is not only fun, but also provides you with many fulfilling career opportunities—so stick with it and make the most of it!"

CHAPTER 7

Physical Implementation on ICs

▶ 7.1 INTRODUCTION

A digital circuit design that has been created but just drawn, perhaps with pencil on paper or as a figure in this book, is merely a drawing. Designers must eventually implement that circuit on a real physical device, so that the device can be placed in an electronic product to carry out the desired function. In other words, how do designers get from Figure 7.1(a), the seat belt warning light circuit that was designed in Chapter 2, to Figure 7.1(b), a physical implementation?

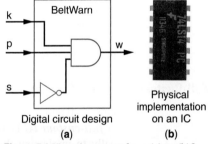

Digital circuit design
(a)

Physical implementation on an IC
(b)

Figure 7.1 How do we get from (a) to (b)?

Most digital circuits today are physically implemented using an integrated circuit device. An *integrated circuit*, or *IC*, refers to a piece of semiconductor material (typically silicon) existing inside of a package (typically plastic) like the package of Figure 7.1(b), with all the components of the circuit being integrated on the surface of the silicon. Such integration is in contrast to those components existing as separate components on a board—hence the term "integrated circuit." Because the piece of silicon is cut ("chipped") from a larger wafer of silicon, an IC is commonly referred to as a *chip*.

Designers can implement a circuit using a variety of available IC types. An *IC type* is a category of IC having specific features. Important features that distinguish IC types are the time and cost required to implement the circuit using that IC type, or in the speed, size, power consumption, and cost of the resulting IC. An analogy can be made with the various available car types, such as a sports car versus a family sedan; a sports car is faster but more expensive. Importantly, IC types differ in the steps required to convert a circuit into an implementation—those steps are known as the *design flow*. For example, Figure 7.2 shows that designers might use an IC type like a full-custom IC or an ASIC (soon to be described) whose design flow requires that the designers spend millions of dollars and several months to manufacture a chip optimized for their circuit, or designers might use an IC type that is premade and that they can program in minutes. This chapter describes and compares several popular IC types for implementing digital circuits, including full-custom ICs, standard cell ICs, gate array ICs, FPGAs, PLDs, and logic ICs.

413

Figure 7.2 Common design flows for different IC types: (a) digital designers first create a desired circuit, (b) some IC types, like full-custom ICs or ASICs, involve manufacturing a new IC, requiring millions of dollars and many months, (c) a programmable IC type is premade and available off-the-shelf, costing tens of dollars and requiring just minutes, but resulting in bigger and slower circuit implementations.

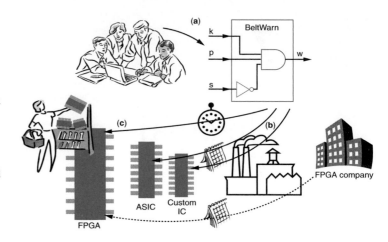

▶ 7.2 MANUFACTURED IC TYPES

If designers are willing to wait months for a physical implementation of a digital circuit, and to spend millions of dollars for that physical implementation, then those designers might consider implementing the circuit using one of several IC types that require the manufacturing of a new IC.

Full-Custom Integrated Circuits

One IC type is known as a full-custom IC. A *full-custom IC* is a chip created specifically to implement the gates (actually, the transistors) of the desired circuit. The design flow for a full-custom IC is shown in Figure 7.3. Digital designers don't usually build full-custom ICs themselves, but rather they send the desired circuit to a group or company whose engineers specialize in transforming digital circuits into full-custom ICs.

Those engineers, assisted by computer-aided design (CAD) tools, convert the desired digital circuit design into a circuit of transistors, and decide where to place each transistor on the surface of the chip, how to orient each transistor (e.g.,

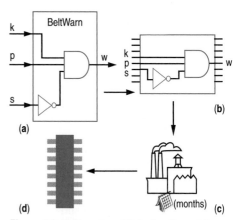

Figure 7.3 Full-custom IC design flow: (a) desired circuit, (b) custom layout of gates and wires, (c) fabrication, (d) IC obtained.

left to right, right to left, top to bottom, etc.), how big to make each transistor, how to place the wires that connect the transistors, and so on. All that information about how the transistors and wires should be layed out on a chip's surface is known as a *layout*. The full-custom IC engineers then send that layout information to a factory that specializes in

A 2006 Samsung fab in Texas cost $3.5 billion; fabs typically cost from $1 billion to over $10 billion.

fabricating ICs, known as a fabrication plant, or **fab** for short. Fabricating an IC is a complex error-prone process utilizing state-of-the-art photographic, laser, and chemical equipment that each can cost hundreds of millions of dollars. The transistors and wires are formed as dozens of **layers** on the surface of a chip; the lower layers define the transistors and connections within logic gates, while the upper layers define the wires that exist between gates. An IC may have tens of layers. Each layer requires a set of **masks** that allow light to reach specific regions of the chip to modify chemicals on the chip surface during the formation of layers. This cost for creating the masks required for IC fabrication is known as **nonrecurring engineering (NRE) cost**. The cost is called non-recurring because it occurs once, before chips are made, and then does not recur, no matter how many chips are subsequently manufactured. Because a full-custom IC type requires masks to be made for every layer of the chip, the NRE cost for a full-custom IC type is very high, typically tens of millions dollars. The NRE cost can be recouped by adding some amount to the selling price of each chip manufactured. Thus, if a particular IC will have 10,000,000 copies made and sold, and the NRE costs totalled $100,000,000, then $10 could be added to the selling price of each chip to recoup the NRE cost.

The time spent waiting for an IC to be manufactured also contributes to cost. In particular, the setup of the layout and masks takes months. During that time, the product for which designers are manufacturing the chip may be losing market share to a competing product already being sold while the designers wait for their chip to be fabricated, translating to lost revenue, which can be thought of as a cost too—"time is money."

The high cost of the full-custom IC type can be further increased due to what are known as respins. Fabricating an IC is referred to as a silicon **spin**, named from the way that the silicon is melted and then spun before slicing the hardened silicon into wafers and then into chips. Because all the chip's layers are custom designed, the probability is high that engineers or tools will make a mistake somewhere in the transistors or wiring, such as placing two transistors too close together, resulting in interference. Therefore, after fabricating a full-custom IC, designers commonly find errors that necessitate refabricating the IC, known as a **respin** (pronounced as "ree-spin"). Respins may happen two or three times or more, each time incuring some additional NRE cost and requiring weeks or months per respin, possibly losing more market share and thus costing even more.

According to one survey, only about 10% of 2002 digital circuits were implemented as custom ICs.

Needless to say, full-custom IC fabrication is uncommon. Designers choose to implement a digital circuit on a full-custom IC when they absolutely require the IC type's small size, low power, or high performance, and when they can recoup the NRE costs due to high volumes, such as chips found inside calculators, wristwatches, mobile phones, or desktop PCs. Alternatively, designers may use a full-custom IC if cost is not tightly constrained but maximum performance is a high priority, as might be the case in military or space applications.

Semicustom (Application-Specific) Integrated Circuits—ASICs

Because physical implementation on full-custom ICs is so costly and time-consuming, semicustom IC types evolved during the 1980s and 1990s to reduce the costs and the time of fabricating a chip. These types are known as **application-specific integrated circuits**, or **ASICs**. An ASIC is somewhat customized, hence the term *semicustom*, and the customization is specific for a particular circuit application, hence the term *application-*

specific. The distinction is akin to that between full-custom and semicustom houses: The former involves custom-designing every aspect of a house and is thus expensive, time-consuming, and rare, while the latter involves adjusting a basic design (e.g., choosing between a larger family room or an additional bedroom) and is thus less costly, faster to build, and far more common. Two common ASIC types are *standard cell* and *gate array*.

Standard Cell ASIC

Standard cell is an ASIC type that reduces physical implementation NRE cost and manufacturing time compared to full-custom ICs. **Standard cell ASICs**, sometimes called **cell-based ASICs**, use a collection (known as a **library**) of previously layed-out gates or pieces of logic, called *cells*, that must be instantiated and connected with wires to implement a circuit.

A cell might be a 2-input AND gate, a 2x1 mux, or a combination of gates like two 2-input AND gates connected to an OR gate connected to an inverter (called an AND-OR-INVERT, or AOI, cell). All cells are typically the same *standard* height (hence

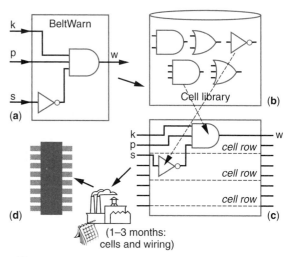

Figure 7.4 Standard cell ASIC design flow: (a) desired circuit, (b) cell library, (c) standard cell layout, (d) IC created by fabricating the cells and wires.

the term *standard cells*), meaning they occupy the same vertical space in Figure 7.4(c), so cells can be placed in standard-height rows on a chip. A standard cell ASIC company pre-designs the layout for each cell, resulting in a collection or "library" of cell designs (the library exists in computer files). The seat belt warning light circuit in Figure 7.4(a) can be implemented as a standard cell ASIC by choosing appropriate cells from a cell library as in Figure 7.4(b), instantiating and wiring those cells as in Figure 7.4(c), and fabricating an IC as in Figure 7.4(d).

Designers themselves don't typically choose standard cells and map their circuits onto those cells. Rather, automated tools convert the desired digital circuits into standard cells and output results in data files that are processed by fabs to control the fabrication process.

A typical cell library might contain hundreds or thousands of cells; the cell library shown in Figure 7.4(b), having just five cells, is *trivially small and for illustrative purposes only*. A typical standard cell ASIC may have millions of cells, not just a few as in the figure.

Compared to the full-custom IC type, the standard cell IC type is less optimized, because the cells are restricted in their size and variety, and their placement is restricted to predetermined standard-height rows. But standard cell ASICs require less NRE cost and time, because no transistor-level design or layout is necessary, as those were done beforehand by the standard cell company. Furthermore, respins, though still occuring, are less frequent than with full-custom ICs.

The task of converting a desired digital circuit into a circuit using only components from a particular library (e.g., a particular standard cell library) is known as ***technology mapping***. The task of determining where to place those components on a chip is known as ***placement***, and the task of connecting those components by wires is known as ***routing***. All three tasks are collectively known as ***physical design***, and are typically carried out today by automated tools.

Example 7.1 Implementing a half-adder using standard cells

Using the standard cell library in Figure 7.4, this example implements a half-adder on a standard cell ASIC. Recall that the equations for a half-adder are: $co = ab$, and $s = a'b + ab'$. Thus, the half-adder can be implemented using two inverter cells, three 2-input AND cells, and one 2-input OR cell from the library.

The half-adder can be implemented using cells as shown in Figure 7.5, assuming each cell row can hold at most three cells.

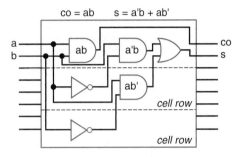

Figure 7.5 Half-adder on standard cells.

Gate Arrays (Structured ASICs)

A standard cell ASIC, while having lower NRE and involving less time than full-custom ICs, must still have all its layers fabricated. A ***gate array*** ASIC involves a chip whose transistors are *predesigned* to form rows ("arrays") of logic gates on the chip, as shown in Figure 7.6(b), meaning that only the wires remain to be fabricated. Creating the wires represents just the last steps of fabrication, and thus gate array technology eliminates much of the time and cost of fabricating a chip for a particular circuit. A gate array company predesigns and mass-produces the gate array chip. When a client wants a circuit on an IC, the company then customizes some of those

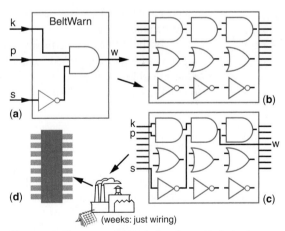

Figure 7.6 Gate array ASIC design flow: (a) desired circuit, (b) gate array before wires are added, (c) gate array after wires are added, thus implementing the desired circuit, (d) IC created by fabricating the wires. Note: real gate array ICs have millions of gates.

chips for the client's circuit by fabricating the metal layers. Figure 7.6 illustrates how the seat belt warning light desired circuit in Figure 7.6(a) might be implemented using the gate array chip in Figure 7.6(b) consisting of a row of 2-input AND gates, a row of 2-input OR gates, and a row of inverters. Figure 7.6(c) shows how to map the desired circuit's 3-input AND gate using two of the gate array's available 2-input AND gates, and how to map the desired inverter to one of the gate array inverters. The figure also shows how the desired wiring among the gate array's pins, the gate array AND gate, and the gate array inverter, might be implemented. The remaining gates and pins on the gate array chip would be unutilized. Fabricating those wires would result in the IC being customized to the seat belt application (Figure 7.6(d)).

The actual mapping of the desired circuit to a gate array would typically be carried out by an automated tool. Designers almost never carry out that mapping manually, and in fact usually don't see that mapping in any form—the mapping is all done by tools, resulting in large data files that can be processed by other tools at a fab to create the necessary masks and to control the fabrication process.

A typical gate array chip may hold *millions of gates*; the gate array shown in Figure 7.6, having about ten gates, is trivially small and is for illustration purposes only—*gate arrays with only 10 gates do not exist*. For designs with only a few gates, logic ICs or PLDs, described in Section 7.4, might be used instead.

Compared to standard cell ASICs, gate array ASICs involve less NRE and require less time. However, gate array ASICs are less optimized. Comparing Figure 7.4(c) and Figure 7.6(c) illustrates that standard cell ASIC flexibility of choosing and placing cells results in a more compact design, with fewer gates and fewer wires, than gate array ASICs. Notice that the gate array implementation in Figure 7.6 utilizes an extra level of logic than the original circuit, has longer wires, and has wasted area due to unused gates and pins. 3x to 5x speed and size differences between standard cells and gate arrays are common.

In the 2000s, the term **structured ASIC** began to replace the term "gate array" in practice. A structured ASIC usually supplements arrays of gates with other components on the chip, such as microprocessors, RAMs, and other higher-level system building blocks. The term **platform ASIC** is also sometimes used.

Example 7.2 Implementing a half-adder on a gate array

This example implements a half-adder circuit on the gate array chip of Figure 7.6. Recall that the equations for a half-adder circuit are: co = ab, and s = a'b + ab'. Thus, one AND gate is needed for co, and two inverters, two AND gates, and one OR gate for s. The gate array chip in Figure 7.6 has three AND gates, three OR gates, and three inverters, so the chip has enough gates to implement the desired circuit.

The implementation of the half-adder circuit on the gate array chip as shown in Figure 7.7.

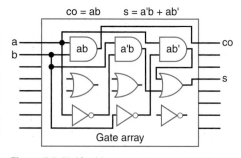

Figure 7.7 Half-adder on a gate array ASIC.

Implementing Circuits Using Only NAND Gates

Recall from Chapter 2 that CMOS transistors more efficiently implement NAND and NOR gates rather than AND and OR gates. The underlying reason was that pMOS transistors conduct 1s well but not 0s, while nMOS transistors conduct 0s well but not 1s. Therefore, gate arrays typically contain NAND or NOR gates rather than AND and OR gates, and standard cell circuits are more efficient if implemented using NAND or NOR cells rather than AND and OR cells. Furthermore, creating a gate array is easier using just one type of gate, like just NANDs, or just NORs, rather than having to decide how many AND gates, OR gates, and NOT gates to pre-instantiate in the arrays. Thus, given the preference for NAND or NOR gates in CMOS ASIC types, a method is needed for converting AND/OR circuits to NAND circuits or to NOR circuits.

Fortunately, converting any AND/OR circuit to a NAND-only circuit is possible because NAND is a universal gate, as was mentioned in Section 2.8. A *universal gate* is a logic gate type that can implement any Boolean function using some number of gates of that one type only. One way to understand NAND's universality is to recognize that a NOT gate, an AND gate, or an OR gate can be implemented by substituting each gate with an equivalent circuit of NAND gates. Therefore any circuit of NOT, AND, or OR gates can be implemented using just NAND gates.

To implement a NOT gate using NAND gates, we can substitute the NOT gate with a two-input NAND gate having its two inputs tied together, as shown in Figure 7.8. The truth table in the figure shows that the NAND gate with its inputs tied together acts the same as an inverter. When the input x is 0, both inputs of the NAND gate are 0, causing the NAND gate to output 1. When the input x is 1, both inputs of the NAND gate are 1, causing the NAND gate to output 0.

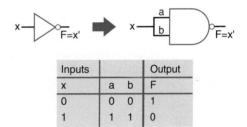

Inputs			Output
x	a	b	F
0	0	0	1
1	1	1	0

Figure 7.8 Implementing NOT using NAND.

An AND gate can be implemented using NAND gates by substituting the AND gate with a NAND gate followed by a NOT gate (implemented as a two-input NAND gate with its inputs tied together), as in Figure 7.9. This works because given inputs a and b, the first NAND computes (ab)', and then the NOT gate computes (ab)'' = ab, which is AND.

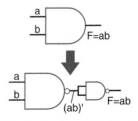

Figure 7.9 Implementing AND using NANDs.

An OR gate can be implemented using NAND gates by substituting the OR gate with a NAND gate having each input inverted (by 2-input NAND gates with inputs tied together), as in Figure 7.10. This works because given inputs a and b, the circuit of NAND gates in the figure computes `(a'b')'`. By DeMorgan's Law, that expression equals `a'' + b''`, which simplifies to a + b, which is OR.

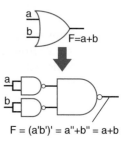

F = (a'b')' = a''+b'' = a+b

Figure 7.10 Implementing OR using NANDs.

When replacing a circuit originally having AND/OR/NOT gates by a circuit having only NAND gates using the above substitutions, some signals may get double-inverted—a signal feeds into an inverter and then immediately into another inverter. Double-inverting a signal yields the original signal, so double inversions can be replaced by a wire, as in Figure 7.11. Such elimination reduces the number of transistors and reduces a circuit's delay, without changing the circuit's function.

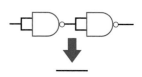

Figure 7.11 Double inversion becomes a wire.

Example 7.3 Implementing a half-adder's sum circuit using only NAND gates

Figure 7.12(a) shows the sum circuit for a half-adder (see Section 4.3), using AND, OR, and NOT gates. We can implement that circuit using only NAND gates by substituting each gate with an equivalent NAND circuit, as shown in Figure 7.12(b).

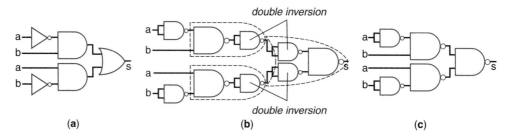

(a)   (b)   (c)

Figure 7.12 Implementing a half-adder's sum circuit using NAND gates only: (a) original AND/OR/NOT circuit, (b) circuit obtained after substituting equivalent NAND circuits for each gate, (c) circuit after eliminating double inversions.

After the substitutions, note that there are two signals that are double-inverted. Eliminating the double inversions results in the circuit shown in Figure 7.12(c).

When converting AND/OR/NOT circuits to NAND circuits by hand, some people find it easier to simply draw inversion bubbles rather than the NAND-based inverters, as shown in Figure 7.13. Then, double inversion bubbles on a signal cancel each other. Any remaining isolated inversion bubbles become a NAND-based NOT gate. Thus, the circuit in Figure 7.13, which uses inversion bubbles, would end up identical to the circuit in Figure 7.12(c).

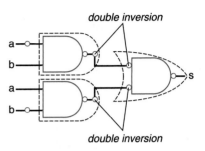

Figure 7.13 Drawing inverters as inversion bubbles during conversion to NAND.

If NAND gates with only a specific number of inputs are available, such as NAND gates with 2 inputs being the only gates available, then we can first modify the AND/OR circuit to use only 2-input AND/OR gates. Such conversion is done by composing larger AND and OR gates from smaller AND and OR gates, respectively, as discussed in Section 5.10. After the conversion to smaller gates, the conversion to NAND gates can proceed as described earlier.

Implementing Circuits Using Only NOR Gates

Converting AND/OR/NOT circuits to NOR gate circuits is similar to converting to NAND circuits, because a NOR gate is also a universal gate. The process of transforming a circuit into NOR gates replaces each AND, OR, and NOT gate with the equivalent NOR-based circuits shown in Figure 7.14. A NOT gate can be replaced with a two-input NOR gate with the inputs tied together. An OR gate is replaced with a NOR gate followed by an inverter, yielding $(a+b)''= a+b$. An AND gate is replaced with a NOR gate having inverted inputs, yielding $(a'+b')' = a''*b'' = ab$ (notice the use of DeMorgan's Law).

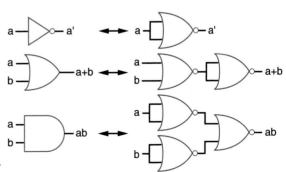

Figure 7.14 NOR gate equivalencies.

Example 7.4 Implementing a half-adder's sum circuit using only NOR gates

An earlier example implemented a half-adder's sum output using NAND gates; this example instead uses NOR gates. The half-adder's sum circuit is shown again in Figure 7.15(a). Each NOT, AND, and OR gate is replaced by its equivalent NOR circuit in Figure 7.15(b), using inversion bubbles instead of NOR-based NOT gates for convenience.

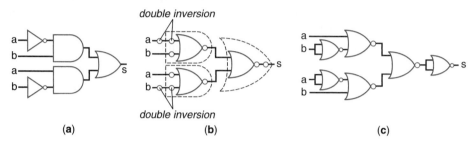

(a) (b) (c)

Figure 7.15 Implementing an AND/OR/NOT circuit using NORs only: (a) original circuit, (b) circuit obtained by substituting AND/OR/NOT gates with equivalent NOR circuits, using inversion bubbles for ease of drawing, (c) final circuit after eliminating double inversions and replacing standalone inversion bubbles with NOR-based NOT gates.

We eliminate double inversions, and replace stand-alone inversion bubbles by NOR-based NOT gates, as shown in Figure 7.15(c)

The half-adder's sum circuit was implemented with fewer NAND gates than NOR gates. Depending on the original circuit, the reverse could be true. NAND gates are well-suited to circuits in the sum-of-products form. NOR gates are well-suited to circuits in product-of-sums form (a level of OR gates feeding into a single AND gate).

Gate array and standard cell libraries typically include additional components, beyond just NAND or NOR gates, that have efficient CMOS implementations. For example, one popular such component is known as AND-OR-INVERT, or *AOI* for short. Such a component has two 2-input AND gates (thus four inputs total), feeding into a 2-input NOR gate. That circuit can be efficiently designed using CMOS transistors. Thus, a tool would strive to utilize AOI components, and other compact available components in a library, as much as possible to improve implementation performance and size.

Example 7.5 Implementing the seat belt warning light on a NOR-based gate array

This example implements the *BeltWarn* circuit of Figure 7.1(a) using the NOR-based gate array of Figure 7.16(a). Noticing that the gate array has only 2-input NOR gates, we first convert the *BeltWarn* circuit to use AND/OR gates with 2 inputs only, as shown in Figure 7.16(b). We then convert the AND/OR circuit to the NOR-only circuit in Figure 7.16(c), using the equivalencies in Figure

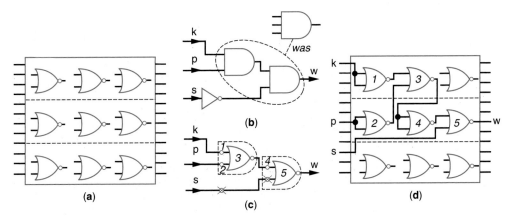

Figure 7.16 Implementing the *BeltWarn* circuit on a NOR-based gate array IC: (a) original gate array, (b)–(c) converting the desired circuit to two-input NOR gates only, (d) final gate array with wires.

7.14, and using inversion bubbles rather than NOR-based inverters. A double inversion exists on the wire from input s, so we eliminate those two inversions. Note that we do not eliminate the double inversion between points 3 and 4 in Figure 7.16(c), because the first inversion is part of a NOR gate—eliminating that first inversion would convert the NOR gate to an OR, defeating our goal of having NOR gates only.

After converting remaining standalone inversions to NOR-based inverters, we map the circuit to the gate array's 2-input NOR gates as in Figure 7.16(d)—we numbered the NOR gates of Figure 7.16(c) and (d) to show the correspondence between the two circuits.

▶ 7.3 OFF-THE-SHELF PROGRAMMABLE IC TYPE—FPGA

Manufactured IC types require at least a few weeks, and often several months, to convert a desired digital circuit design into a physical IC. What if a designer is developing a circuit that should be implemented *today*, or the designer simply does not wish to incur the NRE cost, complexity, and risk of manufacturing an IC? In those cases, the designer can use one of several off-the-shelf programmable IC types. An *off-the-shelf* IC is pre-manufactured and available for purchase, from a store or more commonly (in the case of ICs) by shipment from a vendor. A **programmable IC** is an off-the-shelf IC that implements a desired circuit simply by storing a particular sequence of bits into the IC's memory. Programmable ICs have the drawback of worse performance, size, and power compared to custom or semicustom manufactured ICs. However, the implementation on a programmable IC can be ready in just minutes, with no NRE cost or other complexities of manufacturing an IC, and these benefits may outweigh the drawbacks.

The most popular type of programmable IC is known as a *field-programmable gate array*, or *FPGA,* which consists of numerous configurable logic blocks and programmable interconnects, which shall be introduced shortly, that can be programmed to implement a desired circuit. An FPGA company prefabricates an FPGA chip, meaning that the chip contains all the transistors and all wires that the chip will ever have, likely using a full-custom IC type. A designer buys those FPGA chips, and then *programs* the chips to implement the desired circuit.

Figure 7.17 FPGA chips.

To *program* in this context means to download a series of bits into the chip's memories—not to be confused with writing high-level software programs like C or C++ code. Programming an FPGA occurs in the *field*, meaning in a designer's lab, or office, or home, as opposed to in a fabrication plant. Hence the words "field-programmable" in the name. Furthermore, programming typically takes only seconds, or perhaps minutes at most. Figure 7.17 shows some FPGA chips. The chip at the top, with its front and back shown, measures about three quarters of an inch on each side. The chip on the bottom is about 1 inch on each side.

Field-programmable gate arrays (FPGAs) have no "gate arrays" inside them—the name is there due to historical reasons.

The term "gate array" is there in the name because, when FPGAs first became popular in the mid-1980s, they were marketed as an alternative to the gate array IC type, which was very popular at that time. Thus, an FPGA was a semicustom IC (nearly synomous with "gate array" at that time) that could be programmed in the field instead of at a fabrication plant. However, be forewarned that the internal design of an FPGA chip looks nothing like a gate array—the naming is somewhat unfortunate.

The two basic types of components inside an FPGA are lookup tables and switch matrices. Those components are replicated thousands of times in regular patterns inside an FPGA. We now describe each type of component.

Lookup Tables

A basic idea underlying FPGAs is that *a memory can implement combinational logic*. More specifically, a 1-bit-wide memory with N address lines, and hence 2^N words, can implement any Boolean combinational function of N variables.

Recall that a memory configured to be read will output the contents of the word corresponding to the present address at the memory's address lines. So if a 4x1 memory's address lines a1a0 are 00, the memory will output the contents of word 0. If the address lines are 01, the memory outputs the contents of word 1. Likewise, 10 outputs word 2, and 11 outputs word 3.

The key idea underlying FPGAs is that a memory with N address lines can implement any combinational function with N inputs.

Implementing a Boolean function with a memory can therefore be done simply by connecting the function's inputs to the memory address lines, and storing a 0 or 1 in each memory word to match the desired function output value for each combination of input values. For example, consider the function F(x,y) = x'y' + xy. The truth table for the function is shown in Figure 7.18(a). To implement the example function, we can connect x and y to a 4x1 memory's address lines a1 and a0, respectively, and based on the truth table, we store a 1 in word 0, a 0 in word 1, a 0 in word 2, and a 1 in word 3—specifically, we

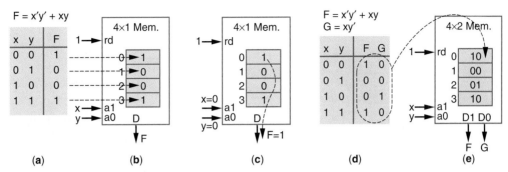

Figure 7.18 Implementing logic functions using a memory: (a) 2-input function truth table, (b) corresponding memory contents and connections, (c) the proper output appears for the given input values, (d) two functions having the same two inputs, (e) memory contents for the two functions.

store the truth table output values in the memory. The memory then implements the desired function, as shown in Figure 7.18(b). For example, when xy=00, we want the output to be 1. Figure 7.18(c) shows that when xy=00, the memory's address lines will be 00, and thus the memory will output the contents of word 0, which is the value 1, as desired.

A memory with *M* bits per word, rather than just 1 bit per word, can implement *M* functions that have the same inputs. For example, consider the two functions F(x,y) = x'y' + xy and G(x,y) = xy'. The truth table for these two functions is shown in Figure 7.17(d). A 4x2 memory, which has 2 bits per word, can implement those two functions, as shown in Figure 7.18(e).

A memory used to implement a combinational circuit is known in FPGA terminology as a ***lookup table***, or LUT. When used as a lookup table, a memory is typically referred to by the number of *inputs* (address lines) and the number of outputs (bits per word), rather than by the number of *words* and the number of outputs. For example, an 8x2 memory being used as a lookup table is referred to as a "3-input 2-output lookup table," rather than as an 8x2 lookup table. An FPGA typically consists of large numbers of same-sized LUTs.

From this point forward, we will assume the memory is configured for read, and thus we won't show the read line set to 1.

Example 7.6 Implementing the seat belt warning light with a lookup table

This example uses a lookup table to implement the seat belt warning light circuit from Figure 7.1, whose circuit appears in Figure 7.19(a) and whose equation is

$$w = kps'$$

We first generate the truth table for the function, which is shown in Figure 7.19(b). Because the circuit has three inputs, the circuit will require a 3-input 1-output lookup table (memory).

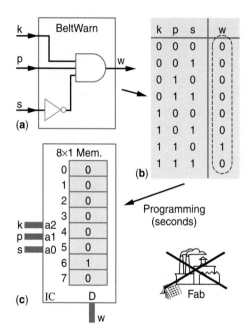

Figure 7.19 FPGA design flow: (a) desired circuit, (b) circuit's truth table, (c) implementing the truth table in an FPGA lookup table.

We connect the inputs to the memory's address lines, and store the truth table in the memory, as in Figure 7.19(c), thus implementing the desired function.

If the 3-input 1-output memory is an IC, then the implementation is complete, and we can insert the IC into the electronic system with which the IC should interact.

You've just seen an example of a very simple programmable IC—a memory. A memory chip with N address lines and hence 2^N words, and with M bits per word, can implement M different Boolean functions of the same N inputs. A designer can purchase a memory chip before it is needed in a design, and then the designer can "program" the memory chip to implement a desired Boolean function.

Mapping a Circuit among Multiple Lookup Tables

Unfortunately, using a memory to implement a Boolean function is inefficient for functions with numerous inputs. For example, while a 4-input function would need only a 16-word memory, a 12-input function would require a 4-Kword memory; a 32-input function would require a 4-billion-word memory. The needed memory size grows the same as the size of the function's truth table, which grows as 2^N, where N is the number of function inputs. In short, a truth table is *not* an efficient Boolean function representation for functions with numerous inputs, and thus a lookup table is not an efficient implementation for functions with numerous inputs. For example, the function F = abc + def + ghi, shown in Figure 7.20(a), has 9 inputs. Implementing the

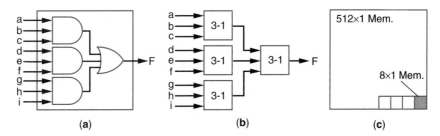

Figure 7.20 Dividing a many-input circuit among smaller lookup tables reduces total lookup table size: (a) a 9-input circuit, (b) the circuit mapped to four 3-input 1-output lookup tables, (c) the four 3-input 1-output lookup tables are much smaller than a 9-input 1-output lookup table.

function on a single lookup table would require a table with $2^9 = 512$ words. However, one can partition the circuit into subcircuits such that each subcircuit has 3 inputs and 1 output—the first subcircuit computes abc, the second def, the third ghi, and the fourth ORs the outputs of the first three subcircuits to generate the output F. Each subcircuit could be implemented using a 3-input 1-output lookup table (i.e., an 8x1 memory). The resulting implementation would have four 3-input 1-output lookup tables, as shown in Figure 7.20(b). The total words for that four-LUT implementation would be a mere $8 + 8 + 8 + 8 = 32$ words—far less than the 512 words required for a single 9-input lookup table. Figure 7.20(c) shows the relative sizes of one 512-word memory and four 8-word memories; the memory sizes are drawn to scale. Notice the reduction in size obtained by using multiple small lookup tables.

As a result, FPGAs typically contain large numbers of small lookup tables, rather than a small number of large lookup tables. Researchers have conducted numerous studies on thousands of typical circuits, and found that lookup tables with 3 to 6 inputs seem to be most efficient for most circuits. An FPGA typically has one size of LUT that is replicated thousands of times.

Therefore, a circuit being mapped to an FPGA must be partitioned into subcircuits such that each subcircuit can be mapped to one of the small lookup tables in an FPGA. Such partitioning is handled by tools and forms part of the *technology mapping* task for FPGAs; we'll consider such partitioning here to gain insight into the behavior of such tools. If an FPGA uses 3-input 1-output lookup tables, then the circuit must be partitioned into subcircuits each having 3 inputs (or less) and 1 output. For example, consider the circuit shown in Figure 7.21(a). That circuit can't be mapped to a 3-input 1-output lookup table because the circuit has 4 inputs. The circuit must therefore be partitioned into two sub-circuits, as shown by the dashed circles in Figure 7.21(b). The first subcircuit's output, labeled as t, computes t = abc. The second subcircuit's output computes F = t + de'. The circuits are mapped to two lookup tables as shown in Figure 7.21(c). The first lookup table is programmed to implement the first subcircuit, namely t = abc. Likewise, the second lookup table is programmed to implement the second subcircuit, namely F = t + de'. The two lookup tables with the shown connections thus implement the desired circuit.

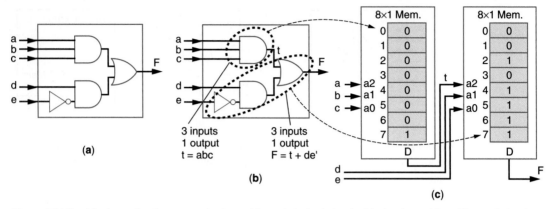

Figure 7.21 Partitioning a circuit onto two lookup tables: (a) desired circuit, (b) circuit partitioned into subcircuits with at most 3 inputs and 1 output, (c) subcircuits mapped to two 3-input 1-output lookup tables.

Example 7.7 Mapping a circuit to 3-input 1-output lookup tables

This example maps the circuit shown in Figure 7.22(a) onto a minimum number of 3-input 1-output lookup tables. The first step is to partition the circuit into subcircuits having three (or fewer) inputs and one output. Such a partitioning is shown in Figure 7.22(b). Subcircuit 1 has three inputs a, b, and c, and one output labeled t. Subcircuit 2 has three inputs c, e, and f, and one output labeled u. Subcircuit 3 has three inputs t, d, and u, and one output Y.

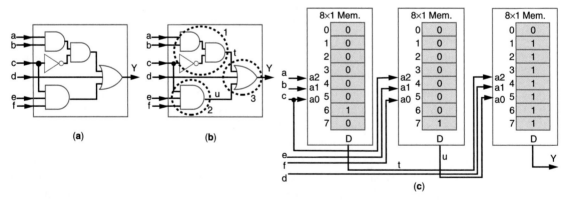

Figure 7.22 Mapping a circuit onto a minimum number of 3-input 1-output lookup tables: (a) desired circuit, (b) circuit partitioned into subcircuits with at most 3 inputs and 1 output, (c) subcircuits mapped to three 3-input 1-output lookup tables.

Figure 7.22(c) shows three lookup tables that implement those three subcircuits. The first lookup table implements t = ab * c' (the 1 in word 6 corresponds to abc'). The second lookup table implements u = cef. The third lookup table implements Y = t+d+u, thus completing the circuit implementation.

A circuit mapped to lookup tables may not always fully utilize the lookup tables. In particular, if partitioning leads to a 2-input subcircuit rather than a 3-input subcircuit, then mapping that subcircuit to a 3-input lookup table will utilize only two of the lookup table's address inputs; the third input, namely a2, can be set to 0, which means that only words 0 to 3 of the lookup table will be used. The following example illustrates such an underutilized lookup table.

Example 7.8 Mapping that results in an underutilized lookup table—Extended seat belt warning light

This example maps the circuit of Figure 7.23(a), which is the extended seat belt example from Example 2.8, onto a minimum number of 3-input 1-output lookup tables. Because the circuit has four inputs, mapping the circuit to 3-input 1-output lookup tables requires first partitioning the circuit into 3-input subcircuits; such a partitioning is shown in Figure 7.23(b). While the first subcircuit has 3 inputs, the second subcircuit has only 2 inputs.

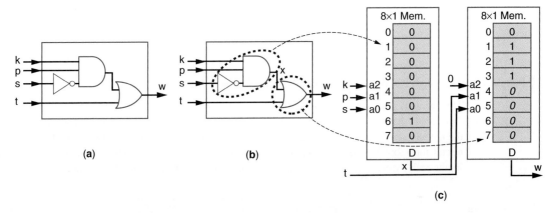

Figure 7.23 Mapping a circuit onto lookup tables sometimes yields underutilized lookup tables: (a) desired circuit, (b) circuit partitioned into two subcircuits, one subcircuit having only two inputs, (c) subcircuits mapped to two 3-input 1-output lookup tables; the second lookup table has its a2 address line set to 0, so only the first four words are used.

Figure 7.23(c) shows the mapping of those subcircuits to lookup tables. The first lookup table implements the first subcircuit, x = kps'. The second lookup table implements the second subcircuit, w = x + t. Because the second subcircuit has only two inputs, we set address line a2 of the lookup table to 0, and connect the two inputs x and t to the lower two address lines. Because a2 is always 0, words 4 to 7 of the lookup table will never be accessed. We've programmed those words as 0s, but they are shown in italics to indicate that those words will *never be accessed*. The values of x and t will cause either word 0, 1, 2, or 3 to be read. Those words have been programmed to implement the OR function to achieve x + t.

Sometimes a circuit has a gate with four or more inputs. Clearly, such a circuit cannot be directly partitioned into subcircuits with three or fewer inputs. The solution is to replace the 4-input gate by an equivalent set of gates having fewer inputs. Technology mapping tools commonly first modify a circuit into a functionality equivalent circuit by decomposing gates having three or more inputs into an equivalent set of 2-input gates, before trying to partition the circuit into subcircuits. Example 7.9 will perform some initial decomposition before partitioning.

Recall that a memory with *M* bits per word can implement *M* functions of the same inputs. Researchers have investigated how many bits per word a lookup table should have to accomodate most circuits efficiently, and have found that two bits per word is efficient for many circuits. The remainder of this chapter will thus use 3-input 2-output lookup tables.

Mapping a circuit onto 3-input 2-output lookup tables is similar to mapping to 3-input 1-output lookup tables, except that when partitioning into subcircuits, each subcircuit may have up to two outputs rather than just one output, as in the following example.

Example 7.9 Mapping a 2x4 decoder to 3-input 2-output lookup tables

This example implements a 2x4 decoder, without enable, using 3-input 2-output lookup tables. A 2x4 decoder has two inputs, `i1` and `i0`, and four outputs, `d0`, `d1`, `d2`, and `d3`. The equations for the outputs are `d0 = i1'i0'`, `d1=i1'i0`, `d2=i1i0'`, and `d3=i1i0`. Figure 7.24(a) shows a circuit for a 2x4 decoder, and also shows a partitioning of the circuit into subcircuits having two inputs each (which is less than the maximum of three inputs) and having two outputs each.

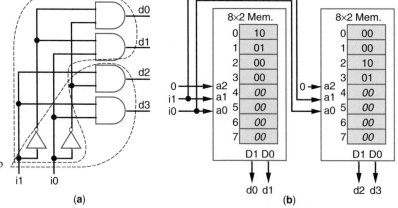

Figure 7.24 Mapping a 2x4 decoder to two 3-input 2-output lookup tables: (a) desired circuit, (b) mapping to two lookup tables. Italicized bits are unused.

Because the two subcircuits in Figure 7.24(a) have only two inputs each, the lookup tables implement those subcircuits using the top halves of the lookup tables' words; the bottom halves are unused, as shown in Figure 7.24(b). For the used words, both bits of each word are used.

Just as earlier examples showed that a subcircuit with fewer than three inputs results in unused lookup table words, likewise a subcircuit with fewer than two outputs will result in an unused lookup table column (meaning an unused LUT output), as in the following example.

Example 7.10 Mapping problem that decomposes a large gate, and that has unused LUT outputs

This example implements the circuit shown in Figure 7.25(a) using two 3-input 2-output lookup tables. The first step is to try to partition the circuit into subcircuits such that each group has at most 3 inputs and 2 outputs. However, the 4-input AND gate prevents such partitioning, because whatever subcircuit that gate is in will have at least four inputs. That problem can be remedied by first decomposing that gate into two smaller gates, while maintaining the same functionality, as shown in Figure 7.25(b). The circuit can then be partitioned into two subcircuits, each with 3 inputs and 1 output, as shown in the figure.

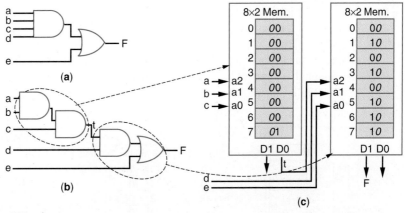

Figure 7.25 Mapping a circuit onto 3-input 2-output lookup tables: (a) original circuit, (b) transformed circuit that decomposes the 4-input AND gate into two-input gates, with the partitioning into 3-input 1-output subcircuits shown, (c) mapping of each subcircuit to a lookup table, with each subcircuit's function converted to programmed bits in the lookup table. Italicized bits are unused.

The subcircuits can then be mapped onto two 3-input 2-output lookup tables as shown in Figure 7.25(c). Notice that the first lookup table's D1 output is unused, and the second lookup table's D0 output is also unused; those columns have been programmed with 0s, and are shown in italics to indicate that those bits will never be accessed. The first table's D0 column implements t = abc. The second table's D1 column implements F = td + e.

An FPGA may have hundreds or thousands of lookup tables, and thus can implement large amounts of combinational logic.

Programmable Interconnects (Switch Matrices)

Earlier examples used custom connections between lookup tables, but the point of FPGAs is that the entire chip is prefabricated, even the wires. FPGAs thus come with ***programmable interconnects***, often called ***switch matrices***, which can be *programmed* to create the connections among lookup tables. Figure 7.26(a) shows a simple FPGA chip with five inputs (*P0–P4*), two 3-input 2-output LUTs, one 4-input 3-output switch matrix, and two outputs (*Q0, Q1*). All three of the left LUT's inputs come from the external inputs *P0, P1,* and *P2*—that LUT's inputs can't be changed. However, the right LUT's inputs may come from either the left LUT's outputs, or from the external inputs *P3* and *P4*. The switch matrix determines which of those connections will be made.

The switch matrix's internal design appears in Figure 7.26(b). It consists of three 4x1 multiplexers (muxes)—the bottom multiplexor is omitted from the drawing to save space. The top mux connects the switch matrix output *o0* to one of the matrix's four inputs. The second mux connects the output *o1* to one of the matrix's four inputs. The bottom mux (not drawn) connects *o2* to one of the matrix's four inputs. A two-bit memory (which is actually a 2-bit register, but called a memory for consistency with the memory inside a lookup table) holds the two bits that set each mux's two select lines. Thus, we can program the desired connections simply by writing the appropriate bits into those two 2-bit memories. Notice that each switch matrix output can be configured independently of the other. In fact, we could even make the same input appear at two or three outputs, though that's probably not useful in this FPGA architecture.

We'll illustrate the use of the switch matrix with an example.

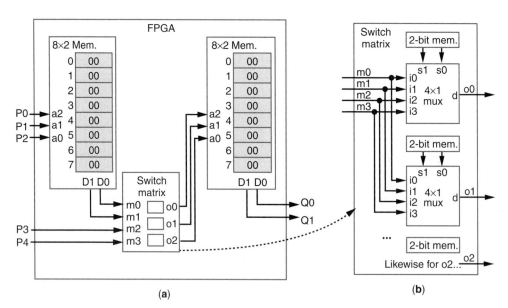

Figure 7.26 A simple FPGA architecture: (a) an FPGA that includes a switch matrix, and (b) the switch matrix's internals showing two 4x1 muxes controlled by two 2-bit registers. Note: real FPGAs have hundreds of lookup tables and switch matrices, not just a few.

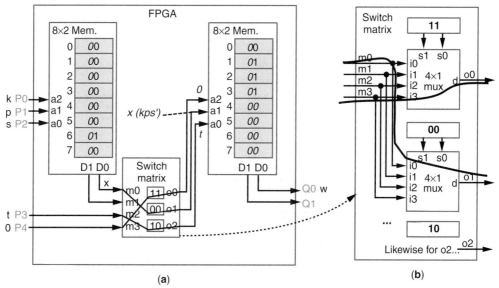

Figure 7.27 Implementing the extended seat belt warning light circuit on the FPGA fabric having a switch matrix: (a) external connections and programmed bits, (b) a look inside the switch matrix, showing the programmed connections. Italicized bits in the lookup tables are unused.

Example 7.11 Extended seat belt warning light on an FPGA with a switch matrix

This example implements the extended seat belt warning light system of Example 7.6, which computes w = kps' + t, on the FPGA in Figure 7.26 having a switch matrix. We connect k, p, and s to the FPGA pins going to the left lookup table, and we program that lookup table to implement the function x = kps', as shown in Figure 7.27(a). The right lookup table should compute w = x + t. This subcircuit has only two inputs, so we need to set the right lookup table's a2 input to 0. We do so by setting pin P4 to 0, and then by passing that 0 to switch matrix output o0, by programming 11 into o0's two-bit memory. o0 is connected to a2, thus causing a2 to have the value 0, as desired.

Likewise, we need to set the right lookup table's a1 input to x, which appears at the D0 output of the left lookup table. We do this by programming 00 into the 2-bit memory for switch matrix output o1. We set the right lookup table's a0 input to t by programming 10 for switch matrix output o2. Figure 7.27(b) shows how the programming of the 2-bit memories inside the switch matrix creates the desired connections. We then program the right lookup table to implement the function x + t, as shown in Figure 7.27(a).

Notice that, in the last few examples, to implement a desired circuit, we merely had to program different bits into the lookup tables and switch matrices. That's the appeal of FPGAs—they implement our circuit just by programming.

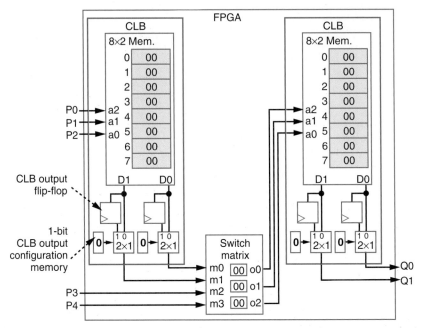

Figure 7.28 An FPGA with configurable logic blocks (CLBs), which contain flip-flops along with a lookup table. The configuration memory bit cells in the figure all contain 0s.

Configurable Logic Block

In the previous section, the illustrated FPGAs were missing a critical element needed to implement general circuits, namely, *flip-flops*. Flip-flops enable implementing sequential circuits on FPGAs.

FPGAs may include a flip-flop with each output of a lookup table—two flip-flops in the case of a 2-output lookup table. The lookup table and its flip-flops together are known as a ***configurable logic block***, or ***CLB***. A simple CLB is shown in Figure 7.28. Each configurable logic block has a 3-input 2-output lookup table, and has two outputs and two flip-flops. Each flip-flop is loaded every clock cycle with the corresponding lookup table output. Each output of the CLB can be configured to come either from the output's flip-flop, or directly from the corresponding lookup table output. That configuration is done by programming a 1-bit memory (which itself is a flip-flop, but we'll call it a memory to avoid confusion), shown in Figure 7.28, that controls a 2x1 mux for each CLB output.

The output flip-flops enable implementation of sequential circuits, such as circuits having registers, on the FPGA. Mapping a circuit onto 3-input 2-output CLBs involves partitioning the circuit into subcircuits having three or fewer inputs and two or fewer outputs, as for LUTs, but with the option that the outputs may come from a flip-flop in the circuit. The partitioning must ensure that the only place that a flip-flop appears in a subcircuit is immediately before the output of the output, because that is where the flip-flops exist in the CLBs.

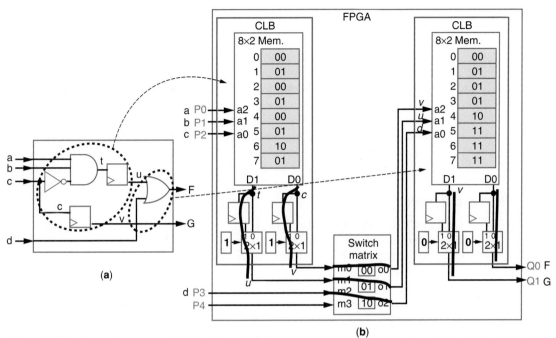

Figure 7.29 Implementing a sequential circuit on an FPGA: (a) desired sequential circuit, partitioned into subcircuits suitable for mapping onto CLBs, (b) programmed FPGA.

Example 7.12 Implementing a sequential circuit on an FPGA

This example implements the sequential circuit shown in Figure 7.29(a), having two flip-flops in the circuit, on the FPGA of Figure 7.28. The first step is to partition the circuit into subcircuits having three or fewer inputs and two or fewer outputs each, ensuring that the circuit's flip-flops only appear at the outputs of subcircuits, as shown in Figure 7.29(a). Based on that partitioning and the shown mapping to CLBs, we connect a, b, and c to the left lookup table in Figure 7.29(b). The left lookup table's D1 output computes abc', labeled as t in the figure. In the desired circuit of Figure 7.29(a), that value t feeds into a flip-flop (whose output is labeled u), and thus in Figure 7.29(b) we program the CLB's D1 output to come from the CLB's D1 flip-flop rather than from D1 directly. The left lookup table's D0 output computes c—note that the wire for c represents a simple "pass through" function, which can be programmed into the LUT just like a more complex function. In this case, because c is connected to address line a0, a 1 is programmed into the D0 column for any word whose address has a0 = 1. In the desired circuit, that value c then feeds into a flip-flop (whose output is labeled v), and thus we program the CLB's D0 output to come from the flip-flop, as shown.

The desired circuit of Figure 7.29(a) shows v connecting directly to external output G. However, the FPGA has no means for directly connecting the left CLB's D0 output to an external output pin. Instead, we can create the desired connection by passing v to the switch matrix output o0, which connects to the right lookup table's a2 input, and we then program that lookup table's D1 column to pass v through, by programming a 1 into any word whose address has a2 = 1. Pin Q1 thus represents output G. Likewise, output F is computed by passing the appropriate value through the switch matrix and programming the D0 column of the right lookup table to implement the desired OR function.

Care should be taken to avoid confusing the output flip-flops themselves and the CLB output configuration "memories." The configuration memories store bits that program the FPGA to implement the desired circuit before circuit operation, while the output flip-flops store the bits that the circuit loads during circuit operation.

The storage elements for the lookup table, the CLB output configuration, and the switch matrices, are collectively known as an FPGA's *configuration memory*, although that "memory" is comprised of numerous smaller memories and even registers or flip-flops.

Overall FPGA Architecture

Grid of CLBs and Switch Matrices

A commercial FPGA contains hundreds or even thousands of CLBs and switch matrices, arranged in a regular pattern on the chip. A sample arrangement is shown in Figure 7.30. CLBs connect with horizontal and vertical routing channels where wires exist, and those wires connect to switch matrices. A sample connection of a CLB to the wires in channels is shown for the top center CLB. The channels consist of tens of wires, represented in the figure just as single bolded wires.

CLBs and switch matrices in commercial FPGAs are more complex than described in this chapter. For example, CLBs may contain two

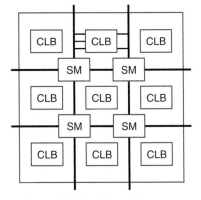

Figure 7.30 FPGA architecture.

lookup tables, or direct connections to adjacent CLBs to support carry chains of carry-ripple adders. Switch matrices may contain more inputs and outputs and more flexible switching options.

Furthermore, commercial FPGAs commonly include large embedded RAM memories for data storage, and embedded multipliers or multiply-accumulate units for fast multiplications. Memory and multiplcation operations are common in digital circuits, and so including RAM and multipliers results in faster and more compact implementation of those operations, and avoids occupying large numbers of CLBs and switch matrices that otherwise would be required to implement those operations. The RAMs and multipliers would be distributed throughout the FPGA fabric of Figure 7.30; there may be tens or hundreds of each in a single FPGA.

Programming an FPGA

One may wonder how to get the program bits into the configuration memories of an FPGA. The configuration memories are all the lookup table memories, the switch matrix memories, and the CLB-output configuration memories. Conceptually, programming is enabled by the FPGA having all the configuration memory bit cells connected as one big shift register (see Chapter 4). That shift register's bit cells are spread out across the chip, so they don't represent a traditional register whose bits are usually in one place, but thinking of them as a shift register helps understand their connectivity. Actually, bit cells connected as a shift register are typically referred to as a ***scan chain***. The FPGA will have an extra input pin for programming that serves as the shift input for the scan chain. Another extra input pin indicates that programming is taking place. During programming, the bits necessary to implement the desired circuit are shifted into the scan chain. Remember that the configuration memory bit cells only get written during programming of the FPGA—during normal FPGA operation, those cells become read-only.

Automated tools that program FPGAs start with a file containing the bits to be shifted into the scan chain—that file is known as a ***bit file*** or ***bitstream***. The tool that creates the bit file obviously must know the purpose of every bit in the scan chain, so such tools will generate a different bit file for different FPGA devices.

Example 7.13 Programming an FPGA

This example demonstrates programming a specific FPGA for the desired circuit of Example 7.12. Figure 7.29 from that example already showed the required contents of the configuration memory on the FPGA to implement the desired circuit. Figure 7.31 replicates the contents, this time illustrating the manner in which the FPGA has the configuration memory bits connected as a scan chain, using a thick dotted line.

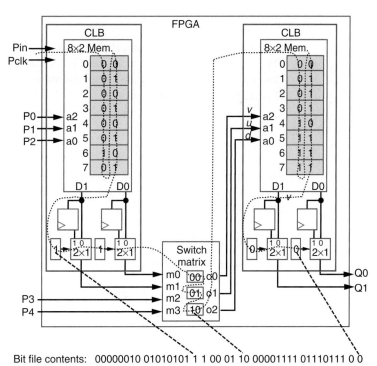

Figure 7.31 Programming an FPGA: all configuration memory bit cells exist in a scan chain. The bottom shows a bit file's contents that would be shifted in during programming—some relationships between the file's bits and configuration memory bit cells are shown.

Bit file contents: 00000010 01010101 1 1 00 01 10 00001111 01110111 0 0

The bottom of the figure shows the contents of a bit file that could be used to program the FPGA to implement the desired circuit. The bit file is determined simply by following the dashed line that represents the scan chain, placing 1s and 0s into the bit file as they appear in the figure. The spaces in the bit file are for readability of the figure, and would not actually exist in a bit file.

_____

How Many Gates Does an FPGA Implement?

We usually think of a digital circuit's size using the notion of "gates" to represent design size. A design with 3000 gates is likely bigger than a design with 2000 gates. Of course, whether that statement is true depends on the type of gates used in each design (e.g., because XOR gates are bigger than NAND gates, 2000 XOR gates may actually be bigger than 3000 NAND gates), as well as the number of inputs to each gate (a 20-input gate is bigger than a 2-input gate). Thus, a common method of indicating design size for a circuit *approximates the number of 2-input NAND gates* that would be required to implement the circuit. So when we say that a circuit consists of 3000 gates or 2000 gates, we typically mean that if those circuits were implemented using 2-input NAND gates, they would require 3000 2-input NAND gates and 2000 2-input NAND gates, respectively.

FPGAs have lookup tables and switch matrices inside, not gates. FPGA sizes are therefore typically reported by considering how large a circuit made up of 2-input NAND gates could be implemented using the FPGA architecture. FPGA vendors may report FPGA size by saying a particular FPGA has a "density of 100,000 system gates" or "100,000 typical gates." These numbers are *approximations*, and many people view such reported numbers very skeptically (because sometimes companies like to exaggerate). FPGA vendors might also describe FPGA size as the number of "logic blocks" or "lookup tables," which is useful when comparing sizes of FPGAs having the same types of logic blocks or lookup tables.

▶ 7.4 OTHER OFF-THE-SHELF IC TYPES

This section describes other IC types for physically implementing digital circuits. Some of those types are older types that are still useful for particular situations. Others are newer types that are beginning to gain popularity.

Off-the-Shelf Logic (SSI) IC

Sometimes a designer needs to implement a circuit having just a few gates. In these cases, using an FPGA may be overkill, as FPGAs typically support thousands or millions of gates. Likewise, using an ASIC would also be overkill. For cases where only a few gates are needed, a designer might instead use one or more off-the-shelf logic ICs.

A *logic IC* typically contains a few, perhaps ten or less, gates connected directly to the IC's pins, as shown in Figure 7.32. The IC shown has four AND gates and 14 pins. One pin is for power to the IC (known as *VCC*), the other for ground (*GND*) (see Chapter 2). The remaining pins connect to the four AND gates in the IC, as shown in the figure. Different logic ICs have gate types other than AND, such as OR, NAND, NOR, or NOT. To build a small circuit from these off-the-shelf logic ICs, we would simply place the ICs on a board and connect the appropriate pins. ICs with only a few gates are known as *small-scale integration* chips, or *SSI* chips.

7400 ICs

The most popular off-the-shelf SSI ICs are known generally as *7400-series* ICs. A 7400 IC typically contains four to six logic gates, and about 14 pins. A particular 7400 IC is shown in Figure 7.31. The IC measures about 1/2 inch across. The IC package shown has two rows, or lines, of pins, and is thus known as a *dual inline package*, or *DIP*.

7400 ICs first became available in the early 1960s. The original 7400 chip had four NAND gates, and cost about $1000 each, in 1962. That's right—$1000. And that's in 1960s' dollars, when a U.S. engineer earned only about $10,000 per year. The price dropped significantly during that decade, thanks in large part to the use of huge numbers of the devices by the U.S. Minuteman Missile and the Apollo rocket programs, and has continued to drop since then due to cheaper transistors and huge volumes. Today, you can buy 7400-series ICs for just tens of cents each.

Parts with different gates have different part numbers. Table 7.1 shows some commonly used 7400 parts from Fairchild's 74LS00 sub-

An Appolo rocket carried astronauts to the moon. Neil Armstrong's famous words upon stepping on the moon, "One small step for man, one giant leap for mankind," were supposed to be "for a man" (NASA claimed that static obscured the word "a"). Most people understood Neil's meaning anyway.

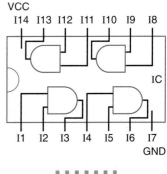

VCC

Figure 7.32 Example logic IC.

Figure 7.31 7400-series IC.

Table 7.1: Commonly used 7400-series ICs.

Part	Description	Pins
74LS00	Four 2-input NAND	14
74LS02	Four 2-input NOR	14
74LS04	Six inverters	14
74LS08	Four 2-input AND	14
74LS10	Three 3-input NAND	14
74LS11	Three 3-input AND	14
74LS14	Six inverters (Schmitt trigger)	14
74LS20	Two 4-input NAND	14
74LS27	Three 3-input NOR	14
74LS30	One 8-input NAND	14
74LS32	Four 2-input OR	14
74LS74	Two D flip-flop, positive edge triggered, with preset and reset	14
74LS83	4-bit binary full-adder	16
74LS85	4-bit magnitude comparator	16

Source: www.digikey.com

family of the 7400 series. In addition to basic gates, the table shows ICs with D flip-flops, full-adders, or a magnitude comparator. Parts also exist for XOR, XNOR, buffers, decoders, multiplexers, up-counters, up-down-counters, and more.

There are several different subfamilies of 7400-series parts—parts from a subfamily can be used with other parts from the subfamily, but generally not with parts from other subfamilies. The reason is that the voltage and current setting of a subfamily are designed such that the ICs can be connected without requiring adjusting the voltage and current between ICs. The **74** series (e.g., 7400, 7402, etc.), is the basic subfamily, based on a type of transistor known as TTL—designers using logic ICs today only use 74-series ICs if they must integrate with old designs, and typically don't use the series for new designs. The **74LS** subfamily (e.g., 74LS00, 74LS02) uses a special type of TTL technology known as Schottky that results in lower power and slightly higher speed than the 74 series—the "L" in the name means "low-power," the "S" means "Schottky." The **74HC** subfamily uses high-speed (denoted by the "H") CMOS (denoted by the "C") transistors. The **74F** subfamily was introduced by Fairchild, consisting of fast (hence the "F") advanced Schottky TTL logic. Numerous other 7400 subfamilies exist.

Furthermore, additional series of off-the-shelf SSI ICs exist in addition to the 7400 series. Another popular series is the **4000 series** of ICs, a CMOS series that evolved in the 1970s as a low-power alternative to the TTL-based 7000 series. More series exist too.

Example 7.14 Seat belt warning implementation using off-the-shelf 7400 ICs

Using 74LS-series ICs shown in Table 7.1, physically implement the seat belt warning light circuit of Figure 7.1, shown again in Figure 7.32(a). We could implement the inverter using a 74LS04. The 74LS08 has 2-input AND gates, and we need a 3-input AND gate. A simple solution is to decompose the 3-input AND into two 2-input ANDs, as shown in Figure 7.32(b). The final implementation is shown in Figure 7.32(c).

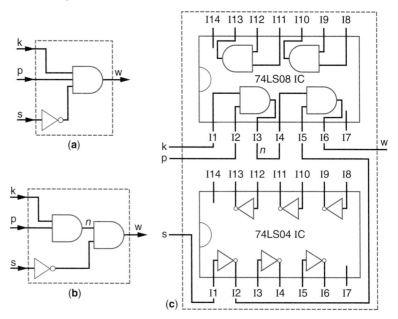

Figure 7.32 Implementing the seat belt warning circuit with 74LS-series ICs: (a) desired circuit, (b) circuit transformed to use 2-input AND gates, (c) circuit mapped to two 74LS ICs. Additional connections not shown would be power to the *I14* pins and ground to the *I7* pins on each IC.

Preferably, we would implement the circuit using just one IC, to reduce board size, cost, and power. Converting the circuit to use only one type of gate, like NAND gates only, or NOR gates only, could result in just one IC. For example, if we could convert to 3-input NOR gates, we could use the 74LS27 chip. We start by converting the circuit to NORs only, as in Figure 7.33(a). We remove the double inversion, and replace the single inversions by 3-input NOR gates. The implementation using a single 74LS27 IC is shown in Figure 7.33(c).

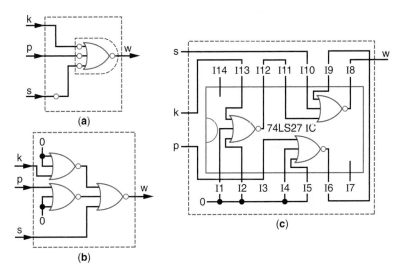

Figure 7.33 Implementing the seat belt warning circuit with one 74LS IC, namely, the 74LS27 consisting of three 3-input NOR gates: (a) desired circuit transformed to NOR gates with inversion bubbles, (b) circuit with double inversions eliminated and single inversions replaced by 1-input NOR gates, (c) circuit mapped to a 74LS27 chip. Additional connections not shown would be power to the *I14* pin, and ground to the *I7* pin.

Simple Programmable Logic Device (SPLD)

A *programmable logic device*, or *PLD*, is an IC that can be configured to implement a variety of logic functions, ranging from tens of gates to thousands of gates. PLDs became popular in the 1970s (thus predating FPGAs), because PLDs could implement far more functionality in a single IC than was possible using SSI ICs.

A PLD device contains a prefabricated circuit with a set of external inputs feeding into a large AND-OR circuit structure, with the special feature of allowing the user to configure (via "programming") which external inputs connect to the AND gates. For example, Figure 7.34 shows a basic PLD with three inputs feeding into three AND gates followed by an OR gate. The inputs feed into the AND gates in both true and complemented forms. Each wire feeding into each AND gate passes through a programmable node, which can either pass the node's input to the node's output, or disconnect the node's input from the node's output. Thus, by programming the nodes, a PLD can implement *any* 3-term function of three inputs.

The programmable node design varies among types of PLDs. Figure 7.35 shows two types. The type shown in Figure 7.35(a) is fuse-based PLD. A fuse conducts like a wire, unless the fuse is "blown," meaning a higher-than-normal current is passed

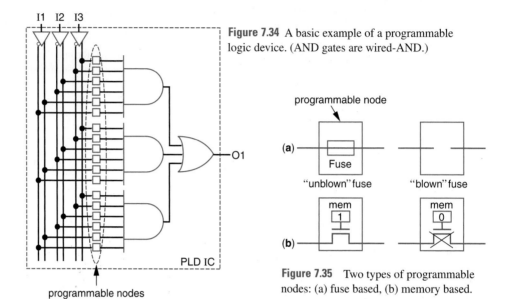

Figure 7.34 A basic example of a programmable logic device. (AND gates are wired-AND.)

Figure 7.35 Two types of programmable nodes: (a) fuse based, (b) memory based.

through the fuse, causing the fuse to literally burn up and break. A blown fuse obviously does not conduct electricity. The type shown in Figure 7.35(b) is based on memory and a transistor—programming a 1 into the memory causes the transistor to conduct, while programming a 0 causes the transistor to not conduct. We omit the details of how to program the fuses or program the memories themselves. Memory-based PLDs can usually be reprogrammed, in contrast to fuse-based PLDs that can only be programmed once, and that are known as ***one-time programmable*** (***OTP***) devices. Fuse-based PLDs are popular in electrically noisy applications, like space applications, since memories can have their contents changed from radiation in space. They are also popular in applications demanding high security, since malicious enemies can't reprogram the device. Memory-based devices are more common, however, since they can be reprogrammed and thus reduce costs when we make design changes. The memories used are almost always nonvolatile, meaning the memories don't need power to retain their stored bits. (See Section 5.7 for more information on nonvolatile memories.)

You might be wondering how those AND gates work when the programmable node is programmed to disconnect an input. In other words, how does the AND gate treat an input with no connection—as a 0, a 1, or something else? Actually, PLDs don't use normal AND gates. Instead, PLDs typically use what is known as "wired-AND." Explaining how wired-AND works is beyond the scope of this book, and instead the subject of a course on transistor-level circuits. For our purposes, we can think of a wired-AND gate as an AND gate that simply ignores unconnected inputs.

Real PLDs have more inputs, gates, and outputs than shown in Figure 7.34. PLD structure drawings thus benefit from a more concise way of drawing the circuits. A concise method of drawing PLDs is shown in Figure 7.36. Such a drawing doesn't show the programmable nodes, and simply utilizes an "x" to indicate a connection. In the drawing, wires that cross each other are *not* connected unless an "x" exists at the crossing. Furthermore, such a drawing uses a single wire to represent all the AND gate inputs, representing the wired-AND. The figure shows how such a drawing would indicate the connections needed to generate the term I3*I2'. The "x" on the left represents I2' feeding into the top AND gate. The "x" on the right indicates I3 feeding into the top AND gate.

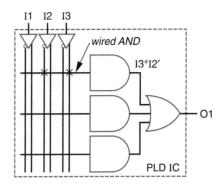

Figure 7.36 Simplified PLD drawing.

Example 7.15 Seat belt warning light using a simple PLD

This example implements the seat belt warning light system of Figure 7.1 using the PLD of Figure 7.36. We can do so by programming the PLD as shown in Figure 7.37. We generate the desired term kps' by programming the connections for the top AND gate as shown.

We want the bottom two AND gates to output 0s so that the OR gate's output equals the top AND gate's output. We can achieve 0s by ANDing an input with its complement—the result of a*a' is always 0. The figure shows two ways of achieving a 0, with the middle gate using just one of the inputs, and the bottom gate using all three inputs.

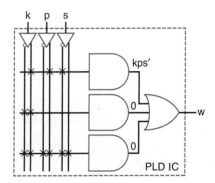

Figure 7.37 Seat belt warning system on a simple PLD.

PLDs typically have more than just one output. Figure 7.38(a) shows a PLD with two outputs instead of just one. Each output is an OR of up to three terms.

Many PLDs have a D flip-flop that stores each output's bit, and the PLD's output pin can be programmed to connect either from the OR gate output or from the flip-flop output, known as combinational or registered output, respectively. A PLD supporting combinational/registered output is shown in Figure 7.38(b).

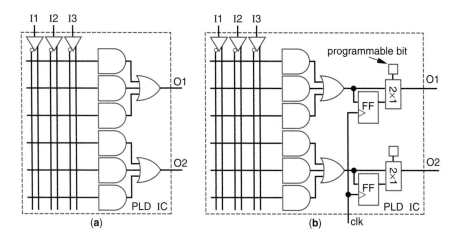

Figure 7.38 PLD: (a) with two outputs, (b) with programmable registered outputs.

Another extension is to allow the PLD output to be either the true or complemented value of the OR gate or flip-flop output, using a 2x1 mux controlled by a programmable bit. Yet another extension is for the output to feed back to the input array. One use of feedback is to implement functions with more terms, achieved by feeding back the combinational output value. Another common use of feedback, achieved by feeding back the registered output, is to implement a state register and control logic (i.e., a controller)—the AND array gets its inputs from the registered outputs and external inputs, and the OR gates then generate the external outputs and the next values for the state register.

Some PLDs have not only a programmable AND array, but also a programmable OR array, meaning the OR gate can get its inputs from any of the AND gates.

SPLD versus PAL versus GAL versus PLA

Like so many names in the rapidly evolving field of computer technology, names for PLDs are somewhat confusing. Originally, in the 1970s, PLDs consisted of programmable AND arrays and programmable OR arrays, and were known as ***programmable logic arrays***, or ***PLAs***. In the mid-1970s, a company named AMD (Applied Micro Devices, Inc.) developed PLDs that instead had OR gates with fixed rather than programmable inputs, as in Figure 7.38 and the other PLD figures in this chapter, and referred to such devices as ***programmable array logic***, or ***PALs*** ("PAL" is a registered trademark of AMD). PALs were originally fuse-based and hence one-time-programmable. A company named Lattice Semiconductor Corporation developed a PLD using a memory-based programming approach rather than fuses, resulting in reprogrammability, and referred to such devices as ***generic array logic***, or ***GAL*** (which are registered trademarks of Lattice Semiconductor Corporation). As PLDs became more complex (as the next section describes), PLDs based on PAL or GAL architectures (PLA architectures seem to be rare) became known as ***simple PLDs***, or ***SPLDs***, to contrast them with the more complex PLD varieties. Today, numerous companies manufacture SPLDs, and often state that their SPLD architecture is based on "PAL" or "PAL/GAL" architectures, with the distinction between PAL and GAL not seemingly relevant in that context. SPLDs typically support tens of logic gates to hundreds of logic gates.

Complex Programmable Logic Device (CPLD)

As IC transistor densities grew in the 1980s, companies began to build PLDs to support thousands of gates. However, the PLD architecture described in the previous section does not scale well to thousands of gates—who needs one big huge circuit of two-level logic? Instead, architectures evolved that consisted of numerous SPLDs on a single device, connected using switch matrices (also known as programmable interconnect)—see Section 7.3 for details on switch matrices. These devices today are known as ***complex PLDs***, or ***CPLDs***. CPLDs can typically implement designs with thousands of gates.

SPLDs versus CPLDs versus FPGAs

What's the difference among SPLDs, CPLDs, and FPGAs? In general, the term SPLD is used for devices that support tens of gates to hundreds of gates, CPLD for devices that support thousands of gates, and FPGAs for devices that support tens of thousands of gates to millions of gates.

Furthermore, today's SPLDs and CPLDs are almost always nonvolatile, meaning they can store their program even after power is removed, whereas FPGAs are almost always volatile, meaning they lose their program when power is removed—and thus must include external circuitry that stores the program in nonvolatile memory and that programs the FPGA from that memory on power up of the FPGA. FPGAs today are volatile in part because nonvolatile memory technology is hard to incorporate with fast logic technology on the same chip, resulting in slower circuit performance and less efficient use of area. However, conceptually, any of SPLDs, CPLDs, and FPGAs could be made to be volatile or nonvolatile, and today some companies do offer nonvolatile FPGAs—those companies focus on low power, and on space applications and other electrically noisy environments that can cause undesired changes in volatile memory.

FPGA-to-Structured-ASIC Flows

An interesting new technology that has evolved in the early 2000s is that of creating an ASIC directly from an FPGA-based design. Many designers use FPGAs for ASIC prototyping. They use automated tools to implement their circuit on FPGAs, and they then extensively test the circuit in the circuit's environment, for example, in a prototype digital video player or a prototype satellite communication chip. The FPGA-based prototype may be larger, costlier, and more power-hungry than an ASIC-based implementation, but can be useful for detecting and correcting errors in the circuit, for creating other components and software that interact with the circuit, and for demonstrating the eventual product. Once satisfied with the circuit, automated tools could be used to reimplement the circuit on an ASIC. The ASIC implementation traditionally did not utilize any information from the FPGA implementation.

Implementing large circuits on ASICs is a difficult task, even with automated tools. Nonrecurring engineering costs may exceed millions of dollars, and fabricating the IC may take months. Furthermore, any problem with the fabricated ASIC may require a second fabrication cycle, requiring additional weeks or months. Problems may arise in the ASIC that didn't appear in the FPGA due to the new implementation of the circuit as an ASIC—perhaps timing problems might arise, for example, due to the circuit being placed and routed in a completely different fashion than was done in the FPGA.

To ease the migration of a circuit from FPGA to ASIC, some FPGA vendors offer a structured ASIC approach. In this particular structured ASIC approach, a tool converts the *FPGA implementation* to an ASIC implementation, in contrast to converting the *original circuit* to an ASIC implementation. In other words, the structured ASIC will reflect the lookup table and switch matrix structure of the original FPGA. However, the structured ASIC will not be programmable, and thus will have faster lookup tables and faster switch matrices, because their contents will have been "hardwired" into the ASIC. The structured ASIC's lower layers can be prefabricated, with only wires left to be completed to implement a particular circuit. The result is less NRE cost (tens of thousands of dollars rather than millions) and shorter time-to-silicon (weeks rather than months), as well as less chance of unforeseen problems. The drawback is that the structured ASIC will be larger, slower, and more power-hungry than a traditional cell-based ASIC, but still better than an FPGA, generally about 2x smaller, faster, lower-power, and cheaper than an FPGA.

▶ 7.5 IC TRADEOFFS, TRENDS, AND COMPARISONS

As is the case when designing a digital circuit (as discussed in Chapter 6), physically implementing a circuit on an IC presents designers with numerous tradeoffs among design metrics. Common metrics include performance, size, power, cost, and time to availability. Figure 7.39 illustrates some of the tradeoffs among various IC types described in this chapter.

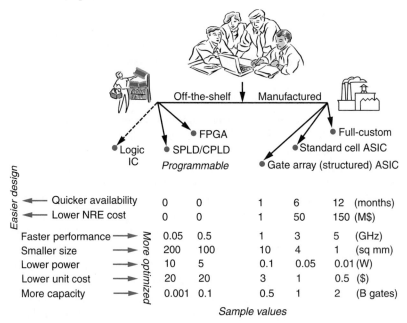

Figure 7.39 Tradeoffs among various IC types. Sample values for various metrics are also shown. For example, performance for an SPLD/CPLD might be 0.05 GHz, but 3 GHz for a standard cell ASIC. Actual values can vary tremendously from those shown.

Tradeoffs Among IC Types

Generally, a circuit implemented on IC types towards the right of the figure will have faster performance, smaller size, lower power, and lower unit cost (meaning lower cost per chip). For example, for a given circuit, a standard cell ASIC will be faster, smaller, and lower power than a gate array ASIC, because the cells can be chosen and placed to match the circuit, meaning there may be fewer cells and shorter wires. Likewise, a gate array ASIC uses gates rather than slower/larger/higher-power lookup tables, and wires rather than slower/larger/higher-power switch matrices. The circuit of Figure 7.24(a) could be implemented in a gate array ASIC with performance involving just a few gate delays from input to output, but when mapped to the FPGA of Figure 7.28, that circuit would have a longer delay—the inputs would pass through the left CLB's lookup table (which may have a delay of two gate-delays), through the left CLB's output muxes (another two gate-delays), through the switch matrix (another two gate-delays), through the right CLB's lookup table (another two gate-delays), and finally through the right CLB's output muxes, resulting in a total of ten gate-delays. In terms of size, a gate array implementation of the circuit of Figure 7.24(a) would require about 20 transistors, whereas the FPGA implementation using two CLBs and a switch matrix would require several hundred transistors. Some studies report that FPGAs are approximately 10 times slower, are 10–30 times bigger, and consume about 10 times more power, than ASIC implementations of the same circuit. However, these overheads are decreased compared to the previous decade, and the overheads are decreasing further as commercial FPGAs continue to mature.

Unit cost (which does not include NRE cost) is reduced towards the right of the figure, in part because IC cost is closely related to silicon size. Furthermore, for a given size chip, IC types to the right can implement larger circuits (i.e., the IC has more capacity) because the chip is optimized for the given circuit.

However, a circuit implemented on IC types towards the left of the figure will generally have quicker availability and lower NRE cost. For example, a gate array ASIC only requires wires to be fabricated and may thus be available in a few weeks and involve NRE costs of perhaps one million dollars, whereas a standard cell ASIC requires all layers to be fabricated, which may require several months and incur NRE costs of tens of millions of dollars. Likewise, an FPGA is prefabricated and thus may be immediately available if already stocked in a lab or may require only a few days to order from a vendor, and has no NRE costs, whereas a gate array ASIC requires a few weeks and NRE costs of perhaps one million dollars.

Figure 7.39 also makes a clear distinction between manufactured versus off-the-shelf IC types, because the difference in metric values between those two categories can be enormous, much like the difference between vehicles in the categories of aircraft versus automobiles. For example, while NRE costs are in the range of millions of dollars in the manufactured IC category, namely full-custom costing perhaps $150 million, standard cell $50 million, and gate array $1 million, they reduce to $0 for the off-the-shelf IC category. Likewise, while time to availability for the manufactured IC category is measured in months or weeks, the off-the-shelf IC types reduce it to just minutes or seconds—effectively zero time.

Example 7.16 Choosing an IC type

Consider a company that has a text encrypter circuit that will be used in three different projects A, B, and C.

- Project A involves putting the circuit into 100 million mobile phones; encryption speed must be 2.5 GHz, and each chip can be priced up to $5.

- Project B involves putting the circuit into 10,000 medical devices; encryption speed must be 1 MHz, and each chip can be priced up to $50.

- Project C involves putting the circuit into 100,000 automobiles; encryption speed must be 10 MHz, and each chip can be priced up to $10.

Suppose that all other factors are ignored, and that the company must choose from among standard cell ASIC, gate array ASIC, or FPGA IC types only. Considering the sample metric values shown in Figure 7.39, which IC type is best for each project?

For project A, the only IC type with at least 2.5 GHz speed is standard cell ASIC. The $50 million in NRE cost can be amortized over the 100 million chips by adding just $0.50 to the price of each chip, which when added to the $1 unit cost results in a price of $1.50 per chip, much less than the limit of $5. Thus, project A should use standard cell ASICs.

For project B, any of the three IC types meets the speed requirement of 1 MHz. The $50 million of NRE for a standard cell ASIC amortized over 10,000 chips would involve adding $5,000 to the price of each chip, which clearly exceeds the limit of $50 per chip. Even the $1 million of NRE for a gate array ASIC would require adding $100 to the price of each chip, which is still too much. Fortunately, the FPGA has no NRE cost, and a unit cost of $20, which is less than the $50 limit per chip. Thus, project B should use FPGAs.

For project C, all three IC types meet the speed requirement of 10 MHz. Amortizing standard cell NRE would result in too high a chip price. Amortizing the gate array ASIC NRE of $1 million over 100,000 chips would add $10 per chip, which when added to the $1 unit cost would result in $11 per chip, slightly exceeding the $10 per chip limit. However, the unit cost per FPGA chip is $20. Thus, none of the three IC types meets project C's price per chip requirement, but the gate array IC type comes very close, and is thus the best implementation choice.

IC Technology Trend—Moore's Law

Understanding the trends of IC technologies requires knowledge of Moore's Law. **Moore's Law** roughly states that IC capacity doubles every 18 months. Figure 7.40 plots such doubling, beginning with about 10 million transistors per IC in 1997. The plot uses a logarithmic scale for the *y*-axis—each tick mark on the *y*-axis represents 10 times more than the previous tick mark. The growth rate is astounding—ICs

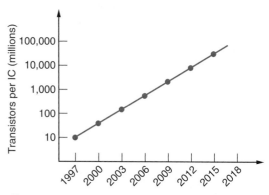

Figure 7.40 The trend of increasing transistors per IC.

In a 2004 speech, an Intel vice-president suggested that we might now consider transistors as essentially free.

are predicted to increase from 10 million transistors in 1997 to over 10 *billion* transistors in 2015. That means that the 2015 IC would hold 1000 times more transistors than the 1997 IC. In other words, the 2015 IC would be as powerful as about 1000 1997 ICs. This increasing capacity trend has also resulted in the cost per transistor dropping at nearly the same astounding rate. The increasing capacity is made possible by decreasing the smallest size of the individual parts within a chip, like the size of a single wire or of a transistor's gate, known as a chip's ***feature size***. Feature sizes in the 1980s were on the order of 1 micrometer (known as a micron), shrinking to 0.35 microns by 1995, and 0.18 microns by 2000 (around which time people began referring to feature size by nanometers rather than micrometers). Feature size shrinking continued to 90 nanometers by around 2003, then 65 nm by 2005, and 45 nm by 2007. Further shrinking may occur down to 32 nm by 2010, and 22 nm by 2012.

The IC capacity trend has many implications. One implication is that digital designers can create massively parallel designs that use huge numbers of functional units and registers, to create high-performance systems not previously practical. The number of required transistors for such designs might have been considered absurd just a decade earlier. Another implication is that the size overhead of FPGAs compared to ASICs (about 10x) becomes less relevant, making FPGAs an increasingly popular choice in more systems. Yet another implication is that designers increasingly need automated tools to help build these multimillion transistor circuits, and may increasingly wish to use RTL and even higher levels of design (e.g., C-based design) as the method for describing circuits, leaving the remaining design steps to tools. Smaller feature sizes also make layout more challenging (the closer items are, the more that can go wrong), which has increased standard cell ASIC NRE costs from tens of thousands of dollars in the 1980s to tens of millions of dollars in the 2010s.

At some point, Moore's Law must come to an end, because transistors cannot shrink to an infinitely small size. When that end will occur has been a subject of debate for many years. Some people claim Moore's Law is already slowing down and will perhaps end a couple decades into the 2000s.

In the early 1980s, many people predicted that feature sizes could not shrink below 1 micron. 2010 feature sizes are about 0.020 microns. As Neils Bohr said, "Prediction is very difficult, especially about the future."

▶ *HOW DOES IT WORK?—INCREMENTALLY SCALING DOWN CHIP FEATURES*

Moore's Law is enabled by chip feature sizes being made smaller every few years. A common question is: "Why don't chip makers just jump forward and make the smallest features now, rather than reducing feature sizes incrementally each year?" Part of the answer is that each incremental reduction creates a new set of problems that must be solved before the next incremental reduction can be considered, such as problems related to reliably creating smaller wires, updating tools to consider more and stricter layout rules when items are placed closer together on a chip, and testing chips for correctness even though there are more components on each chip and those components are less accessible from the chip's pins. These problems are tackled by thousands of researchers and engineers around the world, and solutions evolve slowly, often by improvements built on

previous solutions. The solutions also require the more powerful computers enabled by a current generation of chips. An analogy is that of building a pyramid—only by standing on what is already built can one proceed to build the next higher level.

"If I have seen further it is by standing on the shoulders of giants." Isaac Newton.

The advent of ICs containing a billion transistors has led to ICs that contain what used to exist on multiple ICs. Thus, a single IC may contain dozens or hundreds of microprocessors, custom digital circuits, memories, buses, etc. An IC with numerous processors, custom circuits, and memories is known as a ***system-on-a-chip***, or ***SOC***.

Relative Popularity of IC Types

One may wonder about the relative popularity of IC types. Several ways exist to measure the popularity of an IC type.

One measure is each type's annual revenues. One 2007 study of IC sales reported $15.3 billion in total revenues with the following revenue percentages for different IC types: Full-custom—19%, standard cell—54%, gate array—3%, FPGA/PLD—24%. Another measure is the number of ***design starts*** for each IC type, which is the number of unique circuits implemented in each IC type, regardless of how many copies are made. A 2008 study reported about 3,000 ASIC design starts, versus about 100,000 FPGA design starts. Numbers from different studies vary, and there are many other measures that could be considered; these numbers are provided just to give a general feel for the popularity of the various IC types.

In 2002 alone, nearly 80 billion ICs (of all types) were produced. (Source: IC Insights McClean Report, 2003.)

The tools used to map digital designs to physical implementations, collectively known as ***electronic design automation*** tools, or ***EDA***, themselves form a market with revenues of $4 billion in 2008, employing about 30,000 people worldwide (source: EDA Consortium, 2009).

ASSPs

Rising ASIC NRE costs (from tens of thousands of dollars in the 1980s to tens of millions of dollars in the 2000s) have lead to the increasing popularity of ASSPs. An ***application specific standard product***, or ***ASSP***, is an off-the-shelf IC that targets a particular application domain, such as the video processing domain or the network processing domain, but that is intended to be sold to a variety of different companies ("users") who each will program and configure the device for their specific products. In contrast, ASICs are typically created by one company ("user") for a single device, and FPGAs are not focused on a particular application domain. For example, an ASSP for video processing might contain custom digital circuits optimized for high-speed low-power video compression and decompression (known as *codecs*)—such ASSPs often contain codecs for a wide variety of protocols (e.g., MPEG 2, MPEG 4, H.264, etc.) because the platform could be used in different products supporting different standards. An example is the Nexperia platform from Philips. One user may program the ASSP for use in a TV set-top box, while another user may place the ASSP in a security camera. As another example, an ASSP may focus on network processing, such as Intel's IXP device, which is programmed by different users to implement network gateways, routers, switches, wireless access points, and more. ASSPs typically include microprocessors and other programmable items (even FPGA fabrics) that can be programmed to customize the ASSP for a particular product.

Thus, the high NRE cost of building the ASSP IC, which may itself be created using full-custom, standard-cell ASIC, or some other IC type, can be amortized by the company that builds the ASSP over larger quantities of ICs due to being used by numerous user companies in numerous products. Furthermore, ASSP users (distinct from the ASSP builder) obtain quicker availability of the IC and incur less risk, with drawbacks including a less optimized design. A 2008 study reported ASSP annual revenue to be about $60 billion, compared to about $20 billion for ASICs.

IC Types versus Processor Varieties

IC types and processor varieties are orthogonal implementation features. Two implementation features are **orthogonal** if we can select each independently (in mathematics, orthogonal means forming a right angle). Several processor varieties can each implement a desired system function, including a custom processor (i.e., a circuit created by a designer to implement a particular function, such as video compression) or a programmable processor (often called a microprocessor).

Figure 7.41 illustrates that the choice of processor variety is independent of the choice of IC type. Point *1* represents the choice of implementing desired system functionality using a custom processor circuit with a full-custom IC type. That choice results in a highly optimized design. Point *2* represents the choice of implementing a custom processor circuit on an FPGA. While the circuit may be optimized, the FPGA IC type results in a less-optimized implementation (compared to full-custom) but easier design overall.

Point *3* represents the choice of implementing system functionality as software executing on a programmable processor, where the programmable processor is implemented in standard cells. Point *4* represents the choice of implementing software on a programmable processor that is implemented on an FPGA. While that concept may seem strange, a programmable processor is just another circuit, so that circuit can be mapped to an FPGA just like any other circuit. Programmable processors mapped to FPGAs, known as **soft core** processors, are in fact becoming quite popular, because a designer can choose how many processors to put on a single IC (perhaps the designer wants 9 programmable processors on one IC),

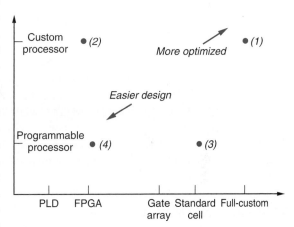

Figure 7.41 IC types and processor varieties are orthogonal implementation features. Four of the above ten possible choices are shown.

and because a designer can put single-purpose processors alongside programmable processors—all without having to fabricate a new IC.

Of course, programmable processors can often be purchased as off-the-shelf ICs, so a designer using a programmable processor may not have to worry about the processor's IC type. But increasingly, designers must place a programmable processor within their own IC, coexisting with other processors. When a programmable processor coexists on an IC along with other processors (programmable or custom), that programmable processor is called a ***core***. A ***hard core*** is built into the chip's hardware, while a soft core (mentioned above) is programmed onto the existing hardware (typically FPGA hardware).

The rise of cores in the 1990s and 2000s has led to a new processor type known as customized programmable processors or ***application-specific instruction-set processors*** (***ASIPs***), wherein a designer can extend a base programmable processor to have custom datapath components and custom instructions that provide improved performance for a particular application or application domain. The newly-created ASIP can then be implemented alongside other circuits or cores on an ASIC or FPGA.

Our discussion of IC types and processor varieties has thus far assumed just one type of each item (e.g., one type of FPGA). In reality, each item itself has many types. For example, dozens of different types of FPGAs are available, varying in their size, speed, power, cost, etc. Likewise, dozens of different types of programmable processors are available, also varying in those features. And we know that we can create different types of custom processors, varying also in their size, speed, power, etc. Thus, each point in Figure 7.39 and Figure 7.41 is actually a large collection of points that spread out in different directions on the plots, and may even overlap with other types. Furthermore, other IC types as well as processor varieties exist and continue to evolve.

We also point out that a single IC may actually incorporate several different IC types. So a single IC may have some circuits created using full-custom IC type, and other circuits created using ASIC or even FPGA types. Likewise, a single processor may have different parts implemented in different IC types. For example, a common situation is for a programmable processor to have its datapath implemented as a full-custom IC type, but its controller implemented in an ASIC type—the reason being that the datapath is very regular, while the controller is mostly unstructured combinational logic.

In short, designers have a *huge* number of choices in choosing processor varieties and IC types to implement their systems.

FPGAs alongside Microprocessors

This chapter has introduced FPGAs primarily as an alternative to manufactured ICs such as ASICs. Today, FPGAs are also viewed as an alternative to microprocessors in computing platforms. In particular, some computations can be performed faster on an FPGA than on a microprocessor. For example, multiplying 20 pairs of 4-bit numbers might require about 200 clock cycles on a microprocessor, as each multiplication requires instructions to fetch, multiply, and store the data and those instructions execute (mostly) sequentially. However, multiplying those 20 pairs of numbers could require just one clock cycle on an FPGA if the FPGA had capacity for 20 multipliers—all 20 multiplications could be done in parallel. Even if the FPGA clock cycle were 10 times slower than the microprocessor's clock cycle, the net result would still be a 20x speedup ((200/1)/10) on the FPGA. Many computing domains, such as biological computing, financial computing, and video processing, process streams of data that lend themselves well to computing on

FPGAs. Thus, computer makers today increasingly provide support for adding FPGAs alongside microprocessors, and thus many desktop computers, server computers, and supercomputers today come with hardware and software support for FPGAs. Furthermore, new compilers exist that can translate high-level program code like C++ code into circuits on FPGAs. Thus, creating digital circuits is no longer just the domain of "hardware" engineers; it is becoming part of the domain of "software" engineers too.

▶ 7.6 PRODUCT PROFILE: GIANT LED-BASED VIDEO DISPLAY WITH FPGAS

In the late 1990s and 2000s, giant color video displays became popular at sport stadiums, car dealerships, casinos, freeway billboards, and various other locations. Most such video displays utilize a huge grid of light-emitting diodes (LEDs) driven by digital circuits.

A *light-emitting diode* (*LED*) is a semiconductor device that emits light when current passes through the device. In contrast, a traditional "incandescent" light bulb emits light when current passes through the bulb's internal filament, which is a high-resistance wire that heats up and glows when current flows through the wire—the wire, however, doesn't burn because it is enclosed in a vaccum or inert gas within the bulb. Because LED light comes from a semiconductor material and not from a hot glowing filament in a bulb, LEDs use less power, last longer, and can handle vibrations that would break a regular light bulb.

LEDs have long been used to display simple device status (e.g., on or off), text messages, or even simple graphics. However, until recently, LEDs were only available in white, yellow, red, and green colors, and were not very bright. Thus, earlier LED video displays were typically small, used only a single color, and were designed for indoor use. However, with the development of the blue LED in 1993, and the development of brighter LEDs, full-color LED displays evolved that can display video in much the same way as a computer monitor or television, even in sunny outdoor environments. In fact, LEDs, being a semiconductor technology, have been improving at a rate similar to transistors (which also use semiconductor technology). The improvement has followed what is known as *Haitz's Law* (the LED equivalent of Moore's Law), stating that the LED "flux per package" doubles every 18–24 months, which has been the case for several decades. Due to this improvement, many people predict that LEDs will replace incandescent light bulbs for home and office lighting. LEDs have already begun to replace incandescent bulbs in traffic lights, as illustrated in Figure 7.42. LED-based flashlights are now commonplace.

Traffic light using incandescent light and red plastic cover

Traffic light made from several hundred red LEDs

Figure 7.42 LEDs are replacing incandescent bulbs in traffic lights, as well as other areas.

Figure 7.43(a) shows a large LED video display capable of displaying full-color video on a 15-yard-by-8-yard screen. Because each LED is relatively large (1/8th of an inch wide, for example) in comparison to the pixels of a computer monitor, one has to stand several feet away from the LED display to view the image without noticing the individual LEDs. If we look closer at the LED display, as seen in Figure 7.43(b), we can see the individual lines of the displays. If we look even closer at the display, we can finally see the individual LEDs within the display, as shown in Figure 7.43(c). That figure shows that the LEDs are clustered into groups of red, green, and blue LEDs—each cluster represents one pixel. For the LED video display shown in Figure 7.43, each cluster of LEDs consists of five LEDs: two red, two green, and one blue LED. Giant video displays are indeed intended to be viewed from a distance, so most viewers don't see the individual LEDs.

Assume we want to create an LED video display capable of displaying a 720x480 pixel video, where each pixel simply consists of one red, one green, and one blue LED. If each LED cluster has a width of just over 3/8 inch (10 millimeters) and a height of 3/8 inch, our display will be roughly 24 feet wide and 16 feet high. Furthermore, our display will contain over one million individual LEDs, because 720 * 480 = 345,600 pixels, and the three LEDs per pixel results in 1,036,800 LEDs.

Controlling every LED using a single digital circuit would require millions of output pins and miles of wire to connect all of the LEDs. Instead, as depicted in Figure 7.44, an LED video display is constructed of smaller and smaller components. The LED display consists of an array of smaller components called *panels*, shown in Figure 7.44(a). The panels are large display components typically designed in a modular fashion such that display manufacturers can easily create custom-size video displays and repair broken components within a display simply by replacing individual panels. The LED display panels are further divided into LED *modules* that control the physical LEDs, shown in Figure 7.44(b). An LED module is the basic display component and, depending on the design of the module, can control anywhere from a few hundred to a couple thousand LEDs. For example, in designing a 720x480 pixel display, we may want to use an array of 6x6 panels, where each panel consists of an array of 5x5 LED modules. Each LED

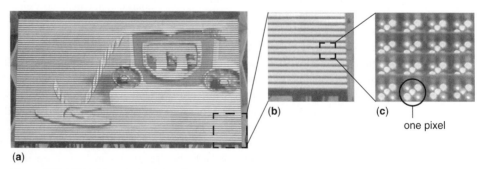

Figure 7.43 LED video display: (a) a large LED display (about 10 yards wide and 5 yards tall), (b) a closer view showing about 1 square yard, (c) a very close view showing about 1 square inch—16 "pixels" can be seen, each pixel having 2 red (upper-left and lower-right of pixel), 2 green (upper-right and lower-left of pixel), and 1 blue LED (center of pixel).

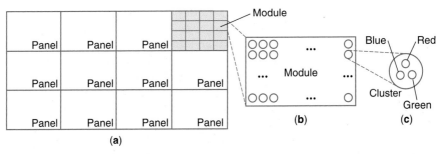

Figure 7.44 LED video displays are designed hierarchically: (a) the LED display consists of several larger panels, which can be composed to create different-sized displays, and which can be individually replaced to repair broken panels, (b) each panel consists of several smaller LED modules, responsible for controlling the individual pixels, and (c) each pixel consists of a cluster of red, green, and blue LEDs.

module would then need to control an array of 24x16 pixels, where each pixel is composed of three LEDs.

The LED video display operates by dividing the incoming video stream into separate streams for each panel. The panels further process the video stream by dividing the incoming video stream into even smaller streams for the LED modules. Finally, the LEDs modules display the video frames by controlling the LEDs to output the correct colors for each pixel, or LED cluster.

LED Module

The LED module controls the individual LEDs within the video display by turning the LEDs *on* and *off* at the proper times to create the final color images. Because each LED module can consist of thousands of LEDs, directly controlling each LED would require too many wires. Instead, as shown on Figure 7.45, the LEDs within the LED module are connected in a matrix with a single control wire for each row and three control wires for each column (one wire for each colored LED

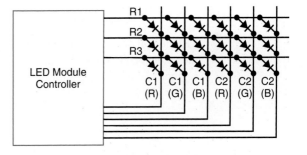

Figure 7.45 LED module circuit consisting of a matrix of red (R), green (G), and blue (B) LEDs controlled by the LED module controller. R1/R2/R3 are rows 1 through 3, and C1/C2 are columns 1 and 2—thus the matrix shown is 2x3 pixels, or 6 pixels total, with 18 LEDs total (3 LEDs per pixel).

within the LED clusters). In the figure, the LED module controller controls an array of 2x3 pixels, where each pixel consists of three individual LEDs, for a total of 18 LEDs. But as shown, the controller uses only 9 wires to control those 18 LEDs. The wire saving using this row and column approach becomes even more significant for more pixels. An LED module with 24x16 pixels and three LEDs per pixel would have 24*16*3 = 1152 LEDs, but the controller would require only 16 wires (one per row) plus 24*3 wires (three per column), for a total of only 88 wires. The LED module controller displays a video image by sequentially scanning, or enabling, each row and displaying the pixel values for each column within the video image. Using this technique, only one row of LEDs is illuminated at any given time. However, the LED module scans the rows quickly enough that the human eye perceives all rows as being illuminated.

The LED module must control the LEDs to create the desired color for each pixel. Each pixel within a video frame is typically represented using an RGB color space. An RGB (red/green/blue) color space is a method to create any color of light by adding specific intensities, or brightnesses, of red, green, and blue colors. Each pixel within a video frame may be represented as three 8-bit binary numbers, where each 8-bit number specifies the intensity of the red, green, or blue colors. Thus, for each color, the LED module must be able to provide 256 distinct brightness levels. However, an LED by itself only supports two values: *on* and *off*, or full intensity and no intensity.

The largest LED display in 2004 was 135 feet wide by 26 feet tall, built using 10 large FPGAs, 323 moderate-size FPGAs, 333 flash memories, and 3800 PLDs.
(Source: Xcell Journal, Winter 2004.)

To support 256 brightness levels, the LED module controller uses pulse width modulation. In ***pulse-width modulation*** (also known as ***PWM***), a controller drives a wire with a 1 value for a specific percentage of a time period—the signal being 1 is known as a pulse, the duration of the 1 is known as the pulse's width, and the percentage of the period spent at 1 is known as the *duty cycle*. When that pulse drives an LED, a wider pulse causes the LED to appear brighter to the human eye. Figure 7.46 illustrates how the LED module controller uses pulse width modulation to support various brightness levels for the LEDs. To illuminate an LED at full brightness, the controller simply drives the LED with 1 for the entire period, as shown in Figure 7.46(a). To illuminate the LED at half brightness, the controller uses a pulse with a 50% duty cycle, as shown in Figure 7.46(b). For 25% brightness, the controller sets the pulse to 1 for 25% of the period, meaning a 25% duty cycle, as shown in Figure 7.46(c). For an LED video display, the LED module controller divides the length of time each row is scanned into 255 time segments, and controls the brightness of the LEDs by turning each LED *on* for 0 to 255 time segments, thereby supporting 256 levels of intensity.

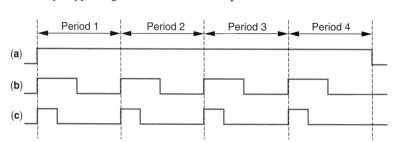

Figure 7.46 Pulse width modulation can be used to create various LED brightness levels: (a) for full brightness, the LED is always on, (b) for half brightness, the LED is turned on 50% of the time, and (c) for quarter brightness, the LED is turned on 25% of the time.

Because an LED module controller must provide precisely timed signals at a fast rate, custom processors are commonly used rather than just microprocessors. FPGAs are a common choice for implementing those custom processor circuits in LED video displays, for several reasons. First, FPGAs are fast enough to support the required scan rates. Second, the circuit on the FPGAs can be easily changed, making it possible for the display manufacturer to fix bugs in the circuit, and even upgrade the circuit, without requiring the high cost of creating a new ASIC. Third, the displays themselves are fairly large, expensive, and consume much power, and therefore the larger size, higher cost, and more power consumption of FPGAs compared to ASICs do not impact the overall display's size, cost, and power too significantly.

▶ 7.7 CHAPTER SUMMARY

Section 7.1 discussed the idea that circuits must be mapped to a physical implementation so that those circuits can be inserted into a real system. Section 7.2 introduced some IC types that require that a new chip be fabricated to implement our circuit. A full-custom IC type gives the most optimized implementation, but is expensive and time-consuming to design. Semicustom IC types give very good implementations while costing less and taking less time to design, through the predesigning of the gates or cells that will be used on the IC. Section 7.3 described the increasingly popular IC type of FPGAs, and showed how a circuit could be mapped onto a set of programmable lookup tables and switch matrices. Section 7.4 highlighted several other IC types, including off-the-shelf SSI/MSI ICs, and programmable logic devices. Section 7.5 provided some data showing the relative popularity of the IC types described in the chapter.

An interesting trend in physical implementation is the trend toward programmable ICs (FPGAs in particular). Implementing functionality on an FPGA involves the task of downloading a bitstream into the FPGA IC device. One might notice the similarity of that task with the task of implementing functionality on a microprocessor, which also involves downloading bits into an IC device. Thus, the difference between software on a microprocessor and custom digital circuits continues to be blurred—especially when one considers that modern FPGAs can also include one or several microprocessors within the same IC. For more information on the blurring, see "The Softening of Hardware," F. Vahid, *IEEE Computer*, April 2003, and also "It's Time to Stop Calling Circuits Hardware," F. Vahid, *IEEE Computer*, September 2007.

▶ 7.8 EXERCISES

SECTION 7.2: MANUFACTURED IC TYPES

7.1 Explain why a gate array IC type has a shorter production time than a full-custom IC type.

7.2 Explain why the use of NAND or NOR gates in a CMOS gate array circuit implementation is typically preferred over an AND/OR/NOT implementation of a circuit.

7.3 Draw a gate array IC having three rows, the first row having four 2-input AND gates, the second row having four 2-input OR gates, and the third row having four NOT gates. Show how to instantiate wires to the gate array to implement the function `F(a,b,c) = abc + a'b'c'`.

7.4 Assume that a standard cell library has a 2-input AND gate, a 2-input OR gate, and a NOT gate. Use a drawing to show how to instantiate and place standard cells on an IC and wire them together to implement the function in Exercise 7.3. Draw your cells the same size as the gates in Exercise 7.3, and be sure your rows are of equal size.

7.5 Draw a gate array IC having three rows, the first row having four 2-input AND gates, the second row having four 2-input OR gates, and the third row having four NOT gates. Show

how to instantiate wires to the gate array to implement the equation F(a,b,c,d) = a'b + cd + c'.

7.6 Assume that a standard cell library has a 2-input AND gate, a 2-input OR gate, and a NOT gate. Use a drawing to show how to instantiate and place standard cells on an IC and wire them together to implement the function in Exercise 7.5. Be sure to draw your cells the same size as the gates in Exercise 7.5, and be sure your rows are of equal size.

7.7 Consider the implementations of a half-adder with a gate array in Figure 7.7 and with standard cells in Figure 7.5. Assume that each gate or cell (including inverters) has a delay of 1 ns. Also assume that every inch of wire (for each inch in your drawing, not on an actual IC) has a delay of 3 ns (wires are relatively slow in the era of tiny fast transistors). Estimate the delay of the gate array and the standard cell circuits.

7.8 For your solutions to Exercise 7.3 and Exercise 7.4, assume that each gate and cell has a delay of 1 ns, and that every inch of wire (for each inch in your drawing, not on an actual IC) corresponds to a delay of 3 ns. Estimate the delays of the gate array and standard cell circuits.

7.9 Draw a circuit using AND, OR, and NOT gates for the following equation: F(a, b, c) = a'bc + abc'. Place inversion bubbles on that circuit to convert the circuit to:
(a) NAND gates only,
(b) NOR gates only.

7.10 Draw a circuit using AND, OR, and NOT gates for the following equation: F(a, b, c) = abc + a' + b' + c'. Place inversion bubbles on that circuit to convert the circuit to:
(a) NAND gates only,
(b) NOR gates only.

7.11 Draw a circuit using AND, OR, and NOT gates for the following equation: F(a, b, c) = (ab + c)(a' + d) + c'. Convert the circuit to a circuit using:
(a) NAND gates only,
(b) NOR gates only.

7.12 Draw a circuit using AND, OR, and NOT gates for the following equation: F(w, x, y, z) = (w + x)(y + z) + wy + xz. Convert the circuit to a circuit using:
(a) NAND gates only,
(b) NOR gates only.

7.13 Draw a circuit using AND, OR, and NOT gates for the following equation: F(a, b, c, d) = (ab)(b' + c) + (a'd + c'). Convert the circuit to a circuit using:
(a) NAND gates only,
(b) NOR gates only.

7.14 Show how to convert the following gates into circuits having only 3-input NAND gates:
(a) A 3-input AND gate.
(b) A 3-input OR gate.
(c) A NOT gate.

7.15 Assume that a standard cell library consists of 2-input and 3-input NAND gates with a delay of 1 ns each, 2-input and 3-input AND and OR gates with a delay of 1.8 ns each, and a NOT gate with a delay of 1 ns. Compare the number of transistors and the delay of an implementation using only AND/OR/NOT gates with an implementation using only NAND gates for the function: F(a, b, c) =ab'c + a'b. For calculating the size of an implementation, assume that each gate input requires two transistors.

7.16 Assume that a standard cell library consists of 2-input AND and OR gates with a delay of 1 ns each, 3-input AND and OR gates with a delay of 1.5 ns each, and a NOT gate with a delay of 1 ns. Compare the number of transistors and the delay of an implementation using only 2-input AND/OR gates and NOT gates with an implementation using only 3-input AND/OR gates and NOT gates for the function: $F(a, b, c) = abc + a'b'c + a'b'c'$. For calculating the size of an implementation, assume that each gate input requires two transistors.

7.17 Assume a standard cell library consisting of 2-input NAND and NOR gates with a delay of 1 ns each, and 3-input NAND and NOR gates with a delay of 1.5 ns each. Compare the number of transistors and the delay of an implementation using only 2-input NAND/NOR gates with an implementation using only 3-input NAND/NOR gates for the function: $F(a, b, c) = a'bc + ab'c + abc'$. For calculating the size of an implementation, assume that each gate input requires two transistors.

SECTION 7.3: PROGRAMMABLE IC TYPE—FPGA

7.18 Show how to implement on a 3-input 2-output lookup table the function $F(a, b, c) = a + bc$.

7.19 Show how to implement on two 3-input 2-output lookup tables the function $F(a, b, c, d) = ab + cd$. Assume you can connect the lookup tables in a custom manner (i.e., do not use a switch matrix, just directly connect your wires).

7.20 Show how to implement on two 3-input 2-output lookup tables the following function: $F(a, b, c, d) = a'bd + b'cd'$. Assume the two lookup tables are connected in the manner shown in Figure 7.47. You may not need to use every lookup table output.

7.21 Show how to implement on two 3-input 2-output lookup tables the following functions: $F(x, y, z) = x'y + xyz'$ and $G(w, x, y, z) = w'x'y + w'xyz'$. Assume the two lookup tables are connected in the manner shown in Figure 7.47.

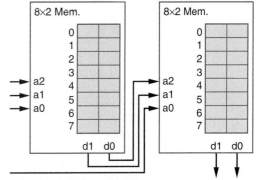

Figure 7.47 Two 3-input 2-output lookup tables implemented using 8x2 memory.

7.22 Show how to implement on two 3-input 2-output lookup tables the following functions: $F(a, b, c, d) = abc + d$ and $G = a'$. You must implement both F and G with only two lookup tables connected in the manner shown in Figure 7.47.

7.23 Implement a 2-bit comparator that compares two 2-bit numbers and has three outputs indicating greater-than, less-than, and equal-to, using any number of 3-input 2-output lookup tables and custom connections among the lookup tables.

7.24 Show how to implement a 4-bit carry-ripple adder using any number of 3-input 2-input lookup tables and custom connections among the lookup tables. Hint: map one full-adder to each lookup table.

7.25 Show how to implement a 4-bit carry-ripple adder using any number of 4-input 1-output lookup tables and custom connections among the lookup tables.

7.26 Show how to implement a comparator that compares two 8-bit numbers and has a single equal-to output, using any number of 4-input 1-output lookup tables and custom connections among the lookup tables.

7.27 Show the bit file necessary to program the FPGA fabric in Figure 7.31 to implement the function $F(a, b, c, d) = ab + cd$, where a, b, c, and d are external inputs.

7.28 Show the bit file necessary to program the FPGA fabric in Figure 7.31 to implement the function $F(a, b, c, d) = abcd$, where a, b, c, and d are external inputs.

7.29 Show the bit file necessary to program the FPGA fabric in Figure 7.31 to implement the function $F(a, b, c, d) = a'b' + c'd$, where a, b, c, and d are external inputs.

SECTION 7.4: OTHER IC TYPES

7.30 Use any combination of 7400 ICs listed in Table 7.1 to implement the function $F(a, b, c, d)$ = ab + cd.

7.31 Use any combination of 7400 ICs listed in Table 7.1 to implement the function $F(a, b, c, d)$ = abc + ab'c' + a'bd + a'b'd'.

7.32 By drawing Xs on the circuit, program the PLD of Figure 7.38(a) to implement a full-adder.

7.33 By drawing Xs on the circuit, program the PLD of Figure 7.38(a) to implement a 2-bit equality comparator. Assume the PLD has an additional I4 input.

7.34 *(a)Design a PLD device capable of supporting a 2-bit carry-ripple adder. By drawing Xs on your PLD circuit, program the PLD to implement the 2-bit carry-ripple adder.
(b) Using a CPLD device consisting of several PLDs from Figure 7.38(a) and assuming you can connect the PLDs in a custom manner, implement the 2-bit carry-ripple adder by drawing Xs on the PLDs.
(c) Compare the size of your PLD and the CPLD by determining the gates required for both designs (make sure you compare the number of gates within the PLD and CPLD and not the number of gates used for your implementation).

SECTION 7.5: IC TYPE COMPARISONS

7.35 For each of the system constraints below, choose the most appropriate technology from among FPGA, standard cell, and full-custom IC types for implementing a given circuit. Justify your answers.
(a) The system must exist as a physical prototype by next week.
(b) The system should be as small and low-power as possible. Short design time and low cost are *not* priorities.
(c) The system should be reprogrammable even after the final product has been produced.
(d) The system should be as fast as possible and should consume as little power as possible, subject to being completely implemented in just a few months.
(e) Only five copies of the system will be produced and we have no more than $1000 to spend on all the ICs.

7.36 Which of the following implementations are *not* possible? (1) A custom processor on an FPGA. (2) A custom processor on an ASIC. (3) A custom processor on a full-custom IC. (4) A programmable processor on an FPGA. (5) A programmable processor on an ASIC. (6) A programmable processor on a full-custom IC. For each, explain your answer.

CHAPTER 8

Programmable Processors

▶ 8.1 INTRODUCTION

Digital circuits designed to perform a single processing task, such as a seat belt warning light, a pacemaker, or an FIR filter, form a common class of digital circuits. A circuit performing a single processing task is a ***single-purpose processor***. Single-purpose processors represent a class of digital circuits enabling tremendously fast or power-efficient computation. However, another class of digital circuits, known as programmable processors, is also popular. Programmable processors are largely responsible for the computing revolution that has taken place in the past several decades, leading to what many call the information age. A ***programmable processor***, also known as a ***general-purpose processor***, is a digital circuit whose particular processing task is stored in a memory rather than being built into the circuit itself. The representation of that processing task in the memory is known as a ***program***. Figure 8.1 illustrates single-purpose versus general-purpose processors. A designer could create a custom digital circuit for a seat belt warning light system (Chapter 2) or an FIR filter system (Chapter 5), or instead could program a general-purpose processor circuit to implement those systems.

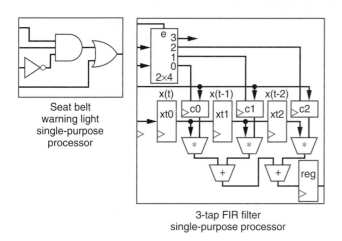

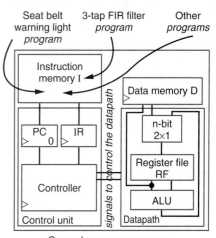

Figure 8.1 Single-purpose versus general-purpose processors.

Some programmable processors, like the well-known Intel Pentium processor or Sun's Sparc processor, are intended for use in desktop computers. Other programmable processors, like ARM, MIPS, 8051, and PIC processors, which are widely known in the design community but less known by the general public, are intended for *embedded computing systems* like cellular telephones, automobiles, video games, or even tennis shoes with blinking lights. Some programmable processors, like the PowerPC, are intended for both desktop and embedded domains.

A benefit of a programmable processor is that its circuit can be mass-produced and then programmed to do almost anything. Thus, a particular programmable desktop processor can run Windows 7, Windows XP, Linux, or some new operating system. That same processor can run application programs like word processors, spreadsheets, video games, and web browsers. Likewise, a particular programmable embedded processor can be used in a cell phone, automobile, video game, or tennis shoe by programming the processor for the desired processing task. Mass-production results in low costs due to amortization of design costs (see "Why such cheap calculators?" in Chapter 4 for a discussion of amortization).

Of course, because programmable processors are mass-produced and then used for a wide variety of applications, there aren't as many unique programmable processor designs as there are single-purpose processor designs. There are also far fewer programmable processor *designers* than there are single-purpose processor designers. Nevertheless, even though you may never design a programmable processor as part of a job, it is interesting and enlightening to understand how such a programmable processor works. Some people argue that designers who understand how a processor works are better software programmers. And technology trends have led to the situation of designers being able to create semicustom processors ("application-specific" processors) that have just the right architecture for one or a small number of applications, making knowledge of programmable processor designs important. Finally, there are indeed people who do design programmable processor architectures.

This chapter shows how to design a simple programmable processor using the previously-described digital design methods. The purpose is mainly to demystify these devices and to provide an insight on how programmable processors work. Real mass-produced processors are designed using different methods, and their designs can be much more complex than the design described in this chapter—learning about those processors' designs is the subject of many textbooks on computer architecture.

▶ 8.2 BASIC ARCHITECTURE

A programmable processor consists of two main parts: a datapath and a control unit. This section provides a general introduction to those two parts, and then a later section provides a more detailed look at those parts.

Basic Datapath

Processing generally consists of transforming input data into output data. For example, a seat belt warning system reads bit data from sensors representing whether a seat belt is fastened and whether a person is sitting in a seat, transforms that data by computing a new bit indicating whether to turn on a warning light, and writes that new data to a warning light. An FIR filter reads data representing the most recent set of input signal samples, transforms that data by performing multiplies and adds, and writes new data to an output representing the filtered signal. The transformations take place inside a processor's *datapath*, which consists of several parts.

A *data memory* contains the programmable processor's input and output data. Components external to the processor, such as sensors or displays, may also access that memory to write or read that data, perhaps through a second memory port (not shown). For example, an FIR filter system may have a component that writes digitized signal values to a particular word in the data memory, which the processor can read. To process that data, a programmable processor needs to be able to *load* data from the data memory into one of several registers (typically a register file) within the processor, needs to be able to feed data from some subset of registers through functional units that can perform *transformation* operations (typically an ALU) with results stored back into a register, and needs to be able to *store* data from a register back into data memory. Therefore, a programmable processor needs the basic circuit shown in Figure 8.2, having a data memory, register file, and ALU, together comprising a datapath. The basic datapath shown in Figure 8.2 can perform the following possible *datapath operations* in a given clock cycle:

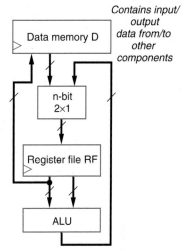

Contains input/ output data from/to other components

Figure 8.2 Basic datapath of a programmable processor.

- *Load operation:* This operation loads (reads) data from any location in the data memory into any register in the register file. A load operation is illustrated in Figure 8.3(a).

- *ALU operation:* This operation transforms register data by passing any two registers through the ALU configured for any of the ALU's supported operations, and back into any register of the register file. An ALU operation is illustrated in Figure 8.3(b). Typical ALU operations include addition, subtraction, logical AND, logical OR, etc.

- *Store operation:* This operation stores (writes) data from any register in the register file to any data memory location. A store operation is illustrated in Figure 8.3(c).

Each such operation requires the appropriate setting of the control inputs of the data memory, mux, register file, and ALU—those control inputs will be shown shortly. For now, just familiarize yourself with the basic datapath's abilities. Notice that the datapath in Figure 8.2 cannot directly operate on data memory locations with the ALU in one clock cycle, because the data must first be read into the register file, which itself requires a clock cycle, before the data can be operated on by the ALU. A datapath that requires all

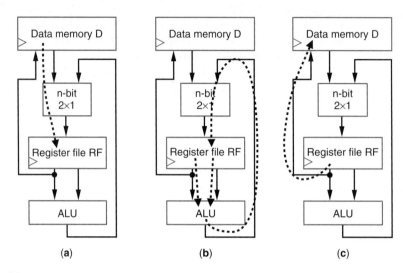

Figure 8.3 Basic datapath operations: (a) load (read), (b) ALU operation (transform), and (c) store (write).

data to first pass through the register file before that data can be transformed by the ALU is known as a ***load-store architecture***.

Example 8.1 Understanding datapath operations

Which of the following are valid single-clock-cycle datapath operations for the datapath of Figure 8.2?

1. Copy data from a data memory location into a register file location.

2. Read data from two data memory locations into two register file locations.

3. Add data from two data memory locations and store the result in a register file location.

4. Copy data from one register file location to another register file location.

5. Subtract data in a register file location from a data memory location, storing the result in a register file location.

(1) is a valid operation, known as a load operation. (2) is *not* a valid operation. The datapath does not support reading more than one data memory location during a datapath operation, and it does not support writing to more than one register file location during an operation. (3) is *not* a valid operation. The datapath does not support reading two data memory locations during one operation, and furthermore does not have connections directly from the data memory to the ALU to perform the add. (4) is a valid operation. The ALU can be configured to simply pass one of its inputs through to the output (perhaps by adding 0) and storing the result in the register file. (5) is *not* a valid operation. A read data memory location cannot be fed directly to the ALU—there is no such connection in the datapath. Values read from data memory must be loaded into the register file first.

Basic Control Unit

Suppose the basic datapath of Figure 8.2 should perform the simple processing task of adding data memory location 0 and data memory location 1 together, and writing the result in data memory location 9—in other words, computing $D[9] = D[0] + D[1]$. This processing task can be achieved by "instructing" the datapath to perform the following operations:

- *load* datapath memory location 0 to register $RF[0]$ (i.e., $RF[0] = D[0]$),
- *load* datapath memory location 1 to register $RF[1]$ (i.e., $RF[1] = D[1]$),
- perform an *ALU* operation that adds $RF[0]$ and $RF[1]$ and writes the result back into $RF[2]$ (i.e., $RF[2] = RF[0] + RF[1]$), and
- *store $RF[2]$ into data memory location 9 (i.e., D[9] = RF[2]).*

Note that any registers in the register file could be used rather than $RF[0]$, $RF[1]$, and $RF[2]$.

If $D[0]$ contained the value 99 (in binary, of course), and $D[1]$ contained the value 102, then after carrying out the above operations, $D[9]$ would contain 201.

You might think that having to instruct the datapath to perform four distinct operations is a rather cumbersome way of adding two data items. A custom digital circuit to implement $D[9] = D[0] + D[1]$ could just feed $D[0]$ and $D[1]$ through an adder whose output connects to $D[9]$, thus avoiding the four operations involving the register file and ALU. This simple example demonstrates the basic tradeoff of single-purpose versus programmable processors—programmable processors have the drawback of computation overhead because they have to be general, but they provide the benefits of a mass-produced processor that can be programmed to do almost anything.

A method is needed to describe the sequence of operations—$RF[0] = D[0]$, then $RF[1]=D[1]$, then $RF[2] = RF[0] + RF[1]$, then $D[9] = RF[2]$—that should execute on the datapath. Such a description of desired processor operations uses **instructions**, and a collection of instructions is known as a **program**. The desired program is stored in another memory called the **instruction memory**. A later section describes how to represent those instructions. For now, assume that the four instructions are somehow stored in locations 0, 1, 2, and 3 of the instruction memory *I* shown in Figure 8.4.

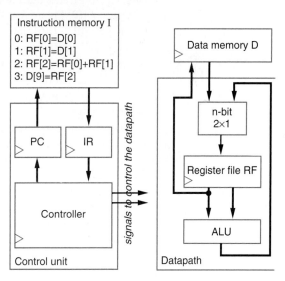

Figure 8.4 The control unit in a programmable processor.

The processor's **control unit** reads each instruction from instruction memory, and executes that instruction using the datapath. To execute the above simple program, the control unit repeatedly performs the following tasks, known as **stages**, each stage requiring one clock cycle.

1. **Fetch**: The control unit starts by reading ("fetching") the current instruction into a local register called the **instruction register** or **IR**. The current instruction's address in the instruction memory is kept in a register called the **program counter** or **PC**. The first instruction fetched for the above example will be $RF[0] = D[0]$, which will be placed into the IR.

2. **Decode**: The control unit then determines ("decodes") what operation this instruction is requesting. For the above example, the decode stage will determine that the instruction in the IR is requesting a datapath load operation.

3. **Execute**: The control unit carries out ("executes") the instruction's requested datapath operation by setting the datapath's control lines appropriately. For the above example's first instruction $RF[0] = D[0]$, the control unit would set the control lines of the datapath to read $D[0]$, set the 2x1 mux in front of the register file to pass the read data, and set the register file to store that data into $RF[0]$.

Thus, the basic stages that the control unit carries out for the first instruction are: *fetch, decode,* and *execute*, requiring three clock cycles to complete just that first instruction.

Because the instruction locations are usually in sequence, the PC can be implemented using a simple up-counter to proceed from one instruction to the next instruction of the program—hence the name "program counter." The processor starts with $PC = 0$, so the instruction in $I[0]$ represents the first instruction of the program.

Figure 8.5 illustrates the three stages of executing the program's first instruction, namely $RF[0] = D[0]$. Figure 8.5(a) shows the first stage fetching $I[0]$'s content, which is the instruction $RF[0] = D[0]$, into the *IR*. Figure 8.5(b) shows the second stage decoding the instruction and thus determining that the instruction is a load instruction. Figure 8.5(c) shows the third stage executing the instruction by configuring the datapath to read the value of $D[0]$ and storing that value into $RF[0]$. If $D[0]$ contained 99, then $RF[0]$ will contain 99 after completion of the execute stage. The first instruction thus required three clock cycles to complete.

The control unit then fetches the next instruction, which is in $I[1]$, decodes that instruction, and executes that instruction. Thus after three more clock cycles, the instruction $RF[1] = D[1]$ completes. The control unit then fetches the next instruction, which is in $I[2]$, decodes that instruction, and executes that instruction. So after three more clock cycles, the instruction $RF[2] = RF[0] + RF[1]$ completes. Finally, the control unit fetches the next instruction, which is in $I[3]$, decodes that instruction, and executes that instruction. So after another three clock cycles, the instruction $D[9] = RF[2]$ completes. The four instructions thus require $4*3 = 12$ clock cycles to run to completion on the programmable processor.

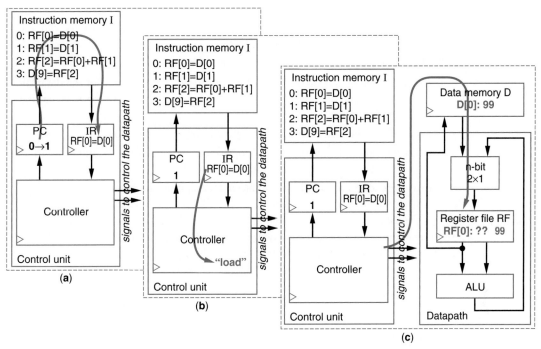

Figure 8.5 Three stages of processing *one* instruction: (a) fetch, (b) decode, (c) execute.

The control unit will require a controller, like those described in Chapter 3. After initializing the *PC* to 0, the controller repeatedly performs the fetch, decode, and execute steps—note that a controller appears inside the control unit in Figure 8.4. Figure 8.6 shows an FSM for that controller. The controller increments the program counter after fetching each instruction in state *Fetch*, so that the next fetch state will fetch the next instruction (notice that *PC* gets incremented at the end of the fetch stage in Figure 8.5(a)). We'll describe the actions of the *Decode* and *Execute* states later.

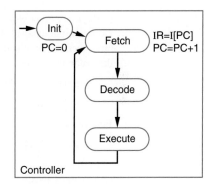

Figure 8.6 Basic controller states.

Thus, the basic parts of the control unit include the program counter *PC*, the instruction register *IR*, and a controller, as illustrated in Figure 8.4. In previous chapters, the nonprogrammable processors consisted only of a controller and a datapath. Notice that the programmable processor instead contains a control unit, which itself consists of some registers and a controller.

To summarize, the control unit processes each instruction in three stages:

1. *Fetching* the instruction by loading the current instruction into *IR* and incrementing the *PC* for the next fetch, then

2. *Decoding* the instruction to determine its operation, and finally

3. *Executing* the operation by setting the appropriate control lines for the datapath, if applicable. If the operation is a datapath operation, the operation may be one of three possible types:

   (a)*loading* a data memory location into a register file location,

   (b)*transforming* data using an *ALU* operation on register file locations and writing results back to a register file location, or

   (c)*storing* a register file location into a data memory location.

Example 8.2 Creating a simple sequence of instructions

Create a set of instructions for the processor in Figure 8.4 to compute $D[3] = D[0] + D[1] + D[2]$. Each instruction must represent a valid single-clock-cycle datapath operation.

We might start with three operations that read the data memory locations into register file locations:

0. $RF[3] = D[0]$

1. $RF[4] = D[1]$

2. $RF[2] = D[2]$

Note that we intentionally chose arbitrary register locations, to make clear that any available registers can be used.

Next, the three values need to be added and the result stored in a register file location, such as in $RF[1]$. In other words, the following operation should be performed: $R[1] = R[2] + R[3] + R[4]$. However, the datapath of Figure 8.4 cannot add three register file locations in a single operation, but rather can only add two locations. Instead, the desired addition computation can split into two datapath operations:

3. $R[1] = R[2] + R[3]$

4. $R[1] = R[1] + R[4]$

Finally, the result can be written into $D[3]$:

5. $D[3] = R[1]$

Thus, the program consists of the six instructions appearing above, which would appear in instruction memory locations 0 through 5.

Example 8.3 Evaluating the time to carry out a program

Determine the number of clock cycles required for the processor of Figure 8.4 to execute the six-instruction program of Figure 8.2.

The processor requires 3 cycles to process each instruction: 1 cycle to fetch the instruction, 1 to decode the fetched instruction, and 1 to execute the instruction. At 3 cycles per instruction, the total cycles for 6 instructions is: 6 instr * 3 cycles/instr = 18 cycles.

▶ 8.3 A THREE-INSTRUCTION PROGRAMMABLE PROCESSOR

A First Instruction Set with Three Instructions

The way instructions are represented in the instruction memory, and the list of allowable instructions, are known as a programmable processor's *instruction set*. Instruction sets typically reserve a certain number of bits in the instruction to denote what operation to perform. The remaining bits specify additional information needed to perform the operation, such as the addresses of the registers that are involved in the operation. This section defines a simple instruction set having just three instructions, each instruction being 16 bits wide (with the processor's instruction memory I being 16 bits wide). The most significant (meaning leftmost) 4 bits identify the operation, and the least significant 12 bits identify the register file and data memory addresses, as follows:

* *Load* instruction—**0000 $r_3r_2r_1r_0$ $d_7d_6d_5d_4d_3d_2d_1d_0$**: This instruction specifies a move of data from the data memory location whose address is specified by the bits $d_7d_6d_5d_4d_3d_2d_1d_0$ into the register-file register whose location is specified by the bits $r_3r_2r_1r_0$. For example, the instruction "0000 0001 00000000" specifies a move of data memory location 0, or $D[0]$, into register file location 1, or $RF[1]$—in other words, that instruction represents the operation $RF[1] = D[0]$. Likewise, "0000 0011 00101010" specifies $RF[3] = D[42]$. We've inserted spaces between some bits for ease of reading by you the reader—those spaces have no other significance and would not exist in the instruction memory.

* *Store* instruction—**0001 $r_3r_2r_1r_0$ $d_7d_6d_5d_4d_3d_2d_1d_0$**: This instruction specifies a move of data in the opposite direction as the instruction above, meaning a move from the register file to the data memory. So "0001 0000 00001001" specifies $D[9]=RF[0]$.

* *Add* instruction—**0010 $ra_3ra_2ra_1ra_0$ $rb_3rb_2rb_1rb_0$ $rc_3rc_2rc_1rc_0$**: This instruction specifies an addition of two register-file registers specified by $rb_3rb_2rb_1rb_0$ and $rc_3rc_2rc_1rc_0$, with the result stored in the register-file register specified by $ra_3ra_2ra_1ra_0$. For example, "0010 0010 0000 0001" specifies the instruction $RF[2] = RF[0] + RF[1]$. Note that *add* is an ALU operation.

None of these instructions modifies the contents of the instructions' source operands. In other words, the *load* instruction copies the contents of the data memory location to the specified register, but leaves the data memory location itself unchanged. Likewise, the *store* instruction copies the specified register to data memory, but leaves the register's contents unchanged. The *add* instruction reads its *rb* and *rc* registers without changing them. Note also that the instruction merely contains the addresses of registers (or memory); the registers themselves are in the register file.

Using this instruction set, the desired computation $D[9] = D[0] + D[1]$ can be written as the program shown in Figure 8.7.

Notice that the first four bits of each instruction are a binary code that indicates the instruction's operation. Those bits are known as the instruction's *operation code* or *opcode*. "0000" means a move from data memory to register file, "0001" means a move from register file to data memory, and "0010" means an add of two registers, based on the instruction set defined in the bulleted list above. The remaining bits of the instruction represent *operands*, which indicate what data to operate on.

The above-defined three-instruction instruction set can be used to write programs to perform other computations, such as $D[5] = D[5] + D[6] + D[7]$. Such a program is shown in Figure 8.8. The number before the colon represents the instruction's address in the instruction memory I. The text following the two forward slashes (*//*) represents a comment, and is not part of an instruction. Examining the program instruction by instruction reveals that the program computes the desired result.

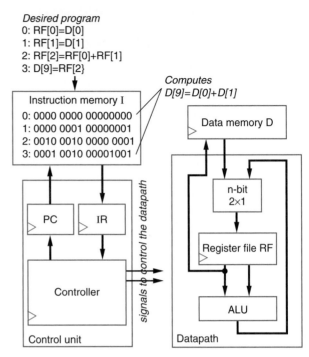

Figure 8.7 A program that computes $D[9] = D[0] + D[1]$ using a given instruction set. The spaces between the instruction memory's bits are for readability only—those spaces don't exist in the memory.

Machine Code versus Assembly Code

The instructions of a program exist in instruction memory as 0s and 1s. A program represented as 0s and 1s is known as *machine code*. Writing and reading programs represented as 0s and 1s are tasks that humans are not particularly good at. We humans can't understand those 0s and 1s easily, and thus will make plenty of mistakes when writing such programs. Thus, early computer programmers developed a tool known as an *assembler* (which itself is just another program) to help humans write programs. An assembler allows us

```
0: 0000 0000 00000101 // RF[0] = D[5]
1: 0000 0001 00000110 // RF[1] = D[6]
2: 0000 0010 00000111 // RF[2] = D[7]
3: 0010 0000 0000 0001 // RF[0] = RF[0] + RF[1]
                       // which is D[5]+D[6]
4: 0010 0000 0000 0010 // RF[0] = RF[0] + RF[2]
                       // now D[5]+D[6]+D[7]
5: 0001 0000 00000101 // D[5] = RF[0]
```

Figure 8.8 A program to compute $D[5]=D[5]+D[6]+D[7]$ using the three-instruction instruction set.

to write instructions using ***mnemonics***, or symbols, that the assembler automatically translates to machine code. Thus, an assembler may support the three-instruction instruction set using the following mnemonics:

*   ***Load*** instruction—**MOV Ra, d**: Specifies the operation $RF[a] = D[d]$. a must be 0, 1, ..., or 15—so $R0$ means $RF[0]$, $R1$ means $RF[1]$, etc. d must be 0, 1, ..., 255.
*   ***Store*** instruction—**MOV d, Ra**: Specifies the operation $D[d] = RF[a]$.
*   ***Add*** instruction—**ADD Ra, Rb, Rc**: Specifies the operation $RF[a] = RF[b] +RF[c]$.

Using those mnemonics, the program in Figure 8.7 for $D[9] = D[0] + D[1]$ could be rewritten as follows:

0: MOV R0, 0
1: MOV R1, 1
2: ADD R2, R0, R1
3: MOV 9, R2

That program is much easier to understand than the 0s and 1s in Figure 8.7. A program written using mnemonics that will be translated to machine code by an assembler is known as ***assembly code***. Hardly anybody writes machine code directly these days. An assembler would automatically translate the above assembly program to the machine code shown in Figure 8.7.

You might be wondering how the assembler can distinguish between the load and store instructions above, when the mnemonics for both instructions are the same—"MOV." The assembler distinguishes those two types of instructions by examining the first character after the mnemonic "MOV"—if the first character is an "R," then that operand is a register, and thus that instruction must be a load instruction.

Control Unit and Datapath for the Three-Instruction Processor

From the definition of the three-instruction instruction set and an understanding of the basic control unit and datapath architecture of a programmable processor as shown in Figure 8.4, a complete digital circuit for a three-instruction programmable processor can be designed. The design process is similar to the RTL design process of Chapter 5.

▶ *COMPUTERS WITH BLINKING LIGHTS.*

Big computers shown in the movies often have many rows of small blinking lights. In the early days of computing, computer programmers programmed using machine code, and they entered that code into the instruction memory by flipping switches up and down to represent 0s and 1s. To enable debugging of the program, as well as to show the computed data, those early computers used rows of lights—on lights meant 1s, off lights meant 0s. Today, nobody in their right mind would try writing or debugging a program by using machine code. So computers today look like big boxes—with no rows of lights. But big plain boxes don't make for interesting backgrounds in movies, so movie makers continue to use movie props with lots of blinking lights to represent computers—lights that are useless, but entertaining.

The process begins with a high-level state machine description of the system, shown in Figure 8.9. Assume that *op* is shorthand for *IR*[15..12], meaning the leftmost four bits of the instruction register. Likewise, *ra* means *IR*[11..8], *rb* means *IR*[7..4], *rc* means *IR*[3..0], and *d* means *IR*[7..0].

The next step in the RTL design process is to create the datapath. The datapath was already created in Figure 8.4, which is refined in Figure 8.10 to show every control signal from the controller. The refined datapath has control signals for

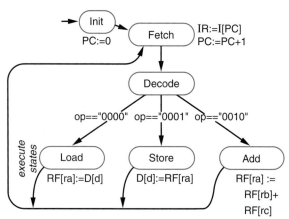

Figure 8.9 High-level state machine description of a three-instruction programmable processor.

each read and write port of the register file. The register file has 16 registers because the instructions have only 4 bits with which to address registers. The datapath has a control signal to the ALU called alu_s0—assume that the simple ALU adds its inputs when alu_s0 = 1, and just passes input *A* when alu_s0 = 0. The datapath has a select line for the 2x1 mux in front of the register file's write data port. Finally, control signals are

---

▶ *"BOOTING" A COMPUTER.*

Turning on a personal computer causes the operating system to load, a process known as "booting" the computer. The computer executes instructions beginning at address 0, which usually has an instruction that jumps to a built-in small program that loads the operating system (the small program is often called the basic input/output system, or BIOS). Most computing dictionaries state that the term "to boot" originates from the popular expression "to pull oneself up by one's bootstraps," which means to pick yourself up without any help, though obviously you can't do this by grabbing onto your own bootstraps and pulling—hence the cleverness of the expression. Since the computer loads its own operating system, the computer is in a sense picking itself up without any help. The term "bootstrap" eventually got shortened to "boot." A colleague of mine who has been around

computing a long time claims a different origin. One way of loading a program into the instruction memory of early computers was to create a ribbon with rows of holes. Each row might have enough room for, say, 16 holes, thus each row would represent a 16-bit machine instruction—a hole meant a 0, no hole a 1 (or vice versa). A programmer would punch holes in the ribbon to store the program on the ribbon (using a special hole-punching machine), and then feed the ribbon into a computer's ribbon reader, which would read the rows of 0s and 1s and load those 0s and 1s into the computer's instruction memory. Those ribbons might have been several feet long, and looked a lot like the straps of a boot, hence the term "bootstrap," shortened to "boot." Whichever is the actual origin, we can be fairly sure the term "boot" comes from the bootstraps on the boots we wear on our feet.

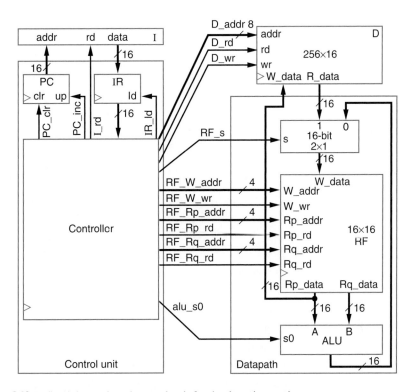

Figure 8.10 Refined datapath and control unit for the three-instruction processor.

included for the data memory, which has a single address port, and can thus support only a read or a write, but not both simultaneously. The data memory has 256 words, since the instruction only has 8 bits with which to address the data memory.

The datapath is now able to carry out all of the load/store operations and arithmetic operations needed for the HLSM from Figure 8.9. The RTL design process proceeds by connecting the datapath with a controller. Figure 8.10 shows those connections, as well as the connections of the controller to the *PC* and *IR* registers in the control unit, and to the instruction memory *I*.

The last step of the RTL design process is to derive the controller's FSM. The FSM is straightforwardly achieved by replacing the high-level actions of the HLSM in Figure 8.9 by Boolean operations on the controller's input and output lines, as shown in Figure 8.11. Remember that *op*, *d*, *ra*, *rb*, and *rc* are shorthand notations for *IR*[15...12], *IR*[7...0], *IR*[11...8], *IR*[7...4], and *IR*[3...0], respectively. The controller's design could be completed by converting the FSM to a state register and combinational logic using the methods from Chapter 3.

The resulting design represents a simple but complete programmable processor.

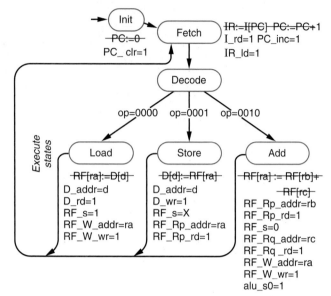

Figure 8.11 FSM for the three-instruction processor's controller.

Let's trace through the controller's FSM behavior to see how a program would execute on the three-instruction processor. Remember the FSM conventions that all transitions are implicitly ANDed with a rising clock edge, and that any control signal not explicitly assigned a value in a state is implicitly assigned a 0.

- The FSM initially starts in state *Init*, which sets PC_clr = 1, causing the *PC* register to be cleared to 0.

- The FSM on the next clock cycle enters the *Fetch* state, in which the FSM reads the instruction memory *I* at address 0 (because *PC* is 0) and loads the read value into *IR*—that read value will be the instruction that was in *I*[0]. At the same time, the FSM increments the *PC*'s value.

- The FSM on the next clock cycle enters the *Decode* state, which has no actions but which branches on the next clock cycle to one of three states, *Load*, *Store*, or *Add*, depending on the values of the highest four bits of the *IR* register (i.e., depending on the current instruction's opcode).

- In the *Load* state, the FSM sets the data memory address lines to the low eight bits of the *IR* and sets the data memory read enable to 1, sets the 2x1 mux's select line to pass the data memory output to the register file, and sets the register file write address to *ra* (which is *IR*[11...8]) and the write enable to 1, causing whatever gets read from the data memory to be loaded into the appropriate register in the register file.

- Likewise, the *Store* and *Add* states set the control lines as needed for the store and add operations.

- Finally, the FSM returns to the *Fetch* state, and begins fetching the next instruction.

Notice that because the *Store* state does not write to the register file, then the value of the register file's mux select lines don't matter, so that state assigns RF_s = X in that state, meaning the signal's value does not matter. Using such don't care values (see Section 6.2) can help to minimize the logic in the controller.

You may wonder why the *Decode* state is necessary when that state contains no actions—couldn't *Decode*'s transitions instead originate from state *Fetch*? Recall from Section 5.2 that register updates listed in a state do not actually occur until the next clock edge, meaning that transitions originating from a state use the previous register values. Thus, we could not have originated *Decode*'s transitions from the *Fetch* state, because those transitions would have been using the old opcode in the instruction register *IR*, not the new value read during the *Fetch* state.

► 8.4 A SIX-INSTRUCTION PROGRAMMABLE PROCESSOR

Extending the Instruction Set

Clearly, having only a three-instruction instruction set limits the behavior of the programs. The only thing instructions can do is add numbers. A typical programmable processor may have 100 or more instructions to support a wider variety of programs. This section introduces three new instructions to illustrate how the programmable processor's instruction set can be expanded with more instructions.

The first new instruction can load a constant value into a register-file register. For example, consider wanting to compute $RF[0] = RF[1] + 5$. The 5 is a constant. A *constant* is a value that is part of a program, not a value to be found in data memory. An instruction is thus needed that can load a constant into a register, e.g., to support an instruction like $RF[2] = 5$. A new instruction can be introduced with the following machine and assembly code representations:

- ***Load-constant*** instruction—**0011** $r_3r_2r_1r_0$ $c_7c_6c_5c_4c_3c_2c_1c_0$: specifies that the binary number represented by the bits $c_7c_6c_5c_4c_3c_2c_1c_0$ should be loaded into the register specified by $r_3r_2r_1r_0$. The binary number being loaded is known as a *constant*. For example, "0011 0010 00000101" specifies the instruction $RF[2] = 5$. The mnemonic for this instruction is:

   MOV Ra, #c—specifies the operation $RF[a] = c$

a can be 0, 1, ..., or 15. Assuming two's complement representation (see Section 4.6), *c* can be –128, –127, ..., 0, ..., 126, 127. The "#" is a special symbol that enables the assembler to distinguish this instruction from a regular load instruction.

Another new instruction performs subtraction of two registers, similar to addition of two registers, having the following machine and assembly code representations:

- ***Subtract*** instruction—**0100** $ra_3ra_2ra_1ra_0$ $rb_3rb_2rb_1rb_0$ $rc_3rc_2rc_1rc_0$: specifies subtraction of two register-file registers specified by $rb_3rb_2rb_1rb_0$ and $rc_3rc_2rc_1rc_0$, with the result stored in the register-file register specified by $ra_3ra_2ra_1ra_0$. For example, "0100   0010   0000   0001" specifies the instruction $RF[2] = RF[0] – RF[1]$. The mnemonic for this instruction is

   SUB Ra, Rb, Rc—specifies the operation $RF[a] = RF[b] – RF[c]$

A third new instruction allows the program to jump to other parts of a program:

- *Jump-if-zero* instruction—**0101 $ra_3ra_2ra_1ra_0$ $o_7o_6o_5o_4o_3o_2o_1o_0$**: specifies that if the contents of the register specified by $ra_3ra_2ra_1ra_0$ are 0, the *PC* should be loaded with the current value of *PC* plus $o_7o_6o_5o_4o_3o_2o_1o_0$, which is an 8-bit number in two's complement form representing a positive or negative offset amount. For example, "0101 0011 11111110" specifies that if the value in *RF*[3] is 0, then the *PC* should be set to *PC* – 2. The mnemonic is

JMPZ Ra, offset—specifies the operation $PC = PC +$ *offset* if *RF[a]* is 0.

Negative jump offsets are commonly used to implement a loop. The 8-bit offset can specify an offset forward by 127 addresses, or backward by 128 addresses (−128 to +127).

Table 8.1 summarizes the six-instruction instruction set. A programmable processor typically comes with a databook that lists the processor's instructions and the meaning of each instruction, using a format similar to the format of Table 8.1. Typical programmable processors have dozens or hundreds of instructions.

TABLE 8.1 Six-instruction instruction set.

Instruction	Meaning
MOV Ra, d	RF[a] = D[d]
MOV d, Ra	D[d] = RF[a]
ADD Ra, Rb, Rc	RF[a] = RF[b]+RF[c]
MOV Ra, #C	RF[a] = C
SUB Ra, Rb, Rc	RF[a] = RF[b]-RF[c]
JMPZ Ra, offset	PC=PC+offset if RF[a]=0

Extending the Control Unit and Datapath

The three new instructions require some extensions, shown in Figure 8.12, to the control unit and datapath of Figure 8.10. First, the *load constant* instruction requires that the register file be able to load data from *IR*[7...0], in addition to data from data memory or from the ALU output. Thus, the register file's multiplexer is widened from 2x1 to 3x1, another mux control signal is added, and a new signal coming from the controller labeled *RF_W_data* is added, which will connect with *IR*[7...0]. These changes are highlighted by the dashed circle labeled "*1*" in Figure 8.12.

Second, the subtract instruction requires using an ALU capable of subtraction, so another ALU control signal is added, highlighted by the dashed circle labeled "*2*" in the figure. Third, the jump-if-zero instruction requires that the ability to detect if a register is zero, and the ability to add *IR*[7...0] to the *PC*. Thus, a datapath component is inserted to detect if the register file's *Rp* read port is all zeros (that component would just be a NOR gate), labeled as dashed-circle "*3a*" in the figure. The *PC* register is upgraded so it can be loaded with *PC* plus *IR*[7...0], labeled as "*3b*" in the figure. The adder used for this also subtracts 1 from the sum, to compensate for the fact that the *Fetch* state already added 1 to the *PC*.

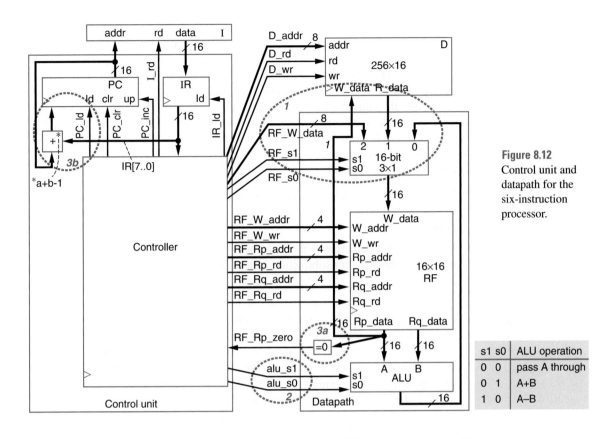

Figure 8.12
Control unit and datapath for the six-instruction processor.

s1	s0	ALU operation
0	0	pass A through
0	1	A+B
1	0	A–B

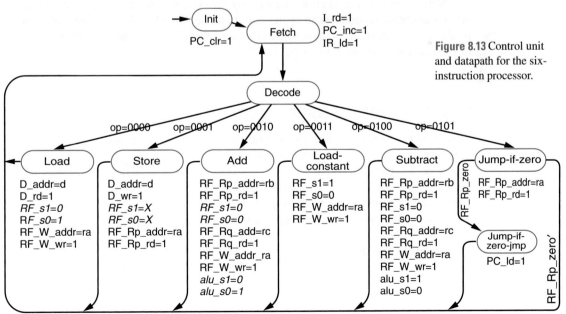

Figure 8.13 Control unit and datapath for the six-instruction processor.

The FSM for the controller within the control unit must also be extended to handle the three additional instructions, as in Figure 8.13. The *Init* and *Fetch* states stay the same. The FSM has three new transitions from the *Decode* state for the three new instruction opcodes. A minor revision was made to the *Load*, *Store*, and *Add* states' actions (the new actions are italicized) because the register file mux now has a mux with two select lines instead of just one. Likewise, the *Add* state actions were revised to configure the ALU with two control lines instead of one. The FSM has four new states, *Load-constant*, *Subtract*, *Jump-if-zero*, and *Jump-if-zero-jmp*, for the three new instructions. Those new states perform the following functions on the datapath:

- The *Load-constant* state configures the register file mux to pass the *RF_W_data* signal, and configures the register file to write to the address specified by *ra* (which is *IR*[11...8]).

- The *Subtract* state performs the same actions as in the *Add* state, except the state configures the ALU for subtraction instead of addition.

- The *Jump-if-zero* state configures the register file to read the register specified by *ra* onto read port *Rp*. If the value of the read register *Rp* is all 0s, RF_Rp_zero will become 1 (and 0 otherwise). Thus, the state has two outgoing transitions. One transition will be taken if RF_Rp_zero is 0, meaning the read register was not all 0s—that transition takes the FSM back to the *Fetch* state, meaning no actual jump occurs. The other transition will be taken if RF_Rp_zero is 1, meaning the read register was all 0s. That transition goes to another state, *Jump-if-zero-jmp*, which actually carries out the jump. That state carries out the jump simply by setting the load line of the *PC*.

Notice that with the addition of a *Jump-if-zero* instruction, the processor may require up to four cycles to complete an instruction. In particular, when the *ra* register of a *Jump-if-zero* instruction is all 0s, then an extra state is needed to load the *PC* with the address of the instruction to which to jump.

▶ 8.5 EXAMPLE ASSEMBLY AND MACHINE PROGRAMS

This section provides an example of assembly-language programming of the six-instruction processor to perform a particular task. The section shows how the assembly code would be converted to machine code by an assembler. An assembler would make use of the table shown in Table 8.2, which summarizes the mapping of instructions to opcodes.

TABLE 8.2 Instruction opcodes.

Instruction	Opcode
MOV Ra, d	0000
MOV d, Ra	0001
ADD Ra, Rb, Rc	0010
MOV Ra, #C	0011
SUB Ra, Rb, Rc	0100
JMPZ Ra, offset	0101

MOV R0, #0; // initialize result to 0	0011 0000 00000000
MOV R1, #1; // constant 1 for incrementing result	0011 0001 00000001
MOV R2, 4; // get data memory location 4	0000 0010 00000100
JMPZ R2, lab1; // if zero, skip next instruction	0101 0010 00000010
ADD R0, R0, R1; // not zero, so increment result	0010 0000 0000 0001
lab1:MOV R2, 5; // get data memory location 5	0000 0010 00000101
JMPZ R2, lab2; // if zero, skip next instruction	0101 0010 00000010
ADD R0, R0, R1; //not zero, so increment result	0010 0000 0000 0001
lab2:MOV 9, R0; // store result in data memory location 9	0001 0000 00001001

(a)   (b)

Figure 8.14 A program to count the number of nonzero numbers in $D[4]$ and $D[5]$, storing the result in $D[9]$: (a) assembly code, and (b) corresponding machine code generated by an assembler. The spaces in the machine code's 16-bit instructions are there for your convenience as you read this book; actual machine code has no such spaces.

Example 8.4 Assembly and machine programs for a simple program

Write a program that counts the number of words that are not equal to 0 in data memory locations 4 and 5, and that stores the result in data memory location 9. Thus, the possible results that would be stored in location 9 are zero, one, or two.

Using the instruction set of Table 8.2, we can write an assembly program as shown in Figure 8.14(a). The program maintains the count in register $R0$, which the program initializes to 0. The program may need to add 1 to this register later, so the program loads the value 1 into register $R1$. The program next loads data memory location 4 into register $R2$. The program then jumps to the instruction labeled as *lab1* if the value of $R2$ is zero. If $R2$ is not zero, the program will execute an add instruction that adds one to register $R0$, and will then proceed to the instruction labeled *lab1* since that instruction is the next instruction. The instruction labeled *lab1* loads data memory location 5 into register $R2$. The program jumps to the instruction labeled *lab2* if $R2$ is zero. If $R2$ is not zero, the program executes an add instruction that adds one to register $R0$, and then proceeds to the next instruction, which is the instruction labeled *lab2*. That instruction stores the contents of register $R0$ to data memory location 9.

In writing the assembly program, we arbitrarily chose the registers used to store the result, the constant 1, and the value read from the data memory. We could have used any registers for those purposes. For example, we could have used register $R7$ to hold the result, meaning all occurrences of $R0$ in the code would instead have been $R7$. Furthermore, in writing the assembly program, we arbitrarily chose the labels *lab1* and *lab2*. Other names for those labels could have been used, such as *skip1* and *done*, or *Fred* and *George*. Descriptive labels are preferred to help people reading the assembly code to understand the program.

An assembler would automatically convert the assembly code to the machine code shown in Figure 8.14(b). For each assembly instruction, the assembler determines the specific instruction type by looking at the mnemonic as well as the operands if necessary, and then outputs the appropriate opcode bits (four bits) for that instruction type, as defined in Table 8.2. For example, the assembler would examine the first instruction "*MOV R0, #0*" and thus know from the first three letters *MOV* that this is one of the data movement instructions. The assembler would examine the operands and, seeing $R0$, would determine this is either a regular load or a load-constant instruction.

Finally, the assembler would detect the "#" and conclude this is a load-constant instruction, thus outputting the opcode 0011 for a load-constant instruction as shown in the first machine instruction of Figure 8.14(b).

The assembler converts the operands to bits also, converting *R0* of the first instruction to 0000, and "#0" to 00000000, as shown in the first machine instruction of Figure 8.14(b).

The JMPZ instruction requires some extra handling. The assembler recognizes this as a *jump-if-zero* instruction and thus outputs the opcode 0101. The assembler converts the first operand *R2* to 0010. The assembler then reaches the second operand *lab1* and does not know what bits to output, since the assembler doesn't yet know the address of the instruction labeled *lab1* because the assembler hasn't reached that instruction yet in the program. To solve this problem, many assemblers actually make *two passes* over the assembly code: during the first pass, the assembler creates a table of all labels and their addresses, and then on the second pass the assembler outputs machine code. Such an assembler would therefore know during the second pass that the instruction labeled *lab1* is at an address two addresses beyond the first *JMPZ* instruction—specifically, that the *lab1* instruction is at address 5, while the *JMPZ* instruction is at address 3 (assuming that the first instruction is at address 0, not 1). Thus, the assembler would output an offset of 2 to jump forward 2 addresses to the instruction labeled *lab1*. Notice that the labels *lab1* and *lab2* do not appear in the machine code—they are merely a convenience construct that the assembler provides for the assembly-language programmer.

▶ 8.6 FURTHER EXTENSIONS TO THE PROGRAMMABLE PROCESSOR

Instruction Set Extensions

Extending the instruction set with further instructions would require similar types of extensions and modifications to the control unit, datapath, and FSM. A programmable processor might contain dozens more **data movement instructions** that move data between data memory and the register file, or between registers. For example, a processor might have instructions for copying the contents of one register to another (e.g., *MOV R0, R1*, which would copy *R1*'s contents into *R0*), and would carry out that instruction using a state that reads the source register, passes the read value through the ALU unchanged, and writes the ALU output to the destination register. As another example, a processor might have instructions that would use the contents of a register as the address from which to read data memory, known as *indirect* addressing.

A programmable processor would also contain dozens of **arithmetic/logic instructions** that perform arithmetic and logic operations on registers in the register file. For example, a processor might include not just add and subtract instructions, but also increment, complement, decrement, AND, OR, XOR, shift left, shift right, and other instructions that could be carried out by an ALU.

A programmable processor would furthermore contain several **flow-of-control instructions** that determine the next value of the *PC*. For example, a processor might include not just a jump-if-zero instruction, but also a jump-if-not-zero, an unconditional jump, an indirect jump, and perhaps even jump-if-negative and similar such instructions. Furthermore, a processor may include instructions that can jump farther than just a small offset from the current *PC*, and perhaps even to an absolute address rather than an offset address.

Input/Output Extensions

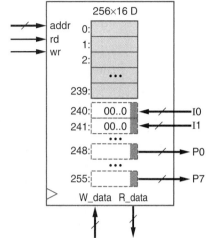

Figure 8.15 Connecting to external pins.

Section 1.3 introduced a basic microprocessor having eight inputs $I0, I1, ..., I7$, and eight outputs $P0, P1, ..., P7$. The basic programmable processor of Figure 8.12 can be extended to implement such external inputs and outputs. One method for such an extension utilizes a specially designed data memory. In that data memory, the last 16 words of the memory are replaced by direct connections to the input and output pins, as illustrated in Figure 8.15. The data memory stores locations 0 through 239 in a normal RAM. Location 240, however, is actually a special word whose high 15 bits are all 0s, and whose lowest bit comes from a flip-flop loaded every cycle with the value on external input pin $I0$. Thus, reading location 240 will result in either `00...01` (integer 1), or `00...00` (integer 0), depending on the value appearing at $I0$. Likewise, location 241 is connected to pin $I1$, location 242 to $I2$, and so on, with location 247 connected to $I7$. Locations 248 through 255 are connected to pins $P0$ through $P7$, except the pins are connected to those locations' flip-flop outputs rather than inputs. For example, writing to location 255 writes the flip-flop with either 0 or 1 (only the low-order bit matters during the write), and that flip-flop drives external output pin $P7$. This approach of accessing inputs and outputs as if they were data memory locations is known as ***memory-mapped I/O***. Thus, an assembly-language programmer can read or write a microprocessor's external data pins simply by reading or writing particular data memory locations.

Example 8.5 Motion-in-the-dark detector in assembly language

Section 1.3 included an example, illustrated in Figure 1.24, that utilized a microprocessor to implement a motion-in-the-dark detector. That section utilized C code to compute the expression `P0 = I0 && !I1`. This example shows the underlying assembly code that implements that C expression. Assuming that the microprocessor's external pins $I0...I7$ and $P0...P7$ are mapped to data memory locations as in Figure 8.15, the expression can be programmed in assembly as follows:

```
0: MOV R0, 240       // move D[240], which is the value at pin I0, into R0
1: MOV R1, 241       // move D[241], which is that value at pin I1, into R1
2: NOT R1, R1        // compute !I1, assuming existence of a complement instruction
3: AND R0, R0, R1    // compute I0 && !I1, assuming an AND instruction
4: MOV 248, R0       // move result to D[248], which is pin P0
```

Performance Extensions

One difference between real processors and the basic processor architecture in this chapter is that many real processors are pipelined (see Section 6.5). The basic three-instruction processor utilized a controller with three stages: *fetch*, *decode*, and *execute*.

By inserting appropriate pipeline registers throughout the design and modifying the controller appropriately, the fetch, decode, and execute stages can be pipelined. In other words, as the control unit decodes instruction 1, the control unit could be simultaneously fetching instruction 2. Next, as the control unit executes instruction 1, the control unit could be decoding instruction 2, and fetching instruction 3. Thus, rather than processing one instruction every 3 cycles, the control unit could be processing one instruction every cycle. Each instruction still takes 3 cycles to process (3-cycle latency), but the pipelining results in single-cycle throughput. The net result would be that programs would execute three times faster.

Another extension involves creating deeper pipelines. Thus, rather than just three stages (fetch, decode, execute), the stages might be divided into stages of even finer granularity (e.g., fetch, decode, read operands, execute, store results). Creating finer grained stages may shorten the longest register-to-register delay, which enables a faster clock frequency. The net result would again be faster program execution.

Another extension involves having multiple ALUs in the datapath. The control unit may then perform multiple ALU operations simultaneously in the datapath. One form of this extension involves a processor whose instruction set uses instructions with multiple opcodes and associated operands in a single instruction, known as a ***very large instruction word (VLIW)*** processor. Another form uses a processor with a control unit that reads in multiple instructions simultaneously and then assigns those instructions to execute simultaneously on available ALUs, known as a ***superscalar*** processor. A high-end desktop processor may support perhaps 5 simultaneous instructions, with perhaps 10 stages of pipelining. Thus, at any moment, such a processor may be in the middle of processing 5*10 = 50 different instructions. Needless to say, modern processor architectures can become quite complex.

This chapter described the basic idea of how a programmable processor's design works and how the design could be extended to support a fuller instruction set. We leave the role of describing a complete processor, as well as modern processor design techniques for improved performance (such as pipelining, caching, etc.), to textbooks on computer architecture.

▶ 8.7 CHAPTER SUMMARY

Section 8.1 stated that programmable processors are widely used for implementing a system's desired functionality, due in part to their easy availability and short design time (design consists of writing programs). Section 8.2 provided the basic architecture of a programmable processor, consisting of a general-purpose datapath having a register file and ALU; a control unit having a controller, *PC*, and *IR*; and memories for storing the program and the data. The control unit would fetch the next instruction from program memory, decode the instruction, and then execute the instruction by configuring the datapath to carry out the instruction's specified operation. Section 8.3 designed a simple three-instruction programmable processor and showed how a program would be represented as 0s and 1s (machine code) in the processor's program memory. Section 8.4 designed a six-instruction processor and discussed how further extensions could be made to add more instructions and hence achieve a more complete processor architecture. Section 8.5 provided an example of assembly and machine code for the six-instruction processor. Section 8.6 discussed a few extensions to the programmable processor architecture such as memory-mapped I/O.

Programmable processors are typically produced in huge quantities, numbering in the tens of millions or even billions, and so tremendous attention is given to their design. Readers should realize that the programmable processor designs in this chapter are extremely simplistic and used for illustration purposes only. Yet, seeing even the simplistic designs hopefully provides an understanding of the principle of how a programmable processor works. Modern commercial processors are based on the same principles—instructions are stored as machine code in program memory, control units fetch, decode, and execute the instructions, and datapaths support the operations of the instructions using register files and ALUs. Modern processors just do a much better job, using concurrency, pipelining, and many other techniques to obtain high clock frequencies and fast program execution.

▶ 8.8 EXERCISES

SECTION 8.2: BASIC ARCHITECTURE

8.1 If a processor's program counter is 20 bits wide, up to how many words can the processor's instruction memory hold (ignoring any special tricks to expand the instruction memory size)?

8.2 Which of the following are legal single-cycle datapath operations for the datapath in Figure 8.2? Explain your answer.
   (a) Copy data from a memory location into another memory location.
   (b) Copy two register locations into two memory locations.
   (c) Add data from a register file location and a memory location, storing the result in a memory location.

8.3 Which of the following are legal single-cycle datapath operations for the datapath in Figure 8.2? Explain your answer.
   (a) Copy data from a register file location into a memory location.
   (b) Subtract data from two memory locations and store the result in another memory location.
   (c) Add data from a register file location and a memory location, storing the result in the same memory location.

8.4 Assume we are using a dual-port memory from which we can read two locations simultaneously. Modify the datapath of the programmable processor of Figure 8.2 to support an instruction that performs an ALU operation on any two memory locations and stores the result in a register file location. Trace through the execution of this operation, as illustrated in Figure 8.3.

8.5 Determine the operations required to instruct the datapath of Figure 8.2 to perform the operation: $D[8] = (D[4] + D[5]) - D[7]$, where D represents the data memory.

SECTION 8.3: A THREE-INSTRUCTION PROGRAMMABLE PROCESSOR

8.6 If a processor's instruction has 4 bits for the opcode, how many possible instructions can the processor support?

8.7 What does the following assembly program, which uses the three-instruction instruction set of this chapter, compute? *MOV R5, 19; ADD R5, R5, R5; MOV 20, R5.*

8.8 What does the following assembly program, which uses the three-instruction instruction set of this chapter, compute? *MOV R4, 20; MOV R9, 18; ADD R4, R4, R9; MOV R5, 30; ADD R9, R4, R5; MOV 20, R9.*

8.9 Using the three-instruction instruction set of this chapter, write an assembly program that updates the data memory *D* as follows: $D[0] = D[0] + D[1]$.

8.10 Using the three-instruction instruction set of this chapter, write an assembly program that updates the data memory *D* as follows: $D[4] = D[1]*2 + D[2]$.

8.11 Convert the following assembly program to machine code based on the three-instruction instruction set of this chapter: *MOV R5, 19; ADD R5, R5, R5; MOV 20, R5.*

8.12 List the basic register/memory transfers and operations that occur during each clock cycle for the following program, based on the three-instruction instruction set of this chapter: *MOV R0, 1; MOV R1, 9; ADD R0, R0, R1.*

SECTION 8.4: A SIX-INSTRUCTION PROGRAMMABLE PROCESSOR

8.13 List the basic register/memory transfers and operations that occur during each clock cycle for the following program, based on the six-instruction instruction set of this chapter, assuming that the content of *D*[9] is 0: *MOV R6, #1; MOV R5, 9; JMPZ R5, label1; ADD R5, R5, R6; label1: ADD R5, R5, R6.* What is the value in *R5* after the program completes?

8.14 Add a new instruction to the six-instruction instruction set of this chapter that performs a bitwise AND of two registers and stores the result in a third register. Extend the datapath, the control unit, and the controller's FSM as needed.

8.15 Add a new instruction to the six-instruction instruction set of this chapter that performs an unconditional jump (jumps always) to a location specified by a 12-bit offset. Extend the datapath, the control unit, and the controller's FSM as needed.

8.16 Add a new instruction to the six-instruction instruction set of this chapter that performs a jump if two registers are equal, to a location specified by a 12-bit offset. Extend the datapath, the control unit, and the controller's FSM as needed.

8.17 Using the six-instruction instruction set of this chapter, write an assembly program for the C code in Figure 8.16, which computes the sum of the first *N* numbers, where *N* is another name for *D*[9]. *Hint:* Use a register to first store *N*

```
i=1;
sum=0;
while (i!=N) {
    sum = sum + i;
    i = i + 1;
}
```

Figure 8.16 C code.

8.18 Using the extended instruction set you designed in Exercise 8.16, write an assembly program for the C code in Exercise 8.17.

SECTION 8.5: EXAMPLE ASSEMBLY AND MACHINE PROGRAMS

8.19 Define two new data movement instructions for the six-instruction instruction set of this chapter. Extend the datapath, the control unit, and the controller's FSM as needed.

8.20 Define two new arithmetic/logic instructions for the six-instruction instruction set of this chapter. Extend the datapath, the control unit, and the controller's FSM as needed.

8.21 Define two new flow-of-control instructions for the six-instruction instruction set of this chapter. Extend the datapath, the control unit, and the controller's FSM as needed.

8.22 Assuming that the microprocessor's external pins *I0...I7* and *P0...P7* are mapped to data memory locations as in Figure 8.15 and an AND instruction has been added to the six-instruction instruction set of this chapter, create an assembly program that will output 0 on *P4* if all eight inputs *I0...I7* are 1s.

▶ *DESIGNER PROFILE*

Carole grew up in a country where the best students went to engineering school, as engineering was highly respected. "I was good in school, so engineering seemed like a natural option. I was also very interested in building things, and very curious about how one builds new things—so I was attracted to engineering at an early age, around 10 years of age."

Carole has worked at Intel for 15 years. She was one of the original architects of the popular MMX (multimedia extension of the Intel architecture) part of Pentium processors. "It was fascinating to learn the algorithms used to compress video and audio, and to invent new instructions for the Intel Architecture to run these applications efficiently. It is not always easy for processor architects to quantify the benefits of new features, and to motivate the expense in silicon area (or chip die size) for new instructions. In the case of multimedia applications, the benefits are well understood: running a video clip at a few frames per second, or running it in real time (about 30 frames per second) makes a huge, visible difference to everyone." As is the case with so many engineers, she is very proud of what she accomplished: "When the first Pentium processor with MMX came up, it was really rewarding to think that a small piece of my mind was in all of these machines running video real time popping up everywhere."

Carole was also one of the architects on the Intel / Hewlett-Packard team that defined the Itanium computer

architecture. "This was a unique opportunity to define a processor 'from scratch.' Technically this was a very challenging project, and working with so many top-notch architects was very enriching. But I also learned what it takes to build something big, involving a very large team, and two large companies. The two companies had different cultures, different methodologies, and reconciling the differences was sometimes more challenging than solving the technical problems. But this is all part of 'building things,' and this was a great lesson in leadership."

What Carole likes most about her career is "the constant change. After 22 years as a computer architect, I am still doing new things every day. Computer science is a work in progress, and it offers new opportunities that one has to grab, and run with. This is where the fun is."

Asked to give some advice to students, Carole suggests two things:

• "Stay at school as long as possible. Get a PhD if you can. To be able to adapt to constant change, you will need a very robust, and theoretical foundation. Only learning how to do things is not enough; it will get you a job for 2 years, but then your skills will be obsolete."

• "Be open for change. It is important to build an in-depth expertise in one area; in my case, it is computer architecture. But one has to be ready to use this expertise in many different projects, with different people, and more and more in different parts of the world. Fifteen years ago multimedia applications were the focus of many computer architects. Today it is bioinformatics and data mining. Change requires a lot of work to learn new domains, but not adapting to change is not an option."

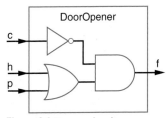

CHAPTER 9

Hardware Description Languages

9.1 INTRODUCTION[1]

Earlier chapters drew circuits that were designed. For example, Chapter 2 designed an automatic door opener circuit and drew the circuit shown in Figure 9.1. A drawing has more information than is necessary to describe the circuit, such as information about the location of the inputs and outputs. In Figure 9.1, the inputs are located on the left and the output is located on the right. The c input is located on the top, the h input in the middle, and the p input on the bottom. The drawing also gives information about

Figure 9.1 Drawn circuit

the size and location of the components in the circuit: the inverter is at the top, the OR gate below the inverter, the AND gate on the right, and each component is about a half inch by a half inch. The drawing gives information about the wires too: the wire from the inverter goes to the right, then down, then to the right again, for example. However, all that information about the drawing is really irrelevant, and has nothing to do with how the design will be physically implemented. When a circuit is drawn, all that information must be defined, even if arbitrarily. A drawing of a circuit is commonly referred to as a circuit *schematic*.

A problem with drawing circuits arises with larger circuits. Does the schematic in Figure 9.2 mean anything to you? That schematic has just a couple dozen components—what if there were a couple thousand components, as is quite common? Drawing a large circuit would require tremendous effort to figure out how to place each component in the drawing, and how to route wires among the components. And if a tool generated the circuit, the tool would have to spend compute time to figure out a visually appealing way to draw the circuit (rather than a spaghetti-like mess), and such computation is time-consuming and still may not result in a readable drawing. Furthermore, the files used to store schematics would be very large, as those files would contain all that extra information about the location and size of every component. All that extra effort, file size, and time,

1 Substantial content of this chapter was contributed by Roman Lysecky.

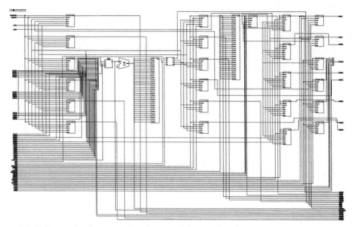

Figure 9.2 Schematics become hard to read beyond a dozen or so components—the graphical information becomes a nuisance rather than an aid.

would be needed for something that is really not very useful—humans can't comprehend circuit drawings of more than perhaps a few dozen gates, so what is the point of drawing such circuits? What is needed is a way to just describe the circuit itself—what are the inputs and outputs, what components exist, and what are the connections, without any of the graphical information like where each component is drawn or how big the component is drawn. Ideally, this description would be in a textual language so that people could type such descriptions with a computer keyboard just like they type email messages and C programs.

The circuit in Figure 9.3(a) could be described using the textual language of English as in Figure 9.3(b). We've given names to each gate in the circuit and to the internal wires in Figure 9.3(a).

Of course, English is not a good language if a computer tool will be used to read in the description—a computer tool requires a language with a precise syntax and precise meaning for every language construct. Computer-readable languages thus evolved in the

(a)

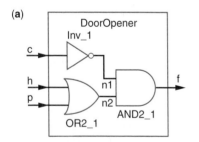

Figure 9.3 Describing a circuit using a textual language rather than a graphical drawing: (a) schematic, (b) textual description in the English language.

(b)

We'll now describe a circuit whose name is DoorOpener.
The external inputs are c, h, and p, which are bits.
The external output is f, which is a bit.

We assume you know the behavior of these components:
An inverter, which has a bit input x, and bit output F.
A 2-input OR gate, which has bit inputs x and y, and bit output F.
A 2-input AND gate, which has bit inputs x and y, and bit output F.

The circuit has internal wires n1 and n2, both bits.
The DoorOpener circuit internally consists of:
An inverter named Inv_1, whose input x connects to external input c, and whose output connects to n1.
A 2-input OR gate named OR2_1, whose inputs connect to external inputs h and p, and whose output connects to n2.
A 2-input AND gate named AND2_1, whose inputs connect to n1 and n2, and whose output connects to external output f.
That's all.

1970s and 1980s for describing hardware circuits. Such languages became known as **hardware description languages**, or **HDLs**. Hardware description languages not only enable describing the structural interconnections of components, but also include methods to describe the behavior of components themselves. Modern digital design relies heavily on the use of HDLs at all stages of design.

This chapter provides a brief introduction to the most popular hardware description languages—VHDL, Verilog, and SystemC—but to thoroughly learn each language, one may want to consult textbooks specifically dedicated to each language. Each section of this chapter can be covered immediately after corresponding earlier chapters (Section 9.2 after Chapter 2, Section 9.3 after Chapter 3, Section 9.4 after Chapter 4, and Section 9.5 after Chapter 5)—or these sections may be covered all at once after completing those earlier chapters. Furthermore, each section has three parts, one for VHDL, one for Verilog, and one for SystemC. Each of those parts is independent of the other parts of the section, so a reader interested only in one of the HDLs, say Verilog, can read only the Verilog parts of each section, skipping the VHDL or SystemC parts.

A reader interested in comparing the three HDLs may read the sections of all three HDLs. In doing so, you may notice that the HDLs have similar capabilities, differing primarily in their syntax. Thus, after learning one HDL thoroughly, a designer can likely learn other HDLs quickly.

► 9.2 COMBINATIONAL LOGIC DESCRIPTION USING HARDWARE DESCRIPTION LANGUAGES

Structure

This chapter's introduction sought to describe a circuit using a textual language. This section shows how some different HDLs describe circuits. The term **structure** is sometimes used to refer to a circuit, with structure meaning an interconnection of component.

VHDL

Figure 9.4(c) shows a VHDL description of the *DoorOpener* circuit of Figure 9.4(a). For convenience, the English description appears in Figure 9.4(b), along with the correspondence between the English description and the VHDL description.

The description begins with an **entity** declaration, which defines the design's name and the design's inputs and outputs, known as **ports**. An entity declaration says nothing about the internals of the design—just the design's name and interface. The description lists the port names and defines their type, which in this case is type **std_logic**. That type means a bit, but isn't built into VHDL (the predefined *bit* type in VHDL is too limited, for reasons beyond this section's scope). Using *std_logic* requires including the statements: "*library ieee; use ieee.std_logic_1164.all;*" at the top of the file, which indicate that a **library** named *ieee* of predefined items will be used, in particular all the items within a package named *std_logic_1164*, which defines *std_logic* among other things.

The description continues with an **architecture** definition, which describes the internals of the design. The description names the architecture *Circuit*, but other names are possible like *DoorOpenerCircuit*, *DoorOpenerStructure*, *Structure*, or even *Fred*. Descriptive names that help in understanding the architecture are preferred. The architec-

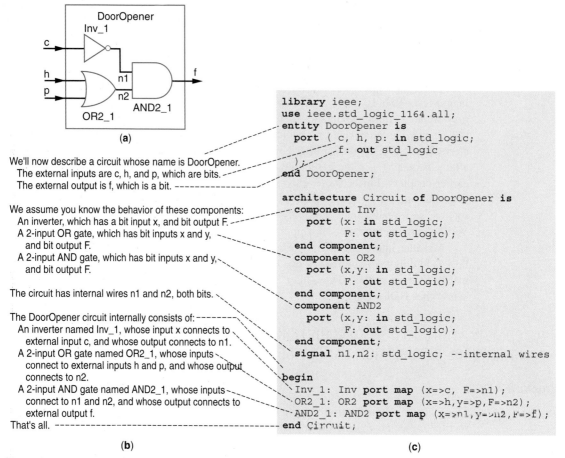

Figure 9.4 Describing a circuit using a textual language rather than a graphical drawing: (a) schematic, (b) textual description in the English language, (c) textual description in the VHDL language. Bolded words are reserved words in VHDL.

ture starts by declaring what *components* the design will be using—those components must be defined elsewhere in the description's file or in another file. Those components' definitions will be discussed later. Each component declaration must define the inputs and outputs of each component, and those inputs and outputs must match the component's entity declaration (found elsewhere) exactly.

The description then includes a declaration of the design's internal *signals n1* and *n2*, which are essentially internal wires. Next to that declaration, the description includes an example of a VHDL *comment*: "*-- internal wires*". Comments start with "--" followed by any text on the rest of the line. That text is ignored by VHDL tools, but is useful to people who read the description.

Finally, the description instantiates the circuit's components and defines those components' connections using **port maps**. For example, the statement "*Inv_1: Inv port map (x=>c, F=>n1);*" instantiates a component named *Inv_1*, which is a component of type

Inv (declared earlier in the VHDL description), and indicates that *Inv_1*'s input *x* connects to *c* and that *Inv_1*'s output *F* connects to *n1*, which is an internal signal. A more concise port map notation omits the port names: "*Inv_1: Inv port map (c, n1);*"—the order of the signals in the port map of *Inv* corresponds to the order of the ports in the component definition of *Inv*. Subsequent examples will use this more concise notation.

The bold words in the description represent **reserved words**, also known as **keywords**, in VHDL. Reserved words cannot be used for names of entities, architectures, signals, instantiated components, etc., as those words have special meaning that guide VHDL tools to understand our descriptions.

Summarizing, the VHDL structural description has an entity that describes the design's name, its inputs, and its outputs; a declaration of what components will be used; a declaration of internal signals; and finally, an instantiation of all components along with their interconnections.

The entity just defined could then be used as a component in another entity.

Verilog

Figure 9.5(c) shows a Verilog description of the *DoorOpener* circuit of Figure 9.5(a). For convenience, the English description also appears in Figure 9.5(b), along with the correspondence between the English description and the Verilog description.

The description begins by defining modules for an inverter *Inv*, a 2-input OR gate *OR2,* and a 2-input AND gate *AND2*. We'll skip discussion of those modules, and begin our discussion with the definition of the fourth module *DoorOpener*.

The description declares a **module** named *DoorOpener*. The module declaration defines a design's name and the names of that design's inputs and outputs, known as ports. The module declaration says nothing about the internals of the design or the ports—just the design's name and interface.

The description then defines the type of each port, assigning the types **input** and **output** in this example.

The description then includes a declaration of the design's internal **wires**, named *n1* and *n2*.

Finally, the description instantiates the circuit's components and defines those components' connections. For example, the statement "*Inv Inv_1(c, n1);*" instantiates a component named *Inv_1*, which is a component of type *Inv*. The connections to the inputs and outputs of the instantiated components are specified in the order in which the component's modules declare the inputs and outputs. In the instantiation of *Inv_1*, the input *c* is connected to the input *x* of the *Inv* component, and the wire *n1* is connected to output *F* of the component. In Verilog, the module does not need to specify the interface of a component within the module instantiating the component. For example, the *DoorOpener* module does not include a declaration of which components it will instantiate or any information regarding those components. The components, of course, must be defined elsewhere, perhaps earlier in the same file as shown in Figure 9.5(c), or perhaps in another file. For reference purposes, the example shown here provides incomplete specifications for the *Inv*, *AND2*, and *OR2* components in order to clearly show the ports and interface for these components. In place of specifying the internal behavior of these components, we simply included an example of a Verilog **comment**. A comments starts with "*//*" and then can be followed by any text on the rest of the line.

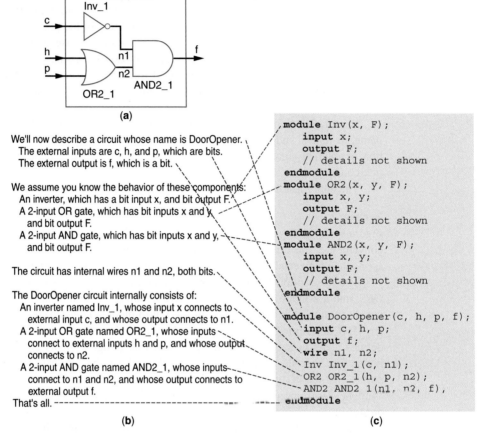

Figure 9.5 Describing a circuit using a textual language rather than a graphical drawing: (a) schematic, (b) textual description in the English language, (c) textual description in the Verilog language. Bold words are reserved words in Verilog.

The bold words in the description represent reserved words, also known as keywords, in Verilog. We cannot use reserved words for names of modules, ports, wires, instantiated components, etc., as those words have special meaning that guide Verilog tools to understand our descriptions.

Summarizing, the Verilog structural description has a module that describes the design name, lists the module's inputs and outputs, and specifies the type for each input and output; a declaration of internal wires; and finally, an instantiation of all components, along with their interconnections.

SystemC

Figure 9.6(c) shows a SystemC description of the *DoorOpener* circuit of Figure 9.6(a). For convenience, the English description also appears in Figure 9.6(b), along with the correspondence between the English description and the SystemC description. The

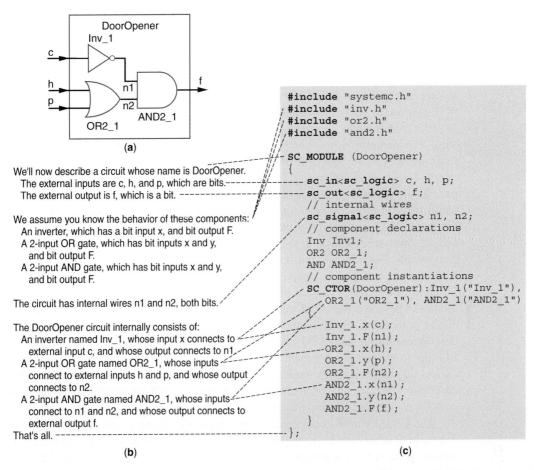

(a)

We'll now describe a circuit whose name is DoorOpener.
   The external inputs are c, h, and p, which are bits.
   The external output is f, which is a bit.

We assume you know the behavior of these components:
   An inverter, which has a bit input x, and bit output F.
   A 2-input OR gate, which has bit inputs x and y,
     and bit output F.
   A 2-input AND gate, which has bit inputs x and y,
     and bit output F.

The circuit has internal wires n1 and n2, both bits.

The DoorOpener circuit internally consists of:
   An inverter named Inv_1, whose input x connects to
     external input c, and whose output connects to n1.
   A 2-input OR gate named OR2_1, whose inputs
     connect to external inputs h and p, and whose output
     connects to n2.
   A 2-input AND gate named AND2_1, whose inputs
     connect to n1 and n2, and whose output connects to
     external output f.
That's all. -

(b)

```
#include "systemc.h"
#include "inv.h"
#include "or2.h"
#include "and2.h"

SC_MODULE (DoorOpener)
{
  sc_in<sc_logic> c, h, p;
  sc_out<sc_logic> f;
  // internal wires
  sc_signal<sc_logic> n1, n2;
  // component declarations
  Inv Inv1;
  OR2 OR2_1;
  AND AND2_1;
  // component instantiations
  SC_CTOR(DoorOpener):Inv_1("Inv_1"),
    OR2_1("OR2_1"), AND2_1("AND2_1")
  {
    Inv_1.x(c);
    Inv_1.F(n1);
    OR2_1.x(h);
    OR2_1.y(p);
    OR2_1.F(n2);
    AND2_1.x(n1);
    AND2_1.y(n2);
    AND2_1.F(f);
  }
};
```

(c)

Figure 9.6 Describing a circuit using a textual language rather than a graphical drawing: (a) schematic, (b) textual description in the English language, (c) textual description in the SystemC language. Bold words are reserved words in SystemC.

SystemC language is built on top of the C++ programming language, but it is not necessary to be an expert C++ programmer to use SystemC. However, it is important to keep in mind that certain restrictions exist as a result, such as not using C++ keywords to name modules, ports, signals, etc.

Before defining the circuit behavior, we must include the statement "#include "systemc.h"" at the top of each SystemC file. The description begins with an **SC_MODULE** declaration, which defines the design's name, in this case *DoorOpener*. The module declaration says nothing about the internals of the design—just the design's name. Within the module description, the input and output ports of the design are specified, using the **sc_in<>** and **sc_out<>** statements respectively. The description lists the port names and defines their types, which in this case is type *sc_logic*, which specifies a single bit.

The description then includes a declaration of the design's internal signals, specified as *sc_signal,* which are essentially internal wires. Next to that declaration, the description includes an example of a SystemC comment: "*// internal wires*". A comment starts with "*//*" and then can be followed by any text on the rest of the line.

The module then declares what components the design will be using. The SystemC module does not need to specify the interface of the components, but rather just the type of component as well as a unique name for each component within the design.

The module defines a constructor function **SC_CTOR** that is responsible for instantiating and connecting the components within the SystemC design. The constructor function takes as an argument the name of the current SystemC module, which in this case is *DoorOpener*. Following the *SC_CTOR* statement after the colon is a list of component instantiations. The SystemC module's instantiations are used to call the constructor functions of each component being instantiated. However, we point out that the connections between the individual components are not specified at this point. Instead, the statements within the constructor finally define the connections between the components. For example, the statement "*Inv_1.x(c); Inv_1.F(n1);*" connect the inverter *Inv_1's* input *x* to external output *c* and the inverter's output *F* to internal signal *n1*. In SystemC, the module does not need to specify the interface of a component within the module. The components, of course, must be completely defined elsewhere, perhaps earlier in the same file or in another file. In our SystemC *DoorOpener* description, the descriptions for the *Inv, AND2,* and *OR2* components are specified in other SystemC files. In order to use those components, we must include a statement at the beginning of the current file, indicating where we can find this description. For example, our *DoorOpener* description includes the statement "*#include "inv.h""*", and the description of the component *Inv* can be found within that file.

The bolded words in the description represent reserved words, also known as keywords, in SystemC and C++. We cannot use reserved words for names of modules, ports, signals, instantiated components, etc., as those words have special meaning that guide SystemC and C++ tools to understand our descriptions.

Summarizing, the SystemC structural description has: a module that defines the design name; a list of inputs and outputs of the module specifying their types, a declaration of internal signals; a declaration of components providing the name for each component, a constructor function instantiating the module's components, and finally, the components' interconnections.

Combinational Behavior

HDLs typically support the ability to describe the internals of a design as behavior rather than as a circuit. This ability enables description of the bottom-level building-block components used in a design, such as the combinational behavior of an AND gate or OR gate.

VHDL

Figure 9.7 contains a behavioral description of a 2-input OR gate, which was used as a component in Figure 9.4(c). The description begins with the declarations necessary to use *std_logic*. It then declares the entity with the name *OR2* as having two input ports *x* and *y* and having output port *F*, all of type *std_logic* which means bit.

The description then defines an architecture named *behavior* for *OR2*. That architecture consists of a ***process***, which is the VHDL construct that describes behavior. The process declaration is "*process(x,y)*", which means the process should execute from beginning to end whenever *x* or *y* changes. In other words, the process is ***sensitive*** to *x* and to *y*, which comprise the process' ***sensitivity list***. A process body (the part between the process's *begin* and *end*) can contain sequential statements, like sequential statements in C but with a different syntax. The process shown has only one such statement, assigning the value of "*x or y*" to *F*. "*or*" is a built-in operator in VHDL, making the internal description of the OR gate simple.

As another example of a behavioral description, let's revisit the *DoorOpener* example from Figure 9.4(c), for which we created an architecture having a structural description. We can alternatively create an architecture having a behavioral description. (In fact, a VHDL entity may have multiple architecture descriptions for that same entity.) Assuming the same entity declaration as in Figure 9.4(c), an alternative architecture definition is shown in Figure 9.8. The behavior consists of a process that is sensitive to inputs *c*, *h*, and *p*. When the process executes (which is whenever *c*, *h*, or *p* changes), then the process executes its one statement, which updates the value of *f*.

```
library ieee;
use ieee.std_logic_1164.all;

entity OR2 is
   port (x, y: in std_logic;
           F: out std_logic
   );
end OR2;

architecture behavior of OR2 is
begin
   process (x, y)
   begin
      F <= x or y;
   end process;
end behavior;
```

Figure 9.7 Behavioral VHDL description of an OR gate.

```
architecture beh of DoorOpener is
begin
   process(c, h, p)
   begin
      f <= not(c) and (h or p);
   end process;
end beh;
```

Figure 9.8 Behavioral VHDL description of the *DoorOpener* design.

In designing the *DoorOpener* circuit, we might start with the behavioral description, and run a simulation to verify correct behavior. We might then create a structural description, and run simulation again to verify that the circuit has the same functionality as the behavior. In fact, tools exist that automatically convert such behavior to a circuit.

When describing a combinational circuit's behavior, care must be taken to include all the circuit's inputs in the process's sensitivity list. Omitting an input is not a VHDL error, but such omission is a mistake that results in different behavior than combinational behavior—with an input omitted, the output does not change when that input changes, meaning there must be some storage in the circuit.

Verilog

Figure 9.9 contains a behavioral description of a 2-input OR gate, which was used as a component in Figure 9.5. The description begins by declaring the module named *OR2* and specifying that the module has three ports named *x*, *y*, and *F*. The description then defines that the ports *x* and *y* are both inputs and the port *F* is an output. The description then defines the output *F* to be a *reg* output. In Verilog, a port is by default assumed to be a **wire**, which does not store values. Instead, wires can only create connections between components. If we want to assign a value to an output port, we must define the port to be a **reg**, which indicates the output port stores the values assigned to the port. The

```
module OR2(x,y,F);
  input x, y;
  output F;
  reg F;

  always @(x or y)
  begin
    F <= x | y;
  end
endmodule
```

Figure 9.9 Behavioral Verilog description of an OR gate.

Verilog code for the design continues with an **always** procedure that defines a block of code that will be repeatedly executed whenever a change occurs on an input in the block's input list. The always procedure declaration is "*always @(x or y)*", which means the procedure should execute from beginning to end whenever *x* or *y* changes. In other words, the procedure is *sensitive* to *x* and *y*. *x* and *y* comprise the procedure's sensitivity list. The *always* procedure's statements (the part between the procedure's *begin* and *end*) can contain sequential statements, like sequential statements in C but with a different syntax. The block shown has only one such statement, assigning the value of "*x | y*" to *F*, where "|" is a built-in Verilog operation to compute an OR.

As another example of a behavioral description, let's revisit our *DoorOpener* example from Figure 9.5(c), for which we created a structural Verilog description. We can alternatively create a behavioral description. Figure 9.10 presents a behavioral Verilog description of the *DoorOpener* circuit. The module declaration is similar to the structural description of Figure 9.5(c), but in the behavioral description we need to declare the output *f* as a *reg*. The behavior consists of an always procedure sensitive to inputs *c*, *h*, and *p*. When the procedure executes (which is whenever *c*, *h*, or *p* changes), then the procedure executes a

```
module DoorOpener(c,h,p,f);
  input c, h, p;
  output f;
  reg f;

  always @(c or h or p)
  begin
    f <= (~c) & (h | p);
  end
endmodule
```

Figure 9.10 Behavioral Verilog description of the DoorOpener design.

single statement that updates the value of *f*, by assigning the value "*(~c) & (h | p)*", where "~" , "&", and "|" perform the invert, AND, and OR operations, respectively.

In designing the *DoorOpener* circuit, we might start with the behavioral description and run a simulation to verify correct behavior. We might then create a structural description and run a simulation again to verify that the circuit has the same functionality as the behavior. In fact, tools exist that automatically convert such behavior to a circuit.

When describing a combinational circuit's behavior, care must be taken to include all the circuit's inputs in the procedure's sensitivity list. Omitting an input is not a Verilog error, but such omission is a mistake that results in different behavior than combinational behavior—with an input omitted, the output does not change when that input changes, meaning there must be some storage in the circuit. Verilog provides a means of avoiding such a mistake. The sensitivity list can be specified merely as "*always @(*)*", which means that the procedure is sensitive to all items that are read in the procedure.

SystemC

Figure 9.11 contains a SystemC behavioral description of a 2-input OR gate, which you'll recall we used as a component in Figure 9.6(c). The SystemC description declares the module with the name *OR2* and has two input ports *x* and *y* and one output port *F*, all of type *sc_logic*, indicating that each input and output is an individual bit. The module defines the constructor function *SC_CTOR* that consists of a single process named *comblogic* defined as a *SC_METHOD*. **SC_METHOD** is one SystemC construct that describes behavior. The process declaration here is "*SC_METHOD (comblogic); sensitive << x << y;*", which means the process will execute the circuit behavior described in the function *comblogic* whenever *x* or *y* changes. In other words, the process is **sensitive** to *x* and *y*. The process body is defined in the function *comblogic* and is declared as "*void comblogic()*". The process function (the part between the open brace "*{*" and close brace "*}*") can contain sequential statements, like sequential statements in C or C++ but sometimes with different syntax. The process shown has only one such statement, writing the value of "*x.read() | y.read()*" to *F*, where "*|*" executes an OR operation. In SystemC, the current value of an input port can be read using the **read()** function and an output port can be written using the **write()** function. While other methods of accessing the input and output ports are possible, the *read()* and *write()* functions are recommended.

```
#include "systemc.h"

SC_MODULE(OR2)
{
  sc_in<sc_logic> x, y;
  sc_out<sc_logic> F;

  SC_CTOR(OR2)
  {
    SC_METHOD(comblogic);
    sensitive << x << y;
  }

  void comblogic()
  {
    F.write(x.read() | y.read());
  }
};
```

Figure 9.11 Behavioral SystemC description of an OR gate.

As another example of a behavioral description, let's revisit our *DoorOpener* example from Figure 9.6(c), for which we created a structural SystemC description. We can alternatively create a behavioral description. Figure 9.12 presents a behavioral SystemC description of the *DoorOpener* circuit. The module declaration is the same as the structural description of Figure 9.6(c). The behavior consists of a single process, named *comblogic*, that is sensitive to inputs *c*, *h*, and *p*. When the process executes (which is whenever *c*, *h*, or *p* changes), then the process executes its one statement, which updates the value of *f* by assigning the value "*(~c.read()) & (h.read() | p.read())*", where "*~*" per-

```
#include "systemc.h"

SC_MODULE(DoorOpener)
{
  sc_in<sc_logic> c, h, p;
  sc_out<sc_logic> f;

  SC_CTOR(DoorOpener)
  {
    SC_METHOD(comblogic);
    sensitive << c << h << p;
  }

  void comblogic()
  {
    f.write((~c.read()) & (h.read() |
            p.read()));
  }
};
```

Figure 9.12 Behavioral SystemC description of the *DoorOpener* design.

forms an invert operation, "&" performs an AND operation, and "|" performs an OR operation.

In designing the *DoorOpener* circuit, we might start with the behavioral description, and run a simulation to verify correct behavior. We might then create a structural description, and run simulation again to verify that the circuit has the same functionality as the behavior. In fact, tools exist that automatically convert such behavior to a circuit.

Testbenches

One of the main uses of an HDL is that of simulating a new design to ensure that the design is correct. To simulate a design, we need to set the design's inputs to certain values, and then check that the design's output values are what we expect them to be. A system that sets input values and checks output values is known as a ***testbench***. We now show how to create an HDL testbench to test our *DoorOpener* circuit.

VHDL

Figure 9.13 shows a VHDL testbench for the *DoorOpener* design of Figure 9.4(c). Notice that the entity, named *Testbench*, has no ports—the entity is self-contained, requiring no inputs and generating no outputs. The architecture declares the component that we plan to test—namely, the *Door-Opener* component. The architecture instantiates one instance of the *DoorOpener* component, which is named *DoorOpener1*. A single process in the architecture sets the inputs of the component and checks for correct output. This testbench tries all possible cases of the three inputs, of which there are eight cases. Many components have too many inputs to try all possible cases—in that situation, we might try border cases (e.g., all 0s, all 1s) and then some random cases.

Each case sets the three inputs of the component to a particular input combination,

```
library ieee;
use ieee.std_logic_1164.all;

entity Testbench is
end Testbench;

architecture behavior of Testbench is
  component DoorOpener
    port ( c, h, p: in std_logic;
           f: out std_logic
    );
  end component;
  signal c, h, p, f: std_logic;
begin
  DoorOpener1: DoorOpener port map (c,h,p,f);

  process
  begin
    -- case 0
    c <= '0'; h <= '0'; p <= '0';
    wait for 1 ns;
    assert (f='0') report "Case 0 failed";

    -- case 1
    c <= '0'; h <= '0'; p <= '1';
    wait for 1 ns;
    assert (f='1') report "Case 1 failed";
    -- (cases 2-6 omitted from figure)
    -- case 7
    c <= '1'; h <= '1'; p <= '1';
    wait for 1 ns;
    assert (f='0') report "Case 7 failed";

    wait; -- process does not wake up again
  end process;
end behavior;
```

Figure 9.13 Behavioral VHDL description of *DoorOpener* testbench.

and waits for those values to propagate through the component—we arbitrarily wait for 1 ns of simulated time, but could have picked any time, since we didn't actually create a time delay within the component. But we do have to wait for some time, as VHDL simulation is defined such that no signal is updated instantaneously, but rather after an infinitely small period of simulated time. After waiting, each case checks for the correct value on the output *f*, using an ***assert*** statement. If the condition of the *assert* statement evaluates to true, simulation proceeds to the next statement. But if the condition evaluates to false, the corresponding error message will be reported and the simulation will terminate.

Verilog

Figure 9.14 shows a Verilog testbench for the *DoorOpener* design of Figure 9.5(c). Notice that the module, named *Testbench*, has no ports—the module is self-contained, requiring no inputs and generating no outputs. The module first declares three registered signals *c*, *h*, and *p* and a single wire *f*. The signals *c*, *h*, and *p* are declared as *reg* because we must assign values to the signals that will be connected to the inputs of the design being tested. However, because we do not need to assign a value to the output being monitored, the signal *f* is declared as a *wire*. The testbench then instantiates one instance of the *DoorOpener* component, named *DoorOpener1*, and connects the inputs and outputs of the

```verilog
module Testbench;
  reg c, h, p;
  wire f;

  DoorOpener DoorOpener1(c, h, p, f);

  initial
  begin
    // case 0
    c <= 0; h <= 0; p <= 0;
    #1 $display("f = %b", f);
    // case 1
    c <= 0; h <= 0; p <= 1;
    #1 $display("f = %b", f);
    // (cases 2-6 omitted from figure)
    // case 7
    c <= 1; h <= 1; p <= 1;
    #1 $display("f = %b", f);
  end
endmodule
```

Figure 9.14 Behavioral Verilog description of *DoorOpener* testbench.

component to the internal wires. The testbench then contains an ***initial*** procedure that defines a block of code that will be executed only once when execution of the testbench begins. The *initial* procedure sets the inputs of the *DoorOpener* component and displays the resulting value of the component's output. This testbench tries all possible cases of the three inputs, of which there are eight cases. Many components have too many inputs to try all possible cases—in that situation, we might try border cases (e.g., all 0s, all 1s) and then some random cases.

Each case sets the three inputs of the component to a particular input combination, and waits for those values to propagate through the component—we arbitrarily wait for 1 unit of simulated time using the delay control statement "*#1*", but we could have picked any length of time, since we didn't actually create a time delay within the component. The Verilog language does not define standard time units, such as nanoseconds, but instead simply defines time in terms of time units, which a designer can use within a simulation environment. We do have to wait for some time, as the assignments within the testbench are nonblocking statements that are not updated until the current simulation time completes. After waiting, each case outputs the value of the output *f* using a *$display* statement. The statement "*$display("f = %b", f)*" outputs the value of *f* in binary. For example, if the value of *f* is 1, then the display statement will output "*f = 1*". The display statement consists of a format string followed by a comma-separated list of wires, registers, or ports. Within the format string of our display statement, the *%b* indicates that the value of the signal specified after the format string will be displayed in binary. After simulation has finished, we can compare the values output during simulation to the expected values, to determine if our circuit is working correctly.

SystemC

Figure 9.15 shows a SystemC test-bench for the *DoorOpener* design of Figure 9.6(c). Notice that the module, named *Testbench*, has three output ports, *c_t*, *h_t*, and *p_t*, and one input port *f_t*. In SystemC, we design the testbench circuit as a separate module that connects to the design we are testing. Therefore, for every input port on the circuit being tested, our testbench will have a corresponding output port. Likewise, for every output port on the circuit being tested, our testbench will have a corresponding input port. The testbench module defines a single process named *testbench_proc*. The testbench process is defined as an *SC_THREAD*, which is similar to an *SC_METHOD* process except that the *SC_THREAD* allows us to use the *wait()* function within the process body to control the timing behavior of the process. In contrast, SystemC does not allow use of the *wait()* function within an *SC_METHOD* process. The testbench process controls the inputs of the circuit being tested and checks for correct output. This testbench tries all possible cases of the *DoorOpener's* three inputs, of which there are eight cases. Many components have too many inputs

```
#include "systemc.h"

SC_MODULE(Testbench)
{
  sc_out<sc_logic> c_t, h_t, p_t;
  sc_in<sc_logic> f_t;

  SC_CTOR(Testbench)
  {
    SC_THREAD(testbench_proc);
  }

  void testbench_proc()
  {
    // case 0
    c_t.write(SC_LOGIC_0);
    h_t.write(SC_LOGIC_0);
    p_t.write(SC_LOGIC_0);
    wait(1, SC_NS);
    assert( f_t.read() == SC_LOGIC_0 );

    // case 1
    c_t.write(SC_LOGIC_0);
    h_t.write(SC_LOGIC_0);
    p_t.write(SC_LOGIC_1);
    wait(1, SC_NS);
    assert( f_t.read() == SC_LOGIC_1 );

    // (cases 2-6 omitted from figure)
    // case 7
    c_t.write(SC_LOGIC_1);
    h_t.write(SC_LOGIC_1);
    p_t.write(SC_LOGIC_1);
    wait(1, SC_NS);
    assert( f_t.read() == SC_LOGIC_0 );

    sc_stop();
  }
};
```

Figure 9.15 Behavioral SystemC description of *DoorOpener* testbench.

to try all possible cases—in that situation, we might try border cases (e.g., all 0s, all 1s) and then some random cases.

Each case sets the three inputs of the *DoorOpener* circuit to a particular input combination, and waits for those values to propagate through the component—we arbitrarily wait for 1 ns of simulated time, but could have picked any time, since we didn't actually create a time delay within the component. But we do have to wait for some time, as SystemC simulation is defined such that no signal or port is updated instantaneously, but rather after an infinitely small period of simulated time. After waiting, each case checks for the correct output by reading the port *f_t* using an **assert** statement. If the condition of the assert statement evaluates to true, simulation proceeds to the next statement. But if the condition evaluates to false, simulation will stop and the corresponding error message will be reported.

In SystemC, values such as 0 and 1 are integer values and not logic values. Instead, SystemC defines the values *SC_LOGIC_0* and *SC_LOGIC_1* that correspond to the logic values of 0 and 1, respectively, which we used in the description.

▶ 9.3 SEQUENTIAL LOGIC DESCRIPTION USING HARDWARE DESCRIPTION LANGUAGES

Register

The most basic component in sequential logic is a register. We now show how to model a basic register in HDLs.

VHDL

Figure 9.16 shows a basic 4-bit register in VHDL. The register is identical to that described in Figure 3.36. The entity defines the data input *I* and the data output *Q*, as well as the clock input *clk*. The input *I* and output *Q* of this design correspond to 4-bit values. Instead of using 4 individual inputs and 4 individual outputs of types *std_logic*, the entity's *I* and *Q* ports are defined as *std_logic_vector*. A *std_logic_vector* is a vector, or array, of multiple *std_logic*

```
library ieee;
use ieee.std_logic_1164.all;

entity Reg4 is
    port ( I: in std_logic_vector(3 downto 0);
           Q: out std_logic_vector(3 downto 0);
           clk: in std_logic
    );
end Reg4;

architecture behavior of Reg4 is
begin
    process(clk)
    begin
        if (clk='1' and clk'event) then
            Q <= I;
        end if;
    end process;
end behavior;
```

Figure 9.16 Behavioral VHDL description of a 4-bit register.

elements. For example, the type declaration "*std_logic_vector(3 downto 0)*" defines a 4-bit vector of *std_logic* elements, where the bit positions within the vector are numbered from 3 to 0. The *downto* keyword defines the ordering of the elements within the vector, indicating that element 3 is located in the leftmost position. The statement *"I<= "1000""* would thus assign the value 1 to position 3 of the vector *I* and the value 0 to the remaining three positions. When assigning a value to a *std_logic_vector*, the vector's value must be specified within double quotations. For example, the decimal value 5 would be specified as a 4-bit *std_logic_vector* as "0101".

The architecture describes the register behaviorally, using a process statement. The process is sensitive to its *clk* input only. Because the process should only update its output during a rising clock edge, the process need not execute if input *I* changes. If *clk* changes, the process begins executing its statements. The first statement checks whether the process began executing due to a rising clock edge (0 to 1), as opposed to a falling clock edge (1 to 0). The statement checks for a rising edge by checking whether the *clk* input just changed (*clk'event*) and that change was to a 1 (*clk='1'*). If the process began executing due to a rising clock edge, then the process updates the register's contents using the statement "*Q <= I*". For a falling clock edge, the process will begin executing, check the *if* statement condition, and then reach the end of the process and hence stop executing without updating *Q*. Ideally, VHDL would have a way to begin executing a process only on a rising clock edge, but VHDL has no such feature.

In VHDL, output ports are a type of signal, and signals have memory in simulation. Thus, assigning *I* to *Q* causes *Q* to retain the new value, even when the process stops executing, thus implementing the storage part of the register.

Verilog

Figure 9.17 shows a basic 4-bit register in Verilog. The register is identical to that described in Figure 3.36. The module defines the data input *I* and the data output *Q*, as well as the clock input *clk*. The input *I* and output *Q* of this design correspond to a 4-bit value. Instead of using 4 individual inputs and 4 individual outputs, the module's *I* and *Q* ports are defined as vectors. For example, the type declaration "*input [3:0] I*" defines a 4-bit input vector where the bit positions within the vector are numbered from 3 to 0. The "*[3:0]*" defines the ordering of the elements within the vector, indicating that element 3 is located in the leftmost position. The statement "*I<=4'b1000*" would

```
module Reg4(I, Q, clk);
   input [3:0] I;
   input clk;
   output [3:0] Q;
   reg [3:0] Q;

   always @ (posedge clk)
   begin
      Q <= I;
   end
endmodule
```

Figure 9.17 Behavioral Verilog description of a 4-bit register.

thus assign the value 1 to position 3 of the vector *I* and the value 0 to the remaining three positions. When assigning a value to a vector, we must specify the number of bits within the value, the base of the value, and the value itself. For example, the decimal value 5 would be specified as the 4-bit binary value *4'b0101*.

The module describes the register behaviorally, using an *always* procedure. The procedure block is sensitive to the positive edge of the *clk* input, specified using the **posedge** keyword. Because the module should only update its output during a rising clock edge, the *always* procedure need not execute if *I* changes. On the positive edge of the clock, the procedure updates the register's contents using the statement "*Q <= I*". Because we defined the output *Q* as a *reg*, assigning *I* to *Q* causes *Q* to retain the new value, even when the procedure is done executing, thus implementing the storage part of the register.

SystemC

Figure 9.18 shows a basic 4-bit register in SystemC. The register is identical to that described in Figure 3.36. The module defines the data input *I* and the data output *Q*, as well as the clock input *clk*. The input *I* and output *Q* of this design correspond to a 4-bit value. Instead of using 4 individual inputs and 4 individual outputs of type *sc_logic*, the module's *I* and *Q* ports are defined as **sc_lv**, which stands for logic vector. An *sc_lv* is a vector of multiple *sc_logic* elements. For example, the type declaration "*sc_lv<4>*" defines a 4-bit vector of *sc_logic* elements where the bit positions within the vector are numbered from 3 to 0. In SystemC, the ordering of the elements within the vector is defined such that the leftmost position is the most significant bit. For example, the statement "*I<="1000"*" would thus assign the value 1 to position 3 of the vector *I* and the value 0 to the remaining three positions. When assigning a value to an *sc_lv*, the vector's value must be specified within double quotations. For example, the decimal value 5 would be specified as a 4-bit *sc_lv* as "*0101*". Notice that in defining the input port for *I*, we included a space between the two closing angle brackets, "*> >*"—that space is required in SystemC.

```
#include "systemc.h"

SC_MODULE(Reg4)
{
  sc_in<sc_lv<4> > I;
  sc_out<sc_lv<4> > Q;
  sc_in<sc_logic> clk;

  SC_CTOR(Reg4)
  {
    SC_METHOD(seq_logic);
    sensitive_pos << clk;
  }

  void seq_logic()
  {
    Q.write(I.read());
  }
};
```

Figure 9.18 Behavioral SystemC description of a 4-bit register.

The module consists of a single process named *seq_logic* that is sensitive to the positive edge of the *clk* input. The positive edge is specified using the **sensitive_pos** statement for defining the sensitivity list. Bcause the module should only update its output during a rising clock edge, the *seq_logic* process need not wake up if *I* changes. On the positive edge of the clock, the register updates the register's contents using the statement "*Q.write(I.read())*".

In SystemC, output ports are a type of signal, and signals have memory. Thus, assigning *I* to *Q* causes *Q* to retain the new value, even when the process is done executing, thus implementing the storage part of the register.

Oscillator

VHDL

The register presented in Figure 9.16 has a clock input. We thus need to define an oscillator component that generates a clock signal. Figure 9.19 illustrates an oscillator described in VHDL. The entity defines one output, *clk*. The architecture consists of a process, but notice that the process does not have a sensitivity list. By default, such a process executes its statements as if they were enclosed in an infinite loop. So the process sets the clock to 0, waits until 10 ns of simulated time passes, sets the clock to 1, waits another 10 ns of simulated time, goes back to the first statement in the process that sets the clock to 0, and so on. The output waveform for such an oscillator will be identical to the waveform shown in Figure 3.29.

The *wait for* statement in VHDL tells the simulator the amount of simulated time that the process should wait. A process *without* a sensitivity list *must* have at least one wait statement, otherwise the simulator will never finish simulating that process (because the process is in an implicit infinite loop), and thus the simulator will never get a chance to update outputs or to simulate other processes. On the other hand, a process *with* a sensitivity list *cannot* include wait statements, because by definition the sensitivity list defines when the process should execute.

```
library ieee;
use ieee.std_logic_1164.all;

entity Osc is
  port ( clk: out std_logic );
end Osc;

architecture behavior of Osc is
begin
  process
  begin
    clk <= '0';
    wait for 10 ns;
    clk <= '1';
    wait for 10 ns;
  end process;
end behavior;
```

Figure 9.19 VHDL oscillator description.

Verilog

The register presented in Figure 9.17 has a clock input. We thus need to define an oscillator component that generates a clock signal. Figure 9.20 illustrates an oscillator described in Verilog. The module defines one output, *clk*. The module consists of an *always* procedure, but notice that the always procedure does not have a sensitivity list. By default, such a procedure executes its statements as if they were enclosed in an infinite loop. Assuming we are using a time scale of nanoseconds, the always procedure sets the clock to 0, delays for 10 ns of simulated time, sets the clock to 1, delays for another 10 ns of simulated time, goes back to the first statement in the procedure that sets the clock to 0, and so on. The output waveform for such an oscillator will be identical to the waveform shown in Figure 3.29.

```
module Osc(clk);
  output clk;
  reg clk;

  always
  begin
    clk <= 0;
    #10;
    clk <= 1;
    #10;
  end
endmodule
```

Figure 9.20 Verilog oscillator description.

The *delay control statement*, specified with the **#** character, tells the simulator the amount of simulated time that the procedure should delay. A procedure *without* a sensitivity list *must* have at least one delay control statement, otherwise the simulator will never finish simulating that procedure (because the procedure is in an implicit infinite loop), and thus the simulator will never get the chance to update outputs or to simulate other procedures. On the other hand, a procedure *with* a sensitivity list *cannot* include delay control statements, because by definition the sensitivity list defines when the procedure should awake.

SystemC

The register presented in Figure 9.18 has a clock input. We thus need to define an oscillator component that generates a clock signal. Figure 9.21 illustrates an oscillator described in SystemC. The module defines one output, *clk*. The module consists of a single process, named *seq_logic*, implemented as an *SC_THREAD*. By default, an *SC_THREAD* process is only executed once. In order to ensure the process executes continuously, we enclose the statements of the process in an infinite loop, implemented using the statement "*while(true)*". Thus, the loop will execute the statement included within the braces forever. During execution, the process sets the clock to 0, suspends execution for 10 ns of simulated time, sets the clock to 1, sleeps another 10 ns of simulated time, sets the clock to 0, and so on. The output waveform for such an oscillator will be identical to the waveform in Figure 3.29.

```
#include "systemc.h"

SC_MODULE(Osc)
{
  sc_out<sc_logic> clk;

  SC_CTOR(Osc)
  {
    SC_THREAD(seq_logic);
  }

  void seq_logic()
  {
    while(true) {
      clk.write(SC_LOGIC_0);
      wait(10, SC_NS);
      clk.write(SC_LOGIC_1);
      wait(10, SC_NS);
    }
  }
};
```

Figure 9.21 SystemC oscillator description.

The **wait()** function in SystemC tells the simulator the amount of simulated time that the process should wait. For example, the statement "*wait(10, SC_NS);*" will suspend the execution of the process for 10 ns. An *SC_THREAD* process explicitly implementing an infinite loop *must* have at least one wait statement, otherwise the simulator would never finish simulating that process (because the process is in an infinite loop), and thus the simulator could not update outputs or simulate other processes.

Controllers

Recall that a common type of sequential circuit is a *controller*, which implements a finite-state machine. The controller consists of a state register and combinational logic.

VHDL

Figure 9.22 shows one way to model a controller in VHDL. The controller modeled is for the FSM shown in Figure 3.47. The VHDL entity, named *LaserTimer*, defines the controller's inputs and outputs.

The VHDL architecture describes the behavior of the entity. The architecture consists of two processes, one modeling the state register, the other modeling the combinational logic, that form the standard controller architecture from Figure 3.59.

The first process describes the controller's state register. That process, named *statereg*, is sensitive to inputs *clk* and *rst*. If the *rst* input is enabled, then the process asynchronously sets the *currentstate* signal to the FSM's initial state, *S_Off*. Otherwise, if the clock is rising, the process updates the state register with the next state.

The *currentstate* and *nextstate* signals are defined as a user-defined type named *statetype*. *statetype* is defined by the **type** statement and specifies the possible values a signal of that type can represent. The *type* declaration of *statetype* consists of the names of all the states in the controller, *S_Off*, *S_On1*, *S_On2*, and *S_On3*.

The second process describes the controller's combinational logic. That process, named *comblogic*, is sensitive to the inputs to the combinational logic of Figure 3.59, namely the external inputs (in this case, *b*) and the state register outputs (*currentstate*). When either of those items change, the process sets the FSM's outputs, in this case *x*, with the appropriate value for the current state. The process also determines what the next state should be, based on the current state and the values of inputs (i.e., the conditions on the FSM transitions). The next state will be loaded into the state register by the state register process on the next rising clock edge.

Notice that the architecture declares two signals, *currentstate* and *nextstate*. Signals are visible across all processes in an architecture. The *currentstate* signal represents the actual storage of the state register. The *nextstate* signal represents the value coming from the combinational logic and going to the state register. Notice also that the architecture declares those signals as type *statetype*, defined in the architecture as a type whose value can be either *S_Off*, *S_On1*, *S_On2*, or *S_On3*.

```vhdl
library ieee;
use ieee.std_logic_1164.all

entity LaserTimer is
   port (b: in std_logic;
         x: out std_logic;
         clk, rst: in std_logic
   );
end LaserTimer;

architecture behavior of LaserTimer is
   type statetype is
      (S_Off, S_On1, S_On2, S_On3);
   signal currentstate, nextstate:
      statetype;
begin
   statereg: process(clk, rst)
   begin
      if (rst='1') then -- intial state
         currentstate <= S_Off;
      elsif (clk='1' and clk'event) then
         currentstate <= nextstate;
      end if;
   end process;

   comblogic: process (currentstate, b)
   begin
      case currentstate is
         when S_Off =>
            x <= '0'; -- laser off
            if (b='0') then
               nextstate <= S_Off;
            else
               nextstate <= S_On1;
            end if;
         when S_On1 =>
            x <= '1'; -- laser on
            nextstate <= S_On2;
         when S_On2 =>
            x <= '1'; -- laser still on
            nextstate <= S_On3;
         when S_On3 =>
            x <= '1'; -- laser still on
            nextstate <= S_Off;
      end case;
   end process;
end behavior;
```

Figure 9.22 Behavioral VHDL description of the *LaserTimer* controller.

Verilog

Figure 9.23 shows one way to model a controller in Verilog. The controller modeled is for the FSM shown in Figure 3.47. The Verilog module, named *LaserTimer*, defines the controller's inputs and outputs.

The module consists of two procedures, one modeling the state register, the other modeling the combinational logic, that together form the standard controller architecture from Figure 3.59.

The state register procedure is sensitive to the positive edge of the *rst* input and the positive edge of the *clk* input. The state register has an asynchronous reset signal and in order to model the asynchronous reset, the state register procedure must be sensitive to the positive edge of the *rst* input. On the positive edge of the *rst* input, the procedure will wake asynchronously and sets the *currentstate* signal to the FSM's initial state, *S_Off*. On the rising edge of the clock input, *clk*, if the reset input is not enabled, the procedure updates the state register with the *nextstate* value determined by the combinational logic procedure.

In Verilog, we explicitly specify the size of the state registers as well as define the FSM's state encodings. Within the *LaserTimer* module, we declare four parameters *S_Off*, *S_On1*, *S_On2*, and *S_On3*, which specify the encodings. For example, "*S_Off = 2'b00*" defines the state name *S_Off* and assigns the 2-bit value "*00*" as the encoding of this state. We can then refer to this state throughout the module using *S_Off* instead of using specific bit values. While not required to define a state machine, using parameters increases the readability of a design and makes revisions to the FSM easier. Because

```verilog
module LaserTimer(b, x, clk, rst);
   input b, clk, rst;
   output x;
   reg x;

   parameter S_Off = 2'b00,
             S_On1 = 2'b01,
             S_On2 = 2'b10,
             S_On3 = 2'b11;

   reg [1:0] currentstate;
   reg [1:0] nextstate;
   // state register procedure
   always @(posedge rst or posedge clk)
   begin
      if (rst==1) // initial state
         currentstate <= S_Off;
      else
         currentstate <= nextstate;
   end
   // combinational logic procedure
   always @(*)
   begin
      case (currentstate)
         S_Off: begin
            x <= 0; // laser off
            if (b==0)
               nextstate <= S_Off;
            else
               nextstate <= S_On1;
         end
         S_On1: begin
            x <= 1; // laser on
            nextstate <= S_On2;
         end
         S_On2: begin
            x <= 1; // laser still on
            nextstate <= S_On3;
         end
         S_On3: begin
            x <= 1; // laser still on
            nextstate <= S_Off;
         end
      endcase
   end
endmodule
```

Figure 9.23 Behavioral Verilog description of the *LaserTimer* controller.

the *LaserTimer*'s FSM has four states, we need a 2-bit state register and thus declare the *currentstate* and *nextstate* signals as 2-bit registers.

The second procedure is the combinational procedure implementing the control logic of the FSM. That procedure is sensitive to all the items it reads (specified by the "***"), which are the inputs to the combinational logic of Figure 3.59, namely the external inputs (in this case, *b*) and the state register outputs (*currentstate*). When either of those items change, the procedure sets the FSM's outputs, in this case *x*, with the appropriate value for the current state. The procedure also determines the next state based on the current state and the values of inputs (i.e., the conditions on the FSM transitions). The next state will be loaded into the state register by the state register procedure on the next positive clock edge.

Notice that the module declares two signals *currentstate* and *nextstate*. Signals are visible across all procedures in a module. The *currentstate* signal represents the actual storage of the state register. *nextstate* represents the value coming from the combinational logic going to the state register.

SystemC

Figure 9.24 shows one way to model a controller in SystemC, for the FSM in Figure 3.47. The module, named *LaserTimer*, defines the controller's inputs and outputs.

The module consists of two processes, one modeling the state register named *statereg*, the other process modeling the combinational logic named *comblogic*, that form the standard controller architecture of Figure 3.59.

The state register process is sensitive to the positive edge of the *rst* input and the positive edge of the *clk* input. The state register has an asynchronous reset signal. In order to model the asynchronous reset, the state register process is sensitive to the positive edge of the *rst* input. On the positive edge of the *rst* input, the process will wake asynchronously and sets the *currentstate*

```
#include "systemc.h"

enum statetype { S_Off, S_On1, S_On2, S_On3 };

SC_MODULE(LaserTimer)
{
  sc_in<sc_logic> b, clk, rst;
  sc_out<sc_logic> x;
  sc_signal<statetype> currentstate, nextstate;

  SC_CTOR(LaserTimer) {
    SC_METHOD(statereg);
    sensitive_pos << rst << clk;
    SC_METHOD(comblogic);
    sensitive << currentstate << b;
  }

  void statereg() {
    if( rst.read() == SC_LOGIC_1 )
      currentstate = S_Off; // initial state
    else
      currentstate = nextstate;
  }
  void comblogic() {
    switch (currentstate) {
      case S_Off:
        x.write(SC_LOGIC_0); // laser off
        if( b.read() == SC_LOGIC_0 )
          nextstate = S_Off;
        else
          nextstate = S_On1;
        break;
      case S_On1:
        x.write(SC_LOGIC_1); // laser on
        nextstate = S_On2;
        break;
      case S_On2:
        x.write(SC_LOGIC_1); // laser still on
        nextstate = S_On3;
        break;
      case S_On3:
        x.write(SC_LOGIC_1); // laser still on
        nextstate = S_Off;
        break;
    }
  }
};
```

Figure 9.24 Behavioral SystemC description of the *LaserTimer* controller.

signal to the FSM's initial state, *S_Off*. On the rising edge of the clock input, *clk*, if the reset input is not enabled, the process updates the state register with the *nextstate* value determined by the combinational logic process.

The *currentstate* and *nextstate* signals are defined as a user-defined type, named *statetype*. *statetype* is defined by the **enum** statement and specifies the possible values a signal of that type can represent. The *enum* declaration for *statetype* consists of the names of all the states in the controller, *S_Off, S_On1, S_On2,* and *S_On3*.

The second process, named *comblogic*, is sensitive to the inputs to the combinational logic of Figure 3.59, namely the external inputs (in this case, *b*) and the state register outputs (*currentstate*). When either of those items change, the process sets the FSM's outputs, in this case *x*, with the appropriate value for the current state. The process also determines what the next state should be, based on the current state and the values of inputs (i.e., the conditions on the FSM transitions). The next state will be loaded into the state register by the state register process on the next rising clock edge. Within the first state, we determine the next state depending on the value of input *b* by performing the comparison "*b.read()* == *SC_ LOGIC_0*". Note that the comparison for equality uses the syntax "==". A common mistake is to use "=" instead, which means assignment rather than equality.

Notice that the module declares two *sc_signals*: *currentstate* and *nextstate*. Signals are visible across all processes in a module. The *currentstate* signal represents the actual storage of the state register. The *nextstate* signal represents the value coming from the combinational logic and going to the state register. Notice also that the architecture declares those signals as a type *statetype*, defined in the architecture as a type whose value can be either *S_Off, S_On1, S_On2,* or *S_On3*.

► 9.4 DATAPATH COMPONENT DESCRIPTION USING HARDWARE DESCRIPTION LANGUAGES

Full-Adders

This section shows how to describe a full-adder behaviorally in an HDL. Recall from Figure 4.31 that a full-adder is a combinational circuit that adds three bits (a, b, and ci) and outputs a sum (s) and a carry-out (co) bit.

VHDL

Figure 9.25 shows a full-adder described behaviorally in VHDL. The VHDL entity, named *FullAdder*, defines the full-adder's three inputs *a, b,* and *ci* and two outputs *s* and *co*.

The architecture describes the behavior of the full-adder. The architecture consists of one process describing the combinational behavior of the full-adder. The

```vhdl
library ieee;
use ieee.std_logic_1164.all;

entity FullAdder is
    port ( a, b, ci: in std_logic;
           s, co: out std_logic
    );
end FullAdder;

architecture behavior of FullAdder is
begin
    process (a, b, ci)
    begin
        s <= a xor b xor ci;
        co <= (b and ci) or (a and ci) or (a and b);
    end process;
end behavior;
```

Figure 9.25 Behavioral VHDL description of a full-adder.

process is sensitive to all three inputs (*a*, *b*, and *ci*) of the full-adder. When any of the inputs change, the process executes its two statements updating the values for the sum (*s*) and carry-out (*co*).

Verilog

Figure 9.26 shows a full-adder described behaviorally in Verilog. The Verilog module, named *FullAdder*, defines the full-adder's three inputs *a*, *b*, and *ci* and two outputs *s* and *co*.

The module describes the behavior of the full-adder and consists of a single *always* procedure describing the combinational behavior of the full-adder. The procedure is sensitive to all items read, which in this case are the three inputs (*a*, *b*, or *ci*) of the full-adder. When any of the inputs change, the procedure executes its two statements updating the values for the sum (*s*) and carry-out (*co*).

```
module FullAdder(a, b, ci, s, co);
  input a, b, ci;
  output s, co;
  reg s, co;

  always @(*)
  begin
    s <= a ^ b ^ ci;
    co <= (b & ci) | (a & ci) | (a & b);
  end
endmodule
```

Figure 9.26 Behavioral Verilog description of a full-adder.

SystemC

Figure 9.27 shows a full-adder described behaviorally in SystemC. The SystemC module, named *FullAdder*, defines the full-adder's three inputs *a*, *b*, and *ci* and two outputs *s* and *co*.

The module describes the behavior of the full-adder and consists of a single process, named *comblogic*, describing the combinational behavior of the full-adder. The process is sensitive to all three inputs (*a*, *b*, or *ci*) of the full-adder. When any of the inputs change, the process executes its two statements updating the values for the sum (*s*) and carry-out (*co*).

```
#include "systemc.h"

SC_MODULE(FullAdder)
{
  sc_in<sc_logic> a, b, ci;
  sc_out<sc_logic> s, co;

  SC_CTOR(FullAdder)
  {
    SC_METHOD(comblogic);
    sensitive << a << b << ci;
  }

  void comblogic()
  {
    s.write(a.read() ^ b.read() ^ ci.read());
    co.write((b.read() & ci.read()) |
             (a.read() & ci.read()) |
             (a.read() & b.read()));
  }
};
```

Figure 9.27 Behavioral SystemC description of a full-adder.

Carry-Ripple Adders

This section shows how to structurally describe the 4-bit carry-ripple adder of Figure 4.32 using the full-adder designed in the previous section.

VHDL

Figure 9.28 is a VHDL description of a 4-bit carry-ripple adder with a carry-in. The VHDL entity, named *CarryRippleAdder4*, has two 4-bit inputs *a* and *b*, and a carry-in input *ci*. The carry-ripple adder outputs a 4-bit sum *s* and a final carry-out *co*.

The architecture structurally describes the carry-ripple adder composed of four full-adders. The architecture begins by declaring the component *FullAdder*, which was described in the previous section. The design has three internal signals, *co1*, *co2*, and *co3*, that are used for internal connection between the full-adders. The architecture then instantiates four *FullAdder* components. In VHDL, each instantiated component must have a unique name. The four *FullAdder* components in this design are uniquely identified by the names *FullAdder1*, *FullAdder2*, *FullAdder3*, and *FullAdder4*.

```
library ieee;
use ieee.std_logic_1164.all;

entity CarryRippleAdder4 is
   port ( a:  in std_logic_vector(3 downto 0);
          b:  in std_logic_vector(3 downto 0);
          ci: in std_logic;
          s:  out std_logic_vector(3 downto 0);
          co: out std_logic
   );
end CarryRippleAdder4;

architecture structure of CarryRippleAdder4 is
   component FullAdder
      port ( a, b, ci: in std_logic;
             s, co: out std_logic
      );
   end component;
   signal co1, co2, co3: std_logic;
begin
   FullAdder1: FullAdder
      port map (a(0), b(0), ci, s(0), co1);
   FullAdder2: FullAdder
      port map (a(1), b(1), co1, s(1), co2);
   FullAdder3: FullAdder
      port map (a(2), b(2), co2, s(2), co3);
   FullAdder4: FullAdder
      port map (a(3), b(3), co3, s(3), co);
end structure;
```

Figure 9.28 Structural VHDL description of a 4-bit carry-ripple adder.

In VHDL, the *std_logic_vector* type provides a convenient method of specifying ports or signals consisting of multiple bits. However, a design may need to access the individual bits of these vectors. The individual bits of a *std_logic_vector* can be accessed by specifying the desired bit position within parentheses after the vector's name. For example, to access bit 0 of the 4-bit input *a* of this design, one would use the syntax "$a(0)$". In defining the connections to the instantiated components in the carry-ripple adder, individual bits of the inputs *a* and *b* and output *s* are accessed using this syntax. The first full-adder, *FullAdder1*, connects bit 0 of the inputs *a* and *b* as well as the carry-ripple adder's carry-in *ci* to the full-adder's three inputs. The *s* output of *FullAdder1* is connected to bit 0 of the 4-bit adder's sum output *s*, represented as $s(0)$. The design then connects the carry-out bit of *FullAdder1* to the internal signal *co1*, which is subsequently connected to the carry-in input of the next full-adder *FullAdder2*. The component connections of the remaining three full-adders are connected in a similar manner, with the exception of the last full-adder in the carry-ripple chain. The carry-out from that last full-adder *FullAdder4* is connected to the carry-out output *co* of the carry-ripple adder.

Verilog

Figure 9.29 is a Verilog description of a 4-bit carry-ripple adder with a carry-in. The Verilog module, which is named *CarryRippleAdder4*, has two 4-bit inputs *a* and *b*, and a carry-in input *ci*. The carry-ripple adder outputs a 4-bit sum *s* and a final carry-out *co*.

The module structurally describes the carry-ripple adder composed of four full-adders. The design has three internal wires, *co1*, *co2*, and *co3*, that are used for internal connection between the full-adders. The module instantiates four *Full-Adder* components. In Verilog,

```
module CarryRippleAdder4(a, b, ci, s, co);
    input [3:0] a;
    input [3:0] b;
    input ci;
    output [3:0] s;
    output co;

    wire co1, co2, co3;

    FullAdder FullAdder1(a[0], b[0], ci,
                         s[0], co1);
    FullAdder FullAdder2(a[1], b[1], co1,
                         s[1], co2);
    FullAdder FullAdder3(a[2], b[2], co2,
                         s[2], co3);
    FullAdder FullAdder4(a[3], b[3], co3,
                         s[3], co);
endmodule
```

Figure 9.29 Structural Verilog description of a 4-bit carry-ripple adder.

each instantiated component must have a unique name. The four *FullAdder* components in this design are uniquely identified by the names *FullAdder1*, *FullAdder2*, *FullAdder3*, and *FullAdder4*.

In Verilog, vectors provide a convenient method of specifying ports or signals consisting of multiple bits. However, a design may need to access the individual bits of these vectors. The individual bits of a vector can be accessed by specifying the desired bit position within brackets after the vector's name. For example, to access bit 0 of the 4-bit input *a* of this design, one would use the syntax "*a[0]*". In defining the connections to the instantiated components in the carry-ripple adder, individual bits of the inputs *a* and *b* and output *s* are accessed using this syntax. The first full-adder, *FullAdder1*, connects bit 0 of the inputs *a* and *b* as well as the carry-ripple adder's carry-in *ci* to the full-adder's three inputs. The *s* output of *FullAdder1* is connected to bit 0 of the 4-bit adder's sum output *s*, represented as *s[0]*. The design then connects the carry-out bit of *FullAdder1* to the internal signal *co1*, which is subsequently connected to the carry-in input of the next full-adder *FullAdder2*. The component connections of the remaining three full-adders are connected in a similar manner, with the exception of the last full-adder in the carry-ripple chain. The carry-out from the last full-adder *FullAdder4* is connected to the carry-out output *co* of the carry-ripple adder.

SystemC

Figure 9.30 is a SystemC description of a 4-bit carry-ripple adder with a carry-in. The SystemC module, named *CarryRippleAdder4*, has two 4-bit inputs *a* and *b*, and a carry-in input *ci*. The carry-ripple adder outputs a 4-bit sum *s* and a final carry-out *co*.

The module structurally describes the carry-ripple adder composed of four full-adders. The design has three internal signals, *co1*, *co2*, and *co3*, that are used for internal connection between the full-adders. The module first instantiates four *FullAdder* components. In SystemC, each instantiated component must have a unique name. The four *FullAdder* components in this design are uniquely identified by the names *FullAdder_1*, *FullAdder_2*, *FullAdder_3*, and *FullAdder_4*.

Previously, we defined multiple-bit inputs as an input vector using the *sc_lv* type. However, SystemC does not support connecting individual bits within a signal or port of type *sc_lv* in a structural description. In our *CarryRippleAdder4* design, we instead defined the inputs and outputs *a*, *b*, and *s* as arrays of *sc_logic* with four elements each, rather than using type *sc_lv*. The individual bits of the array can be accessed by specifying the desired bit position within brackets after the array's name. For example, to access

```
#include "systemc.h"
#include "fulladder.h"

SC_MODULE(CarryRippleAdder4)
{
  sc_in<sc_logic> a[4];
  sc_in<sc_logic> b[4];
  sc_in<sc_logic> ci;
  sc_out<sc_logic> s[4];
  sc_out<sc_logic> co;

  sc_signal<sc_logic> co1, co2, co3;

  FullAdder FullAdder_1;
  FullAdder FullAdder_2;
  FullAdder FullAdder_3;
  FullAdder FullAdder_4;

  SC_CTOR(CarryRipple4):
    FullAdder_1("FullAdder_1"),
    FullAdder_2("FullAdder_2"),
    FullAdder_3("FullAdder_3"),
    FullAdder_4("FullAdder_4")
  {
    FullAdder_1.a(a[0]); FullAdder_1.b(b[0]);
    FullAdder_1.ci(ci); FullAdder_1.s(s[0]);
    FullAdder_1.co(co1);

    FullAdder_2.a(a[1]); FullAdder_2.b(b[1]);
    FullAdder_2.ci(co1); FullAdder_2.s(s[1]);
    FullAdder_2.co(co2);

    FullAdder_3.a(a[2]); FullAdder_3.b(b[2]);
    FullAdder_3.ci(co2); FullAdder_3.s(s[2]);
    FullAdder_3.co(co3);

    FullAdder_4.a(a[3]); FullAdder_4.b(b[3]);
    FullAdder_4.ci(co3); FullAdder_4.s(s[3]);
    FullAdder_4.co(co);
  }
};
```

Figure 9.30 Structural SystemC description of a 4-bit carry-ripple adder.

bit 0 of the 4-element input array *a* of this design, one would use the syntax "*a[0]*". In defining the connections to the instantiated components in the carry-ripple adder, individual bits of the inputs *a* and *b* and output *s* are accessed using this syntax. The first full-adder *FullAdder_1* connects bit 0 of the inputs *a* and *b* as well as the carry-ripple adder's carry-in *ci* to the full-adder's three inputs. The *s* output of *FullAdder_1* is connected to bit 0 of the 4-bit adder's sum output *s*, represented as *s[0]*. The design then connects the carry-out bit of *FullAdder_1* to the internal signal *co1* that is subsequently connected to the carry-in input of the next full-adder *FullAdder_2*. The component connections of the remaining three full-adders are connected in a similar manner, with the exception of the last full-adder in the carry-ripple chain. The carry-out from the last full-adder *FullAdder_4* is connected to the carry-out output (*co*) of the carry-ripple adder.

Up-Counter

This section shows how to structurally describe the 4-bit up-counter of Figure 4.66.

VHDL

Figure 9.31 is a VHDL description of a 4-bit up-counter. The entity, named *UpCounter*, defines the counter's inputs and outputs, consisting of a clock input *clk*, a count enable control input *cnt*, the 4-bit count value *C*, and a terminal count output *tc*.

The *UpCounter's* architecture structurally describes the design consisting of three components, namely *Reg4*, *Inc4*, and *AND4*. *Reg4* is a 4-bit parallel-load register with a load control input *ld*. *Inc4* is a 4-bit incrementer. *AND4* is a four-input AND gate that will output 1 when all four inputs are 1. The architecture further specifies two signals, *tempC* and *incC*, used as internal wires within the structural description.

The architecture instantiates each of the three components and specifies the connections among them. *Reg4* is the only

```
library ieee;
use ieee.std_logic_1164.all;

entity UpCounter is
    port ( clk: in std_logic;
           cnt: in std_logic;
           C: out std_logic_vector(3 downto 0);
           tc: out std_logic
    );
end UpCounter;

architecture structure of UpCounter is
    component Reg4
        port ( I: in std_logic_vector(3 downto 0);
               Q: out std_logic_vector(3 downto 0);
               clk, ld: in std_logic
        );
    end component;
    component Inc4
        port ( a: in std_logic_vector(3 downto 0);
               s: out std_logic_vector(3 downto 0)
        );
    end component;
    component AND4
        port ( w,x,y,z: in std_logic;
               F: out std_logic
        );
    end component;
    signal tempC: std_logic_vector(3 downto 0);
    signal incC: std_logic_vector(3 downto 0);
begin
    Reg4_1: Reg4 port map(incC, tempC, clk, cnt);
    Inc4_1: Inc4 port map(tempC, incC);
    AND4_1: AND4 port map(tempC(3), tempC(2),
                          tempC(1), tempC(0), tc);

    outputC: process(tempC)
    begin
        C <= tempC;
    end process;
end structure;
```

Figure 9.31 Structural VHDL description of 4-bit up-counter.

sequential component within the up-counter and thus the *clk* input only needs to be connected to the clock input of the register. The up-counter's counting is controlled by connecting the count enable input *cnt* to the load enable *ld* of the register. The output *Q* of *Reg4_1* is connected to the internal signal *tempC*, which connects the register's output to both the *Inc4_1* and *AND4_1* components. *Inc4_1* receives the current count from the *tempC* connection and outputs the incremented count on its output *s*, which is connected to the other internal signal *incC*. The *incC* signal connects the incremented count from *Inc4_1* to the parallel load input *I* of *Reg4_1*. The current count is also connected to the four inputs of the *AND4_1* component. *AND4_1*'s output *F* is connected to the counter's terminal count output *tc*.

The *UpCounter* design must connect the output of the 4-bit register to the incrementer, the AND gate, and the counter's output port *C*. VHDL does not allow connecting multiple signals or ports within the *port map* of an instantiated component. Therefore, the architecture uses the *tempC* signal to connect *Reg4_1*'s output to both the *AND4_1* and *Inc4_1* components. We still need to connect the register's output to the output port *C*. The architecture makes this connection by specifying a process, named *outputC*, that is used to connect the output of the register to the output port *C*. The *outputC* process is sensitive to the signal *tempC*, previously used as an internal wire between the three components. Whenever *tempC* changes, which corresponds to a change in the up-counter's stored count, the *outputC* process assigns the new count to the output port *C*.

Verilog

Figure 9.32 is a Verilog description of a 4-bit up-counter. The module *UpCounter* defines the counter's inputs and outputs, consisting of a clock input *clk*, a count enable control input *cnt*, the 4-bit count value *C*, and a terminal count output *tc*.

The *UpCounter*'s module structurally describes the design using three components *Reg4*, *Inc4*, and *AND4*. *Reg4* is a 4-bit parallel load register with a load control input *ld*. *Inc4* is a 4-bit incrementer. *AND4* is a four-input AND gate that will output 1 if and only if all four inputs are 1. The module further specifies two 4-bit wires, *tempC* and *incC*, used as internal wires within the structural description.

The module instantiates each of the three components and specifies the connections between them. *Reg4* is the only sequential component within the up-counter, and thus the *clk* input only needs to be connected to the clock input of the register. We control the up-counter's counting by connecting the count enable input, *cnt*, to the load enable, *ld*, of the register. The output *Q* of *Reg4_1* is connected to the internal signal *tempC*, which connects the register's output to both the *Inc4_1* and *AND4_1* components. *Inc4_1* receives the current count from the *tempC* connection and outputs the incremented count on its output *s*, which is

```verilog
module Reg4(I, Q, clk, ld);
    input [3:0] I;
    input clk, ld;
    output [3:0] Q;
    // details not shown
endmodule

module Inc4(a, s);
    input [3:0] a;
    output [3:0] s;
    // details not shown
endmodule

module AND4(w,x,y,z,F);
    input w, x, y, z;
    output F;
    // details not shown
endmodule

module UpCounter(clk, cnt, C, tc);
    input clk, cnt;
    output [3:0] C;
    reg [3:0] C;
    output tc;

    wire [3:0] tempC;
    wire [3:0] incC;

    Reg4 Reg4_1(incC, tempC, clk, cnt);
    Inc4 Inc4_1(tempC, incC);
    AND4 AND4_1(tempC[3], tempC[2],
                tempC[1], tempC[0], tc);

    always @(tempC)
    begin
        C <= tempC;
    end
endmodule
```

Figure 9.32 Structural Verilog description of 4-bit up-counter.

connected to the other internal signal *incC*. The *incC* signal connects the incremented count from *Inc4_1* to the parallel load input *I* of *Reg4_1*. The current count is also connected to the four inputs of the *AND4_1* component. The *AND4_1*'s output *F* is then connected to the counter's terminal count output *tc*.

The *UpCounter* design must connect the output of the 4-bit register to the incrementer, the AND gate, and the counter's output port *C*. Therefore, the module uses the *tempC* signal to connect *Reg4_1*'s output to both the *AND4_1* and *Inc4_1* components.

We still need to connect the register's output to the output port *C*. The module makes this connection by specifying a procedure that is used to connect the output of the register to the output port *C*. The procedure is sensitive to the signal *tempC*, previously used as an internal wire between the three components. Whenever *tempC* changes, which corresponds to a change in the up-counter's stored count, the procedure assigns the new count to the output port *C*.

SystemC

Figure 9.33 is a SystemC description of a 4-bit up-counter. The SystemC module, named *UpCounter*, defines the counter's inputs and outputs, consisting of a clock input *clk*, a count enable control input *cnt*, the 4-bit count value *C*, and a terminal count output *tc*.

The *UpCounter's* module structurally describes the design consisting of three components *Reg4*, *Inc4*, and *AND4*. *Reg4* is a 4-bit parallel load register with a load

```
#include "systemc.h"
#include "reg4.h"
#include "inc4.h"
#include "and4.h"

SC_MODULE(UpCounter)
{
  sc_in<sc_logic> clk, cnt;
  sc_out<sc_lv<4> > C;
  sc_out<sc_logic> tc;

  sc_signal<sc_lv<4> > tempC, incC;
  sc_signal<sc_logic> tempC_b[4];

  Reg4 Reg4_1;
  Inc4 Inc4_1;
  AND4 AND4_1;

  SC_CTOR(UpCounter) : Reg4_1("Reg4_1"),
                       Inc4_1("Inc4_1"),
                       AND4_1("AND4_1")
  {
    Reg4_1.I(incC); Reg4_1.Q(tempC);
    Reg4_1.clk(clk); Reg4_1.ld(cnt);

    Inc4_1.a(tempC); Inc4_1.s(incC);

    AND4_1.w(tempC_b[0]); AND4_1.x(tempC_b[1]);
    AND4_1.y(tempC_b[2]); AND4_1.z(tempC_b[3]);
    AND4_1.F(tc);

    SC_METHOD(comblogic);
    sensitive << tempC;
  }

  void comblogic()
  {
    tempC_b[0] = tempC.read()[0];
    tempC_b[1] = tempC.read()[1];
    tempC_b[2] = tempC.read()[2];
    tempC_b[3] = tempC.read()[3];
    C.write(tempC);
  }
};
```

Figure 9.33 Structural SystemC description of 4-bit up-counter.

load control input *ld*. *Inc4* is a 4-bit incrementer. *AND4* is a four-input AND gate that will output 1 if and only if all four inputs are 1. The module further specifies two 4-bit signals, *tempC* and *incC*, used as internal wires within the structural description. Additionally, the module defines a four-element array of *sc_logic* signals named *tempC_b* used to access the individual bits within the 4-bit vector *tempC*.

The module first instantiates each of the three components and then specifies the connections between them. *Reg4* is the only sequential component within the up-counter, and thus the *clk* input only needs to be connected to the clock input of the register. We control the up-counter's counting by connecting the count enable input, *cnt*, to the load enable, *ld*, of the register. The output *Q* of *Reg4_1* is connected to the internal signal *tempC*, which connects the register's output to *Inc4_1*. *Inc4_1* receives the current count from the *tempC* connection and outputs the incremented count on its output *s*, which is connected to the internal signal *incC*. The *incC* signal connects the incremented count from *Inc4_1* to the parallel load input *I* of *Reg4_1*. The current count is also connected to the four inputs of the *AND4_1* component using the *tempC_b* array to access the individual bits. The *AND4_1*'s output *F* is then connected to the counter's terminal count output *tc*.

The *UpCounter* design must connect the output of the 4-bit register to the incrementer, the AND gate, and the counter's output port *C*. Therefore, the module uses the *tempC* signal to connect *Reg4_1*'s output to the *Inc4_1* component and uses the *tempC_b* array to connect *Reg4_1*'s output to the *AND4_1* component. Thus, we still need to connect the register's output to the output port *C* and assign the individual bits of the register's output to the *tempC_b* array. The module makes these connections by defining a process, named *comblogic*, that is sensitive to the signal *tempC*. Whenever *tempC* changes, which corresponds to a change in the up-counter's stored count, the *comblogic* process assigns the new count to the output port *C*. Additionally, the process assigns the bits within vector *tempC* to the individual *sc_logic* signals within the *tempC_b* array. In order to access the individual bits of the vector signal *tempC*, we use the syntax, "tempC.read()[0]".

▶ 9.5 RTL DESIGN USING HARDWARE DESCRIPTION LANGUAGES

This section demonstrates how to create RTL descriptions using HDLs. HDLs will describe the starting point of RTL design, namely high-level state machines (HLSMs), and the ending point of RTL design, namely connected controllers and datapaths (processors). RTL designers will commonly create a testbench to test the HLSM description, and then use that same testbench for the controller/datapath description, thus helping to verify that the designer created a correct controller/datapath implementation.

High-Level State Machine of the Laser-Based Distance Measurer

This section shows how to create an HDL description for the laser-based distance measurer HLSM from Figure 5.12.

VHDL

Figure 9.34 presents a VHDL description of an HLSM for the laser-based distance measurer. Two new *ieee* library packages are used, *std_logic_arith* and *std_logic_unsigned*, which support arithmetic operations (like addition) on *std_logic_vector* items representing unsigned binary numbers. The entity, named *LaserDistMeasurer*, defines the

```vhdl
library IEEE;
use IEEE.STD_LOGIC_1164.ALL;
use IEEE.STD_LOGIC_ARITH.ALL;
use IEEE.STD_LOGIC_UNSIGNED.ALL;

entity LaserDistMeasurer is
  port (
      clk, rst : in  std_logic;
      B, S     : in  std_logic;
      L        : out std_logic;
      D        : out std_logic_vector
                        (15 downto 0)
);
end LaserDistMeasurer;

architecture behavior of
      LaserDistMeasurer is

   type statetype is (S0,S1,S2,S3,S4);
   signal State, StateNext : statetype;

   signal Dctr, DctrNext:
       std_logic_vector(15 downto 0);
   signal Dreg, DregNext:
       std_logic_vector(15 downto 0);

   constant U_ZERO :
       std_logic_vector(15 downto 0)
               := "0000000000000000";
   constant U_ONE  :
       std_logic_vector(15 downto 0)
               := "0000000000000001";

begin

Regs: process(clk, rst)
begin
   if(rst = '1') then
      State <= S0;
      Dctr <= U_ZERO;
      Dreg <= U_ZERO;
   elsif(clk'event and clk='1') then
      State <= StateNext;
      Dctr  <= DctrNext;
      Dreg  <= DregNext;
   end if;
end process;
```

```vhdl
CombLogic: process(State, Dctr, B, S)
   begin
      case State is
         when S0 =>
            L <= '0'; -- laser off
            DregNext <= U_ZERO; --clr D
            DctrNext <= U_ZERO; --clr Dctr
            StateNext <= S1;
         when S1 =>
            DctrNext <= U_ZERO; --clr Dctr
            L <= '0'; -- laser off

            if(B = '1') then
               StateNext <= S2;
            else
               StateNext <= S1;
            end if;
         when S2 =>
            L <= '1'; --laser on
            DctrNext <= U_ZERO;
            StateNext <= S3;
         when S3 =>
            L <= '0'; -- laser off
            DctrNext <= Dctr + 1;

            if( S = '1') then
               StateNext <= S4;
            else
               StateNext <= S3;
            end if;
         when S4 =>
            DctrNext <= Dctr;
            DregNext <= SHR(Dctr, U_ONE);
            L <= '0';
            StateNext <= S1;
         when others =>
            DregNext <= U_ZERO;
            DctrNext <= U_ZERO;
            L <= '0';
            StateNext <= S0;
      end case;
   end process;

--assign Dreg output to D output
D <= Dreg;

end behavior;
```

Figure 9.34 Behavioral VHDL description of an HLSM of the laser-based distance measurer.

inputs and outputs, including a user-pressed button input *B*, a laser sensor input *S*, a laser control output *L*, and a 16-bit output *D* for the distance measured.

The **use** statement specifies which packages will be used within a design. The package *ieee.std_logic_arith* defines the *unsigned* type as well as a set of operations and functions that can be performed on *unsigned* values.

The entity also defines a clock input *clk* and reset input *rst*. We assume that the clock input is 300 MHz, as was assumed in the laser-based distance measurer design from

Chapter 5. We omit details of generating the 300 MHz oscillator (see Section 9.3 for an example of describing an oscillator).

The VHDL architecture describes the behavior of the entity. The description defines constants *U_ZERO* and *U_ONE* for 16-bit numbers 0 and 1, respectively. As was the case for an FSM, the description for the HLSM defines two signals for the state register: a current state signal *State*, and a next state signal *StateNext*. Furthermore, the description declares current and next signals for every other register too, thus declaring signals *Dctr* and *DctrNext*, and *Dreg* and *DregNext*.

As was the case for describing an FSM, the description for the HLSM uses two processes, one for all registers, and one for all combinational logic. The register process is sensitive to the reset and clock inputs, and has an asynchronous reset that clears all the current register signals. On a rising clock, the register process updates the current register signals with the next register signals.

The combinational logic process is sensitive to all items that it reads. The process consists of a case statement carrying out the HLSM's actions and transitions. The process reads the current register signals and writes the next register signals; current register signals are never written and next register signals are never read by the process.

The HLSM for the laser-based distance measurer performs two arithmetic operations, addition and shifting. Incrementing the counter signal *Dctr* in state *S3* is done using the syntax "*DctrNext <= Dctr + 1;*". State *S4* calculates the distance *D* by dividing the value of *Dctr* by 2. However, this division is achieved using a right-shift-by-one operation. Performing the shift and assigning the value to the output *D* is done using the statement "*DregNext <= SHR(Dctr, U_ONE);*". The function **SHR()**, defined within the *ieee.std_logic_arith* package, shifts the first parameter *Dctr* by the amount specified by the second parameter *U_ONE*, where *U_ONE* is a constant defined earlier in the architecture.

Finally, the output of *Dreg* is permanently assigned to the output *D* using the statement "*D <= Dreg;*". Note that the statement is not contained inside a process. The statement is known as a ***concurrent signal assignment***. The statement executes whenever a signal on its right side changes.

The two-process approach to describing an HLSM can be thought of as follows. The combinational logic process computes the inputs of all registers by reading current register values, performing combinational operations like addition, and writing to the next register signals. When a rising clock arrives, the register process updates the current contents of all registers with the next register values.

Verilog

Figure 9.35 presents a Verilog description of an HLSM for the laser-based distance measurer. The module, named *LaserDistMeasurer*, defines the inputs and outputs, including a user-pressed button input *B*, a laser sensor input *S*, a laser control output *L*, and a 16-bit output *D* for the distance measured.

The module also defines a clock input *clk* and reset input *rst*. We assume that the clock input is 300 MHz, as was assumed in the laser-based distance measurer design in

```
module LaserDistMeasurer(clk,rst,B,S,L,D);
    input clk, rst, B, S;
    output L;
    output [15:0] D;
    reg L;
    reg [15:0] D;

    parameter    S0 = 3'b000,
                 S1 = 3'b001,
                 S2 = 3'b010,
                 S3 = 3'b011,
                 S4 = 3'b100;

    reg [2:0] State, StateNext;
    reg [15:0] Dctr, DctrNext;
    reg [15:0] Dreg, DregNext;

    //Registers
    always@(posedge clk, posedge rst) begin
        if(rst == 1) begin //asynchr. reset
            State <= S0;
            Dctr  <= 0;
            Dreg  <= 0;
        end
        else begin
            State <= StateNext;
            Dctr  <= DctrNext;
            Dreg  <= DregNext;
        end
    end

    always @(Dreg) begin
        D <= Dreg;
    end
```

```
    //Combinational logic
    always@(State, Dctr, B, S) begin
        case (State)
            S0: begin
                L <= 0; //Laser off
                DregNext <= 0; //clr D
                StateNext <= S1;
                DctrNext  <= 0;
            end
            S1: begin
                DctrNext <= 0;
                L <= 0;

                if(B == 1)
                    StateNext <= S2;
                else
                    StateNext <= S1;
            end
            S2: begin
                L <= 1;      //Laser on
                DctrNext <= 0;
                StateNext <= S3;
            end
            S3: begin
                L <= 0;      //Laser off
                DctrNext <= Dctr + 1;

                if(S == 1)
                    StateNext <= S4;
                else
                    StateNext <= S3;
            end
            S4: begin
                DregNext <= Dctr >> 1;
                StateNext <= S1;
            end
        endcase
    end
endmodule
```

Figure 9.35 Behavioral Verilog description of an HLSM of the laser-based distance measurer.

Chapter 5. We omit details of generating the 300 MHz clock (see Section 9.3 for an example of describing an oscillator).

The Verilog module behaviorally describes the *LaserDistMeasurer's* HLSM. As was the case for describing an FSM, the module declares two signals for the state register: *State* for the current state, and *StateNext* for the next state. Furthermore, the description declares current and next signals for every other register too, thus declaring *Dctr* and *DctrNext*, and *Dreg* and *DregNext*.

As was the case for describing an FSM, the description for the HLSM uses two procedures, one for all registers, and one for all combinational logic. The register procedure is sensitive to the reset and clock inputs, and has an asynchronous reset that clears all the current register signals. On a rising clock edge, the register procedure updates the current register signals with the next register signals.

The combinational logic procedure is sensitive to all items that it reads. The procedure consists of a case statement carrying out the HLSM's actions and transitions. The procedure reads the current register signals and writes the next register signals; current register signals are never written and next register signals are never read by the procedure.

The HLSM for the laser-based distance measurer performs two arithmetic operations, addition and shifting. Incrementing the counter signal *Dctr* in state *S3* is done using the syntax "*DctrNext <= Dctr + 1;*". State *S4* calculates the distance *D* by dividing the value of *Dctr* by 2. However, this division is achieved using a right-shift-by-one operation. Performing the shift and assigning the value to the output *D* is done using the statement "*DregNext <= Dctr >> 1*". The operator ">>" shifts the value of left parameter *Dctr* by the amount specified by the right parameter 1.

Finally, the output of *Dreg* is permanently assigned to the output *D* using an *always* procedure sensitive to *Dreg* and executing the statement "*D <= Dreg;*". Thus *D* is updated whenever *Dreg* changes, so *D* will always equal *Dreg*.

The two-procedure approach to describing an HLSM can be thought of as follows. The combinational logic procedure computes the inputs of all registers by reading current register values, performing combinational operations like addition, and writing to the next register signals. When a rising clock arrives, the register procedure updates the current contents of all registers with the next register values.

SystemC

Figure 9.36 presents a SystemC description of an HLSM for the laser-based distance measurer. The module, named *LaserDistMeasurer*, defines the inputs and outputs, including a user-pressed button input *B*, a laser sensor input *S*, a laser control output *L*, and a 16-bit output *D* for the distance measured.

The module also defines a clock input *clk* and reset input *rst*. We assume that the clock input is 300 MHz, as was assumed in the laser-based distance measurer design in Chapter 5. We omit details of generating the 300 MHz clock (see Section 9.3 for an example of describing an oscillator).

The SystemC module behaviorally describes the *LaserDistMeasurer's* HLSM. As was the case for describing an FSM, the module declares two signals for the state register, *State* for the current state, and *StateNext* for the next state. Furthermore, the description declares current and next signals for every other register too, thus declaring *Dctr* and *DctrNext*, and *Dreg* and *DregNext*.

As was the case for describing an FSM, the description for the HLSM uses two processes, one for all registers, and one for all combinational logic. The register process is sensitive to the reset and clock inputs, and has an asynchronous reset that clears all the current register signals. On a rising clock, the register process updates the current register signals with the next register signals.

The combinational logic process is sensitive to all items that it reads. The process consists of a case statement carrying out the HLSM's actions and transitions. The procedure reads the current register signals and writes the next register signals; current register signals are never written and next register signals are never read by the procedure.

The HLSM for the laser-based distance measurer performs two arithmetic operations, addition and shifting. Incrementing the counter signal *Dctr* in state *S3* is done using the syntax "*DctrNext.write(Dctr.read() + 1);*". State *S4* calculates the distance *D* by dividing

```
#include "systemc.h"

enum statetype { S0, S1, S2, S3, S4 };

SC_MODULE(LaserDistMeasurer)
{
    sc_in<sc_logic> clk, rst;
    sc_in<sc_logic> B, S;
    sc_out<sc_logic> L;
    sc_out<sc_uint<16> > D;

    sc_signal<statetype> State, StateNext;
    sc_signal<sc_uint<16> > Dctr, DctrNext;
    sc_signal<sc_uint<16> > Dreg, DregNext;

    SC_CTOR(LaserDistMeasurer)
    {
        SC_METHOD(Regs);
        sensitive << clk.pos();

        SC_METHOD(CombLogic);
        sensitive << State << B << S << Dctr;

        SC_METHOD(Output);
        sensitive << Dreg;
    }

    void Regs(){
        if (rst.read() == SC_LOGIC_1){
            State.write(S0);
            Dctr.write(0);
            Dreg.write(0);
        }
        else{
            State.write(StateNext.read());
            Dctr.write(DctrNext.read());
            Dreg.write(DregNext.read());
        }
    }
}
```

```
void CombLogic(){
    switch (State) {
        case S0:
            L.write(SC_LOGIC_0);//laser off
            StateNext.write(S1);
            break;
        case S1:
            DctrNext.write(0); // clr count
            if (B.read() == SC_LOGIC_1){
                StateNext.write(S2);
            }
            break;
        case S2:
            L.write(SC_LOGIC_1);//laser on
            StateNext.write(S3);
            break;
        case S3:
            L.write(SC_LOGIC_0);//laser off
            DctrNext.write(Dctr.read()+1);
            if (S.read() == SC_LOGIC_1)
                StateNext.write(S4);
            else
                StateNext.write(S3);
            break;
        case S4:
            DregNext.write
                ((Dctr.read()>>1));
            StateNext.write(S1);
            break;
    }
}

void Output(){
    D.write(Dreg.read());
}
};
```

Figure 9.36 Behavioral SystemC description of an HLSM of the laser-based distance measurer.

the value of *Dctr* by 2. However, this division is achieved using a right-shift-by-one operation. Performing the shift and assigning the value to the output *D* is done using the statement "*DregNext.write(Dctr.read()>>1);*". The operator ">>" shifts the value of the left parameter *Dctr.read()* by the amount specified by the right parameter 1.

Finally, the output of *Dreg* is permanently assigned to the output *D* using a process sensitive to *Dreg* and executing the statement "*D.write(Dreg.read());*". Thus *D* is updated whenever *Dreg* changes, so *D* will always equal *Dreg*.

The two-process approach to describing an HLSM can be thought of as follows. The combinational logic process computes the inputs of all registers by reading current register values, performing combinational operations like addition, and writing to the next register signals. When a rising clock arrives, the register process updates the current contents of all registers with the next register values.

Controller and Datapath of the Laser-Based Distance Measurer

VHDL

Figure 9.37 is a VHDL description of the laser-based distance measurer controller/datapath from Figure 5.24. The entity, named *LaserDistMeasure* defines the inputs and outputs, including a user-pressed button input *B*, a laser sensor input *S*, a laser control output *L*, and a 16-bit output *D* for the distance measured. The entity also defines a 300 MHz clock input *clk* and reset input *rst* for the design's controller.

The *LaserDistMeasurer*'s architecture structurally describes the connections of the controller and datapath components. The architecture instantiates two components. *LDM_Controller_1* is the controller for the laser-based distance measurer, and *LDM_Datapath_1* is the datapath for this design. The architecture connects the entity's *clk*, *rst*, *B*, and *S* inputs to the inputs of *LDM_Controller_1* and connects the controller's laser control output to the corresponding output port

```vhdl
library IEEE;
use IEEE.STD_LOGIC_1164.ALL;

entity LaserDistMeasurer is
    port (
        clk, rst : in  std_logic;
        B, S     : in  std_logic;
        L        : out std_logic;
        D        : out
            std_logic_vector(15 downto 0)
        );
end LaserDistMeasurer;

architecture structure of LaserDistMeasurer is
    component LDM_Controller
    port ( clk, rst : in std_logic;
           B, S     : in std_logic;
           L        : out std_logic;
           Dreg_clr, Dreg_ld : out std_logic;
           Dctr_clr, Dctr_ld : out std_logic
         );
    end component;

    component LDM_Datapath
    port ( clk : in std_logic;
           Dreg_clr, Dreg_ld : in std_logic;
           Dctr_clr, Dctr_ld : in std_logic;
           D : out std_logic_vector(15 downto 0)
         );
    end component;

    signal Dreg_clr, Dreg_ld : std_logic;
    signal Dctr_clr, Dctr_ld : std_logic;

  begin
    LDM_Controller_1 : LDM_Controller
       port map ( clk, rst, B, S, L,
                    Dreg_clr, Dreg_ld, Dctr_clr,
                       Dctr_ld);

    LDM_Datapath_1 : LDM_Datapath
       port map ( clk, Dreg_clr, Dreg_ld,
                    Dctr_clr, Dctr_ld, D);
end structure;
```

Figure 9.37 Structural description of top-level VHDL description of laser-based distance measurer.

L. Additionally, the four signals *Dreg_clr*, *Dreg_ld*, *Dctr_clr*, and *Dctr_ld* connect the controller's four control signals to the four inputs of *LDM_Datapath_1*. The *LaserDistMeasurer* datapath has a single output *D*, providing the distance measured, that is connected to the output port *D* of the entity.

Figure 9.38 is a VHDL description of the *LaserDistMeasurer's* datapath component shown in Figure 5.23. The entity, named *LDM_Datapath*, defines a clock input *clk*, four control inputs *Dreg_clr*, *Dreg_ld*, *Dctr_clr*, and *Dctr_ld*, and a 16-bit distance output *D*.

The architecture defines three components, a 16-bit register, a 16-bit right shifter that shifts right by one position, and a 16-bit adder. The architecture instantiates a register component named *Dctr*, an adder component named *Add1*, a shifter component *ShiftRight*, and another register *Dreg*. *Dctr's* instantiation connects the datapath's *Dctr_clr* and *Dctr_ld* inputs to *Dctr's* clear and load control inputs. *Dctr's* output *Q* is

```vhdl
library IEEE;
use IEEE.STD_LOGIC_1164.ALL;

entity LDM_Datapath is
   port ( clk : in std_logic;
          Dreg_clr, Dreg_ld : in std_logic;
          Dctr_clr, Dctr_ld : in std_logic;
          D : out std_logic_vector(15 downto 0)
        );
end LDM_Datapath;

architecture structure of LDM_Datapath is

   component Reg16
     port ( I : in std_logic_vector(15 downto 0);
            Q : out std_logic_vector(15 downto 0);
            clk, clr, ld : in std_logic
          );
   end component;
   component ShiftR1_16
     port ( I: in std_logic_vector(15 downto 0);
            S: out std_logic_vector(15 downto 0)
          );
   end component;
   component Add16
     port ( A, B: in std_logic_vector(15 downto 0);
            S: out std_logic_vector(15 downto 0)
          );
   end component;

   signal tempC:  std_logic_vector(15 downto 0);
   signal addC :  std_logic_vector(15 downto 0);
   signal shiftC : std_logic_vector(15 downto 0);

   constant U_ONE: std_logic_vector(15 downto 0)
      := "0000000000000001";

begin
Dctr: Reg16
   port map(addC, tempC, clk, Dctr_clr, Dctr_ld);
Add1 : Add16
   port map(U_ONE, tempC, addC);
ShiftRight: ShiftR1_16
   port map(tempC, shiftC);
Dreg: Reg16
   port map(shiftC, D, clk, Dreg_clr, Dreg_ld);

end structure;
```

Figure 9.38 Structural VHDL description of the laser-based distance measurer's datapath.

```
library ieee;
use ieee.std_logic_1164.all;

entity LDM_Controller is
   port ( clk, rst: in std_logic;
          B, S: in std_logic;
          L: out std_logic;
          Dreg_clr, Dreg_ld: out std_logic;
          Dctr_clr, Dctr_ld: out std_logic
          );
end LDM_Controller;

architecture behavior of LDM_Controller is

type statetype is (S0, S1, S2, S3, S4);
signal currentstate, nextstate: statetype;

begin
statereg: process(clk, rst)
begin
   if (rst='1') then
      currentstate <= S0; -- initial state
   elsif (clk='1' and clk'event) then
      currentstate <= nextstate;
   end if;
end process;
```

```
comblogic: process(currentstate, B, S)
begin
   L <= '0';
   Dreg_clr <= '0';
   Dreg_ld <= '0';
   Dctr_clr <= '0';
   Dctr_ld <= '0';
   case currentstate is
      when S0 =>
         L <= '0'; -- laser off
         Dreg_clr <= '1'; -- clr Dreg
         nextstate <= S1;
      when S1 =>
         Dctr_clr <= '1'; -- clr count
         if (B='1') then
            nextstate <= S2;
         else
            nextstate <= S1;
         end if;
      when S2 =>
         L <= '1'; -- laser on
         nextstate <= S3;
      when S3 =>
         L <= '0'; -- laser off
         Dctr_ld <= '1'; -- count up
         if (S='1') then
            nextstate <= S4;
         else
            nextstate <= S3;
         end if;
      when S4 =>
         Dreg_ld <= '1'; -- load Dreg
         Dctr_ld <= '0'; -- stop count
         nextstate <= S1;
   end case;
end process;

end behavior;
```

Figure 9.39 Behavioral VHDL description of laser-based distance measurer's controller.

then connected to the architecture's internal signal *tempC* that connects the count value to the *ShiftRight* shifter's input. The shifted count is then connected to the input of the *Dreg* register using the internal signal *shiftC*. The instantiation of the *Dreg* register connects the register's clear and load control inputs to the datapath's *Dreg_clr* and *Dreg_ld* input ports. Finally, the register's data output *Q* is connected to *LDM_datapath*'s measured distance output *D*.

Figure 9.39 is the VHDL description of the laser-based distance measurer's FSM controller described in Figure 5.26. The entity, named *LDM_Controller*, defines a clock input *clk*, a reset signal *rst*, a user-pressed button input *B*, a laser sensor input *S*, and five output control signals, *L, Dreg_clr, Dreg_ld, Dctr_clr,* and *Dctr_ld*. The output *L* is used to turn the laser on and off, where if *L* is 1, the laser is on. The four other output signals are used to control the RTL design's datapath components.

The VHDL architecture describes the behavior of the entity. Similar to the controller design shown in Figure 9.22, the architecture consists of two processes, one modeling the state register, the other modeling the combinational logic. The state register process, named *statereg*, is sensitive to inputs *clk* and *rst*. If *rst* is 1, then the process asynchronously sets the *currentstate* signal to the FSM's initial state, *S0*. Otherwise, if the clock is rising, the process updates the state register with the next state.

The second process, named *comblogic*, is sensitive to the inputs to the combinational logic, namely, the external inputs *B* and *S*, and the state register output *currentstate*. When either of those items change, the process sets the FSM's outputs—in this case *L*, *Dreg_clr*, *Dreg_ld*, *Dctr_clr*, and *Dctr_ld*—with the appropriate value for the current state. In the controller example of Figure 9.22, the FSM's output *x* was defined within the case statement for all possible states. With five outputs that must be defined in the *LDM_Controller* and five possible states, assigning the values to all outputs in each state would be cumbersome. Furthermore, finding a mistake and making corrections or modifications to the controller would become difficult in a larger FSM consisting of more states and having many more outputs. The *comblogic* process uses a different approach, in which a default value for the outputs is first assigned and only the deviations from the defaults are assigned later. The *comblogic* process first assigns a default value of 0 to all five outputs. The process then evaluates the current state and assigns the values to the outputs only when the output should be 1. The process also assigns the value 0 to several signals when these assignments are needed to clearly indicate the behavior of the controller (they are redundant but help make the description easier to understand).

The process also determines what the next state should be, based on the current state and the values of inputs *B* and *S*. The next state will be loaded into the state register by the state register process on the next rising clock edge.

Verilog

Figure 9.40 is a Verilog description of the laser-based distance measurer controller/datapath from Figure 5.24. The module, named *LaserDistMeasurer*, defines the inputs and outputs, including a user-pressed button input *B*, a laser sensor input *S*, a laser control output *L*, and a 16-bit output *D* for the distance measured. The module also defines a 300 MHz clock input *clk* and reset input *rst* for the design's controller.

```
module LaserDistMeasurer(clk,rst,B,S,L,D);
   input clk, rst, B, S;
   output L;
   output [15:0] D;

   wire Dreg_clr, Dreg_ld;
   wire Dctr_clr, Dctr_ld;

   LDM_Controller
      LDM_Controller_1(clk, rst, B, S, L,
                       Dreg_clr, Dreg_ld,
                       Dctr_clr, Dctr_ld);
   LDM_Datapath
      LDM_Datapath_1(clk, Dreg_clr, Dreg_ld,
                     Dctr_clr, Dctr_ld, D);
endmodule
```

Figure 9.40 Structural description of top-level Verilog description of laser-bsed distance measurer.

The *LaserDistMeasurer* structurally describes the connections of the controller and datapath components. The module instantiates two components. *LDM_Controller_1* is the controller for the laser-based distance measurer, and *LDM_Datapath_1* is the datapath for this design. The architecture connects the module's *clk*, *rst*, *B*, and *S* inputs to the inputs of *LDM_Controller_1* and connects the controller's laser control output to the corresponding output port *L*. Additionally, the four internal wires, *Dreg_clr*, *Dreg_ld*,

Dctr_clr, and *Dctr_ld*, connect the controller's four control signals to the four inputs of *LDM_Datapath_1*. The *LaserDistMeasurer* datapath has a single output *D*, providing the distance measured, that is connected to the output port *D* of the module.

Figure 9.41 is a Verilog description of the *LaserDistMeasurer's* datapath component shown in Figure 5.23. The module, named *LDM_Datapath*, defines a clock input *clk*, four control inputs *Dreg_clr*, *Dreg_ld*, *Dctr_clr*, and *Dctr_ld*, and a 16-bit distance output *D*.

The datapath defines three components, a 16-bit register, a 16-bit adder, and a 16-bit right shifter that shifts right by one position. The datapath module instantiates a register named *Dctr*, an adder named *Add1*, a shifter named *ShiftRight*, and another register named *Dreg*. The module connects the datapath's *Dctr_clr* and *Dctr_ld* inputs to *Dctr's* clear and load control inputs, respectively. The counter's count output *C* is then connected to the 16-bit internal wire *tempC* that connects the count value to the *ShiftRight* shifter's input. The shifted count is then connected to the input of the *Dreg* register using the internal 16-bit wire *shiftC*. The module connects the *Dreg* register's clear and load control inputs to the datapath's *Dreg_clr* and *Dreg_ld* input ports. Finally, the register's data output *Q* is connected to *LDM_datapath's* measured distance output *D*.

```verilog
module Add16(A, B, S);
    input [15:0] A, B;
    output [15:0] S;
    //details not shown
endmodule

module Reg16(I, Q, clk, clr, ld);
    input [15:0] I;
    input clk, clr, ld;
    output [15:0] Q;
    // details not shown
endmodule

module ShiftR1_16(I, S);
    input [15:0] I;
    output [15:0] S;
    // details not shown
endmodule

module LDM_Datapath(clk, Dreg_clr, Dreg_ld,
                    Dctr_clr, Dctr_ld, D);
    input clk;
    input Dreg_clr, Dreg_ld;
    input Dctr_clr, Dctr_ld;
    output [15:0] D;

    wire [15:0] addC, tempC, shiftC;

    Reg16 Dctr(addC,tempC,clk,Dctr_clr,Dctr_ld);
    Add16 Add1(1, tempC, addC);
    ShiftR1_16 ShiftRight(tempC, shiftC);
    Reg16 Dreg(shiftC,D,clk,Dreg_clr,Dreg_ld);
endmodule
```

Figure 9.41 Structural Verilog description of the laser-based distance measurer's datapath.

Figure 9.42 is the Verilog description of the laser-based distance measurer's FSM controller described in Figure 5.26. The module, named *LDM_Controller*, defines a clock input *clk*, a reset signal *rst*, a user-pressed button input *B*, a laser sensor input *S*, and five output control signals, *L, Dreg_clr, Dreg_ld, Dctr_clr,* and *Dctr_ld*. The output *L* is used to turn the laser on and off, where if *L* is 1, the laser is on. The four other output signals are used to control the RTL design's datapath components.

The Verilog module behaviorally describes the *LaserDistMeasurer's* FSM. Similar to the controller design shown in Figure 9.23, the module consists of two procedures, one

```
module LDM_Controller
    (clk, rst, B, S, L, Dreg_clk,
     Dreg_ld, Dctr_clr, Dctr_ld);
    input clk, rst, B, S;
    output L;
    output Dreg_clk, Dreg_ld;
    output Dctr_clr, Dctr_ld;
    reg L;
    reg Dreg_clr, Dreg_ld;
    reg Dctr_clr, Dctr_ld;

    parameter S0 = 3'b000,
              S1 = 3'b001,
              S2 = 3'b010,
              S3 = 3'b011,
              S4 = 3'b100;

    reg [2:0] State;
    reg [2:0] StateNext;

    always @(posedge rst or posedge clk)
    begin
        if (rst==1)
            State <= S0; // initial state
        else
            State <= StateNext;
    end
```

```
    always @(State or B or S)
      begin
        L <= 0;
        Dreg_clr <= 0;
        Dreg_ld <= 0;
        Dctr_clr <= 0;
        Dctr_ld <= 0;
        case (State)
          S0: begin
            L <= 0; // laser off
            Dreg_clr <= 1; // clr Dreg
            StateNext <= S1;
          end
          S1: begin
            Dctr_clr <= 1; // clr count
            if (B==1)
                StateNext <= S2;
            else
                StateNext <= S1;
          end
          S2: begin
            L <= 1; // laser on
            StateNext <= S3;
          end
          S3: begin
            L <= 0; // laser off
            Dctr_ld <= 1; // count up
            if (S==1)
                StateNext <= S4;
            else
                StateNext <= S3;
          end
          S4: begin
            Dreg_ld <= 1; // load Dreg
            Dctr_ld <= 0; // stop count
            StateNext <= S1;
          end
        endcase
      end
endmodule
```

Figure 9.42 Behavioral Verilog description of laser-based distance measurer's controller.

modeling the state register, the other modeling the FSM's control logic. The state register procedure is sensitive to the positive edge of the reset input, *rst*, and the positive edge of the clock input, *clk*. If the *rst* input is enabled, then the procedure asynchronously sets the *currentstate* signal to the FSM's initial state, *S0*. Otherwise, on the rising edge of the clock, the procedure updates the state register with the next state.

The second procedure is sensitive to the inputs to the combinational logic, namely, the external inputs *B* and *S*, and the state register output *currentstate*. When either of those items change, the procedure sets the FSM's outputs, in this case *L, Dreg_clr, Dreg_ld, Dctr_clr,* and *Dctr_ld*, with the appropriate value for the current state. In the controller example of Figure 9.22, the FSM's output *x* was defined within the case statement for all possible states. With five outputs that must be defined in the *LDM_Controller* and five possible states, assigning the values to all outputs in each state would be cumbersome. Furthermore, finding a mistake and making corrections or modifications to the controller would become very difficult in a larger FSM consisting of more states and having many more outputs. Instead, the procedure uses a different approach, in which a default value for all the outputs is first assigned and only the deviations from the defaults are assigned later. The procedure first assigns a default value of 0 to all five outputs. The procedure then evaluates the current state and assigns the values to the outputs only when the output should be 1. The procedure also assigns the value 0 to several signals within the *case* statements to clearly indicate the behavior of the controller (those assignments are redundant but help make the description easier to understand).

The procedure also determines what the next state should be, based on the current state and the values of inputs *B* and *S*. The next state will be loaded into the state register by the state register procedure on the next positive clock edge.

SystemC

Figure 9.43 is a SystemC description of the laser-based distance measurer shown in Figure 5.24. The module, named *LaserDistMeasurer*, defines the inputs and outputs, including a user-pressed button input *B*, a laser sensor input *S*, a laser control output *L*, and a 16-bit output *D* for the distance measured. The module also defines a 300 MHz clock input *clk* and reset input *rst* for the design's controller.

The *LaserDistMeasurer* structurally describes the connections of the controller and datapath components. The architecture instantiates two components. *LDM_Controller_1* is the controller for the laser-based distance measurer, and *LDM_Datapath_1* is the datapath for this design. The module connects the module's *clk*, *rst*, *B*, and *S* inputs to the inputs of *LDM_ Controller_1* and connects the controller's laser control output to the corresponding output port *L*. Additionally, the four internal wires, *Dreg_clr*, *Dreg_ld*, *Dctr_clr*, and *Dctr_ld*, connect the

```
#include "systemc.h"
#include "LDM_Controller.h"
#include "LDM_Datapath.h"

SC_MODULE(LaserDistMeasurer)
{
    sc_in<sc_logic> clk, rst;
    sc_in<sc_logic> B, S;
    sc_out<sc_logic> L;
    sc_out<sc_uint<16> > D;

    sc_signal<sc_logic> Dreg_clr, Dreg_ld;
    sc_signal<sc_logic> Dctr_clr, Dctr_ld;

    LDM_Controller LDM_Controller_1;
    LDM_Datapath LDM_Datapath_1;

    SC_CTOR(LaserDistMeasurer) :
        LDM_Controller_1("LDM_Controller_1"),
        LDM_Datapath_1("LDM_Datapath_1")
    {
        LDM_Controller_1.clk(clk);
        LDM_Controller_1.rst(rst);
        LDM_Controller_1.B(B);
        LDM_Controller_1.S(S);
        LDM_Controller_1.Dreg_clr(Dreg_clr);
        LDM_Controller_1.Dreg_ld(Dreg_ld);
        LDM_Controller_1.Dctr_clr(Dctr_clr);
        LDM_Controller_1.Dctr_ld(Dctr_ld);
        LDM_Datapath_1.clk(clk);
        LDM_Datapath_1.Dreg_clr(Dreg_clr);
        LDM_Datapath_1.Dreg_ld(Dreg_ld);
        LDM_Datapath_1.Dctr_clr(Dctr_clr);
        LDM_Datapath_1.Dctr_ld(Dctr_ld);
        LDM_Datapath_1.D(D);
    }
};
```

Figure 9.43 Structural description of top-level SystemC description of laser-based distance measurer.

controller's four control signals to the four inputs of *LDM_Data-path_1*. The *LaserDist-*

Measurer datapath has a single output *D*, providing the distance measured, that is connected to the output port *D* of the module.

Figure 9.44 is a SystemC description of the *LaserDistMeasurer's* datapath component shown in Figure 5.23. The module, named *LDM_Datapath*, defines a clock input *clk*, four control inputs *Dreg_clr*, *Dreg_ld*, *Dctr_clr*, and *Dctr_ld,* and a 16-bit distance output *D*.

The datapath includes three components, a 16-bit adder, a 16-bit register, and a 16-bit right shifter that shifts right by one position. The datapath module instantiates an adder named *Add1*, a register named *Dctr*, a register named *Dreg,* and a shifter named *ShiftRight*. The module connects the datapath's *Dctr_clr* and *Dctr_ld* inputs to *Dctr*'s clear and load control inputs, respectively. The counter's count output *C* is then connected to the 16-bit internal signal *tempC* that connects the count value to the *ShiftRight* shifter's input. The shifted count value is then connected to the input of the *Dreg* register using the internal signal *shiftC*. The module connects the *Dreg* register's clear and load control inputs to the datapath's *Dreg_clr* and *Dreg_ld* input ports. Finally, the register's data output *Q* is connected to *LDM_datapath*'s measured distance output *D*.

```cpp
#include "systemc.h"
#include "add16.h"
#include "reg16.h"
#include "shiftr1_16.h"

SC_MODULE(LDM_Datapath)
{
    sc_in<sc_logic> clk;
    sc_in<sc_logic> Dreg_clr, Dreg_ld;
    sc_in<sc_logic> Dctr_clr, Dctr_ld;
    sc_out<sc_uint<16> > D;

    sc_signal<sc_uint<16> > tempC;
    sc_signal<sc_uint<16> > addC;
    sc_signal<sc_uint<16> > shiftC;

    Add16 Add1;
    Reg16 Dctr;
    Reg16 Dreg;
    ShiftR1_16 ShiftRight;

    SC_CTOR(LDM_Datapath) :
        Dctr("Dctr"),
        Dreg("Dreg"),
        Add1("Add1"),
        ShiftRight("ShiftRight")
    {
        Add1.A(1);
        Add1.B(tempC);
        Add1.B(addC);

        Dctr.I(addC);
        Dctr.Q(tempC);
        Dctr.clk(clk);
        Dctr.clr(Dctr_clr);
        Dctr.ld(Dctr_ld);

        ShiftRight.I(tempC);
        ShiftRight.S(shiftC);

        Dreg.I(shiftC);
        Dreg.Q(D);
        Dreg.clk(clk);
        Dreg.clr(Dreg_clr);
        Dreg.ld(Dreg_ld);
    }
};
```

Figure 9.44 Structural SystemC description of the laser-based distance measurer's datapath.

```
#include "systemc.h"

enum statetype { S0, S1, S2, S3, S4 };
SC_MODULE(LDM_Controller)
{
    sc_in<sc_logic> clk, rst, B, S;
    sc_out<sc_logic> L;
    sc_out<sc_logic> Dreg_clr, Dreg_ld;
    sc_out<sc_logic> Dctr_clr, Dctr_ld;

    sc_signal<statetype> State, StateNext;

    SC_CTOR(LDM_Controller)
    {
        SC_METHOD(statereg);
        sensitive << clk.pos();

        SC_METHOD(comblogic);
        sensitive << State << B << S;
    }

    void statereg() {
        if ( rst.read() == SC_LOGIC_1 )
            State = S0; // initial state
        else
            State = StateNext;
    }
```

```
void comblogic() {
    L.write(SC_LOGIC_0);
    Dreg_clr.write(SC_LOGIC_0);
    Dreg_ld.write(SC_LOGIC_0);
    Dctr_clr.write(SC_LOGIC_0);
    Dctr_ld.write(SC_LOGIC_0);

    switch (State) {
        case S0:
            L.write(SC_LOGIC_0); // laser off
            Dreg_clr.write(SC_LOGIC_0);
            StateNext.write(S1);
            break;
        case S1:
            Dctr_clr.write(SC_LOGIC_1);
            if (B.read() == SC_LOGIC_1)
                StateNext.write(S2);
            else
                StateNext.write(S1);
            break;
        case S2:
            L.write(SC_LOGIC_1); // laser on
            StateNext.write(S3);
            break;
        case S3:
            L.write(SC_LOGIC_0); // laser off
            Dctr_ld.write(SC_LOGIC_1);
            if (S.read() == SC_LOGIC_1)
                StateNext.write(S4);
            else
                StateNext.write(S3);
            break;
        case S4:
            Dreg_ld.write(SC_LOGIC_1);
            Dctr_ld.write(SC_LOGIC_0);
            StateNext.write(S1);
            break;
    }
}
};
```

Figure 9.45 Behavioral SystemC description of laser-based distance measurer's controller.

Figure 9.45 is the SystemC description of the laser-based distance measurer's FSM controller described in Figure 5.26. The module, named *LDM_Controller*, has a clock input *clk*, a reset signal *rst*, a user-pressed button input *B*, a laser sensor input *S*, and five output control signals, *L, Dreg_clr, Dreg_ld, Dctr_clr,* and *Dctr_ld*. The output *L* is used to turn the laser on and off; where is *L* is 1, the laser is on. The four other output signals are used to control the RTL design's datapath components.

The SystemC module behaviorally describes the *LaserDistMeasurer's* FSM. Similar to the controller design shown in Figure 9.24, the module consists of two processes, one modeling the state register, the other modeling the FSM's control logic. The state register process, named *statereg*, is sensitive to the positive edge of the reset input *rst* and the positive edge of the clock input *clk*. If the *rst* is enabled, then the process asynchronously sets the *currentstate* to the FSM's initial state, *S0*. Otherwise, on the rising edge of the clock, the process updates the state register with the *nextstate*.

The second process, named *comblogic*, is sensitive to the inputs to the combinational logic, namely, the external inputs *B* and *S*, and the state register output *currentstate*. When either of those signals changes, the process sets the FSM's outputs, in this case *L*, *Dreg_clr*, *Dreg_ld*, *Dctr_clr*, and *Dctr_ld*, with the appropriate value for the current state. In the controller example of Figure 9.24, the FSM's output *x* was defined within the case statement for all possible states. With five outputs that we must define in the *LDM_Controller* and five possible states, assigning the values to all outputs in each state would be cumbersome. Furthermore, finding a mistake and making corrections or modification to the controller would become very difficult in a larger FSM consisting of more states and having many more outputs. Instead, the process uses a different approach, in which a default value for the all outputs is first assigned and only the deviations from the defaults are assigned later. The process first assigns a default value of 0 to all five outputs. The process then evaluates the current state and assigns the values to the outputs only when the output should be 1. The process also assigns the value 0 to several signals within the **case** statements; however, these assignments are included only to clearly indicate the behavior of the controller (they are redundant but help make the description easier to understand).

The process also determines what the next state should be, based on the current state and the values of inputs *B* and *S*. The next state will be loaded into the state register by the state register process on the next positive clock edge.

► 9.6 CHAPTER SUMMARY

This chapter stated that hardware description languages (HDLs) are widely used in modern digital design. The chapter introduced three popular HDLs: VHDL, Verilog, and SystemC. The chapter introduced those HDLs primarily through the use of examples, illustrating how each HDL might be used to describe combinational logic, sequential logic, datapath components, and RTL behavior and structure. To become proficient at the use of HDLs, a more thorough study of a particular HDL might be helpful. This chapter also illustrated the point that the three different HDLs have several aspects in common.

► 9.7 EXERCISES

The following exercises can be completed using any of the HDLs described in this chapter. The solution to Exercise 9.1 is needed in order to solve many of the remaining exercises.

SECTION 9.2: COMBINATIONAL LOGIC DESCRIPTION USING HARDWARE DESCRIPTION LANGUAGES

9.1 (a) Create combinational behavioral HDL descriptions of *Inv*, *AND2*, *AND3*, *OR2*, and *OR3* gates, such that those gates can then be used as components in another design. Use names *a*, *b*, and *c* for inputs (as needed) and *F* for the output. (b) Create a testbench for the *AND3* gate to test its correctness.

9.2 (a) Create combinational behavioral HDL descriptions for *NAND2* and *XOR2* gates, where each gate has two inputs a and b and a single output F. (b) Create a separate testbench for each.

9.3 Show that the parity generator equation of Example 2.19 correctly generates the desired parity bit, by first capturing the equation as combinational behavior in an HDL, creating a testbench that tests all possible input combinations, and then showing that simulation yields correct output value for each input combination.

9.4 For the seat belt warning light system in Example 2.7: (a) create a combinational HDL description using the given equation, (b) create a testbench to test the description, checking all possible combinations of input values, (c) simulate the system using your testbench, and verify that the output values are correct (d) create a structural HDL description of the given circuit, (e) reuse the testbench to test the structural description.

9.5 Example 2.12 algebraically transformed one equation into another. Show that those two equations represent the same function by using simulation. First, create a combinational behavioral description of the initial equation. Second, create a combinational behavioral description of the final equation. Third, create a testbench that tests all possible combinations of input values and show that simulation yields identical output values for both equations.

9.6 For the 2x4 decoder in Figure 2.62, but extended with an enable input: (a) create a structural HDL description of the given circuit, (b) create a testbench to test the structural description, testing all possible input combinations, (c) simulate to verify correct behavior.

9.7 For the 4x1 mux in Figure 2.67: (a) create a structural HDL description of the given circuit, (b) create a testbench to test the structural description; do not test all possible input combinations, but rather a few input cases for each possible combination of the select control inputs, (c) simulate to verify correct behavior.

9.8 Create a behavioral HDL description of a 2x1 multiplexor described in Figure 2.54. Then, create a structural HDL description that combines three 2x1 multiplexors to create a 4x1 multiplexor as shown in Figure 9.46.

9.9 Create a combinational behavioral description of an 8-bit 4x1 multiplexor. Be sure to specify the input and output ports using a multiple-bit data type.

9.10 Clearly explain the difference between a structural HDL description and a behavioral HDL description. Explain the benefits of using each.

9.11 Explain why a combinational behavioral HDL description must include all the combinational circuit's inputs in a sensitivity list. In particular, explain why omitting an input actually describes a sequential circuit.

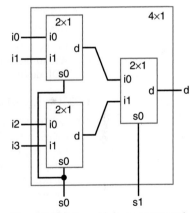

Figure 9.46 4x1 multiplexor composed of three 2x1 multiplexors.

SECTION 9.3: SEQUENTIAL LOGIC DESCRIPTION USING HARDWARE DESCRIPTION LANGUAGES

9.12 (a) Create a behavioral HDL description of a 32-bit basic register (no load or clear control inputs). (b) Create a testbench to test the description for some random data input values. (c) Simulate the system to demonstrate correct behavior.

9.13 (a) Create a behavioral HDL description of the sequence generator of Figure 3.66. (b) Create a testbench; with no inputs, the testbench will not have to set input values and instead will just let the clock run. (c) Simulate the system to show that it generates the correct repeating sequence.

9.14 (a) Create a behavioral HDL description of the flight attendant call button system of Figure 3.53. (b) Create a testbench to test various sequences of the call and cancel buttons being pressed (there are many possibile sequences; you can't test all of them). (c) Simulate the system to show correct behavior.

SECTION 9.4: DATAPATH COMPONENT DESCRIPTION USING HARDWARE DESCRIPTION LANGUAGES

9.15 (a) Create a behavioral HDL description of an 8-bit parallel load register with load and clear control inputs (both synchronous; clear has priority over load). (b) Create a testbench to test the description, testing load, clear, simultaneous load/clear, and holding the register value. (c) Simulate the system to demonstrate correct behavior.

9.16 Create a behavioral HDL description of an 8-bit register with two control inputs $s0$ and $s1$ having the control behavior described in Figure 9.47.

9.17 Create a structural HDL description of a half-adder.

9.18 Create a structural HDL description of a 4-bit carry-ripple adder without a carry input. First create a behavioral description of a full-adder, and then use the full-adder component in your carry-ripple adder description.

s1	s0	Operation
0	0	Maintain present value
0	1	Parallel load
1	0	Shift right
1	1	Rotate right

Figure 9.47 Register operation table.

9.19 Create a structural HDL description of the counter circuit in Figure 4.69. Be sure to first create a behavioral HDL description of each component used in your structural HDL design.

9.20 Create a structural HDL description of the 4-bit adder/subtractor circuit in Figure 4.54(b). Be sure to first create a behavioral HDL description of each component used in your structural HDL design.

SECTION 9.5: RTL DESIGN USING HARDWARE DESCRIPTION LANGUAGES

9.21 (a) Create a behavioral HDL description of the high-level state machine for the cycles-high counter of Example 5.1. (b) Create a testbench and simulate the system for some sample input sequences and verify correct behavior. (c) Create a structural HDL description for the datapath of the cycles-high counter in Figure 5.16(d). (d) Create a controller FSM and connect it to the datapath as in Figure 5.16(d). (e) Use the earlier testbench to simulate the controller/datapath system to verify correct behavior.

9.22 For the soda dispenser example used throughout Chapter 5: (a) create a behavioral HDL description of the HLSM, (b) create a testbench and simulate the system for some sample input sequences and verify correct behavior, (c) create a structural HDL description for the datapath, (d) create a controller FSM and connect it to the datapath, (e) use the earlier testbench to simulate the controller/datapath system to verify correct behavior.

9.23 Starting from the C description shown in Figure 9.48, create an RTL design of a greatest common divisor (GCD) calculator that takes as input two 16-bit inputs a and b, an enable input go, and a 16-bit output D. When go is '1', the GCD calculator will compute the greatest common divisor and output the GCD on the output D. (a) Convert the C to a high-level state machine captured behaviorally in an HDL, (b) create a testbench and simulate for various input values, (c) create a controller and datapath HDL description, (d) simulate using the same testbench.

```
uint GCD(uint a, uint b) // not quite C syntax
{
   while ( a ! = b ) {
      if( a > b ) {
         a = a - b;
      } else {
         b = b - a;
      }
   }
   return(a);
}
```

Figure 9.48 C program description of a greatest common divisor calculator.

Boolean Algebras

This appendix is reproduced with permission from the textbook Introduction to Digital Systems *by Ercegovac, Lang, and Moreno, ISBN 0-471-52799-8, John Wiley and Sons publishers, 1999.*

Boolean algebras is an important class of algebras that has been studied and used extensively for many purposes (see Section A.5). The **switching algebra**, used in the description of switching expressions discussed in Section 2.4, is an instance (an element) of the class of Boolean algebras. Consequently, theorems developed for Boolean algebras are also applicable to switching algebra, so they can be used for the transformation of switching expressions. Moreover, certain identities from Boolean algebra are the basis for the graphical and tabular techniques used for the minimization of switching expressions.

In this appendix, we present the definition of Boolean algebras as well as theorems that are useful for the transformation of Boolean expressions. We also show the relationship among Boolean and switching algebras; in particular, we show that the switching algebra satisfies the postulates of a Boolean algebra. We also sketch other examples of Boolean algebras, which are helpful to further understand the properties of this class of algebras.

▷ A.1 BOOLEAN ALGEBRA

A **Boolean algebra** is a tuple $\{B, +, \bullet\}$, where

- B is a set of elements;
- $+$ and $\bullet$ are binary operations applied over the elements of B,

satisfying the following postulates:

P1: If $a, b \in B$, then

(i) $a + b = b + a$

(ii) $a \cdot b = b \cdot a$

That is, $+$ and $\bullet$ are commutative.

P2: If $a, b, c \in B$, then

    (i) $a + (b \cdot c) = (a + b) \cdot (a + c)$

    (ii) $a \cdot (b + c) = (a \cdot b) + (a \cdot c)$

P3: The set B has two distinct **identity elements**, denoted as 0 and 1, such that for every element in B

    (i) $0 + a = a + 0 = a$

    (ii) $1 \cdot a = a \cdot 1 = a$

The elements 0 and 1 are called the **additive identity element** and the **multiplicative identity element**, respectively. (These elements should not be confused with the integers 0 and 1.)

P4: For every element $a \in B$ there exists an element a', called the **complement** of a, such that

    (i) $a + a' = 1$

    (ii) $a \cdot a' = 0$

The symbols $+$ and $\bullet$ should not be confused with the arithmetic addition and multiplication symbols. However, for convenience $+$ and $\bullet$ are often called "plus" and "times," and the expressions $a + b$ and $a \cdot b$ are called "sum" and "product," respectively. Moreover, $+$ and $\bullet$ are also called "OR" and "AND," respectively.

The elements of the set B are called **constants**. Symbols representing arbitrary elements of B are **variables**. The symbols a, b, and c in the postulates above are variables, whereas 0 and 1 are constants.

A precedence ordering is defined on the operators: $\bullet$ has precedence over $+$. Therefore, parentheses can be eliminated from products. Moreover, whenever single symbols are used for variables, the symbol $\bullet$ can be eliminated in products. For example,

$$a + (b \cdot c) \text{ can be written as } a + bc$$

▶ A.2 SWITCHING ALGEBRA

Switching algebra is an algebraic system used to describe switching functions by means of switching expressions. In this sense, a switching algebra serves the same role for switching functions as the ordinary algebra does for arithmetic functions.

The switching algebra of the set of two elements $B = \{0, 1\}$, and two operations AND and OR defined as follows:

AND	0	1
0	0	0
1	0	1

OR	0	1
0	0	1
1	1	1

These operations are used to evaluate switching expressions, as indicated in Section 2.4.

Theorem 1

The switching algebra is a Boolean algebra.

Proof We show that the switching algebra satisfies the postulates of a Boolean algebra.

P1: Commutativity of (+), (•). This is shown by inspection of the operation tables. The commutativity property holds if a table is symmetric about the main diagonal.

P2: Distributivity of (+) and (•). Shown by **perfect induction**, that is, by considering all possible values for the elements a, b, and c. Consider the following table:

abc	$a + bc$	$(a + b)(a + c)$
000	0	0
001	0	0
010	0	0
011	1	1
100	1	1
101	1	1
110	1	1
111	1	1

Because $a + bc = (a + b)(b + c)$ for all cases, P2(i) is satisfied. A similar proof shows that P2(ii) is also satisfied.

P3: Existence of additive and multiplicative identity element. From the operation tables

$$0 + 1 = 1 + 0 = 1$$

Therefore, 0 is the additive identity. Similarly

$$0 \cdot 1 = 1 \cdot 0 = 0$$

so that 1 is the multiplicative identity.

P4: Existence of the complement. By perfect induction:

a	a'	$a + a'$	$a \cdot a'$
1	0	1	0
0	1	1	0

Consequently, 1 is the complement of 0, and 0 is the complement of 1.

Because all postulates are satisfied, the switching algebra is a Boolean algebra. As a result, all theorems true for Boolean algebras are also true for the switching algebra.

▶ A.3 IMPORTANT THEOREMS IN BOOLEAN ALGEBRA

We now present some important theorems in Boolean algebra; these theorems can be applied to the transformation of switching expressions.

Theorem 2 Principle of Duality

Every algebraic identity deducible from the postulates of a Boolean algebra remains valid if

- the operations + and • are interchanged throughout; and
- the identity elements 0 and 1 are also interchanged throughout.

Proof The proof follows at once from the fact that for each of the postulates there is another one (the dual) that is obtained by interchanging + and • as well as 0 and 1.

This theorem is useful because it reduces the number of different theorems that must be proven: every theorem has its dual.

Theorem 3

Every element in B has a **unique** complement.

Proof Let $a \in B$; let us assume that a'_1 and a'_2 are both complements of a. Then, using the postulates we can perform the following transformations:

$$a'_1 = a'_1 \cdot 1 \qquad \text{by P3(ii)} \qquad \text{(identity)}$$
$$= a'_1 \cdot (a + a'_2) \qquad \text{by hypothesis } (a'_2 \text{ is the complement of } a)$$
$$= a'_1 \cdot a + a'_1 \cdot a'_2 \qquad \text{by P2(ii)} \qquad \text{(distributivity)}$$
$$= a \cdot a'_1 + a'_1 \cdot a'_2 \qquad \text{by P1(ii)} \qquad \text{(commutativity)}$$
$$= 0 + a'_1 \cdot a'_2 \qquad \text{by hypothesis } (a'_1 \text{ is the complement of } a)$$
$$= a'_1 \cdot a'_2 \qquad \text{by P3(i)} \qquad \text{(identity)}$$

Changing the index 1 for 2 and vice versa, and repeating all steps for a'_2, we get

$$a'_2 = a'_2 \cdot a'_1$$
$$= a'_1 \cdot a'_2 \text{ by P1(ii)}$$

and therefore $a'_2 = a'_1$.

The uniqueness of the complement of an element allows considering ′ as a unary operation called **complementation**.

Theorem 4

For any $a \in B$:

1. $a + 1 = 1$
2. $a \cdot 0 = 0$

Proof Using the postulates, we can perform the following transformations:

Case (1):

$$
\begin{array}{llll}
a + 1 & = 1 \cdot (a + 1) & & \text{P3(ii)} \\
& = (a + a') \cdot (a + 1) & & \text{P4(i)} \\
& = a + (a' \cdot 1) & & \text{P2(i)} \\
& = a + a' & & \text{P3(ii)} \\
& = 1 & & \text{P4(i)}
\end{array}
$$

Case (2):

$$
\begin{array}{llll}
a \cdot 0 & = 0 + (a \cdot 0) & & \text{P3(i)} \\
& = (a \cdot a') + (a \cdot 0) & & \text{P4(ii)} \\
& = a \cdot (a' + 0) & & \text{P2(ii)} \\
& = a \cdot a' & & \text{P3(i)} \\
& = 0 & & \text{P4(ii)}
\end{array}
$$

Case (2) can also be proven by means of Case (1) and the principle of duality.

Theorem 5
The complement of the element 1 is 0, and vice versa. That is,

1. $0' = 1$
2. $1' = 0$

Proof   By Theorem 4,

$$0 + 1 = 1 \text{ and}$$
$$0 \cdot 1 = 0$$

Because, by Theorem 3, the complement of an element is unique, Theorem 5 follows.

Theorem 6 Idempotent Law
For every $a \in B$

1. $a + a = a$
2. $a \cdot a = a$

Proof
(1):

$$
\begin{array}{lll}
a + a & = (a + a) \cdot 1 & \text{P3(ii)} \\
& = (a + a) \cdot (a + a') & \text{P4(i)} \\
& = (a + (a \cdot a')) & \text{P2(i)} \\
& = a + 0 & \text{P4(ii)} \\
& = a & \text{P3(i)}
\end{array}
$$

(2): duality

Theorem 7 Involution Law

For every $a \in B$,

$$(a')' = a$$

Proof From the definition of complement $(a')'$ and a are both complements of a'. But, by Theorem 3, the complement of an element is unique, which proves the theorem.

Theorem 8 Absorption Law

For every pair of elements $a, b \in B$,

    1. $a + a \cdot b = a$

    2. $a \cdot (a + b) = a$

Proof

(1):
$$
\begin{aligned}
a + ab &= a \cdot 1 + ab &&\text{P3(ii)}\\
&= a(1 + b) &&\text{P2(ii)}\\
&= a(b + 1) &&\text{P1(i)}\\
&= a \cdot 1 &&\text{Theorem 4 (1)}\\
&= a &&\text{P3(ii)}
\end{aligned}
$$

(2): duality

Theorem 9

For every pair of elements $a, b \in B$,

    1. $a + a' b = a + b$

    2. $a(a' + b) = ab$

Proof

(1):
$$
\begin{aligned}
a + a' b &= (a + a')(a + b) &&\text{P2(i)}\\
&= 1 \cdot (a + b) &&\text{P4(i)}\\
&= a + b &&\text{P3(ii)}
\end{aligned}
$$

(2): duality

Theorem 10

In a Boolean algebra, each of the binary operations $(+)$ and $(\cdot)$ is associative. That is, for every $a, b, c \in B$,

    1. $a + (b + c) = (a + b) + c$

    2. $a(bc) = (ab)c$

The proof of this theorem is quite lengthy. The interested reader should consult the further readings suggested at the end of this appendix.

Corollary I

1. The order in applying the + operator among n elements does not matter. For example,

$$a + \{b + [c + (d + e)]\} = \{[(a + b) + c] + d\} + e$$
$$= \{a + [(b + c) + d]\} + e$$
$$= a + b + c + d + e$$

2. The order in applying the • operator among n elements does not matter.

Theorem 11 DeMorgan's Law

For every pair of elements $a, b \in B$:

1. $(a + b)' = a' b'$
2. $(ab)' = a' + b'$

Proof

We first prove that $(a + b)$ is the complement of $a' b'$. By the definition of the complement (P4) and its uniqueness (Theorem 3), this corresponds to showing that $(a + b) + a' b' = 1$ and $(a + b) a' b' = 0$. We do this proof by the following transformations:

$$
\begin{aligned}
& && \text{by} \\
(a + b) + a' b' &= [(a + b) + a'][(a + b) + b'] && \text{P2(i)} \\
&= [(b + a) + a'][(a + b) + b'] && \text{P1(i)} \\
&= [b + (a + a')][a + (b + b')] && \text{associativity} \\
&= (b + 1)(a + 1) && \text{P4(i)} \\
&= 1 \cdot 1 && \text{Theorem 3 (1)} \\
&= 1 && \text{idempotency}
\end{aligned}
$$

$$
\begin{aligned}
& && \text{by} \\
(a + b)(a' b') &= (a' b')(a + b) && \text{commutativity} \\
&= (a' b')a + (a' b')b && \text{distributivity} \\
&= (b' a')a + (a' b')b && \text{commutativity} \\
&= b'(a' a) + a'(b' b) && \text{associativity} \\
&= b'(aa') + a'(bb') && \text{commutativity} \\
&= b' \cdot 0 + a' \cdot 0 && \text{P4(ii)} \\
&= 0 + 0 && \text{Theorem 3 (2)} \\
&= 0 && \text{Theorem 5 (1)}
\end{aligned}
$$

By duality, $(a \cdot b)' = a' + b'$

Theorem 12 Generalized DeMorgan's Law

Let $\{a, b, ..., c, d\}$ be a set of elements in a Boolean algebra. Then, the following identities hold:

1. $(a + b... + c + d)' = a'\,b'...\,c'\,d'$
2. $(ab..cd)' = a' + b' + ... + c' + d'$

Proof By the method of **finite induction**. The basis is provided by Theorem 11, which corresponds to the case with two elements.

Inductive step: Let us assume that DeMorgan's Law is true for n elements, and show that it is true for $n + 1$ elements. Let $a, b, ..., c$ be the n elements, and d be the $(n + 1)$st element. Then, by associativity and the basis,

$$(a + b + ... + c + d)' = [(a + b + ... + c) + d]'$$
$$= (a + b + ... + c)'\,d'$$

By the induction hypothesis

$$(a + b + ...c)' = a'\,b'...c'$$

Thus

$$(a + b + ...c + d)' = a'\,b'...c'\,d'$$

DeMorgan's theorems are useful in manipulating switching expressions. For example, finding the complement of a switching expression containing parentheses is achieved by applying DeMorgan's Law and the Involution Law repeatedly to bring all $(')$ inside the parentheses. That is,

$$[(a + b')(c' + d') + (f' + g)']' = [(a + b')(c' + d')]'\,[(f' + g)']'$$
$$= [(a + b')' + (c' + d')']'\,(f' + g)$$
$$= (a'\,b + cd)(f' + g)$$

The symbols $a, b, c, ...$ appearing in theorems and postulates are **generic variables**. That is, they can be substituted by complemented variables or expressions (formulas) without changing the meaning of these theorems. For example, DeMorgan's Law can read as

$$(a' + b')' = ab$$

or

$$[(a + b)' + c']' = (a + b)c$$

We have described a general mathematical system, called Boolean algebra, and established a basic set of algebraic identities, true for any Boolean algebra, without actually specifying the nature of the two binary operations, (+) and (•). In Chapter 2, we presented an algebra useful for the representation of switching functions by switching expressions.

▶ A.4 OTHER EXAMPLES OF BOOLEAN ALGEBRAS

There are other algebras that are also instances of Boolean algebras. We now summarize the two most commonly used ones.

Algebra of Sets. The elements of B are all subsets of a set S (the set of all subsets of S is denoted by $P(S)$), and the operations are set-union ($\cup$) and set-intersection ($\cap$). That is,

$$M = (P((S), (\cup, \cap)))$$

The additive identity is the empty set, denoted by ϕ, and the multiplicative identity is the set S. The set $P(S)$ has $2^{|S|}$ elements, where $|S|$ is the number of elements of S.

It can be shown that every Boolean algebra has 2^n elements for some value $n > 0$.

Venn diagrams are used to represent sets as well as the operations of union and intersection. Consequently, since the algebra of sets is a Boolean algebra, Venn diagrams can be used to illustrate the theorems of a Boolean algebra.

Algebra of Logic (Propositional Calculus). In this algebra, the elements are T and F (true and false), and the operations are LOGICAL AND and LOGICAL OR. It is used to evaluate logical propositions. This algebra is isomorphic with the switching algebra.

▶ A.5 FURTHER READINGS

The topic of Boolean algebras has been extensively studied, and many good books on the subject exist. The following is a partial list, in which the reader can obtain additional material that goes significantly beyond the limited treatment of this appendix: *Boolean Reasoning: The Logic of Boolean Equations* by F. M. Brown, Kluwer Academic Publishers, Boston, MA, 1990; *Introduction to Switching and Automata Theory* by M. A. Harrison, McGraw-Hill, New York, 1965; *Switching and Automata Theory* by Z. Kohavi, 2nd. ed., McGraw-Hill, New York, 1978; *Switching Theory* by R. E. Miller, Vols. 1 and 2. Wiley, New York, 1965; *Introduction to Discrete Structures* by F. Preparata and R. Yeh, Addison-Wesley, Reading, MA, 1973; and *Discrete Mathematical Structures* by H. S. Stone, Science Research Associates, Chicago, IL, 1973.

B

Additional Topics in Binary Number Systems

▶ B.1 INTRODUCTION

Chapter 1 introduced the concept of *binary* or base two numbers. The chapter showed how one could convert a decimal integer to binary through the *addition method* or the *divide-by-two method*. However, numbers used in digital design may not always be whole numbers.

Consider a doctor who uses an in-ear digital thermometer that works in Celsius units to check whether a patient's body temperature is normal. We know that a human's normal body temperature is 37 degrees C (98.6 degrees F). If the thermometer's temperature sensor outputs integer values, then a readout of 37 C corresponds to an actual temperature anywhere between 36.5 C and 37.4 C, assuming the temperature sensor rounds its output to the nearest integer. Clearly, a more precise temperature readout is preferable to tell if a patient's temperature is abnormal. A readout of 37 C may mean that the patient has a normal body temperature or it may mean that the patient is close to having a fever. In order to be useful, the thermometer should output fractional components of the temperature so that the doctor can differentiate between 37.0 C and 37.9 C, for example.

This appendix discusses how *real* numbers (as opposed to just whole numbers) are represented in binary, and discusses methods that modern digital designers use to work with real numbers.

▶ B.2 REAL NUMBER REPRESENTATION

Just as Chapter 1 looked closely at how integers are represented in decimal before moving on to binary numbers, understanding how real numbers are represented in decimal can illuminate how real numbers are represented in binary.

Chapter 1 showed that each digit in a number had a certain weight that was a power of 10. The ones place had a weight equal to $10^0 = 1$, the tens place had a weight equal to $10^1 = 10$, the hundreds place had a weight equal to $10^2 = 100$, and so on. If a decimal number had an 8 in the hundred's place, a 6 in the ten's place, and a 0 in the one's place, the value of the number can be calculated by multiplying each digit by its weight and adding them together: $8*10^2 + 6*10^1 + 0*10^0 = 860$. This calculation is easy since people commonly manipulate decimal numbers.

The same concept of weights for each digit can be extended to the fractional components of the number. Consider the decimal number "923.501." The dot in the middle of the digits is the **decimal point**. The decimal point separates the fractional component of the number from the whole part. While the weights of each digit in the whole part of the number

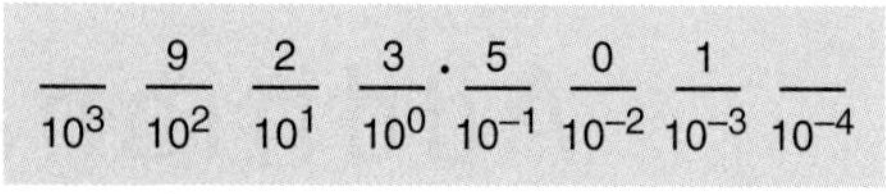

Figure B.1 Representing real numbers in base 10.

are increasing powers of 10, the weights of the fractional digits are decreasing powers of 10, so the digits have fractional weights (e.g., $10^{-1} = 0.1$ and $10^{-2} = 0.01$). Therefore, the digits "923.501" represent $9*10^2 + 2*10^1 + 3*10^0 + 5*10^{-1} + 0*10^{-2} + 1*10^{-3}$, as shown in Figure B.1.

Generally, the point used to separate the whole part of the number from the fractional part is called a **radix point**, *a term applicable to any base.*

We can represent real numbers in binary in a similar manner. Instead of a decimal point, real binary numbers feature a **binary point**. Digits to the right of the binary point are weighted with negative powers of 2. For example, the binary number 10.1101 equals $1*2^1 + 0*2^0 + 1*2^{-1} + 1*2^{-2} + 0*2^{-3} + 1*2^{-4}$, or 2.8125 in decimal, as shown in Figure B.2.

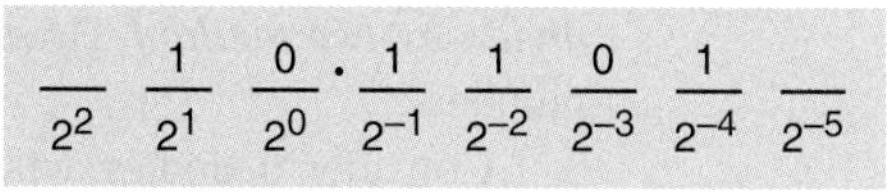

Figure B.2 Representing real numbers in base 2.

You may be comfortable counting up by powers of two (1, 2, 4, 8, 16, 32, etc.). Counting down by powers of two may be difficult to memorize, but the numbers can be derived by dividing by 2: 1, 0.5, 0.25, and so on. Table B.1 illustrates this pattern.

The addition method used in Chapter 1 to convert decimal integers to binary is also a suitable method for converting real numbers, requiring no modifications other than needing to work with negative powers of two.

Table B.1 Powers of two.

Power	Value
2^2	4
2^1	2
2^0	1
2^{-1}	0.5
2^{-2}	0.25
2^{-3}	0.125
2^{-4}	0.0625
2^{-5}	0.03125

Example B.1 Converting real numbers from decimal to binary with the addition method

Convert the number 5.75 to binary using the addition method.

To perform this conversion, we follow the process described in Chapter 1. The conversion is detailed in Figure B.3.

			Binary			
Put 1 in highest place	1	0	0 . 0	0	*(current value: 4)*	
Place 8 too big, but 4 works, put 1 there.	4	2	1	0.5	0.25	

1 in place 2 too big (4+2>5.75), put 0.	1	0	1 . 0	0	*(current value: 5)*	
1 in place 1 is OK (4+1 < 5.75), put 1.	4	2	1	0.5	0.25	

1 in place 0.5 is OK (5+0.5 < 5.75), put 1	1	0	1 . 1	0	*(current value: 5.5)*	
	4	2	1	0.5	0.25	

1 in place 0.25 is OK (5.5+0.25 = 5.75)	1	0	1 . 1	1	*(current value: 5.75)*	
5.75 reached, so done.	4	2	1	0.5	0.25	

Figure B.3 Converting the decimal number 5.75 to binary using the addition method.

The alternative method in Chapter 1 for converting a decimal number to a binary number, namely the divide-by-2 method, can be adapted to work with decimal numbers. We first separate the whole part of the number from the fractional part, and perform the divide-by-2 method on the whole part by itself. Second, we take the fractional part of the number and *multiply* it by 2. After multiplying the fractional part by two, we append the digit in the one's place of the product after the binary point in the converted number. We continue multiplying the fractional part of the product and appending one's place digits until the fractional part of the product is 0.

For example, let's convert the decimal number 9.8125 to binary using the divide-by-2 method variant. First, we convert 9 to binary, which we know is `1001`. Next, we take the fractional part of the number, 0.8125, and multiply by 2: 0.8125*2 = 1.625. The one's digit is a 1, therefore we write a `1` after the binary point of the converted number: `1001.1`. Since the fractional part of the product is not 0, we continue multiplying the fractional part of the product by 2: 0.625*2 = 1.25. We append a `1` to the end of our converted number, giving us `1001.11`, and we continue multiplying by 2: 0.25*2 = 0.5. Now we append a `0` to the end of our converted number, yielding `1001.110`. We multiply by 2 again: 0.5*2 = 1.0. After appending the `1` to our converted number, we are left with `1001.1101`. Since the fractional part of the last product is 0, we are finished converting the number and thus obtain $9.8125_{10} = 1001.1101_2$.

A decimal real number can often require a very long sequence of bits after the binary point to represent the number in binary. In digital design, we are typically constrained to a finite number of bits available to store a number. As a result, the binary number may need to be truncated, and the binary number becomes an approximation.

► B.3 FIXED POINT ARITHMETIC

If we fix the binary point of a real number in a certain position in the number (e.g., after the 4th bit), we can add or subtract binary real numbers by treating the numbers as integers and adding or subtracting normally. The process is known as *fixed point arithmetic*. In the resulting sum or difference, we maintain the binary point's position. For example, assume we are working with 8-bit numbers with half of the bits used to represent the fractional part of the number.

```
    1 1 1   1 1
  1 0 0 1 . 0 0 1 0
+ 0 0 1 1 . 1 1 1 1
  ─────────────────
  1 1 0 1 . 0 0 0 1
```

Figure B.4 Adding two fixed point numbers.

Adding `1001.0010` (9.125) and `0011.1111` (3.9375) can be done simply by adding the two numbers as if they were integers. The sum, shown in Figure B.4, can be converted back to a real number by maintaining the binary point's position within the sum. Converting the sum to decimal verifies that the calculation was correct: $1*2^3 + 1*2^2 + 0*2^1 + 1*2^0 + 0*2^{-1} + 0*2^{-2} + 0*2^{-3} + 1*2^{-4} = 8 + 4 + 1 + 0.0625 = 13.0625$.

Multiplying binary real numbers is also straightforward and does not require that the binary point be fixed. We first multiply the two numbers as if they were integers. Second, we place a binary point in the product such that the precision of the product is the sum of the precisions of the multiplicand and multiplier (the two numbers being multiplied), just like what is done when we multiply two decimal numbers together. Figure B.5 shows how we might multiply the binary numbers 01.10 (1.5) and 11.01 (3.25) using the partial product method described in Chapter 4. After calculating the product of the two numbers, we place a binary point in the appropriate location.

```
        0 1 . 1 0
      × 1 1 . 0 1
      ───────────
        0 1 1 0
        0 0 0 0
      0 1 1 0
  +   0 1 1 0
  ───────────────
    0 1 0 0 . 1 1 1 0
```

Figure B.5 Multiplying two fixed point numbers.

Both the multiplier and multiplicand feature two bits of precision; therefore the product must have four bits of precision, and we insert a binary point to reflect this. Converting the product to decimal verifies that the calculation was correct: $0*2^3 + 1*2^2 + 0*2^1 + 0*2^0 + 1*2^{-1} + 1*2^{-2} + 1*2^{-3} + 0*2^{-4} = 4 + 0.5 + 0.25 + 0.125 = 4.875$.

The previous example was convenient in that we never had to add four 1s together in a column when we summed up the partial products. To make the calculations simpler and to allow for the partial product summation to be implemented using full-adders, which can only add three 1s at a time, we add the partial products incrementally instead of all at once. For example, let's multiply `1110.1` (14.5) by `0111.1` (7.5). As seen in Figure B.6, we begin by generating partial products as done earlier. However, we add partial products immediately into partial product sums, labeled *pps* in the figure.

```
        1 1 1 0 . 1     multiplicand
      × 0 1 1 1 . 1     multiplier
      ───────────       
        1 1 1 0 1       partial product 1 (pp1)
    +  1 1 1 0 1        pp2
    ─────────────       
      1 0 1 0 1 1 1     pps1 = pp1 + pp2
    +  1 1 1 0 1        pp3
    ───────────────     
    1 1 0 0 1 0 1 1     pps2 = pps1 + pp3
  +  1 1 1 0 1          pp4
  ─────────────────     
  1 1 0 1 1 0 0 1 1     pps3 = pps2 + pp4
+  0 0 0 0 0            pp5
───────────────────     
0 1 1 0 1 1 0 0 . 1 1   product = pps3 + pps5
```

Figure B.6 Multiplying two fixed point numbers using intermediate partial products.

Eventually, we find that the product is `01101100.11`, which corresponds to the correct answer of 108.75. You may want to try adding the five partial products together at once instead of using the intermediate partial product sums to see why this method is useful.

Before proceeding to binary real number division, we will introduce binary integer division, which was not discussed in previous chapters.

We can use the familiar process of long division to divide two binary integers. For example, consider the binary division of 101100 (44) by 10 (2). The full calculation is shown in Figure B.7. Notice how the procedure is exactly the same as decimal long division except that the numbers are now in binary.

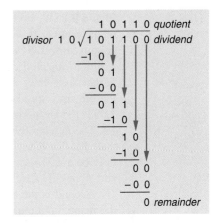

Dividing binary real numbers, like multiplication, also does not require that the binary point be fixed. However, to simplify the calculation, we shift both the dividend and divisor's binary points right until the divisor no longer has a fractional part. For example, consider the division of 1.01_2 (1.25) by 0.1_2 (0.5). The divisor, 0.1_2, has one digit in its fractional part; therefore we shift the dividend and divisor's binary points right by one digit, changing our problem to 10.1_2 divided by 1_2. We now treat the numbers

Figure B.7 Dividing two binary integers using long division.

as integers (ignoring the binary point) and can divide them using the long division approach. Trivially, $101_2/1_2$ is 101_2. We then restore the binary point to where it was in the dividend, giving us the answer 10.1_2 or 2.5.

Why does shifting the binary point not change the answer? In general, shifting the radix point right by one digit is the same as multiplying the number by its base. For binary numbers, shifting the binary point right is equivalent to multiplying the number by 2. Dividing two numbers will give you the ratio of the two numbers to each other. Multiplying the two numbers by the same number (by means of shifting the binary point) will not affect that ratio, since doing so is equivalent to multiplying the ratio by 1.

Fixed point numbers are simple to work with, but are limited in the range of numbers that they can represent. For a fixed number of bits, increasing the precision of a number comes at the expense of the range of whole numbers that we can use, and vice versa. Fixed point numbers are suitable for a variety of applications, such as a digital thermometer, but more demanding applications need greater flexibility and range in their real number representations.

▷ B.4 FLOATING POINT REPRESENTATION

When working with decimal numbers, we often represent very large or very small numbers by using scientific notation. Rather than writing a googol as a 1 with a hundred 0s after it, we could write $1.0*10^{100}$. Instead of 299,792,458 m/s, we could write the speed of light as $3.0*10^8$ m/s, as $2.998*10^8$, or even $299.8*10^6$.

If such notation could be translated into binary, we would be able to store a much greater range of numbers than if the binary point were fixed. What features of this notation need to be captured in a binary representation?

First is the whole and fractional part of the number being multiplied by a power of 10, which is called the **mantissa** (or **significand**), as shown in Figure B.8. We do not need to store the whole part of the number if we make sure the number is in a certain form. We call a number written in scientific notation **normalized** if the whole part of the number is greater than 0 but less than the base. In the previous speed of light examples, $3.0*10^8$ and $2.998*10^8$ are normalized since 3 and 2, respectively, are greater than zero but less than 10. The number $299.8*10^6$, on the other hand, is not normalized because 299 is greater than 10. If a *binary* real number is normalized, then the whole part of the mantissa can only be a `1`. To save bits, we can safely assume that the whole part of the mantissa is 1 and store only the fractional part.

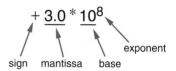

Figure B.8 Parts of a number in scientific notation.

Second is the base (sometimes referred to as the **radix**) and the exponent by which the mantissa is multiplied, shown in Figure B.8. Calling 10 the base is no accident—the number is the same as the base of the entire number. In binary, the base is naturally 2. Knowing this, we do not need to store the 2. We can simply assume that 2 is the base and store the exponent.

Third, we must capture the sign of the number.

The IEEE 754-1985 Standard

The Institute of Electrical and Electronic Engineers (IEEE) 754-1985 standard specifies a way in which the three values described above can be represented in a 32-bit or a 64-bit binary number, referred to as single and double precision, respectively. Though there are other ways to represent real numbers, the IEEE standard is by far the most widely used. We refer to these numbers as *floating point* numbers.

The IEEE standard assigns a certain range of bits for each of the three values. For 32-bit numbers, the first—most significant—bit specifies the sign, followed by 8 bits for the exponent, and the remaining 23 bits are used for the mantissa. This arrangement is pictured in Figure B.9.

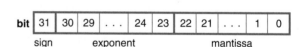

Figure B.9 Bit arrangement in a 32-bit floating point number.

The sign bit is set to 0 if the number is positive, and the bit is set to 1 if the number is negative. The mantissa bits are set to the fractional part of the mantissa in the original number. For example, if the mantissa is `1.1011`, we would store `1011` followed by 19 zeroes in bits 22 to 0. As part of the standard, we add 127 to the exponent we store in the exponent bits. Therefore, if a floating point number's exponent is 3, we would store 130 in the exponent bits. If the exponent was –30, we would store 97 in the exponent bits. The adjusted number is called a ***biased*** exponent. Exponent bits containing all 0s or all 1s have special meanings and cannot be used. Under these conditions, the range of biased exponents we can write in the exponent bits is 1 to 254, meaning the range of unbiased exponents is –126 to 127. Why don't we simply store the exponent as a signed, two's complement number (discussed in Section 4.8)? Because it turns out that biasing the exponents results in simpler circuitry for comparing the magnitude (absolute value) of two floating point numbers.

The IEEE standard defines certain special values if the contents of the exponent bits are uniform. When the exponent bits are all 0s, two possibilities occur:

1. If the mantissa bits are all 0s, then the entire number evaluates to zero.

2. If the mantissa bits are nonzero, then the number is not normalized. That is, the whole part of the mantissa is a binary zero and not a one (e.g. 0.1011).

When the exponent bits are all 1s, two possibilites occur:

1. If the mantissa bits are all 0s, then the entire number evaluates to + or – infinity, depending on the sign bit.

2. If the mantissa bits are nonzero, then the entire "number" is classified as not a number (NaN).

There are also specific classes of NaNs, beyond the scope of this appendix, that are used in computations involving NaNs.

With this information, we can convert decimal real numbers to floating point numbers. Assuming the decimal number to be converted is not a special value in floating point notation, Table B.2 describes how to perform the conversion.

Table B.2 Method for converting real decimal numbers to floating point

	Step	Description
1	Convert the number from base 10 to base 2.	Use the method described in Section B.2.
2	Convert the number to normalized scientific notation.	Initially multiply the number by 2^0. Adjust the binary point and exponent so that the whole part of the number is 1_2.
3	Fill in the bit fields.	Set the sign, *biased* exponent, and mantissa bits appropriately.

Example B.2 Converting decimal real numbers to floating point

Convert the following numbers from decimal to IEEE 754 32-bit floating point: 9.5, infinity, and $-52406.25 * 10^{-2}$.

Let's follow the procedure in Table B.2 to convert 9.5 to floating point. In Step 1, we convert 9.5 to binary. Using the subtraction method, we find that 9.5 is 1001.1 in binary. To convert the number to scientific notation per Step 2, we multiply the number by 2^0, giving 1001.1 * 2^0 (for readability purposes, we write the 2^0 part in base 10). To normalize the number, we must shift the binary point left by three digits. In order not to change the value of the number after moving the binary point, we change the 2's exponent to 3. After Step 2, our number becomes $1.0011 * 2^3$.

In Step 3, we put everything together into the properly formatted sequence of bits. The sign bit is set to 0, indicating a positive number. The exponent bits are set to $3 + 127 = 130$ (we must bias the exponent) in binary, and the mantissa bits are set to 0011_2, which is the fractional part of the mantissa. Remember that the 1 to the left of the binary point is implied since the number is normalized. The properly encoded number is shown in Figure B.10.

Now let's convert infinity to a floating point number. Since infinity is a special value, we cannot employ the method we used to convert 9.5 to floating point. Rather, we fill in the three bit fields with special values indicating that the number is infinity. From the discussion of special values above, we know that the exponent bits should be all 1s and the mantissa bits should be all 0s. The sign bit should be 0 since infinity is positive. Therefore, the equivalent floating point number is 0 11111111 00000000000000000000000.

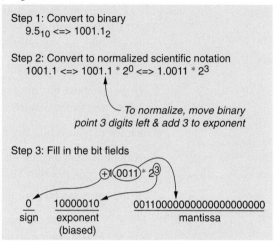

Figure B.10 Representing 9.5 as a 32-bit floating point number, most significant bit first.

Converting $-52406.25 * 10^{-2}$ to floating point is straightforward using the method in Table B.2. For Step 1, we convert the number to binary. Recall that we represent the sign of the number using a single bit and not using two's complement representation, so we only need to convert $52406.25 * 10^{-2}$ to binary and set the sign bit to indicate that the number is negative. The number $52406.25 * 10^{-2}$ evaluates to 524.0625. Using the subtraction or divide-by-2 method we know that 524 is 1000001100 in binary. The fractional part, 0.0625, is conveniently 2^{-4}. Thus 524.0625 is 1000001100.0001 in binary. In Step 2, we write the number in scientific notation: $1000001100.0001 * 2^0$. We must also normalize the number by shifting the binary point left by 9 digits and compensating for this shift in the exponent: $1.0000011000001 * 2^9$. Finally, we combine the sign (1 since the original number is negative), biased exponent ($9 + 127 = 136$), and fractional part of the mantissa into a floating point number: 1 10001000 00000110000010000000000.

Example B.3 Converting floating point numbers to decimal

Convert the number 11001011101010100000000000000000 from IEEE 754 32-bit floating point to decimal.

To perform this conversion, we first split the number into its sign, exponent, and mantissa parts: 1 10010111 01010100000000000000000. We can immediately see from the sign bit that the number is negative.

Next, we convert the 8-bit exponent and 23-bit mantissa from binary to decimal. We find that 10010111 is 151. We unbias the exponent by subtracting 127 from 151, giving an unbiased exponent of 24. Recall that the mantissa in the pattern of bits represents the fractional part of the mantissa and is stored without the leading 1 from the whole part of the mantissa (assuming the original number was normalized). Restoring the 1 and adding a binary point gives us the number 1.0101010000000000000000000, which is the same number as 1.010101. By applying weights to each digit, we see that $1.010101 = 1*2^0 + 0*2^{-1} + 1*2^{-2} + 0*2^{-3} + 1*2^{-4} + 0*2^{-5} + 1*2^{-6} = 1.328125$.

With the original sign, exponent, and mantissa extracted, we can combine them into a single number: $-1.327125 * 2^{24}$. We can multiply the number out to $-22,265,462.784$, which is equivalent to $-2.2265462784 * 10^7$.

The format for double precision (64-bit) floating point numbers is similar, with three fields having a defined number of bits. The first, most significant bit represents the sign of the number. The next 11 bits hold the biased exponent,

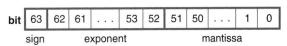

Figure B.11 Bit arrangement in a 64-bit floating point number.

and the remaining 52 bits hold the fractional part of the mantissa. Additionally, we add 1023 to the exponent instead of 127 to form the biased exponent. This arrangement is pictured in Figure B.11.

Floating Point Arithmetic

Floating point arithmetic is beyond the scope of this text, but we will provide a brief overview of the concept.

Floating point addition and subtraction must be performed by first *aligning* the two floating point numbers so that their exponents are equal. For example, consider adding the two decimal numbers $2.52*10^2 + 1.44*10^4$. Since the exponents differ, we can change $2.52*10^2$ to $0.0252*10^4$. Adding $0.0252*10^4$ and $1.44*10^4$ gives us the answer $1.4652*10^4$. Similarly, we could have changed $1.44*10^4$ to $144*10^2$. Adding $144*10^2$ and $2.52*10^2$ gives us the sum $146.52*10^2$, which is the same number as our first set of calculations. An analogous situation occurs when we work with floating point numbers. Typically, hardware that performs floating point arithmetic, often referred to as a *floating point unit*, will adjust the mantissa of the number with the smaller exponent before adding or subtracting the mantissas (with their implied 1s restored) together and preserving the common exponent. Notice that before the addition or subtraction is performed, the exponents of the two numbers are compared. This comparison is facilitated through the use of the sign bit and the biased exponent as opposed to representing the exponent in two's complement form.

Multiplication and division in floating point require no such alignments. Like in decimal multiplication and division of numbers in scientific notation, we multiply or divide the mantissas and add or subtract the two exponents, depending on the operation. When multiplying, we add exponents. For example, let's multiply $6.44*10^7$ by $5.0*10^{-3}$. Instead of trying to multiply 64,400,000 by 0.005, we multiply the two mantissas together and add the exponents. $6.44*5.0$ is 32.2 and $7+(-3)$ is 4. Thus the answer is $32.2*10^4$. When dividing, we subtract the exponent of the divisor from the dividend's exponent. For example, let's divide $31.5*10^{-4}$ (dividend) by $2.0*10^{-12}$ (divisor). Dividing 31.5 by 2.0 gives us 15.75. Subtracting the divisor's exponent from the dividend's gives

$-4 - (-12) = 8$. Thus the answer is $15.75 * 10^8$. Floating point division defines results for several boundary cases such as dividing by 0, which evaluates to positive or negative infinity, depending on the sign of the dividend. Dividing a nonzero number by infinity is defined as 0, otherwise dividing by infinity is NaN.

▶ B.5 EXERCISES

SECTION B.1: REAL NUMBER REPRESENTATION

B.1 Convert the following numbers from decimal to binary:
   (a) 1.5
   (b) 3.125
   (c) 8.25
   (d) 7.75

B.2 Convert the following numbers from decimal to binary:
   (a) 9.375
   (b) 2.4375
   (c) 5.65625
   (d) 15.5703125

SECTION B.3: FIXED POINT ARITHMETIC

B.3 Add the following two unsigned binary numbers using binary addition and convert the result to decimal:
   (a) `10111.001 + 1010.110`
   (b) `01101.100 + 10100.101`
   (c) `10110.1 + 110.011`
   (d) `1101.111 + 10011.0111`

SECTION B.4: FLOATING POINT REPRESENTATION

B.4 Convert the following decimal numbers to 32-bit floating point:
   (a) $-50{,}208$
   (b) $42.427523 * 10^3$
   (c) $-24{,}551{,}152 * 10^{-4}$
   (d) 0

B.5 Convert the following 32-bit floating point numbers to decimal:
   (a) `01001100010110110101100001011000`
   (b) `01001100010110110101001000000000`
   (c) `01111111111000110000000000000000`
   (d) `01001101000110101000101000000000`

C

Extended RTL Design Example

▶ C.1 INTRODUCTION

Chapter 5 included an RTL design example of a soda dispenser processor. The example started with a high-level state machine, created the datapath's structure, and then described the controller using a finite-state machine. The controller was not further design to structure, as such design was the subject of Chapter 3. This appendix completes the RTL design by designing the controller's FSM down to a state register and gates, resulting in a complete custom-processor implementation of a controller and a datapath. The appendix traces through the behavior of the complete implementation. The purpose of demonstrating this complete design is to give the reader a clear understanding of how the controller and datapath work together.

The block symbol for the soda dispenser processor appears in Figure C.1. Recall that the soda dispenser has three inputs c, s, and a. The 8-bit input s represents the cost of each bottle of soda. The 1-bit input c is 1 for one clock cycle when a coin is inserted. Additionally, the value on 8-bit input a indicates the value of the coin that was inserted. The soda dispenser features one output d used to indicate when soda should be dispensed. The 1-bit output d is 1 for one clock cycle after the value of the coins inserted into the soda dispenser is greater than or equal to s. The soda dispenser does not give change.

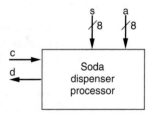

Figure C.1 Soda dispenser block symbol.

Chapter 5 developed the high-level state machine seen in Figure C.2. The HLSM was then converted into a controller (represented behaviorally as an FSM) and datapath, shown in Figure C.3.

The datapath supports the data operations necessitated by the high-level state machine, including resetting the value of *tot* (*tot* = 0 in the *Init* state), comparing whether *tot* is less than s (for the transitions from the *Wait* state), and adding *tot* and a (in the *Add* state).

557

The controller FSM is similar to the high-level state machine, but is modified to control the datapath and accept status input from the datapath (i.e., `tot_lt_s`) rather than performing data operations directly. The controller and datapath are shown in Figure C.3.

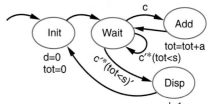

Figure C.2 Soda dispenser high-level state machine.

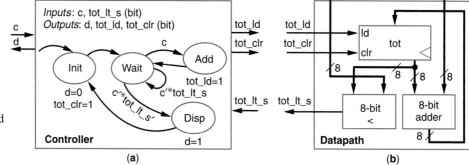

Figure C.3 Soda dispenser: (a) controller (described behaviorally) and (b) datapath (structure).

(a)

(b)

► C.2 DESIGNING THE SODA DISPENSER CONTROLLER

Using the controller design process introduced in Chapter 3, we can complete the design of the controller. The steps are as follows:

Capture the FSM. The FSM for the soda dispenser's controller was created during Step 4 of the RTL design method. The controller's FSM is shown in Figure C.3(a).

Set up the architecture. As indicated by the controller's FSM, the state machine's architecture has 2 inputs (c and `tot_lt_s`) and 3 outputs (d, `tot_ld`, and `tot_clr`). We will use two bits to represent the controller's states, naming the current state signals s1 and s0, and the next state signals n1 and n0. The corresponding controller architecture is shown in Figure C.4.

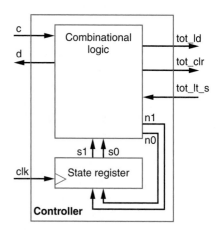

Figure C.4 Standard controller architecture for the soda dispenser.

Encode the states. A straightforward encoding of the soda dispenser's four states is: *Init*: 00, *Wait*: 01, *Add*: 10, and *Disp*: 11.

Fill in the truth table. From the controller architecture set up above, we know that the truth table must have 4 inputs (c, tot_lt_s, s1, and s0) and 5 outputs (d, tot_ld, tot_clr, n1, and n0). With 4 inputs, the table will have $2^4 = 16$ rows as in Figure C.5.

		Inputs			Outputs				
	s1	s0	c	tot_lt_s	d	tot_ld	tot_clr	n1	n0
Init	0	0	0	0	0	0	1	0	1
	0	0	0	1	0	0	1	0	1
	0	0	1	0	0	0	1	0	1
	0	0	1	1	0	0	1	0	1
Wait	0	1	0	0	0	0	0	1	1
	0	1	0	1	0	0	0	0	1
	0	1	1	0	0	0	0	1	0
	0	1	1	1	0	0	0	1	0
Add	1	0	0	0	0	1	0	0	1
	1	0	0	1	0	1	0	0	1
	1	0	1	0	0	1	0	0	1
	1	0	1	1	0	1	0	0	1
Disp	1	1	0	0	1	0	0	0	0
	1	1	0	1	1	0	0	0	0
	1	1	1	0	1	0	0	0	0
	1	1	1	1	1	0	0	0	0

Figure C.5 The soda dispenser controller's truth table.

By examining the outputs specified in the controller FSM, duplicated for convenience in Figure C.6, we can fill in the d, tot_ld, and tot_clr columns in the truth table. For example, Figure C.6 shows that when the controller FSM is in state *Init*, d=0, tot_clr=1, and tot_ld is implicitly 0. Thus, for rows in the truth table that correspond to state *Init* —namely the four rows where s1s0=00, since we chose "00" as the encoding for the *Init* state—we set the d column to 0, the tot_clr column to 1, and the tot_ld column to 0.

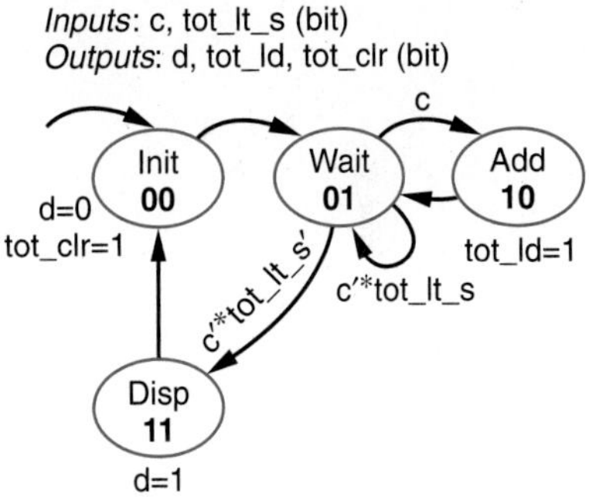

We fill in the next state columns n1 and n0 based on the transitions specified in the con-

Inputs: c, tot_lt_s (bit)
Outputs: d, tot_ld, tot_clr (bit)

Figure C.6 Soda dispenser controller FSM with state encodings.

troller FSM and the state encoding chosen in the earlier step. For example, consider the *Wait* state. As indicated in Figure C.6, the FSM transitions to the *Add* state when c=1. Thus, for rows where s1s0c=011 (s1s0=01 corresponds to the *Wait* state), we set the n1 column to 1 and the n0 column to 0 (n1n0=10 corresponds to the *Add* state). When c=0, the FSM transitions to the *Disp* state if tot_lt_s=0 or remains in the *Wait* state of tot_lt_s=1. We represent the transition from *Wait* to *Disp* in the truth table by setting n1 to 1 and n0 to 1 (*Disp*) in the row where s1s0=01 (*Wait*), c=0, and tot_lt_s=0. Similarly, we represent the transition from *Wait* back to *Wait* by writing n1n0=01 where s1s0=01, c=0, and tot_lt_s=1. We then examine the remaining transitions in a similar way, filling in the appropriate values for n1 and n0 until all transitions are accounted for. The completed truth table is shown in Figure C.5.

Implement the Combinational Logic. For each of the truth table's outputs, we write the corresponding Boolean equation. From the truth table we obtain the following equations:

```
d = s1s0
tot_ld = s1s0'
tot_clr = s1's0'
n1 = s1's0c'tot_lt_s' + s1's0c
```

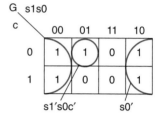

```
n0 = s1's0' + s1's0c' + s1s0'
n0 = s0' + s1's0c'
```

Figure C.7 K-map for output n0.

Note that the first four equations derived from the truth table are already minimized. The fifth equation, corresponding to n0, can be minimized to s0' + s1's0c' through algebraic methods, or by using a K-map as shown in Figure C.7. K-maps were discussed in Chapter 6.

Using techniques discussed in Chapter 2, we convert the above Boolean equations into an equivalent two-level gate-based circuit. This conversion is straightforward since the Boolean equations are already in sum-of-products form. The final sequential controller circuit and the datapath for the soda dispenser is shown in Figure C.8.

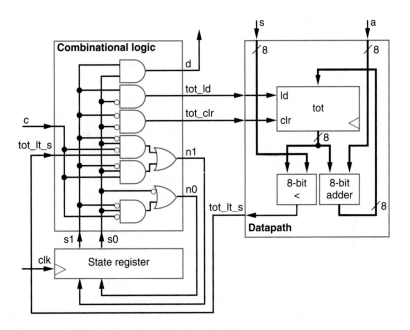

Figure C.8 Final implementation of the soda machine controller with datapath.

▶ **C.3 UNDERSTANDING THE BEHAVIOR OF THE SODA DISPENSER CONTROLLER AND DATAPATH**

This section examines how the controller and datapath designed for the soda dispenser interact to form a working implementation of the initial high-level state machine.

Figure C.9 illustrates the behavior of the soda dispenser controller and datapath, including initialization and how the soda dispenser behaves when a user inserts a quarter into the system. The 5 clock cycles shown are labeled 1 through 5 in Figure C.9(a). We'll assume that the cost of a soda can is 60 cents and that the soda dispenser's controller is in the *Init* state during the first clock cycle. Let's examine what occurs in each clock cycle:

- Initially, in clock cycle 1, the controller is in the *Init* state, shown in Figure C.9(b). When in state *Init*, the controller sets d to 0, tot_ld to 0, and tot_clr to 1. Additionally, the controller sets the next state signals n1n0 to 01, corresponding to the *Wait* state. In the datapath, the value of *tot* and *tot+a* is unknown, denoted by "*??*". Notice that even though the controller set tot_clr to 1 during this clock cycle, the *tot* register will not be cleared immediately (asynchronously). Rather, *tot* will be cleared shortly after the next clock cycle, a synchronous behavior. Finally, notice that the price of the soda, s, is set to 60 cents and the coin input signals, c and a, are initially 0 and 0, respectively.

- Figure C.9(c) shows the soda dispenser in clock cycle 2. The controller is now in the *Wait* state. Accordingly, the controller sets d, tot_ld, and tot_clr to 0. The value of *tot* is cleared, and shortly afterwards, two signals, tot_lt_s and *tot+a*, take a known value. The datapath's comparator sets tot_lt_s to 1 since the total, 0, is less than the price of soda, 60. The datapath's adder sets intermediate signal *tot+a* to 0 since *tot* and a are now known. The next state signals remain set to 01 (*Wait*) since c is 0 and tot_lt_s is 1.

- Figure C.9(d) shows the soda dispenser in clock cycle 3. During the third clock cycle, the user inserts a quarter into the soda dispenser, as indicated by c becoming 1 and a becoming 25. Shortly after a changes, the adder's output *tot+a* changes to 25, the sum of *tot* and a. Since c is 1, the controller sets the next state to 10 (*Add*). The values of d, tot_ld, and tot_clr remain the same since the controller's state has not changed since the previous (2nd) clock cycle.

- In clock cycle 4, shown in Figure C.9(e), the controller is in the *Add* state and sets tot_ld to 1 while keeping d and tot_clr at 0. As was the case with tot_clr during the *Init* state, *tot* will not be updated until the next clock cycle. The controller will unconditionally return to state *Wait*, setting n1n0 to 01 (*Wait*).

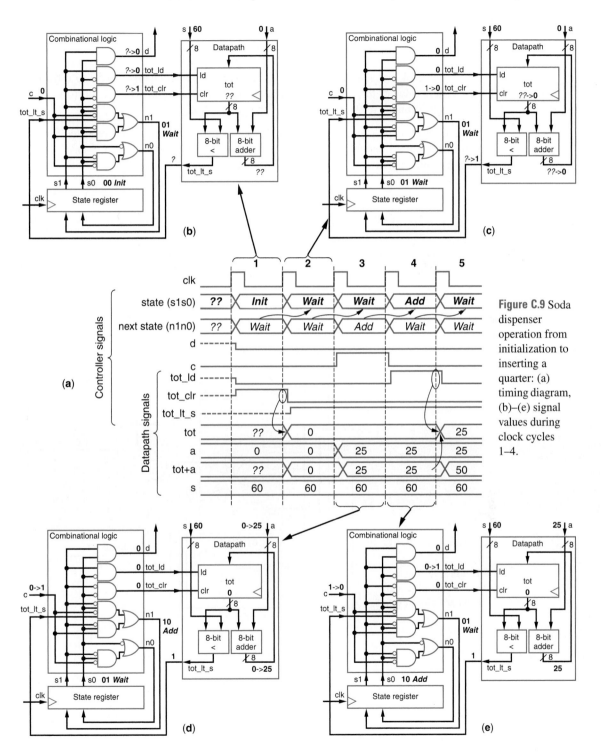

Figure C.9 Soda dispenser operation from initialization to inserting a quarter: (a) timing diagram, (b)–(e) signal values during clock cycles 1–4.

- In clock cycle 5, shown in Figure C.10, the controller sets d, tot_ld, and tot_clr to 0 since the controller is in the *Wait* state. The *tot* register loads the value of *tot+a*, storing 25. Shortly afterwards, *tot+a* changes to 50 to reflect the new value of *tot*; however, 50 is not loaded into *tot*, as *tot* will only perform a load synchronous to the rising edge of the clock signal.

The addition procedure demonstrated in clock cycles 3 through 5 is repeated for each coin inserted until enough change has been inserted to cover the cost of a soda, as indicated by input signal s.

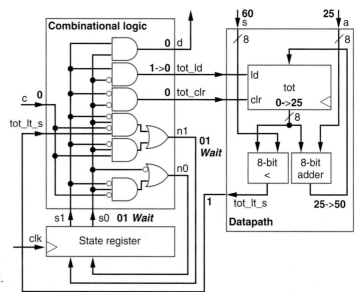

Figure C.10 Operation of the controller and datapath: clock cycle 5.

Figure C.11 details the behavior of the soda dispenser when the user has inserted enough change into the machine to cause a soda to be dispensed. In the timing diagram shown in Figure C.11(a), we duplicate clock cycle 5 from Figure C.9(a) as a point of reference. During the next few dozen clock cycles, we assume that the user has inserted a nickel followed by a quarter. As a result, the register *tot* will contain the value 55 $(25 + 5 + 25$ cents). Let's examine the behavior of the soda dispenser when the user inserts a dime into the machine:

- In Figure C.11(b), corresponding to clock cycle 100, the soda dispenser's controller is in the *Wait* state. Assuming the user inserts a dime into the soda dispenser, the c input will become high for one clock cycle and the a input will change to 10, the value of a dime. Shortly after a changes, the intermediate signal *tot+a* changes to 65 (55+10). With c asserted, the next state signals n1n0 become 10 (*Add*).

- In clock cycle 101, shown in Figure C.11(c), the controller is in the *Add* state and asserts tot_ld. The register *tot* will not load a new total until the rising edge of the next clock cycle. The controller unconditionally sets the next state to 01 (*Wait*).

- Figure C.11(d) shows the status of the soda dispenser in clock cycle 102, where the controller is in the *Wait* state. As indicated by the arrows in Figure C.11(a), tot_ld being asserted on the rising edge of the clock causes *tot* to load the value on its input, which is 65. Shortly after *tot* loads a new value, the comparator's output tot_lt_s changes from 1 to 0 to reflect the fact that *tot* (65) is not less than s (60). Since the controller is in the *Wait* state, and since both c and tot_lt_s are 0, the controller sets the next state signals to 11 (*Disp*). Notice that prior to the next state signals settling on the *Disp* state, the next state was *Wait* for a brief period of time. Depending on the time required for signals to propagate through the datapath and controller, certain signals may initially contain unexpected values, but these signals will eventually settle to their expected values. We can avoid any problems associated with this period of uncertainty by selecting a clock period that is long enough to allow our circuit's intermediate signals to settle into a stable state and stay stable long enough to comply with any setup times required by our circuit's sequential components.

- In Figure C.11(e), the controller is in the *Disp* state. The controller asserts d, indicating to some outside component that a soda should be dispensed. The controller will unconditionally transition to the *Init* state, where the initialization procedure shown in Figure C.9 is repeated (partially shown in clock cycle 104 of Figure C.11(a)).

We see that the controller and datapath work together to implement the behavior of the original high-level state machine.

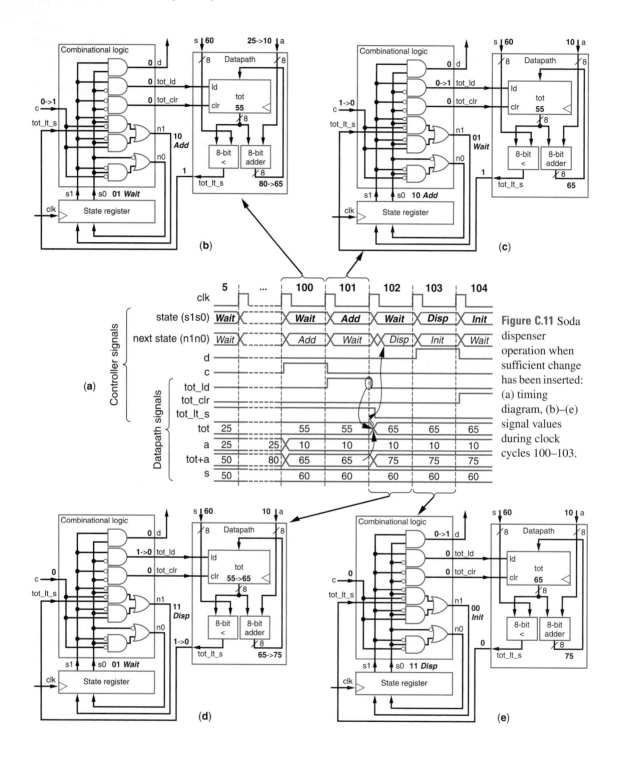

Figure C.11 Soda dispenser operation when sufficient change has been inserted: (a) timing diagram, (b)–(e) signal values during clock cycles 100–103.

Index